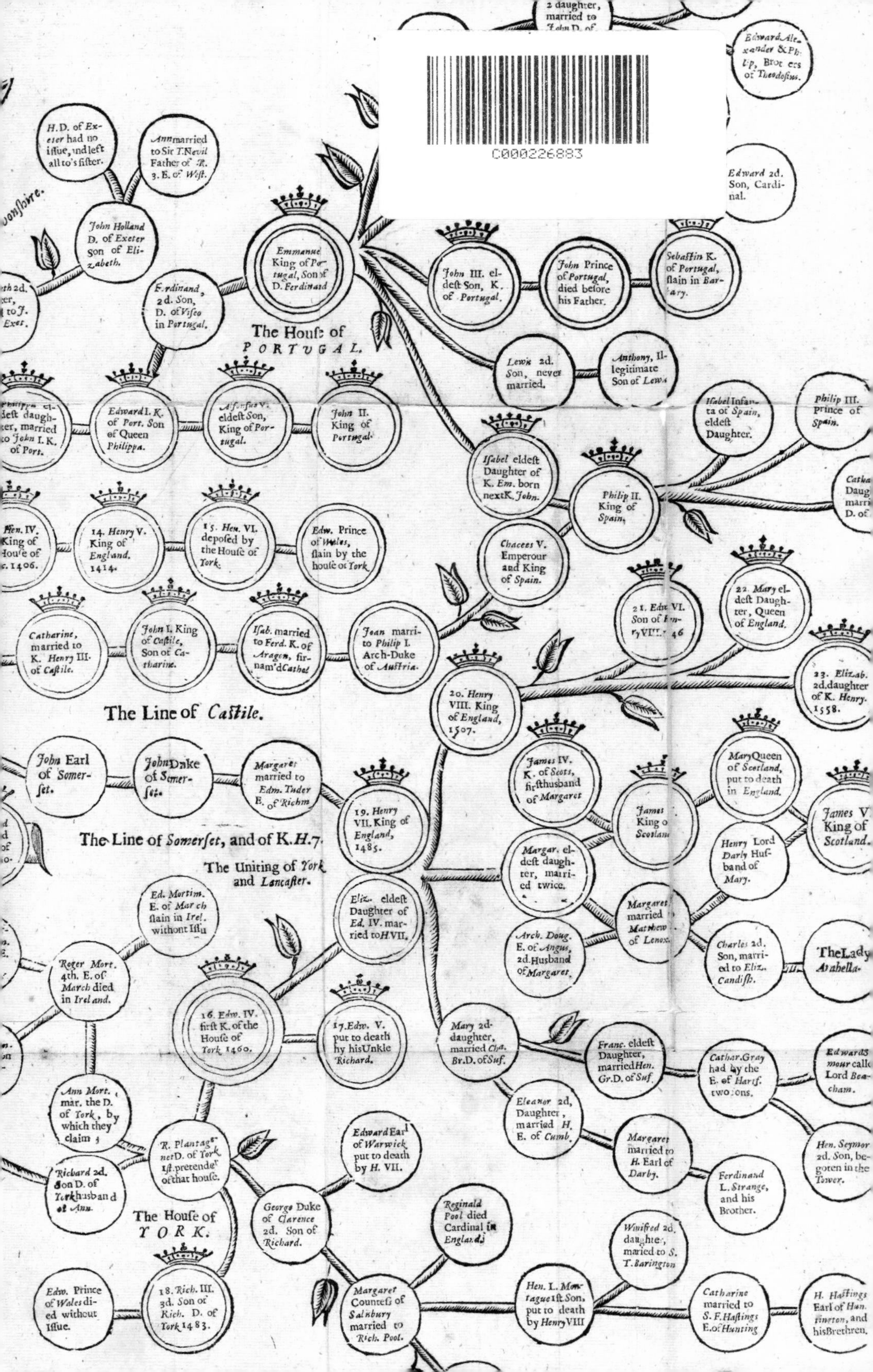

The House of PORTUGAL.
Emmanuel King of Portugal, Son of D. Ferdinand
John III. eldest Son, K. of Portugal.
John Prince of Portugal, died before his Father.
Sebastian K. of Portugal, slain in Barbary.
Lewis 2d. Son, never married.
Anthony, Illegitimate Son of Lewis
Edward 2d. Son, Cardinal.
H. D. of Exeter had no issue, and left all to's sister.
Ann married to Sir T. Nevil Father of R. 3. E. of West.
John Holland D. of Exeter Son of Elizabeth.
Ferdinand, 2d. Son, D. of Viseo in Portugal.
Edward I. K. of Port. Son of Queen Philippa.
Alfonsus V. eldest Son, King of Portugal.
John II. King of Portugal.
Isabel eldest Daughter of K. Em. born next K. John.
Philip II. King of Spain.
Isabel Infanta of Spain, eldest Daughter.
Philip III. prince of Spain.
Chacees V. Emperour and King of Spain.
14. Henry V. King of England. 1414.
15. Hen. VI. deposed by the House of York.
Edw. Prince of Wales, slain by the house of York
Catharine, married to K. Henry III. of Castile.
John I. King of Castile, Son of Catharine.
Isab. married to Ferd. K. of Aragon, sirnam'd Cathol
Joan married to Philip I. Arch-Duke of Austria.
21. Edw. VI. Son of Henry VIII. 1546
22. Mary eldest Daughter, Queen of England.
23. Elizab. 2d. daughter of K. Henry. 1558.
20. Henry VIII. King of England, 1507.
The Line of Castile.
John Earl of Somerset.
John Duke of Somerset.
Margaret married to Edm. Tuder E. of Richm
19. Henry VII. King of England, 1485.
The Line of Somerset, and of K. H. 7.
The Uniting of York and Lancaster.
James IV. K. of Scots, first husband of Margaret
Mary Queen of Scotland, put to death in England.
James V. King of Scotland
Margar. eldest daughter, married twice.
Henry Lord Darly Husband of Mary.
Margaret married to Matthew of Lenox.
Arch. Doug. E. of Angus, 2d. Husband of Margaret.
Charles 2d. Son, married to Eliz. Candish.
The Lady Arabella.
Ed. Mortim. E. of March slain in Irel. without Issu
Eliz. eldest Daughter of Ed. IV. married to H. VII.
Roger Mort. 4th. E. of March died in Ireland.
16. Edw. IV. first K. of the House of York. 1460.
17. Edw. V. put to death by his Unkle Richard.
Mary 2d. daughter, married Cha. Br. D. of Suf.
Franc. eldest Daughter, married Hen. Gr. D. of Suf.
Cathar. Gray had by the E. of Harts. two sons.
Edward Seymour called Lord Beacham.
Ann Mort. mar. the D. of York, by which they claim
Eleanor 2d, Daughter, married H. E. of Cumb.
Margaret married to H. Earl of Darby.
Hen. Seymor 2d. Son, begoten in the Tower.
R. Plantagenet D. of York 1st. pretender of that house.
Edward Earl of Warwick put to death by H. VII.
Richard 2d. Son D. of York husband of Ann.
Ferdinand L. Strange, and his Brother.
The House of YORK.
George Duke of Clarence 2d. Son of Richard.
Reginald Pool died Cardinal in England.
Winifred 2d. daughter, maried to S. T. Barington
Edw. Prince of Wales died without Issue.
18. Rich. III. 3d. Son of Rich. D. of York 1483.
Margaret Countess of Salsbury married to Rich. Pool.
Hen. L. Montague 1st Son, put to death by Henry VIII
Catharine married to S. F. Hastings E. of Hunting
H. Hastings Earl of Huntington, and his Brethren.

Devil-Land

CLARE JACKSON

Devil-Land

England under Siege, 1588–1688

ALLEN LANE
an imprint of
PENGUIN BOOKS

ALLEN LANE

UK | USA | Canada | Ireland | Australia
India | New Zealand | South Africa

Allen Lane is part of the Penguin Random House group of companies
whose addresses can be found at global.penguinrandomhouse.com

First published 2021
001

Set in 10.2/13.87 pt Sabon LT Std
Typeset by Jouve (UK), Milton Keynes
Printed and bound in Great Britain by Clays Ltd, Elcograf S.p.A.

The authorized representative in the EEA is Penguin Random House Ireland,
Morrison Chambers, 32 Nassau Street, Dublin D02 YH68

A CIP catalogue record for this book is available from the British Library

ISBN: 978-0-241-28581-7

www.greenpenguin.co.uk

Penguin Random House is committed to a sustainable future for our business, our readers and our planet. This book is made from Forest Stewardship Council® certified paper.

For Mark and Julius

Contents

List of Illustrations

(Photographic credits are given in italics.)

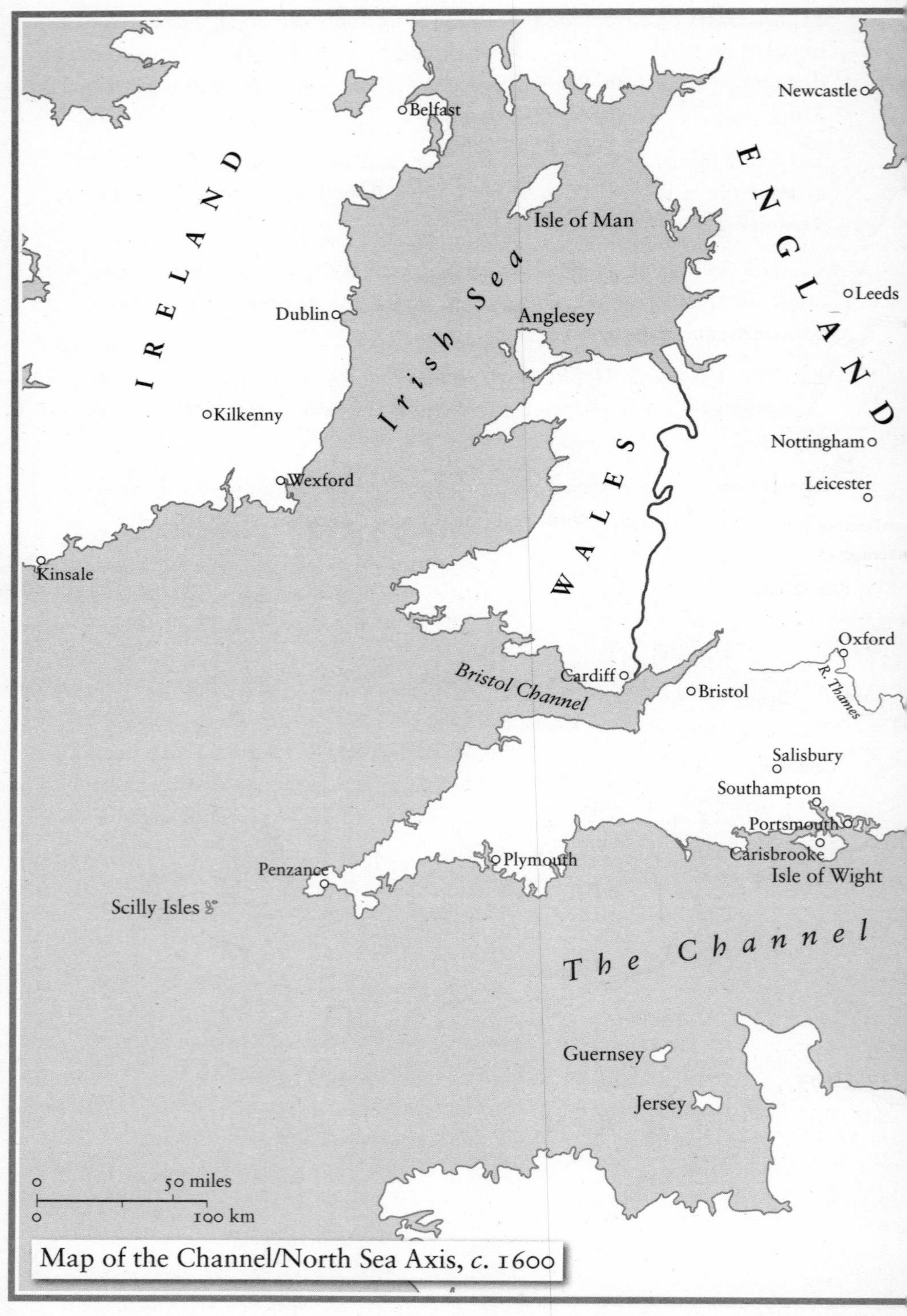

Map of the Channel/North Sea Axis, *c.* 1600

N
North Sea
King's Lynn
Norwich
Peterborough
Yarmouth
theringhay
Cambridge
Harwich
London
Margate
Canterbury
The Downs
Dover
Calais
Dunkirk
Gravelines
Boulogne
Ostend
Amsterdam
The Hague
HOLLAND
Hellevoetsluis
Rotterdam
ZEELAND
Breda
Bergen-op-Zoom
Antwerp
UNITED PROVINCES
Wesel
Maastricht
LIÈGE
Cologne
Aachen
Liège
Brussels
FLANDERS
SPANISH NETHER-LANDS
Cambrai
Amiens
Trier
Luxembourg
Le Havre
FRANCE
R. Seine
R. Meuse
Paris

The Dutch Republic in 1672

Descendants of Henry VII

Henry VII of England 1457–1509, reigned as King 1485–1509 *m.* Elizabeth of York 1466–1503

- James IV of Scotland 1473–1513, reigned as King 1488–1513 *m.* Margaret 1489–1541
  - James V of Scotland 1512–42, reigned as King 1513–42 *m.* 1 Madeleine of Valois 1520–37; *m.* 2 Mary of Guise 1515–60
    - Mary, Queen of Scots 1542–87, reigned as Queen of Scotland 1542–67 *m.* 1 Francis II of France 1544–60, reigned as King 1559–60; *m.* 2 Henry Stuart, Lord Darnley 1545/6–67; *m.* 3 James Hepburn, Earl of Bothwell *c.* 1534/5–78
      - James VI of Scotland and I of England 1566–1625
- Arthur, Prince of Wales 1486–1502 *m.* Catherine of Aragon 1485–1536
- Henry VIII of England 1491–1547, reigned as King 1509–47 *m.* 1 Catherine of Aragon
  - Mary I of England 1516–58, reigned as Queen 1553–8 *m.* Philip II, of Spain 1527–98, reigned as King of Spain 1556–98
  - *m.* 2 Anne Boleyn *c.* 1500–36
    - Elizabeth I of England 1533–1603, reigned as Queen 1558–1603
  - *m.* 3 Jane Seymour 1508/9–37
    - Edward VI of England 1537–53, reigned as King under a regency council 1547–53
  - *m.* 4 Anne of Cleves 1515–57
  - *m.* 5 Catherine Howard *c.* 1518/24–42
  - *m.* 6 Catherine Parr 1512–48
- Mary 1496–1533 *m.* 1 Louis XII King of France 1462–1515, reigned as King 1498–1515; *m.* 2 Charles Brandon, Duke of Suffolk *c.* 1484–1545

The Stuarts

- James IV of Scotland 1473–1513, reigned as King 1488–1513 *m.* Margaret Tudor 1489–1541
  - James V of Scotland 1512–42, reigned as King 1513–42 *m.* 1 Madeleine de Valois 1520–37; *m.* 2 Mary of Guise 1515–60
    - Mary, Queen of Scots 1542–87, reigned 1542–67 *m.* 1 Francis II of France 1544–60, reigned 1559–60; *m.* 2 Henry Stuart, Lord Darnley 1545/6–67; *m.* 3 James Hepburn, Earl of Bothwell *c.* 1534/5–78
      - James VI & I 1566–1625, reigned as James VI of Scotland 1567–1625 and James I of England 1603–1625 *m.* Anna of Denmark 1574–1619
        - Henry, Prince of Wales 1594–1612
        - Elizabeth Stuart, Electress Palatine, briefly Queen of Bohemia 1596–1662 *m.* Frederick V, Elector Palatine, briefly King of Bohemia 1596–1632
          - Frederick Henry 1614–29
          - Karl Ludwig, 1618–80 Elector Palatine 1660–80 *m.* Charlotte of Hesse-Kessel, Electress Palatine 1627–86
            - Karl, 1651–85 Elector Palatine 1680–5
            - Elisabeth Charlotte, Duchess of Orléans 1652–1722 *m.* Philippe 'Monsieur', Duke of Orléans 1640–1701
          - Elisabeth 1618–80
          - Rupert, Prince Palatine, Duke of Cumberland 1619–82
          - Maurice, Prince Palatine of the Rhine 1621–52
          - Louise Hollandine 1622–1709
          - Edward, Count Palatine of Simmern 1625–63 *m.* Anna Marie de Gonzague, Princess Palatine 1616–84
          - Henrietta Maria 1626–51 *m.* Sigismund Rákóczi Prince of Transylvania 1622–52
          - 2 others (died in infancy)
          - Sophia, Electress of Hanover, Heiress of Great Britain 1630–1714 *m.* Ernst Augustus, Elector of Hanover 1629–98
            - George Louis 1660–1727, reigned as George I of Great Britain 1714–27 *m.* Sophia Dorothea 1666–1726
          - Philip Frederick, Prince Palatine 1627–50
          - Gustavus Adolphus, Prince Palatine 1632–41

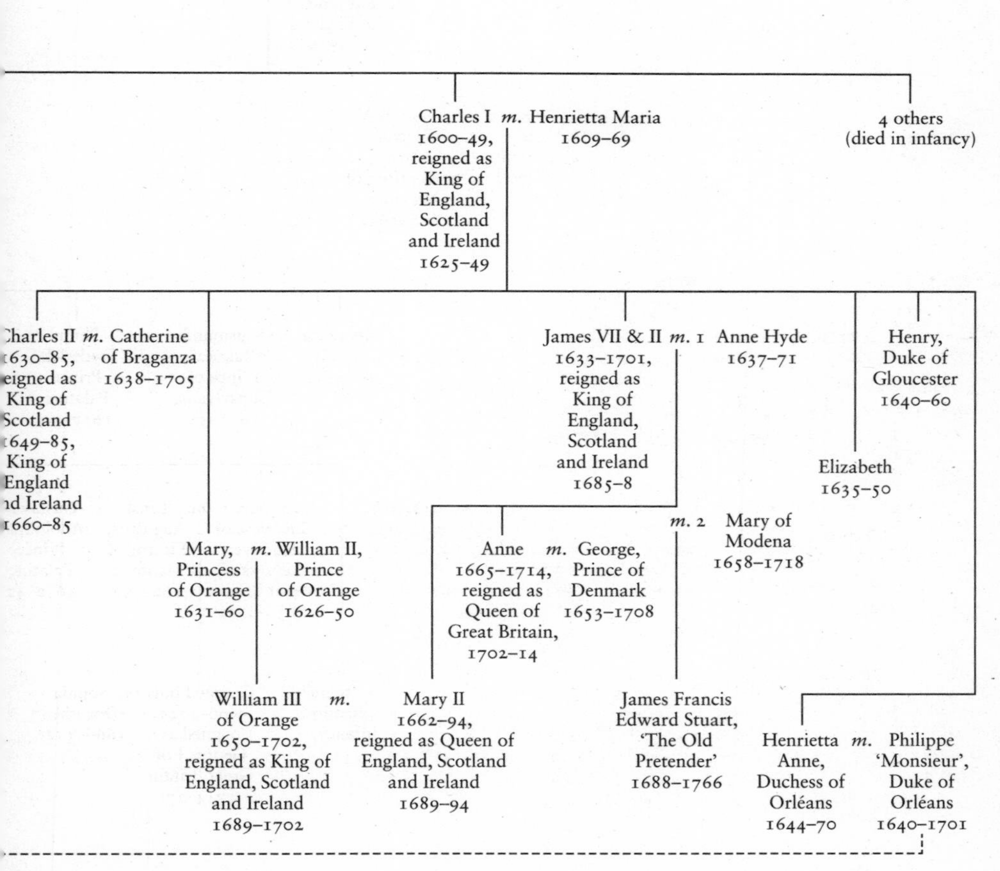
Charles I m. Henrietta Maria
1600–49, reigned as King of England, Scotland and Ireland 1625–49
1609–69
4 others (died in infancy)
harles II m. Catherine of Braganza
630–85, eigned as King of Scotland 649–85, King of England nd Ireland 1660–85
1638–1705
James VII & II m. 1 Anne Hyde
1633–1701, reigned as King of England, Scotland and Ireland 1685–8
1637–71
Henry, Duke of Gloucester
1640–60
Elizabeth
1635–50
m. 2 Mary of Modena
1658–1718
Mary, Princess of Orange m. William II, Prince of Orange
1631–60
1626–50
Anne m. George, Prince of Denmark
1665–1714, reigned as Queen of Great Britain, 1702–14
1653–1708
William III of Orange m. Mary II
1650–1702, reigned as King of England, Scotland and Ireland 1689–1702
1662–94, reigned as Queen of England, Scotland and Ireland 1689–94
James Francis Edward Stuart, 'The Old Pretender'
1688–1766
Henrietta Anne, Duchess of Orléans m. Philippe 'Monsieur', Duke of Orléans
1644–70
1640–1701

The House of Bourbon

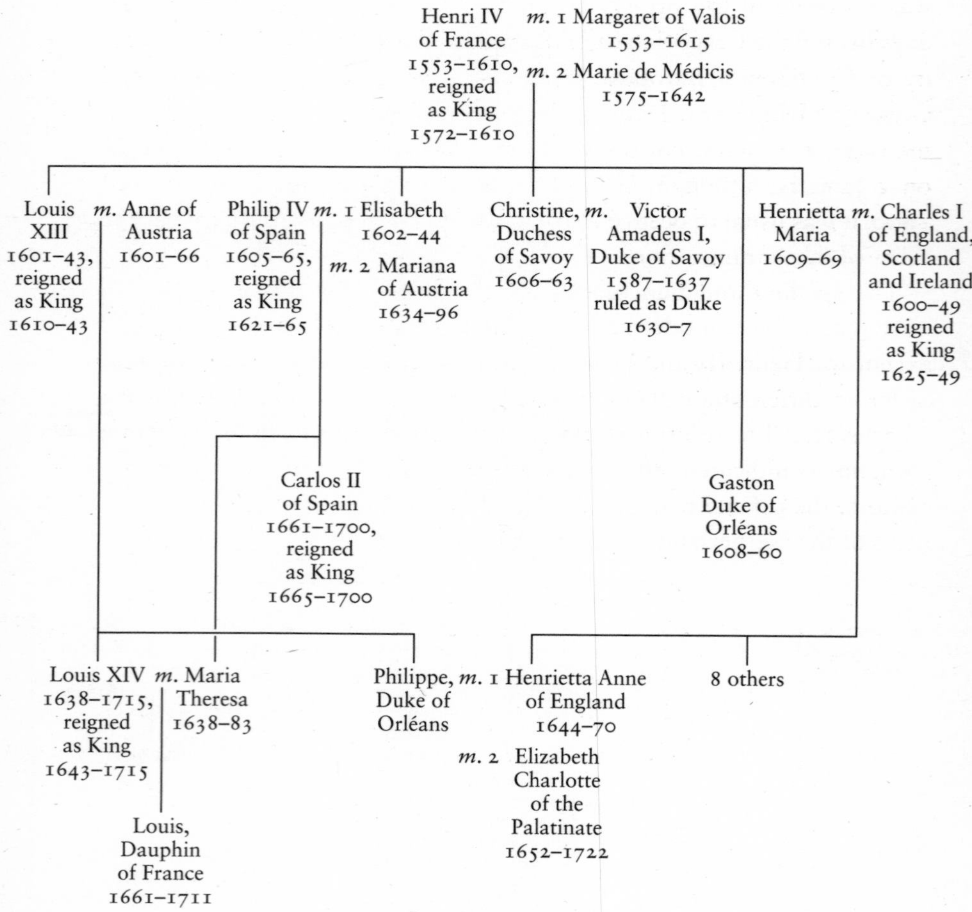

Author's Note

Dates in the text appear in 'Old Style' as per the Julian calendar that was observed in the British Isles until 1752 and, until 1700, was ten days behind the Gregorian calendar that had been adopted in the majority of Continental European countries after its introduction by Pope Gregory XIII in 1582. Dates in the endnotes remain as they appeared in the original sources. For convenience, each new year is taken to begin on 1 January, although, in England until 1752, and in Scotland until 1600, it was usual to deem each new year as starting on 25 March at the Feast of the Annunciation.

The spelling and punctuation of quotations and publication titles have mostly been modernized and the names of monarchs Anglicized, except for Henri III and Henri IV of France and Carlos II of Spain in order to differentiate them from their English Tudor namesakes and Charles II. All translations from French, Latin or Spanish texts are my own, unless indicated otherwise in the endnotes. During the seventeenth century, the official name of the Dutch Republic was the United Provinces of the Netherlands.

Introducing Devil-Land

In 1652, an anonymous Dutch pamphleteer advised that England should no longer be known as 'Angel-land', but instead be rechristened 'Devil-land'.[1] Reversing familiar Latin puns whereby the '*Anglorum*' (English) could be cherished as cherubic '*angelorum*' (angels), Dutch denigration of 'devil-land' drew on xenophobic suspicions, dating back to medieval times, that Englishmen had tails. Diabolic and dreadful, the English were fallen angels: rebellious king-killers who had murdered their monarch, Charles I, three years earlier, and whose republican leaders, most prominently Oliver Cromwell, had declared war against their Dutch commercial rivals. A Dutch print, also published in 1652 and entitled *The Horrible Tail-Man*, depicted Cromwell sporting a strong, scaly tail that was made of gold coins and proved resistant to blows inflicted by his English Royalist, Scottish and Dutch enemies (Plate 16). Nor were denunciations of *duyvel-landt*, or devil-land, confined to foreign critics. A former chaplain to Charles I, Peter Heylyn, repeated a familiar seventeenth-century adage that, while the Spanish monarch was popularly known as '*Rex Hominum*, the king of men', comfortably reliant on his subjects' loyalty, and his French counterpart commonly termed '*Rex Asinorum*, the king of asses' for levying exorbitant taxes on his suffering subjects, the English monarch's relationship to his people was that of '*Rex Diablorum*, the king of devils, by reason of their many rebellions'. Twenty years earlier, an Essex apothecary, Dr Conyers, had been imprisoned for publicly claiming that, since the Holy Roman Emperor was styled 'king of kings', and his Spanish and French counterparts kings of men and asses, 'so the king of England is king of devils'.[2]

To contemporaries and foreigners alike, seventeenth-century England was a failed state: a discomfiting byword for seditious rebellion, religious extremism and regime change. Revisiting English history's most turbulent and radical era, *Devil-Land* re-explores Stuart England's dynastic politics and diplomatic dealings, the leitmotifs of which were instability, mistrust and contingency. In the mid-1670s, the experienced diplomat Sir William Temple declined Charles II's offer of promotion to a Secretaryship of State, admitting to his father that he remained sceptically mindful of the disdain, expressed by the recently assassinated Grand Pensionary of Holland, John de Witt, for the 'fluctuation perpetuelle dans la conduite d'Angleterre' – the unending flux of English affairs – 'which, of all things in the world, I am not made for . . . wrenching myself continually with sudden turns'.[3] In the 1830s, the Whig historian and essayist Lord Macaulay denounced Temple's 'extreme dread of all responsibility' and his readiness 'rather to leave his country in a scrape than to run any chance of being in a scrape himself'. While England 'resounded with tumult' and 'the din of civil wars', Temple 'amused himself by writing memoirs and tying up apricots' in his orchard.[4] But Macaulay's Victorian verdict was delivered secure in the knowledge of a 'Glorious' Revolution that would take place in 1689 and eighteenth-century Britain's emergence as a Great Power. Before 1689, de Witt's disparaging denigration was all too accurate. Seventeenth-century England remained Europe's adventure playground: a troubled nation, by turns too endemically unstable to influence with confidence, but simultaneously tempting as a pawn to be strategically ventured on the chessboard of Continental diplomacy.

Four centuries ago, Edmund Garrard predicted that readers of his *Country Gentleman Moderator* (1624) could plausibly complain 'that in my discourse I have been squint-eyed, as not looking or bending my course any ways direct'; *Devil-Land*'s readers might feel similarly.[5] Like turning a jumper inside out to reveal the untidy seams, tied-off threads and disordered fabric of Stuart rule, this account emphasizes confusion, distrust and trepidation, rather than confidence, buoyancy and assurance. Acknowledging the inevitably selective content of all books, the Elizabethan playwright John Lyly penned a dedication to female readers of his two-part prose romance *Euphues and His England* (1580), pointing out that viewers only ever saw a single side of two-dimensional paintings or arras-hangings. By the same logic, Lyly explained that, if *Euphues*'s readers felt 'some sleights are wanting, I must say they are noted on the backside of the book'.[6] In the prologue to his tragicomedy *Midas* (1592), Lyly developed his textile metaphor by maintaining that, in England, 'traffic and travel hath woven the nature of all nations into ours, and made this land like Arras, full of device, which was broad-cloth, full of workmanship'. Global commerce and overseas travel had prompted the demise of dense, durable and plain English broadcloth, as fashion now favoured intricate foreign tapestries with figurative designs, named after the northern French town of Arras. Detecting similar trends in literary form, Lyly warned that voguish hybridity was replacing traditional pastoral, comedy and tragedy: what had previously appeared as 'several dishes for a feast, is now minced in a charger for a gallimaufrey'. If play-goers found distasteful the resulting 'mingle-mangle, our fault is to be excused, because the whole world is become a hodge-podge'.[7] Less like a thickly woven plush arras-hanging, *Devil-Land*'s metaphorical texture more closely echoes the deliberate 'openwork' of a seventeenth-century doily, designed precisely to expose Stuart England's unstable fissures and vulnerable fragilities.

I

The 'hodge-podge' of external perspective is central to *Devil-Land*'s emphasis on the remarkable degree to which seventeenth-century English history was determined, in Alexander Pope's phrase, 'by foreign hands', who saw recurrent and irresistible opportunities for interference, involvement and even invasion.[8] At the outset of our story, England's narrow escape from the Spanish Armada in 1588 may have prompted hysterical gratitude for the nation's 'miraculous' deliverance, but the biological bankruptcy of its Tudor monarchs led to a foreign dynasty – the Scottish Stuarts – acceding to the English and Irish thrones in 1603. While James VI & I articulated ambitious plans to create a new unitary kingdom of 'Great Britain', his son Charles I relied on foreign policy advisers who were characterized by one critic as variously 'Hispanolished, Frenchified, Romanised or Neutralised'.[9] As bitter internecine divisions spawned civil wars throughout England, Scotland and Ireland during the 1640s, foreign intervention was alternately sought and feared by Royalist and Parliamentarian contingents alike. In 1645, for instance, an Italian archbishop, Giovanni Battista Rinuccini, arrived as a papal nuncio in County Kerry with plentiful finances and arms, seeking to spearhead the creation of an independent, Catholic-controlled Ireland.

Following the English Parliament's trial and execution of Charles I in 1649, the new republic's leaders trod dangerously when trying to evangelize overseas. In early 1651, Philip IV of Spain's ministers were understandably incensed by reports that the Commonwealth's General-at-Sea, Admiral Robert Blake, had arrived in the Andalusian port of Cadiz and brazenly announced 'in the public square there, that, with the example afforded by London, all kingdoms will annihilate tyranny and become republics'. With England's regime change completed, and France convulsed by internal rebellions, Blake recognized that 'the natural gravity of Spaniards rendered them somewhat slower in their operations', but he nevertheless 'gave them ten years for the revolution in this country'.[10] But a decade later, it was Charles I's heir who, after a prolonged and peripatetic exile in a succession of foreign Continental courts, was invited to return to England as King Charles II by the same army that had engineered his father's removal. Over the next quarter of a century, fears that England risked being overrun by an aggressive neighbouring Catholic superpower persisted as traditional Hispanophobia transmuted into frenzied Francophobia, culminating in James VII & II's dramatic attempts to re-Catholicize the British Isles in the late 1680s. Foreign conquest then became a reality when, rather than Spanish or French forces, it was James's Dutch son-in-law and nephew, William of Orange, who spearheaded a successful seaborne invasion that landed at Torbay in Devon in November 1688 and rendered England, as one pamphleteer put it, 'a blank apt to receive any kind of impression'.[11]

England's chaotic predicament was not unique. Amid a 'global crisis', the mid-seventeenth century witnessed the collapse of political authority and the outbreak of popular rebellion engulf not only Continental Europe, but also Ming China, Japan and the Mughal Empire. Shortly before Charles I's execution, the Welsh Royalist James Howell marvelled that so many 'monstrous things' had occurred, 'it seems the whole world is off the hinges'.[12] In 1655, the French ambassador to London, Antoine de Bordeaux-Neufville, doubted the likelihood of his imminent recall, admitting to a colleague that 'one must still apprehend some revolution in a country more subject to change and alteration, than any other in the world that is known'.[13] Eight months later, Bordeaux's long-serving Spanish counterpart in London, Alonso de Cárdenas, warned a newly arrived Venetian envoy, Giovanni Sagredo, that 'I had come to a sea in which a knowledge of the compass and experience of navigation were insufficient for avoiding the rocks'.[14] As an alternative to discredited royal and parliamentary precedents, the republican theorist James Harrington imagined a utopia which he dedicated to England's Lord Protector, Oliver Cromwell, in *The Commonwealth of Oceana* (1656). As Harrington rhetorically wondered,

> What is become of the princes . . . in Germany? Blown up. Where are the estates, or the power of the people, in France? Blown up. Where is that of the people in Aragon, and the rest of the Spanish kingdoms? Blown up. On the other side, where is the king of Spain's power in Holland? Blown up. Where is that of the Austrian princes in Switz? Blown up.[15]

Despite the Stuart monarchy's peaceful restoration in 1660, renewed revolt and rebellion could not be discounted. In 1673, one of Charles II's chaplains, the French-born Huguenot Pierre Du Moulin, acclaimed recent history as 'an age of wonders', and suggested that readers divert their attention from Continental Europe and look 'towards this island' to 'find that this little British world is a small enchiridion or epitome of all the stupendous events that ever happened in the great one'.[16] While Du Moulin feared that Restoration England risked becoming a satellite state of Louis XIV's France, to foreign eyes more generally England's Stuart kings – and their Danish, French, Portuguese and Italian queen consorts – ruled an anxious, fractious and erratic people with a volatile constitutional history and complex confessional politics.

II

Devil-Land places the succession of Stuart rulers centre-stage to illustrate how a nation's insecurities and apprehensions were refracted through their monarchs' diplomatic agendas, different personalities and political associates. To many of their English subjects, the Stuarts were regarded as an alien, imported dynasty that could not be securely relied upon to promote the national interest. Indeed, *Devil-Land* opens with the spectacle of a state execution, as Elizabeth I signed the death warrant of her cousin Mary, Queen of Scots, who was not even one of her subjects, but a former queen consort of France and deposed queen regnant of Scotland, with a strong hereditary claim to the English throne and a track record of fomenting Catholic conspiracies to undermine the Elizabethan regime. Mary Stuart's demise left the vexed question of Elizabeth's eventual succession unresolved and banned from public discussion. But for audiences attending the first performances of William Shakespeare's *Hamlet* around 1600, the anxious fears of a royal court, anticipating imminent regime change and fearing military aggression from foreign enemies hoping to exploit dynastic weakness, were only too resonant.

Although James VI of Scotland's peaceful accession as James I in 1603 averted fears of a bloody war of succession, he had only been on the English throne for fifteen months when MPs in the House of Commons presented a draft *Form of Apology and Satisfaction* disabusing their new king of any 'misinformations' he might have received and firmly denying that 'kings of England have any absolute power in themselves' regarding religious or civil legislation.[17] In the public arena, English MPs, lawyers and polemicists decisively rejected James's unionist vision of 'Great Britain' on the grounds that 'England' would thereby be eradicated as a separate and ancient constitutional entity. On the international front, it was as brother-in-law to Christian IV of Denmark that James successfully acted as mediator – in a role unthinkable for Elizabeth I – to broker the Treaty of Knäred that ended the Kalmar War between Denmark-Norway and Sweden in 1613. That same year, the marriage of James's daughter Elizabeth to the Protestant Palatine Elector Frederick V rendered inevitable England's eventual entanglement in the Thirty Years War which broke out in 1618, following Frederick's misjudged decision to accept the Bohemian crown. A self-styled '*rex pacificus*', James's reluctance to enter the Continent-wide conflict on his daughter's behalf, while simultaneously seeking a Catholic bride for her brother, Prince Charles, was criticized both as a father's dereliction of dynastic duty and for undermining England's international responsibilities to promote Protestant interests.

Although popular rejoicing greeted the failure of Prince Charles's projected 'Spanish Match' in 1623, he went on to marry the French Catholic Princess Henrietta Maria the following year. Residual suspicions that Charles I was 'popishly inclined' gained credence through artistic installations that included the splendidly baroque ceiling of the Banqueting House in Whitehall, painted by the Flemish artist Peter Paul Rubens, who secured the commission while acting as an envoy of Philip IV of Spain during a nine-month diplomatic mission to London in 1629.[18]

As civil wars engulfed England, Scotland and Ireland during the 1640s, the poet John Milton rued that Stuart foreign policy had left England 'naked of our firmest, and most faithful neighbours abroad, by disparaging and alienating from us all Protestant princes and commonwealths' and 'preferring the Spaniard, our deadly enemy, before them'.[19] Resenting continued interference and serial invasions by Scottish Presbyterians and Irish Catholics, the civil wars stimulated a rhetoric of English exceptionalism, championed by 'God's own Englishman', Oliver Cromwell, who denounced Charles I's alliance with Scottish 'Engagers' in 1648 as an attempt 'to vassalise us to a foreign nation'.[20]

Dividing the Stuart dynasty as it divided families across England, the civil wars pitted Charles's Palatine nephews, Prince Rupert and his younger brother Prince Maurice, who served as Royalist commanders, against the siblings' eldest brother Charles Louis, who in 1644 accepted the English Parliament's invitation to travel to London, where he resided in the king's former residence at Whitehall until shortly after his uncle's execution in 1649. Thereafter, the English monarchy was officially abolished as an institution, prompting one propagandist to point out that 'forty years were the English under the government of two Scottish kings', which was 'just as many years as the children of Israel did wander in the wilderness before they came unto rest'.[21] Although the English had successfully thrown off their alien subjugators, the Scots' determination to re-export Charles II as England's rightful king soon posed a new security threat.

After the Stuart monarchy's restoration in 1660, fears that England's national interests risked liquidation only intensified during the second half of the seventeenth century when Charles II relied on secret French subsidies to avoid negotiating with a truculent English Parliament. When renewed conflict broke out between England and the Dutch Republic, a string of English naval defeats culminated in one of the most daring exploits in naval history: the Dutch raid on the River Medway in June 1667 and the humiliating capture of the Royal Navy's flagship, the *Royal Charles*, the carved stern piece of which remains on prominent display in Amsterdam's Rijksmuseum (Plate 25). In Whitehall, Charles insisted to Louis XIV's envoy, Henri de Massue, marquis of Ruvigny, that he was 'standing up for France's interests against his entire kingdom' in 1674. Five years later, he confirmed to Ruvigny's successor, Paul Barillon d'Amoncourt, marquis of Branges, that he would prefer to rely on financial subsidies from the French king than accede to demands from opposition Whig MPs to exclude his Catholic brother, James, duke of York, from the royal line of succession. Hence it was up to Louis to decide 'whether he wanted a republic or a monarchy in England'.[22]

During the short reign of James VII & II – himself a veteran of Louis's French army – the fortunes of Continental Catholicism and Stuart kingship became more inextricably linked than ever. Determined to reverse James's pro-Catholicizing agenda, a group of seven prominent English nobles invited the king's Dutch son-in-law and nephew, William of Orange, to intervene in domestic politics. After William successfully landed a massive invasion fleet at Torbay, Dutch, Danish and Hessian troops occupied London during Christmas in 1688, with all English regiments barred from approaching within twenty miles of the city for over a year thereafter.[23]

In 1687, a Scots Presbyterian exile in the Netherlands, Patrick Hume, Lord Polwarth, had warned William to court English opinion carefully and beware his Stuart credentials, admitting that 'the far greater part, even of those who like monarchy, of that nation carry to this hour a dislike of the race and branches of the Scots family, and if they could fix elsewhere, would certainly reject it'.[24] As Polwarth predicted, even this form of Protestant deliverance posed new risks to the national interest as William thereafter voraciously drained England's resources for Dutch ends to prosecute a Continental war against Louis XIV on an unprecedented scale. Accusing a resuscitated 'William the Conqueror' of having illegally seized the English crown, in 1692 a French polemicist, Eustache Le Noble, compared William of Orange to 'a guilty second Cromwell, under whose power . . . enslaved Albion is moaning'.[25]

By the time of George I's accession two decades later, England's domestic security remained on a knife-edge. Defensive about its legitimacy, the new Hanoverian dynasty feared constant challenge from determined supporters of the exiled James VII & II, known as Jacobites, and found itself obliged to maintain an unpopular standing army at a time of ostensible peace. Once again, England's national priorities were in the grip of a foreign – German – dynasty, but this time permanently.

III

If the Stuarts were regarded as alien foreigners by their own, more critical, English subjects, one priority of this book is to reveal how they were perceived by foreign observers, especially by the large cast of overseas ambassadors and envoys dispatched to seventeenth-century England. Having ruled Scotland as an adult king for almost two decades before succeeding Elizabeth I as English monarch, James VI had already developed extensive diplomatic relations with states including France, Spain, the United Provinces, the Spanish Netherlands, Denmark-Norway and the papacy. His accession to the English throne attracted a visibly enlarged resident diplomatic community in London. Between 1603 and 1625, James received more than 250 diplomatic delegations from over thirty different states while the number of English ambassadorial missions dispatched abroad also increased significantly.[26]

It was, moreover, through foreign eyes that incisive critiques of Stuart rule emerged, since it was precisely those characteristics most distrusted by domestic critics – such as insisting on the absolute power of divinely ordained monarchy and concealing the secret arts of successful statecraft, known as the *arcana imperii* – that were instinctively appreciated by foreign envoys trained in dissimulation and deception. Personifying their own rulers' dignity and authority, seventeenth-century ambassadors continually calibrated the standing of their own country vis-à-vis that of other states through interactions at court, official royal audiences, intelligence-gathering and unofficial patronage. At the same time, ambassadors' assessments were inescapably subjective and distorted, since diplomats deployed a double vision, observing events in their host country in terms of their domestic impact, but primarily as the basis for reports to be returned to their own country. But as Louis XIV reminded his newly dispatched representative to London, Gaston Jean-Baptiste, count of Cominges, in 1663, 'there is nothing in the whole world that does not come under the cognisance and fall within the sphere of an ambassador'.[27]

Although no seventeenth-century government had its own professional consular service, diplomatic ceremonial, codes, techniques and practice were becoming more formalized. Promoted as England's first Historiographer Royal under Charles II, James Howell published a treatise on ambassadorial practice in 1664 which confirmed 'the absolute and indispensable necessity of ambassadors'. Insisting that 'mankind cannot subsist without them', Howell explained that 'if it were not for ambassadors, wars would be endless and enmities everlasting'. Although commenting on royal policy was 'a ticklish and tremendous task' – akin to a man 'walking upon the ridge of a high house, or dancing upon a rope . . . in danger to break his neck' – Howell criticized Charles II's father for notoriously disregarding diplomatic protocol by travelling to the Spanish court incognito when Prince of Wales in 1623. Well-intentioned, but naïve, the prince's presence in Madrid had only 'distracted and retarded' objectives that Howell claimed would, if negotiated by ambassadors, have 'been brought to perfection'.[28]

If sometimes seeming hyperbolic, the intense jealousies attaching to matters of diplomatic ceremonial – such as the hierarchy of seating arrangements at royal events or the perceived quality of royal coaches placed at the disposal of different retinues – reflected the proxy roles that ambassadors performed for their rulers and states. The long-standing rivalry between the ambassadors of France and Spain even bloodied London's streets in 1661 as struggles for precedence in a public procession to welcome a new Swedish delegation resulted in gunfire, French fatalities and threats of renewed Franco-Spanish warfare. Three years later, Secretary of State Henry Bennet (later earl of Arlington) reminded Charles II's representative in Madrid, Sir Richard Fanshawe, of new protocols designed to avoid such clashes; most monarchs preferred 'to have their business done by their ambassadors, than punctilios disputed' ensuring that, only when diplomacy had been exhausted, was it 'fit they rather fight them out with their armies than their ambassadors'.[29] In an era when sovereigns more often ventured overseas at the head of invading armies than enjoyed ceremonial state visits, ambassadors provided peacetime proxies for face-to-face summits. Leading an English delegation resident at Tsar Aleksei Mikhailovich's court in Moscow in 1663, Charles Howard, earl of Carlisle, had tried to circumvent obstructive Russian courtiers and gain a personal audience with the Tsar. Only then, as Carlisle had explained to Aleksei, would he be able to represent Charles II's 'words upon this occasion, as if he and you could meet together' and perceive, through 'that glass of friendship, the most clear eyes of one another'.[30]

Early modern diplomacy's inherently theatrical character provided the Stuarts with regular opportunities to magnify their majesty for domestic and foreign audiences. Yet early modern diplomacy also depended as much on artifice and disguise as decorum. Serving as James VI & I's ambassador to Venice for three terms between 1604 and 1623, Sir Henry Wotton first came to the king's attention when he arrived at

James's court in Edinburgh in 1601, posing as a Florentine envoy named 'Octavio Baldi', ostensibly sent to warn James of an imminent plot to poison him and prevent his accession to the English throne, with Baldi also helpfully bringing the requisite Italian antidote. Having successfully maintained the fiction for three months in Edinburgh, Wotton's reward was prolonged diplomatic service for James. Royal patience was tested, however, when Wotton's witty inscription in a friend's commonplace book – that an ambassador was an 'honest man sent to lie abroad for the good of his country' – backfired when the English pun (whereby 'to lie' could also denote 'to reside') failed to translate into Latin and the epigram was cited in print by a Catholic controversialist as evidence that the English king routinely posted mendacious representatives to lie on his behalf overseas.[31] At the same time, James's pacifist preference for dispatching envoys to negotiate, rather than armed battalions to fight, incurred mocking censure from Continental critics. Visiting the Low Countries to research materials involved in glass-making in the early 1620s, Howell reported news of a satirical play staged by Jesuits in Antwerp in which reports were received of the imminent arrival of extensive supplies for the defeated Protestant Elector Palatine from Christian IV of Denmark, 'the Hollanders' and James. Further enquiries revealed, however, that the Danes were actually intending to 'send 100,000 red herrings', while the Dutch authorities would provide '100,000 cheeses' and the English king would dispatch '100,000 ambassadors'.[32]

Amid growing recognition that a diplomat's official duties might risk compromising an individual's private integrity, the Dutch-born envoy Abraham de Wicquefort produced a popular manual of diplomatic practice, first published in French in 1681 and translated into English as *The Embassador and His Functions* (1716). To define an ambassador's role, Wicquefort cited instructions given to Francis Walsingham before a delegation to France in 1570. While the ostensible purpose of Walsingham's mission had been to seek a formal Anglo-French alliance, Elizabeth I had further tasked him with observing 'all the actions of the king, and the queen regent, as well private as public' that 'might be prejudicial to us and to our state'. 'These few lines' wherein Elizabeth succinctly confirmed 'the two first functions of an ambassador . . . as a messenger of peace on one side and as an honourable spy on the other' were singled out for admiration by Wicquefort – who was himself later convicted of selling state secrets.[33] Although often deployed ironically, Wicquefort's characterization of the 'honourable spy' captured the shadowy boundaries between an ambassador's duty to gather intelligence and the potential for illicit espionage.

During the 1660s, Charles II's special ambassador in The Hague, Sir William Temple, confessed to enjoying his role as a 'moderate intelligencer' while his counterpart in Paris, Ralph Montagu, frankly admitted to Arlington that since 'the part of an ambassador is to be a spy and a tell-tale', he would 'tell you all I hear and learn in this country'.[34] Twice sent to England to represent Charles II of Spain's interests in 1674 and 1680, Don Pedro Ronquillo acknowledged that his ambassadorial role amounted to 'an honourable mode of deception', according to a manual of diplomatic procedure penned by a member of Ronquillo's entourage. While Ronquillo knew that 'flattery is the magnet which everywhere attracts goodwill', all foreign embassies were haunted by 'certain busybodies' that acted as 'conduits and gutter-spouts of political gossip' and were denounced by the Spanish commentator as 'moths and woodlice of the state'.[35]

Inherent within any diplomat's role was also the risk of going native. Having served as Florentine ambassador to Ferdinand V of Aragon's court in the 1510s, Francesco Guicciardini observed that 'ambassadors often take the side of the prince at whose court they are'. Expected blandishments would include valuable gifts and flattering compliments, but Guicciardini also warned about the possibility of a distorted perspective. Since envoys were naturally preoccupied with the politics of a foreign court, 'the ambassador has the affairs of that prince constantly before his eyes', often meaning that 'they assume greater importance than they really have'.[36] In London, James VI & I had only been on the English throne for nine months when reports circulated that he had already spent over £25,000 on gifts to foreign ambassadors, contemporaries particularly distrusting his companionable sharing of bibliophile, oenophiliac and hunting interests with Philip III's representative, Diego Sarmiento de Acuña, count of Gondomar.[37]

By the same token, however, ministers naturally welcomed evidence that domestic events were being reported abroad to English advantage. In 1679, Charles II's Secretary of State, Sir Henry Coventry, apologized to the Irish Lord Deputy, James Butler, duke of Ormond, for forwarding a letter intercepted in the Dutch Republic which observed, in passing, that Ormond's son, Thomas, earl of Ossory, 'has not much brains'. Coventry was, however, more interested in the anonymous correspondent's claim that members of the Dutch States-General were alarmed that their ambassador in London, Conrad van Beuningen, 'gives more credit to the king and his directions, than he does to them'. As the writer acknowledged, if Van Beuningen could be persuaded to 'write with a little more guard it would do well, for we live in an age that even blockheads can see day at the least crevice'.[38]

IV

If its English subjects regarded its Stuart court as suspiciously foreign, they were justified in doing so, not least since successive queens consort at Whitehall each brought different networks of political patronage, confessional complexities and foreign entanglements. James VI & I's consort Anna, for example, could write fluently in Danish, German, Latin, French, Scots, English and Italian. Often overlooked, too, are the cosmopolitan dimensions to the Stuart dynasty's extended family and consorts whose numerous tentacles yielded extensive foreign contact and influence. While the English court had not known a functioning royal family for over half a century at the time of Elizabeth I's death, James's credentials to succeed his English cousin had been strengthened by both his Protestant faith, as well as future heirs in his children, Henry, Elizabeth and Charles. Progeny not only assured posterity, but also diplomatic potential. As James's ambassador in Madrid, Sir Charles Cornwallis, observed in 1608, contemporary political wisdom admired 'princes with large posterity' for 'as many children as any king has, so many more baits they have' to tempt prospective partners in an international marriage market.[39] Acclaiming the Stuart–Bourbon alliance achieved by the marriage of James's son Charles and Princess Henrietta Maria in 1624, one French commentator marvelled that 'two of the most mighty and potent kingdoms of Christendom should be united together, by the most glorious marriage that ever was seen in the world'.[40] But just as the French Valois and Bourbon dynasties faced regular threats from semi-sovereign 'foreign princes' – or *princes étrangers* – notably from the House of Guise, in an English context members of the Palatine branch of the Stuart dynasty provided a parallel destabilizing influence on domestic affairs as a result of the marriage of Charles I's sister Elizabeth to Elector Frederick V in 1613. Several of Charles's overseas ambassadors became confidants and frequent correspondents of Elizabeth, supplying critical commentaries of Caroline foreign policy. From the diplomat Sir Thomas Roe, for instance, Elizabeth received numerous letters, variously sent from Moghul India, Constantinople, Poland, Denmark, Vienna and England. While Elizabeth often started her letters to Roe with the salutation 'honest, fat Tom', she teasingly addressed another ambassador, John Hay, earl of Carlisle, as 'ugly, filthy camel's face'.[41]

Although the marriages of both Charles and Henrietta Maria, and Elizabeth and Frederick, proved remarkably fecund, the Stuarts were not a family renowned for dynastic reliability. Between 1603 and 1700, over twenty-five of their legitimate offspring died before the age of twenty-one including, notably, Charles I's popular older brother, Prince Henry, for whom James had written a manual of kingship, *Basilikon Doron* (1599), but who died at the age of eighteen in 1612. After chronic dynastic insecurity had ended the Tudor royal line, James VI & I became the only one of thirteen English monarchs between Henry VII and George I who lived to see a grandchild born.[42] With the post-Reformation English crown also came Supreme Governorship of the established church, but following the covert conversion to Catholicism of James's Danish wife, Anna, both James's son, Charles I, and grandsons Charles II and James VII & II, all took Catholic consorts in the forms, respectively, of Queens Henrietta Maria, Catherine of Braganza and Mary of Modena, and each queen maintained separate Catholic religious establishments at court. Following the Williamite Revolution in 1688, the English political establishment's startling decision to elevate Protestant confessional conformity over actual patrilineal descent ensured that, by the Act of Settlement in 1701, succession to the English crown was diverted from James VII & II's Catholic descendants to James VI & I's Protestant grandchild through the Palatine branch, Electress Sophia of Hanover, who then died in June 1714. On Queen Anne's death the following August, the era of Stuart rule ended when Sophia's son and heir, Georg Ludwig, became King George I and the first Hanoverian monarch to rule over a united Great Britain and Ireland.

To some extent, the Stuart court's confessional complexities reflected the heterogeneity of religious belief throughout its territories. Although a

Protestant, Episcopalian church was established in all three kingdoms of England, Scotland and Ireland, the majority population in Ireland remained Roman Catholic, while opposition to the Church of England's ecclesiastical hierarchy of archbishops and bishops by a significant proportion of Scots prompted the eventual re-establishment of Presbyterianism in 1690, whereby the Church of Scotland was governed by representative assemblies of church elders. During the mid-century civil wars, the collapse of state-controlled religious conformity had unleashed an explosion of new and radical religious sects, including Quakers, Baptists, Fifth Monarchists and Ranters, while Oliver Cromwell's Protectorate reversed the thirteenth-century expulsion of Jews from England and oversaw their readmittance in 1656. Responsibility for England's growing religious sectarianism was inevitably attributed to foreign influence. The former Thames boatman and Royalist water-poet John Taylor bewailed the extent to which 'religion is made a hotch-potch and, as it were, tossed in a blanket, and too many places of England, Amsterdamnified by several opinions'.[43] As Dutch practices of religious toleration threatened to gain ground, the title-page of Taylor's *Religion's Enemies* (1641) bore a woodcut illustration of an Anabaptist, Brownist, Familist and Papist, each holding a corner of a blanket, bearing a large Bible.

Concerns about English Protestantism's capacity to accommodate myriad doctrinal differences compounded anxieties regarding long-standing fears of domestic rebellion or foreign intervention undertaken to promote Catholic interests. Between 1590 and 1690, Counter-Reformation military victories and missionaries reduced the geographical extent of Protestantism from one-half to one-fifth of Continental Europe's land area.[44] To foreign envoys in London representing Catholic states, Stuart England was now one of a reduced handful of countries inhabited by obstinate heretics. Nonetheless, the Venetian Resident, Francesco Giavarina, was alarmed by the Cromwellian Protectorate's deployment of troops in Flanders in 1658, objecting that 'this mad dog nation, which professes such false and wicked doctrines, keeps gaining a firmer footing in the Catholic states'.[45] While Giavarina's fears proved alarmist, ambassadors representing Catholic states were regularly disconcerted by the variety of worship encountered in England. In 1663, Louis XIV's ambassador, Cominges, winced to see 'this nation, so deeply gnawed and ruined by false religions that nothing short of a miracle will be wanted to save it'.[46]

For their part, English administrations distrusted the influence exerted by Catholic chapels attached to foreign embassies that recruited English-speaking priests and attracted congregations of English recusants who were protected, on extra-territorial grounds, while worshipping inside the embassy's walls, but whose immunity evaporated once they returned to London's streets. At the royal court, the sung Masses held in Catherine of Braganza's chapel drew regular attendance by the diarist Samuel Pepys, who in 1667 was given a private tour of the lodgings for the queen's Franciscan friars by her Grand Almoner and later cardinal, Philip Howard. As well as viewing 'a crucifix given by a pope to Mary, Queen of Scots', Pepys so admired the friars' comfortable living quarters that he 'wished myself one of the Capuchins' (actually Franciscans), while Howard referred 'in mirth' to Pope Alexander VII as 'the Antichrist' and ended the visit by sharing a coach with Pepys, 'talking merrily about the difference in our religions'.[47] But when James VII & II's queen, Mary of Modena, bore a son in June 1688, the 'differences' were no longer those of musical taste or jovial banter. Protestant propagandists, alarmed by the sudden prospect of a perennial Catholic dynasty on the English throne, tried to deny the new Prince of Wales's legitimacy, claiming that he had been surreptitiously smuggled into the royal apartments in a warming-pan, before the king summoned over forty prominent witnesses to Whitehall in October to provide sworn depositions to dispel such rumours. While James worried about reports that his Dutch nephew and son-in-law, William of Orange, 'with the first eastwardly wind, will invade this kingdom', the Lord Chancellor, George, Baron Jeffreys, was among those who formally testified to having attended the queen's delivery where he had observed the baby prince 'black and reeking, so that it plainly seemed to this deponent to have been newly come from the womb'.[48]

Living in constant terror of an international popish plot, whether through dynastic coup, political assassination, foreign invasion or domestic subversion, Protestant polemicists preached a need for constant vigilance. Although medieval fears of physical demons had receded, the godly remained vulnerable to more insidious forms of spiritual corruption. With pernicious priests 'demonised as diabolic servants in Christian camouflage', Protestants feared that susceptible souls might yet be seduced by Catholicism's claims to theological certainty or tempted by the alluring ceremonial, images and incense of its false worship.[49] In

1588, James VI of Scotland published *A Fruitful Meditation* on verses in the biblical Book of Revelation that identified the imminent descent of the Antichrist in the Spanish galleons currently 'prepared and come forward against this isle'.[50] Four years later, the Elizabethan satirist John Nashe likewise invoked the precarity of the 'Narrow Seas' that separated England from its Continental neighbours as a means of imagining the propinquity of Hell. As Nashe suggested, just 'as a man standing upon Calais sands may see men walking on Dover cliffs, so easily may you discern Heaven from the farthest point of Hell'.[51] While James VI's *Fruitful Meditation* was translated into French, Dutch and Latin and published in Amsterdam, La Rochelle, Basle, Halle and Jena during the 1590s, the Scottish king also provided articulations of the theoretical basis and practical workings of divinely ordained monarchical power in *The True Lawe of Free Monarchies* (1598) and *Basilikon Doron*.

Fundamental to James's supernatural conception of the divine right of kings was a parallel appreciation of the concomitant dangers posed by satanic forces and his printed dialogue entitled *Daemonologie* (1597) was the only work by an early modern monarch on the demonic presence in politics and society. Deploying an oppositional rhetoric of contrarieties, the character 'Epistemon' ventriloquized James's warning that he 'who denies the power of the Devil, would likewise deny the power of God' and insisted that, 'since the Devil is the very contrary opposite to God, there can be no better way to know God, than by the contrary'.[52] Two years after James's accession as English king, discovery of the Catholic Gunpowder Plot in 1605 supplied terrifyingly tangible proof of how demonic potential might be activated to wreak destruction.

Yet although providential deliverance preserved both the royal court and Westminster Parliament from Catholic plotters, Devil-land's constitutional practices remained disorderly. After more than a decade of disillusionment, James candidly vented his frustration to Philip III of Spain's ambassador, Gondomar, describing the English House of Commons in 1614 as a rambunctious and unmanageable body, whose meetings comprised only 'cries, shouts and confusion'. Surprised 'that my ancestors should ever have permitted such an institution to come into existence', James admitted, 'I am a stranger, and found it here when I arrived, so that I am obliged to put up with what I cannot get rid of'.[53] Towards the end of James's reign in 1624, the Venetian ambassador Alvise Valaresso wearily reported that, in London, 'matters are in a state of fluctuation, not to say decadence; every day brings its novelty, and the novelties are all but detestable. Nothing is more stable than instability.' Three months later, following the impeachment and conviction of the Lord High Treasurer Lionel Cranfield, earl of Middlesex, Valaresso reported that Middlesex's imprisonment had only lasted a few days, despairingly observing that 'this is the way in England: hardly has the ink dried of a sentence fulminated by parliament than the king annuls it . . . yet it all happens without exciting disgust'.[54]

Even when the Stuarts set Parliament aside in favour of 'personal rule', perceptions of a pervasive arrogance, combined with fatal indecisiveness, exacerbated foreigners' frustrations. In 1637, another Venetian envoy, Anzolo Correr, visited the sickbed of his Spanish counterpart, Íñigo Vélez de Guevara, count of Oñate, who railed 'in a very contemptuous manner about this court', insisting 'there was no school in the world where one could learn how to negotiate with the English' and denying that he was 'capable of understanding their humours'.[55] To some minds, endemic instability was the natural result of Britain's offshore insular geography. In his first-century BC *Eclogues*, the Roman poet Virgil had described Britain as *penitus toto divisos orbe* – 'that land completely separated from the world' – while the Jacobean poet Anthony Nixon referred to 'this sea-walled isle' in 1613.[56] Dispatched to London to congratulate James on his accession as king in 1603, the Protestant Huguenot Maximilien de Béthune, marquis of Rosny, insisted that 'no nation in Europe is more haughty and disdainful, nor more conceited in an opinion of its superior excellence'. Inclined 'to adore all their own opinions, and despise those of every other nation', the English, he speculated, had 'contracted all the instability of the element by which they are surrounded', namely water. For this reason, Rosny insisted that any future French ambassador must be someone 'of understanding and authority, who may compel them to hear him, and force them to be reasonable'.[57]

Prolonged mid-century civil wars and successive republican regimes only perpetuated diplomatic vexations. Resident in London in 1646, the French ambassador, Pomponne de Bellièvre, objected to Louis XIV's Secretary of State, Henri-Auguste de Loménie, count of Brienne, that 'affairs here change so fast that one no longer reckons time by months and weeks, but by hours and even by minutes'.[58] In a tract entitled *A German Diet* (1653), James Howell gave voice to a vitriolic German noble who likewise observed of Britain that 'as the sea tumbles perpetually about the country, so their brains do fluctuate in their noddles [heads], which makes them so variable and unsteady'.[59] Christer Bonde, serving as Sweden's representative in London two years later, complained to Charles X that 'I go round in circles with these irresolute people: sometimes I blaze away at them, at others I take them to my bosom', adding that 'they cannot produce a single argument which I cannot show to be palpably erroneous'. Unlike many of his diplomatic colleagues, Bonde spoke fluent English which he acknowledged 'comes in extremely handy', narrating a conversation with the Lord Protector in which Cromwell had confessed 'that it was a matter of grief to him that he had been so ill-educated that he scarcely ventured to speak any other language than English'.[60]

Cromwell's monolingualism served him poorly given that, as the London-based language teacher, translator and sometime spy John Florio had observed in 1578, English was 'a language that will do you good in England, but past Dover, it is worth nothing'.[61] Just over a century later, a Spanish commentary on diplomatic etiquette recommended that ambassadors learn the vernacular language of their host country 'or at least the language most in use there, as is French in London'.[62] As Louis XIV's ambassador, Gaston Jean-Baptiste, count of Cominges, confirmed to a colleague in Paris, he refused to 'nettle myself by listening to English and I will never learn it'. As Cominges insisted, 'it can only be spoken after long practice in the habit which the English have of flapping their lips, but neither pronouncing nor articulating effectively'.[63]

Not that maintaining Francophone communications muted the diplomatic chorus of confusion and crossness. As Cominges admitted to Louis XIV in 1663, 'it seems to me, every moment, I have been transferred to the antipodes'. Baffled by English politics, the French envoy ventured that, even were Aristotle – famed for his precise and detailed constitutional analyses – 'to come again to this world, he could not find words to explain the manner of this government'. For Cominges, England's government 'has a monarchical appearance, as there is a king, but at bottom it is very far from being a monarchy', prefiguring the famous description of eighteenth-century Britain as 'a nation where the republic hides under the form of a monarchy' by the Enlightenment *philosophe* Charles-Louis de Secondat, baron de Montesquieu, in his *Spirit of the Laws* (1748).[64]

England's unpredictable climate only compounded Gallic gloom.

Whereas Rosny had identified strength of character as the essential attribute for future French envoys, when the plague afflicted London in 1665, Honoré Courtin advised Louis XIV 'to cast his eyes on some broad-shouldered person' and prioritize physical robustness when appointing ambassadors to England. While Courtin hoped 'not to die in London', he warned one of Louis's ministers in Paris that, concerning his fellow envoy Henri de Bourbon, duc de Verneuil, unless a speedy replacement was dispatched, 'French travellers will be one day shown the tomb of Monsieur de Verneuil in Westminster Abbey', while their colleague, Cominges, also suffered 'a chronic rheum which will follow him to his grave'. Having been afflicted by scurvy the previous year, Cominges plaintively feared that 'I shall go home without one single tooth left', after London doctors had dismissively offered 'a pretty piece of consolation' when predicting that the ambassador would 'only lose five or six' teeth with each outbreak.[65]

Visiting Charles II's court from his native Florence in the late 1660s, Lorenzo Magalotti likewise found Restoration England to be a 'perturbed and disorderly machine'. Denying that his bewilderment derived from being a foreigner, Magalotti instead blamed 'the perpetual changeableness with which everything is directed and governed'. He objected that even if 'one tries hard to understand the necessary rules, they change before one can finish getting them into one's head', and equated his experiences to reading a particular time on a clockface, only to find that such a time had already passed.[66]

V

Dominating Devil-land was London, which had around 200,000 inhabitants in 1600, but by 1700 had rapidly expanded to become Europe's largest city, with a population of around 575,000, eclipsing Paris and Naples. Accommodating over 10 per cent of the country's inhabitants by the start of the eighteenth century, London was also around twenty times larger than any other sizeable English city, such as Bristol, Exeter, Norwich or York. The Stuart royal court was not, however, located in the ancient City of London, following Henry VIII's decision to relocate his principal royal residences from the Tower of London and Bridewell Palace west towards Whitehall and St James's Palace in Westminster, close to the Houses of Parliament, the courts of justice and Westminster Abbey. Unlike the French Bourbons, Spanish Habsburgs or Danish Oldenburg dynasties, the Stuarts owned no property in the heart of their capital city, which limited the potential for royal majesty to be showcased through extensive and elegant civic improvement. By contrast, the spectacularly wealthy City of London retained its own jurisdiction and municipal structures, including a Court of Common Council, which was the largest representative body in England after the House of Commons. Moreover, whereas the walled City of London was easily secured with defensible gates and England's premier fortress, the Tower of London, the royal court at Westminster lay dangerously unprotected from the west.

Throughout the seventeenth century, royal policy tried unsuccessfully to deter further development in London to curb the capital's inflated rents and prices and protect against threats alliteratively cited in a Star Chamber prosecution in 1606: 'death, dearth, depopulation, disorder'.[67] A decade later, James VI & I justified legislation that restricted new buildings to existing foundations, arguing that, otherwise, 'with time, England will only be London, and the whole country be left waste'. Monstrously over-sized, England's capital was, in its king's eyes, 'a general nuisance to the whole kingdom . . . like the spleen' which inflated in proportion as the rest of an invalid's body wasted away.[68] Yet recurrent outbreaks of bubonic plague could quickly render London's prosperity precarious: one epidemic that broke out shortly after Charles I's accession in 1625 claimed the lives of over 26,000 Londoners, or a fifth of the city's population. Appealing to the rich seeking rural sanctuary 'in your orchards and pleasant gardens', the dramatist Thomas Dekker described a 'desolate and forsaken city' where 'if one shop be open, sixteen in a row stand shut up together, and those that are open, were as good to be shut; for they take no money'. While a scene of 3,000 armed troops prepared for combat would be viewed with approbation, Dekker wondered what reactions might be provoked 'if we should behold 3,000 coffins piled (in heaps) one upon another, or 3,000 corpses in winding-sheets, laid in some open place, one on the top of each other'?[69]

Although plague mortality failed to derail the capital's long-term demographic expansion, images of armed troops became common during the mid-century civil wars, when the City's resources proved decisive in facilitating Parliamentarian victories and London's rebellious credentials were confirmed. Charles I's disastrous decision to flee from the capital in January 1642 saw the monarch excluded from London until he returned, seven years later, for his trial and execution. As one Royalist pamphleteer warned in 1643, when posterity wondered who had 'pulled the crown from the king's head, taken the government off its hinges, dissolved monarchy, enslaved the laws and ruined their country', the answer would be 'the proud, unthankful, schismatical, rebellious, bloody city of London'.[70] That same year, Howell concurred in attributing chief blame for the civil wars to the City of London, objecting that the swollen metropolis 'bears no proportion with the size of this island'. Exchanging James's splenetic metaphor for an anserine alternative, Howell likened London 'to the liver of a crammed Italian goose, whose fattening emaciates the rest of the whole body, and makes it grow lean and languish'.[71]

Following the Great Fire that ravaged the city in 1666, London's rebuilt streets accommodated growing numbers of coffee-houses whose clientele was dangerously well informed and keenly interested in state affairs. The year before the Fire, the delegation of three French envoys attending Charles II's court had objected to Louis XIV's secretary for foreign affairs that, in England, 'everybody thinks it his right to speak of the affairs of state, and the very boatmen want the milords to talk to them about such topics while they row them to Parliament'.[72] In a world of garrulous Thames boatmen, coffee-house debate, town-criers, local scriveners and politicized Sunday pulpits, the political punditry of England's citizens did not depend on formal capacities to read and write.[73] Named after French *courants*, serial 'corantos' and regular newsletters were themselves foreign imports that dated from the *Mercurius Gallobelgicus*'s publication in Cologne in 1594, before other titles had appeared in cities including Amsterdam, Antwerp, Paris, Venice and Vienna. In the late-Elizabethan era, pamphlets bearing titles such as *News from Spain and Holland, containing an information of English Affairs in Spain* (1593) avoided offering overt polemic but were, rather, framed as fortuitous opportunities for English readers to eavesdrop on overseas debates about their own country. Despite a well-established market in manuscript newsletters, the printed reporting of domestic news remained forbidden in England while attempts to ban the import of foreign newsletters were largely unsuccessful. In 1622, the prolific letter-writer John Chamberlain objected to the English ambassador in

The Hague, Sir Dudley Carleton, that in London 'we know not what to believe of that [which] is done here under our nose, and what is given out today for certain is tomorrow contradicted'. Chamberlain lamented that, in the 'two years that the forge or mint was set up at Amsterdam, we have never left off coining, so apish are we in imitation of what is worst'.[74] Once licences to publish foreign news were granted, English readers could follow Continental events closely. In 1632, Charles I's Master of the Revels, Sir Henry Herbert, apologized to his Herefordshire-based friend, John, Viscount Scudamore, for failing to keep him fully updated with the latest news, but complained that 'the corantos of this time are like the Thames at a full water, or a spring tide rather, with this difference, that the one monthly, the other weekly, overflows'.[75]

For Stuart administrations, the popular addiction to news was a destabilizing threat that encouraged subjects to interest themselves in matters of state and tended to prize novelty over attestation. During the mid-century civil wars, the collapse of pre-publication censorship provoked an explosion of print. For whereas a yearly average of 624 titles had been published in Britain during the 1630s, with additional English volumes printed overseas, when armed hostilities broke out between crown and Parliament, that figure rocketed to 4,038 items printed in 1642 alone.[76] Moreover, all information – whether audaciously printed or whispered rumour – could be denounced as erroneous, misleading and damaging. Royal courtiers and foreign ambassadors alike detected an unwelcome rise in 'false news', fearing that London's Royal Exchange could rival the Rialto in Venice, or the Piazza Navona in Rome, as a notorious site for rumour-mongering. Advising his counterparts in London from the Dutch embassy in Paris, the envoy Willem Boreel recalled in 1653 how, 'when we were last in England, we could hardly trust . . . our own eyes and ears, so much were all things then disfigured unto us, through the conduct of the parliament; so much daubing and colouring over'. The Commonwealth regime had inserted so many 'spies among our domestics, and false informers', that the Dutch delegation had needed to recruit 'secret and confiding correspondents on the other side' to understand 'affairs in their true colours'.[77]

After Charles II's restoration, the Licensing Act (1662) made press censorship a matter of statutory authority rather than royal prerogative, and the king's Licenser of the Press, Roger L'Estrange, made clear his opposition to greater press freedom. In the government-backed

Intelligencer's first issue, L'Estrange warned that undue coverage of domestic politics made 'the multitude too familiar with the actions and counsels of their superiors . . . and gives them not only an itch, but a kind of colourable right and licence to be meddling with the government'.[78] Visiting England three years later, the French physician Samuel de Sorbière doubted the scope of English independence of mind, but recognized that freedom of expression was a cherished shibboleth. As Sorbière ventured, 'the English may be easily brought to anything, provided you fill their bellies, let them have freedom of speech, and do not bear too hard upon their lazy temper'.[79] Habituated to turbulent constitutional change, the English had indeed become incurable coffee-house commentators. Several years earlier, an exhausted Venetian Resident, Francesco Giavarina, had refused to be drawn into political speculation, given that England's 'variations and instability have continued without interruption for so many years'. To foreign observers, Giavarina admitted that 'such constant motion must appear incredible and excite laughter at such a long comedy which must infallibly be turned, one day, into a tragedy'.[80] It is time to visit Devil-land for ourselves.

1

So Strange a Precedent, 1587

In her end is the beginning of our story. Mary, Queen of Scots's execution at Fotheringhay Castle in Northamptonshire on 8 February 1587 was sanctioned by a death warrant bearing Elizabeth I's signature and followed Mary's conviction for plotting harm to the English queen. Embroidered into the canopied cloth of state under which she had sat during various forms of house arrest in different English strongholds for nearly two decades, Mary's motto, *en ma fin gît mon commencement* – 'in my end is my beginning' – had once offered hope that, after her forced deposition as queen of Scotland in 1567, Mary might, one day, regain her Scottish throne and she and her heirs might also realize their hereditary claim to the English crown. But, once Elizabeth decided to put her fellow queen and close relative to death, Mary's motto became a martyr's text.

In Catholic eyes, Mary Stuart should have reigned as rightful queen of England since 1558. Refusing to recognize the dissolution of Henry VIII's marriage to Catherine of Aragon, Catholics regarded Elizabeth's birth in 1533 to Henry's second wife, Anne Boleyn, as illegitimate. Following Boleyn's execution in 1536, and the annulment of Boleyn's marriage to Henry, Elizabeth was also formally declared a bastard by her own father in the Succession Act passed that year. Another Succession Act (1543) then restored Elizabeth to the English royal line – after her Protestant younger brother, Edward, and Catholic older sister, Mary – but legally she remained a bastard when she succeeded her sister, Mary Tudor, as queen of England in 1558. Thereafter, Elizabeth's long reign as England's 'Virgin Queen' was endured by Catholics as the illegitimate tyranny of a Protestant heretic bastard that simultaneously deprived Henry VIII's legitimate great-niece, Mary Stuart, of her rightful English crown.

Nine years younger than Elizabeth, Mary Stuart had acceded to the Scottish throne at only six days old after the death of her father, James V, in December 1542. Although once identified as a potential bride for Elizabeth's half-brother, Edward VI, Mary had instead married the French dauphin and briefly became queen consort of France between 1559 and 1560, before the death of her husband, Francis II, prompted her return to Scotland as the Catholic sovereign of a country undergoing a radical Protestant Reformation. After a second marriage to Henry Stuart, Lord Darnley – a distant cousin who, like Mary, also had hereditary claims to both the English and Scottish thrones – Mary was forcibly removed as queen of Scotland in July 1567 and succeeded by her infant son, James VI, who was thereafter raised as a Protestant.

The following year, Mary escaped from her detention in the island fortress of Lochleven Castle and sought refuge in England where she was initially detained at Tutbury Castle in Staffordshire. In February 1569, Mary was visited at Tutbury by an Irish lawyer, Nicholas White, who noticed the motto '*en ma fin gît mon commencement*' embroidered on the queen's canopied cloth of state, but admitted to Elizabeth's chief minister, Sir William Cecil, that it was 'a riddle he understands not'. White further warned Cecil that 'very few should have access to, or conference with, this lady', given his own susceptibilities to what he described as 'a goodly personage' with 'an alluring grace, a pretty Scottish speech, and a searching wit, clouded with mildness'.[1]

Over the next two decades, Mary's prolonged presence on English soil magnetically attracted serial Catholic conspiracies, which claimed greater legitimacy after Pope Pius V's excommunication of Elizabeth in 1570. But Mary's eventual execution created a dangerous English precedent for Stuart regicide that sent shock waves across Catholic Europe and reverberated for decades thereafter. The international significance of Mary's death was confirmed by the insistence of both the Elizabethan regime and Mary's supporters that her execution must be explained, justified and described 'to the world'. At the same time, both Mary and Elizabeth had been equally as keen to proclaim consistently – if wholly disingenuously – their innocence: in Mary's case, her innocence of the charge that she had ever intended harm against the English queen and, in Elizabeth's, that she was innocent of sanctioning the execution itself.

I

The trial of Mary, Queen of Scots took place over two days in October 1586 and investigated her alleged complicity in the 'Babington Plot': a conspiracy that had envisaged a potential Spanish invasion of England, together with Elizabeth's assassination and Mary's installation as queen. The previous month, the plot's convicted ringleader, a young Catholic named Anthony Babington, and thirteen associates had been executed in London, where the Elizabethan chronicler, Raphael Holinshed, described how, through dismembering, disembowelling and decapitation, 'these venomous vipers' were 'hewn in pieces, their tigers' hearts burned in the fire' and their heads and quartered corpses 'fixed upon poles and set over the gates of London, that all the world might behold the just reward of traitors'.[2] At the same time, Cecil (now Lord Burghley) demanded that parliamentary sanction be attached to official investigations into Mary's complicity 'to make the burden better borne and the world abroad better satisfied'.[3]

Having deemed the Tower of London too risky a venue to try such a prominent suspect, Elizabeth's ministers ordered that Mary be moved from Chartley Hall in Staffordshire, where she had been held since the previous December, to Fotheringhay Castle in Northamptonshire to be tried under legislation passed in 1584 that had rendered involvement in any plot to harm, shorten or threaten Elizabeth's life a capital offence. But Mary denied the right of any English tribunal to try her on the grounds that she was 'an absolute prince and not within the compass of your laws', being solely accountable to God and 'equal to any prince of Europe'. Despite being 'ignorant of the laws and statutes' of England, 'destitute of counsel' and fearful that 'nobody dares or will speak' on her behalf, Mary protested that she was 'innocent and had not procured or encouraged any hurt against' Elizabeth. She further warned the commission of thirty-six Privy Councillors, nobles and judges appointed to question her to consider their actions 'in regard of the world; for England is not all the world'.[4] Mary's claims regarding immunity from prosecution were endorsed by her erstwhile brother-in-law, Henri III of France, who confirmed to his ambassador in London, Guillaume de l'Aubespine, baron of Châteauneuf, that, even were Mary to be tried and convicted of a capital crime, her status as 'a born sovereign princess' would ensure that she remained 'exempt from human jurisdiction and subject only to the judgement of God'. In practical terms, Elizabeth could not proceed in a prosecution 'without offending all the kings and sovereign princes of Christendom'.[5]

Undeterred, the commissioners persevered, alleging that Mary had supplied tacit approval of the plot in an encrypted letter that she had dictated to Babington in July 1586 from Chartley Hall. Cited as the prosecution's main evidence, Mary's letter had been intercepted and decoded by Elizabeth's spymaster, Thomas Phelippes, who had forged a damning postscript to the queen's letter. Making a separate copy for Elizabeth's principal secretary, Sir Francis Walsingham, Phelippes had also drawn a gallows cartoon on the envelope, indicating the likely destination of its royal sender. This was not the first time that the queen's opponents had resorted to forgery, for shortly after her deposition in 1569 a cache of Mary's sonnets and papers – the notorious 'Casket Letters' – was tampered with, if not fabricated entirely, in an attempt to implicate the queen in adulterous complicity in Darnley's murder. While Mary objected that resorting to forms of invisible ink for communication was 'very hazardous and vulgar', in 1584 she had recommended the use of alum (hydrated potassium aluminium sulphate) in covert correspondence with the French ambassador to Elizabeth's court, Michel de Castenau. As Mary had advised, when engaging in 'secret writing', the alum needed to be 'soaked in a little clear water twenty-four hours before one wishes to write' and, to read messages penned in alum, 'it is only necessary to damp the paper in some basin of clear water', while the 'secret writing' would disappear when the paper dried again.[6]

Following the hearings at Fotheringhay, the commissioners adjourned to London where review of the evidence generated a unanimous guilty verdict. A new English parliament met at the end of October 1586 and, equally unanimously, endorsed a motion petitioning Elizabeth to pass a sentence of execution on the Scottish queen. Maintaining that her very existence posed a threat to the English commonwealth, the radical Puritan MP for Warwick, Job Throckmorton, denounced Mary as 'the daughter of sedition, the mother of rebellion, the nurse of impiety, the handmaid of iniquity' and 'the sister of unshamefastness'. She was, moreover, a loathsome foreigner: 'Scottish of nation, French of education, papist of profession, a Guisian of blood, a Spaniard in practice' and 'a libertine in life'.[7] As MPs knew, the Babington Plot was only the latest in a succession of foiled Catholic conspiracies that had sought to eject Elizabeth in favour of Mary, including the 'Ridolfi Plot' of 1571 (spearheaded by a Florentine banker, Roberto Ridolfi) and the 'Throckmorton Plot' of 1583 (revealed by an English Catholic, Francis Throckmorton, and prompting expulsion of Spain's ambassador in London, Bernadino de Mendoza, for his alleged involvement).

Given that Mary was, as indicated, also widely suspected of involvement in the murder of her second husband, Darnley, MPs reasoned that so long as the Scottish queen lived Protestant lives were endangered. Within a single state it was simply untenable, invoking an image later used in Shakespeare's play *Richard II* (1597) to deny 'the fear that is conceived of two suns in one firmament, and of the one rising and the other setting'. The House of Commons Speaker, Thomas Puckering, insisted that Elizabeth must confirm the capital penalty attaching to Mary's conviction, warning that 'to spare her, is to spill us'. Since thousands of ordinary subjects, and even Mary herself, had sworn a Bond of Association in 1585, pledging themselves to defend the English queen's life and to revenge anyone who threatened her, Elizabeth risked divine wrath if justice was not done. Mercy should not be extended to 'this enemy of our felicity' that sought 'to undermine the religion' and 'to supplant us and plant strangers in the place', while lying 'in continual wait to take your life'.[8] In a play written in the late 1590s and initially entitled *L'Écossaise, ou le Désastre* (1601) – 'The Scotswoman, or the Disaster' – the French playwright Antoine de Montchrestien, imagined a 'Counsellor' (presumably Burghley) warning that, for England's Catholic neighbours, Elizabeth's assassination at popish hands would be 'the wish of kings fulfilled, the end of our faith, and the death of our laws'. By contrast, securing Mary's removal would extinguish 'the barbarous plots of those proud, swarthy Spaniards' and would 'bring security to us, injury to Scotland, and terror to France'.[9]

Confirming the death sentence on Mary nevertheless entailed executing another royal woman who, like Elizabeth herself, was a granddaughter of Henry VII and also an anointed queen and former queen consort. In mid-November 1586, Elizabeth was confronted at Richmond Palace by a joint delegation from the Houses of Commons and Lords, bearing a parliamentary petition demanding the death sentence, and she warned them that 'princes, you know, stand upon stages' with their actions scrutinized. Since her 'doings will come to the scanning of many fine wits, not only within the realm, but in foreign countries', they should 'look to persons as well abroad as at home'. Confessing a wish that tensions between Mary and herself might have remained private, Elizabeth offered to 'become a blab' (gossip) and claimed to have written directly to Mary before the trial, offering to protect her in return for a confession and supply of detailed intelligence. As Elizabeth daintily – if implausibly – ventured, had it 'pleased God to have us both milkmaids with pails on our arms', she would have accepted Mary's determination to 'seek my destruction still, yet could I not consent to her death'.[10] Faced by a second visitation twelve days later, Elizabeth remained anxious as to how her actions would be 'sifted and finely scanned by good fellows abroad' only too willing 'to publish pamphlets, libels and books against me, with detestation of me and my government'. Yet she refused to be rushed, or to let parliamentary pressure dictate royal (in)action, and beseeched her Privy Councillors, rather, to 'take in good part my answer answerless'.[11]

On the same day that Elizabeth sought to justify procrastination to baleful MPs, Mary wrote from Fotheringhay to her cousin and leader of the Catholic League in France, Henri of Lorraine, duke of Guise, protesting horrified disbelief that her conviction might result in death and her fate being entrusted to the hands of a common executioner: 'such a death as no-one of our race, thank God, has ever received, still less one of my quality'. Yet if such a hideous eventuality were to result, Mary also recognized the potential potency of what would be acclaimed throughout Continental Europe as an honourable Catholic martyrdom, acknowledging to Guise that 'we, both men and women, may be ready to shed our blood to maintain the fight of the faith'.[12] The previous day, Mary had confided to the Spanish diplomat Mendoza her suspicion that building works in her apartments at Fotheringhay were 'for the purpose of erecting a scaffold on which I am to perform the last act of the tragedy'.[13]

On 4 December, Elizabeth issued a royal proclamation confirming the sentence of death against Mary, explaining that royal consent had been given only after visitations from MPs and peers who had been obliged to fall 'upon their knees, pray, beseech, and with many reasons of great force and importance, move and press us' to pursue this course of action.[14] Two weeks later, the condemned queen wrote her last letter to Elizabeth, requesting that, should she be executed, her body might thereafter be buried in France to lie alongside relatives, particularly her mother, Mary of Guise, who lay in the Convent of Saint-Pierre-les-Dames in Reims. Unwilling to lie in heretic soil, Mary Stuart reminded Elizabeth that, in 'our religion, we set great store by being interred in holy ground'.[15]

As news of the death sentence quickly spread to Continental Europe, Dutch, German and Latin translations of Elizabeth's proclamation were published in Cologne, Middelburg and Leiden, and in the Bavarian city of Ingolstadt.[16] From Frankfurt, the English envoy Sir Horatio Palavicino advised Elizabeth's secretary Sir Francis Walsingham 'to make clear to the world the business of the Queen of Scots' to ensure that 'it may in all times hereafter be by all most fully justified'.[17] Elizabeth's dilemma was outlined in a pamphlet entitled *The Copy of a Letter to the Earl of Leicester* (1586), which was translated into Latin, French, Dutch and German editions that also reproduced the parliamentary petitions demanding Mary's execution as well as Elizabeth's replies in a way that presented the English queen as facing political pressure to confirm the death sentence while being consumed by personal anguish. Yet Elizabeth's signature under the Great Seal was still required before any execution could take place. In Madrid, the Venetian ambassador, Hieronimo Lippomano, took little notice of Elizabeth's rumoured determination to remove Mary, insisting that 'there is no reason in the world why England should commit an act which would rouse all Christendom in wrath against her'.[18]

Setting the whole of Christendom to one side, Elizabeth was also mindful of the likely reaction of Mary's relatives sitting on the thrones of England's neighbours, Scotland and France. In Scotland, Mary's twenty-year-old son, James VI, had recently concluded a league of amity with England via the Treaty of Berwick, which, in July 1586, had guaranteed Scottish neutrality should England be invaded by a foreign power, in return for James's receipt of an English annuity of £4,000 sterling – albeit one that was paid irregularly – and a commitment from Elizabeth that she would take no action to obstruct James's hereditary claim to the English throne on her death.

When first informed of Mary's alleged involvement in the Babington Plot in October 1586, James – who had been an infant when he had last seen his mother – opined, in a conversation reported to Henri III's ambassador to Scotland, Monsieur de Courcelles, that Mary 'might well drink the ale and beer which herself had brewed'. Having sworn the Bond of Association to preserve Elizabeth's life, 'she ought to have kept her promise'. But as a formal trial appeared more likely, Courcelles warned that many of the Scots nobility opposed James's diplomatic rapprochement with England and were ready 'to declare open war against' Elizabeth if she proceeded against Mary. Discussing his mother's case with Courcelles in November, James described it as 'the strangest that ever was heard of, the like not to be found in any story of the world' and asked the Frenchman if 'he had ever read of a sovereign prince that had been detained prisoner so long time without cause, by king or prince her neighbour', that 'in the end would put her to death'?[19] Writing to a Scots agent in London, William Keith, James admitted that 'whole Scotland [was] incensed with this matter'. In a spiteful swipe at Elizabeth's parentage, James suggested that, even if Henry VIII had become infamous for 'beheading of his bedfellow', he still reckoned 'that tragedy was far inferior to this'. Directing Keith to ensure that Elizabeth saw his letter, he nevertheless ventured that, if the English queen could 'see the inward parts of my heart', she would find 'a great jewel of honesty toward her locked up in a coffer of perplexity' to which her future actions would hold the key.[20]

Two months later, Elizabeth replied directly to James, asking him to 'transfigure yourself into my state, and suppose what you ought to do': given the evidence adduced against his mother, should she 'keep the serpent that poisons me?'[21] Yet James still accounted the execution of one divinely ordained and anointed monarch – as well as a woman and blood relative – by another of equal status as unthinkable. Writing to Elizabeth in January 1587, he described the very prospect as a 'monstrous thing' and refused to credit that 'my nearest neighbour, being in straightest friendship with me, shall rigorously put to death a free sovereign prince and my natural mother, alike in estate and sex to her . . . and touching her nearly in proximity of blood'. He reminded Elizabeth that monarchs remained solely accountable to God, and beseeched a change of mind that would render him and 'all other princes in Europe eternally beholden unto you'.[22]

Elizabeth deployed the same tactic of inviting Mary's former brother-in-law, Henri III of France, to imagine himself in her position when considering the Scottish queen's fate. Before Mary's trial, Elizabeth had instructed her envoy to Paris, Edward Wotton, to explain to the French king that, since the Scottish queen's 'long continued malice' daily put Elizabeth's life 'into continual peril', her English subjects were impelled 'importunately to require that some course should be taken' to ensure their sovereign's safety.[23] After the hearings at Fotheringhay, the Venetian ambassador in Madrid, Lippomano, reported that Elizabeth had also offered to send Henri 'the minutes of the trial' to show, bitterly, 'how she had been recompensed for sparing the queen's life before, owing to a dislike of shedding royal blood'. Acclaiming Henri as 'a judge in this case', Elizabeth was convinced that, when the French king had 'examined the crimes' serially committed by Mary, 'he, himself, would pass upon her the sentence which he now, in his want of information, begged her to quash'.[24]

But instead, Henri dispatched to London his most experienced diplomat, Pomponne de Bellièvre, who, in a series of audiences with Elizabeth, unsuccessfully offered a monetary ransom for Mary's life, along with pledges as to her future good conduct, in the hope that the capital sentence might be commuted. In early December, Bellièvre reported that Elizabeth had confessed to him 'that nothing had ever touched her heart so keenly as this last accident' and that she had shed 'more sighs and tears' for Mary than for 'the loss of all her kinsfolk' – in an allusion to the deaths of her father Henry VIII, mother Anne Boleyn, half-sister Mary and half-brother Edward.[25]

II

In the event, false rumours of both an imminent Spanish invasion and Mary's escape from Fotheringhay prompted a panicked response. Although Elizabeth later protested that the document had not been intended for imminent use, she put her signature to Mary's death warrant on 1 February 1587, in the presence of her secretary Sir William Davison. She also instructed Davison to inform his senior colleague, Walsingham, who was ill at the time, quipping in ironic jest that 'the grief thereof would go near . . . to kill him outright'.[26] In turn, Walsingham confirmed to the English ambassador in Paris, Sir Edward Stafford, that the warrant for Mary's death had been signed and sealed. As Walsingham explained, the decision had been taken amid widespread unrest, as 'bruits were spread abroad' that 'the Queen of Scots was broken out of prison, that the City of London was fired, that many thousand Spaniards were landed in Wales' and that prominent English nobles had mysteriously left the capital. Indeed, the general 'stir and confusion' seemed more threatening than at any point in the last hundred years – i.e. since the Battle of Bosworth Field and the start of Tudor rule.[27]

Terrified by the prospect of sanctioning what would widely be seen as sacrilegious regicide, Elizabeth had evidently already requested that Walsingham and Davison write to Mary's keeper, the Puritan diplomat Sir Amias Paulet, requesting the quiet dispatch of the former queen as a pragmatic means of achieving her permanent removal without incurring royal responsibility. But an appalled Paulet had responded by refusing to commit murder and objecting that 'God forbid that I should make so foul a shipwreck of my conscience, or leave so great a blot to my poor posterity, to shed blood without law or warrant'.[28] Unable to secure Mary's demise on the quiet, Elizabeth's only option remained the death warrant. Having surrendered control of events after entrusting the signed document to Davison's custody, the queen did not know that the earls of Shrewsbury and Kent, the Privy Council's Clerk, Sir Robert Beale, and a sheriff, Thomas Andrews, had already set off for Fotheringhay, on the 'apt and colourable pretext' of investigating local disturbances, accompanied by a public executioner who was disguised as their servant.[29]

In the early hours of 8 February – 'this morning of my death' – Mary wrote to Henri III and drew up a final will.[30] Later that morning, her execution took place, attended by around 300 observers, comprising state officials, local gentry and a handful of Mary's personal servants, in a scene of pathos that was constantly replayed in contemporaries' imaginations and provided creative inspiration to later generations of composers, dramatists and writers including Robert Burns, Gaetano Donizetti, Alexandre Dumas, Friedrich Schiller, Richard Wagner and Stefan Zweig. In a contemporaneous account submitted to Burghley, Sir Robert Wingfield of Upton reported that Mary had refused to listen to admonitions delivered by the Protestant Dean of Peterborough Cathedral, Richard Fletcher, and had stated to those attending that she was 'cousin to your queen, and descended from the blood of Henry VII, a married queen of France, and the anointed queen of Scotland'. To her personal servants, Mary had emphasized her unjust betrayal at the hands of foreign persecutors as she continued to protest her innocence, while enjoining them to 'tell my friends, that I die a true woman to my religion, and like a true Scottish woman, and a true French woman'.

After her death, Mary's ladies-in-waiting were denied access to the queen's clothing to minimize any potential martyrological capital, since Elizabeth's ministers were familiar with the searches for relics that customarily attended public executions of Catholic priests. As Wingfield observed, the queen's small lap-dog had, however, refused to 'depart from the dead corpse, but came and laid between her head and shoulders'; having becoming 'imbrued with her blood', the dog was thereafter 'carried away and washed', while the queen's other effects were 'either burned or clean washed'.[31] Mary's embalmed body then remained at Fotheringhay for nearly six months before its interment – contrary to her wishes – in the local Protestant cathedral at Peterborough in the early hours of 1 August, or Lammas Day: a day customarily reserved for settling accounts. Mary's former confidant, Mendoza, denounced the outrageous burial arrangements to the Spanish king while observing that buried alongside Mary in Peterborough was Henry VIII's first wife, Catherine of Aragon, 'who was no less a martyr in her life than the queen of Scotland in her death'.[32] The affront to Philip II – as the most powerful monarch in sixteenth-century Europe – was both confessional and personal; in addition to being a member of Catherine of Aragon's family, he was also the widower of Elizabeth's half-sister and predecessor as queen, Mary Tudor.

Once the execution of Mary Stuart had taken place, Elizabeth protested her innocence in its realization. Enraged, the English queen refused to see close advisers and dispatched Davison to the Tower of London, since he had been the official entrusted with the death warrant's safekeeping. Designated the regime's sacrificial scapegoat, Davison was charged before the Star Chamber with misprision (deliberately concealing a treasonable act) and contempt, for having allowed the warrant to leave his possession. Although acquitted of 'evil intention', Davison was fined heavily, sentenced to indefinite imprisonment and never again served Elizabeth in person. On 11 February, the queen delivered a raging rebuke to her Privy Councillors, prompting Burghley to draft an entreaty to Elizabeth on the Councillors' behalf, which seemed to suggest that the English queen had suffered some form of breakdown. Burghley confirmed, 'with sobbing hearts, our desire to have your grief of mind to cease and to give yourself to your natural food and sleep to maintain your health without which we have no comfort to live or breathe'. Whether or not Burghley actually sent this draft is unknown.

Its emotive appeal was accompanied by justification of Mary's execution on the grounds that 'there was never any worldly act that could bring more surety to your own life, more strength to all your good subjects at home, and your friends abroad'. Meanwhile, Elizabeth's enemies had also been permanently discouraged, 'seeing the anchor of their hold lost, and the foundation of all their intended machinations dissolved'.[33] Defending the English queen's agitated response, the poet George Puttenham admitted that Elizabeth nevertheless remained incredulous 'to think that she, of all Christian princes, should be made the first author of so strange a precedent in justice'.[34] In the version of events presented to the outside world, Mary's execution was an unfortunate 'accident' for which Elizabeth was not directly responsible.

When news of Mary's execution reached London, the bells of City churches were rung and bonfires blazed: such civic festivities were usually ordered to mark royal births rather than a death. Finding himself coerced into supplying firewood for a celebratory bonfire outside his official residence, Henri III's ambassador, Châteauneuf, was disgusted. In Paris, the Spanish ambassador Mendoza denounced this unprecedented 'piece of insolent intolerance' to Philip II, regarding it as insensitive to expect a French dignitary to share in any English triumph, but entirely unacceptable 'to force him to rejoice over the death of a queen of France'.[35] Only days after the execution, Elizabeth also faced implicit censure for shamefully trying to shift responsibility for Mary's death to her advisers in a sermon preached in her presence at Greenwich Palace by Dean Fletcher, who had officiated at Fotheringhay. Taking as his text Matthew 2:19–20, which described the aftermath of King Herod's death, Fletcher allegorically urged Elizabeth to desist from indulging in unjustified mourning and making unworthy claims of innocence. Instead, the queen was advised to focus on the 'land of Israel' and direct her energies to further Protestant evangelism, especially in Ireland and the 'cold parts' of northern England, where her subjects remained 'frozen in their dregs' of popery.[36] On 23 February the Puritan MP Throckmorton, echoing sectarian interpretations of Mary's removal, renewed his warnings in the House of Commons about England's encirclement by Catholic states, denouncing the repugnant 'litter' produced by Mary's mother-in-law Catherine de'Médicis and attacking Philip II's territorial ambitions – even belittling Mary's son James as 'the young imp of

Scotland'. As Throckmorton advised, England needed to strengthen its diplomatic and military support for the Protestant Dutch, there being 'no hope of Spain, no trust in France, cold comfort in Scotland'.[37]

III

Not even cold comfort awaited the English delegation sent to inform James of his mother's death. In late December 1586, Courcelles had reported mounting pressure on the Scottish king by nobles who opposed his apparent appeasement of Elizabeth's murderous intentions. 'In choler', James had responded by denying culpability for his mother's fate: were she to die unnaturally, 'her blood should be upon them [the English], and not upon him'.[38] The following month James had written to Elizabeth, acknowledging that his mother's judicial execution could 'peril my reputation among my subjects'.[39] The English queen's disregard of his entreaties to spare Mary's life obliged James to tread a difficult tightrope between acknowledging incensed calls for vengeance in order to satisfy the honour of both the Stuart dynasty and Scotland's independent sovereignty, while also trying to preserve the recent achievement of Anglo-Scottish amity and his own claim to the English throne on Elizabeth's death.

When news of Mary's demise reached Edinburgh, crowds reacted angrily to the English execution of a Scottish Stuart, albeit one whose queenship they had forcibly overthrown twenty years earlier. The courtier Robert Carey, dispatched by Elizabeth to inform James in person, was denied entry at the Scottish border, aware that if he 'had gone in', he would 'have been murdered'.[40] On 14 February, Elizabeth wrote directly to James, wishing he could know 'the extreme dolour that overwhelms my mind, for that miserable accident, which far contrary to my meaning' had befallen his mother, beseeching him to acknowledge 'how innocent I am in this case'.[41] Several weeks later, Walsingham was informed by an Edinburgh correspondent, Robert Carvell, that James continued to refuse audience to English envoys, being as yet unclear 'that the queen is as sorry for his mother's death as he was informed she was'.[42] Circulating anti-English verses reflected popular anger and Carvell enclosed a halter of hemp that had accompanied a libel addressed

To Jezebel, that English whore
Receive this Scottish chain
As presages of her great malheur
For murdering our queen.[43]

According to the Scots lawyer David Moysie, several Scots Privy Councillors were eventually sent to meet Elizabeth's envoy in mid-March, when Carey confirmed that, since 'the queen was very sorry for taking Queen Mary's life', if James were to indicate an appropriate form of satisfaction, 'it should be granted'. Disconcertingly for Carey, he was nevertheless informed that, by 'the custom of Scotland', it was not for James to make such a suggestion; rather, the party responsible for a murder should make a compensation offer to be considered by the victim's family and friends. Given Mary's eminent lineage, the councillors added that any offer from Elizabeth would not only need to be reviewed by James, but also by the Scottish nobility and Parliament, as well as by James's relatives in foreign royal houses who were 'as well interested as he'.[44]

Depictions of Elizabeth as Jezebel – the wicked female ruler incarnate – also circulated in Paris, where one poet objected that 'from the cradle, there has not been a day' that Elizabeth had not 'vomited some outrage'. In this instance, she had proceeded 'against all law, made a prisoner and killed' a queen who 'excelled your own lineage'.[45] Despite mounting a propaganda campaign to publicize the reasons for passing sentence on Mary throughout Europe, the Elizabethan regime was equally determined to suppress accounts of the execution itself. In mid-January, all English ports had been closed to forestall communications with the Continent and Mary's servants were detained at Fotheringhay for six months. Accordingly, as the Gallicized Scot Adam Blackwood later acknowledged, 'not knowing what had happened', verse-writers, hagiographers and artists 'could only publish what they conjectured and imagined' had occurred at Fotheringhay.[46] Blackwood himself composed at least one of fifty or more short verses, collectively termed the 'De Jezabelis', poems that reviled Elizabeth as an immoral, heretic bastard, responsible for Mary's death.

In Paris, the English ambassador, Stafford, reported that 'truly, I find all men here in a fury', with ubiquitous predictions of 'some great harm' likely to redound on Elizabeth. A month later, Stafford confirmed to Burghley that he had never known an event more detested by 'little, great, old, young and of all religions, than the Queen of Scots's death, and especially the manner of it'. Weeks later, Stafford restated to Walsingham his alarm, as those of 'what religion, state, passion, affection or age soever' continued to debate the execution 'in public or in private, speaking against it and in hard terms, especially against the manner of it'. But the ambassador's litanies drew only rebuke from Walsingham who demanded that Stafford stop supplying Elizabeth with pretexts to become 'so much the more exasperated' with her councillors. Rather, Walsingham directed Stafford to find evidence to support rumours in Paris regarding James VI's likely absolution of Elizabeth from blame, since that type of report 'did wonderfully content her Majesty, who desires nothing more than to have it generally conceived that she had least part in the action'.[47] Stafford's hysterical reports of French outrage may also have been deliberately exaggerated to deflect attention from Spanish antipathy towards England, since, by March 1587, Stafford had become a double agent, receiving, via Mendoza, at least one substantial payment of 2,000 crowns for the first of serial supplies of English intelligence to Madrid.[48]

Convincing Continental Europe of Elizabeth's personal innocence was challenging. In Madrid, Philip II acknowledged to Mendoza that he had been 'deeply hurt' by news of Mary's death and judged it 'very fine' for Elizabeth 'now to want to give out that it was done without her wish, the contrary being so clearly the case'.[49] In the Spanish Netherlands, a member of Philip's Council of State, Charles, count of Aremburg, informed Henry Stanley, fourth earl of Derby, that it would have 'been better done to have poisoned' Mary 'or to have choked her with a pillow, but not to have put her to so open a death'.[50] From Ostend, Walsingham received reports that English and Scottish soldiers, currently assisting the Dutch in their struggle to secure independence against Spain, had been outraged at news of Mary's death, making 'lewd speeches' and claiming 'that they desired to serve against the English as well as against the Spaniards to revenge their queen'.[51] In Rome, the Venetian envoy, Giovanni Gritti, confirmed that Pope Sixtus V 'shows great grief' at news of Mary's death, but was consoled by the expectation that Henri III would 'desire to avenge this deep injury' on his former sister-in-law's behalf or, at the very least, would not impede other powers intent on attacking England.[52] In Paris, Mendoza confirmed the indignation expressed by Henri's normally placid and restrained councillor

Bellièvre that Elizabeth seemingly believed 'that monarchs' heads were laced on, to have done such a knavish thing as to dare to lay hands on the queen of Scotland'.[53] In his *Historia de lo Sucedido en Escocia e Inglaterra en cuarenta años que vivió María Estuardo* (1589) ('History of Events in Scotland and England during the forty-four years Mary Stuart lived'), the Spanish chronicler Antonio de Herrera y Tordesillas predicted that 'the day of punishment will come for this monster Elizabeth, who has not only turned Great Britain upside down, but also by extending her diabolic fury beyond its borders, has unsettled her neighbours'. Invoking classical mythology to find comparable instances of royal wickedness, Herrera compared Elizabeth to the Egyptian king Busiris, who welcomed strangers to his home 'only to murder them afterwards'.[54]

While Mary's body remained unburied in England, Henri organized a memorial service at the French court, within a month of the queen's execution, to which all foreign ambassadors were invited and instructed to appear in mourning dress. With foreign envoys also invited to special vespers and a morning Mass, 'the ceremony was truly regal' in the view of Venice's representative, Giovanni Dolfin.[55] In another memorial Mass held at Nôtre-Dame Cathedral in Reims, Archbishop Renaud de Beaune of Bourges delivered an emotional eulogy, later published, that acclaimed Mary's links to the Guise dynasty and exhorted the congregation to interpret her death as a martyrdom. In Normandy, Mary's confidante and former Catholic Bishop of Ross, John Leslie, preached a funeral oration in Scots – later published in French translation – that emphasized Mary's martyred commitment to Catholicism and her innocence of involvement in any conspiracies. As the Parisian diarist Pierre de L'Éstoile observed, by preachers across the city, Mary was 'canonized daily in their sermons', with sympathizers 'loudly' insisting that she had been executed solely on account of her Catholicism.[56]

Graphic visual reconstructions of Mary's last moments – as she placed her head before the executioner – were also soon circulating in the *Theatre of the Cruelties of the Heretics of our Time* (1587), produced in Antwerp by the Anglo-Dutch Catholic publisher, Richard Verstegan, with captions acclaiming Mary as 'the most serene queen of Scotland' and 'the legitimate heir to the English throne', before putting 'into the hands of Christian princes' the duty to seek revenge against the 'barbarian tyrant' responsible for the queen's death.[57] In scenes of mounting grisliness, Verstegan's illustrations depicted the many arrests, interrogations, imprisonments, condemnations and executions of Catholics in England, of whom Mary was now the most distinguished victim. From Paris, Stafford complained to Walsingham in June that pictures of the gruesome manner in which the English executed 'traitors, Jesuits and priests, which they call Catholics and martyrs' were prominently displayed in the cloister of Saint-Séverin church in Paris. According to Stafford, around 'five thousand people a day come to see' the images, to which exiled English recusants 'point with a rod and show everything; affirm it to be true and aggravate it'. Six months later, Walsingham received similar reports from an English agent in Venice, Stephen Powle, who had seen 'sundry pictures of the Scottish Queen to be sold' in the city, together with verses – apparently by a Scottish Jesuit, William Crichton – extolling Mary's virtues with 'an exhortation to all princes of the earth to endeavour a revenge against her royal person and estate'.[58]

IV

Rather than permanently eliminating a problematic rival queen, Mary's execution left unfinished business. In the long term, Elizabeth's reluctance to invoke parliamentary authority to proceed against Mary, and her attempts to disregard the statutory penalties attaching to the queen's conviction, inevitably diluted the prerogatives of clemency and mercy traditionally claimed by divinely ordained monarchs. A dangerous precedent had been created that would be dramatically extended, over six decades later, when Mary's grandson, Charles I, was placed on trial by that same English Parliament and sentenced to death by a warrant signed by fifty-nine commissioners, later denounced as regicides. In the short term, the emotive resonances unleashed by Mary's execution inspired English writers such as Henry Constable who – despite serving as 'a courtier maintaining a solid Protestant façade', commissioned to rebut Counter-Reformation polemic – penned manuscript 'spiritual sonnets' shortly after the execution, acclaiming Mary as a 'blessed martyr' who 'as a queen became a sacrifice / Like to a lamb unto a scaffold led'.[59] In a poem entitled 'Decease, Release', the English Jesuit Robert Southwell imagined Mary as an anonymous narrator called 'N.', insisting that

Alive a Queen, now dead I am a Saint,
Once 'N.' called, my name now Martyr is,
From earthly reign debarred by restraint,
In lieu whereof I reign in heavenly bliss.
. . .
By death from prisoner to a prince enhanced,
From Cross to Crown, from thrall to throne again.
My ruth, my right, my trap, my stile advanced,
From woe to weal, from Hell to Heavenly reign.[60]

Overseas, the teenage Maffeo Barberini, who would become Pope Urban VIII in 1623, penned a Latin funeral elegy for Mary which expressed confidence that, although 'the axe strikes you undeservingly' and appropriate funeral rites had been disregarded, 'don't let Scotland cry in sorrow', heavenly reward would follow.[61] Around the same time, an elaborate and colourful funerary monument was erected in Sint-Andrieskerk (St Andrew's Church) in Antwerp, then part of the Spanish Netherlands, carved from black marble and alabaster and sumptuously gilded. The monument marked the final resting-places of 'two noble British matrons' who had been erstwhile members of the queen's entourage before 'flying from their homeland to the protection' of the Spanish king, but also included a detailed portrait of Mary, painted on copper. The accompanying inscription confirmed that the queen's 'martyrdom' arose as a result of 'the perfidy of her kinswoman Queen Elizabeth, reigning there, and through the hatred of an heretical parliament'.[62]

But in 1587, others demanded more immediate justice. In France, members of the Catholic League, led by Mary's Guise cousins, insisted that her execution made plain the urgent need to end Henri III's toleration of Protestant Huguenots. The brutal images of Protestant persecutors presented in Verstegan's *Theatre of the Cruelties* were taken to prefigure the horrors likely to be unleashed on Catholics should the childless Henri III be succeeded by the Protestant Henri of Navarre. As the number of polemical Catholic tracts printed in France increased fourfold between 1586 and 1589, around a quarter focused on accounts of Mary's execution and the persecution suffered by English Catholics.[63] Moreover, when Mary's personal servants were released from arrest and arrived in France during the autumn of 1587, further personal testimonies of her final days and details of the posthumous autopsy performed on her body were incorporated into Blackwood's *Martyrdom of the Scottish Queen* (1587) and *The Death of the Scottish Queen and Dowager Queen of France* (1588), which went through at least twelve editions by 1589.

In Edinburgh, when the Scottish Parliament convened in July 1587, Henri III's ambassador, Courcelles, reported that all the assembled commissioners had knelt down before James 'and prayed him to revenge the injury which he had received, with them, by the murder of the late queen his mother' and 'promised him, with one voice, to employ their lives and goods' to this end.[64] The following January, one of Mary's attendants, Jane Kennedy, who had witnessed the execution, met James in Edinburgh. From Berwick-upon-Tweed, the town's English governor, Henry Carey, Baron Hunsdon, reported that Kennedy was declaring 'openly how the queen was martyred and mangled by the executioner' and did so 'with such speeches and gestures as moved everybody to mislike greatly' what they were hearing. Dismissing the Scottish king's reassurances of restraint as 'plain dissembling', Hunsdon warned Elizabeth that, since James intended 'to revenge the death of his mother if ever he be able', urgent military reinforcements should be sent to 'make her borders presently strong'.[65]

The most immediate likelihood of imminent revenge emanated, however, from Spain, where Philip II now seemed the most likely Catholic claimant to succeed Elizabeth on the English throne. In August 1587, the Venetian envoy in London, Lippomano, relayed reports that Philip had requested documents from the royal archives in Simancas in order to review his dynastic right to the English throne amid speculation 'that his claims are extremely well founded'.[66] Writing to Mendoza in May 1586, Mary had indicated her intention – if her son James remained a Protestant – to 'cede and grant by will my right to the succession of this crown' to Spain, if Philip undertook to advance Catholic interests in England.[67] Although Mary's claim later fuelled fruitless searches for the queen's 'phantom will' confirming these arrangements, Philip was, in any event, already incensed by the English on account of their support for the rebellious Dutch against Spain, as well as the activities of notorious English corsairs, such as Sir Francis Drake, who harried Spanish ships and coastal ports.

Ten days after news of Mary's execution reached Madrid, longstanding plans for an attack on England were resuscitated and orders were sent to naval officers throughout Spain's Iberian and Mediterranean territories, demanding that resources be directed towards marshalling a sizeable fleet. As Philip's secretary Don Juan d'Idíaquez observed to the future commander of the Armada that sailed in 1588, Alonso Pérez de Guzmán, duke of Medina Sidonia, Philip now judged the English threat to be such that 'defensive measures cannot deal with everything. Rather, it obliges us to put their house to the torch.'[68]

Auspicious conditions were confirmed by a newsletter from England, received by Philip's court in November 1587, claiming that 'the people have never been so alarmed before, nor so little prepared to defend themselves as they are now'. Further intelligence indicated that Elizabeth was now convinced that 'the Pope and the kings of Spain and France were in league to ruin her' and confessional warfare was unavoidable. Although Elizabeth regarded James VI as 'neither fish nor flesh himself' when it came to siding unilaterally with Protestant or Catholic powers, among her advisers 'it is said secretly that if the Spanish Armada comes, he will welcome it'. Put simply, one execution necessitated another. The unnatural death of Mary, Queen of Scots could now legitimate the delayed realization of Pope Pius V's sentence of execution issued against Elizabeth. Among Medina Sidonia's papers was a document intended to inspire confidence among those involved in the Armada's preparations. Accompanying in spirit all those setting sail for English shores would be 'the blessed and innocent, Mary, Queen of Scotland, who, still fresh from her sacrifice, bears copious and abounding witnesses to the cruelty and impiety of this Elizabeth, and directs her shafts against her'.[69]

2

The Enterprise of England, 1588

Non Sufficit Orbis – 'the world is not enough' – read the ominous legend on a triumphant Spanish medal struck in 1583 to celebrate the global extent of Philip II's dominions. After the death of Sebastian I of Portugal in 1578, Philip had annexed the Portuguese imperial territories to create a vast Catholic empire that included the renamed, now eponymous Philippine Islands, and extended 'from Madrid through Mexico, Manila, Macau and Malacca to India, Mozambique and Angola, and so back to Madrid'.[1] But following Francis Drake's remarkable circumnavigation of the globe between 1577 and 1580, Philip II needed a defensive strategy to protect his possessions from incursion. The Spanish no longer had the world to themselves. After suppressing residual resistance to Spanish rule on the Azorean island of Terceira in 1583, Álvaro de Bazán, marquis of Santa Cruz, had advised Philip to 'follow up this victory by making arrangements for the invasion of England next year'.[2]

To the English, the threat of Spanish conquest was not new. Nor was Philip an unknown quantity, having been granted the title 'King of England' by Parliament during his marriage to Mary Tudor between 1554 and 1558. Indeed, Philip's own Lancastrian lineage had been publicly acclaimed when the newlyweds had witnessed a London pageant in 1554 that depicted the couple's shared genealogical descent from Edward III.[3] During his first year in England, Philip had not only survived a major Protestant rebellion and an assassination attempt, but had also started to acquire a library of works describing seaborne invasions that had threatened successive English administrations since the time of William I's successful conquest in 1066. After Mary Tudor's death in 1558 and with the accession of her Protestant half-sister, Elizabeth I, Philip maintained a keen interest in English affairs. When Pope

Pius V excommunicated Elizabeth in 1570, and issued the papal bull *Regnans in Excelsis*, releasing all subjects from allegiance to the queen's orders, mandates and laws, Philip protested that Pius should have consulted him first, knowing 'I could give him better information and advice on that kingdom, and on its affairs and people, than anyone else'.[4] As Philip's anti-English animus grew, serial conspiracies aimed at removing Elizabeth and installing a Catholic replacement often involved some form of Spanish-sponsored invasion, which became known in Madrid as *la empresa de Inglaterra*: 'the Enterprise of England'.

I

The execution of Mary, Queen of Scots on Elizabeth I's order provoked a Continental chorus of calls for the execution of Pius's papal bull. In 1588, the Spanish Jesuit Pedro de Ribadeneyra insisted that Mary's recent execution supplied 'so heinous and so extreme an exemplar of cruelty as was never yet seen of or heard among barbarians, infidels or madmen'. Ribadeneyra's *Historia Eclesiástica del Cisma del Reino de Inglaterra* (1588) ('Ecclesiastical History of the Schism of the Kingdom of England') was published simultaneously in six Habsburg-ruled cities – Madrid, Valencia, Zaragoza, Barcelona, Antwerp and Lisbon – and warned readers that there could be 'no security or foundation in crowns, sceptres or territories' if an anointed queen of Scotland and France could be put to death 'at the hands of the executioner of London'. In a private letter intended as an exhortation to Spanish soldiers taking part in a future Armada, Ribadeneyra deemed it no less urgent for Spain to prioritize 'casting the Devil out of England than in having cast him out of the Indies'. Incensed by the heretical and sacrilegious dimensions of Mary's execution, he urged Spanish forces to mete out due punishment and 'behead a woman' (Elizabeth) who had 'ordered the beheading of a queen of France and Scotland for being a Catholic, her own niece and successor, who entered her realm under her devilish word'. Under Elizabeth, England was 'a nest of vipers, a den of thieves, [and] a ditch and cesspit of poisons and noxious vapours'.[5]

Outside Spain, however, Philip needed to convince foreign powers, including a sceptical papacy, that his 'enterprise of England' was not simply yet another expansionist bid to swell Spain's territories or to promote his own hereditary claim to succeed the childless Elizabeth. It was, rather, a pious crusade to eradicate Protestant heresy and avenge Mary Stuart's death: his infantry units known as *tercios* would land on English shores as Catholic liberators, not Spanish conquerors. Accepting this rationale, in 1587 Pope Sixtus V offered Philip's ambassador in Rome, Enrique de Guzmán, count of Olivares, a papal subsidy of 1 million escudos, one half of which would be paid when Spanish troops landed on English, Scottish or Irish soil, with the remainder to be paid by instalment. The following June, Elizabeth's administration were alerted to reports that 12,000 copies of a broadsheet repeating the *Declaration of the Sentence and Deposition of Elizabeth, the Usurper and Pretended Queen of England* (1588) had been printed in Antwerp, renewing the papal sentence of excommunication.[6]

A rhetoric of confessional crusade notwithstanding, Spanish aggression was also fuelled by damage sustained to Philip's reputation by the recurrent activities of English privateers. The apparent ease with which Sir Francis Drake had attacked Spanish possessions in Galicia, the Canary and Cape Verde islands, present-day Colombia and Spanish Florida in 1585 had only been compounded by Drake's recent attack on the Andalusian harbour of Cadiz in April 1587, resulting in the destruction of twenty-four Spanish ships, intended as part of a future Armada against England. As the Venetian ambassador in Madrid, Hieronimo Lippomano, observed the following month, Drake's depredations would 'raise many considerations in the minds of other princes' regarding the vulnerability of Philip's possessions, and could also foment rebellious thoughts among Spaniards themselves. As Lippomano reported, it was generally remarked that 'this woman has shown the world how they can strike at the Spaniard in Flanders, in the Indies and in his own house'.[7]

In northern Europe, Elizabeth had directly undermined Spanish sovereignty in the Low Countries by supplying financial, military and political support to Protestant Dutch rebels seeking to overthrow Spanish Habsburg rule. Through a series of agreements known as the Treaty of Nonsuch in 1585, the queen's ministers had supplied 4,000 soldiers, 400 horse and an annual subsidy of 600,000 florins, together with an English Governor in the form of Robert Dudley, earl of Leicester. By way of security, the Dutch had ceded English control over the Zeeland fortress of Rammekens, two 'Cautionary Towns', Briel and Vlissingen, and agreed to lend twenty ships if England was attacked by Habsburg forces.

To hostile Spanish minds, exterminating Elizabeth was essential to preserve their country's potent reputation. Invoking Aesopian imagery, Ribadeneyra insisted that since 'the entire world fears our power and hates our greatness', defeating 'this mad and perverse boldness' would ensure that other enemies would 'make no move, nor will the beetles seek to do battle with the eagles, nor the rats with the elephants'. By contrast, 'so long as this wicked spider lives in England, weaving her plots and spinning webs of treason and chaos in Flanders' and elsewhere, perceptions of Philip's puissance were damagingly compromised.[8]

Bellicose warmongering between England and Spain was nevertheless accompanied by serial attempts at diplomatic resolution with at least five separate peace negotiations started between 1585 and 1588. Elizabeth also sustained alliances with neighbouring powers, Henri III of France and James VI of Scotland, finding a common cause in resisting Spanish expansionism. Writing to Walsingham in early 1588, the English Lord High Admiral, Charles Howard, Baron Effingham, wearily concluded that he had 'made of the French King, the Scottish King, and the King of Spain, a Trinity that I mean never to trust to be saved by'. Howard distrusted Habsburg diplomatic initiatives, doubting that 'there was never, since England was England, such a stratagem and mask made to deceive England withal as this is of the treaty of peace'.[9] The previous month, Walsingham had been warned by an English agent sent to Venice, Stephen Powle, that 'a Spanish peace is more dangerous than manifest hatred', suspecting that Philip was 'following that devilish advice of Machiavelli, to join the lion and fox in one body, in making show of peace and carrying secretly in heart, war'.[10] In late 1586, Lippomano had opined from Madrid that, despite Philip's well-known desire to menace Elizabeth, 'two considerations of great weight present themselves: the questions of how and when'. In Lippomano's view, 'the French, from thinking too little, often fail', while 'the Spanish, from thinking too much, often miss their opportunity'.[11] Over a year later, the Holy Roman Emperor's ambassador in Madrid, Hans Khevenhüller, admitted to Emperor Rudolf II that, whereas in 1587 he had been 'right when I predicted the Armada would not leave that year, now in 1588, I do not trust myself to make a prediction'. Unable to fathom Spanish intentions towards England, Khevenhüller sensed that 'all these preparations are more to facilitate and preserve a good peace than for any other reason'.[12]

Unfortunately for the English, while the English embassy in Paris was

Elizabeth's only permanent diplomatic presence in Catholic Europe, the English ambassador, Sir Edward Stafford, had, by early 1587, started selling intelligence to Spain as a means of tackling mounting personal debts. In April, Stafford warned Philip's representative in Paris, Bernadino de Mendoza, that it had been 'suggested to Drake that Cadiz was a suitable port' to attack since 'anyone who arrived in force might burn any ships that were there'. Stafford's accurate alert was hurriedly passed on to Madrid, and reached Philip's court only the day after Drake's raid on Cadiz, suggesting that – had Drake been delayed by adverse weather – his attack might have been forestalled. As well as sharing state secrets, Stafford collaborated with Mendoza to spread false information, informing Elizabeth's ministers in January 1588 that Philip's Armada had been disbanded, although this claim was distrusted by Lord High Admiral Howard (who happened to be Stafford's brother-in-law), suspecting a deliberate 'device, knowing that a little thing makes us too careless'.[13]

The following April, Stafford reported apparent scepticism in Paris that Philip would launch his Armada, citing rumours that 'their great elephant will bring forth but a mouse'. According to Stafford, it was rumoured that the Spanish king 'in his sleeve laughs at the Pope, that he can make such a fool of him', organizing processions and promising papal jubilees for an enterprise 'which he durst never think of in deed, but in show, to feed the world'.[14] As speculation regarding the Armada's intended destination shifted from north Africa to the Indies, obtaining reliable information became even more difficult following the 'Day of the Barricades' in May 1588, when Philip's ally, Henri of Lorraine, duke of Guise, seized political control in Paris, prompting Henri III's panicked flight from the city. With effective power wielded by the Catholic League and Guise – cousin to the executed Mary, Queen of Scots – Philip hoped that, rather than France remaining neutral during any Anglo-Spanish hostilities, strategically important Channel ports might now be controlled by pro-Spanish interests.

II

Information, misinformation and disinformation combined to create pervasive uncertainty regarding the likely scale and direction of any Spanish attack on England. In April 1586, an English agent at the Grand

Duke of Tuscany's court in Florence, Sir Anthony Standen – who operated under the alias 'Pompeo Pellegrini' – is thought to have been the means by which Elizabeth's ministers were supplied with a copy of a draft invasion strategy, drawn up by the marquis of Santa Cruz, only weeks after it had first been proposed to Philip. With clandestine copies also circulating in Paris, Rome, Venice and Urbino, the plan envisaged a colossal amphibian invasion of around 260 warships, escorting an army of 60,000 soldiers to land in Ireland where English governors would be overthrown before a threatened move to mainland Britain, if peace terms were not agreed by Elizabeth.[15] Although this scheme was rejected by Philip's ministers as overly ambitious, other intelligence reports identified several southern English ports and the Isle of Wight as likely targets, as well as Milford Haven in Wales, Waterford in Ireland and Kirkcudbright in Scotland.

As Lord Admiral Howard lamented to Walsingham in June 1588, it was 'a hard matter and a thing impossible for us to lie in any place, or to be anywhere to guard England, Ireland and Scotland'. An alternative scenario envisaged England being invaded from Flanders, using the large number of veteran Habsburg troops already stationed in the Low Countries and commanded by Philip's nephew Alexander Farnese, duke of Parma. That same month, the experienced English admiral Sir William Wynter recalled, as a young man, serving in a fleet of 260 ships 'when we burned Leith and Edinburgh' in 1544. Although Henry VIII's ships had sailed greater distances than the Spanish fleet would need to reach vulnerable eastern ports such as Sheppey, Harwich or Yarmouth from Flanders, Wynter suggested to Walsingham that rumours of Parma's forces landing in England seemed 'rather a scarecrow', primarily aimed at securing Habsburg advantage in parallel peace negotiations.[16]

Given Elizabethan England's strategic vulnerability, the plethora of ports identified as potential Spanish landing sites was nevertheless alarming. On land, there was no standing army, few fortified towns and reliance was primarily placed on voluntary 'trained bands' in each county, with militias under no obligation to serve outside their own localities. Although compliance with official requirements was patchy, all physically able Englishmen between sixteen and sixty were, in principle, required to present themselves regularly at local musters, together with armour and arms (such as pikes and muskets) to confirm their ammunition was in working order. Equipment that failed, or was used incorrectly, did not 'pass muster' and rendered individuals liable to fines or other punishments. The cost of supplying weapons for those without their own arms was borne by counties. Each year, numerous beacons along the English coasts were guarded twenty-four hours a day, by two men, between early March and late October. If an invading force was sighted, beacons were lit and musters assembled, commanded by local gentry and nobles. But maintaining an effective coastal defence was complicated by different territories falling under competing and overlapping jurisdictions that included the Admiralty Court, the archdiocese of Canterbury, the Constabulary of Dover Castle and the medieval confederation of south-eastern towns between Hastings and Sandwich, known as the Cinque Ports. Surveying defences on the Isle of Wight, the island's Captain, George Carey, warned Walsingham in April 1588 that he was 'utterly unprovided of any warlike ships or vessels fit for employment' but was loath to 'terrify the minds of this country with so great a charge, neither usual nor accustomed' as would be needed to improve security.[17] In London, Elizabeth's principal adviser, William Cecil, Lord Burghley, admitted to Walsingham in July that he had spent 'a painful and restless' night worrying about the city's defences, while an expensive floating boom of chains and cables was erected across the River Thames between Tilbury and Gravesend.[18] Designed by the Italian military engineer Federigo Giambelli, the boom then collapsed under its own weight during the first flood-tide.

The ignominy attaching to England's primitive infrastructure became particularly acute in the light of propaganda publicizing Philip's preparations. A pamphlet entitled *La Felicissima Armada que el Rey Don Felipe* ('The Fortunate Armada of King Philip') – originally printed in Lisbon in May 1588 as information for Philip and the Armada's captains – was translated into English and appeared as a compact quarto.[19] Printed in cities including Paris, Nuremburg, Cologne, Ghent, Delft, Rome, Naples, Milan, Bologna and Venice, the pamphlet provided details – that subsequently proved accurate – of 130 Spanish ships ready to attack England, as well as nearly 20,000 soldiers, 8,000 sailors and specified amounts of artillery, shot and rope, together with stipulated quantities of victuals including biscuit, wine, bacon, rice, beans, oil, vinegar and cheese.

If England's physical defences were precarious, it was also unclear if Elizabeth's regime could count on the loyalty of Protestant co-religionists elsewhere in mainland Britain. In March 1588, Henry Radclyffe, earl of Sussex, sent Walsingham a report supplied by the master of a small ship that had brought a cargo of coal into the Sussex port of Newhaven. Encountering a group of over fifty Scots in the port, the ship's master, Robert Keble, had been forced to hand money over and warned that 'if they might catch him at sea, they would heave him and his [crew] overboard, and all other Englishmen, and would pull their hearts out of their bodies, calling them "English dogs", saying they would be revenged of the blood of their queen'.[20] At the same time, England's sizeable community of recusant Catholics was targeted by prominent exiles, such as Cardinal William Allen, whose *Admonition to the Nobility and People of England and Ireland* (1588) cited the belated need to execute the papal sentence of deposition against Elizabeth as justification for the 'present wars' between England and Spain. Despite its being printed under conditions of tight security in Antwerp, Burghley received a smuggled copy of Allen's *Admonition* from his brother-in-law Henry Killigrew, who was one of three English representatives on the Council of State, which advised the Dutch States General. Denouncing Elizabeth as a heretic usurper, Allen's pamphlet charged that she had abused papal patience in postponing execution of the sentence with ever-greater cruelties and abuses, culminating in the consummation of her 'devilish desires against the lady Mary, Queen of Scotland'. Allen exhorted English Catholics to perform the Pope's pious duty in resisting Elizabeth's authority, alleging that scriptural delineations of Jezebel 'do so much resemble our Elizabeth, that in most foreign countries and writings of strangers, she is commonly called by the name of Jezebel'.[21]

The English administration responded by promoting patriotism among its citizens. On 1 July, a proclamation warned that, to prevent the danger whereby Elizabeth's 'people should be seduced or their simplicity abused' by false and seditious publications, stringent penalties would be imposed on anyone possessing such material. The proclamation warned that Philip's motivation in attacking England was not to improve the condition of the country's Catholics, but 'utterly to overthrow our most happy estate and this flourishing commonwealth, and to subject the same to the proud, servile, and slavish government of foreigners and strangers'.[22] In July, Privy Councillors approved publication of a manuscript by 'G. D.', written after an English Catholic, Sir William Stanley, had surrendered the Dutch city of Deventer to Parma's forces in January 1587. 'G. D.' averred that, whatever his religion, no Englishman could bear 'to see his wife forced, his sisters ravished, his daughters deflowered, his house sacked, his goods pillaged and spoiled by a stranger . . . and his own throat cut' if he tried to defend himself. Aside from a few subversive 'scum and dregs' found in every nation, the English were inherently loyal, 'especially against foreign enemies, in a case of invasion'.[23] Entitled *A Brief Discovery of Dr Allen's Seditious Drifts*, copies of this pamphlet were sent to Lord Lieutenants as Elizabeth's representative in each English county, to be circulated to justices of the peace and mayors in a bid to promote local loyalty. Meanwhile, foreigners fell under xenophobic suspicion as lurid rumours started spreading. Despite having lived in England for nearly four decades, the Tuscan Protestant Petruccio Ubaldini observed how a credulous populace developed 'a mortal and dangerous hatred of all foreigners', fearing that cargoes of invading Spanish ships would include 'many instruments of torture'. As Ubaldini later recalled, it had seemed easier 'to find flocks of white crows than one Englishman (and let him believe what he will about religion) who loves a foreigner'.[24]

While they endorsed a mindset that axiomatically assumed the Spanish threat to be overwhelming, clerics also sought to rally English resistance against the impending colossus. In January 1588, Edmond Harris preached to gentry responsible for training soldiers in Hertfordshire, imploring his listeners to trust that Providence would assist them in defeating the Spaniards, in the same way that 'little David did set upon the great giant Goliath and prevailed'.[25] The Suffolk Puritan Thomas Tymme likewise urged 'every true Englishman' to 'be in a readiness with bows, bills, morris pikes, and guns, to march on in a warlike array, like true soldiers'. Since God had 'placed us Englishmen here in one commonwealth, also in one Church, as in one ship together', Tymme warned that there was 'no storm so dangerous to a ship on the sea, as is discord' in society.[26] Within days of the Armada being sighted in the English Channel in July, the Admiral of the Narrow Seas, Lord Henry Seymour, wrote to Walsingham from aboard the *Rainbow*, quietly confident that Spanish hopes of 'conquering little England' would be frustrated, since the country was now 'united with thousands [of] resolute civil minds'. Even in previous centuries, when England had been 'divided with many kings, the people barbarous and uncivil', its populace had always 'resisted mightily long before they could be conquered'.[27]

Foreign observers were not necessarily convinced of the Armada's assured success. In March 1588, the Venetian ambassador in Rome, Giovanni Gritti, reported residual papal scepticism regarding Philip II's intentions as well as – ironically – the explicit esteem in which Sixtus V evidently held Elizabeth. Declaring that 'she certainly is a great queen' and 'were she only a Catholic, she would be our dearly beloved', Sixtus publicly admired how 'she makes herself feared by Spain, by France, by the Empire, by all', despite being 'only a woman' and 'only mistress of half an island'. The following month, Gritti's Parisian counterpart, Giovanni Mocenigo, denied the likelihood that Philip would risk so much for 'a doubtful battle', especially since 'the English are men of another mettle from the Spaniards, and enjoy the reputation of being, above all the Western nations, expert and active in all naval operations, and great sea dogs'. The Messianic scale of Spanish ambitions also ensured, as Mocenigo presciently predicted, that 'if the English are successful, there is no doubt but that the Queen will acquire such fame and glory that the fruits of the victory will continue to appear greater and greater as time goes on'.[28] In Rome, the perversity of papal praise for Elizabeth was especially frustrating for Philip II's ambassador, Olivares, who warned the Spanish king in March 1588 that he 'might as well cry for the moon as to ask for' the promised financial subsidy from Sixtus. By August, Olivares had all but abandoned hope, complaining that 'when it comes to getting money out of him, it is like squeezing his life-blood'. According to the ambassador, 'the moment my back is turned, he babbles the most ridiculous nonsense at table, such as would not be said by a baby of two years old'. Insisting that 'the Armada business is nothing but a trick', Sixtus was claiming that Philip's fleet was only being assembled 'for brag, and to frighten the queen of England into making peace'.[29]

Members of Elizabeth's administration would have been further reassured had they known of the internal dissension and misgivings among those tasked with achieving the enterprise of England. Aware that his uncle envisaged an ambitious amphibious attack, whereby the Armada would rendezvous with his 'Army of Flanders', Parma protested to Philip in January 1588 that he had 'done my best to perform the impossible' by trying to raise vast numbers of experienced troops with insufficient resources. Nevertheless, Parma complained that 'everything has turned out the reverse of what I expected and hoped', since 'secrecy, which was of the utmost importance, has not been maintained;

and from Spain, Italy, and all parts come, not only news of the expedition, but full details of it'. Further delays were incurred when the Armada's commander, Santa Cruz, died and was replaced by a reluctant Alonso Pérez de Guzmán, duke of Medina Sidonia. Claiming to possess 'neither aptitude, ability, health, nor fortune, for the expedition', Medina Sidonia warned that his unfamiliarity with the project's preparation meant that he 'would be simply groping in the dark'. Despite insisting he did not wish to 'attempt a task of which I have no doubt I should give a bad account', the duke's protestations went unheeded.[30]

Although Parma was advising his uncle in March that 'it would be better to conclude peace' with England than risk 'the danger of some disaster', Philip continued to instruct Medina Sidonia to sail through the Channel 'as far as Cape Margate, where you will join hands with the duke of Parma, my nephew', who would provide barges for an invasion force of around 27,000 soldiers to land in Kent, before entering the River Thames to facilitate a rapid descent on London. Aware that tactical success depended on calm weather, the enemy being surprised, precise timing and clear communications between the Armada and Parma's forces, Philip advised Medina Sidonia that if the first strategy failed, one contingency might be to 'seize the Isle of Wight, which is apparently not so strong as to be able to resist and may be defended, if we gain it'.[31] Should the mission fall short of entire success, Philip counselled Parma to improvise pragmatic peace terms that could still yield significant gains, such as securing religious toleration for English Catholics, agreeing the evacuation of English forces from the Netherlands, securing Spanish control of a deep-water Channel port, such as Vlissingen, or agreeing financial compensation for the depredations of Drake and other English corsairs.

III

In late May 1588, the vast Spanish fleet set sail from Lisbon, comprising over 130 ships, 7,000 sailors, 17,000 soldiers and around 1,300 officials. But forced to shelter from storms in the Galician port of La Coruña, Medina Sidonia's despair deepened. In mid-June he wrote to Philip, insisting that, compared to the Spanish forces that had assembled to attack Portugal in 1580, 'I assure you that we are very weak'.

Denying that 'we can attack so great a country as England with such a force as ours is now', Medina Sidonia advised Philip to make 'honourable terms with the enemy'.[32] The following month, Elizabeth's envoy, Valentine Dale, tried to maintain constructive peace talks with Parma outside Dunkirk, despite Parma's gleeful statement that a single battle 'lost by the English might bring loss of the kingdom as well'. Refusing to be intimidated, Dale alluded to Spanish travails in the Netherlands as evidence that Philip knew he 'could not invade a realm and conquer it in a single battle'. But as Dale admitted to Burghley, the Habsburgs' military preparations were clearly in evidence as invasion troops were being massed 'without any dissimulation whither, but professing it as openly as if they were to go to a fair or market'.[33] After leaving La Coruña on 22 July 1588, the Armada was sighted off the Cornish coast seven days later, prompting skirmishes in which, as Howard reassured Walsingham, 'their force is wonderful, great and strong; and yet we pluck their feathers by little and little'.[34] Having anchored at Calais on 6 August to await arrival of Parma's forces, the English Navy attacked and forced the Spanish fleet into open waters, resulting in a day-long battle the following day, off Gravelines, fifteen miles south-west of Dunkirk. Meanwhile Parma's forces failed to rendezvous with the Armada as planned and remained in port, while the Spanish fleet was forced into the North Sea to escape bombardment.

Within a fortnight of its first sighting in the Channel, the challenge was over, as the scattered Armada was forced by the prevailing wind to embark on a circuitous return journey along the coasts of northern Scotland and western Ireland and the Bay of Biscay, during which a third of its ships sank and over half of its sailors and soldiers drowned or died from disease, starvation or from being captured and killed as prisoners. After finally reaching sanctuary in Flanders, one surviving captain, Francesco de Cuéllar, presented Philip II with such a harrowing and protracted narrative of shipwreck, beatings, strippings, malnourishment, exposure and imprisonment in Ireland and Scotland that Cuéllar admitted, 'you will almost think it taken from some book of chivalry'.[35]

What had long been anticipated as a titanic and decisive military clash thereby resulted in a seemingly inconclusive and unresolved encounter. From an English perspective, 'the danger was not really understood until it was past'.[36] Unaware of naval engagements that had already occurred, including the decisive encounter at Gravelines two days earlier, Elizabeth set sail on 9 August, in a procession of barges, from Whitehall to inspect troops camped at West Tilbury under the command of Robert Dudley, earl of Leicester. In a speech that came to epitomize popular memories of 'Good Queen Bess', Elizabeth reportedly declaimed that she had 'the heart and stomach of a king, and of a king of England too, and think foul scorn that Parma or Spain, or any prince of Europe should dare to invade the borders of my realm'. Since the first printed account of her speech appeared more than seventy years later, and no definitive record of the words spoken on the day survives, Elizabeth's actual turn of phrase may have been rhetorically less sparkling. She was nevertheless likely to have acknowledged that, although her enemies 'may challenge my sex for that I am a woman', the rectitude of English resistance meant that the soldiers had no 'need to fear what Rome or Spain can do against us'.[37] In the visual arts, despite the uncertain contingency of events in the English Channel, the national victory quickly assumed iconic status in the different surviving versions of Elizabeth's 'Armada portrait' on display at the National Maritime Museum, the National Portrait Gallery and Woburn Abbey. With the resplendent queen positioned between two seascape windows – one depicting the Spanish invasion force on approach and the other its vanquished flight – the portraits confirmed England's own imperial ambitions as the queen's hand was placed possessively on a terrestrial globe.

But in 1588, a more edgy mood prevailed and Elizabeth's language remained pugnacious in confirming to James VI of Scotland that, although the Spanish fleet had been 'well-beaten in our narrow seas', the Armada was now set for Scotland. Although Elizabeth claimed to doubt not a 'whit but that all this tyrannical, proud and brainsick attempt will be the beginning, though not the end, of the ruin' of Philip, she reminded James that any potential show of Scottish support for Spain's forces would fatally ruin his reputation in England.[38] As James sought to extract maximal diplomatic advantage from Elizabeth's vulnerability, the English ambassador in Edinburgh, William Ashby, reported that the Scottish king was seeking conferral of a rare English duchy, an annual pension of £5,000 and a royal guard funded by England. Warning Burghley in mid-August that there were 'many malcontents and papists' in Scotland susceptible to Spanish influence, Ashby recommended that Elizabeth should keep 'an eye to the back door' into England, surmising that 'every pound her Majesty sends hither now will save twenty later, and many a life'.[39] On the same day that Ashby was soliciting subsidies to secure Scots fidelity, the Lord High Admiral, Howard, was informing Burghley of the pitiful effects of English penury closer to home. Seeking refuge on the Kent coast, Howard recounted the 'most pitiful sight to see, here at Margate': English sailors, with no food or shelter, left to 'die in the streets'; as Howard rued, 'it would grieve any man's heart to see them that have served so valiantly to die so miserably'.[40] Still waiting in Tilbury a week later, Walsingham worried that, with incoming reports indicating that the majority of Spanish ships had escaped, 'our half-doing doth breed dishonour and leaves the disease uncured'.[41]

Since the English authorities were unsure whether the dispersed Armada might regroup and return, or if reinforcements had been dispatched from Spain, examination of captured prisoners at least offered them the chance to ask questions likely to have been pondered across Continental Europe. At Bridewell Prison on 2 August, the captain of a wrecked galleon, the *Nuestra Señora del Rosario*, Vincente Alvarez, confirmed that the fleet's mandate had been to enable Parma to undertake 'the conquest of England' and that it had been resolved that 'in what place soever they should enter within the land, to sack the same, either city, town, village or whatsoever', including London. In terms of potential support from the native population, Alvarez reported that it had been 'commonly bruited amongst them that a third part or one half of the realm of England would join to their aid so soon as they should enter on the land'. When asked who would have assumed sovereignty of a conquered England, Alvarez ventured that the ensuing rivalry between Philip and his nephew Parma suggested 'it would breed a new war between them'. Interrogated two days later, the Andalusian general, Don Pedro de Valdés, likewise confirmed that the purpose of the expedition had been to enable Parma to 'land in this kingdom and conquer it', but denied that instructions had been given to land in Scotland or Ireland. De Valdés claimed ignorance when asked questions about Philip's justification for attacking England, his hereditary claim to the English crown, how Spanish forces intended 'to have dealt with the King of Scots' and the extent of assistance received from France and other Catholic powers.[42]

In England, there seemed more cause for concern than public celebration. Eleven captured Spanish ensigns were displayed in St Paul's Cathedral in early September to offer thanks for England's deliverance, before the banners were moved to London Bridge to please crowds attending Southwark Fair. Two months later, a Genoese spy, Marco Antonio Messia, returned reports to Madrid indicating that the general mood in London remained one of 'such alarm and terror'. He detected 'no sign of rejoicing amongst the Councillors' who 'look rather like men who have a heavy burden to bear' and described the queen as 'much aged and spent, and is very melancholy'. Messia also claimed that Elizabeth had intended to go to St Paul's Cathedral to offer public thanks for the victory, but had been dissuaded by her advisers 'for fear that an arquebus might be fired at her'.[43]

Over three months after the two fleets' encounter in the Channel, an official thanksgiving service was held at St Paul's on 24 November to coincide with the thirtieth anniversary of Elizabeth's accession. Although the queen travelled to the service in a Roman-style horse-drawn chariot, ballad evidence implied that, notwithstanding Henri III's alliance with Elizabeth, the French delegation, headed by Guillaume de l'Aubespine, baron de Châteauneuf, wore 'velvet black', as if in mourning, while the English Jesuit Henry Garnet returned an account of the thanksgiving to the Jesuit General in Rome, Claudio Acquaviva. Rumours that 'the queen was afraid to show herself in public' were, Garnet explained, confirmed by an official injunction that 'in every single household along the route, no-one should be allowed to look out from the windows while she was passing' unless the householder was willing 'to stake his life and entire fortune' on the residents' integrity.[44]

Although fear of further incursion was endemic, Elizabeth's ministers were relieved that the strategic threat posed by Scotland remained unrealized. In the Fife fishing community of Anstruther, the minister James Melville recorded in his diary how 'terrible was the fear' and 'zealous and fervent were the prayers' while 'that monstrous navy [was] about our coasts' as Spanish galleons approached Scottish 'islands, rocks and sands'. As he recalled, 'the news was credibly told, sometimes of their landing at Dunbar, sometimes at St Andrews, and in Tay, now and then at Aberdeen and Cromarty'. Melville himself had been surprised when woken, one morning in late summer, to learn that a contingent of shipwrecked Armada refugees had arrived in Anstruther seeking food and shelter. While local dignitaries assembled in the town's Tolbooth, Melville informed Commander Jan Gomes de Medina that although, as Catholics, Philip II and his subjects were unavoidably enemies of the Scottish nation, he wanted the sailors to 'know by experience, that we were men, and so moved by human compassion'. Indeed, the alms provided by Fife townspeople would provide a Protestant contrast to the violent injustices regularly suffered by Scots merchants who fell foul of the Inquisition when trading in Spain.[45]

Concerned about the exposure of England's 'back door', north of the border, in May 1588 Elizabeth had invoked Homer's *Odyssey* when advising James to 'take Ulysses's wax to save you from such sirens' on the grounds that succumbing to tempting Spanish inducements could only prove fatal for his long-term interests.[46] Four months later, the new English envoy in Edinburgh, Sir Robert Sidney, relayed reassurance received from James that 'he had not carried himself as a neutral', but as 'an open enemy to the Spaniards'. Pursuing Elizabeth's classical trope, James had grimly recognized that, were Spain to conquer England, Philip's 'favours towards him would have been like Polyphemus to Ulysses' – i.e. 'that he should be the last man he would eat'.[47] After being shipwrecked off the Irish coast, the Armada captain de Cuéllar then spent over six months in Scotland where he was disappointed to find James's administration seemingly slavish in its submission to Elizabeth's sway. As de Cuéllar later informed Philip, 'the King of Scotland is a nobody, and has neither the authority nor the bearing of a king, and he doesn't budge an inch or eat a morsel unless by order of the Queen'.[48] Although de Cuéllar's impressions were distorted – in that James's independent actions regularly alarmed Elizabeth's ministers – the Spaniard's claim served to confirm, as the Jesuit Ribadeneyra put it, that 'the world is ruled by opinion, and matters of war even more so . . . opinion often determines things more than arms and armies'.[49]

IV

Elizabeth's administration was determined to control how the Armada's defeat was understood in Continental Europe. In October 1588, Burghley authored the *Copy of a Letter sent out of England to Don Bernardin Mendoza*, which was published anonymously and purportedly written to Philip II's ambassador in Paris by an English seminary priest, Richard Leigh, who had, in reality, been executed for treason two months earlier. Posing as 'Leigh', Burghley articulated the extent to which English

Catholic hopes of 'imagined conquest' had been 'built but in the air, or upon waves of the sea' since they were now 'utterly overthrown, and as it were with an earthquake, all our castles of comfort brought to the ground'. 'Leigh' denounced Spanish hubris that had blithely boasted to English Catholics that the Armada would arrive with 'such mighty strength, as no Navy of England, or of Christendom, could resist, or abide their force'. Cleverly incorporating claims made by Spaniards currently in English custody, Burghley also had 'Leigh' inform Mendoza that those captured from the Armada had confirmed dishonest Spanish assurances 'that this country was so open to march in, and so weak to withstand any force, and the people so miserable, as they thought the conquest thereof had been of no more difficulty than the overcoming [of] a number of naked Indians'.[50] While Burghley's pamphlet appeared in French, Italian, Dutch and German translations, readers skilled in sowing misleading stories of their own quickly realized the ruse. In early November, the Genoese spy Messia informed Mendoza that the English had published a tract which 'in their usual cunning way, pretended had been written by a Catholic to your lordship', but had in fact been 'done by the Lord Treasurer [Burghley]'.[51]

Official thanksgiving services were haunted by renewed fears of invasion. In London, the French ambassador was warned in October of the need to ensure that Elizabeth 'keeps her foot upon the neck of the Spaniard' since there was 'no certainty of a similar success a second time'.[52] In Madrid, Lippomano confirmed that, 'in spite of everything', Philip was 'quite determined to carry on the war; and the other evening sitting at his table and, talking of this subject, he said, "We will sell these candlesticks if no other way of raising money can be found"'.[53] Austerity was even more urgent, given that promised papal funds seemed unlikely ever to materialize. While the fate of the Armada had remained unknown that summer, the Spanish ambassador in Rome renewed his entreaties for financial assistance, but, as Olivares reported, Pope Sixtus 'heard me without interruption, although he writhed about a good deal with inward impatience, but when I finished, his anger leapt out' with a refusal to entertain any claim on papal funds as matters stood. Olivares admitted despairingly, 'it becomes daily more evident that when he offered the million he did so in the belief . . . that the undertaking would never be carried through'. In Paris, Mendoza continued to encourage Philip to 'keep up the talk of war and great armaments, even if you do not carry them out', since 'publicity is as important now as secrecy was before'.[54]

In December 1588, Admiral Wynter wrote to Walsingham, venturing that, now that it was known that Philip and Parma had planned to attack London via the Thames, this 'plot being then in their heads, no doubt but that it remains there still, and will hardly be removed until they see their hope made void'. Wynter therefore recommended urgent fortification, not only of London, but also of vulnerable port towns such as Sandwich, Harwich and Yarmouth. Since 'ships are subject to wind, weather, and other haps', Wynter also doubted the future strategic wisdom of entrusting England's defences entirely to the Navy.[55] In January 1589, the first day of national thanksgiving to be held in Ireland generated a divided response. From Kinsale, Elizabeth's Lord Deputy, Sir William Fitzwilliam, received reports that the local Protestant church had been too small to accommodate the multitude of worshippers seeking to give thanks for the Armada's defeat, with many obliged to remain outside and 'hang upon the walls and windows to hear the sermon'. By contrast, Ireland's Lord Chancellor, Archbishop Adam Loftus of Armagh, admitted to Walsingham that, even though the national day of thanksgiving had been held while the courts were sitting in Dublin, the city's lawyers had resolved 'to leave the town of purpose to absent themselves from that godly exercise', evincing a 'great want of duty and loyalty unto her Majesty, and giving just occasion unto us, to conceive a doubtful opinion of them'.[56]

In England, eulogies celebrating the country's providential escape poured from printing presses. In September 1588, the young Calvinist and future bishop of Down and Connor, Robert Humpston, preached a sermon in Norfolk, acclaiming England's preservation from savage papal enemies who would have 'turned our floods of peace into channels of blood' and 'murdered the honourable councillor and grave judge, the reverend bishop and venerable magistrate, the wealthy citizen and painful craftsman, the aged matron and chaste virgin, the infant in the cradle and the cripple at the gate'. Deliverance should not, however, induce sinful complacency: Humpston warned that England still harboured plenty of 'bloody fields, bloody vineyards, bloody cities, bloody houses, bloody magistrates, bloody ministers, bloody merchants, bloody lawyers, bloody men and bloody women'.[57]

In *Meditations* published to commemorate the Armada's defeat, the

Puritan Oliver Pigge cautioned that 'the hatred and malice of the Spaniard' was 'not yet quenched, but rather we may be assured, much more increased, so as they will but wait opportunity to set upon us again'.[58] In 1589, James VI of Scotland published a series of *Meditations* on the Book of Chronicles, likening God's delivery of the Israelites from Philistine attack to Scotland's preservation from Spanish invasion. Just as 'God, by blowing in the tops of the trees with his mighty wind, put the Philistines to flight', so 'in like manner, by brangling with his mighty wind, their timber castles scattered and shaken them asunder, to the wreck of a great part and confusion of the whole'. Regarding Anglo-Scottish amity as essential to Protestantism's survival, James reminded his readers that there was 'now one sincere profession of the truth among us in this isle, assailed by the nations about, haters of the Holy Word'.[59]

Praise also came, in inventively octolingual form, from the Genevan Calvinist Théodore Bèza whose antithetical Latin epigram celebrated how 'the swollen waters overwhelmed you swollen ones (Spaniards!)' and 'the deep pit of the inexhaustible sea swallowed up the greedy raptors of the whole world!'[60] Dedicated to Elizabeth, Bèza's poem was, remarkably, printed as an expensive vellum broadside in imitation of royal and parliamentary proclamations and papal indulgences, while the international significance of the English victory was confirmed by parallel translations into English, Hebrew, Greek, Dutch, French, Italian and the 'enemy' vernacular, Spanish. Victory was all the sweeter on account of England's vulnerability. The propagandist James Lea reflected that Spain's 'huge and mighty ships', supported by French Guise interests and united with Parma's army, seemed so powerful 'that in a moment they might swallow up little England, as the ravenous crocodile doth the smallest fish'.[61] Elsewhere, the rhyming *Skeletonical Salutation, or Condign Gratulation and Just Vexation of the Spanish Nation* (1589) satirized the piscatorial theme, wondering whether 'for this year / It were not best to forbear' eating fish that might have feasted on Spanish corpses. On reflection, the anonymous author was confident that the public health risk was probably minimal since 'the Devil of Hell, / Loved Spaniards so well' that they would already have been transferred to 'the place appointed / For the Pope's anointed'.[62]

A silver medal commemorating the Armada's repulse was struck in the Dutch city of Middelburg and bore the motto '*Venit, Ivit, Fuit*' ('It

Came, It Went, It Was No More') in a clever adaptation of Julius Caesar's epigram.[63] By contrast, the motto 'the world is not enough', with which this chapter began, was a reminder that the enterprise of England remained unfulfilled. In France, Elizabeth's ally Henri III reasserted his authority and, in December 1588, ordered the murder of his rivals (and Mary Stuart's relatives) the duke of Guise and his brother, the cardinal of Lorraine. In May 1589, Elizabeth's trusted adviser Burghley, aged nearly seventy, wearily admitted that 'the state of the world is marvellously changed' to a time 'when we true Englishmen have cause for our own quietness to wish good success to a French king, and a king of Scots'. In his twenties, Burghley had participated in Henry VIII's 'rough wooing' and had contributed to the decisive English defeat of the Scots at the Battle of Pinkie (1547). But four decades later Burghley's reasoning was predicated on the rationale that, since both Scotland and France were 'enemies to our enemies, we have cause to join with them in their actions against our enemies'.[64]

While Drake and Sir John Norris led an unsuccessful expedition to attack Spanish ships in La Coruña, Peniche and Lisbon in April and May 1589, the Venetian ambassador in Madrid, Tomaso Contarini, confirmed that Philip was 'resolved on attacking England again, in order to show the Queen that though she began the war like a man she will have to end it like a woman'.[65] In 1590, it was reported that the entire crew aboard Elizabeth's *Vanguard* warship had seen 'in the air over the moon the shape of a man, with a crown on his head and the King of Spain's arms plainly displayed'.[66] Meanwhile, claiming to care not *A Fig for the Spaniard* (1591), another anonymous author marvelled that, despite controlling 'more large territories, and greater store of wealth' than any Christian monarch in history, Philip was now confronted by domestic uprisings in Aragon, Catalonia, Portugal and Valencia. Despite being repulsed by 'our simple fleet of fish-boats' in 1588, the Spanish king remained clearly determined to attack 'little England'.[67] But so long as the identity of Elizabeth I's eventual successor remained unsettled, the enterprise of England could yet be achieved dynastically, rather than militarily.

3
An International Succession Debate, 1589–1601

In 1593, an anonymous pamphlet, published in Antwerp and entitled *News from Spain and Holland* (1593), reported a recent gathering in Amsterdam of 'diverse gentlemen, captains, scholars, and others' from England, Scotland, Ireland, France, Italy and the Dutch Republic, keen to discuss who was likely to succeed the childless Elizabeth I, now in her mid-fifties, as sovereign of England and Ireland. One discussant – a lawyer – admitted that the unsettled state of the English succession posed 'a terrible threatening of extreme calamity to the commonwealth to have so many lie in wait to assail her'. Lamenting that 'the matter is so doubtful, ambiguous and disputable, on every side, as God only and the sword must make the conclusion', the 'lawyer' knew that contemporaries could readily identify at least ten potential claimants to the English throne. Among the Stuart branch of Henry VII's cognatic descendants were James VI of Scotland and his English-born cousin Arbella Stuart, while the Suffolk branch of the Tudor dynasty encouraged claims by Edward Seymour, Lord Beauchamp and William Stanley, earl of Derby, at the same time as Lancastrian claims were energetically promoted by Philip II of Spain on behalf of his daughter, the Infanta Isabella Clara Eugenia.[1] In reality, the captains, scholars and other gentlemen had never gathered together in person: *News from Spain and Holland* was a fictional fabrication by the English-born Jesuit Robert Persons. Yet the widespread apprehension it described was real. Discussion of Elizabeth I's successor was statutorily prohibited in England. Legislation enacted in 1571 had rendered it a treasonable – and therefore capital – crime to discuss the royal succession in terms of 'any such claimer, pretender, usurper, utterer, declarer, affirmer, usurper, publisher or not-acknowledger'.[2]

For Catholics, an uncertain succession offered the alluring prospect that regime change might yet bring confessional reversal as it had under

Mary Tudor: a papist successor to Elizabeth seemed potentially the last chance for England to return to the Catholic fold. Yet acute anxieties were also articulated at the other end of the religious spectrum by Puritans such as the Northampton MP, Peter Wentworth, who questioned Elizabeth's wisdom in remaining silent and resolving 'to leave us your people wittingly and willingly, at random, to the rage and fury of hell and hellhounds'. In a manuscript that circulated from around 1587, Wentworth daringly called for all claims to the English crown 'thoroughly to be tried and examined' by Parliament, insisting that the only way to end endemic Catholic plotting was through statutory confirmation that Elizabeth's successor would be a Protestant, and preferably one who 'shall then beat them [Catholics] with whips, as slaves and dogs'.[3]

While Wentworth suffered serial imprisonment in the Tower of London for his temerity in raising the subject, Continental publications readily considered it. In 1589, *The Copy of a Letter, Lately written by a Spanish Gentleman to his Friend in England* was published in Antwerp by the English-born Catholic Richard Verstegan and was purportedly authored by an Armada veteran recently released from detention in England. The 'Spanish Gentleman' denounced restraints on free speech as 'a very evident and sufficient sign of a tyrannous estate', governed by a monarch who selfishly prioritized preserving his or her own power but left 'the people in such possibility to be killed, in the confusion of so many competitors'. The trepidation bred by such endemic insecurity was palpable, with the English described as a people 'who in seeming to fear nothing, are seen to start at their own shadows'. As the author ventured, 'this intolerable fear is more manifested in your English government, than in any state else in the whole world'.[4] Successive harvest failures, rising prices and popular unrest, combined with recurrent threats of foreign invasion and Catholic encirclement, generated a national mood of perturbation. Meanwhile, Elizabeth's subjects were silenced by an ageing queen who remains unique among all English monarchs in recklessly refusing to make explicit provision for the stable continuation of royal authority after her death.

I

The principles governing succession to the English crown were unhelpfully ambiguous.[5] Common law prohibited foreigners from inheriting property in England and a fourteenth-century statute of Edward III excluded anyone born outside the monarch's allegiance from the line of succession. Although common law likewise restricted the inheritance rights of children born illegitimately, Tudor legislation had declared both Henry VIII's daughters, Mary and Elizabeth, to be bastards, but had then also confirmed their place in the royal line of succession. In testamentary wills from 1544 onwards, Henry had also disregarded primogeniture to confirm the hereditary rights attaching to the offspring of his younger sister Mary, duchess of Suffolk, while ignoring the progeny of his older sister Margaret, who would prove to be great-grandmother to James VI of Scotland. In 1561, five years before James's birth, Elizabeth had informed a Scottish ambassador, William Maitland of Lethington, that 'when I am dead, they shall succeed that has most right', supplying tacit recognition that James's mother, Mary, Queen of Scots, retained the strongest hereditary claim, but refusing to name any successor.[6]

Four decades later, Elizabeth's position remained unchanged as she compelled silence on the subject. Following his mother's execution in 1587, James VI had inherited the Stuart dynastic claim, with the additional credentials of being male, Protestant, an English pensioner and already a sovereign monarch in Scotland. But despite vocal protestations of support for Elizabeth during the Armada crisis, James had failed to extract from the English queen public affirmation that he possessed the strongest hereditary right to the English throne or reassurance that his claim had not been impaired by his mother's conviction for treason. James's requests to be granted an English dukedom, or some landed estate, had likewise fallen on deaf ears. Yet as the fictional debate in *News from Spain and Holland* confirmed, contemporaries could cite up to a dozen alternative claimants with rival hereditary rights, differing religious inclinations and varying potential to attract foreign backing.

With attachments to Catholicism particularly strong in northern England, Elizabeth's ministers feared that a future Spanish invasion attempt might be routed through Scotland, since James's court at Edinburgh included a significant number of Catholic nobles with longstanding Spanish connections. In early 1589, Elizabeth's ambassador in Edinburgh, William Ashby, presented James with deciphered copies of letters, sent by the Catholic earls of Huntly, Erroll and Crawford to Philip II's nephew Alexander Farnese, duke of Parma, and intercepted in England. The earls commiserated over the Armada's failure, regretted that a Scottish landing site had not been used and hoped for a fresh Habsburg assault against England. Correspondence from a Scots Catholic activist, Robert Bruce, confirmed to Parma that, when the Armada's ships had returned to Spain via Scottish coasts the previous summer, those 'of the faction of England, were in a marvellous fear' and 'confessed plainly, if it had landed here, they had been all utterly wrecked'.[7]

For his part, James aimed to steer a middle course, besieged by demands for religious toleration from Catholic factions on the one hand and resisting Presbyterian attempts to curb royal power on the other. Accordingly, James's perceived leniency in confronting the Catholic signatories provoked a predictably irate response from Elizabeth who warned the Scottish king to 'seize your opportunity, and to take action while your traitors are at hand' and, in a potentially veiled allusion to his mother's fate, advised James to 'learn from recent experience how dishonourable it is to postpone doing right until forced by necessity'. As matters stood, Elizabeth warned that 'your behaviour is so exasperating that if I did not love you better than you deserve, I should not mind to see you ruined'.[8] Days earlier, meanwhile, an English agent in Edinburgh, Thomas Fowler, had described to Elizabeth's principal secretary Sir Francis Walsingham the vehemence with which aggrieved Scots berated their king for apparent pusillanimity in the face of English browbeating. As well as asking James 'have they not cut off your mother's head?', his disgruntled subjects resented English ministers' attempts 'to keep you unmarried, besides stirring up factions in your country'.[9] In April, the volatile factionalism of Scottish politics was underscored when James went in person to confront an armed rising, led by Huntly, at the Brig O'Dee near Aberdeen. Although Huntly's resistance arose from domestic rivalries among James's courtiers, as opposed to foreign-sponsored Catholic agitation, the king's public role in restoring order further reminded Elizabeth's advisers that the pro-English inclinations in James's administration should not be taken for granted.[10]

English security concerns increased when, in October 1589, James absented himself from Scotland for over six months after stormy weather had forced the fleet accompanying his Danish bride, Anna, to Edinburgh to take shelter in Oslo. Having heard rumours that the king intended to travel to Norway in person, Fowler informed Elizabeth's chief adviser William Cecil, Lord Burghley, that 'there is so extreme secrecy used in this voyage as not any nobleman in Scotland knows of his stealing away, more than by conjecture'. Since the king had prepared 'no order for the government here but in writing, to be delivered when he is gone, and many blanks', Fowler feared that 'surely here will be shortly a confused state as ever was', admitting he was 'at my wit's end where to stay myself'.[11] On leaving Scotland, James issued a proclamation, read at market crosses across the country, deflecting criticism for travelling abroad by emphasizing the dynastic and political importance of his marriage. Describing himself as 'alone, without father or mother, brother or sister, king of this realm and heir apparent of England', James admitted that 'my nakedness made me to be weak and my enemies stark' and, with a pointed jibe in Elizabeth's direction, warned that 'the want of hope of succession bred disdain'.[12]

At the age of twenty-three, the king made the decision to marry Anna after careful adjudication: as he explained to his Privy Councillors, he had spent a fortnight in seclusion, seeking God's direction 'to move his heart the way' that seemed most fit, considering the physical portraits, as well as rival diplomatic benefits, of marrying either the fourteen-year-old Anna, daughter of Frederick II of Denmark, or Henri of Navarre's thirty-year-old sister, Catherine of Bourbon.[13] After his visit to Edinburgh the previous year, Navarre's envoy, Guillaume de Salluste, seigneur du Bartas, had reassured Henri of James's attractiveness as a suitor, since he was 'already in possession of one crown and in very certain hope of those of England and Ireland'. Writing to Henri on St Valentine's Day 1588, du Bartas added that, in person, James was also 'handsome, brave, eloquent, active and discreet – in short, your own image and picture'.[14]

While both prospective brides were Protestant, James's marriage to Catherine would have renewed the traditional Franco-Scottish 'auld alliance' but thereby incurred instant Spanish enmity. A Franco-Bourbon match would likewise have harmed lucrative Scottish–Iberian trade and required expensive involvement in France's religious wars, with the added disadvantage that any dowry payment would be deferred until peacetime. By contrast, the Danish-Oldenburg match – confirmed by James's proxy marriage to Anna in Edinburgh in August 1589 – secured an immediate dowry and Scottish retention of the Orkney and Shetland islands during James's lifetime.[15] In 1472, the islands had been given to Scotland as a pledge for the dowry to be paid for James III's Danish queen, Margaret, but since the dowry had never been paid, the islands had remained under Scots ownership.

Since James had initially intended to return from Norway to Scotland within three weeks, his prolonged absence alarmed Elizabeth's administration. Writing to Walsingham in December 1589, Ashby confirmed that 'no word is come of the king', adding that it was being 'muttered in hugger mugger' that James was using his nuptial expedition 'to enter into confederation' with his new Danish in-laws and other Protestant princes in Germany 'to strengthen himself against all occasions'.[16] As English ministers were aware, one reason for keeping the identity of Elizabeth's eventual successor a taboo subject of debate was the risk that, were an alternative English candidate to be named, the Scottish king would immediately ask foreign princes for diplomatic and military support to challenge any such nomination. Ashby's inklings regarding James's foreign policy ambitions were accurate as, after Frederick II's death in April 1588, James had tried to include a clause in his marriage contract by which he and Anna's younger brother Christian IX would 'enter into an alliance against the Catholic princes' to provide mutual defence against hostile incursions, although this request had been politely declined on the grounds that Denmark's new king was a twelve-year-old minor.[17]

While away from Scotland, James also attended the wedding in Copenhagen in April 1590 of Anna's older sister Elisabeth to Duke Henry Julius of Brunswick-Lüneburg and, at Kronborg Castle in Elsinore, admired a forceful visual endorsement of hereditary monarchy in the display of over forty Flemish tapestries, commissioned by Frederick in the early 1580s, that depicted all Danish kings from the biblical times of the mythical King Dan to Frederick's own reign and that of his designated successor, Christian.[18] Despite the formally elective principles governing succession to his country's crown, Frederick's success in obtaining recognition for his son as prince-elect denoted the kind of public endorsement that James repeatedly (if unsuccessfully) sought from Elizabeth. But Elizabeth – who never once left her own kingdom – deeply disapproved of James's expedition. In March 1590 she sent another scolding letter, denouncing James for undertaking such an 'untimely' and 'evil-seasoned journey' overseas and describing Scotland as 'your broken country, too much infected with the malady of strangers' humours'.[19]

In late 1592, Scottish susceptibility to Spanish interference resurfaced when a well-connected Catholic agitator, George Kerr, was arrested on the Scottish west coast, and found to be carrying eight otherwise blank sheets of paper, signed by the earls of Angus, Erroll and Huntly, with separate heraldic seals. Under torture, Kerr admitted that the 'Spanish blanks' had been intended to confirm details of Scottish support in a future Spanish invasion. An accompanying document, also seen by Elizabeth's administration, enumerated 'certain reasons which may be used to prove it meet, or unmeet, the executing of this enterprise this summer or not, 1592', supplying pro and contra arguments for attempting another 'enterprise of England', evidently compiled by James himself for future overtures to Madrid. The Scottish king had counselled caution, mindful of the proverbial warning that 'the higher and suddener a man climb, the greater and sorer shall his fall be, if his purpose fail'. James's instinct had, rather, been to continue negotiating with Elizabeth, 'fair and pleasantly for my title to the crown of England, after her decease', judging it 'not impossible, however unlikely' that the queen could yet be induced to confirm his right whereby he would have 'attained our design without stroke of sword'. With astonishing audacity, James had also indicated that recourse could yet be made, 'when I like hereafter', to join Philip II in a military offensive, as an alternative means to 'attain to our purpose, she not suspecting such [a] thing, as now she does'.[20]

Aside from James's clear willingness to jettison his official alliance with Elizabeth, English alarm was exacerbated by the seemingly dilatory response in Edinburgh to the latest discoveries. James's administration offered the Catholic earls implicated in the 'Spanish blanks' affair the choice of going into exile or, if they remained in Scotland, swearing allegiance to the established church and renouncing their Catholicism. Elizabeth's exasperation was evident, as she rebuked her royal godson for believing that his actions 'would have satisfied anyone in her four senses, let alone five'. Reminding the king that English legislation debarred anyone from succeeding who had plotted against her interests, stronger retribution was required. As the queen warned, should James be thought 'weak, then "bold spirits" will seize the helm, and drive the ship to destruction'.[21]

Fortunately for Elizabeth, Philip's attention was distracted by the international succession war that had erupted in France after Henri III had been assassinated by a Catholic zealot, Jacques Clément, in August 1589. In the months that followed, the Spanish-backed Catholic League refused to recognize Henri's nominated successor, Henri of Navarre, as king, on the grounds that he was an excommunicated Protestant heretic. Intense sectarian strife in France coincided with turbulent papal politics following the death in August 1590 of Elizabeth's grudging admirer, Sixtus V. The twelve-day tenure of Sixtus's successor, Urban VII, became the shortest papacy on record, while Gregory XIV's pontificate between 1590 and 1591 was followed by the two-month tenure of Innocent IX in 1591, before the Florentine cardinal Ippolito Aldobrandini was elected as Pope Clement VIII in February 1592 and papal politics stabilized.

As the Spanish-backed Catholic League's influence increased in northern France and confirmed the vulnerability of England's south coast to invasion, Elizabeth's administration agreed to supply Navarre's forces with soldiers and funds to prevent French Channel ports coming under Catholic-Habsburg control. In early 1591, Sir William Stanley – the English Catholic who had surrendered the Dutch town of Deventer to Spanish forces in 1587 – unsuccessfully tried to interest Philip in seizing Alderney in the Channel Islands as a strategic base. Describing Alderney's shape as 'exactly like an animal's kidney', Stanley envisaged a well-trained force of around 600 English Catholics taking possession of the island, thereby offering both the potential to launch reprisal raids in southern England, as well as to support the Spanish invasion of Brittany started by Don Juan del Águila in October 1590.[22]

As Navarre's forces struggled to dislodge the League's control of northern France and Paris, rumours started to circulate that Navarre might convert to Catholicism. Initially sceptical, Pope Clement had objected to the Venetian agent in Rome, Paolo Paruta, in early 1592, 'how can we believe in Navarre?' Evidently one of Navarre's supporters had warned that 'even if Saint Peter himself declared that the king would become a Catholic, we had better not believe it, for he had reached an age when it was ridiculous to think that he would change his faith', having been 'born and bred a heretic'. To Clement's mind, rumours regarding Navarre's new-found piety savoured of 'a ruse suggested to him by the Queen of England, who saved her own life by a like deception', recalling how Elizabeth had ostensibly abided by Mary Tudor's attempted re-Catholicization of England, before becoming, as queen, 'the source of all those ills and misfortunes which have fallen upon Catholics'. Navarre's public abjuration of Protestantism and his reception into the Catholic Church in July 1593 preceded his coronation as a consecrated king at Chartres the following February and his re-entry into Paris through the same city gates that Henri III had fled through on the 'Day of the Barricades' six years earlier. In July 1594, however, Henri IV declined Elizabeth's advice to offer a position at the French court to his Bourbon relative and heir presumptive, Henri, Prince of Condé, on the grounds that 'her Majesty was not inclined to follow a similar course in her own case, for she still refused to name her successor'.[23]

Although Henri's notorious rationale for his conversion – that 'Paris was worth a Mass' – was an apocryphal attempt to discredit his actions by malicious League opponents, many Catholics in the British Isles hoped that James VI of Scotland might yet follow a similar course. As the son of Mary, Queen of Scots, James had, after all, been born and baptized a Catholic and – unlike Henri – had never been formally excommunicated. There was also growing speculation in Edinburgh that James's queen, Anna, had secretly converted to Catholicism; in 1593, she had referred to Calvinist forms of communion as something 'she could very aptly liken . . . to a tavern breakfast'.[24]

II

In February 1594, James and Anna acquired a significant advantage in the succession stakes with the birth of a healthy son, Prince Henry Frederick, whose names honoured Henri IV of France, the prince's illustrious Tudor ancestors in England, and his maternal grandfather, Frederick II of Denmark. The lawyer David Moysie recorded how news of the prince's birth prompted widespread celebrations, bonfires and dancing in Scotland, 'as if the people had been daft for mirth'.[25] To showcase Scotland's international reputation and to reinforce his claim to succeed Elizabeth as the next English monarch, James staged sumptuous baptismal celebrations in August for which an elaborate new Chapel Royal was built at Stirling Castle, architecturally modelled on the Temple of Solomon in Jerusalem.[26] Scottish ambassadors had been dispatched to courts in England, France, Denmark, the Low Countries and German duchies to request representation at Prince Henry's christening. As the Venetian envoy in Regensburg, Tomaso Contarini, inferred, 'the occasion is considered important on account of the understanding which may then be reached', implying that James also hoped to form alliances to enhance his international standing.[27] From The Hague, one of Elizabeth's representatives on the Dutch Council of State, Thomas Bodley, informed Burghley that the States General intended to offer as a gift 'two standing cups of pure gold, worth £1200' and a patent conferring on the young prince an annual pension of £500, 'but this they are unwilling to have publicly known'.[28]

During the service, Prince Henry's claim to the English throne was reinforced when Robert Radclyffe, earl of Sussex – serving as proxy for the prince's godmother, Elizabeth – symbolically carried the infant into the new Chapel Royal and later returned him to his apartments. As Elizabeth's ambassador in Edinburgh, Robert Bowes, reported to Burghley, the Latin sermon preached by Bishop David Cunningham of Aberdeen had 'discoursed of the genealogies, alliances, leagues and amities contracted between the King of Scots and every one of the princes sending their ambassadors hither', adding that Cunningham had 'laboured much to make known how this prince was descended from these princes', especially 'from the kings of England'.[29]

A True Reportarie of the most Triumphant, and Royal Accomplishment of the Baptism ... (1594), compiled by William Fowler, but published anonymously in London and Edinburgh, described events for those unable to attend. In the entertainment that followed the baptismal service, Fowler explained that the goddess-bearing chariot which entered Stirling Castle's Great Hall was originally meant to have been drawn by a lion, before concerns had arisen that the lion's 'presence might have brought some fear, to the nearest' or that the lion itself might be startled by the 'sight of the light and torches'. An eighteen-foot replica ship, with thirty-six guns and flagged forty feet high with the arms of Scotland and Denmark, had 'sailed' across a twenty-four-foot 'sea', recalling James's seaborne journey to meet Queen Anna and echoing the Greek mythological heroism of Jason, leader of the Argonauts, who had retrieved the Golden Fleece, assisted by Medea. The third course of the baptismal banquet was served from the replica galleon and comprised herrings, whiting, flounders, oysters, limpets, lobsters, crabs, razorfish and clams, all in the form of sugared confectionary. According to Fowler's account, three full days of entertainment had initially been envisaged, with opportunities for guests to admire 'lion, elephant, hart, unicorn, and the gryphon, together with the camel, hydra, crocodile, and dragon', before the celebrations had been scaled back to a single day.[30]

Elsewhere in Scotland, the prince's birth was celebrated in Latin verses composed by the Presbyterian Rector of the University of St Andrews, Andrew Melville, who eagerly anticipated the time when 'a prince born of a Scoto-Britannic king' would unite subjects of Scotland and England into 'a single body of Scoto-Britannic people'. The new British prince, Melville predicted, would, assisted by Danish arms, 'press under your foot the triple crown of the papacy', defeating 'Iberian pride', 'Italian intrigue' and the 'Roman Jupiter'.[31] Published in Edinburgh by the royal printer, Melville's verses illustrated the extent to which images of Henry as a future martial, pan-Protestant champion circulated from the time of his birth. When James was taxed by the English ambassador, Bowes, that Melville's designation of him as 'king of all Britain in possession cannot but breed offence' to Elizabeth, 'considering her portion is the greatest part of Britain, and his the less', the king claimed – implausibly – not to have read Melville's printed tribute.[32]

James's determination to defend his right to succeed Elizabeth acquired additional urgency following publication in Antwerp of *A Conference about the Next Succession to the Crown of England* (1595). Its pseudonymous author 'R. Doleman' denoted Robert Persons, either as sole author or a collaborator; it enjoyed an unusually large initial print run of 2,000 copies.[33] Circulating in manuscript from the late summer of 1593, Persons's *Conference* was set in the aftermath of the English parliament that had met earlier that year, when MPs who had dared to raise the question of Elizabeth's successor had been censured and imprisoned.

Purporting to offer an objective analysis, the *Conference* identified real dangers posed by popular ignorance of the unsettled succession. As well as adjudicating among the rival claimants, Persons denied that royal succession was determined by hereditary right alone, regarding elective models as a safer means of ensuring that subjects did not inadvertently 'set up public murderers, ravishers, thieves and spoilers to devour us instead of kings, and governors to defend us'. Persons was also clear that the English succession was a matter of international concern, given that rival contenders would receive offers of support from 'foreign princes and states round about us' which could prove crucial 'when the forces at home be divided, and when there shall be different ports, harbours and holds, ready within the land, to receive and harbour them'. Reviewing earlier English succession crises, Persons denied that the crown had always passed to the strongest hereditary claimant, judging John of Gaunt's right to have succeeded Edward III in 1377 as stronger than that of Richard II. Accompanying genealogical tables and commentaries also showed that Philip II of Spain's daughter Isabella Clara Eugenia was a descendant of Philippa, oldest child of John of Gaunt and his first wife Blanche, whereas James VI of Scotland's Lancastrian lineage only dated back to the illegitimate children of John of Gaunt's third wife, Katherine Swynford. Persons's *Conference* also evaluated the strength of rival claims on behalf of James's cousin Arbella Stuart (great-granddaughter of Henry VII's eldest daughter, Margaret Tudor) and Katherine Grey (granddaughter of Henry VII's younger daughter, Mary Tudor). Despite its ostensibly neutral stance, the *Conference* concluded by identifying the Infanta Isabella Clara as 'likest to bear it away', having devoted considerable energy to denying that, in terms of 'the public good of the English commonwealth', significant benefit would accrue from James's accession. Large numbers of Scots would seek 'the commodities and riches of England', without offering reciprocal benefits. Moreover, any Anglo-Scottish regal union 'would not long endure', given the Scots' 'aversion and natural alienation' from their English neighbours 'and their ancient inclination to join with the French and Irish against us'.[34] Rather, Persons's *Conference* suggested to hopeful Catholic readers that the uncertain succession presented a crucial opportunity. At the two Catholic seminaries recently established to train future English priests at Valladolid and Seville, the *Conference* was read aloud during mealtimes.[35]

Once an explicitly pro-Catholic author had impugned James's hereditary right, a Protestant backlash ensued. In 1596, the Scots Jesuit William Crichton rued Persons's intervention by citing 'a French proverb: you don't catch a hare by a drum'. As Crichton observed, 'ministers are now beating it in the pulpits both of England and Scotland' and the more emphasis that was placed on the dangers of a Catholic alternative – endorsed by the Jesuits, Spain and the papacy – the more James's attractions were appreciated as a legitimate, male, Protestant sovereign, with not only an heir, but also a spare, following Princess Elizabeth's birth that same year.[36] In November 1595, the Scots king had gone on record before his Privy Councillors to confirm that he would take 'all the means he could against the practice of Spain and their invasion here', being resolved 'not only to defend his own realm but [also] the realm of England which he esteemed more dear to him than his own'. Temporarily in England, and absent from his post in Edinburgh, Elizabeth's ambassador, Bowes, was reassured by a colleague, Roger Ashton, who 'heard the same myself', that James was determined to assert his claim to the English crown peacefully, keeping his 'hands clean of practice and blood' and giving international observers 'no cause to think' that he 'meant by Scotland to conquer England but, by the contrary, by England to conquer Scotland'.[37]

James was also determined to provide counter-arguments to Persons's *Conference*. The following February, Burghley was informed by another Edinburgh correspondent that he had approached a courtier to request sight of the *Conference* and its loan had been agreed for 'a night and half a day, in which time it was sent for thrice by the king'.[38] Back in Edinburgh in April, Bowes confirmed that James remained visibly agitated about the succession. Discussing the threat posed by Catholic nobles in Scotland, the king had suddenly made a 'solemn protestation that, to gain the crown of England, he would not wish the shortening of her Majesty's reign or days or justly grieve or offend her during her life'. Although a shocked Bowes had instantly warned James that discussion of the English succession was 'so holy' a matter that 'I durst not let my ears, tongue or hands be touched therewith, whereupon he ceased', Bowes added that he had been 'credibly informed that publicly at his table and privately in his bedchamber', the Scottish king 'used oftentimes like speeches and protestations'.[39]

The statutory prohibition placed on discussion of Elizabeth's successor also saw succession debates displaced into imaginative works focusing on dynastic competition, civil war, legitimacy, rebellion and usurpation. Plays written and performed in London by Shakespeare's company of 'Queen's Men' during the 1590s included *Titus Andronicus*, *Julius Caesar*, *Richard II*, *Richard III*, *King John*, the *Henry VI* trilogy and the two parts of *Henry IV*. Meanwhile James was so insulted by transparently allegorical similarities between the trial of his mother, Mary Stuart, and the fictional trial of Duessa in Edmund Spenser's *The Faerie Queene* (1596) that he banned the epic poem from being sold in Scotland. The reading public also evinced a keen appetite for news of hostilities in France, haunted by fears that, on Elizabeth's death, England might again descend into the type of dislocation suffered during the Wars of the Roses or the sectarian strife currently dividing French society. In the autumn of 1596, a Venetian aristocrat, Francesco Gradenigo, spent a fortnight in London where he found the English 'in great alarm about the enemy' as new controls on individuals seeking to enter or leave the country had revealed the presence of numerous foreign spies. As Gradenigo observed, Elizabeth remained 'little disposed to name a successor', despite it being 'a step which her subjects greatly desire, though they do not dare to speak about it'.[40]

III

Had Spanish forces launched a successful invasion of southern England, Elizabeth's crown might yet have been forcibly seized. After English raiders had sacked the Spanish settlement of Pernambuco in north-eastern Brazil in April 1595, Philip II launched a reprisal raid the following August, dispatching galleons from Brittany to attack Cornwall: the towns of Mousehole, Penzance and Newlyn were plundered and burned and several local inhabitants were killed. In Paul, outside Mousehole, the expedition's commander Don Carlos de Amézola noted that 'the mosque, where they gather for their conventicles' was spared destruction after an English renegade reminded the Spaniards of the church's pre-Reformation history of Mass worship.[41] Although similar reasoning did not spare other sites, describing a Cornish church as a *mezquita* (mosque) reflected the ways in which Habsburg attacks on Elizabethan England could be justified in terms of holy war. Denounced as schismatics and heretics, the English were regarded as equally legitimate objects of crusade as infidel Ottoman Turks.

The following June, over a hundred English ships attacked the strategic Andalusian port of Cadiz, occupying the town for a fortnight of looting and destruction. Watching the blazing inferno in Cadiz harbour, the English fleet's rear-admiral Sir Walter Ralegh ventured that 'if any man had a desire to see Hell itself, it was there most lively figured', while a Spanish officer, Don Luis Fajardo, lamented to Philip II 'the prestige that is destroyed' as he watched English troops sack the city 'with as much security and pleasure as though they had been in the river of London'.[42] In July, the Governor of the Scilly Isles, Sir Francis Godolphin, warned Elizabeth's adviser Robert Devereux, earl of Essex, that, despite a new eight-pointed Star Castle having been built on the island of St Mary's two years earlier, the fortress needed 'a stronger garrison'. As Godolphin feared, 'the gathering of these Spaniards seems as a cloud that is like to fall shortly in some part of her Majesty's dominions'.[43] In October 1597, Philip attempted the enterprise of England again, sending an armada of 136 ships, and over 12,000 soldiers and mariners, which approached the English Channel near Lizard Point and only narrowly missed intercepting Elizabeth's fleet before autumnal storms forced its dispersed retreat. In the event of the fleet's landing in England, Philip had authorized an English-language proclamation, denying aggressive intent and explaining that he was 'merely endeavouring to maintain in their accustomed peace those who for confession of our holy faith and the good of their native land are being persecuted'.[44]

English nervousness regarding imminent Spanish incursions was exacerbated by the outbreak of rebellion in Ulster in 1594, led by two Gaelic Irish lords, Hugh O'Neill, earl of Tyrone, and Hugh O'Donnell, which saw English forces heavily defeated at the battle of Clontibret in County Monaghan the following summer. As Irish resistance mobilized across the country, a beleaguered English administration engaged in serial parleys and truces. In July 1596, the English-born Bishop William Lyon of Cork and Ross wrote despairingly to Elizabeth's cousin Henry Carey, Baron Hunsdon, describing how the local population denounced the established Church of Ireland's Protestant services as 'the Devil's Service, and the professors thereof, devils'. Visiting a local school, Lyon had 'found to my great grief Her Majesty's style and title torn out of all the grammars' that had been newly provided, while one schoolmaster had denied Elizabeth's right to rule Ireland, but had acknowledged the lawful title of her Tudor forbears. Although Lyon had imprisoned the recalcitrant teachers, he wondered 'what good shall be looked for in this commonwealth, where the youth are taught by such schoolmasters?'[45] That autumn, Captain Alonso Cobos was dispatched to Ireland to discuss providing Spanish support to Tyrone's forces. At a meeting with

Irish earls in Donegal, a request was made for 6,000 Spanish troops and arms for 10,000 soldiers and it was suggested that the Habsburg Governor of the Low Countries, Archduke Albert of Austria, should be named Governor of Ireland.[46]

Meanwhile, across Continental Europe, James VI's sympathetic intentions towards Catholics were energetically promoted by Scottish agents with differing degrees of accreditation. One of James's more duplicitous agents, John Pury of Ogilvy, travelled through the Low Countries to Venice, Milan, Florence and Rome before heading to Spain where he presented 'Memorials' to Philip II at Toledo in June 1596. Insisting that James was seeking vengeance for his mother's execution, Pury acknowledged that 'for certain causes he has dissembled and deferred acting until now'. But, according to Pury, the Scottish king was now so committed to forming an anti-English alliance with Spain that he would even be willing to 'give into the hands of the King of Spain, his son', Prince Henry, 'as greater security'. Pury's overtures were closely watched by an English secular priest, John Cecil, who denied their credibility, pointing out that since James 'with his own hand [had] written books against the Catholic religion . . . how then is it possible that this man should become a Catholic all of a sudden?'[47]

Yet residual suspicions remained regarding the king's susceptibility to Catholic approaches. Henri IV's shift from Protestant hero to loyal Catholic provided a perturbing model for Protestants fretting about their rulers' potential mutability. Earlier that year, the English agent in Edinburgh, George Nicolson, had reported an instance in which James had railed that, even if he agreed 'to hear and know the devices of the enemy, yet he shall never consent to them, nor change his religion and do as the French king has done to gain any kingdom or save his own [kingdom] or yet his own life'.[48] Although Cecil dismissed Pury's overtures as 'very shifty, sharp and open to suspicion', the English administration remained more concerned by James's own diplomatic initiatives.[49] After all, of the ten or so potential claimants to the English crown, James was the only one that could negotiate with other sovereigns, Protestant or Catholic, on equal terms. At the opening of the Scottish Parliament in December 1597, Nicolson reported to Burghley's son, Sir Robert Cecil, that James had unleashed a litany of grievances against Elizabeth to the crown-appointed committee of nobles, known as the Lords of the Articles. Although 'loath to do evil offices between the princes', Nicolson reported that James had protested 'how far he was wronged by the death of his mother', cited repeated delays in receiving his English annuity and 'scornful answers' offered if the matter was raised; he also objected to being blamed 'wrongfully as a stirrer-up of Poland and Denmark', 'for the late accidents in Ireland' and for disturbances in the Anglo-Scottish borders. According to another English observer, the Scottish Estates had then advised James to 'send ambassadors to all his foreign friends and brother kings and princes to complain' and encourage fellow sovereigns to 'send their ambassadors to England for this effect'.[50]

The royal court in Edinburgh also regularly received foreign embassies, including a surprise visit from Queen Anna's younger brother Ulric, duke of Schleswig-Holstein, in the spring of 1598. The lavish reception accorded to Ulric discomfited the pro-English courtier Roger Aston, who lamented that 'the god Bacchus is a great guider among us at this time', warning Sir Robert Cecil that Elizabeth's 'good health will not be drunk here', since James's brother-in-law 'professes himself a great enemy to England and marvels much that the king suffers me to be about him'.[51] Ulric was accompanied home by Bishop Cunningham of Aberdeen and Sir Peter Young who then undertook diplomatic missions to the Danish court and to various German Protestant states including Mecklenburg, Brandenburg, Saxony and Hesse. Cunningham and Young were tasked with informing James's fellow Protestant rulers 'more clearly and fully as to his right to the English throne', since other 'competitors and their instigators are leaving no stone unturned at home or abroad to prejudice the title of the King of Scots and his children'. The envoys' instructions also included reassurances to foreign rulers that since James 'loves and cherishes the whole English people even as the Scots', they should 'importune' Elizabeth to declare formally that James and his children were 'by indubitable right the nearest heirs and successors to the crown' in order to forestall counter-claims by any foreign-backed Catholic candidate.[52] Although supportive responses were elicited, formal commitments of military support were avoided, on the grounds of internal dissensions within the Empire and around the Baltic region.

James also endorsed hereditary rights of royal succession in his *Trew Law of Free Monarchies* which was published anonymously in Edinburgh in 1598. Firmly denying the capacity of statutes or other testamentary provision to deprive rightful claimants to any throne, the king reminded readers of the bloody war of succession that had followed Henri III's assassination. As James observed, the 'whole [of] France acknowledges the superstitious rebellion of the Leaguers, who upon pretence of heresy, by force of arms held so long out, to the great desolation of their whole country, their native and righteous king'.[53] That same year saw the posthumous publication of the manuscript of the royal succession by the Puritan MP Peter Wentworth, which challenged Robert Persons's claims regarding the unsuitability of a Scottish successor. Anticipating James's accession as king, Wentworth had reassured readers that, with 'both his parents descended of English blood', James would 'in England become English and a favourer chiefly of Englishmen'. Since 'the meanest Scotsmen that are settled in England are content to forget their country, kindred and parents', James would soon be 'Englished with us'.[54]

IV

By the late 1590s, shifting Continental geopolitics were rendering James VI's claim to succeed Elizabeth increasingly compelling as a means by which England might resist Catholic or Habsburg encirclement. In April 1598, Henri IV issued the controversial Edict of Nantes, effectively ending France's internal sectarian strife by permitting confessional coexistence. While Catholicism remained the country's state religion, Huguenot churches received legal recognition and Henri's former co-religionists were accorded surety towns in which freedom of Protestant worship was guaranteed. Weeks later, papal mediation secured an end to the long-running Franco-Spanish war through the Treaty of Vervins, whereby Philip II recognized Henri as French king, withdrew Spanish forces from French soil and returned the port of Calais to French control. Fears that England risked diplomatic isolation were compounded by the prospect of future Habsburg encirclement as, before concluding the Vervins treaty, Philip had donated joint sovereignty of the territories that broadly approximate to modern Belgium, known as the Spanish Netherlands, to his daughter Isabella, and her future husband, Archduke Albert of Austria. In Madrid, the Venetian ambassador, Agostino Nani, claimed that a government minister, Don Juan d'Idíaquez, had confirmed Spanish satisfaction at concluding peace with France, notwithstanding Elizabeth's attempts to dissuade Henri from signing, 'even to the length of threatening war'. The French king had, however, responded by indicating that 'he wished to free himself, first from the [Habsburg] lion's paws, and then he could easily protect himself from the [English] cat's claws'.[55]

As Henri's ally, Elizabeth was granted a six-month diplomatic window to decide whether or not an end to Anglo-Spanish hostilities should accompany the Vervins treaty. Ministers thereby needed to consider whether or not to continue English financial and military support of the Dutch Republic to preserve its recent independence from Spanish Habsburg rule. In the summer of 1598, the earl of Essex, Elizabeth's adviser, penned an *Apology*, strongly arguing against any Anglo-Spanish peace. For Essex, it was simply too risky to move 'from a doubtful war, to an unsafe treaty', given powerful Catholic factions keen to promote the claims of Archduchess Isabella to succeed Elizabeth as the daughter of the queen's erstwhile brother-in-law. Isabella's husband, Archduke Albert, might now regard 'the Low Countries [as] the rise by which he must leap into England'.[56] In such an outcome, a composite monarchy joining England with the Spanish Netherlands offered a Catholic alternative to a Protestant regal union that joined England with Scotland under James VI.

Following Philip II's death in September, his successor, Philip III, welcomed peace with France on the grounds that it enabled Spanish forces to concentrate on regaining control of the Dutch Republic and attacking England. As the Spanish navy regrouped and attacked English and Dutch shipping in the Atlantic, there was palpable panic in England. In August 1599, the London letter-writer John Chamberlain informed his diplomat friend, Dudley Carleton, of 'news (yet false) that the Spaniards were landed in the Isle of Wight, which bred such a fear and consternation in this town'. The rumoured invasion had provoked 'such a cry of women, chaining of streets, and shutting of the gates, as though the enemy had been at Blackwall'.[57]

Together with perennial fears of a Spanish descent, the Elizabethan regime was discomfited by James VI's continued attempts to convince Catholic powers to support his claim to the English throne. In September 1599, the Scottish king initiated direct contact with the papacy by writing to Clement VIII, addressing the Pope as 'most blessed father' and signing himself as Clement's 'most obedient son'. A year later Sir Robert Cecil warned George Nicolson that, however much James might try to cover his tracks, 'the king is deceived if he do not conclude that all Italy rings of it', with no rumour 'so common as that the king will follow the French king's example' by converting to Catholicism. Although Cecil had no way of 'believing that the king hath done all this', he nevertheless inferred 'that these lewd persons whom he hath employed do either counterfeit his hand or else this is a truth'.[58] James himself later disavowed knowledge of the letter's content and few Catholics in Scotland regarded his imminent conversion as likely. A 'memorial on the state of Scotland' in 1601, sent to Rome by the Jesuit superior in Scotland, Robert Abercrombie, confirmed of James that 'the single object of his ambition is the crown of England, which he would gladly take, to all appearance, from the hand of the Devil himself'. Lamenting that James's 'language consists almost entirely of blasphemy or heresy', the memorial's author accepted that the Scottish king might well be moved to act as 'a hypocrite, but only a miracle of God's power, and an extraordinary inspiration, will ever make him a Catholic in reality'.[59]

In the spring of 1599, a regular informer to Elizabeth's court, John Petit, warned that James was relying on his Danish brother-in-law to supply 10,000 soldiers should he seek 'to gather grapes before they are ripe'. With Catholics convinced that 'for a kingdom, he [James] will become a counterfeit Catholic, like the King of France', Petit advised that 'means should be taken to prevent that king cutting the grass under Her Majesty's feet'. Suspicions also arose that Henri IV might have his own designs on the English throne. From Liège, Petit observed the following April that, although 'the French King gives the King of Scotland fair words, promising to assist his pretences to England', royal reassurances potentially belied ulterior motives. For Petit, 'the smoke does not rise without some fire, though covered with ashes of deep dissimulation'.[60]

In Paris, Henri resisted appeals from Clement VIII in 1601 to lend French support to an alternative, Catholic candidate to succeed Elizabeth. Speaking from personal experience, Henri claimed to believe that 'it would be more equitable, easier and more useful' to hope for the Scottish king's conversion.[61] Unsurprisingly, James remained suspicious of Henri's encouragement. As an English informant, Thomas Douglas, had informed Sir Robert Cecil earlier that year, the Scottish king's sense of humour had failed when told that, 'in his merriment', Henri had acclaimed the birth of his new son César – by his Norman mistress, Gabrielle d'Estrées – by recalling an earlier Norman conquest to suggest 'it may be we find a bastard of Normandy to conquer those chalk hills shining in the eyes of France'.[62]

Whereas Henri might fancifully jest about landing French troops in Kent, the prospect of a Spanish landing in Ireland remained all too plausible. English forces had been defeated at the Battle of the Yellow Ford in County Armagh in August 1598, as Tyrone's rebellion extended beyond Ulster and Connaught into Leinster and Munster, where the English planter community feared imminent extinction. A manuscript 'Supplication', composed that autumn, exhorted Elizabeth's administration to 'weep England, mourn, lament, not the loss of us, but the loss of thy honour; not our destruction, but thine own disgrace'. Attributed to Edmund Spenser, or another member of the New English planter community, the tract's author could not credit that although English troops had previously triumphed in France and supported the Dutch overthrow of Spanish rule in Flanders, they were now 'by a crew of contemptible rebels controlled in thine own territories, in thine own dominions'. Aware that 'Little England hath many great enemies', the author knew that Tyrone's forces were only too keen to 'let in the enemies of England upon her back, yea and to join with them'. Amid rumours that 15,000 Spanish soldiers had been promised, 'their coming is bruited every day, expected certainly by the Irish, greatly feared by all the English'.[63]

To quell Irish disturbances, the earl of Essex was appointed as Lord Lieutenant and arrived in Dublin with an army of over 17,000 soldiers in April 1599. But as serial English humiliations continued, the English queen upbraided Essex in July, pointing out that, despite her success in putting 'down the greatest enemy she had' in Philip II, 'a base bush kern' – Tyrone – remained obdurate.[64] After Essex had attempted to negotiate privately with Tyrone, Elizabeth berated her Lord Lieutenant's naïvety, insisting that 'to trust this traitor upon oath is to trust a devil upon his religion'. Essex then incurred further royal disapproval by quitting his post and returning to England without permission.[65] Suspicions that Essex had encouraged Irish ambitions were reinforced by prospective peace terms, presented by Tyrone shortly afterwards, that envisaged Ireland being ruled by an English viceroy with the Catholic Church, under papal control, restored as the country's established religion. While Tyrone's peace proposals were brusquely dismissed in Sir Robert Cecil's handwritten marginalia as 'Utopia', Essex wrote to James

VI on Christmas Day 1600, warning the Scottish king that Cecil and other ministers were dangerously 'juggling with our enemies', promoting the succession claims of Philip III's daughter Isabella and fomenting 'devilish plots with your Majesty's own subjects against your person and life'.[66] But Essex's own downfall was sealed, weeks later, when he despairingly attempted to provoke a popular rising in London among his supporters and was subsequently convicted and executed for treason.

In September 1600, a Spanish armada had finally made landfall on Elizabeth's territories when twenty-eight ships, carrying around 3,700 soldiers and commanded by the veteran Don Juan del Águila – who had led Philip II's invasion of Brittany a decade earlier – landed at Kinsale in County Cork, which was awkwardly a couple of hundred miles away from the rebellion's leaders in Ulster. As Tyrone's forces embarked on an unseasonal march across Ireland to rendezvous with the Spanish forces besieging Kinsale, another six ships and 650 soldiers landed at Castlehaven, in west Cork, commanded by Pedro de Zubiaur, in early December. Perceiving his mission as that of a glorious conquistador, Zubiaur promised Philip III that 'just as the Basques went to Rome to fight and as Hernán Cortés sunk his ships in the New World with full zeal and contentment, so I am serving God and Your Majesty on this good occasion'. In mid-December, the new Lord Deputy, Charles Blount, Lord Mountjoy, wrote to Cecil, requesting urgent supplies and reinforcements for English forces trying to break the siege at Kinsale. Mountjoy was convinced that 'the king of Spain means to make this place the seat of the war', not only to conquer Ireland, but also 'to push for England'. Interrogations of captured Spanish soldiers had revealed Philip's hope that Ireland's population would unite against England 'to get that liberty (as they call it) that they have so long fought for'. As Tyrone's forces arrived to support the Spaniards, Mountjoy still hoped that English force would prevail and 'the war both of Ireland and Spain might have an end together here'.[67]

On Christmas Eve 1601, an attack by Mountjoy's forces successfully broke the siege of Kinsale, incurring Irish and Spanish losses of around 1,200 soldiers, while English casualties were minimal. Amid mutual recriminations among the confederate rebels and their Spanish allies, the veteran naval commander Martín de Padilla y Manrique rued a systemic failure by successive administrations in Madrid to offer adequate support to the Irish. As Padilla had insisted to Philip, reinforcements must be sufficient to 'end the business for once and for all, and not driblets, like sips of broth, that will only prolong the agony, and allow the invalid to die after all'. Having been part of a failed attempt to seize the Cornish port of Falmouth in 1597, Padilla denounced the extent to which 'from motives of economy, expeditions are undertaken with such small forces, that they principally serve to irritate our enemies, rather than to punish them'.[68] But nor was Elizabeth's administration able to quell Irish resistance by force, given that Tyrone remained in arms and the prospect of further Spanish assistance could not be discounted; accordingly, Mountjoy was authorized to seek a negotiated end to hostilities. Remarkably generous terms attached to the Treaty of Mellifont that was agreed between Mountjoy and Tyrone on 30 March 1603. As well as formally submitting to Mountjoy, Tyrone agreed to abjure all dependency on foreign powers and renounce his title to any lands other than those granted by the English crown. Unbeknown to Tyrone – but known to Mountjoy – Elizabeth I had died six days earlier at Richmond Palace.

4
Uniting this Sea-Walled Isle, 1601–1605

In a posthumously published memoir, the English diplomat Sir Henry Wotton recalled an instance towards the end of Elizabeth I's reign when a packet of letters arrived at Blackheath, piquing the interest of the ageing queen. Her chief adviser, Sir Robert Cecil, had deflected Elizabeth's curiosity by warning that, since the packet's contents 'looked and smelled ill-favouredly, coming out of a filthy budget', it was always necessary 'to open and air' letters from Scotland.[1] Cecil had feared that the packet might contain items of the clandestine correspondence that he had started with James VI of Scotland in the spring of 1601, amid the reconfiguration of political alliances that had followed the downfall of Robert Devereux, earl of Essex. With the correspondence known to only half-a-dozen individuals, secret letters were placed in the ordinary diplomatic post for the unsuspecting English agent in Edinburgh, George Nicolson – nicknamed 'the pigeon' – while return missives from James's court were addressed to French Huguenot nobles in London.[2] In one coded letter to James, Cecil acknowledged that Elizabeth had designated him as her successor *in corde* ('in her heart'), though not *in ore aperto* ('by public utterance'). Accordingly, Cecil reassured James that, following the English queen's eventual death, 'your ship shall be steered into the right harbour without cross of wave or tide that shall be able to turn over a cockboat, for which many that will talk now, and brave it, will be fitter pilots' than they might appear at present. Henry Percy, earl of Northumberland, likewise advised the Scottish king against any premature action, recognizing that, to 'a prince of spirit, the time may be long-seeming where expectation of such a fortune is at hand'. Although 'men look rather for the sun rising than after the sun setting', Northumberland warned James not to jeopardize his chances of a peaceful succession by distracting Elizabeth's administration at a time when its energies were concentrated on suppressing rebellion in Ireland, its finances strained by supporting the Dutch and its military defences focused on repulsing another armada.[3]

Elizabeth died in the early morning on 24 March 1603 and, an hour after her death, a proclamation was read aloud at Richmond Palace, confirming that James was 'by law, by lineal succession, and undoubted right' king of England, being 'lineally and lawfully descended' from Henry VII. Enjoining the loyalty of local officials, the proclamation warned that measures would be taken to prevent any 'word or deed against the public peace' or attempt to impugn 'our only undoubted and dear Lord and Sovereign that now is James'.[4] At 10 a.m. the proclamation was read publicly at Whitehall, St Paul's, Ludgate, Cheapside and Cornhill, amid tightened security measures that included alerting the English Navy, closing the nation's ports, detaining prominent Catholics in the localities, withholding troop consignments intended for the Low Countries and placing the crown jewels and royal silver collection under special guard.

In a later account of English affairs, the Venetian ambassador in London, Nicolo Molin, recalled that James 'came to the throne as quietly as could possibly be desired' after Elizabeth, on her deathbed at Richmond, had 'indicated rather than actually declared him as her successor' by silently nodding assent.[5] While tales of the dying queen's nomination may have been apocryphal, the mid-seventeenth-century Anglican cleric George Lawson suggested that – setting aside the question of whether or not Elizabeth had any right to signify her successor – 'her wise council did foresee, that this was an effectual, if not the only way to prevent greater mischiefs and effusion of blood' that might otherwise have ensued. As Lawson added, although 'in an extraordinary case, some extraordinary thing, tending to the public good, may lawfully be done yet this is not to be made an ordinary rule'.[6] Among contemporaries, the uncontested nature of James's accession prompted one writer, Thomas Dekker, to marvel that, 'upon Thursday it was treason to cry "God save King James, King of England", and upon Friday high treason not to cry so'.[7] Another diarist, John Manningham, observed in London 'no tumult, no contradiction, no disorder in the city'; rather, 'every man went about his business as readily, as peaceably, as securely, as though there had been no change, nor any news ever heard of competitors'.[8] From the Midlands, the diplomat Sir George Carew wrote to Cecil three days after Elizabeth's death, confessing relief at the universal recognition of James's succession. Carew admitted that while he had anxiously envisaged 'many distempers in the state', his fears only reflected 'the opinions of the wisest, who for many years past, trembled to think of Her Majesty's decease, as if instantly upon it, the kingdom would have been torn asunder'.[9]

At this crucial juncture, coordinated foreign support for an alternative claimant failed to materialize. In Edinburgh, James learned of Elizabeth's death coincidentally with entertaining an envoy, Nicolas Scorza, who had been sent by the Habsburg rulers of the Spanish Netherlands, Archduke Albert and Archduchess Isabella, to offer financial and military assistance to uphold James's claim.[10] A few weeks earlier, Philip III's chief adviser, the count of Olivares, had advised the Spanish Council of State to support an alternative candidate from among the English Catholic community in return for the Isle of Wight being ceded to Spain. If an undesirable successor to Elizabeth seemed likely to gain power, a Spanish presence on the island would allow 'an invasion of England necessary to stop it'. But Olivares advised against demanding Spanish control of a mainland English port, which 'would offend everyone in England, and in France', and counselled Philip to 'take no heed of Ireland, which is a noisy business, and more trouble than advantage' for Spanish interests.[11]

I

The peaceful accession of the thirty-six-year-old king of Scotland, James Stuart, as king of England astonished foreign observers. The French panegyrist Thomas Pelletier contrasted the tranquil upshot of the unsettled English succession with the protracted French wars of succession that had eventually ended with Henri IV's conversion to Catholicism. As Pelletier conceded, many in Continental Europe had anticipated that, on Elizabeth's death, England would become 'a theatre filled with the most horrible and bloody tragedies which one could expect in an entirely disordered and ravaged state'.[12] Writing to his Spanish counterpart, Henri's ambassador in London, Christophe de Harlay, count of Beaumont, confessed surprise at the placid turn of events, given that, 'for years, all Christendom held for certain that it must be attended with trouble and confusion'. Despite the 'rooted and ancient hostility of the English to the Scottish', Beaumont ascribed popular acceptance of James's accession to his strong hereditary claim, prior royal experience, positive character reports and the welcome novelty of a secure succession in the form of the king's three surviving children, Henry, Elizabeth and Charles. Beaumont alluded to 'the alarm, that everyone feels lest discord should open the door to foreigners' – more foreign, evidently, than James – but added that 'we shall see him here in a few days, and we will observe how he proceeds in his ideas'.[13]

From Paris, the English diplomat Dudley Carleton observed that 'the statists here who, in the depth of their judgements, presaged our ruin and confusion' were now seen to 'shrink up their shoulders', offer grudging admiration for the English succession's smooth management and 'begin to feel their own pulse' instead.[14] Having heard that James had acceded as king 'with great applause, calm and with contradiction from no-one', Philip's ambassador to the French court, Juan Bautista de Tassis, reported that both he and Pope Clement VIII's nuncio had already congratulated James's representative in Paris, Cardinal David Beaton, with Tassis reassuring the Scot that Anglo-Spanish enmity had always been 'solo personal' – purely personal.[15] In the new Spanish capital of Valladolid, the Venetian envoy Simon Contarini observed that Philip III's ministers 'show great relief at the death of the Queen of England', as 'a few days have sufficed to change the aspect of matters from one of despair to one of hope'. As Contarini conceived, 'the whole question' of future Anglo-Spanish relations depended on whether James would continue English military and financial support of the Dutch in their struggle for independence from Habsburg rule.[16] In Brussels, the Archduchess Isabella greeted news of James's accession with the wry observation that, following serial false reports of her demise, Elizabeth had 'enraged us nearly as much in death as she did in life'. Writing to Philip's favourite, Francisco Gómez de Sandoval, duke of Lerma, Isabella remarked that James had succeeded to the English throne 'in such a notably calm and peaceful manner that, so they say, his mother must be rolling over in her grave!' Nevertheless, the archduchess urged Lerma to impress on her brother the importance of securing James's goodwill, insisting that they should 'lose no time in winning him over, in order that others may not do it first, as they will try'. James was now joint monarch of both England and Scotland and, allied with his Danish brother-in-law Christian IV, had also 'come to be lord of the Ocean Sea'.[17]

James's accession coincided with a critical juncture in Spain's long-running war with the Dutch Republic, prompting equal anxiety for the Habsburg archdukes and Dutch leaders regarding the likelihood of future English assistance to either side. In the only Dutch-controlled region of Flanders, the city of Ostend had been under siege since July 1601 and had relied on extensive English support, initially supervised by the city's English governor, Sir Francis Vere. In what became one of history's bloodiest sieges, the situation was increasingly precarious, prompting Dutch requests for an additional 10,000 soldiers, while the Habsburgs' envoy, Scorza, had been sent to Edinburgh specifically to try to forestall future recruitment from Scotland. Having had an audience with the Scottish king five days before Elizabeth's death, Scorza reported that James had evinced an instinctive antipathy to the Dutch on account of their rebellious republicanism, but had asked that his view remain confidential.[18] Dutch hopes seemed likely to be further frustrated by reports that, when travelling south from Edinburgh and pressed about the urgent situation in the Low Countries, the new king was reported to be unconcerned by imminent Dutch losses, having asked, 'What of it? Was not Ostend originally the King of Spain's, and therefore, now, the Archduke's?'[19]

But since effective policy could not be formulated until James arrived in London, his English Privy Councillors wrote to their new king in early April, admitting that 'we know not upon what terms your Majesty means to stand with those princes'. Confirming that they 'dare not wade any further' into diplomatic complexities, the Councillors knew that, as king of Scotland, James had always maintained amity with the Habsburgs, but, as England's new king, he had now inherited financial and other commitments to the Dutch.[20] Among the most vocal advocates of maintaining English support for the Dutch was the poet and soldier Sir Walter Ralegh, who perceptively warned James that the two states' conjunction of interests in Protestantism, naval power and trade competition suggested they should be natural allies, but could equally render them fatal foes. Denying there were any other peoples 'so fitted by art and nature as to annoy these kingdoms as they', Ralegh reminded James that the Dutch were, after all, 'so near us, as they will be in our ports in a summer's day'.[21]

The timing of James's arrival in the English capital was designed to ensure that Elizabeth's funeral had been held by the time the new king entered London. Court etiquette required the burial of a former monarch before any public appearance by their successor, enabling subjects to mourn one sovereign without conflicted loyalties detracting from the new ruler's accession. To Northumberland, James had confirmed his wish to avoid any act that might 'diminish part of that honour and dignity' attaching to the English queen 'as long as her body is above ground'.[22] Accordingly, James spent the day of Elizabeth's funeral on 28 April 1603 being entertained at the Huntingdonshire home of Sir Oliver Cromwell, uncle to his infant namesake who, in 1649, would sign a death warrant for the execution of James's son Charles.

Foreign commentators suspected, however, that personal animus also explained the new king's absence. The Venetian envoy in London, Giovanni Carlo Scaramelli, claimed that James could 'never expel from his memory the fact that his mother was put to death at the hands of the public executioner, with great disgrace and cruelty'. As James approached the English capital for the first time in his life, Scaramelli reported frantic activity to ensure that 'Elizabeth's portrait is being hidden everywhere, and Mary Stuart's shown instead', alongside official protestations that the only reason that James's mother had been executed had been her stubborn adherence to Catholicism.[23] Before leaving Edinburgh, James had also undertaken some damage limitation of his own by clarifying the content of published advice given to Prince Henry in *Basilikon Doron* (1599). Alluding to the divisive legacy attaching to his mother's memory, James had warned Henry not to tolerate 'the false and irreverent writing or speaking of malicious men against your parents and predecessors', deeming it 'a thing monstrous, to see a man love the child, and hate the parents'. Preparing a new edition of *Basilikon Doron* for publication in London and Edinburgh in 1603, James hastily dismissed any apprehension that, by offering such advice to his son, 'it should appear, that I do nourish in my mind, a vindictive resolution against England, or some principals there', insisting that his comments had been made within a domestic, Scottish context and 'without using any persuasion to him of revenge'.[24]

Described by its royal author as supplying 'the true image of my very mind', *Basilikon Doron* was also translated into Welsh, Latin, French, German, Dutch, Swedish and Hungarian. In England, the lawyer and MP Sir Francis Bacon recalled in 1609 how the king's published treatise 'falling into every man's hand filled the whole realm as with a good perfume or incense' before his arrival.[25] On the diplomatic front, James's accession in 1603 prompted an unprecedentedly large gathering of ambassadors in London with envoys sent by the courts of France, Spain, the Spanish Netherlands, the Dutch Republic, Venice, Savoy, Florence, the count Palatine of the Rhine, Württemberg, Pfalz-Neuburg, Brunswick, Brandenburg, Lorraine, the Hanseatic Towns, Denmark and Poland, while envoys were also dispatched from James's court to Rome and Persia.[26] As Henri IV's ambassador extraordinary, Maximilien de Béthune, marquis of Rosny, marvelled, 'it appeared as though all the princes in Europe considered the gaining England in their interests, as of the utmost consequence'.[27] Keen to secure the diplomatic initiative, the delegation from the Dutch Republic arrived in London even before James himself, headed by Frederick Henry of Nassau (son of the Dutch Revolt's assassinated leader, William the Silent) and the Republic's most senior statesman, John van Olden Barnavelt. The large number of missions simultaneously arriving not only landed the English court with mounting entertainment costs, but also posed logistical challenges on account of unpredictable Channel crossings. In June, the entourage attached to Archduke Albert's envoy, Charles de Ligne, count of Aremburg, was met by barge at Gravesend, the day before Rosny's French delegation of around 120 individuals arrived, while across London James's court funded the accommodation and victualling at Richmond of Christian IV of Denmark's entourage of around 140 attendants. Presented to James for the first time at Greenwich in May, Scaramelli encountered 'such a crowd . . . upwards of ten or twelve thousand persons', including Privy Councillors and an 'infinity' of English nobles, arranged 'almost in an attitude of adoration' around their new king.[28]

Rosny could not, however, detect any attitude of adoration among the new king's subjects. Rather, he found the English court 'full of suspicion, mistrust, jealousy, secret and even public discontents'.[29] While Rosny's main objective was to prevent conclusion of any Anglo-Spanish peace, persuading James to continue hostilities required a compelling answer to the question that foreign observers argued should be posed of Henri: 'how can you ask me to live at war in order that you may live in peace?'[30]

In private audiences with the English king, Rosny admired James's recognition that it was 'necessary to preserve an equilibrium' among the Habsburg, Bourbon and Stuart dynasties, but feared that the new king's chief characteristic was a 'dissimulation' that 'constantly consisted in giving hopes to all, but never anything farther to any'. In later years, and ennobled as the duke of Sully, Rosny expounded a 'Grand Design' to promote international peace which envisaged 'a general Council, representing all the States of Europe' as 'the happiest invention that could have been conceived', drawing on legal concepts of international arbitration and collective security. But serving as Henri's ambassador in 1603, Rosny suspected that James's apparent 'disposition to peace' was, in fact, 'rather to indolence and inaction', and 'having promised a little, he should perform nothing'. Toasting the king's health over dinner at Greenwich in June, Rosny also confessed surprise when James 'told me softly' that he would drink a health to 'the double union, which he meditated between the royal houses', envisaging a double marriage between Prince Henry and Princess Elizabeth and two of Henri IV's children, despite having 'never till now said a single word to me about this'.[31]

These discussions of potential future French spouses occurred the night before Prince Henry and Princess Elizabeth, together with Queen Anna, arrived at Windsor, with an entourage of 250 carriages and over 5,000 horses. Having left the sickly Prince Charles in Scotland, Anna and her older children had undertaken a separate progress south, staying in various English towns including Berwick-on-Tweed, Alnwick, Newcastle, Durham, York, Doncaster, Nottingham, Leicester, Northampton and Great Missenden.[32] Evoking memories of Elizabeth I's popular provincial progresses, the royal journeys to England undertaken by both James and Anna enabled their English subjects to enjoy rare glimpses of monarchical pageantry and offered local nobility and gentry a chance to offer hospitality in return for hope of future preferment.

The Stuarts' accession to Elizabeth's crown signalled the novel prominence of a royal family. The last royal heir to be born at the English court had been the future Edward VI, whose birth in 1537 was followed, within days, by the death of his mother and Henry VIII's third queen, Jane Seymour. In the absence of any institutional memory of a functioning family court in England, the Stuarts' accession in 1603 brought opportunities for dynastic diplomacy, as evidenced by the whispered Anglo-French marriage discussions shared by James and Rosny at Greenwich. But royal heirs could also prove a liability. Judicial examinations undertaken during the summer of 1603 revealed a series of domestic conspiracies among discontented subjects who doubted their new king's capacity to promote their interests. What became known as the 'Bye Plot' – instigated by Catholic priests, but also involving Protestants – envisaged a large number of Catholics assembling at Greenwich on Midsummer Night in June 1603 in order to kidnap James and imprison him in either the Tower of London or Dover Castle until a guarantee of religious toleration for Catholics could be extracted. In a separate 'Main Plot' – which initially alleged the treasonable involvement of Archduke Albert's ambassador, Count Aremburg – plans were hatched to install James's English cousin, Arbella Stuart, on the throne in a conspiracy that necessitated, as one plotter George Brooke admitted, destruction of 'the king and his cubs'.[33] Against a destabilizing background of serial attempts to seize their thrones, James and Anna were crowned in Westminster Abbey on 25 July 1603 in the first joint English coronation for nearly a century, since that of Henry VIII and Catherine of Aragon in 1509.

Compared to French overtures to England's new king, Habsburg approaches were tardier. A kinsman and namesake of the Spanish ambassador in Paris, Philip's appointed envoy to London, Juan de Tassis, count of Villamediana, procrastinated on the Continent, hoping that Ostend's anticipated fall might strengthen Spain's position in any future peace talks. The promotion of Habsburg interests was thus left to Aremburg, of whom James disdainfully objected to Rosny that the archdukes had 'sent me an ambassador, who can neither walk nor talk', citing Aremburg's incapacitating gout and lack of facility in foreign languages.[34] Moreover, Aremburg's cordial discussions about 'dogs and ambling mares and such like things' with Cecil's brother-in-law, Henry Brooke, Lord Cobham, assumed sinister overtones once it became known that Cobham and his younger brother George were participants in the 'Main Plot'.[35] Indeed, when Sir Walter Ralegh appeared in court in Winchester that autumn, on a charge of high treason for encouraging Spanish-sponsored plotting against James, Attorney General Sir Edward Coke cited evidence (later retracted) from Cobham that would convince 'the world, that there never lived a viler viper upon the face of the earth'. After Coke had informed Ralegh that 'thou hast a Spanish heart, and thyself art a Spider of Hell', Ralegh escaped death on the scaffold following his conviction for treason and was instead imprisoned in the Tower of London.[36] Meanwhile, although Villamediana's ambassadorial delegation had finally arrived at Dover in August 1603, a plague outbreak obliged the Spanish entourage to undertake an improvised tour of southern England before a royal audience could be arranged a month later, also in Winchester. Leading the first Spanish embassy to England since the expulsion of Bernadino de Mendoza in 1584 for promoting Mary Stuart's interests against Elizabeth, Villamediana admitted to Philip he had arrived in 'a kingdom where in almost thirty years no Spaniard has entered with his face uncovered'.[37]

Unsurprisingly, the simultaneous presence in London of so many ambassadorial missions prompted heated disputes over diplomatic precedence. In private, Cecil noted that Villamediana carried himself so as to 'conform *a la gravedado Espanola*' and was 'very inquisitive' to learn how Rosny's French entourage was treated 'lest he should digest any usage inferior to his'.[38] As Christmas loomed in 1603, Cecil wearily admitted to Edward Talbot, earl of Shrewsbury, that 'we are to feast seven ambassadors; Spain, France, Poland, Florence and Savoy, besides masques, and much more' and wished 'with all my heart' that he was instead enjoying the company of Shrewsbury's wife 'by her turf fire'.[39] By mid-January, the English diplomat Carleton reported from Hampton Court that 'we have had here a merry Christmas and nothing to disquiet us save brabbles amongst our ambassadors'.[40] A major rupture had occurred when Queen Anna had invited Villamediana to attend a performance of Samuel Daniel's masque *The Vision of Twelve Goddesses* on Twelfth Night 1604, in which Anna herself had appeared as the goddess Pallas. When the resident French envoy Beaumont then had his invitation to the same event retracted and substituted with an alternative, the Frenchman had been so incensed at the perceived slight to Henri IV's dignity that he had unleashed 'unmannerly expostulations' to James and had threatened 'at the hazard of my life to kill the Spaniard . . . at the feet of the king'.[41]

II

In an address to both Houses of Parliament at Westminster in March 1607, James would later recall the large gathering of distinguished ambassadors that had been sent from royal courts across Europe to congratulate him on his accession. In James's view, the diplomats had 'saluted me as monarch of the whole isle, and with much more respect of my greatness, that if I were king alone of one of these realms'.[42] As

King James VI & I, he was indeed the first British ruler of a Stuart multiple monarchy that comprised England, Scotland and Ireland, with the euphemistic addition of France in its royal title. In April 1603, when James was still travelling south from Edinburgh, Scaramelli reported that he was evidently 'disposed to abandon the titles of England and Scotland, and to call himself King of Great Britain'. Emulating 'that famous and ancient King Arthur', James seemingly sought 'to embrace under one name the whole circuit of one thousand seven hundred miles' as a single 'United Kingdom now possessed by his Majesty in that one island'.[43] The Venetian's intelligence was correct: James regarded the Stuart dynasty's succession to the English crown as the providential fulfilment of timeworn prophecies that had long predicted Britain's eventual union. After arriving in London, the new king issued a proclamation from Greenwich in May 1603, claiming to have 'found in the hearts of all the best-disposed subjects' in both England and Scotland 'a most earnest desire, that the said happy union should be perfected'.[44] In the ensuing months, a plethora of proclamations, pamphlets and parliamentary speeches debated the merits and demerits of creating a 'Great Britain' that potentially encompassed a much closer union of the two countries' parliaments, national churches and economies than would eventually be achieved by the Anglo-Scottish union negotiated in 1707 under James VI & I's great-granddaughter Queen Anne.

Aside from rhetorical grandiloquence, a strong motivation for closer Anglo-Scottish union was James's desire to entrench the strictly limited regal and dynastic union that had occurred. Both the 'Bye' and 'Main' Plots and the extensive outbreak of plague that had coincided with James's accession offered alarming reminders that it would only take the death of four individuals – James and his three children – to sever the Anglo-Scottish connection achieved by his accession. Given the two countries' traditions of mutual enmity and rivalry, calls for greater Anglo-Scottish union could not necessarily assume axiomatic approval. Having hastened to meet his new king, Francis Bacon wrote to Northumberland, describing James as 'a prince the farthest from the appearance of vain-glory that may be' with a 'swift and cursory' style of speech. At the same time, Bacon worried that James 'hastens to a mixture of both kingdoms and nations, faster perhaps than policy will conveniently bear'.[45] Foreign observers also remained sceptical, with Rosny deeming it 'a material doubt, whether so haughty a people as the

English would submit to be governed by foreigners, and more especially by the Scots, who at all times had been the object of their aversion'.[46] By June 1603, rising tensions at Whitehall regarding the extent of new patronage and preferment extended to Scots courtiers led Scaramelli to warn that 'the ill-will between English and Scottish goes on rising rapidly'. Three months later, the Venetian regretted that, as the British union 'question becomes burning, the hatred between the two races grows more intense'. Observing how the 'French, Spanish, and Flemish all begin to see that the power of the two kingdoms is not what they thought it', Scaramelli added that James's Scots subjects were insisting that 'they will never consent to abandon their name'.[47]

Seeking support from his administration north of the border, James wrote to his Privy Councillors in Edinburgh in January 1604, requesting that measures to promote British union be debated in the Scottish Parliament. Since Scotland and England were now united under his rule 'in one isle disjointed from the great Continent of the world', James wanted subjects in both countries to 'join and coalesce together in a sincere and perfect union, and as two twins bred in one belly, love one another as no more two, but one estate'.[48] Although the Scottish Parliament did not meet until July, James's English ministers were sufficiently alarmed by the potential for unionist initiatives to discourage attendance at the king's first English parliament. In December 1603, Cecil had worried that 'whosoever is absent I will protest they do it purposely because they would say "No" to the Union' being sought between England and Scotland.[49]

James's first English parliament was held directly after the king's ceremonial entry into London on 15 March 1604, which had been postponed from the previous summer on account of a plague epidemic. In England, royal entries into London occurred before a new monarch's coronation, in contrast to the custom of most Continental countries. On the deaths of previous English kings and queens, Lord Mayors of London usually assumed a prominent political role in first accommodating the successor in the city's prime fortress – the Tower – from where the new monarch would depart for their coronation, offering a chance for citizens to confer ritual approval in a residual echo of Saxon England's traditions of elective monarchy. But James's position was unique, since not only did he firmly reject notions of elective kingship as irrelevant to his hereditary claim, but he had also acceded peacefully to the English throne as a reigning monarch of an independent kingdom. Moreover, far from offering a symbolic point of departure for his new reign as England's king, London had been the geographical terminus to James's progress south from Edinburgh the previous summer, as he had visited Berwick-on-Tweed, Newcastle, York and other English cities en route.

Nevertheless, in a ceremony lasting five hours and scripted by Thomas Dekker and Ben Jonson – but beset by cold, driving rain – James admired an elaborate series of pageants and passed under prefabricated structures up to seventy feet high, forming seven triumphal arches. While the entry cost around £36,000 to stage, the city's conduits flowed with wine and expatriate mercantile communities supplied an Italian arch at Gracechurch Street and a Dutch arch at the Royal Exchange. To avoid disputes over diplomatic precedence, foreign ambassadors were not invited to form part of the official cavalcade. But in his report of the royal entry to Philip III, Villamediana confirmed that the king and queen had stopped the procession when it had reached the Spanish delegation's vantage point and had 'greeted him with great courtesy and demonstration', especially Anna, 'who rose from her chair in the litter three times, with a laughing face and kissing the hands many times'.[50]

In his first speech to peers in the House of Lords shortly afterwards, James confirmed his intention to seek 'peace abroad with all foreign neighbours' in order to end the 'great and tedious war' against Spain that England had waged under Elizabeth. To complement the cessation of foreign hostilities, domestic harmony would also be achieved through the natural logic of uniting England and Scotland, which James described as 'two countries being separated neither by sea, nor great river, mountain, nor other strength of nature, but only by little small brooks, or demolished little walls, so as rather they were divided in apprehension, than in effect'. Echoing John of Gaunt's speech in Shakespeare's *Richard II* (1595) – wherein England was described as 'this little world', a 'precious stone set in the silver sea' and 'a fortress built by Nature for herself' – James reminded peers that God had 'made us all in one island, compassed with one sea, and of itself by nature so indivisible'. Scotland and England had 'now become like a little world within itself, being entrenched and fortified round about' by the sea, eradicating ancient rivalries and enhancing national security. Envisaging a new Great Britain which would dissolve former borders, James reassured peers that, just 'as little brooks lose their names by their running and fall into great rivers', so too 'the very name and memory of the great rivers swallowed up in the ocean' had vanished. 'By the conjunctions of diverse little kingdoms in one', similar processes allowed new states to emerge with 'all these private differences and questions swallowed up'. Invoking his own genealogical descent from Henry VII of England, James concluded his exhortation to national unity by recasting geopolitical ambition in the language of holy matrimony: 'I am the husband, and all the whole isle is my lawful wife. I am the head, and it is my body; I am the shepherd, and it is my flock.' While James warned that no 'Christian king under the Gospel, should be a polygamist and husband to two wives', his marital imagery remained notably Protestant with 'the whole island' denoting mainland Britain, to the exclusion of Catholic Ireland.[51]

Reinforcing royal exhortations to Anglo-Scottish unity were lawyers and other writers who promoted the advantages of territorial consolidation achieved through dynastic succession. In a tract written in Latin in 1605, the Scots jurist Thomas Craig of Riccarton warned that there was 'no land whose teeming prosperity has so often invited invasion, and sometimes suffered it, as England'. Seeing James as 'walking in the footprints of his predecessors on the English throne, who were ever animated by the ambition to unite the two kingdoms into one powerful state', Craig regarded Stuart dynastic expansion in the same light as Habsburg military might. Admiring how, over centuries, 'the kings of Spain bent all their energy' to uniting the Iberian peninsula into a single state, Craig pointed out that 'at the present time, Spain is known simply as Spain', as the names of former kingdoms, including Castile, Aragon and Portugal, assumed provincial connotations.[52]

Presenting a different geopolitical analysis, the English lawyer Sir Francis Bacon insisted on a need for thorough integration, contrasting the strength of unions achieved via an entire '*mistio*' of two states with weaker forms of '*compositio*', whereby one state was simply appended to another with no transformation of traditional divisions and rivalries into new loyalties. The former served as 'the mother of sedition and alteration', while the latter facilitated 'peace and continuance: the one rather a confusion, than a union, the other properly a union'.[53] Reimagining Britain's geography, Bacon suggested that the Anglo-Scottish borders could become an exemplar of integration, if courts in Carlisle and Berwick were to assume local jurisdictional authority in both countries and not 'proceed precisely or merely according to the laws and customs either of England or Scotland, but mixtly'.[54] Several years later, James echoed Bacon's hope that, reconceived as 'Middle Shires' rather than 'Borders', the region would be converted from marginal and lawless peripheries to 'the navel or umbilic of both kingdoms, planted and peopled with civility and riches'.[55]

Manifestos for union nevertheless unleashed remarkably emotive reactions from those among James's subjects who feared that the creation of Great Britain signalled the inevitable eradication of separate English and Scottish identities, laws and influence. The English antiquarian Sir Henry Savile, citing Iberian parallels, insisted that when the Spanish territories of Castile and Aragon had been united under Ferdinand and Isabella 'a new name was refuted' and, to this day, Spain's monarch was known as 'King of Castile, of Leon and Aragon'.[56] The Keeper of the English Exchequer Records, Arthur Agard, ascribed considerable cultural value, as well as legal authority, to a country's name and warned that abandoning 'that sweet name of England' would dilute the respect in which the country was held internationally, pointing out that even William I had not considered changing England's name following the Norman Conquest in 1066.[57]

Amid fears that England's vaunted liberties faced imminent extinction, a bill seeking confirmation of Magna Carta's provisions was placed before the Commons in March 1604, while a 'Form of Apology and Satisfaction' purporting to explain the English Parliament's customary privileges to 'a foreign king' was read aloud in the Commons in June, although not formally presented to James.[58] English resistance was further animated by anxiety over longstanding Franco-Scottish fraternity. In 1604, another English antiquarian, Sir Henry Spelman, warned that, if British union went ahead, the Scots would be 'as the Canaanites were to the Israelites, pricks in our sides, always galling and vexing us, and as hooks in our nose to pull us back and divert us from our attempts against France'. Resisting royal insistence, Spelman contended that 'the honourable name of England [would] be buried in the resurrection of Albion or Britannia', needlessly resuscitating 'the memory of an obscure and barbarous people', which would liquidate England's venerated history and international influence, and simply change 'the golden beams of the sun for a cloudy day'.[59]

Frustrated by the hostile reception his unionist vision had generated, James had written to English MPs in May, acclaiming Anglo-Scottish union as a divine blessing and suggesting that to disregard 'God's benefit so freely offered unto us is to spit and blaspheme in his face by preferring war to peace, trouble to quietness, hatred to love, weakness to strength and division to union'. To avoid appearing overly prescriptive, the king approved the appointment of bilateral English and Scottish Commissioners to agree a means of 'perfecting' union and allowing commissioners to 'be your own cook so dress it as you list'.[60] A fortnight later, the new Venetian envoy Nicolo Molin observed that, although James was visibly 'daily more and more eager for the union' and did 'not cease to labour, argue, plead', among MPs 'every day fresh and insurmountable difficulties arise'. As Molin feared, the king's energetic promotion of union seemed 'in vain, for in truth these two nations nourish an inextinguishable hate for each other'.[61]

On the day scheduled for the first bilateral meeting of union commissioners in October 1604, James issued a proclamation, announcing a formal change in his royal style as 'King of Great Britain'. Since England and Scotland now constituted, territorially, 'a little world within itself', he defended proposals to perfect the union as measures 'which justly and safely we may by our absolute power do'. In replacing the names of England and Scotland with that of Great Britain, the king insisted that 'we do not innovate or assume to us any new thing, but declare that which is and hath been evident to all'.[62] The English diplomat Dudley Carleton nevertheless feared that 'the misconceiving vulgar' were likely to misinterpret James's proclamation as an intention 'to cross the proceedings in Parliament', lending credence to those who 'scoffingly have given out that so the king had the name, he would not care much for the matter'.[63] Days before proclaiming the change in royal style, James had also authorized a new coinage for both England and Scotland, regarding the 'reducing of the gold and silver of both the said kingdoms to one perfect equality' as a 'necessary preparation for the union of the said kingdoms'. English sovereign coins were renamed 'unites' and bore a Latin legend from Ezekiel that promised 'I will make them one nation'. As one MP confirmed during a parliamentary debate, 'if we put our hand in our purse, and can feel a twenty-shilling piece of gold, we may perceive on it, *Faciamus eos in gentem unam*' ('Let us make ourselves into one people').[64]

That same month, Dean John Gordon of Salisbury preached a sermon in James's presence that acclaimed Anglo-Scottish union as providential destiny and urged popular compliance with Britain's new Constantine, who ruled by divine will. Avoiding references to either England or

Scotland, Gordon insisted that the king's subjects in 'South Britain' should recognize James's 'great and laudable modesty' in promoting the creation of 'Great Britain', given that he could rightfully have extended the name of Scotland to cover 'this kingdom, [England] which is last fallen in his power'.[65] Scots pamphleteers were likewise mindful that their country was widely regarded as the most ancient monarchy in the world, ruled by an unbroken succession of more than a hundred of James's royal ancestors since 330 BC. Given that Scotland was 'much more free of foreign conquests' than its southern neighbour, one commentator inferred that 'England would appear to be accessory to Scotland, and so to deserve the second place only in his Majesty's style'.[66]

Over six weeks between October and December 1604, forty-eight English and thirty-one Scots commissioners met regularly and agreed a limited set of proposals, formalized as an 'Instrument' of union. The commissioners recommended the abolition of mutually hostile laws, identified measures to promote free trade and suggested clarifications regarding questions of mutual naturalization. But without an English parliament in session, discussion of the 'Instrument' was delayed until November 1606. In the meantime, it was not only the English and Scots who had reservations about becoming 'one nation'. In November 1604, Cecil learned that Henri IV of France remained 'very inquisitive' about a proposed British union, doubting if the Scots 'would be so base as to lose the dignity of a kingdom', and wondering if they might instead choose to retain James's younger son, Prince Charles, in Scotland as their king.[67] In London, the resident French ambassador, Beaumont, advised Henri that the goodwill of the notoriously 'poor and parsimonious' Scots could be secured through 'pensions and gratifications'.[68] Resuscitating the Franco-Scottish 'Auld Alliance' might not only offer a means of thwarting British union, but could also promote French interests by undermining moves towards an Anglo-Spanish peace.

III

On Elizabeth's death in 1603, the English had averted a bloody war of succession, but had acquired a foreign king who seemed intent on eradicating his new country's name and invalidating its ancient laws, while simultaneously insisting on the need for peace with England's sworn enemy, Spain. Accordingly, just as MPs and peers at Westminster were unconvinced that closer political, legal, religious and economic union with Scotland did not threaten the national interest, English opponents of peace rejected James's claims that proposed negotiations with Spain were simply intended to confirm his pre-existing amity, rather than end a long-running war. Congratulating James on his accession, the Dutch States General had appended a plea that any formal peace could not be contemplated 'until the Spaniards and their followers were removed from the government of, and domination over, the Low Countries'.[69] Meanwhile, the Spanish ambassador Villamediana objected to characteristic English arrogance, protesting to Philip that 'this king and kingdom and the Council are exceedingly vain' in appearing to assume that the choice between 'peace or the universal discord of the world will be in their hand and power'.[70] In the autumn of 1603, Philip had named Juan Fernández de Velasco, duke of Frías and Constable of Castile, as the ambassador extraordinary tasked with negotiating an Anglo-Spanish peace, but the Constable delayed his journey to London and remained in the Spanish Netherlands, intent on acquiring sufficient material inducements to assist negotiations. From Antwerp, the English diplomat Ralph Winwood reported to Cecil that the Constable had been seen trying to purchase 'many and sundry jewels of great price', but only if the city's vendors 'would be content to receive them again at the same price' if his mission to England proved unsuccessful.[71]

After reassurances that negotiations could take place without the Constable present, Anglo-Spanish peace talks started in May 1604 while James's first English parliament remained in session, and against a background of escalating hostilities in the Low Countries. Anglo-Dutch forces were mounting an effective siege of the Flemish port of Sluys and foreign observers reported 'heavy betting that the Dutch will capture Sluys before the Spanish get Ostend'.[72] Among Commissioners appointed to negotiate on the English side was the Lord Admiral Charles Howard (now earl of Nottingham), who had commanded the fleet in its defeat of Philip II's Armada in 1588 and had jointly led the English expedition that had sacked Cadiz in 1596. Another commissioner was Charles Blount, Baron Mountjoy (now earl of Devonshire), who had fought Spanish forces in the Low Countries, during the Armada and in the Azores, before coordinating the English victory over Spanish-Irish forces at Kinsale in 1602.

Formalities opened with speeches in Latin by Nottingham, to which a Milanese adviser to the Constable, Alessandro Rovida, responded on the Habsburg side, regarding the mutual amity of Philip and James as resembling that '"rushing of a mighty wind" which preceded the descent of the Holy Spirit on the Apostles'.[73] In an official account of the negotiations published in Spain, concerns about potential disadvantage arising from the talks being held in London were defused by reassurances regarding 'the straightforwardness of the king [James], and how much his presence would matter, as well as that of the queen, for the good outcome of the treaty, since both were so inclined to peace'. Adding that James and Anna were 'not yet well seated' on their thrones, emphasizing the new English king's personal investment in securing peace implicitly provided Spanish ministers with a face-saving reason for ending hostilities that would not have applied under Elizabeth.[74]

After seven weeks of negotiations, thirty-four articles were agreed in what was one of the first major peace treaties between warring Protestant and Catholic states in the post-Reformation era. The conclusion of peace was immortalized in a famous painting of the eleven English, Spanish and Flemish commissioners, seated around the conference table in Somerset House, surviving versions of which are displayed in London's National Portrait Gallery and the National Maritime Museum at Greenwich (Plate 6). As James had intended, the Treaty of London was construed primarily as an agreement of friendship regularizing relations between two previously hostile nations and English negotiators had resisted pressure to conclude a closer offensive and defensive alliance that would have negated their pre-existing amity with France. Following the precedent set in the Franco-Spanish Treaty of Vervins (1598), English rights to trade in the Spanish Indies were neither explicitly permitted nor prohibited. Likewise, although both England and Spain undertook to desist from providing official support to 'rebels', such as the Dutch or Irish, unofficial military recruitment could continue. Since the Treaty of London's conclusion denoted Philip's de facto recognition of James's legitimate rule over all his English, Scottish and Irish subjects, it effectively abandoned those Irish Catholics who had traditionally appealed to Spain for assistance in overthrowing English rule in Ireland. The treaty did not mention Spain's large expatriate Irish community and, as the Constable later warned in 1605, 'the option of transplanting the whole of Ireland to Spain should not be allowed'.[75]

More immediately, the Treaty of London's conclusion encouraged the Constable of Castile's delayed arrival in England in August with an entourage of around 200 attendants, who witnessed the formal signing of the treaty's terms at Whitehall. As it coincided with Princess Elizabeth's eighth birthday, James acknowledged to the Constable that the signing ceremony represented an especially happy day. Deploying the same tactic of spontaneously mooting future marriage alliances that had surprised Rosny the previous year, the English king confided his hope that – as the Constable recorded their conversation – through Princess Elizabeth's 'name, that she might be the means of preserving the kingdoms of Spain and England in friendship and union, unlike that other hostile Elizabeth who had caused so much mischief'. During the celebratory banquet, James presented the Constable with 'a melon and half a dozen of oranges on a very green branch, telling him that they were the fruit of Spain transplanted into England', whereupon the Spaniard responded by kissing the king's hand and dividing the melon into three parts to share with James and Queen Anna.[76]

Habsburg suavity was accompanied by conspicuous largesse, as Molin reported that Villamediana had disbursed over 200,000 crowns' worth of jewels, ensuring that 'the Spaniards are lauded to the skies' since England was a country 'where only those that are lavish are held in account'.[77] After leaving London, the Constable advised Philip from Bordeaux that 'great care' should be taken to identify the right sort of ambassador to promote Spanish interests at James's court. A future envoy should, ideally, be 'likeable, Christian, experienced with the world and the courts of rulers and men, a fine courtier with ladies, sparkling and talkative, frank and generous, a man to dance at the mansions and masques where, at this court, there are better opportunities for business than at formal audiences'.[78] But at the Escorial Palace, a monk named Fray Jerónimo de Sepúlveda deplored the national disgrace whereby Spain had entered into negotiations with a heretic nation and concluded a peace 'with such infamy to ourselves, even going to the extreme of begging for it in their house'.[79]

Reciprocal Spanish ratification of the Treaty of London occurred the following year when Nottingham, as Lord High Admiral, arrived at the Galician port of La Coruña in April 1605, accompanied by an entourage of around 600 mostly Protestant Englishmen and Scots, constituting the first official mission sent to Spain since the ignominious recall of

Elizabeth I's last ambassador, John Man, in 1568. The party remained in the country for over two months, and included a herald, Robert Treswell, whose published account of the expedition showed appreciation for the warm welcome extended by villagers in northern Spain's mountainous interior. As locals admired 'our civility and good behaviour', Treswell suspected that such impressions were 'clean contrary to that which had been formerly preached unto them by their churchmen and friars'.[80]

The party's destination was the capital, Valladolid, into which an elaborate ceremonial entrance was arranged. Although festivities were partly derailed by a sudden downpour – the first rainfall for nine months – Nottingham earned admiration from a Spanish observer for 'this good omen of water'. Nottingham went on to lead by example and stoically remained uncovered on horseback during the deluge.[81] In the ensuing weeks, James's legation was entertained by a series of magnificent festivities, designed as public spectacles to celebrate Habsburg power and prestige and comprising courtly and civic pageants, elaborate masques, bull-fights, chivalric jousts, *juegos de cañas* (games with canes), religious processions, military reviews and lavish banquets. Funded by the Spanish court, the sumptuous entertainment enjoyed by Nottingham's embassy marked a striking new orientation in English foreign relations after decades of enmity with Spain, reflecting Philip's determination to enhance his country's *reputacíon*, which had risked dilution after his decision to negotiate peace, first with France and then with England.

Philip III signed the Treaty of London in Valladolid on 30 May 1605, the day after the English delegation had witnessed the baptismal celebrations arranged for Philip's baby son. Having been born on the day of Christ's crucifixion, Good Friday, the future Philip IV was baptized on Pentecost Sunday, coinciding with the anniversary of the founding of the Catholic Church and celebrated by an assembly of over 600 Dominican friars gathered from across Continental Europe. With the baptism of the king's first son and heir delayed until Nottingham's party had arrived in Valladolid, the lavish festivities accompanying the baptism vividly reinforced the sacrality of Spanish kingship and the close relationship between the Catholic Church and the Habsburgs. Since springtime denoted the main festive period in the church's liturgical year, Nottingham's legation also witnessed several religious processions, including observation of Corpus Christi, as well as spontaneous revels prompted by news received that the pro-Habsburg Camillo Borghese had been elected as Pope Paul V.

During a thanksgiving procession to mark Queen Margaret's 'churching' – when the queen attended Mass for the first time after giving birth – crowds observed Philip look up to the vantage point reserved for Nottingham and remove his hat, in a clear gesture of respect to the man who had commanded the fleet that had defeated his father's Armada in 1588 and jointly directed the expedition that had burned Cadiz eight years later. Appreciating the esteem, Nottingham noted that every time the name of England's new king was mentioned, Philip had always removed his hat in a gesture of distinction hitherto unknown at the Spanish court. As Nottingham informed James, no previous envoy, including those sent by the Holy Roman Emperor or the papacy, had been accorded the privilege that he had enjoyed of sitting beside the Spanish king under his cloth of state. He added that Philip 'himself told me he would have it appear to the world that he made more estimation' of James 'and his love to him, than of all the kings in the world besides'.[82] In a coincidental echo of the theatre choreographed for Prince Henry Stuart's baptism at Stirling Castle a decade earlier, at the farewell masque and banquet for 3,000 attendees held in June, the infant Habsburg Prince Philip 'sailed' across an allegorical ocean, aboard a constructed 'ship of 'state', symbolically accompanied by doves to confirm the new *Pax Hispanica*.

5
Gunpowder, Treason and Scots, 1605–1610

More than four centuries after the event, the English are exhorted, every autumn, to 'Remember! Remember! The Fifth of November!' and reimagine a catastrophe that did not happen. Discovered on the night of 4 November 1605, the Gunpowder Plot was foiled when authorities at the Palace of Westminster, alerted by a tip-off, arrested a Yorkshire-born Catholic, Guy Fawkes, hiding in a cellar underneath the House of Commons, together with thirty-six barrels of gunpowder to be detonated when James VI & I opened his second session of parliament the following day. As ministers frantically sought to discover the Plot's provenance and personnel, a proclamation issued on 7 November ordered the arrest of named individuals, while exonerating foreign powers from suspicion of involvement on the grounds that no 'prince, of what religion soever, could give ear to so savage and barbarous an imagination'.[1] Attention was instead focused on a militant group of Midlands-based English Catholics whose disillusionment with James's seeming determination to maintain the statutory framework of Elizabethan persecution had led them to attempt mass murder. As the government tried to pre-empt further plots and Catholic uprisings, the principal secretary, Sir Robert Cecil (now earl of Salisbury), explained to James's ambassador in Madrid, Sir Charles Cornwallis, that 'martial men' had been sent 'to those countries where the Robin Hoods are assembled, to encourage the good and to terrify the bad'.[2] Unbeknown to Salisbury, only the previous day the Plot's charismatic ringleader Robert Catesby had been killed in a dramatic shoot-out at Holbeach House in Staffordshire which had resulted in the death or arrest of most of the remaining plotters.

In London, James addressed both Houses of Parliament on 9 November, proroguing the session on account of the national emergency and describing the Plot as 'a roaring, nay a thundering sin of fire and brimstone' from which divine providence had ensured their miraculous delivery. To the peers and MPs who would have perished in the carnage, alongside James and the royal family, the king confirmed that the venue had been deliberately chosen. Interrogation of Fawkes had indicated that, since Parliament was where England's anti-Catholic legislation had been framed, the plotters had resolved that 'both place and persons should all be destroyed and blown up at once'. At least, James conceded, posterity would have learned that he had not 'died ingloriously in an ale-house, a stews [tavern], or such vile place', but alongside 'the most honourable and best company', discharging his constitutional duties. At the same time, although peers and MPs were understandably 'so burned up with zeal' that instant revenge was demanded, the king warned that he 'would be sorry that any being innocent of this practice, either domestic or foreign, should receive blame or harm' as a result.[3]

The next day, William Barlow, bishop of Rochester, preached a sermon from London's most prominent pulpit, at St Paul's Cross, describing the conspiracy as evincing 'a hyperdiabolical devilishness' that had enabled Fawkes 'to have beheld as (he said) the houses and bodies flying up; he living and laughing at it'. Politically, the explosion would have left England like a 'hedge lying open for the wild boar of the forest to enter – a foreigner to invade – or the sly fox of the wood to climb – a domestic usurper to intrude'.[4] After Barlow had denounced Fawkes as 'this devil of the vault', 'J. H.' published a poem entitled 'The Devil of the Vault', deploring the plotters as 'tigerish blood-sworn Jesuits / Spanished British slaves' and imagined

To see such royal and noble shapes
Blown up in the whisking air,
Here arms, there legs, dissevered quite,
Lie mangled everywhere.[5]

Reporting Fawkes's death in January 1606 – when the plotter broke his neck after falling from the scaffold on which he was to have been hanged – another pamphleteer saw diabolism literally personified. Fawkes had indeed been 'justly called, the Devil of the Vault; for had he not been a Devil incarnate, he had never conceived so villainous a thought, nor been employed in so damnable an action'.[6] In his Latin poem *Pietas Pontificia* (1606), a London physician, Francis Herring, likewise imagined Fawkes as the diabolic offspring of Lucifer, sent to England to impress on Catesby the need 'to destroy the root and the branches at the same time with one blow'. Assassinating James alone would have been insufficient for Catholic purposes: inclined 'to shudder at the deadly name and omen of Henry', Herring's 'Fawkes' had warned that the royal heir, Prince Henry, would only emulate his namesake, Henry VIII, in undermining the papacy. Herring's 'Fawkes' insisted that 'we should utterly eradicate the heretical and loathsome offspring' and envisaged the 'great procession ... closely packed throng' and 'thickly-packed crowds' that would attend Parliament's opening, before the gunpowder explosion would send the assembled company 'into the breezes above in a tornado of sulphur'. As Herring's poem narrated, although 'England was now no more than a mere twelve hours away from its lethal wound and bitter death', divine intervention had forestalled the Plot's realization, while 'Fawkes' himself had 'confessed the brilliant crime and is only vexed at the fact that his purpose had not been achieved'.[7]

While poets and pamphleteers detailed the Plot's intended apocalyptic annihilation, an official *King's Book* was published in December 1605 that reprinted James's speech in Parliament and presented an account of the Plot based on the confessions of the two principal protagonists: Fawkes and Thomas Winter. The narrative's author (possibly Francis Bacon) evocatively described the conspiracy to confirm that, had it succeeded, not only would 'the king our head, the queen our fertile mother, and these young and hopeful olive plants' – Princes Henry and Charles – have been killed, but so too would England's nobility, judiciary, episcopate and countless innocent citizens, the Houses of Parliament, Westminster Abbey and the state's records also being destroyed. The result would have been 'such sulphured smoke, furious flames, and fearful thunder' that the plotters, 'by their diabolical Domesday', would have 'destroyed and defaced, in the twinkling of an eye, not only our present living princes and people, but even our insensible monuments reserved for future ages'.[8]

Writing to his Danish brother-in-law Christian IV, James himself condemned 'the most horrid and detestable of all treasons either undertaken anywhere in the world within the memory of man, or conceived in thought and mind'.[9] Days after the Plot's discovery, the Venetian ambassador in London, Nicolo Molin, reported an audience in which the king's younger son, Prince Charles, recently elevated as the duke of

York and 'about five years old, came into the chamber', prompting James to marvel that 'this poor boy's innocence', as well as that of other intended targets, had prevailed with God to thwart the plotters' 'perfidious malignity'.[10] But although James and his sons would have perished, intelligence revealed that the plotters had also envisaged exploiting the subsequent confusion to abduct James's nine-year-old daughter, Princess Elizabeth, from Coombe Abbey in Warwickshire with the aim of marrying her to a Catholic consort and installing a second Queen Elizabeth as a puppet sovereign to rule over a re-Catholicized England.

I

The Plot's discovery dashed any hopes of English Catholics that James's accession as king might imminently improve their civil and religious position. James's relatively lenient treatment of Scots Catholics before 1603, the inclusion of prominent Catholic nobles among his Scots state officers, his amicable overtures to Catholic states when promoting his claims to succeed Elizabeth I, his mother's posthumous status as an unofficial Catholic martyr, and reports of Queen Anna's pro-Catholic proclivities had all afforded grounds for optimism. From northern France, the professor of theology at the English Catholic College of Douai, Matthew Kellison, had conjured James to imagine 'your glorious mother, as if she were living on earth', reassuring him that English Catholics 'will never be false to the son, who have been so true to the mother'. In a tract published in 1603, Kellison had ventured that English Catholics would readily 'bind ourselves by corporal oath, to obey your laws in all temporal causes, and to defend your royal person' and family 'with the last drop of our blood' in a commitment they would willingly 'divulge to all the princes of Europe, yea all the Christian world'. At the very least, Kellison had hoped that memory of Mary Stuart's 'glorious martyrdom' would 'move your heart, if not to admit wholly the Catholic religion, at least to permit it, at least not to persecute it'.[11]

Yet even before the Gunpowder Plot provided irrefutable evidence of papist perfidy, there had been little prospect of any major policy reversal. Aware that 'the ink is hardly dry on the articles of peace' concluded between England and Spain by the Treaty of London, the Spanish ambassador extraordinary, Juan Fernández de Velasco, Constable of

Castile, had warned Philip III in November 1604 that 'at least several years of friendship will have to pass first' before longstanding fears of hostile Spanish intervention on behalf of England's Catholics might dissipate. Writing from Brussels after leaving London, the Constable had surmised that James would probably wait until his tenure on the English throne was more secure before introducing significant measures to relieve restrictions on Catholics. For 'the one poison, flowing from the nettles of malice' was James's concern that, were he to offer Catholics freedom of conscience, he would risk being perceived as endorsing papal calls for heretic or excommunicated sovereigns to be deposed from power, placing him in a 'dangerous likelihood of losing his crown and his life'.[12]

Accordingly, although devastation had been narrowly averted, the atmosphere in London in the weeks and months after the Plot's detection remained extraordinarily tense. Fawkes's actions had exacerbated James's long-held fear of gunpowder after his father, Lord Darnley, had been murdered in a mysterious gunpowder explosion in 1567, as well as reviving memories of the 'Gowrie Conspiracy' in 1600 when, having been lured to Gowrie House in Perth, James had survived an assassination attempt by John Ruthven, earl of Gowrie. Addressing Parliament four days after the Gunpowder Plot's discovery, James acknowledged that, since 'these two great and fearful Domesdays' had occurred on the same day of the week (Tuesday), he feared 'it was the same Devil that still persecuted me'.[13] Later that month, Molin described the king as still 'in terror', refusing to appear in public, dining in private, and making it 'known that he wished to have the Scots about his person, as he has not much confidence in the English, who know this, and are greatly annoyed'.[14]

Additionally alarming was evidence that xenophobic hatred of the Scots had infused the plotters' zeal. As the courtier Sir Edward Hoby informed the English ambassador in Brussels, Thomas Edmondes, when asked how he could contemplate such a horrendous atrocity, Fawkes had replied that 'a dangerous disease required a desperate remedy'. With several Scots present during his interrogation, Fawkes had indicated 'his intent was to have blown them back again into Scotland'.[15] In December 1605, Molin reported that a list of London houses inhabited by Scots had been discovered among the plotters' papers, proving their determination 'to massacre all the Scots in this country'. Molin added, 'publication of this news has increased the hatred' between the Scots and English 'and rendered them quite irreconcilable', with many Scots now 'thinking of returning home, for they fear that, some day a general massacre may take place'.[16]

Despite James's government disavowing theories of Continental sponsorship, popular suspicion fell on the French ambassador Christophe de Harlay, count of Beaumont, who had suddenly left London on 4 November and sailed from Dover the next day, only hours before a Privy Council order had arrived at the port, requesting that he remain in England. In London, despite the fact that the Spanish ambassador Baltasar de Zúñiga was himself to have attended Parliament's opening on 5 November, circulating rumours linked the Spanish government to the Plot, and the Lord Mayor was directed to protect Zúñiga's residence to prevent damage to the ambassador's person or property.[17] When news of the Plot reached Philip's court, the English ambassador Cornwallis reported that the horrified reaction of ministers and people alike so 'much inclined me in my own heart unto them' that he now believed the Spanish would become 'fast and faithful friends to his Majesty and our country'. Shortly before learning of the Plot's discovery, Cornwallis had dispatched secret instructions to England, confident that a mantra attributed to the sixteenth-century 'Iron Duke', Fernando Álvarez de Toledo, duke of Alba – *guerra con toda la tierra y paz con Inglaterra* (that Spain should be 'at war with all the world but at peace with England') – 'hath now gotten the force and reputation of a general rule and maxim amongst them'.[18]

Cornwallis's Venetian counterpart in Valladolid, Francesco Priuli, confirmed that Spanish officials had ordered publication of the English government's proclamation denying foreign involvement and 'sold it publicly in the streets, in order to counteract the accusation that they have had a hand in the Plot'. In Italy, James's ambassador, Sir Henry Wotton, told the Venetian authorities that one plotter, Thomas Winter, had admitted under interrogation that, although there had been 'talk, but very late in the day, of foreign help', this option had been discounted since 'Spain was too far off, France not to be trusted, the German princes slow and phlegmatic, the Archduke occupied by his own wars'.[19]

But in the Spanish Netherlands, Thomas Edmondes was frustrated by the reluctance of the archduke's administration to accede to English requests to extradite a Welsh-born spy, Hugh Owen, and an English-born

Jesuit priest, William Baldwin, who were both suspected of complicity in the Plot. As Edmondes explained to Cornwallis, Habsburg ministers in Brussels had initially been inclined to deny any Catholic dimension to the Plot, alleging that it was either 'an artifice of the Puritans against those sanctified persons' or 'a design of the Hollanders' to convert England into a republic. When supplied with compelling evidence, such that 'they can no longer dispute the doubtfulness and uncertainty' of Catholic involvement, the archduke's advisers had then insisted 'that it is a work of the Devil's expressly to banish and extirpate the Catholic religion out of England'.[20]

Back in London, as more information about the Plot emerged, Molin observed in December 1605 that 'both Court and City are more than ever in a bubbub [hubbub], nor can they quiet down; everyone is armed and ready for any event'. Following Molin's recall, his replacement, Zorzi Giustinian, remained nervily apprehensive, reporting in February that 'some other outbreak is so confidently expected that, on the smallest rumours in the City, one hears of reports and of deeds which indicate a deep-rooted suspicion and mistrust of the Catholics'. The next month, rumours spread through the city that James had been assassinated during a hunting trip to Woking. As the royal court doubled its guard and the Tower of London's drawbridge was raised, Giustinian observed that 'the uproar was amazing', and as a foreigner he feared imminent violence as 'everyone flew to arms, the shops were shut, and cries began to be heard against papists, foreigners and Spaniards', before a proclamation reassured subjects of the false alarm.[21] Although Henri IV's ambassador, Beaumont, had incurred suspicion for returning to France shortly before the Plot's discovery, Salisbury wrote to him in March 1606, trusting that he was enjoying more tranquillity than if he had been in London. With the country continually threatened by 'such vile and barbarous practices', Salisbury considered England 'less at rest than we have been from the time of war'.[22]

Confronted by calls for more stringent penalties to be imposed on Catholics, in June 1606 the government expanded Elizabethan legislation directed against 'recusants' who refused to attend Church of England services by permitting the royal seizure of recusant land. A new oath was also levied on indicted or suspected recusants as well as any adult who had not taken Anglican communion at least twice within the previous year. The 'Oath of Allegiance' comprised seven clauses but did not require its swearers formally to deny the Pope's spiritual authority, instead obliging those taking the oath 'from my heart [to] abhor, detest and abjure as impious and heretical this damnable doctrine' that heretical or excommunicated sovereigns 'may be deposed or murdered by their subjects or any other whatsoever'.[23] While Pope Paul V issued a brief against the new oath, ordering English Catholics to desist from swearing it and from attending Protestant services, the effective leader of England's recusant community, Archpriest George Blackwell, refused to distribute the papal brief and swore the oath, regarding acceptance of James's temporal authority, albeit as a 'heretic' ruler, as compatible with adherence to Catholicism.

Copies of the new legislation were published in Madrid where 'a more than ordinary congregation of caterpillars', as Cornwallis put it, accused James's administration of passing 'most bloody cruel laws' against all Catholics, however loyal. At Philip III's court, Cornwallis formed a controversial friendship with the expatriate English Jesuit Joseph Creswell, whose *Carta Escrita al Embaxador de Inglaterra* (1606) ('Letter written to the English Ambassador') denounced the Gunpowder Plot, but deemed it 'a notable and unconscionable injustice' to use the Plot as a pretext for increased persecution since the majority of English Catholics 'had no more to do with the conspiracy than those Catholics which live in Japan'.[24] Meanwhile, Cornwallis reported that Philip's ministers had started searching anew for the elusive will reportedly penned by Mary, Queen of Scots, in which she claimed to have bequeathed her dynastic claim to the English throne to the Spanish Habsburgs, if James remained a Protestant. But as Cornwallis surmised, amid so many challenges to their military might and colonial conquests, the Spanish 'would now, as it seems, perfume themselves with smoke of title to those of other princes'. Lost 'in an intricate labyrinth', Cornwallis predicted that they 'will fall like froth, as they arose like dough'.[25]

II

James was not so sanguine. In late December 1605, Molin described how, after chapel and dinner one Sunday, the king had suddenly unleashed an hour-long harangue, objecting to reports from Rome that warned of his likely excommunication while 'Catholics threaten to dethrone me and to take my life unless I grant them liberty of conscience'. Although James acknowledged that he would, 'most certainly, be obliged to stain my hands with their blood, though sorely against my will', he was 'amazed' that other Christian princes did not offer stronger resistance to deposition theories that he believed were framed solely to increase the papacy's temporal power and further papal ambitions to be 'lords of the whole world'.[26]

Coincidentally, events in Molin's home state of Venice presented a republican parallel when the Italian city rejected what it regarded as the Catholic Church's illegitimate intrusion into its secular authority. In April 1606, Paul V had issued a papal bull of Interdict and Excommunication after Venetian legislation forbade bequests of secular property to the Church and restricted the construction of new churches and monasteries. As the English ambassador in Venice, Wotton, explained to his Brussels counterpart, the papacy had also been angered by the state arrest and conviction, in its criminal courts, of one 'abbot accused of many foul crimes' and 'a Canonico of Vicenza for dishonouring a virgin' as the city authorities disregarded the accused's claims of clerical immunity from prosecution.[27]

Under the Interdict, the Vatican denied local churches the right to conduct Mass or to perform the sacraments of baptism and marriage, although the Venetian authorities responded by declaring the papal bull null and void and ordering priests to continue services on pain of death. As the only Protestant ambassador in Italy, Wotton tried to promote shared anti-papal interests between Catholics and Protestants and approached Venice's rulers to propose a 'secret and defensive' league to resist papal encroachments that might potentially include England, France and German and Swiss states, alongside Venice. From London, Molin's successor as Venetian envoy to England, Zorzi Giustinian, reported to the Doge and Senate in June that he had 'never dreamed of seeing this Court so moved, so full of longings and hopes' of making manifest its support for Venice's resistance to the papacy. Indeed, Giustinian could 'hardly protect myself from the continual offers of men and of ships, made me by great and small alike, English and Scots'. Venice's response to the Interdict formed 'the sole topic of conversation at Court' amid rumours of an imminent, large-scale war in Italy in which 'England, France and Venice will take one side, the Pope and Spain the other'.[28]

Although French intervention resolved the Interdict crisis the following spring, by that stage James was suffering unfavourable comparisons, in terms of royal style, with a fellow Protestant sovereign. In 1606, Christian IV of Denmark-Norway's visit to his sister Queen Anna marked the first state visit to England by a foreign ruler since the Holy Roman Emperor Charles V had visited Henry VIII in the 1520s. The twenty-nine-year-old king, who was fast enhancing Danish military and naval capabilities, had changed markedly from the twelve-year-old minor that James had met during his nuptial visit to Denmark in 1589. Arriving at Tilbury in July, Christian received James publicly aboard his heavily armed flagship, the *Tre Kroner* ('Three Crowns'), before the Danish party was entertained at Greenwich, Richmond, Windsor, Hampton Court and Nonsuch Palace, as well as at Salisbury's estate at Theobalds (which James acquired in exchange for Hatfield Palace the following year). With free wine flowing from London's fountains, James and Christian processed in pomp through the city's streets on 31 July, prompting the dramatist John Ford to pen 'The Monarchs' Meeting, or The King of Denmark's Welcome into England', one verse of which ran:

> Two kings in England have been rarely seen,
> Two kings for singularity renowned:
> The like before hath hardly ever been,
> For never were two with more honour crowned.[29]

Differences between James and his brother-in-law were, however, soon observed by foreign envoys, including Giustinian, who reported that the Danish king and his entourage quickly became 'bored with this country, and more especially with the chase, which is so feverishly pursued' by James.[30] Having denounced hunting as 'a sport wherein were more horses killed in jest than the Low Country wars consumed in earnest', Christian's superior chivalric skills in the tilting ring at Greenwich were widely admired. When both kings ran at the ring, Christian had the 'good hap never almost to miss' targets, while James had 'the ill luck scarce ever to come near', before the Danish king went one further by tilting against armed opponents.[31] Following the tilting debacle, the new French ambassador, Antoine le Fèvre de la Boderie, reported the discovery of an anonymous letter at Hampton Court that advised James to direct his attention to his subjects' welfare and threatened that 'if he did not moderate his way of living, all of his dogs would be poisoned'. Unflattering comparisons were being drawn between James's style of kingship and that of 'this brave Danish king . . . who indulges in truly royal and martial exercises'. Suspecting that the letter had been penned by a hostile Puritan, Boderie acknowledged popular esteem for 'this paragon of a Danish king' whose admired sporting successes had prompted regret among English spectators 'that we do not have such a king'.[32]

In conspicuous contrast to the controlled, remote formality of Elizabeth I's court, its Jacobean successor could be chaotic and dishevelled, with one masque dramatizing the Queen of Sheba's meeting with King Solomon becoming notorious. As the courtier Sir John Harington related to a correspondent, the actor playing the Queen had tripped and bespattered Christian – who was playing Solomon – with 'wine, cream, jelly, beverages, cakes, spices and other good matters'. The female players embodying virtues of 'Hope' and 'Faith' were observed 'sick and spewing', while an inebriated 'Peace' had resisted attempts at restraint and 'most rudely made war with her olive branch'. Admitting that 'the gunpowder fright is got out of all our hearts', Harington feared instead that 'the Devil were contriving every man should blow up himself by wild riot, excess, and devastation of time and temperance'. Surveying the carnage, Harington ventured that 'the Dane hath strongly wrought on our good English nobles'.[33] Preservation of fraternal royal accord was nevertheless maintained until Christian's departure, which was preceded by a farewell feast aboard a Danish warship at Gravesend, as guests enjoyed an imaginative aquatic firework display, in which the figure of a lion unleashed flames to ignite a cube-shaped structure depicting the deadly sins of anger, deceit, envy, gluttony, injustice, luxury, pride and decadence.[34]

When the English Parliament reconvened in November 1606, the potentially deadly sin of xenophobia became evident as MPs were asked to approve the 'Instrument' of Anglo-Scottish union drawn up two years earlier by bilateral commissioners. The 'Instrument' proposed abolishing mutually hostile statutes; instigating new administrative and judicial arrangements for the Anglo-Scottish Borders; expanding free trade arrangements – the *post-nati* (individuals born after James's accession in 1603) being declared natural subjects in both kingdoms and *ante-nati* being naturalized with a royal declaration against preferment in the other kingdom, pending full and perfect union. But fears of an instant influx of impoverished Scots into England moved the MP for the Cornish constituency of St Mawes, Nicholas Fuller, to warn that, since 'trees removed from a hard and barren soil to a rich and fruitful' environment would quickly flourish, the reverse was also true, meaning that the Scots 'doubtless will thrive here; as we doubtless shall waste there'. Accordingly, Fuller preferred to 'wish everyone to remain in that place'. A fellow MP denounced England's northern neighbours as 'the most base, peasant-like, perfidious people of the world' and another attacked 'the beggarly Scots'.[35] The Buckinghamshire MP Sir Christopher Pigott unleashed a vituperative attack in February 1607, the 'outrageousness' of which, 'both in words and actions', put MPs 'into an astonishment', although, as Sir Edward Montagu noted, Pigott's outburst was 'passed over with silence' rather than formally censured.[36]

Jealousy also attached to residual commercial and naturalization privileges available to Scots in France, prompting complaints that the 'auld alliance' represented 'the back door to let in what poison their French sweetheart' might choose to 'spit upon us'.[37] As one critic objected, just as with women, 'a nation cannot stand in firmer inwardness with two men, or nations' and another feared that the more the Scots 'love the French our enemies, the less they love us'.[38] From Paris, Ambassador Boderie was directed by Henri IV's court to pursue whatever underhand – '*sous main*' – practices might be necessary to protect French interests in any future British union.[39]

The question of mutual naturalization provoked particular resistance among those who objected to admitting individuals to the benefits of each country's laws despite the distinctly different status of the Scottish and English legal systems. In response, Sir Edwin Sandys MP speciously argued that discussions should, rather, be directed towards achieving an entire and perfect union, describing limited, imperfect union as 'a crooked and knotty piece of wood' that would require 'much hewing and paring before it can be made fit for use'. Yet in the House of Lords, James's Attorney General, Sir Henry Hobart, rejected such reasoning on the grounds that 'it will give jealousy to the Scottish nation that, having done nothing these three years in the imperfect union, we will delude them in our new project'. As Hobart feared, 'foreign nations' would suspect that stalling in order to discuss more 'perfect' ways of achieving union was only a cynical 'stratagem to delude the Scots, and do nothing'.[40] Writing to Philip III, Spanish ambassador Zúñiga described how 'disturbed' James was over the lack of progress as MPs 'keep speaking out freely and hostilely against the Scots'. With the king apparently claiming that 'those wretches not only do not want to enact the union but they would like to kill me', Zúñiga judged it 'unbelievable how much ill-will the English have for him, and the harm he would like to do them'.[41]

Trying to expedite matters, James addressed both Houses of Parliament in March 1607, frustrated at 'finding many crossings, long disputations, strange questions, and nothing done'. Citing 'many Pigotts', the king denounced xenophobic attacks and claimed that no Scot 'ever spoke dishonourably of England' in their Parliament. To allay suspicion, James reiterated the national security advantages that would accrue from Anglo-Scottish union, patiently explaining that, just as 'two snowballs put together, make one the greater; two houses joined, make one the larger; two castle walls made in one, makes one as thick and strong as both'. Disregarding the likely reaction among Scottish spies at Westminster, James also offered reassurance that England would naturally remain the dominant partner in any British union. Invoking his favoured rhetoric of conjugal concord, the king explained that 'you are to be the husband, they the wife: you conquerors, they as conquered, though not by the sword, but by the sweet and sure bond of love'.[42] Royal blandishments did not, however, stem the multitude of perceived difficulties and obstacles. By May, Giustinian inferred that James was 'now forced to desire the union, not only because it is useful, but also for his own reputation's sake. Like all great minds, opposition fires him.'[43]

Compliance with royal wishes was more forthcoming in Scotland, where the parliament approved most of the Instrument's provisions in August 1607, including naturalization of both *post-* and *ante-nati* with the caveat that naturalized subjects in Scotland could not hold royal, judicial or parliamentary appointments without royal dispensation. As the legislation confirmed, the parliament's members wanted to supply 'all possible proof of their devotion' to James's 'royal designs and projects' in order to secure to the king's 'posterity this flourishing, worthy and great empire'.[44] James's Privy Councillors in Edinburgh were nevertheless dissatisfied with the first union flag that had been flown at sea in April 1606, displaying the English cross of St George superimposed upon the Scottish cross of St Andrew, or saltire. Between James's accession and the introduction of the 'Union Jack' – nicknamed after 'Jacobus' (James) – British ships had been obliged to fly both national flags from the same mast which, unfortunately, implied that some sort of hostile encounter had occurred in which the flag flown higher had triumphed. Heraldically, the new union flag was intended to denote the parity of both states, for although the cross of St George overlay the saltire, it was the Scottish patron saint's colours that were nearest the hoist, in the most honourable quarter of the flag. But the Scots Privy Councillors objected that the flag's design was 'very prejudicial to the freedom and dignity of this Estate and will give occasion of reproach to this nation', given that the cross of St Andrew appeared in fragmented form, while that of St George remained entire.[45] As a result, two designs were thereafter approved for use at sea, with English ships using the original design and Scottish ships flying a reverse arrangement in which the saltire was superimposed upon the cross of St George, with both designs remaining in use until the nineteenth century.

Although the English Parliament had grudgingly enacted legislation to remove 'hostile laws' between England and Scotland, it had rejected the Instrument's recommendations regarding naturalization. Accordingly, as English Privy Councillors were informed in October, the king now intended that 'learned counsel should this term bring the question properly into debate in some of His Majesty's courts'.[46] In what was clearly envisaged as a test case, an English estate would be conveyed to a Scots child born after 1603, but land would then be forcibly possessed by another party, prompting a recovery action by the child's parents. Assuming the defendant would claim that, as an alien, the plaintiff was ineligible to plead, a judicial ruling to confirm the child's status would be required. In what became known as *Calvin's Case*, two estates in London were duly transferred in October 1607 to Robert Colville (also known as 'Calvin'), prompting suits that were transferred to the Exchequer Chamber where the case was heard the following June.

By a majority decision, *Calvin's Case* determined that a subject's allegiance was owed to the sovereign as a natural person, rather than as a distinct political body, strengthening the idea of monarchs ruling by a law of nature superior to common or municipal law. Enshrining a principle of birthright citizenship, the judgment in *Calvin's Case* ensured that anyone born in Scotland after James's accession as English king in March 1603 – the '*post-nati*' – owed their allegiance to the sovereign of England, as well as of Scotland, and should be regarded as natural-born English subjects and could inherit English land. By contrast, those born before James's accession as English king – the '*ante-nati*' – only owed allegiance to James as sovereign of Scotland, retained alien status in England law and could only become naturalized English citizens by statute. Considerable jurisprudential tergiversation was nevertheless required to reach this decision and Sir Edward Coke, as Chief Justice of the Common Pleas, later admitted the deceptively momentous nature of *Calvin's Case*. Although it appeared 'the shortest in syllables', the case proved 'the longest in substance . . . both for the present, and for all posterity'. Wryly observing that whereas gold-digging involved searching for *parvum in magno* ('a little in much'), Coke suggested that 'of this short plea, it might truly be said (which is more strange) that here was *magnum in parvo* ('much in miniature').[47]

III

The year before *Calvin's Case* resolved questions of mutual naturalization legally, the sudden 'Flight of the Earls' from Ulster to mainland Europe in September 1607 had presented James's government with a seemingly providential opportunity to promote Anglo-Scottish cooperation in practice, through plantation in Ireland. The exodus had been led by Elizabeth I's erstwhile antagonist, Hugh O'Neill, earl of Tyrone, whom Henri IV of France had described as 'the third soldier of his age' after himself and Philip II of Spain's nephew Alexander Farnese, duke of Parma.[48] Accompanied by another veteran of the long-running rebellion against Elizabethan rule in Ireland, Rory O'Donnell, earl of Tyrconnell, a party of around ninety had left Rathmullen in County Donegal for the Spanish port of La Coruña before being diverted by storms to land at Quillebeuf in Normandy. Tyrone's attempt to flee to Spain had been motivated by tighter anti-recusancy measures after the Gunpowder Plot, as well as threats to his local standing and jurisdiction by the rumoured intention of James's administration in Dublin to appoint a Protestant President in Ulster.

Mindful of Tyrone's military successes during the 1590s, the English government had hitherto adopted a policy of appeasement towards the earl. As the courtier Sir Thomas Lake admitted to Salisbury, James had not wanted to give Tyrone too much cause 'of just complaint, considering what a dependency the Irish have on him and how ticklish their disposition is towards the state'. But in July 1607, Tyrone had been summoned to Whitehall for adjudication of a long-standing territorial dispute with another Ulster magnate. The following month, an envoy sent to Ireland by Archduke Albert of the Spanish Netherlands had informed Tyrone that he was unlikely to return to Ulster if he went to London and had warned Tyrconnell that he faced imminent imprisonment. The envoy advised the earls to 'be in readiness for the coming of a ship, which would soon be sent for them'.[49]

Surprised by the Irish earls' accidental arrival in France, Henri IV initially prevaricated, ostensibly willing to offer asylum to any Catholic nobles fleeing Protestant persecution, but reluctant to encourage the earls' protracted presence on French soil. Having refused to grant permission for the party to travel overland to Spain, Henri instead offered safe passage to the Spanish Netherlands. In early November, James's government issued a proclamation in English and Latin, describing Tyrone, Tyrconnell and their companions as a 'pack of rebels' and denying that asylum was warranted. Foreign states were warned to disregard protestations that the earls had 'withdrawn themselves for matter of religion (a cloak that serves too much in these days to cover many evil intentions)'; rather, the proclamation explained that the disloyal earls had 'entered into combination for stirring sedition and intestine rebellion' in Ireland and were hoping to secure foreign assistance.[50]

Salisbury alerted the English ambassador in Brussels, Edmondes, to the earls' likely arrival in Habsburg territory, confirming that 'His Majesty esteems them but as silly worms of the earth, unless they be assisted by any foreign power'. But should any Catholic state offer support, James would 'make it known that he is a Prince of power, and will revenge himself against them'.[51] From Paris, the Venetian envoy, Piero Priuli, reported that Henri's refusal to accede to English demands for the earls' arrest and extradition had been partly motivated by their claims of seeking asylum on religious grounds, 'but much more by his natural dislike for the king of England, though he tries to hide it'.[52] Moreover, when the Irish party arrived in Brussels, Edmondes relayed his indignation at being invited to a celebratory feast for the Catholic earls, hosted by the Habsburg military-general, Ambrogio Spínola.

In London, Zúñiga observed the acute nervousness of James's ministers at Tyrone's presence in Flanders, explaining to Philip III that 'their fear of him gnaws at their entrails'. Recommending that the earls be furnished with a guard, Zúñiga further reported that 'I know that they wish to kill him [Tyrone] by poison or by any possible means.' Evidently James's government believed that, if the Spanish king were to 'send a hundred men with him to Ireland, all of that kingdom would rise against them'.[53] From Brussels, the Irish party travelled overland to Italy and finally reached Rome in April 1608, where Tyrconnell died in July, leaving Tyrone to continue soliciting foreign assistance for an anticipated – if ultimately chimerical – descent on Ireland.

In England, anxiety regarding potential Continental support for the fugitive Irish earls coincided with concerns that the Oath of Allegiance was not deterring domestic recusancy. Indeed, the de facto tolerance of Catholic worship had been remarked upon by Zúñiga the previous year, when over 600 worshippers had queued outside his residence to attend Good Friday Mass in the Spanish embassy chapel. As Zúñiga admitted to Philip, had they been 'in Spain, they could not be acting more publicly'.[54] If objections were raised, the ambassador indicated that he would simply confirm that he had neither invited, nor turned away, any individual wanting to worship. But in what James regarded as unacceptable interference in civil affairs, Paul V issued a second papal brief in August, reiterating instructions to English Catholics to refuse to swear the Oath of Allegiance. Whereas Archpriest Blackwell had justified subscription as a means for Catholics to 'shake off the false and grievous imputations of treason and treacheries' and prevent seizure of their estates, Paul V denounced the craven and misguided motivations of recusants who swore the oath, having been ensnared by 'the deceit of the enemies of human salvation' – namely, James's heretical government.[55] Observing the king's furious response, the Dean of the Chapel Royal, James Montagu, confirmed to Salisbury that the king had, over four days in December, penned twenty-four sheets rebutting the Pope's interference. Punning that James was embracing the new sport of (papal) 'bull'-fighting, Montagu ventured that now 'he should neither speak of hawking nor hunting'.[56]

In February 1608, James anonymously published his *Triplici Nodo, Triplex Cuneus: or, an Apology for the Oath of Allegiance* – known as the *Apology* – which defended the Oath of Allegiance's rationale as simply seeking to 'make distinction between the sheep and goats in my own pasture': that is, differentiating between the majority of subjects who, despite being 'popishly affected', remained loyal to their temporal ruler, and a minority, infected by the same 'fanatical zeal' as the 'powder-traitors', who sought to make 'diversity of religion a safe pretext for all kinds of treasons, and rebellions against their sovereign'. James also insisted that he had treated English Catholics more leniently than Elizabeth I, having avoided sustained persecution while conferring knighthoods on 'known and open recusants' and offering royal access 'to both sides, bestowing equally all favours and honours' on Protestants and Catholics alike. James particularly resented his adversaries' failure to appreciate that, unlike the Elizabethan Act of Supremacy (1558), the Oath of Allegiance introduced in 1606 had not denied the Pope's spiritual authority over Catholics. Incensed by Paul V's attempt to sow differences between his Catholic subjects and their king, James objected that 'the Devil could not have devised a more malicious trick for interrupting this so calm and clement a course'.[57]

But foreign observers were unconvinced. When the *Apology* was published, James reassured Giustinian that 'the book did not touch the question of religion, nor of ecclesiastical jurisdiction at all', but only discussed the Oath of Allegiance requiring subjects to offer lawful obedience to their sovereigns.[58] Unsurprisingly, James's restrictive interpretation of the oath was rejected by Catholic envoys, such as Zúñiga, who lamented to Philip in July 1608 that 'we keep saying again and again that this oath was the most disgraceful thing there was here'. Accordingly, Zúñiga welcomed the intervention of the Italian and English Jesuits Cardinal Robert Bellarmine and Robert Persons who countered the king's arguments in print, 'by indicating his mistakes fully, but without offending him in sharp words, since he has the world's biggest temper'.[59] Responding to James's *Apology* later that year, Bellarmine also pointed out that, when trying to deter papal interference in his campaign to succeed Elizabeth on the English throne, James had written to Clement VIII in 1599, requesting the appointment of a Scottish cardinal as an official channel of communication with the papacy. Having ordered an investigation into Bellarmine's claim, James admitted to the English Privy Council that the allegation was potentially as damaging to his 'reputation as any one that ever happened unto us in all our life'.[60] A scapegoat was, however, found in the king's former Scottish secretary, the Catholic Sir James Elphinstone (now Lord Balmerino), who conveniently confessed to having asked James to sign the letter without necessarily making the king aware of its content. In Paris, the diarist and book-collector Pierre de L'Éstoile had bought a copy of *Triplici Nodo* in April, two hours after pressure from the papal nuncio had led to its being banned from sale in a move that, as L'Éstoile wryly remarked, proved 'a good means' of boosting sales.[61]

Stung by the virulent attacks mounted against the anonymous author of *Triplici Nodo*, James sought to reclaim royal dignity by admitting his authorship in the work's second edition, produced in 1609 and accompanied by a *Premonition*, or warning, to the Holy Roman Emperor, Rudolf II, and other Continental princes regarding the papacy's repeated encouragement of rebellions against temporal monarchs. The singular willingness of England's Stuart king directly to engage the papacy and an army of Continental theologians across Europe in printed controversy contrasted sharply with an Elizabethan era often characterized by a determined royal silence on sensitive matters such as religious reform or royal succession. Marc'Antonio Correr, having replaced Giustinian as the Venetian representative in London, reported that James's 'Court is very ill affected to this child-birth of his Majesty', correctly suspecting that the *Premonition* 'may not prove acceptable to the world'. Undeterred, James ordered presentation copies of the *Premonition* for his fellow sovereigns to be bound in velvet and adorned with solid-gold corners stamped with images of a rose, thistle, lion and (French) lilies. In Venice, the authorities politely received James's *Premonition*, before instantly locking it away in the state archives. In Paris, Henri IV likewise accepted the gift, but claimed that he did not 'hold himself capable of understanding theological subjects', while quietly overlooking the description of James as 'King of Great Britain, France and Ireland' on the work's title-page. While Henri acknowledged James's aim of encouraging fellow rulers to reject papal theories of excommunication and deposition, he informed Correr's Parisian counterpart, Antonio Foscarini, that 'those who held their tongues knew better still how to preserve their authority and dignity; referring to himself'.[62]

Elsewhere in Paris, L'Éstoile read a borrowed copy of the *Premonition* but judged *Triplici Nodo* – penned in Latin prose that was 'pretty good for a king' – a superior work. Indeed, L'Éstoile welcomed James's polemical interventions at a time when he felt himself to be living 'in a century in which it is as monstrous to see a learned king as it was in Rabelais's time, for a monk to be learned'.[63] Certainly, when preparing the king's works for publication several years later, James's editor and dean of the

Chapel Royal, Bishop James Montagu, suggested that many subjects had looked 'upon his Majesty's books, as men look upon blazing-stars, with amazement, fearing they portend some strange thing' and liable to exert 'a certain influence to work great change and alteration in the world'. When James had openly engaged the Pope and Bellarmine in printed warfare, Montagu recalled 'Good Lord, what a stir we had; what roaring of the wild bulls of Basan, what a commotion in every country.' With 'scarce a people, language or nation in Christendom' not returning a response, James's defence of his monarchical rights had nevertheless firmly placed Stuart England on the map of international polemic and controversy.[64]

But in May 1610, James's worst nightmares were realized when Henri IV was assassinated in central Paris. Although the French king had survived at least twenty-three previous assassination attempts, when Henri's coach was detained by traffic in the rue de la Ferronnerie, a knife-wielding former monk, François Ravaillac, leapt onto a wheel of the stationary coach and fatally stabbed the king twice in the chest. Ravaillac later justified his actions on the grounds that, as an erstwhile excommunicate, Henri was an illegitimate usurper who was not only failing in his divine duties by tolerating heretic Huguenots, but was also about to declare war on the papacy by attacking the Holy Roman Emperor in the Rhineland territory of Jülich-Cleves-Berg. On the day before the assassination, Henri's queen, Marie de'Médicis, had undergone a coronation ceremony to invest her with formal power to govern France while her husband went on campaign.

While Marie de'Médicis retained control of the regency government appointed on behalf of the infant Louis XIII, Henri's assassination provoked fears of renewed civil war between Huguenots and the remnants of the pro-Spanish Catholic League. Describing how 'one saw, in an instant, the face of Paris completely changed', L'Éstoile was nevertheless relieved that, rather than instantly taking up arms against one another, 'all the fury of the people was turned only against this villainous parricide'.[65] Staying in Royston, James was informed of Henri's assassination and, according to a report received by the French ambassador, Boderie, 'turned whiter than his shirt', declaring himself ready to have his right hand removed if he failed to pledge instant enmity to any power involved in Henri's murder. James was so dazed and filled with despair that he was observed entering and leaving through the wrong doors to his chamber and he returned to London 'surrounded by his bodyguard, a thing he has not been accustomed to do'.[66]

In the English Parliament, Lord Treasurer Salisbury tried to extract political capital from the French king's assassination by insisting to a Commons committee on the need, in 'foreign dispatches, to advertise how careful we are of our king' while recognizing that 'money is the only antidote for future mischief'. MPs had nevertheless opposed the crown's levying of additional customs duties – known as impositions – that James had vigorously defended in terms of similar fiscal freedoms enjoyed by the monarchs of France and Spain. Judging James to be 'in truth very wise, yet he is a stranger to this government', Nicholas Fuller MP rejected Continental comparisons and resisted pressure placed on MPs to approve emergency funds. In a speech delivered in Parliament on 21 May, James insisted that, as a king, 'I was born to be begged of, not to beg', before reminding MPs that, among the regicidal Catholics from whom Henri's assassin had emerged, 'their aim was not at him alone, but at other princes too, whereof I assure you I was one'.[67] The king's claim was endorsed by his new ambassador at Archduke Albert's court in Brussels, William Trumbull, who informed Lord Salisbury that, since Henri's assassination had 'loosened the reins of men's tongues', he had learned that 'passionate and Jesuited people' locally had confirmed their hostility towards James's regime in England, although they were unsure, strategically, 'whether it were more convenient to take away his Majesty's sacred person or your Lordship's'. A week later, Trumbull reported rumours that James had 'been murdered by the hands of a carpenter' while inspecting new buildings at his Whitehall court. Later that summer, the English consul in Lisbon, Hugh Lee, cited Portuguese claims that James had died, either from illness or a 'bloody action', shortly before James received an urgent warning from Naples about a lethal 'russet satin doublet and hose, or jerkin and hose, which if he touches or receives, he dies by poison'.[68]

In June 1610, the English state's unequivocal rejection of Catholic deposition theory was confirmed in a proclamation denouncing 'the papists' bloody doctrine, that make martyrs and saints of such as kill their own kings', observing in Henri IV's murder 'that butcherly theory and practice so linked together'.[69] Measures to enhance royal security included barring all Catholics from living within ten miles of London, ordering all priests and Jesuits to leave the country within a month and confirming that the Oath of Allegiance would now be levied on all adults, rather than solely suspected or convicted recusants. In effect, all Catholics remaining in England were now identified as potential terrorists. In September, the University of Paris issued a 'Remonstrance' that denounced religious defences of regicide as a 'pestilential doctrine' and recalled the serial Catholic assassination plots against Elizabeth I and the Gunpowder Plot against James, as well as the murders of Henri III and Henri IV in France. As the University authorities insisted, all sovereigns remained 'holy and sacred', whether 'Christian, pagan, heretic, idolaters, infidels, excommunicate or apostate'.[70]

6

Dynastic Marriage, Death and Debts, 1610–1618

As part of the Jacobean court's New Year festivities in 1610, Prince Henry Stuart made a dramatic public debut playing the lead role in a masque and mock battle at Whitehall, admired by the king and queen, nobles and foreign dignitaries. Scripted by Ben Jonson, with a set design by Inigo Jones, the masque presented the fifteen-year-old prince as 'Meliadus – Lord of the Isles' and drew on medieval legend to celebrate his father as King Arthur *redivivus* who had gloriously fulfilled Merlin's prophecy by reuniting Britain. The masque's theme was the prince's duty to rehabilitate chivalric virtues of honour and courage; it deliberately emphasized the complementarity of James's kingly ideals of peace and unity with the martial image projected by his eldest son and heir. Merlin reminded Meliadus that responsible knighthood would ensure that 'his arts must be to govern, and give laws / To peace no less than arms', replacing outdated traditions that required 'antique knights, to catch their fellows' steeds, / Or ladies' palfries rescue from the force / Of a fell giant' or other implausible romantic catastrophes. Reviewing past English military successes, nostalgic tribute recalled defeat of 'the proud Armada, styled by Spain / "The Invincible"' that had appeared as if 'half of Norway with her fir-trees came / To join the continents' of England and Continental Europe. Jonson's masque was followed by 'barriers' in which Henry and knightly assistants engaged in one-to-one pike and sword combat across a waist-high barrier. Sir Charles Cornwallis, recently returned from his ambassadorial posting in Madrid to become Treasurer in the prince's household, later recalled how Henry 'did admirably fight his part, giving and receiving that night, thirty-two pushes of pikes, and about 360 strokes of swords, which is scarce credible, in so young years'.[1]

Several months later, Henry's parliamentary installation as Prince of Wales on 4 June 1610 marked another bid to inculcate national loyalty to the Stuart dynasty. The first investiture of a Prince of Wales in England since Henry VIII's installation in 1504, the lavish ceremony was funded by a loan of £100,000 from the City of London.[2] The robes, sword, ring, golden wand and cap of state presented to Henry denoted his ducal status and obligations to deliver justice impartially, act righteously and triumph over the country's enemies. Admiring the sartorial splendours sported by colleagues, the Wiltshire MP John Noyes ventured that 'the very panes of their breeches were nothing else but laces embroidered with gold'. More soberly attired, Noyes felt 'myself to be like a crow in the midst of a great many golden-feathered doves'.[3] The ceremony was followed by a tilting contest, firework display, flotilla of barges and a mock naval battle on the Thames. In constitutional terms, although James would firmly have denied any implied role for Parliament in his son's creation as Prince of Wales, the installation echoed the Spanish Habsburg ceremony of *juramento*, whereby the Cortes of Castile was specifically summoned to swear fealty to the royal heir, as witnessed by Cornwallis in 1608, three years after he had celebrated the future Philip IV's baptism in Valladolid.[4]

Evoking memories of Accession Day tilting contests and other Elizabethan festivities, Prince Henry's technical successes with the sword encouraged more militant Protestant spectators to hope that, in contrast to his father, James's heir might lead England to future military triumphs over its Catholic neighbours. In Continental Europe, geopolitical tensions had increased after the death of the childless Duke John William of Jülich-Cleves-Berg in 1609 had provoked a succession dispute for control of confessionally mixed territories strategically located in the lower Rhineland, close to France and the Dutch Republic. After two claimants – the sons of John Sigismund, Elector of Brandenburg and the Count Palatine of Neuburg, known as the 'Prince Possessors' – had agreed a system of joint administration, the Holy Roman Emperor Rudolph II had intervened on behalf of the former duke's widow by appointing his cousin Leopold, Archduke-Bishop of Strasbourg, as interim governor to sequestrate the duchy. Spanish Habsburg troops, under Leopold, had then seized the fortified city of Jülich in July. Trying to deter Habsburg territorial acquisitiveness, Henri IV of France had failed to remove Leopold's occupying forces. Having requested English and Dutch assistance in preparing a counter-invasion army, Henri's apparent readiness to ally with Protestant heretics in order to displace Catholic foes had provoked his assassination.

While James had been willing to mount an intervention, to do so would require funds. As Lord Treasurer Robert Cecil, earl of Salisbury, had warned James back in 1608, 'all princes are poor and unsafe' if they were insufficiently solvent 'to defend themselves upon any sudden offence or invasion' or to assist allies and neighbours when needed, 'for foreign amity depends on treaties, and treaties break upon slight causes'.[5] To secure funds for the Jülich-Cleves expedition, a new English parliament met in February 1610 and was addressed by Salisbury, who advised that mounting royal debts and a rising annual deficit rendered England vulnerable to foreign aggressors at a time when James wanted to relieve the 'island of Cleves, likely to be overcome by the papists'. Acknowledging that the new English king's 'first three years were his Christmas', in terms of significant royal expenditure, Salisbury confirmed that Parliament's purpose was nevertheless to grant 'supply of wants, not of wantonness' and counselled MPs contemplating resisting fiscal requests to ask themselves 'what sound will this have in Spain?'[6] The following month James addressed both Houses of Parliament, acknowledging that funds 'cannot be supplied out of the air or liquid elements', but advising against any response that might undermine his domestic or foreign reputation. Presenting his audience with the rare gift of 'such a mirror, or crystal, as through the transparentness thereof, you may see the heart of your king', James exhorted peers and MPs not to regard his mirror in a distorted light, nor 'to soil it with a foul breath and unclean hands' by misinterpreting his demands for supply, nor, finally, to disregard his request and thereby risk letting the mirror 'fall or break; (for glass is brittle)'.[7]

As Treasurer, Salisbury hoped to remodel English crown finance through what became known as the 'Great Contract', whereby MPs would agree an annual parliamentary subsidy, raised through a land tax, in return for the crown surrendering unpopular prerogative revenues, such as wardship (by which monarchs managed the estates of minors whose lands were held by the crown) and purveyance (which enabled the crown to obtain provisions for the royal household at preferential rates). Although Salisbury had impressed on the Lords in February that 'we must not look only to put the king out of debt but have sufficient supply to maintain and support his yearly and annual charge', peers and MPs remained cautious when trying to calibrate the value of a future annual supply against existing crown revenues.[8]

Following protracted negotiations, Salisbury asked a committee of peers in June whether, amid Habsburg expansionism, 'the state of Europe is like to change . . . shall England lie in a lethargy?' As the longest summer days of the year approached, Salisbury regretted that, for four months, speeches had been made, 'some square, some *ex diametro*, some as long, but all so circular that the sun has changed his circles, while we are yet in our station', with no agreement reached on royal revenues.[9] MPs nevertheless remained determined to avoid agreeing a substantial subsidy without political and religious grievances being addressed, and presented a petition to the king in July. According to the French ambassador Boderie, James remained uncharacteristically taciturn with 'a pretty bad expression', while the king himself described the MPs' petition enumerating their grievances – which measured more than forty by thirty inches square – as 'big enough to hang a little room'.[10]

Although a substantial subsidy was agreed in principle before the summer recess, the increasing number of caveats attached by Parliament led Salisbury to moan, in October, that the crown was being offered 'a contract and no contract, for a power is left to add, diminish and explain'.[11] Incensed by Parliament's obduracy, James adjourned Parliament the following month, and wrote to Privy Councillors in December, denouncing 'unjust complaints' adduced against royal requests and venturing that 'no house, save the House of Hell, could have found so many' objections. Having left Scotland in 1603 'with an unstained reputation, and without any grudge in the people's hearts', James was exasperated by the extent to which his 'fame and actions have been daily tossed like tennis balls amongst them' with so much 'spite and malice'.[12]

I

Following collapse of the 'Great Contract', Salisbury advised James in January 1611 that since 'the Parliament hath left your Majesty to stand upon your own foundation . . . it is not now a work to repair some small defects, but to raise a new building', capable of rendering the English crown financially viable.[13] In addition to maximizing income from traditional commercial revenues such as customs, and devising new fiscal 'impositions', James also turned to marriage and dowry negotiations to see if his new financial building might be constructed on foreign foundations. The difficulties in Jülich-Cleves had been resolved without English involvement after Henri IV's assassination in May 1610 had (ironically) reduced international tensions when the new queen regent, Marie de'Médicis, swiftly reorientated French foreign policy by opening secret negotiations with the Spanish court that produced the Treaty of Fontainebleau in April 1611. As the first Franco-Spanish treaty of mutual assistance for a century and a half, the Treaty committed the erstwhile enemies to a ten-year defensive pact against foreign and domestic adversaries and agreed preliminary arrangements for a double marriage between Philip III's eldest daughter, the Infanta Ana María Mauricia (later known as Anne of Austria), to the future Louis XIII, alongside a union between Marie de'Médicis's eldest daughter, Elisabeth, to the future Philip IV. To confirm that these were marriages between equal powers, identical dowries were agreed and both princesses renounced their rights of inheritance to avoid potential inequities posed by Salic law that barred the French crown being transmitted through the female line.[14]

While the Spanish Habsburgs offered a spectacular example of a dynasty that had achieved significant territorial expansion through strategic nuptial unions, critics of marriage diplomacy included the Dutch humanist Desiderius Erasmus, who, many years before, had denounced both its cynical rationale and practical effectiveness. In his *Education of a Christian Prince* (1516), Erasmus had attacked as callous the customary way in which monarchs dispatched their young daughters 'to remote regions, to men entirely different in language, appearance, character, and thought, as if they were being sent into exile'. Alleging that dynastic marriages only created 'iron chains of concord between states', Erasmus also demonstrated their practical ineffectiveness by citing the Stuart dynasty's history to show that the so-called 'Treaty of Perpetual Peace', concluded in 1502, had not prevented James IV of Scotland invading England in 1513 to support France against England's Henry VIII.[15]

A century later, as James VI & I reviewed the international marriage market for his two elder children, Sir Walter Ralegh advised Prince Henry against precipitate action. Describing royal marriages as a form of noble deception – 'the fairest and most unsuspected trade of betraying' – Ralegh warned that 'these marriages of France and Spain may vanish away in smoke'. Conversely, although the French were now 'fastened to Spain but with cords of cobweb', Ralegh accepted that they could 'perchance chain themselves with steel'.[16] Indeed, since the Bourbon–Habsburg double marriage did not actually take place until November 1615, everything remained to play for. In France, Marie de'Médicis had kept proposals for the Spanish Habsburg marriages secret to avoid hostile Huguenot reaction. Seven months after the Fontainebleau treaty, she asked her son if he would prefer a dynastic alliance with England or Spain, to which the ten-year-old Louis XIII had reassuringly responded, 'Spain, Spain' since there was 'more greatness there'.[17]

Ralegh's charge of cynical duplicity was, moreover, confirmed by Spanish actions. For in the same month as the Treaty of Fontainebleau was covertly concluded, Philip's ambassador in England, Don Alonso de Velasco, revived the idea that had been mooted after the Treaty of London's conclusion in 1604 of a possible match between Prince Henry and the Infanta Ana María Mauricia, hinting that difficulties over confessional differences could be accommodated. At a court performance of Ben Jonson's *Masque of Beauty* in January 1608, Queen Anna had pointedly reminded the assembled company – which included the Spanish and Venetian ambassadors – of a previous Anglo-Spanish nuptial match by wearing the gold and diamond collar, bearing two jewelled ciphers 'P' and 'M', that Philip II had given to Mary Tudor on their marriage, half a century earlier.[18]

In 1611, Velasco's proposals were taken sufficiently seriously by James's court for Sir John Digby to be dispatched to continue negotiations in Madrid. Despite a lavish welcome, Digby was perturbed by the Spanish court's evasiveness and confronted Philip's favourite, Francisco Gómez de Sandoval y Rojas, duke of Lerma, in August. Admitting that the eldest Infanta was already promised to the French crown, Lerma mooted a possible marriage with her younger sister, the Infanta María Ana. Although Digby saw 'little purpose to argue, or expostulate' when Lerma's colleague, Don Rodrigo Calderón, suggested that minimal account should be made of seniority among royal daughters, Digby emphasized the perversity of regarding the eighteen-year-old Prince Henry of Wales as a suitable partner for the six-year-old Infanta, given that her elder sister was already betrothed to the nine-year-old French heir, Louis.[19] Lerma, Calderón and Digby parted acrimoniously, with Digby later confirming that he could 'only compare the attitude of the Spanish towards us to the weather we have had here this season – one or two days of extreme heat and many days of excessive cold'.[20]

Spanish deception further extended to fabricating rumours regarding a potential match between James VI & I's daughter, Princess Elizabeth, and Philip III after the king's consort, Margaret of Austria, died in childbirth in September 1611. To suspicious colleagues in Madrid, Digby rejected reports that Philip intended to 'demand the Lady Elizabeth' as Spanish courtiers tried 'to blind the world' by confidently insisting that James's daughter would convert to Catholicism to facilitate the marriage. To his counterpart in Brussels, Sir Thomas Edmondes, Digby admitted that he had been 'forced to use so plain and direct speeches' to deny the rumours since the alleged Stuart–Habsburg match was not only in 'the mouth of the multitude', but also 'spoken with much assurance and confidence even amongst the best and greatest'. Customs officials in Spanish-controlled Lisbon had even offered Digby 40,000 to 50,000 ducats if he could ensure the princess's arrival through their port.[21] A member of Digby's household also reported rumours circulating among Madrileños that a municipal project involving extensive demolition of houses was to create a new avenue to the royal palace 'to let in the greatness of our Lady Elizabeth which they hope is to be their next queen'.[22]

In 1611, another double marriage proposal was mooted by the bellicose Duke Charles Emmanuel of Savoy by which his eldest son, Victor Amadeus, Prince of Piedmont, would marry Princess Elizabeth, with Savoy's third daughter, Maria, marrying Prince Henry. Discussed in Turin by James's ambassador to Venice, Sir Henry Wotton, the nuptial proposal reflected the Savoyard duke's determination to avoid isolation after the death of Henri IV with whom he had agreed an anti-Habsburg alliance in 1610. With their territories straddling unstable confessional fault-lines, Savoy's Catholic rulers still hoped – despite a failed attempt in 1602 – to reclaim Geneva after the city had achieved independence from Savoyard control during the Reformation. From London, Wotton was advised that only one Savoyard–Stuart match should be envisaged, together with confirmation that James would not countenance any alliance that did not accord his daughter free exercise of her religion: even 'to make her Queen of the World'.[23] Dispatched twice to London in

1611, the Savoyard envoy, Claudio Cambiano di Ruffia, count of Cartignano, brought gifts of four horses and 'a tame leopard of great beauty' that followed James 'like a dog' and ably assisted by dispatching 'any deer red or fallow that the king shall point out' to the king's 'great delight'.[24] Cartignano confirmed Charles Emmanuel's proposal of '*La Carta Bianca* as he termed it' between Princess Elizabeth and the Prince of Piedmont or, alternatively, an offer of 700,000 crowns (around £210,000 sterling) as a dowry for the Infanta Maria if she married Prince Henry.[25] Meanwhile, Ralegh advised Henry to bide his time as an eligible bachelor – both to secure maximum diplomatic advantage and to avoid incurring the enmity of disappointed suitors – insisting that 'while the prince is unmarried, all the eyes of Christendom are upon him' as rival states vied for an English alliance.[26]

Among other overseas bidders for a Stuart match was Cosimo II, Grand Duke of Tuscany, who offered his sister Catherine de'Médicis as a prospective bride for Henry. Tacitly supported by Catherine's first cousin, the French queen regent, Marie de'Médicis, Cosimo's offer was promoted in London by the Tuscan Resident Ottaviano Lotti, prompting Savoyard alarm that, despite the lack of dynastic prestige, James's notorious penury might incline him to lucrative Tuscan offers, which had now reached a million crowns. But Queen Anna – who was, after all, the daughter, sister and wife of different kings – objected that, as a prospective daughter-in-law, 'she would prefer a Princess of France without a dower to a Florentine Princess with any amount of gold they might offer'.[27] While Henry exploited negotiations to acquire distinctive Tuscan artworks that included fifteen bronze statuettes, Cornwallis also warned him against such a disadvantageous dynastic match, reminding Henry that a Protestant wife would be popular among his subjects and, when it came to parliamentary requests for supply, would attract 'a permanent and continual treasure, not to be equalled by any portion of Florence'.[28]

Given Prince Henry's militantly Protestant image, a Catholic marriage seemed instinctively unlikely. Indeed, in his *Basilikon Doron* (1599) – the handbook of advice written for Henry – James had insisted that he would 'rather have you to marry one that were fully of your own religion' on the grounds that 'disagreement in religion brings ever with it disagreement in manners' alongside the need to establish rival ecclesiastical establishments in the same court and likely tensions regarding the raising of royal children.[29] Following Henri IV's assassination, militant Protestant hopes and impatient demands for vengeance had, moreover, been transferred to Prince Henry, who had been the French king's godson and namesake. In a tract entitled *The French Herald* (1611), the French Huguenot Jean Loiseau de Tourval warned James that the 'time is now past writing; forbearance, longanimity [patience], clemency, pardon, and all pen-work are now out of season: the sword, the sword must cut the knots of this business'. Reassuring the pacific James that he 'need not stir out of your royal Whitehall', Tourval called, rather, for Prince Henry, beseeching the English king to 'let him go for the public good of all Christendom, for your interest, for his own: we have no one else to be the head of our crusade'. Tourval further directed James's heir not to 'mould any longer among your books, no not among your tiltings and feigned combats', but to recall his French ancestry and lead a holy war against the Catholic murderers of his godfather, Henri IV.[30]

Across Continental Europe, Protestants were in increasingly bellicose mood, alarmed by the detente in Franco-Spanish relations after Henri IV's assassination and fearing rupture of the military truce agreed between Spain and the Dutch Republic. In March, James joined the 'Evangelical Union', formed in 1608, which committed England to a six-year defensive alliance with Protestant princes from the Holy Roman Empire. The following month, the Huguenot Henri de La Tour d'Auvergne, duke of Bouillon, arrived in London, ostensibly to reassure James that English interests had not been undermined by the double Habsburg–Bourbon marriage that was now public knowledge. Bouillon also wanted to promote a match between Princess Elizabeth and the German Elector Palatine, Frederick, who was head of the Evangelical Union and had been raised in Bouillon's household in Sedan. Although the Palatinate was not an extensive territory, its Elector had sole responsibility for judging any Holy Roman Emperor accused of misconduct and, together with the Saxon Elector, shared the imperial vicariate responsible for governing the Empire during any imperial interregnum.

By May 1612, marriage terms had been agreed between Elizabeth and Frederick who – unusually for early modern royal marriages – were the same age, having been born within days of each other in August 1596. To deflect persistent offers of a Savoyard bride for Prince Henry, Bouillon also suggested a French marriage with Marie de'Médicis's second daughter, Christine, although James dismissed the suggested dowry of 500,000 crowns (around £150,000) as insufficient and the six-year-old princess as too young. From Paris, Edmondes indicated that Marie de'Médicis's ministers, suspicious of Savoy as a traditional ally of Spain, might yet significantly increase their offer to 800,000 crowns (around £240,000) in what would have become the largest dowry the French court had ever proposed.

Although marriage diplomacy appeared an attractive option for an impoverished royal treasury, James's Chancellor, Sir Julius Caesar – who had assumed responsibility for crown finances after Salisbury's death in May 1612 – calculated the royal debt to stand at £500,000, with the crown running an annual deficit of £160,000.[31] That summer, the new Venetian ambassador to England, Antonio Foscarini, marvelled at the conspicuous expenditure that characterized the Stuart court when he travelled to Belvoir Castle in Lincolnshire to congratulate the English king on the anniversary of his delivery from the Gowrie conspiracy, knowing that James always observed 'the day when his life was miraculously saved'. To the Doge and Senate, Foscarini reported that 'the sumptuous food and the abundance of comfits which they consume is amazing; nor could the greatest monarch in the world, inside his own royal palace, shine with greater pomp'. Taken aback by the costs borne by James's noble hosts, with private estates catering for over a thousand guests, Foscarini felt obliged to distribute equivalent largesse on the Venetian Republic's behalf, admitting that his outgoings would 'infinitely supersede the ordinary expenses of a journey staying at inns'.[32]

As plans for Princess Elizabeth's nuptials gathered pace, the sixteen-year-old Elector Palatine Frederick V arrived in Gravesend in October, having stayed, en route, with James's ambassador in The Hague, Sir Ralph Winwood, where his visit had coincided with Lady Winwood's safe delivery of twins who were named – at the Elector's suggestion – Frederick and Elizabeth, and for whom the Elector became a godfather.[33] Before his daughter's wedding, James also directed the dean and chapter of Peterborough Cathedral to oversee the transfer of his mother's body to Westminster Abbey, being 'the place where the kings and queens of this realm are usually interred'.[34] As the Catholic earl of Northampton, Henry Howard, described, 'many in the streets and windows' then watched Mary, Queen of Scots's body entering London in October, a quarter of a century after her execution, before it was 'buried with honour, as dead rose-leaves are preserved, whence the liquor that makes the kingdom sweet has been distilled'.[35] Having commissioned a similar marble vault for Elizabeth I, James ostensibly granted the two queens equality in royal status, although his mother's tomb was visibly longer, more elaborate and cost at least £600 more than Elizabeth's.[36]

II

Disaster then struck when Prince Henry became ill and died on 6 November 1612, aged eighteen. He was cut down 'at the very flower of his high hopes', and Foscarini predicted that the prince's 'death will certainly cause great changes in the course of the world', while one of Edmondes's correspondents lamented that 'our rising sun is set ere scarcely he had shone' and 'with him all our glory lies buried'.[37] Aged twelve, Henry had been affectionately described by a visiting Italian prince as '*piccolo, bianco, biondo, disposto*' ('small, white, blond, talented'), while a miniature portrait by Isaac Oliver, painted when the prince was around seventeen, depicted him dressed in armour at a military encampment, ready for battle. In another miniature by Oliver, the prince's unusual presentation in classical armour and toga once led the National Portrait Gallery to misidentify this representation of Prince Henry as the Roman general and statesman Pompey the Great.[38] Together with a carefully cultivated martial image that betokened future military success, Henry was fascinated by overseas exploration and had sponsored the first expedition of the Northwest Passage Company in North America, where he is remembered today, in Virginia, at 'Cape Henry, Forty Henry, Henricopolis, [and] Henrico College'.[39] Back in London, at the time of his death the prince had been actively discussing the possible construction of the first bridge to cross the Thames from Westminster.

Although the cause of Henry's death in 1612 was probably typhoid fever, the suddenness of his demise provoked suspicions that the prince had been poisoned in a court intrigue or Catholic conspiracy. The prince's unexpected passing also encouraged conjectures as to his likely nuptial destiny and the spectacular – if speculative – renaissance of cultural splendour confidently prophesied to have accompanied his future reign as Henry IX. As Foscarini presciently observed, since 'many predictions centred around his person, and he seemed marked out for great events', the prince's posthumous memory became a palimpsest for others' ambitions, hopes and expectations, exacerbated by Henry's deathbed order to destroy many of his private papers.[40] Foscarini's claim that Henry had an ulterior motive for intending to accompany his sister to the Palatinate after her wedding – possibly to recruit a Protestant bride – was corroborated by Robert Naunton, MP, who confided to Winwood that Henry had meant to visit Germany and was 'hatching some such secret design'.[41]

Across Continental Europe, Henry's death was seen as a significant setback for Protestant interests. In Paris, the Venetian ambassador Zorzi Giustinian described French shock at hearing the news, especially among Huguenots, who had 'built their hopes on the Prince, and had already chosen him as their chief support and head'.[42] In Brussels, James's ambassador William Trumbull learned from a correspondent in Stuttgart that, since Henry's death was also 'a very great loss to us Germans', prayers were being offered for the preservation of James, Anna and the rest of the Stuart dynasty, 'which we consider as a bridle to the Spaniard'.[43] In Florence, the Venetian Resident Domenico Domenici observed Spanish satisfaction at news of Henry's death: since James's remaining son, Prince Charles, was 'weak and may not live long', anticipation was mounting that 'the king of Spain may one day find the way to place his foot in that kingdom'.[44]

Indeed, from Rome, the fugitive Ulster noble Hugh O'Neill, earl of Tyrone, answered Philip III's enquiries regarding Catholic discontent in Britain by volunteering – if Spanish naval support was forthcoming – 'to risk my life and the lives of all those who will join me in this enterprise'. With an invasion attempted 'suddenly, with great speed and with even greater secrecy', Tyrone advised that 'England itself is the best place at which to aim first'.[45] Confirming prevalent fears, one officer in Prince Henry's household pondered privately, 'now that our hedge is broken down, all passers-by will pull off our grapes; our sea banks be overwhelmed and who or what shall defend us from the over-flowing, all-devouring tyranny, of Pope and Spaniard?' Writing to Digby in Madrid, the prince's Household Comptroller Sir John Holles feared that Princess Elizabeth's marriage to Frederick might be in jeopardy, after Henry's death had placed his sister 'one degree nearer the crown'. Invoking Greek mythology, Holles wondered if Habsburg interests might yet 'venture by force or surprise to snatch this golden fleece from Jason'.[46]

For a month after his death, Henry's encoffined body lay in state in

St James's Palace, where his corpse was attended by ten courtiers at a time with the 'same service and order of meals as when he was alive'.[47] In contrast to the somewhat lukewarm popular esteem in which James was held, one observer described how the prince's sudden death led stunned London pedestrians to pass one another 'as if they had been come out of the graves', with nearly a third of the city's inhabitants donning mourning garments for the dead royal heir.[48] On 7 December, simultaneous funeral ceremonies were held in London, Bristol, Cambridge and Oxford, as a procession of 2,000 mourners accompanied the prince's coffin to Westminster Abbey, accompanied by a fife and drums, normally reserved only for military heroes who had died in action. The mourners were led by Henry's twelve-year-old brother, Prince Charles, since neither the grief-stricken King James nor Queen Anna attended the funeral, which was described by one of Trumbull's correspondents as 'a sight full of royal state, but full of calamity to the state'.[49] A life-sized wooden effigy, dressed in robes that Henry had worn for his creation as Prince of Wales two years earlier, was laid on the coffin: the first royal effigy made of an individual who was not a reigning monarch. In the ensuing weeks, Foscarini reported that James remained overwhelmed by grief and 'even in the midst of the most important discussions, he will burst out with "Henry is dead, Henry is dead"'.[50]

Official mourning for Prince Henry's death ended just before Princess Elizabeth's marriage to the Elector Palatine, Frederick V, on St Valentine's Day, 14 February 1613. Promising a pan-Protestant bulwark against Catholic Habsburg domination, the royal wedding was invested by militant Protestants with eschatological significance after Henry's demise had dramatically docked the line of succession. Given that James's own health was doubtful and Prince Charles was known to be physically frail, there was a plausible prospect that the princess might, one day, reign as Queen Elizabeth II. With her husband's imperial electoral dignities and Palatine territories, the couple could rule a single Protestant state with territories strategically situated in the centre of the Holy Roman Empire with Atlantic, colonial and maritime access.

Unsurprisingly, therefore, the weeks before the wedding were haunted by fears of likely Catholic sabotage. Writing from Brussels at the start of 1613, Trumbull counselled vigilance, warning his counterpart in The Hague that Habsburg supporters 'want not spies and informers out of England, Ireland and Scotland, who resort here in shoals, like cormorants against a tempest'.[51] Night-watches were set up in London and court security tightened, while a royal proclamation issued in January banned the carrying of small, easily concealed wheel-lock pistols, known as 'pocket-dags' to frustrate 'those devilish spirits, that maligning the quiet and happiness of this estate, may use the same to more execrable ends'.[52] Disarmament measures were directed against Catholics and accompanied what one bewildered priest described as 'such buzzes and fears put in our heads and such strange reports cast abroad'. Circulating rumours alleged that papists planned to set fire to Chichester, Winchester and other English towns and that Spanish forces, accompanied by Tyrone, had landed in Ireland where over thirty towns had been burned.[53] In London, Frederick's secretary, Pierre Dathenes, simply confessed to Trumbull, 'I wish the wedding was over, so much do I fear the evil designs of the desperate.'[54]

But in the event, all went smoothly. The first royal wedding in England since Mary Tudor had married Philip II of Spain back in 1554, the ceremonial spectacle cost the Stuart court over £93,000 and included a mock naval battle as well as banquets, masques and a firework display on the Thames. In Wiltshire, George Webbe published the celebratory sermon he had preached in Steeple Ashton, near Trowbridge, insisting that it was not 'ridiculous, or presumptuous, for us that live here in the country' to share in the official celebrations, since 'not court alone, but country also, and (if I not much mistake myself) whole Christendom is interested in this day's business'. Celebrating James's union of the English and Scottish crowns, Webbe recalled how Princess Elizabeth's ancestors had reconciled the dynastic houses of York and Lancaster and predicted that this new alliance would generate 'the friendship of confederate nations confirmed, Britain and Germany combined'.[55]

Providential significance was also attached to the fact that Princess Elizabeth's wedding to Frederick occurred on the twenty-fifth anniversary of the victory over the Spanish Armada, secured by the princess's namesake and godmother, Elizabeth I. The day before the wedding, the new French ambassador, Samuel Spifame, sieur des Buisseaux, described to his predecessor, Boderie, how spectators along the Thames had watched over twenty simulated sea battles between Christians and Turks, with the former sailing in 'twenty-five or thirty well-equipped ships bearing the flags of England, Scotland, Ireland, Venice and the Palatinate'.[56] In his published account of the festivities, the Thames waterman-cum-poet John Taylor explained that, while these mock encounters recalled the famous Christian victory at the Battle of Lepanto in 1571, fought in similar 'bloody manner was the memorable battle betwixt us and the invincible (as it was thought) Spanish Armada in the year 1588'.[57] Persuaded to assume the captaincy of an old pinnace, reinvented as an argosy for the spectacle, the Chatham shipwright Phineas Pett recalled that in such 'jesting business I ran more danger than if it had been a sea service in good earnest'.[58] Awe-inspiring pyrotechnics also served, metonymically, to project a puissant message to potential adversaries. Amid exploding rockets, mortars and fireballs at the top of a multi-storey temporary castle, a distressed maiden appeared, attracting the attention of a brave St George who triumphed over an evil necromancer to save the lady, just as it was hoped that James's new son-in-law, Frederick V, would save Continental Protestantism.

Among the foreign dignitaries who declined the court's official invitation was Velasco, who refused to attend any event with the Dutch envoy, Noel Caron, since Spain did not recognize the sovereignty of Caron's state. But although Velasco could excuse his absence on the grounds that the wedding date fell within Lent – at least according to the Gregorian calendar – Spifame reported that Philip's ambassador was 'much in evidence around town' during the celebrations, even managing 'to find his way into someone's house to watch the opening festivities on the water as a private citizen'.[59] It was nevertheless fortunate that Velasco did not attend the wedding banquet, for, decorating the temporary structure accommodating the dinner guests, there were tapestries celebrating England's defeat of the Spanish Armada. Commissioned in the 1590s by the Navy's Lord High Admiral, Charles Howard, earl of Nottingham, the tapestries had been produced by the renowned Spiering tapestry manufactory in Delft at a cost of nearly £1,600 and had been acquired by James for the royal collection in 1612.[60] Deeming the décor an outrageous insult, the London-based Catholic missionary Luisa de Carvajal y Mendoza wrote to the duke of Lerma's associate Calderón objecting to the tapestries' depictions of Englishmen 'killing Spaniards and triumphing over them ignominiously ... how nice of them to invite the Spanish ambassador to eat there!'[61]

In mid-April, Elizabeth and Frederick departed from Margate on a fifty-eight-day journey along the Rhine to Heidelberg, through The Hague, Amsterdam, Düsseldorf, Cologne and Bonn, involving a procession of thirty-four vessels and an entourage that variously attracted between 650 and 2,000 attendants.[62] The riverine theme appealed to poets who envisaged a glorious union of the Thames and the Rhine swelling to form a Protestant ocean so large that it would deluge the Catholic Tiber in Rome. As one poet put it 'Make this Rhine and Thames an ocean, / That it may with might and wonder / Whelm the pride of Tiber under'.[63] Hopes of pan-Protestant dynastic fulfilment would be further boosted when Elizabeth gave birth to a son, Prince Henry Frederick, on New Year's Day 1614, named in honour not only of his deceased uncle, but also of his German father, Frederick, and Danish grandfather, Frederick II. Henry Peacham's *Prince Henry Revived* (1615) saw the infant Palatine as a replacement for his mourned uncle, combining the royal blood of the Protestant states of Scotland and Denmark, as well as 'the Saxon line' and 'Norman ancestors'. Through the new royal baby, Peacham predicted

> Now Germany, and Britain, shall be one,
> In League, in Laws, in Love, Religion:
> 'Twixt Dane, and English, English and the Scot,
> Old grudges (see) for ever are forgot.[64]

The infant prince's right to succeed to the English throne was, moreover, recognized by parliamentary legislation drawn up in 1614 confirming the naturalization and succession rights of Elizabeth, Frederick and their heirs in the event of Prince Charles's death. Opening Parliament in April 1614, James acknowledged to MPs and peers that, although God had removed Prince Henry, 'he has given me now, not long after, a grandson'. Moreover, English dominance in any future succession, through his daughter, would ensure that 'England will bring the Palatine, but impossible that that [state] should carry England to it'.[65] The king's pledge echoed his commitment to peers and MPs, seven years earlier, that in promoting closer Anglo-Scottish union he would not 'respect the lesser, and neglect the greater' by preferring Scots, who were 'absent, less powerful and farther off', to the richer, more populous English.[66] Such logic was sourly endorsed by the new Spanish ambassador, Don Diego Sarmiento de Acuña, who recorded James's assurances that a Palatine succession 'would be very convenient' for England, 'since it would increase its provinces and subject states without becoming itself a province'. By contrast, had Princess Elizabeth concluded a more prestigious Spanish or French match that had produced offspring, 'England would have become subject to Spain or France, thus losing its soul and body'.[67] A future Palatine succession to the English crown remained a real possibility. It was not until 1630 that Henry's younger brother – by then Charles I – produced an heir (later Charles II), by which point Frederick and Elizabeth had already borne eight children.[68]

III

When James convened a new English parliament in the spring of 1614, it was the first time that MPs had met since Salisbury's 'Great Contract' had foundered four years earlier. With royal debts larger than ever, James addressed both Houses on 9 April, deploying the same metaphor that he had used when opening Parliament in 1610, presenting his royal wishes as 'a mirror which is clear and unpolluted' and hoping that his requests for supply would be more favourably received. Emphasizing the reciprocal importance of parliaments for monarchs and subjects alike, James optimistically trusted that 'this parliament, I hope, shall be called the parliament of love' and dismissed unhelpful rumours that he disdained parliamentary procedure. The king explained that, just as someone who 'overmuch strains and blows his nose will cause blood, so if a prince should stretch his prerogative, it would cause his people to bleed'.[69] But MPs refused to sanction royal requests for supply without receiving reassurances regarding the legality of additional customs duties, known as impositions. Drawing on their diplomatic experience, MPs including Winwood, Wotton and Sir Thomas Roe tried to support the crown by confirming that similar royal exactions were levied in states such as France and Spain, but hostile critics quickly refuted the relevance of foreign practice to English debates.

On 4 May, James returned to the Commons to defend the historic right of all English monarchs to levy impositions and warned MPs that 'he would die a 100 deaths before he would infringe his prerogative'. As parliamentary rhetoric became provocative, Thomas Wentworth – whose father Peter had incurred Elizabeth's wrath for urging debate of the royal succession in the 1590s – quoted scriptural texts from Daniel and Ezekiel to warn of the fatal ends that befell monarchs who levied excessive taxes. Wentworth recalled of Henri IV that 'in the midst of his glory, he died like a calf that had his throat cut by a butcher', but hurriedly expressed his hope that James might avert such a fate.[70] Although Wentworth's analogy drew complaint from the French ambassador, Spifame, fellow MPs absolved their colleague of speaking disrespectfully. But Scots royal ire was incited when another lawyer, John Hoskins MP, admired King Canute's eleventh-century decision to return his Danish advisers to Denmark on becoming English king and commended the Elector Palatine's recent choice of German attendants for Princess Elizabeth in Heidelberg. The anti-Scottish implications of Hoskins's additional reference to the Sicilian Vespers – a rebellion in 1382 against a French-born king in which around 3,000 French settlers had been massacred by native Sicilians – were deemed sufficiently offensive for Hoskins to be detained in the Tower of London for over a year. By 3 June, Roe urged that 'speedy resolution' was required to avoid 'the ending, not only of this, but of all parliaments'. Three days later, Roe warned that if MPs could 'but see the letters that are come from beyond seas lately from diverse ministers to other princes, how they joy in the fraction between the king and his people', they would alter their approach. In response, however, Edwin Sandys confirmed his colleagues' refusal 'not to have the liberties of the House to run through our fingers': it was not the extent of impositions that was disputed, but the monarch's insistence on 'his sole authority to impose them'. After sitting for only forty-three days with no legislation passed, the assembly – later dubbed 'the Addled Parliament' by a newsletter-writer – was dissolved by James on 7 June.[71]

Parliament's precipitate dissolution was detrimental to both royal finances and to James's international image. Ambassadors representing Philip III, Archduke Albert and Christian IV of Denmark had attended its ceremonial opening, sitting – as recounted by the new Spanish ambassador Sarmiento – behind 'a crimson taffeta curtain' by the king's throne, which had 'slits through it so that everything could be seen'.[72] Less than a week after the dissolution, James met Sarmiento at Greenwich and directed the ambassador to report events to Philip 'as he should relate them himself, and not as they were talked about in the streets'. Comparing the challenges of managing a Parliament comprised of nearly 500 with that of the much smaller Castilian Cortes, James had objected that, within the House of Commons, 'there was no head, and they voted without order, nothing being heard but cries, shouts and confusion'. As Sarmiento described, James had ventured that 'he was astonished that the kings his predecessors had consented to such a thing', but having 'himself come to England as a stranger' felt obliged to tolerate its unruliness. To Philip, Sarmiento also relayed James's insistence that any prospect of improving matters was 'now in your Majesty's hands' as a sizeable foreign dowry seemed the most likely means of remedying royal finances. Since James's surviving son was aged thirteen, marriage negotiations might be pursued less urgently than had been the case for Prince Henry, although Sarmiento reported James's irritation at 'the batteries brought to bear upon him by the Scots' to conclude a match between Prince Charles and the eight-year-old French Bourbon Princess Christine, for which a Privy Council committee had already been established.[73]

Financial woes further weakened the English government's capacity to withstand any foreign-backed dissension that might occur in Ireland. Beseeching MPs to agree urgent funds, James's Secretary of State Winwood denied popular claims that the island was 'not a thorn in our foot but a lance in our side' that, left alone, 'will sooner or later show us an Irish trick'. Were an Irish rebellion to break out, Winwood warned that 'the shame would be great and the danger as great' if the English crown could not fund its rapid suppression; in the eyes of other nations, it would 'make us *opprobrium et ludibrium mundi* [the disgrace and mockery of the world]'.[74] When the first Irish parliament of James's reign convened in Dublin in April 1614, the refusal of Catholic 'Old English' MPs to recognize the legitimacy of MPs from eighty-four new constituencies, created to represent Protestant plantation boroughs, prompted the separate election of two Speakers. Having summoned a delegation of 'Old English' MPs to London, James deplored their obstructionism as 'rude, disorderly, inexcusable and worthy of severe punishment', judging them a 'recusant party' who were 'but half-subjects' with 'an eye to me one way and to the Pope another way'.[75] In a report compiled that year on the country's condition, the former President of Munster Sir George Carew identified a new generation of native Irish 'more politic, and able to manage a rebellion with more judgement and dexterity' than their predecessors. Although Carew believed that a serious rebellion would only break out with foreign assistance, he feared 'a displantation being thus effected', having 'often heard fall from the lips of protected rebels' the (ironic) inspiration that Irish Catholics derived from the Dutch Republic whose English-backed revolt against Spain had secured independence from Habsburg rule. Although James had no foreign foes at present, Carew deemed it 'wisdom to trust the worst', fearing that 'the modern English and the Scots' settled in new Protestant plantations were so dispersed that 'the natives' swords will be in their throats in every part of the realm, like the Sicilian Vespers'.[76]

As international tensions resurfaced in the Rhineland duchies of Jülich-Cleves, the idea that James's government would be able to take meaningful action seemed unlikely. From Brussels, Trumbull reported in July 1614 that the city was 'filled with an expectation and rumour of an open rebellion in England', amid speculation that James was 'in some danger of a new powder plot'. Knowledge of the English king's penury, combined with 'the lamentable issue of our parliament', had encouraged Archduke Albert, as ruler of the Spanish Netherlands, to raise Habsburg troops to support the German Catholic League.[77]

From London, Winwood asked Trumbull to avoid including, in reports seen by James, 'any disgraceful or contemptible speeches' heard locally, since 'the knowledge of such reports are grievous unto his spirit', unconsciously echoing directions formerly issued by Elizabethan councillors to overseas envoys, similarly anxious to shore up royal morale. At home, in an attempt to find alternatives to parliamentary subsidies, a voluntary collection of silver plate and ready cash raised around £23,000 for royal coffers. Writing to Trumbull in Brussels, Archbishop George Abbot of Canterbury asserted that the donations had 'stopped the mouths of the malicious, and choked some ambassadors who did infinitely rejoice at the distraction between king and people'. Rumours of an imminent national disaster had suggested to Abbot that 'some of the ambassadors here are no better than practising spies'. But as contributions slowed, Abbot feared that some of James's own courtiers had become 'enchanted by the siren-like songs of Spain'. While the English suffered royal penury, national enervation and popular distraction, 'the adversary insults over us and scorns us abroad'.[78]

Sent to The Hague as an ambassador extraordinary, Wotton had returned reassurances that the Genoese military commander Ambrogio Spínola would not use Habsburg forces to occupy the strategically significant city of Wesel. But events proved otherwise: in a blizzard of attacks unleashed over one fortnight in August 1614, Spínola's forces seized the free imperial city of Aachen (also known as Aix-la-Chapelle), before taking and garrisoning fifty-five towns and forts, culminating in Wesel's capture. Situated on the Dutch union's fragile south-eastern border, the garrisoned town was located at a crossing-point on the Rhine and offered tempting entry into the Dutch Republic.[79]

James's international image came under further hostile scrutiny when the first French Estates General to be convened since 1588 met in Paris. Having achieved his majority in October 1614, Louis XIII confronted endemic factionalism and serial noble rebellions opposing the double Bourbon–Habsburg marriage alliance contracted two years earlier. In December, the 'First Article of the Third Estate' was tabled before the Estates General, requesting Louis to confirm, as 'a fundamental law' of France, that there was 'no power on earth whatever, spiritual or temporal' that could deny, on any pretext, the sacred nature of French kingship nor absolve subjects from loyal obedience to the country's monarch.[80] Intended to buttress the regency government of Marie de'Médicis against domestic challenge, the article's simultaneous undermining of papal authority within France bore echoes of James's controversial Oath of Allegiance (1606). The article was eventually rejected by the Estates General, following vociferous opposition from the clerical First Estate that included a lengthy 'harangue' by Cardinal Jacques Davy du Perron, who insisted that it had 'come by sea and swum from England'. From Rome, Paul V sent a papal brief to the First Estate of clerics that denounced the article as a flammable spark emanating '*ex miserabili Anglicano incendio ad conflagrationem et destructionem*' ('from the deplorable English fire that brought only fire and destruction').[81]

James responded in print, assisted by the French Huguenot pastor Pierre Du Moulin, via a detailed *Remonstrance*, admitting his reluctance 'to furnish foreign kingdoms and people with counsels' but insisting that, in pious duty to the memory of his murdered relatives, Henri III and Henri IV, it remained vital to refute the 'pernicious opinion; that Popes may toss the French king his throne like a tennis ball'. Appearing first in French, and then in English, the *Remonstrance* reminded readers that, since God created monarchs, it was not for the papacy to serve sentences of excommunication and deposition that left sovereigns 'blasted with Roman lightning, and stricken with papal thunder'. As James explained, 'let a cat be thrown from a high roof to the bottom of a cellar or vault, she lights on her feet and runs away, without taking any harm'. But although 'a cat may look upon a king', an excommunicate monarch 'cannot fall from the lofty pinnacle of royalty' to 'the hard pavement of a private state, without crushing all his bones in pieces'. James also rejected claims of nefarious English influence, denying that the French needed any such reminder 'to come swimming with a fish's tail out of an island to the main Continent, when they had before their eyes the murders of two kings, with diverse civil wars' and serial noble conspiracies offering clear internal justification.[82]

According to Edmondes, James's ambassador in Paris, Louis XIII's administration nevertheless suspected the English king of seeking to 'blow the coals for the stirring up of these broils within this state', given James's longstanding correspondence with the leading Huguenot noble Bouillon and his family connections to the Guise dynasty.[83] But any fear that English assistance might be offered to French anti-government rebels was soon dismissed in Spain. As Digby reported from Madrid in September 1615, it was comfortably assumed by Philip's court that no action was likely in light 'of your Majesty's great wants and the discontent of the parliament which has the only power to relieve you'. Recounting ways in which Spanish ministers blatantly mocked James's impecuniousness, Digby cited jocular recommendations that 'alms money should be taken from the Sub-Almoner to buy your Majesty your dinner'.[84] Knowing that all monarchies, especially the Spanish Habsburgs, attached prime importance to *reputacíon*, Sir Thomas Lake insisted to other Privy Councillors in September that 'reputation is as essential, and of as great moment to a prince's well-doing as is his means': mounting royal debts and an unfortunate record of 'breaches' between the king and his parliaments had 'detracted from his Majesty's reputation, both at home, and abroad'.[85]

Taking opportunistic advantage of the king's desperation to raise funds without calling Parliament, the Dutch ambassador Sir Noel Caron was instructed to offer £250,000 if James wished to sell the two 'Cautionary Towns' of Briel and Vlissingen entrusted to England during the Elizabethan wars with Spain. Although the Dutch debt stood at £600,000, the proposal was sufficiently tempting for James, in consultation with his Privy Councillors, to agree the towns' sale for £213,000 in May 1616. Although Winwood reassured Sir Dudley Carleton 'that this business has not been carried on in hugger mugger, by the practice of one or two men', concern prevailed at such a stark reversal of Elizabethan foreign policy.[86] A veteran of the Elizabethan wars in the

Netherlands, the English-born Governor of Utrecht, Sir John Ogle, lamented to Trumbull in July that 'a blind man may see that we are much weakened' by the towns' ignominious sale. Predicting that Anglo-Dutch amity would wane, Ogle observed that, just as the Dutch were no longer 'looked upon with the old English eye, neither do they put that confidence in England where they see a Spanish ambassador so powerful, whom they know to plot and practise nothing more than the ruin of their state'.[87]

Accusations that James and his entourage appeared suspiciously 'English-Popish' surfaced the following summer when the king returned to Scotland for the first time since leaving Edinburgh in 1603.[88] The previous year, James had sought to counter 'false rumours either maliciously or foolishly spread abroad' regarding his motives for the trip by assuring Scottish Privy Councillors that his 'salmon-like instinct' to return to his native land had long 'stirred up our thoughts and bended our desires', both 'when we were awake and many times in our sleep'.[89]

The following March, the Venetian secretary in London, Giovanni Battista Lionello, reported that, at Whitehall, 'the whole Council went on their knees to beg him to put it off' – but to no avail. Arriving in Scotland in mid-May 1617 with an entourage of 700–800 attendants, the king had ordered refurbishment of the royal chapel at Holyroodhouse where an altar, candles and an organ were reintroduced for the first time since the Reformation, although James had been dissuaded from installing gilded wooden carvings of the apostles and evangelists. When James tried to confirm the Kirk's recognition of royal supremacy and enjoin certain ceremonial forms of worship, however, opposition emerged in the Scottish Parliament and among the Church of Scotland's ministers. Later dubbed the 'Five Articles of Perth', the ceremonial requirements included kneeling at communion, which was regarded by some Protestants as deferentially popish and contrary to Christ's practice at the Last Supper of communally breaking bread at a table. Having followed the king's party to Edinburgh, Lionello observed that, by the time James dissolved Parliament after only a month in session, 'the king's dissatisfaction with the parliament was as evident as that of the parliament with the king'.[90]

After leaving Scotland in August, James spent several days in Cumbria, where Bishop Robert Snowden of Carlisle 'preached Robin Hood' to the king, lamenting the lawlessness and endemic poverty prevalent within his diocese.[91] But to English minds, James's northern troubles had a silver lining. Encountering Scottish obstructionism might, as one of Trumbull's London correspondents surmised, not only encourage James to 'hasten his retreat' south, but also incline him to recognize that the English were not 'the only refractories of the world in accommodating their sovereign's desires'.[92]

Indeed, when the Church of Scotland's General Assembly refused to encourage observation of the controversial articles that autumn, James wrote to the Archbishops of St Andrews and Glasgow, objecting that 'since your Scottish Church hath so far condemned my clemency, they shall now find what it is to draw the anger of a king upon them'. Before another General Assembly was convened at Perth in August 1618, James warned its commissioners, 'do not think, that we will be satisfied with refusals, or delays, or mitigations': rather, the king demanded 'a simple and direct acceptance of these articles in the form by us sent unto you, now a long time past'.[93] With an armed guard placed outside the Perth Assembly and a close voting record maintained, observance of the articles was eventually secured. Meanwhile, having arrived in London as Venetian ambassador the previous October, Piero Contarini detected a general lack of esteem for the Stuart monarchy and palpable nostalgia for the Elizabethan era. During his stay, Contarini had 'heard great lords deplore the present state of affairs with bitter tears and complain that England, which once stood high in the world', feared by foreign foes, 'had now forgotten her past glories and almost fallen into oblivion of herself'.[94]

7

Crisis in the Palatinate, 1618–1623

In May 1618, the 'Defenestration of Prague' saw two regents of the Holy Roman Empire and a secretary forcibly ejected from a top-floor window of Prague's Hradčany Castle by Protestant members of the Bohemian Estates in an attempt to halt pro-Catholic policies being pursued by the country's Austrian Habsburg king-elect, Ferdinand of Styria. Denounced for suppressing religious freedoms, the regents had been summarily sentenced to a ritualized form of punishment that invoked both the scriptural instance of Queen Jezebel being fatally flung from a window in the Book of Kings and classical Roman precedents of throwing convicted traitors from the Capitoline Hill's steep Tarpeian Rock. While the three imperial officials unexpectedly survived their seventy-foot descent from the castle, a printed *Apologia* sent by the Bohemian Estates to Holy Roman Emperor Matthias insisted that the punishments had been a necessary 'act of defence' and had not been intended to undermine imperial authority. Meanwhile, in his capacity as neighbouring head of the Evangelical Union, the Elector Palatine Frederick V offered the Bohemian Estates military and diplomatic support and advised against ending the rebellion without first securing their religious freedoms.

Since 'all eyes are directed upon Bohemia' – as the English ambassador in Venice, Sir Henry Wotton, put it in August 1618 – James VI & I found his determination to uphold the inviolable authority of all monarchs brought into direct conflict with his Stuart family loyalties.[1] In early 1619, a Palatine envoy, Baron Christoph von Dohna, arrived in England at Frederick's behest to seek financial and armed assistance from his father-in-law, but James indicated that a negotiated settlement should be sought. Hoping that tensions would not escalate beyond

Bohemia's borders, James's favourite, George Villiers, marquess of Buckingham, wrote to Philip III's ambassador, Don Diego Sarmiento de Acuña (recently elevated as Count Gondomar), intimating that, if the Bohemians proved 'obstinate and pertinacious', James would 'beg his son-in-law and the other Princes of the Union in Germany not to give them aid or assistance of any kind'.[2] In doing so, James was following directions to his late son in *Basilikon Doron* (1599): to treat all other princes 'honestly and kindly', to be 'plain and truthful' in his dealings, even if it harmed his own national interest and 'especially, in counting rebellion against any other prince, a crime against your own self'. Having produced a corpus of published works that repeatedly intoned the iniquity of resistance against monarchical authority, which included a warning to Prince Henry to 'trust not other princes' rebels', James 'needed no more than a bookmark to answer his son-in-law', given the direct applicability of this counsel to the Bohemian situation that emerged in 1618.[3]

While the Bohemian rebels remained in arms, the childless Holy Roman Emperor Matthias died in March 1619 and, as prescribed, Elector Frederick joined Elector Johann Georg of Saxony in assuming the imperial regency, pending election of Matthias's successor, who was expected to be Matthias's cousin, Ferdinand of Styria. From London, James dispatched James Hay, Viscount Doncaster, to central Europe to attempt mediation, although Doncaster soon found himself 'perplexed with many crabbed thoughts' when staying with Frederick and Elizabeth in Heidelberg, after the Elector forcibly impressed on him the imminent danger faced by Protestants across the Empire. Doncaster was nevertheless determined to discharge James's pacific instructions such that even 'the most punctilious critical Spaniard shall have no just cause to complain'.[4] From the perspective of the Austrian and Spanish Habsburgs, attention could not be solely directed towards the Bohemian crisis, since the Empire was also facing simultaneous uprisings in Moravia, Silesia, Upper and Lower Lusatia, and Upper and Lower Austria, while a Calvinist prince from Transylvania, Bethlen Gábor, who had allied himself to the Bohemian cause, conquered most of Hungary and captured Bratislava that summer.

In a history of Continental Europe written later in the century, the Venetian Giovan Battista Nani identified 1618 as the year in which 'war, creeping like a cancer' wrought such extensive devastation that the ensuing years 'might justly be called the Age of Iron and Blood'.[5] In Prague, the Bohemian Estates remained deeply concerned by the threat of Ferdinand of Styria's Catholic militancy and deposed him as their king-elect on 22 August 1619. Four days later, on his twenty-third birthday, the Estates voted to offer Frederick the crown of Bohemia. Together with Frederick's personal qualities and leadership of the Evangelical Union, the Estates noted that 'the King of Great Britain is his father-in-law' and he also had family ties to Christian IV of Denmark and the heads of other Protestant territories and duchies.[6] Six days later, Ferdinand was elected Holy Roman Emperor in Frankfurt, reluctantly endorsed by Frederick's Palatine delegation. Frederick's wife, Elizabeth, however, sarcastically decried Ferdinand as 'a blind Emperor for he hath but one eye' as he lacked the Bohemian crown that usually accompanied the imperial title.[7]

I

Across Europe, Frederick's likely response to the offer of the Bohemian crown provoked apprehension, with opinion divided as to whether the Bohemians were rebelliously engaged in unlawful usurpation or fighting a religious war to protect fundamental rights of free worship. Responses were calibrated in terms of constitutional rectitude and confessional loyalty, military, diplomatic and financial capability and differing appetites for bellicose intervention or pacific abstention. In Paris, James's ambassador Sir Edward Herbert initially protested to Secretary of State Sir Robert Naunton, 'God forbid he [Frederick] should refuse it, being the apparent way His providence hath opened to the ruin of the papacy'. But hearing that James might advise his son-in-law to refuse the crown, Herbert admitted that 'some of this court take occasion to laugh'.[8] The English ambassador in Brussels, William Trumbull, feared that Frederick might 'be so badly advised as to accept this dignity, which will bring him a cruel, and an almost eternal war'.[9] Yet Trumbull also admitted to Sir Dudley Carleton in The Hague, that 'my best friends in England write in a doleful style' of the cool reception accorded to Frederick's envoy Dohna, since nothing would more encourage Catholic 'adversaries than the slackness of his nearest allies'. Trumbull further confided to Carleton that, if he could hear what was being said about

James in Brussels, 'it would make your hair stand upright, and your eyes (as mine do many times) gush out with streams of tears'. Given the general view that the English 'neither can nor have the courage to do anything', Trumbull worried that a reluctance to support Protestants in central Europe would only encourage expatriate Catholics and 'ill-affected subjects [to] cut us out new work in Ireland, and Scotland'.[10]

Yet James was determined to preserve his integrity as a peacemaker and an honest broker. Days before receiving confirmation of Frederick's decision to accept the offer from Prague, James admitted to Doncaster that the situation would result in an offensive war since the Bohemian crown had been 'taken from one head and set upon another'. Since not 'the least blemish or stain' must be suspected, the 'first care must be to vindicate and to clear' the English response. Disingenuously downplaying his delayed responses to Frederick's repeated requests for advice and assistance, James wondered aloud, 'who would imagine that our son-in-law would ever have entertained any such thing' without having informed the English court and followed its counsel? Even so, James hoped that other states would not believe him capable of 'so unworthy a deed, as publicly to profess mediation of peace between a king and his subjects' while secretly conspiring to depose a legitimate ruler.[11] Refusing to recognize any new Bohemian royal titles, James forbade the Church of England's clergy from praying for his daughter and son-in-law as rulers of Bohemia and denied permission for celebratory bonfires, bell-ringing or other forms of public thanksgiving.

In October 1619, Frederick and Elizabeth left Heidelberg for Prague, with their progress enthusiastically acclaimed as a quasi-confessional crusade by the militantly Protestant pamphleteer John Harrison. Describing five-year-old Prince Henry Frederick's visible excitement, Harrison trusted that 'he will one day make good all those great hopes which were dead in Prince Henry, but revived again in him'. Of the prince's mother, Elizabeth Stuart, Harrison watched her 'march forward: showing herself like that Virago at Tilbury in 1588, another Queen Elizabeth for so now she is'. After describing the couple's coronation in Prague the following month, Harrison breathlessly predicted that future military successes would 'run along still, like a train of gunpowder, till at length, we hear the final report, of the sudden downfall of that great city Babylon [Rome] even to the ground'.[12] In London, however, the new Venetian ambassador Girolamo Lando observed of

James's court that, even by late December, 'at least in appearance, they still pretend not to know anything about the coronation' in Prague, suspecting that 'this long procrastination' reflected the king's 'not knowing how to find money, since he has none, and detests the only proper way of obtaining any, namely summoning parliament, although many ministers strongly urge this step'.[13]

James's sombre mood also pervaded a religious *Meditation* on verses from St Matthew's Gospel which he published in 1619 and dedicated to Prince Charles. Describing royal crowns, James recalled that Henry IV of England had 'protested that he was never a day without trouble since it was first put upon his head' and warned Charles that Christ's crown of plaited thorns represented 'the anxious and intricate cares of kings' who encountered 'knotty difficulties' so intrinsically complex that 'they can scantly be touched without smarting'.[14] Seeking support for Frederick's fragile tenure as ruler of Bohemia, a new Palatine envoy, Baron Achatius von Dohna, renewed the earlier attempts of his younger brother Christoph to secure material support from England. Although Dohna 'engaged in incessant disputation with the king' to advance Frederick's case, Lando reported that James 'continued to interrupt him, laying stress upon the reasoning of the Austrians' and denouncing the Bohemians' 'practice of dethroning kings and princes'.[15] At Newmarket, the Flemish envoy Jean Baptiste van Male contemptuously denounced Frederick as 'a winter king who would last one season only', before an elderly courtier warned Van Male that 'if he did not show respect, none would be shown to him and threatened to throw him out of the window'.[16]

Indeed, rather than raising funds and deploying soldiers to protect Protestant interests and support his daughter and son-in-law, the message from James's court remained that of peaceful diplomacy. Following Queen Anna's death from consumption and dropsy in March 1619, James had arranged a sumptuous state funeral that had cost more than double the amount spent on Elizabeth I's obsequies in 1603 and also more than that expended for Prince Henry's funeral in 1612. A vivid panoply of embroidered banners and gilded escutcheons reminded international observers of Anna's extensive armigerous alliances, which encompassed the Protestant kingdoms of England, Scotland, Denmark, Norway and Sweden, together with the duchies of Saxony, Mecklenburg and Pomerania, and additional smaller territories and historic

Danish tribes. While Prince Charles led the cortège of over 1,300 mourners, it was James's motto – *Beati Pacifici* ('Blessed are the Peacemakers') – that adorned the queen's hearse.[17]

James's apparent concern to avoid antagonizing Habsburg interests mystified many. From the Spanish embassy in London, the Dominican friar Diego de Lafuente wrote to Philip III in November 1619 to report that, during Gondomar's absence from London, he had 'successfully caused to suspend the performance here of a play' – Thomas Dekker's *The Whore of Babylon* – which had been 'full of thousands of blasphemies against the Pope and Spain'.[18] As the apocalyptic allegories of Dekker's play (first performed in 1606) assumed new potency amid heightened international tensions, *The Whore of Babylon* had been revived by 'The Elector Palatine's Men' as the successor theatrical company to 'Prince Henry's Men', royal patronage of which had symbolically been entrusted to Frederick after Henry's death in 1612. Meanwhile, James insisted that neutrality was essential to preserve his own independence as a mediator in any future peace settlement and, following Gondomar's return to England in March 1620, repeatedly cited the ambassador's assurances that Habsburg forces would not attack the Palatinate in revenge for Frederick accepting the Bohemian crown.

Furthermore, James continued to contemplate a Spanish marriage for Prince Charles as a means of reducing confessional tensions in central Europe. In May, Lando reported the court's opinion that no obstacles remained to impede such a match, but although the English king visibly delighted in 'Gondomar's suave and plausible demeanour', Lando feared 'that some poisonous snake of artifice lurks hidden beneath these lovely flowers'. More worryingly, James seemed 'to do everything against the grain', disregarding his Councillors' advice and ignoring the national mood. Lando himself suspected that any Anglo-Spanish marriage remained 'nothing but make believe', observing how Gondomar 'laughs about it with his intimates, rejoices at the gain of time and boasts of having so far kept his Majesty's hopes so well buoyed up through his devices'.[19]

Lando's assessment tallied with fictitious claims advanced in Thomas Scott's *Vox Populi, or News from Spain* (1620) which was published anonymously and purported to contain a transcript of a Spanish Council of State debate before Gondomar's return to England. Depicting James's administration as desperate to secure a lucrative Spanish dowry to remedy royal finances, 'Gondomar' welcomed the marriage negotiations as a cynical 'cover for much intelligence, and a means to obtain whatsoever I desired'. He further claimed not only to have sowed so much distrust between James and MPs that no further English parliament would be summoned, but also to have boosted Spain's chances of recovering its former Dutch territories by overseeing James's ignominious sale of the Cautionary Towns of Briel and Vlissingen in 1616. Depicting the English populace as so enfeebled that, at irregular military musters 'of a thousand soldiers, scarce one hundred dare discharge a musket, and of that hundred, scarce one can use it like a soldier', 'Gondomar' insisted that such 'stands the state of that poor miserable country, which had never more people and fewer men'.[20] Going through seven editions in 1620 alone, *Vox Populi* was also translated into French while the real Gondomar was so outraged by the temerity of the pamphlet's claims that he 'foams with wrath in every direction'.[21]

James's reliance on Gondomar's assurances was indeed misplaced. Following a diplomatic mission in which Sir Edward Conway and Sir Richard Weston had failed to dissuade the Habsburg ruler of the Spanish Netherlands, Archduke Albert, from supporting an invasion of the Lower Palatinate, forces led by Ambrogio Spínola conquered several Palatine towns in August 1620, including Oppenheim and Alzey, which had been part of Elizabeth's marital jointure seven years earlier. From Prague, Elizabeth implored Buckingham to entreat her father to desist from futile diplomacy, take military action and 'show himself a loving father to us, and not suffer his children's inheritance to be taken away', adding that 'the enemy will more regard his blows than his words'.[22] On the same day that Elizabeth petitioned Buckingham, Lando reported from London that 'the whole court is boiling over with rage at the news' of the Palatinate's invasion, although a royal audience with Dohna had only yielded 'a rigmarole of phrases and inconclusive promises'.[23]

To foreign onlookers and his own subjects, James's attempts to maintain neutrality in central Europe, while negotiating a Spanish marriage, seemed disastrous and incomprehensible. Trying to explain the ostensibly unintelligible was especially difficult for English ambassadors such as Trumbull who complained that, in Brussels, he was 'looked upon like an owl, [and] interrogated upon such terms' that he was 'compelled to hide my head, and . . . dare not appear in the streets'.[24] In London,

Lando watched pro-Palatine ministers citing letters from noble friends, overseas contacts and ordinary subjects 'who write that they wish they were dead, so that they might not hear the opprobrium and the unworthy attributes cast upon their nation throughout the world'.[25] In Prague, Frederick's brief tenure as king of Bohemia was terminated by a disastrous military defeat at the Battle of White Mountain in November 1620. Placed under an imperial ban by Ferdinand II, Frederick became a rebel and an outlaw as he and his family fled hurriedly towards pro-Protestant Silesia, while the Bohemian Estates sued for mercy less than a fortnight later. In a significant reversal for Continental Protestantism, Bohemia's lands were occupied by imperial troops and its inhabitants subjected to forcible re-Catholicization.

Detecting an unprecedented popular keenness to debate foreign affairs, Lando wondered if, hitherto, 'this kingdom has never had its eyes so wide open', judging the English never 'so teeming and pregnant with ideas and grievances as now'. Indeed, James had 'recently remarked wrathfully that his people are becoming too republicanising'.[26] Amid the febrile mood unleashed by news of Frederick's defeat in battle, a proclamation against excessively 'lavish and licentious speech' was issued on Christmas Eve in 1620, in which the government defended its record in allowing free speech, but cautioned subjects not to 'intermeddle by pen, or speech, with causes of state, and secrets of empire, either at home, or abroad'. The French ambassador Samuel Spifame judged the popular mood to be disturbingly ominous, surmising that 'the hatred in which this king is held, in free speaking, cartoons, defamatory libels' usually constituted 'the ordinary precursors of civil war'.[27] Under pressure from James, the Dutch States General issued a proclamation in January 1621, lambasting unlicensed publications in 'Latin, French, English, Scots, and various other languages' and prohibiting their overseas export, 'especially none against the King of Great Britain and his principal ministers'.[28]

While English contemporaries were dismayed by the Jacobean court's impotent failure to prevent Frederick and Elizabeth's humiliation, the royal couple's plight offered irresistible inspiration for Continental satirists who mocked the Palatine Elector whose single-season tenure as a 'Winter King' unhappily echoed the carnivalesque Twelfth Night custom of electing ordinary subjects as 'kings for a day'. In one poem which featured England's King James as the *hofmeester*, or court steward, who first raised the alarm, Frederick was derided as *Coninck Lappeken van corte rijcken*: literally, 'the fake king of short empire'.[29]

II

The meeting of a new English parliament in January 1621 ended James's seven-year period of 'personal rule'. Opening Parliament, the king once again offered peers and MPs 'a true mirror of my mind and free thoughts of my heart', despite recalling previous occasions when, 'through a spice of envy', critics had spitefully criticized his words, turning them 'like spittle against the wind upon mine own face and contrary to my expectation'. James warned that he neither wished to hear reports of 'lion-like speakers that dare speak of anything that pertains to princes' nor of 'fox-like speakers that seem to speak one thing and intend another'.[30] When Parliament adjourned for the summer recess in June, approval had been secured for a Commons declaration confirming MPs' willingness to raise sufficient funds, should diplomatic attempts to secure peaceful restitution of the Palatinate prove unsuccessful and armed intervention become unavoidable. But when Parliament reconvened later that year, MPs articulated concerns about the likely size of subsidies, the apparent illogicality of seeking a Spanish Habsburg bride for the heir to the throne while simultaneously contemplating warfare against Habsburg forces in central Europe, and uncertainty as to whether funds would be used to wage a military campaign restricted to the Palatinate or a general diversionary war against Spain and the Holy Roman Empire. Despite supporting James's right to declare war, by November Sir James Perrot MP cited practical anxieties regarding 'poverty and impossibility', being loath 'to discover the nakedness of my country' and hoping 'it were not too well known to foreign ambassadors'. Days later, Thomas Wentworth MP was characteristically outspoken in opposing the proposed Spanish marriage for Prince Charles, when he reminded colleagues of 'the Gunpowder Treason' and 'those thirty-six barrels of gunpowder' stored underneath the Commons chamber less than twenty years earlier, suspecting that 'these walls (methinks) do yet shake' at the prospect.[31]

From Newmarket, James nevertheless thundered displeasure at reports that MPs even dared to discuss his son's marriage and to draft petitions requesting that the heir to the throne be found a Protestant bride instead. Although precedents for similar directives included the parliamentary pressure that had been placed on Elizabeth I in 1586 to sanction the death sentence against the king's mother, Mary, Queen of Scots, when James returned to London in December 1621, he summoned the Commons' clerk, John Wright, his Privy Councillors and six judges and angrily tore the MPs' 'Protestation' from the House's journal, declaring it 'fit to be razed out of all memorials and utterly to be annihilated'.[32]

Deciding, yet again, to end the session of parliament precipitately by dissolution the following month, James published a declaration, brusquely insisting, '*ne sutor ultra crepidam*' ('the cobbler should stick to his last'). MPs constantly 'intermeddling' in prerogative concerns, such as the heir to the throne's marriage plans and matters of war and peace, diluted the integrity with which he, as king, could negotiate diplomatically. Foreign powers would be deterred from trusting any royal undertakings unless always 'assured by the assent of parliament'. Furthermore, James insisted that the origins of 'this miserable war, which hath set all Christendom on fire' had been 'only caused by our son-in-law's hasty and rash resolution, following evil counsel' to accept the Bohemian crown. Denouncing as dangerous attempts to convert the conflict into a confessional crusade, James pointed out that those who claimed the protection of Protestant interests as 'a good pretext for dethroning of kings, and usurping their crowns' were, rather, following standard Jesuit practice.[33] But to bewildered observers, the fact that James was acceding to Spanish pressure and simultaneously permitting recruitment of English and Scots soldiers into Habsburg regiments that were fighting Palatine forces seemed a conspicuous sacrifice of national interests and family loyalties. Unsurprisingly, Gondomar acclaimed Parliament's premature dissolution as 'the best news in a century' for Spanish interests, removing any likelihood that England could launch meaningful military action on the Continent.[34]

Diplomatic missions remained the Jacobean regime's default alternative to promoting bellicosity and seeking parliamentary subsidies: as Lando's successor, Alvise Valaresso, put it, 'so they go on weaving this spider's web by constant travelling'.[35] Between 1619 and 1622, ten different diplomatic missions to the German states in central Europe were undertaken on James's behalf while, between 1621 and 1623 alone, special envoys arrived in London from Bohemia, Denmark, France, the

Holy Roman Empire, Muscovy, the Palatinate, Poland, Spain, the Swiss cantons, the Dutch Republic and Venice.[36] But sumptuous court ceremonial could not compensate for strategic incapacity. In April 1622, a Whitehall banquet for Emperor Ferdinand's envoy, Georg Ludwig, count of Schwarzenberg, concluded with 'a confection of sugar soldiers in array' that only provoked surreptitious mutterings that 'other muskets and pikes were required now'. When over twenty Spanish ships were sighted in the English Channel near Portsmouth six months later, Valaresso warned that England's coastal fortresses were 'so denuded that some have not powder to fire a single arquebus' and, although the English Navy boasted a sizeable fleet of warships, 'they remain like corpses, without the soul of sailors, and languish idly' at Rochester on the River Medway.[37]

In the wake of several failed harvests and a collapse in the domestic cloth trade, James issued a proclamation in November that ordered all nobles, knights and gentry to leave London and return to their country estates to promote traditional 'housekeeping and hospitality' in the provinces. Observing the exodus, the Flemish ambassador Ferdinand de Boischot, baron of Zaventem, reported that 'there has never been seen so much murmuring', with so many seeking to 'contest and dispute the king's authority' that Boischot feared 'it may prove necessary to avert an imminent revolution'.[38] Around the same time, Valaresso's predecessor, Lando, concluded his posting to London by compiling an account of English politics that described a perennially cash-strapped monarch who did not command popular affection and could not work with Parliament. Attributing the lack of serious challenge to James's rule to the fact that there were 'no leaders of royal blood, claiming the crown, as at previous times', Lando warned that the English populace nevertheless seemed so frustrated that 'they would flare up like straw the moment the slightest fire was applied'. Amid suspicions that England had unwittingly become a pawn of Habsburg interests, Lando distrusted James's over-reliance on Gondomar, pitying what 'one might almost call his captivity'. Indeed, a despairing minister had lamented to the Venetian that 'every day we grow more Hispanophile, and our government is become greatly changed', while Lando's counterpart in The Hague, Christoforo Surian, reported that, locally, James was 'spoken of little to his advantage and reputation' for being so palpably in thrall to those 'they call the Hispanomaniacs'.[39] In Andalusia, the English adventurer

Sir Anthony Sherley sought preferment from the sixteen-year-old Philip IV, who had succeeded as king of Spain after Phillip III's death in 1621. Having previously – and sometimes simultaneously – worked for Elizabeth I, Shah Abbas I of Persia, Emperor Rudolf II and Philip III, Sherley published a survey of global politics entitled *Peso Político de Todo El Mundo* (1622) ('Political power in the whole world') that downplayed any threat posed by England, insisting of James that 'the realm hates him', as he had succeeded Elizabeth as 'a foreign king from a hated nation'.[40]

James's desire to secure a Habsburg marriage for Prince Charles may have been conceived as an enlightened equilibrium to balance Princess Elizabeth's marriage to a champion of Continental Protestantism, but current geopolitics rendered his strategy seemingly inconsistent. Ejected from Bohemia, Frederick, Elizabeth and their retinue (comprising around 200 individuals, fifty horses and a menagerie of pet dogs and monkeys) had arrived in The Hague in April 1621, having been deterred from travelling to England. Given the residual charisma attaching to his daughter and son-in-law, James feared that domestic politics could easily be destabilized, especially when Parliament was in session, if Elizabeth, Frederick and their family were to arrive at the English court and command sympathy as fugitive Protestant victims of Catholic Habsburg aggression.

James's suspicions of his offspring's popularity were also well known overseas. In Rome, the Venetian envoy Ranier Zen reported a conversation with a visiting Englishman who believed that James sought 'to keep the Palatine down and at low water', not only denying him financial and military support, but also refusing a request for one of the Palatine princes to be raised at his court, lest there be 'some understanding with his people to proclaim the boy king one day and depose him'. Speculation also emerged as to whether James – as an eligible widower after Queen Anna's death – might remarry, with rumours in The Hague suggesting that he wished to sire more sons, precisely 'in order to exclude the Palatine's children from all hopes of succession'.[41] But despite repeated pleas to assist beleaguered Protestant forces, there was minimal response from James's court and Habsburg military successes multiplied. At the same time, hopes of a Spanish match for Prince Charles were dented by rumours that, on his deathbed, Philip III had directed his son to abandon ideas of marrying his sister to a heretic English prince, encouraging an alternative marriage between the Infanta María Ana and one of Emperor Ferdinand's sons. The following spring, the Royalist writer James Howell found himself in Madrid, trying to negotiate the release of an impounded English ship. Despite detecting little overt enthusiasm for a Stuart–Habsburg union, Howell assured his father that, 'notwithstanding all these traverses, we are confident here that the match will take, otherwise my cake is dough'.[42]

III

By 1623, the twenty-two-year-old Prince Charles cut a much more confident and assured figure than the shy and physically frail twelve-year-old who had unexpectedly become heir to the Stuart thrones of England, Scotland and Ireland on Prince Henry's death in 1612. Having overcome a range of childhood ailments, Charles retained a lifelong stutter but remained committed to promoting his family's interests amid growing calls for English military intervention to expel Habsburg troops from the Palatinate. As he had explained to Gondomar in October 1620, 'you must know that at bottom this concerns my sister'.[43]

In February 1623, however, Charles provoked universal perplexity when, accompanied by his father's favourite, Buckingham, he travelled to Madrid in person – both men donning wigs and false beards and using the aliases of 'Jack and Tom Smith'. Having only informed James and a few confidantes of their plan, Charles and Buckingham defied every punctilio of diplomatic protocol. Before the prince and the marquess had even left English shores, they were nearly recognized by two visiting Germans who were persuaded otherwise by Buckingham's groom. As the diplomat Sir Henry Wotton later admitted, imagining 'so great a prince and favourite so suddenly metamorphosed into travellers, with no greater train, was enough to make any man living unbelieve his five senses'.[44] In London, Valaresso described the prince's disguised departure as 'an abyss of marvels; a monster among decisions; a labyrinth without head or way out'. As Valaresso reminded the Venetian Doge and Senate, on his arrival in England, 'I at once recognised, and in my letters I have always represented, the evil state of this government, but I confess that this last blow has gone beyond all my calculations.'[45]

After sailing from Dover to Boulogne, Charles and Buckingham arrived in Paris on 21 February 1623, where they lodged at an inn on the Rue St Jacques. Ironically, Charles's elder brother, Henry, had once confided to a French ambassador his dream of travelling to Paris incognito in order to observe the royal court of his godfather and namesake, Henri IV, but knew that his father would never have permitted such a scheme.[46] While Charles and Buckingham covertly visited the Louvre and observed Louis XIII and Queen Ana – the Spanish Infanta's sister – dining in public, James's ambassador in Paris, Sir Edward Herbert, decided not to visit the prince to prevent discovery. As Herbert confirmed, the prince and the marquess spent two days in the city without coming to official attention, although 'a maid that had sold linen' in London 'seeing him pass by, said, certainly this is the Prince of Wales'.[47] But once the French authorities were informed, Louis XIII's court confirmed its displeasure at 'the prince having come so freely to the Louvre' without identifying himself, deeming his audacity 'an affront and a great insult'.[48]

Shocked stupefaction was the general reaction to news that James's only son and heir had decided, first, to undertake a dangerous and risky overland journey and, secondly, to place himself voluntarily at the Spanish court's disposal while marriage negotiations remained incomplete. From London, John Beaulieu admitted to his brother-in-law at the English embassy in Brussels, William Trumbull, that 'we are in a deplorable condition', warning that he 'could tell you such things that would make your hairs stand at an end'.[49] As prayers were said throughout the Stuart kingdoms for the prince's safe return, hostility was directed towards Buckingham amid suspicions that, if the escapade misfired, the marquess was potentially guilty of high treason for having taken the prince and royal heir out of the kingdom. Concerns also attached to the uncomfortable reality that, assuming Charles reached Madrid, both of James's children would – ironically – be staying as uninvited guests at the courts of the two most diametrically opposed and mutually hostile states in Europe: Spain and the United Provinces. To baffled Privy Councillors, James lamely observed that, by venturing to woo the Infanta in person, Charles was simply following family tradition, since James himself had travelled to Denmark to bring Queen Anna to Scotland in 1589 while Charles's great-grandfather, James V, had voyaged to France to meet his first and second wives. Disregarding a crucial difference – that those journeys had only occurred once the nuptial negotiations and proxy marriages had been successfully concluded – James's natural indulgence towards his son and favourite justified in verse their impulsive actions. Using their adopted aliases, the king recalled that:

Thy grandsire, godsire, thy father too,
Were thine examples, so to do.
Their brave attempts in heat of love,
France, Scotland and Denmark did approve.
So Jack and Tom do nothing new
When love and fortune they pursue.[50]

On 7 March 1623, Charles and Buckingham arrived at the English ambassador's residence in Madrid, known as the 'House of the Seven Chimneys' in the Plaza del Rey. The Spanish writer Andrés de Almansa y Mendoza described the prince's sudden appearance as 'without precedent ancient or modern': what in other countries would be 'an imagined dream' was 'given substance and made reality here by the most serene Prince Charles Stuart'.[51] Recording events for posterity, Almansa provided journalistic coverage of the prince's six-month stay in the Spanish capital in serial *relacións* that were later translated into English. Fearing the effects of such an 'excessive risk and labour for such a young and delicate prince', another court chronicler, Gil González de Avila, acclaimed Charles's arrival 'a singular mark of confidence in Spain that has astonished the entire world'. Philip IV and his advisers were, however, 'not a little embarrassed by the surprise', which prompted urgent meetings of the Council of State, 'since this event has no parallel in history, it was hard to know how to deal with it'.[52] If nothing else, the prince's arrival prompted a speedy decision to rescind stringent austerity measures, known as the *Capitulos de Reformación* ('chapters of reformation'), that had been promulgated the previous month, comprising sumptuary and other regulations, including a ban on gold and silver thread to make garments. Charles's official entry into Madrid occurred on 16 March and, once the Lenten season was over, Philip's court focused its energies and finances on organizing splendid courtly and civic entertainments for its unexpected English visitors, reminiscent of the displays of Habsburg magnificence enjoyed by the earl of Nottingham's delegation in 1605.

To mitigate the astonishing breach of etiquette created by the prince's uninvited arrival, a charitable construction that could be placed on his actions was that of a spontaneous act of chivalric knight errantry. Indeed, in the first letter James wrote to Charles and Buckingham after they left England, he saluted them as 'my sweet boys, and dear venturous knights, worthy to be put in a new romance'.[53] Encountering the Lord Keeper of the Great Seal, John Williams, the next month, the 'smiling' king had asked if Williams 'thought this knight errant pilgrimage would be lucky to win the Spanish lady, and to convey her shortly to England'.[54] In Spain, Howell admitted that ordinary Madrileños 'do mightily magnify the gallantry of the journey', maintaining that Charles 'deserved to have the Infanta thrown into his arms the first night he came'.[55] Both in Spain and England, the widespread popularity of Miguel de Cervantes's novel *Don Quixote* – published in two parts in 1605 and 1615 – did not necessarily render such chivalric references wholly flattering, given the impossible, foolhardy and disastrous enterprises undertaken by the book's eponymous hero. One Spanish poet satirically derided the way in which the 'British prince, without light or guide, claims, although a heretic, that he is a lover, and that his honourable aspirations made him a knight errant'.[56] In Paris, Herbert recorded Duke Charles Emmanuel II of Savoy's view that, since Philip's court really intended to marry the Infanta to Emperor Ferdinand's son, Charles's journey was indeed 'a trick of those ancient knights errant, who went up and down the world after that manner to undo enchantments'.[57]

More seriously, Charles's impromptu arrival at the Spanish court also generated mutually mismatched expectations that ultimately served to liquidate, rather than expedite, the marriage negotiations. In an eyewitness account, the Spanish cleric Francisco de Jesús observed that not only Philip and his chief adviser, Gaspar de Guzmán, count-duke of Olivares, but also ordinary Madrileños instinctively explained the prince's journey by 'the very reasonable conclusion' that 'he had come with the resolution of submitting to the Catholic church'. By Spanish reasoning, had Charles resolved to become a Catholic, not only would his conversion significantly increase the future likelihood of England and Scotland abandoning Protestant heresy, but it would also remove any need to secure papal dispensation for his marriage to the Infanta. As de Jesús recounted in a meeting with Charles, Olivares had cited the example of the prince's grandmother Mary, Queen of Scots, claiming that her martyred blood would 'not cease to cry to Heaven' until her descendants came to 'the true knowledge of that faith', eliciting only Charles's courteous promise to supply Olivares with a portrait of his grandmother and a recent account of 'those extraordinary events'.[58]

Days after the prince's arrival, the Venetian ambassador in Spain, Alvise Cornaro, met the papal nuncio at Philip's court, Bishop Innocent Massimi of Bertinoro, 'when we ambassadors jokingly asked him in the chapel if the prince had any intention of becoming a Catholic', to which Massimi had 'answered coldly that he did not know'. By early April, Cornaro confirmed that the Castilian populace, having initially been reluctant to bestow the Infanta on a heretic prince, 'now displays more and more gladness about it every day, as almost everyone feels certain that the prince will become a Catholic'.[59] Charles and Buckingham were, after all, both sons of mothers who had abandoned Protestantism for Catholicism. At the end of Lent, the Spanish court also arranged for its English visitors to share in traditional Holy Week observances, as one local account described a Good Friday procession of monks walking

> . . . their heads and faces covered with ash; others with crowns of thorns and thistles, with much blood flowing from them. Others with ropes and chains around their bodies and necks, carrying crosses, with shackles and fetters on their feet; others entwined and tied up with ropes, others beating their chests with stones, and others with gags and bones of the dead in their mouths.[60]

Despite the Spanish court's assumption that such sights would promote pious sentiments of edification and compunction, Valaresso relayed rumours reaching London that watching the processions of flagellants had, instead, 'seemed strange to the prince, and the horror of it had increased his detestation of the Catholic rites', adding that he was 'scarcely less certain of all this news than if it came from the prince's own pen'.[61] During the Corpus Christi procession in early June, involving around 2,000 clergy and over 4,000 participants, Charles was nevertheless observed kneeling before the passing monstrance. Insisting that Philip IV had, with 'valour and heroic zeal', secured a greater triumph over 'fierce heresy and the German error' than his grandfather, Charles V, had achieved on the battlefield, the court poet Antonio Hurtado de Mendoza marvelled that 'today, great Philip, in peace you have bent the knee of the greatest Briton'.[62]

While Charles remained a Protestant, any 'Spanish match' required papal dispensation and Philip convened a junta of theologians to discuss specific terms, while Charles engaged in private theological debates with senior friars. For the papacy, there was little point sanctioning the Infanta's marriage to a heretic without guarantees of material improvements in the religious and political position of Catholics within the Stuart kingdoms. For his part, James refused to accept any conditions that compromised his authority, as a temporal ruler, to determine domestic matters of religious observance in Britain. He was therefore justifiably concerned when, within a fortnight of arriving in Madrid, Charles and Buckingham asked James to acknowledge that – notwithstanding his notorious disputes with Cardinal Bellarmine and other Catholic controversialists – he recognized the Pope as God's chief spiritual authority on earth. Echoing the citation of his own published precepts regarding non-resistance against lawful monarchs to his son-in-law Frederick, James now cautiously confirmed his willingness, 'if the Pope would quit his godhead, and usurping over kings, to acknowledge him for chief Bishop, to which all appeals of churchmen ought to lie *en dernier resort* [as a last resort]'. Pointedly alluding to Henri IV of France's pragmatic conversion to Catholicism, James nevertheless insisted that 'this is the furthest that my conscience will permit me to go upon this point; for I am not a Monsieur who can shift his religion as easily as he can shift his shirt, when he comes from tennis'.[63]

When the papal dispensation arrived in early May, its terms confirmed predictions that Charles's uninvited visit to Spain had resulted in more stringent conditions being attached to any marriage. James's earlier informal undertakings to reconsider the position of Catholics in his realms had now been replaced by an insistence on freedom of worship for all English Catholics, statutory repeal of all anti-Catholic legislation and the Infanta's right to supervise the religious education of any children arising from the marriage. To some extent, extracting inflexible demands from the papacy may have served the Spanish court's interests in prolonging unlikely negotiations, rather than effecting any marriage. At the same time, memoranda expounding the likely advantage of an English royal marriage for Continental Catholics suggested that if Henry VIII's 'love for a lady not of royal birth' had led to England's original break from Rome, God's divine plan might yet be that 'the Catholic religion may return with a Spanish queen as it was driven out with one'. Since Spaniards' religious fidelity was so strong, there was minimal risk of the Infanta succumbing to Protestant heresy and the Habsburgs 'may well venture a queen to catch a king who may bring with him two or three whole kingdoms'.[64] Within England, however, precisely the reverse arguments were being adduced: the writer Edmund Garrard reassured 'country people, who in state affairs see no further than the Rhine', that if Charles married the Infanta there was 'not so much likelihood, as probability, she may come to be a Protestant'. Not only would the young princess be far from home, but even if permitted to worship privately, she and her attendants would soon encounter 'such a siege and battery laid to their Romish religion' that prompt conversion was likely.[65]

Charles's household thereafter undertook shuttle diplomacy between Madrid and London, as couriers passed between the two cities 'up and down like a well with two buckets'.[66] In Spain, the prince and his entourage enjoyed a summer of Habsburg hospitality that included bullfights, *cañas* tournaments, jousts, tilting, visits to the Aranjuez Palace south of Madrid, walks along the Manzanares river, fireworks, masques, music and dancing. During public entertainments, Howell observed how Charles's eyes remained 'immovably fixed upon the Infanta half an hour together in a thoughtful, speculative posture', reporting that Philip's favourite, Olivares, had opined that the prince 'watched her as a cat doth a mouse'.[67] Providing a dazzling stage for courtly and civic entertainments was the newly transformed Plaza Mayor in Madrid, which had been reconfigured into a rectangular square, surrounded by balconies and able to accommodate around 50,000 spectators, or half of the capital's inhabitants (see Plate 10).

While Nottingham's delegation had witnessed the celebrations accompanying the baby Prince Philip's baptism in Valladolid in 1605, Charles and Buckingham now shared in festivities to mark Philip IV's eighteenth birthday on 5 April 1623. Three days earlier, Olivares's brother-in-law, Manuel de Fonseca y Zuñiga, count of Monterrey, had celebrated being appointed Lord Chamberlain in Charles's household by hosting a banquet for Buckingham and English guests involving four musical ensembles and over ninety-nine different courses.[68] Charles also accepted a generous array of gifts that included five camels and an elephant, which required complex arrangements to ship the animals from Santander to stables in St James's Park. Valaresso noted the elephant's arrival in London in July, but admitted that he did 'not know whether it comes as an earnest of the Infanta or instead of her'.[69]

As the impoverished Spanish administration eschewed economy for displays of Habsburg munificence, the Venetian agent in Florence relayed reports 'that the prince of England has sacked Madrid without an army and produced an extreme scarcity of everything there', including a total dearth of silver specie, while 'the ocean is swarming with pirates and Dutch'.[70] The Madrid-based artist Vicente Carducho later recalled the voracious cupidity of Charles's art agents, which had put works by Titian, Velázquez, Rubens and others 'at great risk when the Prince of Wales (today the King of England) was here', as his English associates had negotiated deals and frequented auctions and estate sales, with 'money being no object in their acquisition'.[71] To honour Charles as his prospective brother-in-law, Philip also presented the prince with major works by Titian, including the erotic *La Venus du Pardo* (1551) and the *Portrait of Charles V with a Dog* (1530), the latter having been painted to celebrate the coronation as Holy Roman Emperor of the Stuart prince's namesake and the Spanish king's great-grandfather.

Among the plays performed in Madrid in June 1623, and likely to have been watched by Charles, was Pedro Calderón de la Barca's *Amor, Honor y Poder* ('Love, Honour and Power'), which revisited the adulterous relationship allegedly conducted between the fourteenth-century English king Edward III and Catherine Grandison, countess of Salisbury. Calderón's play included a sub-plot involving the arrival at court of a foreign prince, Teobaldo – whose name was evocatively reminiscent of James's favourite residence, Theobalds – who sought to woo the young English king's sister, but found that constant deferral of his romantic hopes only induced melancholy.[72] Among members of Charles's entourage, the jester Archibald Armstrong became especially popular with members of Philip's court, as Howell ventured that Armstrong was accorded 'more privileges than any . . . with his fool's coat', including frequent access to the Infanta and her attendants, among whom he 'keeps a-blowing and blustering'. After the Infanta's ladies discussed a recent military victory by Maximilian I of Bavaria over Charles's Palatine brother-in-law, Frederick, Armstrong had even voiced innocent surprise 'that in the year 1588, there should come a fleet of 140 sails from Spain, to invade England', which had been defeated so heavily that not even ten ships remained to 'go back to tell what became of the rest'.[73]

But neither audacious jest nor courtly grandeur could detract from the impasse reached regarding Charles's marriage negotiations. In London, restrictions on the dissemination of information had provoked Valaresso to complain in April that 'the Court has become an echo which emits no other sound than events from Spain'.[74] Meanwhile, in addition to conferring a dukedom on Buckingham, James reported to his son and his favourite that, at Whitehall, court curiosity about events in Madrid was so intense that Buckingham's rival, James, marquess of Hamilton, 'would needs peer over my shoulder' when their letters arrived, constantly offering 'to help me to read any hard words'.[75] Since Charles and Buckingham had been accommodated in Philip's palace in Madrid, lodgings could not be found for many of the attendants who had followed the prince to Spain, obliging their humiliating return to London. Although the official line remained that the marriage negotiations were nearing completion, Valaresso noticed that returning courtiers talked only of 'the future, nothing of the present' and observed that 'one reads in their faces a truth different from what their tongues express'.[76] With little news arriving from Madrid during May and early June 1623, lurid speculation filled the vacuum. Rumoured conditions attaching to the Pope's dispensation included requirements that Virginia and Bermuda be surrendered to Spain; Portsmouth, Plymouth and the Isle of Wight be garrisoned with Spanish soldiers; liberty of conscience be imposed in England; a Jesuit college opened in England to educate the prince's children; and, in one account, that Philip had also demanded 'Scotland and Wales in dowry'.[77]

Limited Stuart comfort could be sought in James's assurances that the Spanish Habsburgs would surely prefer their own Infanta and her children to become Britain's eventual rulers than risk Frederick, Elizabeth and their children succeeding James, should Charles die unmarried. As anticipation of an imminent Habsburg–Stuart alliance mounted, the Venetian ambassador in The Hague, Christoforo Surian, relayed reports that Charles's sister Elizabeth was being encouraged by ministers in London to move her household-in-exile to Habsburg-controlled, Catholic Brussels, ostensibly to ensure she received the 'honourable treatment' suitable for her royal status that seemed unlikely among 'Dutch boors and rebels'. But a staunchly resistant Elizabeth had warned that 'if my father writes to me to that effect, I have my answer ready, that the first of April is past'. In Rome, Ambassador Zen reported that

Jesuit speculation regarding the English king's physical frailty and likely demise was encouraging predictions that, were James to die while Charles remained in Madrid, 'a revolution will certainly take place' and, 'finding themselves without a king', English ministers might well 'send for the king's daughter and the Palatine as their sovereign, leaving the prince to Spain to marry as he pleases'. As Zen added, in such an eventuality the Habsburgs would 'have their turn of experiencing a son-in-law without dominions, and decide whether it is advantageous or their duty to recover them for him'.[78]

In Antwerp, the *Nieuwe Tijdinghen* newspaper reported rumours from Zeeland that both James VI & I and Charles had been murdered and were to be succeeded by Frederick; even after its retraction, the false claim resurfaced in journals in Frankfurt and Strasbourg.[79] Among Frederick's supporters, frustration persisted that James – as the perceived head of European Protestantism – still remained visibly reluctant to take up arms on his son-in-law's behalf to inspire a significant pro-Palatine coalition. In July, Charles's cousin, Duke Christian of Brunswick-Lüneburg, unleashed a mealtime diatribe against James's pusillanimity, blaming the whole Palatine disaster on England's king. Compared to historical figures such as Alexander the Great, Julius Caesar and Henri IV of France – 'esteemed and celebrated as the most outstanding heroes of the world' – Christian insisted that 'the old pants-shitter, the old English bed-shitter is, because of his stupidity, the greatest ass in the world'.[80]

In Madrid, Charles provoked renewed bafflement in early July by confirming to Philip's court that he would accept all conditions attached to the papal dispensation. Three days of fireworks and illuminations were ordered by way of official celebrations before Charles and Philip swore an oath, binding themselves to observe the marriage treaty's terms. Since the terms of the treaty had been framed in such a way as to render their acceptance by the English court unthinkable, speculation swirled as to whether Charles's apparent readiness to reverse entirely his father's religious policies denoted either the besotted submissiveness of a lovestruck suitor or a desperate expedient to conclude negotiations and escape from Spain. Philip's court nevertheless refused to permit the Infanta's marriage to take place immediately in order to allow sufficient time for the English Parliament to ratify repeal of all anti-Catholic legislation, fearing that, if the Infanta went directly to London with Charles, her new father-in-law might renege on agreed obligations.

Moreover, when the papal dispensation's terms were then voided by Pope Gregory XV's death in early July, additional delays became inevitable as a new dispensation was required from Gregory's successor, Urban VIII.

The previous month, Charles and Buckingham had tried to appease James by casuistically downgrading the treaty's requirement to revoke all anti-Catholic legislation within three years. Since James was only being asked to signify his good intention, 'although it take not effect, you have not broken your word, for this promise is only as a security that you will do your best'. In response, however, James told Charles and Buckingham bluntly that their decision to accept the dispensation's conditions had 'struck me dead', warning that the shock of what had been agreed would 'very much shorten my days'. With no idea how he could justify the marriage treaty's terms to his own Privy Councillors, let alone to the public, James also wondered 'what reason I shall pretend' for explaining why the Infanta would not be returning with Charles in the fleet prepared to fetch her from Spain. He nevertheless advised his son and favourite 'in a word, to come speedily away': if they could not secure permission to leave, they should 'give over all treaty'. Insisting that now he did not 'care for match, nor nothing', the king simply wanted to 'have you in my arms again; God grant it, God grant it, God grant it, amen, amen, amen'.[81]

Determined only to secure Charles's safe return, on 20 July 1623 James attended a service to ratify the marriage terms in the Chapel Royal at Whitehall, accompanied by Philip IV's ambassadors in London, Juan de Mendoza, marquis de la Hinojosa, and Don Carlos Coloma, Spanish embassy priests and Privy Councillors. As Secretary of State Sir Edward Conway reported to Buckingham, James had sworn to observe the treaty's terms in a way that 'freely foreshadowed the impossibilities of the exact performance of the literal part concerning the Parliament, but in the sense of doing his best'.[82] Observing James's palpable disgruntlement, Valaresso identified in the English king 'a peculiar genius for damaging himself'.[83]

Meanwhile, James specifically instructed Charles, regarding the Infanta, that he must 'lie not with her in Spain, except ye be sure to bring her with you', and also directed his son and Buckingham to 'treat for the Palatinate' and ensure that Philip's ministers adhered to 'their former conditions anent [about] the portion [dowry], otherwise both my Baby and I are bankrupts for ever'. But it was not until the day that they left Madrid, on 30 August, that Charles and Buckingham admitted two major impediments 'discovered' in response to English demands regarding the restitution of Frederick's Palatine territories from Habsburg control. First, the Spanish court had demanded another dynastic marriage as grounds for restitution: this time between Frederick's heir, Prince Frederick Henry, and Emperor Ferdinand's daughter, 'with this condition, that your grandchild be bred up in the Emperor's court'. Secondly, while Philip's ministers seemed willing for Frederick to return to his former territories, they would only restore the actual Palatine Electoral dignity to his son. As Charles and Buckingham appreciated, it was unlikely that agreement to the first condition – a Palatine–imperial marriage – could be 'obtained of the father, when they will discontent him in the latter'.[84]

Having agreed that Philip would act as his proxy for the marriage ceremony, Charles and Buckingham finally left the Spanish court in September, after their six-month residence. The Venetian envoy in Madrid, Alvise Cornaro, reported that Charles's physician was offering odds of eight to one that the marriage would be abandoned, suspecting that the prince 'might not remain so much in love' once he returned to London and 'saw the rejoicing of the people because he had not brought her with him'.[85] Shortly to become brothers-in-law, Charles and Philip nevertheless bid a mutual farewell near the Escorial Palace, and, within months, a monument was erected, known as *La Columna del Adiós* ('The Column of Farewell') – still standing today – with a legend extolling the glorious future of the anticipated Stuart–Habsburg liaison. As the legend described, Philip IV and Prince Charles of Wales confirmed the marriage, offered their right hands and, amid loving embraces, pledged eternal treaties of peace and friendship. 'O great and unconquered pair of kings without equal! By Jove, no Hercules could stand against the two of them. Rather, they themselves stand against all ... Stop here, Fame, there is nothing more than this.'[86]

8

All Hell against England, 1623–1628

When Prince Charles and the duke of Buckingham returned to Portsmouth from Santander on 5 October 1623, a spontaneous frenzy of celebration ensued. Venturing that 'London never before saw so many bonfires at one time', a young Puritan law student, Simonds D'Ewes, counted over 330 fires blazing between Whitehall and the City of London's entrance at Temple Bar. Compared to the 'thin and poor' bonfires ordered by the Privy Council to celebrate Charles's safe arrival in Madrid the previous March, D'Ewes observed that those freely lit at the prince's unexpected return 'were many and great'.[1] In what would later be remembered as the zenith of Charles's popular acclaim, the impromptu revelries that greeted him were more carnivalesque than official royal entries or processions. Not only had the date and route of the prince's homecoming been unknown, but the fact that Charles had returned *without* the Infanta only fuelled festivities, as 'church bells rang, in a symphony of tintinnabulation' across the country 'in a communal exorcism of the Spanish threat'.[2] Amid the general rejoicing, the Venetian ambassador Alvise Valaresso reported that 'twenty condemned criminals received an unexpected pardon in the midst of the general rejoicing while actually on their way to the scaffold'.[3]

Among militant Protestants, Charles's escape from Madrid was acclaimed as evidence of God's continued providential delivery of England from popish snares, following the defeat of the Spanish Armada in 1588 and the Gunpowder Plot's discovery in 1605. In London, further divine favour was claimed by Protestants when, less than three weeks after Charles's return, around a hundred Catholics were killed after gathering illegally in a London garret adjoining the French ambassador's residence in Blackfriars to hear a sermon preached by the Jesuit

Robert Drury. When beams supporting the building's gatehouse floor collapsed, the congregation plummeted through a second floor beneath them, with additional eschatological significance arising from the fact that – by the Gregorian calendar used in Continental Europe – the accident occurred on the anniversary of the Gunpowder Plot's discovery on 5 November. Preaching in Blackfriars two years later, Theodore Hering counselled eternal vigilance against the Catholic threat, recalling how, 'on the morning of our fifth of November, they would have blown us up; on the evening of their fifth of November, God beat them down'.[4]

While jubilant Protestants providentially interpreted both the prince's return without a Spanish wife and the Blackfriars tragedy as dual deliverances, the diplomatic situation was less clear. Certainly, as Valaresso confirmed, Charles had returned without a bride, marriage ceremony or clear contract: 'as he went without reason, so he reasonably returns without results'.[5] Before leaving Spain, Charles had directed the resident English ambassador in Madrid, John Digby, earl of Bristol, not to deliver the formal marriage proxy to Philip IV without receiving assurances that, after the ceremony, the Infanta would not enter a nunnery in order to avoid nuptial consummation with a heretic. Bristol had nevertheless dismissed rumours of nunneries as risible, reporting that both the wife of Philip's favourite, the countess of Olivares, and the Infanta herself fell 'a-laughing extremely' when the idea was suggested, with the Infanta protesting that 'she never in all her life had any mind to be a nun'. On the contrary, Bristol reassured Charles, she 'much more avowedly declares her affection to your Highness than ever she did at your being here': as well as being officially styled 'Princess of England', she was diligently learning English.[6]

But with his son and favourite now safely back home, James instructed Bristol to inform Philip that the marriage could only proceed once satisfactory agreement regarding delivery of the Palatinate from Habsburg occupation had been secured. To this end, James would continue negotiations in London with Philip's ambassadors, Juan de Mendoza, marquis de la Hinojosa, and Don Carlos Coloma, trusting that the Spanish king would appreciate that the English court could not simultaneously 'give joy to our only son', but 'give our only daughter her portion [dowry] in tears'.[7] Describing Philip's envoys, Sir John Finet, James's Master of Ceremonies, later remembered Coloma as being of 'a good disposition' while Hinojosa was 'sour and harsh, so that they were compared to oil and vinegar'.[8] True to form, when Hinojosa learned of this unexpected turn of events, he 'blurted out that he would give his son's head to be out of this embassy' in London.[9]

In Madrid, Bristol was equally disturbed by the English court's apparent volte-face. Having understood the marriage to have been agreed before Prince Charles left Spain, Bristol knew that the ceremony could not be delayed for more than ten days after the new papal dispensation from Urban VIII arrived. Furthermore, Bristol shared the Spanish court's scepticism regarding the likely cooperation of James's son-in-law, Frederick V, in any proposed settlement of the German situation as too complex a matter to be hastily appended to a marriage treaty. As Bristol protested to James, when Charles and Buckingham were in Madrid, they had discussed the Palatinate's restitution within the context of the marriage negotiations, but had deemed 'it fit to treat of them distinctly', recognizing 'that the marriage should precede as a good pawn for the other'. Philip and his chief adviser, the count-duke of Olivares, had endorsed their approach, appreciating that 'otherwise they might give a daughter, and have a war within months' without satisfactory resolution of the Palatine problem. To this end, Bristol warned James to avoid needless 'staggering in former resolutions' that had already been agreed and celebrated.[10]

Although a new proxy, valid until March 1624, was sent from London, ostensibly giving Bristol time to pursue English concerns regarding the Palatinate, many contemporaries were bemused. Not knowing 'what to judge of the match', the London letter-writer John Chamberlain likened proceedings to the Spanish slow dance, the pavan, in which James and his court moved 'backward and forward'.[11] Over five days in November 1623, Valaresso counted five separate expresses sent to Spain, suspecting that they contained 'as many different commissions as couriers', while regretting that Prince Charles 'continues in his dissimulation, or stupidity, whichever it may be'.[12] In a desperate intervention to forestall the marriage of the heir to the English throne, James's court dispatched a missive unambiguously insisting on its postponement which arrived in Madrid only three days ahead of the planned ceremony on 29 November. Angered by the affront, the Spanish court swiftly dismantled the temporary galleries erected in preparation, no longer referred to the Infanta as an English princess and regarded the marriage as indefinitely postponed, if not aborted entirely.

The following spring, Bristol received his recall to London, voicing a grim certainty that he would become the sacrificial scapegoat for the collapse of the Spanish match. Describing the English ambassador as 'very melancholy and full of undisguised sadness', the Venetian envoy in Madrid Alvise Cornaro reported Bristol's 'willingness to submit himself to the judgement of the [Venetian] Senate or the Parliament of Paris', regarding either as more objective tribunals than the feared vengeance of James's favourite, Buckingham.[13] When Bristol took his leave of the Spanish court the following January, Olivares even offered him 'a sheet of white paper', inviting the Englishman to 'ask either for lands or honours, with the full assurance that nothing would be denied him'. Declining the offer, Bristol admitted that since such favours 'forced him to consider whether he had not been serving Spain rather than his own country', he 'would rather offer himself to the slaughter of England than be Duke of Infantado in Spain'.[14]

Meanwhile, Charles and Buckingham were now driving a diplomatic reversal that increasingly called for armed hostilities against Spain and its Habsburg allies, as they hastily recast their Hispanic experiences as a felicitous escape from certain popish ensnarement. First-hand experience of living in Madrid had dissipated Buckingham's fears of Spanish invincibility: as he informed foreign envoys in London, 'without going to Spain one would never believe her weakness'.[15] *Arma* – not *amor* – was now held as the only means to secure restitution of the Palatinate and restrict Habsburg expansionism. With James's Secretary of State Sir Edward Conway, Buckingham devised a 'three-year plan' to secure military victory over Spain, envisaging a pan-European coordinated attack whereby French, Savoyard and Venetian forces would reclaim the strategic Valtelline Pass in the Grisons from Habsburg occupation, before launching assaults in Milan and Naples, while Danish and German forces would attack Habsburg interests in northern Europe, and English and Dutch fleets would create naval diversions and intercept Spanish treasure ships returning from the New World. Yet James remained unconvinced by such warmongering ambitions, being a monarch for whom, as Valaresso observed, 'fear is always the predominating sentiment'. With England's king 'now divided between fear of his son and fear of the Spaniard', England was gripped by so palpable a mood of indecision and apprehension that 'these days may be called critical for the salvation or ruin of the kingdom'.[16]

I

At a new English parliament summoned in February 1624, James hinted to MPs and peers that he might, finally, be willing to abandon his long-standing pacifism. Having received repeated assurances regarding the restitution of the Palatine territories and dignities from Habsburg control, James had instead 'found foul and empty performances, being fed only with delays', before his son's journey to Spain served 'as it were, to awake him out of a dream which his credulities had formerly brought him into'.[17] Days later, Buckingham offered MPs unprecedented access into matters normally regarded as *arcana imperii* (state secrets) by leaving the House of Lords to deliver a speech in the Commons that, over several hours, selectively recounted the marriage negotiations in a way that emphasized Charles's shrewdness in thwarting Spanish duplicity and robustly defending English interests. In Buckingham's view, Philip's court had 'intended not a match, but a rebellion', as evidenced by reassurances that, after Charles converted to Catholicism, Spanish arms would have been used to quell any opposition to religious toleration being imposed in England. Frustrated by Charles's refusals to be coerced into conversion, the Spaniards had then found 'a back door to leap out' from the negotiations by ensuring new and unacceptable conditions were attached to the papal dispensation.[18]

Momentum towards war at Westminster prompted Continental speculation that England might, eventually, be considering an armed offensive to secure the Palatinate's restitution. The English ambassador in The Hague, Sir Dudley Carleton, confirmed to Chamberlain that 'all our discourses' concerned events in the English Parliament, admiring how 'the speeches there are scarcely out of men's mouths when they are here in Dutch'. From a correspondent in Mainz, Carleton learned that 'everything remains in suspense', since everyone 'has their eyes fixed on the Parliament of Great Britain' where reliance on God's Holy Spirit would serve as the assembly's 'President and Director'.[19]

While MPs may have been willing retrospectively to approve abandonment of the Spanish match, not all were convinced that declaring war was the logical corollary, especially given the unprecedented (albeit realistic) scale of financial assistance requested, which Sir Edward Coke confirmed was '£900,000, almost a million'.[20] Moreover, even if supply was granted in full, James made it clear that he would not tolerate royal intentions being 'ordered by a multitude', but instead would be directed by 'a secret and faithful Council of War'. He would not be asking MPs if he should 'send 20 or 10,000, by sea or land, east or west, by diversion or otherwise, by invasion upon the Bavarian or Emperor'. While James reminded MPs that 'he had broken the necks of three parliaments' in previous attempts to secure funds, Buckingham warned a House of Lords committee in April that Philip IV had assembled a 'great Navy in Spain as in 1588', with '120 flat-bottomed boats to land men' currently in Dunkirk, dangerously poised were an enterprise to be launched against England.[21]

A grant of around £300,000 was eventually approved, with provisos that the Spanish marriage negotiations would be abandoned and that a Council of War, accountable to Parliament, would approve any monies spent. Meanwhile, Philip's ambassadors, Hinojosa and Coloma, remained in London amid increasing popular bellicosity, hoping to extract improved proposals from Madrid regarding the Palatinate's restitution. Marvelling that the Spanish envoys 'display little or no apprehension about a rupture' with England, Valaresso concluded that such indifference confirmed the extent to which 'they despise this kingdom as unwarlike, poor, disunited, under a timid king, with an inexperienced prince'. Dismissively contemptuous of attempts by Charles and Buckingham to pressurize James into declaring war, Valaresso reported that the Spaniards 'have called this movement the revolt of the mice against the cats', also placing 'great reliance upon the trouble they can cause in Ireland'.[22] Meanwhile, rather than warships, in March 1624 the countess of Olivares sustained a charm offensive towards Prince Charles and sent him an epicure's consignment of 'forty-eight gammons of bacon, diverse vessels of great olives', capers, 'special figs, many sweet lemons, and 300 weight of dried or candied melicotons' and large quantities of 'sweetmeats, besides forty-eight melons'.[23]

Above popular Hispanophobia hovered spirits from a more glorious past. In a pamphlet entitled *Vox Coeli, or News from Heaven* (1624), an Exeter merchant John Reynolds imagined a celestial dialogue involving the ghosts of Henry VIII, Edward VI, Mary Tudor, Elizabeth I, Prince Henry and Queen Anna. Concerned by England's apparent incapacity to defend its national interests, Elizabeth's spirit nostalgically recalled her reign as a time when 'Spain felt that English were soldiers;

when my Drake beat them on my seas and coasts in 1588, my Norris at Croyden in 1594, my Essex at Calais in 1596 and my Mountjoy at Kinsale in 1600'. While Edward VI's wraith wished that Englishmen of the 1620s were 'more martial and less effeminate', the ghost of Prince Henry feared that, if Charles's Spanish match went ahead, not only would it preclude English support of the Dutch, but 'the Pope, the King of Spain, Gondomar, the Jesuits, and English recusants' would speedily 'so shuffle and deal the cards, as England shall not be able to assist herself, much less her neighbours'. When Queen Anna's ghost heard rumours that Don Diego Sarmiento de Acuña, count of Gondomar, was intending to return to London for a third embassy and to be accommodated in her former residence at Greenwich, it surmised that 'the air of London and Islington is not sweet enough, either for his fistula, or perfumed brain', while that of Elizabeth sourly deemed it 'far better, that Prince Charles were married to an English milkmaid, and the Infanta of Spain mewed up for a nun in a cloister'.[24]

In another tract published in 1624, Reynolds beseeched James to effect an immediate military intervention on the Continent, insisting that 'the rightest and shortest way for you to recover the Palatinate will be by your sword'. To avoid misunderstanding, Reynolds reiterated that 'it must be your sword, not your tongue, not your treatises, not your letters, not your ambassadors which must re-fetch it'.[25] In a sequel to his highly successful *Vox Populi* (1620), the Puritan Thomas Scott published a *Second Part of Vox Populi* in 1624 that again imagined Gondomar – now depicted as Machiavelli – appearing before the Spanish Council of State to confirm England's subjugation (see Plate 9). Through pretences of 'taking the air' in order to explore, 'Gondomar' boasted of having acquired a 'perfect knowledge' of the country's weak defences: 'there was no fortification, haven, creek, or landing-place about the coast of England, but I got a platform and draught thereof, I learned the depth of all their channels, I was acquainted with all sands, shelves, rocks, rivers that might impeach or make for invasion'. Given Spain's strategic priorities in mainland Europe, 'Gondomar' counselled against 'awaking a sleepy lion', confident that the English were 'content to let us alone, so that they may enjoy their peace and quiet'.[26] As speculation mounted that the real Gondomar was indeed likely to return to England on another diplomatic mission, the Scots-born Puritan pamphleteer Alexander Leighton published a tract in Amsterdam, deploring

Gondomar's success in having 'so easily entered the Cabinet of Secrets' at James's court, 'where he lay so long like an old rat, feeding on a Parmesan' cheese.[27]

Boundaries between conspiratorial intrigue and routine diplomacy were nevertheless tested when Hinojosa and Coloma accused Buckingham of not only plotting James's removal from the throne in favour of Charles, but also of sabotaging the prince's marriage prospects in order to advance his own dynastic ambitions. In a secret meeting with James in April 1624, with neither Charles nor Buckingham present, Coloma's religious confessor, Don Francisco de Carondelet, informed an aghast king of England that, notwithstanding James's categorical denials of any official overtures to the French court regarding his son's marriage, Buckingham had already authorized nuptial proposals for submission in Paris. Believing that 'his Majesty was a prisoner, or at least besieged and closed up, so as no man could be admit to come at him', Carondelet admitted that James's situation resembled that of the medieval French king, John II, who had been imprisoned in London during the 1350s. Hence the confessor beseeched James to assert his royal authority and demonstrate that he was 'the oldest and wisest king in Europe' by 'freeing himself from this captivity and eminent danger'.[28]

In another audience several weeks later, Gondomar's former confessor, Diego de Lafuente, alleged 'a plot that involved the extinction of the very House of Stuart', claiming that Buckingham had frustrated Charles's marriage negotiations in order to advance a match between his only daughter Mary and the Electress Elizabeth's eldest son (and James's grandson), Frederick Henry. Having persuaded Charles to revoke the agreed marriage proxy in Spain, Buckingham had sought to cover his own dynastic ambitions by cynically starting marriage negotiations with Louis XIII's court, knowing they could not succeed after Charles had publicly sworn that alleviating England's penal laws would never form part of any marriage agreement with a Catholic bride.[29] Hearing reports regarding her son's rumoured alliance with Buckingham's daughter in The Hague, Elizabeth wrote to James to protest that she 'never had a thought of it' until she saw 'such a thing in a book of news printed of Paris' and then heard the same claim relayed via her husband, Frederick. Having initially 'laughed at it as a folly which nobody would believe', the rumour's persistence was, Elizabeth assumed, a cynical Spanish attempt to sow discord between herself and her father.[30] In London, Valaresso reported that James had seen Continental news-books citing the allegations and, indeed, suspected false news had been deliberately placed by the Spaniards, masquerading as independent verification.[31]

Although James demanded that all his Privy Councillors swear an oath denying knowledge of the conspiracy alleged by Hinojosa and Coloma, an impasse was reached when the envoys refused to provide further substantiation of their charges against Buckingham. Treating their claims as those made by private individuals, rather than official Spanish instructions, James nevertheless refused to accede to demands by Buckingham's supporters to arrest the ambassadors for suspected diplomatic misconduct. James confirmed that he 'had no intention of following the example of what had been done with the Queen, his mother' by Elizabeth I, who had expelled one of Philip II's ambassadors for complicity in Catholic plotting.[32] Given leave to return to Spain, Hinojosa left London ignominiously, at his own expense in a merchant ship, 'cast down, and bursting with wrath, his mouth full of fire'. With the ambassadorial residence at Exeter House left in 'a foul stink', members of Hinojosa's retinue were reported to have 'damaged some pictures of former sovereigns, and Queen Elizabeth in particular'.[33] As Hinojosa passed through Paris, an English agent who was trailing him reported the ambassador's furious public declaration that, having succumbed to pressure from Charles and Buckingham, James's decision to abandon marriage negotiations agreed with the mighty House of Habsburg denoted an unacceptable insult by a lesser dynasty. Outraged, Hinojosa had thunderously vowed that he 'would stir heaven, earth, and all hell against England'.[34]

Further insults were directed at the remaining Spanish ambassador in London, Coloma, when Thomas Middleton's play *A Game at Chess* was performed at the Globe Theatre in August 1624. Presenting recent political events through a chess allegory, Middleton's play narrated serial attempts by the Black House (Spain) to ensnare members of the White House (England), with the White King (James) helplessly in thrall to the Black Knight (Gondomar). Warned by a pawn at one juncture that 'your plot's discovered', the Black Knight is obliged to ask, 'which of the twenty thousand, nine hundred, three score and five?', as Middleton's drama envisaged England swarming with multiple conspiracies and Jesuitical designs. Directly echoing lines in Scott's *Second Part of*

Vox Populi, the Black Knight confirms that he has spent his 'summer recreations' in England, learning

> . . . the state
> And strength of the White Kingdom? No fortifications,
> Haven, Creek, Landing-Place 'bout the White Coast
> But I got draught and plot-form, learned the depth
> Of all the Channels, knowledge of all Sands,
> Shelves, Rocks, and Rivers for invasion.

With the visit of the White Knight (Prince Charles) to Madrid forming the play's denouement, the Black Knight was, however, finally checkmated, admitting that 'what we have done has been dissemblance ever'.[35] *A Game at Chess* was performed while James was on a royal progress and staying at Belvoir Castle in Leicestershire and, as John Woolley informed William Trumbull at the English embassy in Brussels, the play's title might as well have been 'a *Vox Populi*' since it was evidently 'six times worse against the Spaniard' in exposing 'Gondomar's devilish plots and devices'.[36] Although John Chamberlain lacked the stamina to join the crowds, he wrote to Dudley Carleton in The Hague, marvelling that those flocking to the Globe Theatre comprised 'all sorts of people, old and young, rich and poor, masters and servants, Papists and Puritans, wise men, churchmen and statesmen . . . and a world besides'.[37]

Indeed, *A Game at Chess* attracted an estimated 30,000 spectators – up to a tenth of London's population – during its nine-day run, before performances were terminated after Coloma had complained to James that the play was 'so scandalous, so impious, so barbarous and so offensive to my royal master', aside from the distinctly unflattering depiction of James himself. With the English king 'forty miles away . . . feasting and fawning upon the French ambassador', Coloma described to Olivares how playgoers 'come out of the theatre so inflamed against Spain that, as a few Catholics have told me who went secretly to see the play, my person would not be safe in the streets'. Expressing 'my sufferings here as a true Hell', Coloma admitted that if he had followed Hinojosa's advice and left London several months ago, at least he would have been spared seeing the 'sacred name of my king outraged in so many ways by such low, vile people, nor his holy and glorious acts so unworthily interpreted'.[38]

Notwithstanding pugnacious parliamentary rhetoric and Hispanophobic theatre, no large-scale military or diplomatic alliances resulted. Sent to London to petition on the Palatine family's behalf, Johann Joachim von Rusdorf lamented that James's continued reluctance to declare a general war on Spain invariably meant that 'the English advance one step and go three backwards'. As James's Secretary of State, Conway, later explained to Rusdorf, since England's interests in central Europe were limited to Frederick and Elizabeth's dynastic and territorial concerns, 'it does not matter to them whether all Germany is set in flames, provided that they might have the Palatinate'. The territory's restitution was nevertheless critical, Conway explained, because 'if we lose the Palatinate first, next we will lose the Low Countries, then Ireland, and finally ourselves'.[39]

That spring, the German mercenary commander, Count Ernst von Mansfeld, had received an unexpectedly warm welcome to London, sumptuously entertained with 'forty dishes a meal' and lodged by Prince Charles in apartments originally prepared for the Infanta.[40] Although James had agreed to supply Mansfeld with 10,000 infantry, 3,000 cavalry, six cannon and a monthly subsidy of £20,000 for a new offensive in central Europe (provided that French supplies of equal strength were also agreed), there was surprise that the renowned *rex pacificus* should readily equip a notorious adventurer with a poor record in military discipline. Even James's own diplomats were sceptical that a single Anglo-French force, commanded by Mansfeld, could simultaneously advance French interests by regaining control of the strategic Valtelline Pass and securing the Palatinate's restitution. From The Hague, Carleton admitted to Conway in November his regret that, despite having long called for more resources to be deployed in central Europe, he could not bring himself to support a bilateral Anglo-French force under Mansfeld's command. Ironically, Carleton found himself like 'one of late Queen Elizabeth's old ladies' who had been reproved 'for withdrawing herself secretly without saying anything when she knew one of the Queen's maids was kissed in a corner behind a hanging' on the grounds that 'since she could make no sport herself she would mar none'.[41] Even after a treaty of mutual defence was concluded between England and the United Provinces in June 1624, which provided up to 6,000 English soldiers for Frederick's use, Valaresso reported Spanish certainty that either the Anglo-Dutch alliance 'will end in smoke' or, if operations commenced, 'half the men will die in the first weeks, as is usual with the English'.[42] Habsburg condescension was duly vindicated when, having sailed from Dover in January 1625 with 13,000 men, Mansfeld's ships were denied permission to land in France and his seaborne force was rapidly decimated by disease and desertion.

Anglo-Dutch amity, suggested by the defensive treaty agreed in June 1624, also remained precarious, having been signed only days after news reached London of what became known as the 'Amboyna massacre'. Over a year earlier, ten English merchants employed by the East India Company in the Indonesian clove trade had been accused by Japanese mercenaries of plotting to overthrow a trading post operated by the rival Dutch East India Company on the neighbouring Ambon Island (now part of the Indonesian Maluku archipelago) and of intending to kill the island's Dutch governor, Herman van Speult. After resorting to torture by fire and water to extract confessions, van Speult had overseen the public beheading of the English merchants. When news of events in the East Indies reached London in late May 1624, James insisted that retribution must be sought through diplomatic channels, but, with luridly emotive accounts of the killings appearing on bookstalls, others recommended summary justice. In Chamberlain's view, the authorities should simply 'stay or arrest the first Indian ship that comes in our way, and hang up upon the Dover cliffs as many as we should find faulty actors in this business, and then dispute the matters afterwards, for there is no other course to be held with such manner of men'.[43] In London, the East India Company commissioned Richard Greenbury to produce an enormous oil painting of events for a fee of £100, although the critic Sir William Sanderson later recalled that Greenbury's visual rendition had 'appeared to me so monstrous, as I then wished it to be burned'. As Sanderson added, 'those in power' evidently agreed, fearing that the painting 'might have incited us then, to a national quarrel and revenge', which led to the painting's hasty delivery into Buckingham's custody and its apparent destruction.[44]

Buckingham's hope was that dynastic diplomacy might be the path to a military alliance that would enable a significant English attack against the Habsburgs. Despite his previous investment in a Habsburg match, the duke now directed his energies towards securing a French Bourbon marriage for Prince Charles with Louis XIII's sister, Henrietta Maria. But the proposal was resisted by Louis's resident ambassador in London, Tanneguy Le Veneur, count of Tillières, who denied that closer union was in French interests. For Tillières, the Stuart dynasty was in 'a miserable state . . . without money, without friends and without reputation', with only 'their glory and their vanity' left. The Stuart monarchy's notorious penury was such that the French court would inevitably find itself obliged, 'not only to support an old House, but also to prop up a falling one'.[45] After Tillières was recalled to France, his replacement in London, Antoine Coiffier de Ruzé, marquis d'Effiat, was besieged by English Catholics demanding that any Bourbon–Stuart marriage must yield equal benefits to the projected Spanish match. In Paris, English diplomats agreed a confidential *escrit particulier*, separate to the marriage treaty, that committed James to ensuring that Roman Catholics in Britain would be accorded 'more liberty and freedom' in relation to their religion than had been 'accorded by the marriage treaty agreed with Spain'.[46] Yielding to French insistence that any military alliance could only be negotiated afterwards, James signed the Anglo-French marriage articles at Newmarket in February 1625.

II

A month later, James VI & I died at his Theobalds estate in Hertfordshire on 27 March 1625 from a form of malaria known as a tertian ague. The first Prince of Wales to succeed to the English throne as an adult since Henry VIII's accession in 1509, Charles I shelved his plans to travel to Paris to marry Henrietta Maria in person and spent an unprecedented sum of around £40,000–£50,000 arranging his father's funeral on 7 May. Whereas neither of his parents had attended Prince Henry's funeral in 1612, and James had also absented himself from Queen Anna's funeral seven years later, Charles had attended both services and now broke with convention by appearing as chief mourner at his father's funeral and leading a procession of thousands to Westminster Abbey. In the funeral sermon, Bishop John Williams of Lincoln acclaimed James as 'Great Britain's Solomon', accounting him 'the most powerful speaker that ever swayed the sceptre of this kingdom'. Extolling the former king's global influence, Williams described James's legacy as witnessing

> . . . all kinds of learning highly improved, manufactures at home daily invented, trading abroad exceedingly multiplied, the Borders of Scotland

> peaceably governed, the north of Ireland religiously planted, the Navy Royal magnificently furnished; Virginia, Newfoundland, and New England peopled; the East Indies well-traded; Persia, China and the Mogul visited; lastly, all the ports of Europe, Africa, Asia and America to our red crosses freed and opened.[47]

In Constantinople, the English ambassador Sir Thomas Roe described the mourning courtesies ordered by the imperial Grand Vizier Hafiz Ahmed Pasha. As Roe recounted to James's daughter, the Electress Elizabeth, even more striking were popular reactions where 'the amazement was such, as if every man had lost a father, as if the pillars of the world had failed, and that peace, the blessing of his days, and the singular gift of his wisdom, had with him, fled to heaven'.[48] Closer to home, the recently created earl of Clare, John Holles, feared that James's death would fuel momentum for military action. As Clare confided to his brother George, 'now are we blotting out the motto of twenty-two years' standing: *Beati Pacifici* (Blessed are the Peacemakers)'.[49]

The week before James's funeral, Charles's marriage to Louis XIII's fifteen-year-old sister, Henrietta Maria, took place at Notre-Dame in Paris, with Charles's kinsman Claude de Lorraine, duke of Chevreuse, acting as his proxy. Before leaving France, Henrietta Maria received strict exhortations to use her new role to promote the interests of British Catholics and, ideally, attempt her husband's conversion, including a direct admonition to this effect from Pope Urban VIII. At a time when sending a young princess to marry and live among heretics remained relatively unusual, Henrietta Maria was also reminded by her mother Marie de'Médicis to remember that God had specifically sent her to Britain to promote the interests of her Catholic co-religionists, 'for these are His people, and His people that have suffered over so many years'.[50] The new king's choice of wife predictably appealed to the Jesuit writer John Fisher, who approved of Charles's decision to marry a Catholic and one whose name revived 'the sweet memory of your right glorious grandmother': a former French queen consort and, in 'princely qualities, the paragon of Europe' during her lifetime, Mary, Queen of Scots.[51]

Opening his first English parliament in June 1625, Charles made clear that, due to his stutter, it was not in 'my nature to spend much time with words', but he urged MPs to approve sufficient financial assistance to facilitate the type of large-scale armed offensive for which he and

Buckingham had been agitating. But, while a severe outbreak of plague necessitated Parliament's relocation from London to Oxford in July, MPs and peers proved no more tractable than they had been under James amid mounting concern regarding Buckingham's monopoly of royal counsel. The Lord Treasurer Richard Weston, earl of Portland, disliked the duke's triumphant claims to have outwitted Philip IV's favourite, Olivares, sabotaged Charles's Spanish match and 'gained a nation', judging Buckingham's language 'so boastful and thrasonical that it seemed most ridiculous, as if nations had been the game and play of favourites who won or lost them after their fortunes or their skills'.[52] To register their concerns, MPs granted Charles the customs revenue yielded by levies of tonnage and poundage for only a year in the first instance, rather than in perpetuity as requested, before Parliament was adjourned in August. Although frustrated by Parliament's parsimony, Buckingham nevertheless resolved to mount England's first major military operation for nearly three decades. Ordering impressment, exploiting royal credit, staking his own jewels as surety and raiding Henrietta Maria's dowry, the duke hoped to recreate past Elizabethan glories by seizing and occupying a Spanish port, while attacking silver-laden Spanish galleons returning from the New World.

Buckingham delegated command of over eighty ships, nearly 10,000 soldiers and 5,000 seamen to Edward Cecil, viscount Wimbledon, and the fleet sailed from Portsmouth on 8 October 1625, arriving at Cadiz a fortnight later. A combination of indecisive strategy, confused communications, inadequate intelligence, disobedient subordinates, defective ships, decayed rations and equinoctial storms conspired to render the expedition a fiasco. There could not have been a more mortifying contrast with Drake's already legendary descent on Cadiz – to 'singe the Spanish king's beard' – for Elizabeth I. After landing at Fort Puntal, near Cadiz, military discipline among the English troops disintegrated as Wimbledon's secretary John Glanville observed untrained soldiers, without weapons or rations, ransacking the Andalusian countryside, 'crying out that they were King Charles's men' and quickly becoming 'all drunken, and in one common confusion, some of them shooting one at another among themselves'.[53] Captured by the Spanish, one Devon soldier, Richard Pike, described the butchery with which his comrades were killed, as 'some heads were spurned up and down the streets like footballs, and some ears worn in scorn in Spanish hats', confirming that he had seen 'Englishmen's ears worn in that despiteful manner' when detained in a Cadiz prison.[54] Easily repulsed by Spanish forces, the remnants of the English fleet limped northwards, although some ships, including the expedition's flagship, the *Anne Royal*, could only reach the southern Irish port of Kinsale where – in an unhappy echo of the defeated Spanish Armada's fate in 1588 – English troops were billeted on a resentful Irish populace for the remainder of the winter.

In Spain, defeat of the English fleet at Cadiz formed part of an *annus mirabilis* in 1625 for Philip IV and Olivares that also saw the strategic Dutch town of Breda come under Habsburg control and Dutch settlers expelled from Spanish settlements in Brazil. To the Spanish Council of State, Olivares demanded that retaliation for the attack on Cadiz should see a fleet of 100 Spanish ships and 20,000 soldiers sent to Ireland, to be supported by the Flanders army, which, as well as ravaging the English coast, could potentially establish a base in England.[55] On the stage, the abject English attempt inspired Rodrigo de Herrera's play *La Fe no ha Menester Armas y Venida del Ingles a Cádiz* (?1626) ('Faith needs no arms, and the coming of the English to Cadiz') which depicted Charles, spurned in his attempt to marry the Infanta, swearing vengeance on Spain. Herrera's 'Charles' bragged that he would 'infest their borders with so many marine monsters that even the sea cannot bear the weight of their roaming hulls . . . the Spanish Armada, burned to ashes, will be but a wretched meal for scaly fish'. But such boasts proved ludicrously hollow when the action in Herrera's play shifted to the English fleet's hapless descent on Cadiz.[56]

On the diplomatic stage, lurid accounts of the English fleet's activities circulated in other Habsburg territories, including Antwerp, where the artist and diplomat Peter Paul Rubens heard rumours (albeit untrue) that Algerian Moors were to have assisted Buckingham's ships. Denouncing the whole expedition as 'bravado on Buckingham's part', Rubens deemed it 'an extreme, unheard of measure, an act of desperation'. Rubens could not credit that Charles's ministers would 'ally themselves with Turks and Moors, for the overthrow of Christians – they who profess a "reformed" religion, as they call it!'[57]

When a new English parliament met in February 1626, strident criticism of Buckingham's disastrous management of the Cadiz expedition bordered on allegations of deliberate sabotage. Having seen the dilapidated fleet returning to Devon in his capacity as the county's Vice Admiral, Sir John Eliot, MP, complained that 'our honour is ruined, our ships are sunk, our men perished, not by the sword, not by an enemy, not by chance; but . . . by those we trust'.[58] Addressing the Lord Mayor, sheriffs and aldermen of 'the famous (though forlorn) City of London', the anonymous author of *Lachrymae Londinenses* (1626) ('London's Tears') recalled 1625 as 'a year full of fatal and memorable accidents' that had included James VI & I's death, Charles I's accession and marriage, 'a mighty and prodigious plague' and the 'setting forth of a mighty Navy'. The coincidence of so many significant events was such that 'no age, no record, no chronicle ever mentioned the like, within this our fairy-land, in this our famous City'.[59] Another author, with the initials 'B. V.', recalled how, before James's death, 'Great Britain stood on the top of her white cliffs triumphing; London on tiptoe, overlooking all other cities in the swelling pride of her approaching fortunes', but 'never was such a sudden joy changed into so sudden a lamentation' as the devastating impact of plague mortality at home was compounded by naval defeat at sea.[60]

Charles's marriage also appeared to have been a costly policy failure for both parties as Anglo-French relations rapidly deteriorated. As the Venetian ambassador in Rome, Anzolo Contarini, put it, the Bourbon–Stuart union 'was hardly consummated before quarrels broke out between the two kings'.[61] Unwilling to participate in a heretic service, Henrietta Maria had refused to attend Charles's coronation in early February while the French court worried about English infringements of the marriage treaty's terms regarding protections for the queen's entourage of around 400 attendants, let alone any signs of fulfilling aspirations regarding the treatment of the queen's Catholic co-religionists in the secret *escrit particulier*. Renewed persecution of England's Catholics had been exhorted in a royal proclamation issued in 1626, while Louis was also angered when Charles's court offered asylum to the rebel Huguenot leader Benjamin de Rohan, duke of Soubise, at the same time as English corsairs were harrying French shipping to seize and sell their cargoes. French antagonism had been further provoked by Buckingham's participation in the Treaty of The Hague in December 1625, whereby England had joined the United Provinces and Denmark in an anti-Habsburg defensive alliance before the Franco-Spanish Treaty of Monzón, signed in March 1626, signalled the end of any envisaged Anglo-French initiatives in central Europe.

In August, Charles gave Buckingham twenty-four hours to expel the majority of Henrietta Maria's French attendants from her household, ideally with minimal fuss but otherwise 'driving them like so many wild beasts until you have shipped them, and so the Devil go with them'.[62]

In London, a lengthy list of misdemeanours, misprisions, offences and other crimes was drawn up by MPs against Buckingham as potential articles of impeachment, while in the streets the 'duke of Fuckingham' became a target for popular libels.[63] Henrietta Maria's chief almoner, Daniel de La Mothe-Houdancourt, bishop of Mende, described diatribes directed at Buckingham as containing 'words more venomous than a viper', as he reported English affairs to his uncle, who was Louis's chief minister, Cardinal Armand Jean du Plessis, duke of Richelieu.[64] Frustrated by caustic attacks on his closest adviser, as well as by delays in granting funds, Charles instructed the Lord Keeper, Sir Thomas Coventry, to direct MPs to 'cease this unparliamentary inquisition', warning that 'his Majesty understands the difference between counsel and controlling, between liberty and the abuse of liberty'. Charles then addressed MPs directly, dissuading them from seeking 'to set the dice and make your own game', by reminding them that 'parliaments are altogether in my power for their calling, sitting and dissolution; therefore as I find the fruits of them good or evil, they are to continue, or not to be'.[65] Notwithstanding royal displeasure, a formal indictment against Buckingham was presented in early May and tensions deepened when Eliot and the MP for Tewkesbury, Sir Dudley Digges, were imprisoned in the Tower for criticizing Buckingham's misrule in terms that had likened the duke to the Roman favourite Sejanus, unfortunately implying that Charles was the tyrannical Emperor Tiberius.

To save Buckingham from formal impeachment proceedings, Charles dissolved Parliament on 15 June 1626, repeating his father's mechanisms for rendering government inoperative at critical junctures. Only the preceding week Buckingham had informed the Privy Council that a fleet of 200 ships and 40,000 men was being prepared to sail from Spain and the Spanish Netherlands to land in either England or Ireland. At the end of June, Privy Council missives warned English port towns of the 'vast ambition and malice of his declared enemy, the king of Spain' and 'what great preparations of sea and land forces are in readiness for the invasion of these kingdoms'.[66] Indeed, memoranda produced six months earlier by the Council of State in Madrid had advised Philip to attack

Charles's dominions 'through Ireland and the north, where the Catholics are more numerous and more friendly towards Spain, and with whom we could enter talks and plan what they themselves have most longed for'.[67] On their arrival in London, two Venetian envoys, Marc'Antonio Correr and Anzolo Contarini, encountered 'a undesirable agitation which is widespread and a feeling of resentment which seems incredible'. Together with a crippling shortage of ready money, the envoys reported 'the common opinion that the Spanish force is about to invade this kingdom'. Struck by the extent of anti-French rancour animating English affairs, the diplomats observed that Buckingham 'never lost an opportunity' of denouncing Louis's government, to which the Venetians evasively admitted that 'the Court of France is a rose with many thorns: one must be careful to pluck what is good, and always fear being hurt by them'.[68]

Frustration was also mounting, among Charles's Protestant allies, at England's failure to honour financial subsidies agreed in the Treaty of The Hague the previous year. In March 1626, a forged letter from Christian IV of Denmark circulated in England, warning Charles that there was 'a subject in your kingdom that rules it more than yourself' and threatening to abandon military activities in Germany unless Buckingham was removed.[69] Meanwhile in Copenhagen, Charles's ambassador Sir Robert Anstruther relayed the Danish king's dismay at his nephew's precipitate dissolution of Parliament. Setting aside James VI & I's record of turbulent crown–parliamentary relations, Christian advised Charles to remember his father's words to MPs in 1624, when he had likened successful parliamentary sittings to meetings 'between man and wife, both in honour and profit', aimed at 'preventing of any mistaking and to understand truly one another'.[70] Regarding Buckingham's anti-French agenda as a fatal distraction, Christian blamed a lack of English support for the disastrous defeat suffered by Danish forces at Lutter-am-Barenberge in August 1626 which ended any imminent chance of securing the Palatinate's restitution to Christian's niece, the Electress Elizabeth, and prompted all remaining German princes still in arms to sue for peace with Emperor Ferdinand.

Manuscript tracts circulating in English political circles purported to offer Frederick 'secret instructions' on how best to retrieve his Palatine territories and dignities. Penned by pro-Habsburg satirists within the Empire, one set of directions, written during the summer of 1626, was translated from Latin into English by the philosopher Thomas Hobbes and firmly impressed on Frederick that 'you cannot be restored by your brother-in-law [Charles I]' who 'hates you out of emulation' and 'hates you out of jealousy'. Denied funds by Parliament, and increasingly distrusted by his subjects, Charles was in no position to mount effective military intervention in central Europe: as the anonymous author insisted, 'he that fears at home, plays no gambols abroad. When London is on fire, will he carry water to Heidelberg?' If Frederick was serious about regaining his former territories and rights, he should, rather, 'attempt England', where he could 'drive out the young king at first dash, as one that is hated by the nobility', especially amid fearsome rumours alleging foul play on Buckingham's part in relation to King James's death the previous year. If Frederick claimed to 'revenge the death of your father-in-law which his son neglects', England 'will take you into her bosom'. Avaricious Puritans tempted by ecclesiastical preferments 'will carry you into the throne upon their shoulders' while similar bribes would likewise secure 'dry and covetous' Scots nobles. Alternatively, Frederick could raise a French Huguenot force in La Rochelle, before heading 'to the coasts of Ireland or Scotland'. Confident in the likely success of such audacious courses, the author advocated decisive action as opposed to Frederick being obliged simply 'to mope, open-mouthed, weighed down by a royal title, reading about other people's deeds, and hearing about the defeats and complaints of your allies'.[71]

Such mocking Habsburg satire hit home since it echoed contemporary diplomatic assessments. An intercepted letter sent by a Palatine administrator, Ludwig Camerarius, to the Swedish Chancellor Count Axel Oxenstierna in October lamented that, in England, 'the young king, is as it were kept a prisoner by one proud man' – Buckingham – whose refusal to support Continental Protestants was proving fatal. As Camerarius warned, 'if God doth not deliver the king of Great Britain from present slavery', and reconcile him with his subjects, the Protestant cause in Europe was doomed.[72] The following April, the Venetian ambassador in Paris, Zorzi Zorzi, reported a meeting in which Richelieu had insisted that the English 'would learn the power of France', adding that he 'spoke in terms of contempt and vituperation of Buckingham, attributing to him all the ills of France, Flanders, Germany and Italy'.[73]

Desperate to remove the impression that he was solely responsible for England's national decay, if not every conflagration in Europe,

Buckingham assumed personal command of a second naval expedition, aimed at relieving French Huguenots besieged in their fortified city of La Rochelle. Sailing from Portsmouth in June 1627, Buckingham's force comprised 7,000 soldiers, transported in around a hundred ships, ironically 'fitted out with the money of the French themselves', from the sale of captured vessels and goods.[74] But as suspected, Buckingham had failed to secure agreement with those he was ostensibly rescuing and the Rochellois initially shunned his relief expedition, reluctant to risk being declared state enemies by joining a foreign force while chances remained of securing peaceful reconciliation with Louis's administration. Having landed instead on the nearby Île de Ré, Buckingham encouraged newsbook reporters to follow his expedition and circulated a printed *Manifestation* that insisted Charles's only aim was to protect the rights of foreign Protestants. From the island's fortified citadel of St Martin, French resistance held out against Buckingham's attacks for sixteen weeks, before an English attempt to storm St Martin failed embarrassingly when scaling-ladders proved too short, incurring heavy losses and the eventual ejection of all English forces from the island in November. From Antwerp, Rubens had been following the expedition's dismal fate and concluded that Buckingham seemed 'by his own audacity, to be reduced to the necessity of conquering or of dying gloriously'. Were he to return to England defeated, Rubens predicted that he would be 'nothing but the sport of fortune and the laughing-stock of his enemies'.[75]

Throughout Europe, Buckingham's bellicose actions provoked bemusement. Trying to promote Charles's diplomatic interests in Venice and Savoy, Sir Isaac Wake did not know how to explain recent hostilities, lamenting that he was 'as ignorant of the affairs of England as Nova Zembla' in the Arctic.[76] In Madrid, the Venetian Alvise Mocenigo reported that Louis's ambassador in the city, Charles d'Angennes, marquis of Rambouillet, 'asked me repeatedly what reasons the English adduce for the rupture with France', with both envoys suspecting Buckingham's influence, although Mocenigo was unsure on 'what frivolous pretext'. Dismayed that French forces were being distracted from tackling Spanish aggression in the simultaneous War of the Mantuan Succession being fought in northern Italy, Contarini warned that 'the upholding or annihilating of the liberty of Europe rests in great measure, I believe, on the decision of the English government'. In Savoy, Contarini's colleague, Marc'Antonio Padavin, regretted that Philip's government successfully pursued 'true policy' that promoted Spanish concerns, while Louis and Charles failed to see that their national interests were being sacrificed in military squabbles provoked by Richelieu and Buckingham's mutual antipathy. Padavin lamented that 'the interests and passions of these two favourites dye red the swords of the two young kings, who allow themselves to be ruled by them, so that this is everywhere called the war of the favourites'.[77] Meanwhile at Philip IV's court, Olivares was indeed convinced that there had never been a better time to attack England. In December 1627, he started planning for the next campaigning season and 'proposed a specific timetable: a diversionary attack on Ireland in March; the capture of one of the Scottish islands in June; and then, in July, an assault on England itself'. That same month, he showed the Genoese ambassador in Madrid 'six very clear and distinct maps' of England and Ireland to demonstrate how easy the invasion would be to effect.[78]

When a new English parliament sat in March 1628, the pervasive national mood was one of abject humiliation. With Charles facing bankruptcy, the MP for Downton in Wiltshire, Sir Benjamin Rudyard, regarded Parliament's continued sitting as vital to hold the court to account. But if his colleagues insisted on demanding redress for constitutional grievances before agreeing the extent of financial subsidies, another dissolution seemed inevitable. As Rudyard memorably warned, 'this is the crisis of parliaments: by this we shall know whether parliaments shall live or die'. Admitting his hope that the 'old decrepit law Magna Carta', which had 'been so long kept and lain bedridden as it were', might 'walk abroad again with new vigour and lustre', Rudyard accepted government justifications of 'intrinsical power' and 'reason of state' as 'matters in the clouds, where I desire we may leave them'.[79]

But Rudyard's colleagues were not so easily deflected and by May a 'Petition of Right' had passed readings in the Commons and Lords, insisting that no subjects could be 'compelled to make or yield any gift, loan, benevolence, tax or such like charge' without parliamentary approval.[80] The following month, MPs rued that recent 'miserable disasters and ill success' had 'extremely wasted that stock of honour that was left unto this kingdom, sometimes terrible to all nations and now declining to contempt beneath the meanest'. Insisting that 6,000 to 7,000 British lives had been lost in the Ré expedition, MPs warned that 'your Majesty is not rightly informed thereof', having 'received information but of a few hundred'.[81] Outside Westminster, one writer bemoaned that England's previous record of triumphs over France had now been liquidated: 'Poitiers, Cressy, Agincourt, all lie buried in one Ile of Ré'.[82] Published anonymously in Amsterdam, John Russell's *The Spy* (1628) insisted that 'All symptoms of a kingdom, that hath been / Declining long, may be in England seen'. Recent actions had left the country 'Unto the rage of all the world exposed' and brought 'our state / Amongst all nations to contempt and hate'.[83] Of Buckingham, one poet simply beseeched, 'And now, just God! I humbly pray, / That thou wilt take that slime away'.[84]

Then, in August 1628, Buckingham was dramatically removed from the political scene when he was fatally stabbed in Portsmouth by an understandably disgruntled demobilized lieutenant, John Felton, who had served in the disastrous expeditions to both Cadiz and Ré. Having travelled to Portsmouth to see Buckingham's preparations for another expedition to La Rochelle, Contarini was stunned by this turn of events, musing how 'in one moment is this great Colossus overthrown, and the greatest and most remarkable favourite whom the world has seen for many centuries dies instantaneously'.[85] When Felton was placed on trial for Buckingham's murder in October, the Attorney General Sir Robert Heath denounced his action as echoing that of the Catholic zealot who had murdered Henrietta Maria's father, Henri IV of France, in 1610. It also emerged that, during the months that followed the retreat from Ré, Felton's appetite for reading works of resistance theory had included borrowing a history of Mary, Queen of Scots.[86] But official censure was belied by the widespread popular celebrations of Buckingham's unexpected demise that prompted the authorities to order a nocturnal funeral for the duke to minimize disruption. Shortly afterwards, the beleaguered Huguenot stronghold of La Rochelle finally fell to French government forces.

9
Between Dons and Monsieurs, 1629–1637

In November 1629, Charles I's government was disturbed to discover copies of a subversive manuscript being sold on London's streets and circulating among MPs, antiquarians, lawyers and clerics. Offering 'Propositions for your Majesty's Service', the anonymous tract – of which more than forty copies survive – identified an urgent need to 'bridle the impertinency of parliaments' and to increase royal revenue. Denounced by Charles's supporters as 'the Devil's project' and a 'Machiavellian plot', the 'Propositions' recommended building fortresses in England's major towns, to be garrisoned by foreign troops who would collect taxes imposed by the monarch's prerogative power without parliamentary approval. Alarmed that unsuspecting readers might readily believe 'that our gracious sovereign has these dangerous plots in his head', Charles's ministers started a seven-month criminal investigation to find the tract's author, before learning that its content derived from proposals first formulated more than a decade earlier, following James VI & I's abrupt dissolution of the English Parliament in 1614.[1]

After his own decision to dissolve Parliament in March 1628 – equally acrimoniously and prematurely – Charles avoided convening the assembly again, leading to more than a decade of 'Personal Rule' during which he resorted to raising revenue through prerogative levies as an alternative to seeking parliamentary supply. Yet in the eyes of a Venetian envoy to England in the mid-1630s, Vicenzo Gussoni, 'parliaments are the Indies and Peru of England', that potentially offered monarchs access to vast funds 'if their goodwill is only cultivated in a tactful and captivating manner'. Royal antipathy towards England's main representative institution was nevertheless so entrenched that Gussoni's ambassadorial colleague, Anzolo Correr, reported in 1637 that Charles 'cannot suffer the mention of parliament, much less its assembling'.[2] Without access to prerogative taxes, such as the *taille* or *gabelle* in Louis XIII's France or the *millions* or *sisa* that funded Philip IV of Spain's military activities, Charles was unable to mount any large-scale military deployment, inevitably compromising his capacity to defend England's national interests and those of its allies. Accordingly, while Gussoni characterized England as 'that great kingdom, overconfident perhaps in its position', he regretted that the nation 'interests itself but little in the present troubles of Europe' since, if marshalled effectively, English resources and influence could potentially 'do much to change the course of affairs in all Christendom'.[3]

To subsequent generations, Charles's 'Personal Rule' during the 1630s was remembered by hostile Parliamentarians as 'eleven years' tyranny' or, conversely, recalled by nostalgic Royalists as England's 'halcyon days' when domestic peace and relative prosperity contrasted with the confessional warfare devastating Continental Europe. Without the distractions of a domestic parliamentary agenda, foreign entanglements provided a key lens by which royal policy might be appraised. Different factions in the Caroline court were described in terms of their partisan support for rival powers, with a dominant 'Spanish faction' including the Lord Treasurer, Richard Weston, earl of Portland; the Chancellor, Sir Francis Cottington, Baron Cottington; the Secretary of State, Sir Francis Windebank; and aristocratic diplomats such as Thomas Howard, earl of Arundel. Seeking to counter the court's Hispanophilic tendencies were Francophile ministers close to Queen Henrietta Maria, including James, marquess of Hamilton, Henry Rich, earl of Holland, and two former associates of George Villiers, duke of Buckingham: Walter Montagu and Henry Jermyn. Other senior ministers, such as the Secretary of State, Sir John Coke, regarded England's interests as best served through amity with the Protestant Dutch, while the diplomat Sir Thomas Roe insisted in 1632 that he had 'anatomised his heart towards every prince and state', being 'neither Swede nor Spaniard, Dutch nor French, but a good Englishman'.[4] Roe was closely allied to another former diplomat and Secretary of State Sir Dudley Carleton, who was created Viscount Dorchester in July 1628 and, like Roe, regularly exchanged political gossip and reading recommendations with the Electress Elizabeth. Acknowledging receipt of a tract referred to as 'The Devil of Milan' in December 1630, Dorchester reciprocated by sending Charles's sister a poem alluding to the recent Puritan exodus from England to America: 'our godly people, who weary

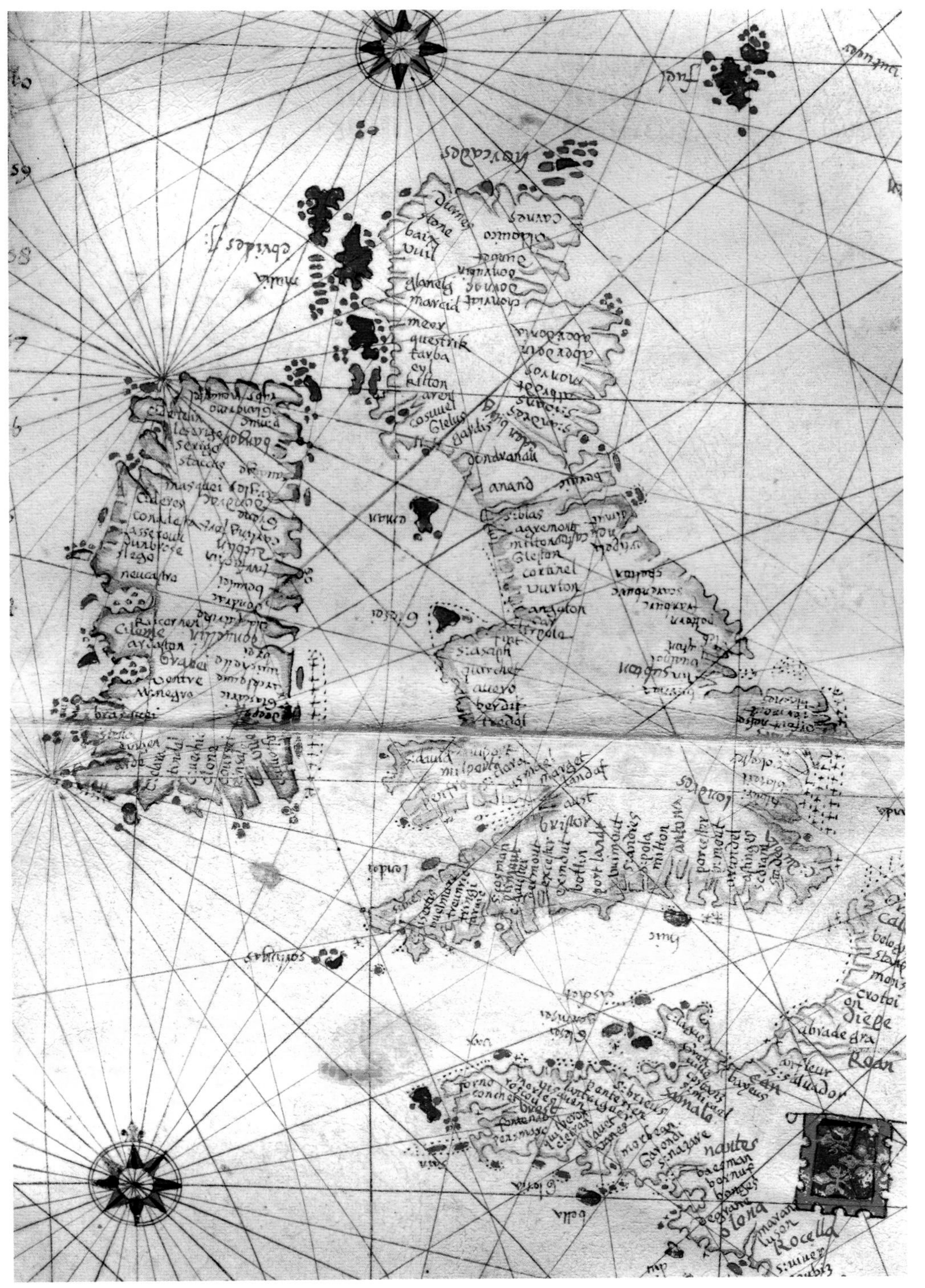

1. A portolan chart of the British Isles, produced by the Calabrian monk and cartographer Domenico Vigliarolo, who worked for Philip II of Spain in Seville, *c.* 1586–96. Read rotationally, portolan charts only note coastal locations.

2. Detail from a full-length memorial portrait of Mary, Queen of Scots, by an unknown Flemish artist *c.* 1604–18, commissioned posthumously by one of Mary's former ladies-in-waiting. The blindfolded queen kneels on the executioner's block, wearing a scarlet bodice under black outer garments.

3. Painted by an unknown artist, this unflattering image of an ageing Elizabeth I emphasizes her wrinkled visage, while pinched cheeks suggest missing teeth.

4. Portrait of Prince Henry, 1598, aged two; in his right hand, Henry holds cherries – signifying innocence and virtue – and, in his left, what appears to be a toy.

5. Designs proposed for a new union flag *c.* 1604 that sought to avoid according precedence to either the English cross of St George or the Scottish saltire. The Lord High Admiral, Charles Howard, earl of Nottingham, favoured the lower central design.

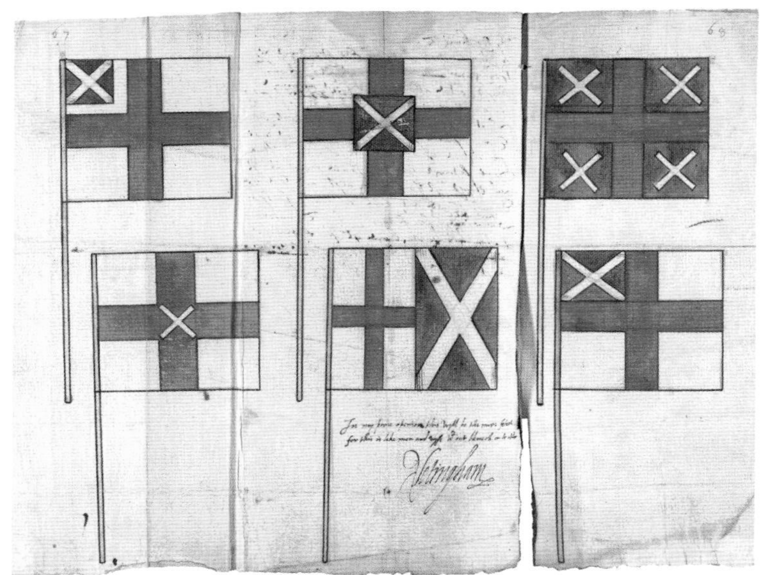

6. This group portrait commemorates the Treaty of London, concluded between England and Spain in 1604, after conference sessions at Somerset House. *On the right*, the English commissioners include Charles Howard, earl of Nottingham, commander of the fleet that had defeated the Armada in 1588, while the Spanish delegation, *on the left*, includes Juan de Velasco, duke of Frias, Constable of Castile, who did not attend the talks on grounds of ill-health.

7. Designed by the Puritan minister of Ipswich, Samuel Ward, and engraved in Amsterdam, *The Double Deliverance* (1621) celebrates England's miraculous escape from the Spanish Armada in 1588, while a furtive Guy Fawkes attempts the Gunpowder Plot in 1605. Beneath a canopy, the Pope consults a Jesuit, monks, a cardinal, a Spaniard and the devil, plotting how best 'Great Britain's state ruinate shall be'.

8. Portrait of James VI & I by an unknown painter, *c.* 1618–20; the curious heads appearing on the king's stockings appear to be remnants of an earlier painting.

9. Engraved illustration for Thomas Scott's *Second Part of Vox Populi* (1624), purporting to relate proceedings in 'the Spanish Parliament'. The Archbishop of Toledo and sixteen Spanish grandees are joined by a smiling devil, partly concealed by a canopy.

10. As canes and bullfighting gradually eclipsed knightly tournaments in popularity, this painting by Juan de la Corte memorializes the elaborate *juegos de cañas* that was staged in Madrid's Plaza Mayor on 21 August 1623 as the Habsburg court anticipated a future royal wedding between the visiting Prince of Wales and the Infanta María Ana.

11. A group portrait of Charles I, Henrietta Maria and the infant Prince Charles, painted *c.* 1632 by the Haarlem-born artist Hendrick Pot. Alongside the crown and sceptre lie sprigs of olive and laurel: classical symbols of peace and triumph.

12. Between Dons and Monsieurs: Crispijn van de Passe's *Den Coninckliicken Morgen-Wecker* (*The Royal Alarm Clock*) (*c.* 1636–41) shows Charles I asleep. Attempts are being made to rouse the English king into taking military action on the Continent by the flute-playing Spanish ambassador (*on the right*) and Louis XIII in armour (*on the left*).

13. Newly restored following an eighteen-month conservation project at Boston's Museum of Fine Arts in 2011, Gerrit van Honthorst's *Triumph of the Winter Queen* (1636) depicts Elizabeth Stuart (Elizabeth of Bohemia) seated on a chariot, drawn by lions. With her three eldest surviving sons on horseback, Elizabeth's crown is restored by her youngest daughter, Sophia. Two of Elizabeth's deceased relatives – her husband Frederick and eldest son Frederick Henry – are shown under a recessed arch.

of this wicked land are gone (man, woman and child) in great numbers to seek new worlds'.[5]

The ceaselessly shifting nature of English factional alliances disconcerted foreign envoys. The artist and diplomat Peter Paul Rubens had been sent to London from Brussels in 1629 by the Habsburg governor of the Spanish Netherlands, Archduchess Isabella; he admitted to Philip IV's favourite, the count-duke of Olivares, that he remained 'very apprehensive as to the instability of the English government'. Objecting that the English 'rarely persist in a resolution, but change from hour to hour, and always from bad to worse', Rubens distrusted the overweening influence of the king's Privy Councillors. Whereas 'in other courts negotiations begin with the ministers and finish with the royal word and signature', Rubens complained that, in England, 'they begin with the king and end with the ministers'.[6]

In dynastic terms, Charles's main foreign policy objective remained consistent: to secure, for his exiled sister and brother-in-law, restitution of their former Palatine dignities and territories and, following the Elector Frederick's death in 1632, the same for their children. But in a Europe defined overwhelmingly by military strength, Charles's lack of money and troops rendered such ambitions largely futile, despite the formation of multiple negotiations and alliances with different Continental powers. Decrying the apparent incoherence of English foreign policy in May 1633, Juan de Necolalde, the Spanish agent in London, complained to Windebank that 'you pull down as fast with one hand as you build up with the other', citing recent negotiations with Emperor Ferdinand II in Vienna that had been followed by talks with Gustavus Adolphus of Sweden and various Protestant princes in Germany, while parallel approaches had also been initiated at the French court. To Necolalde's mind, such serial initiatives seemed 'diametrically opposite, and what appearance can there be of success when you fix upon nothing' in terms of concrete alliances, and 'in seeking to please both' only sowed pervasive distrust?[7]

To some extent, England's seemingly contradictory tactics reflected tensions between the Stuart court's narrow concern to secure restitution for the Palatine family and a broader, predominantly Puritan view of the Palatine family's plight as symbolic of a confessional war that required England to protect Protestant interests internationally. Dispatching Sir Walter Aston as a special ambassador to Madrid in August

1635, Windebank nevertheless emphasized the need for Philip IV to know that England had 'no ambitions but the righting of our nephews, rather by peace and treaties than by the sword'.[8] A year later, Robert Dudley, earl of Leicester, likewise insisted to Louis XIII's Secretary of State, Léon Bouthillier, count of Chavigny, that English interests in German affairs were motivated only by 'affection and nearness in blood', in contrast to French 'reason of state and nearness of situation . . . as our care is only for the Palatine, yours for the Palatinate'.[9] Yet English attempts to harness national interests to the vicissitudes of Continent-wide warfare often conveyed the impression merely of military weakness and diplomatic vacillation. As John, Viscount Scudamore, moaned to Windebank in late 1637, after three years serving as Charles's ambassador in Paris, 'O, that the affairs of the Palatinate were settled, that we might have nothing to do with these Dons or Monsieurs!'[10]

I

Charles's 'Personal Rule' started when the English parliament which had met in January 1629 was abruptly dissolved after two months. Detecting a mood of apprehension even before the assembly met, the Venetian Resident in London, Alvise Contarini, feared that, if MPs' resistance to royal wishes prompted another premature dissolution, 'England may be considered as no longer existing in the world, for she will be impotent for good or harm, and will have to attend to domestic affairs, and the means for raising money'.[11] Once MPs convened, criticism of Charles's religious policy as well as his right to demand certain customs duties, such as tonnage and poundage, once again derailed requests for financial subsidies. Fearing an early termination to their deliberations, on 10 March several MPs forcibly held down the Commons Speaker, Sir John Finch, in his chair until a 'Protestation' was read aloud, declaring anyone who either promoted religious innovation or abetted payment of controversial fiscal levies to be 'a capital enemy to this kingdom and commonwealth'. Dissolving Parliament that afternoon, Charles issued a declaration denouncing the unacceptable conduct of a minority of MPs and drawing parallels between events at Westminster and the destruction of one of the seven wonders of the ancient world. For Charles, the firebrands had sought 'to get themselves a name, by setting Diana's Temple on fire, and make themselves popular by putting all the kingdom in combustion'. Nine MPs were identified as intent on 'blasting our government' and arrested, including the jurist John Selden and another outspoken government critic, Sir John Eliot. Despite vigorously defending free speech as a sacrosanct parliamentary privilege, Eliot and two colleagues, Denzil Holles and Benjamin Valentine, were convicted of sedition and conspiracy at the Court of King's Bench, fined and imprisoned until they acknowledged their offences.[12]

One consequence of the parliamentary disruption was, as Charles pointed out, a failure to agree English assistance to alleviate 'the distressed extremities of our dearest uncle, the King of Denmark'.[13] Christian IV had indeed been desperate for funds to support Protestant interests in Scandinavia and the Baltic, but following military defeat by Habsburg forces at the Battle of Wolgast the previous August, and his nephew's dissolution of the English Parliament, Christian was obliged to conclude terms with Emperor Ferdinand at the Peace of Lübeck in May 1629. Back in England, the Puritan lawyer Sir Simonds d'Ewes deemed Parliament's dissolution 'the most gloomy, sad and dismal day for England that happened in five hundred years last past'. D'Ewes denounced the grounds on which MPs had frustrated royal wishes as 'so immaterial and frivolous', lamenting in his diary the appearance of 'Machiavellian politics' and regretting that 'diverse fiery spirits in the House of Commons were very faulty, and cannot be excused'.[14] Sir Francis Kynaston, who had represented Shropshire in the Commons, later likened the English king to a 'blind, lame, impotent beggar' seeking financial support from an MP who, before making any grant, demanded to 'know how he became poor, whether by chance or unthriftiness' and 'how lame, whether by God's visitation, or by playing at football'.[15] On his return from serving as English ambassador in Constantinople, Sir Thomas Roe was likewise appalled that MPs' destructive activities only served to realize Spanish Habsburg hopes of scuttling the session and preventing any large-scale military deployment. Writing to Sir Horace Vere, the commander of English forces in the Low Countries, Roe rued 'the funeral of our parliament', accurately predicting that, by its dissolution, 'not only all mouths are stopped, but the Parliament doors sealed for many years'.[16]

Dissolution only confirmed Contarini's pessimism regarding the English king's limited capacity to function without substantial funds, fearing that 'to bark without being able to bite brings a government into discredit'. Consequently, 'everything possible is being done to screen reputation', including Charles's dispatch of Sir Henry Vane to the Netherlands that autumn to try to prevent Stuart crown jewels being ignominiously sold at auction, after they had formerly been pawned in Amsterdam to fund Buckingham's wars.[17] While the jewels were duly purchased and returned to England by a London-based French Huguenot, Philip Burlamachi, the extent to which the Stuart crown relied on private credit was evidenced by the fact that, in 1629 alone, it borrowed over £128,000 from Burlamachi whose own indebtedness led to bankruptcy four years later.[18]

Despite the country's external image as impotent and impoverished, England remained technically at war with France in what were, effectively, purposeless hostilities that only benefited Habsburg interests by diverting Louis's attention from central Europe. To negotiate a peaceful resolution, Venetian ambassadors in London and Paris were appointed as mediators. Observing the alacrity with which previously strident English concerns for the welfare of their Protestant co-religionists in France were suddenly jettisoned, Contarini suspected that interest in the Huguenots 'might never have been mentioned' had it 'not been necessary to cloak Buckingham's passions'. In Paris, Contarini's counterpart, Zorzi Zorzi, warned that Charles's negotiators were hardly in a position to expect favourable peace terms, given that England had been the aggressor and the wars 'all began with the folly of an individual who thought he would measure the world by the astrolabe of his chimeras'.[19]

The Treaty of Susa, agreed in April 1629, restored Anglo-French freedom of trade and confirmed the terms of Charles's marriage contract, while French domestic tensions were addressed, two months later, in the Grace of Alais whereby Louis permitted Protestant worship, but ordered the demolition of Huguenot fortifications. That autumn, Contarini's successor, Girolamo Soranzo, observed how Louis's ambassador extraordinary, Charles de l'Aubespine, marquis of Châteauneuf, routinely referred to England's capacity to intervene in Continental affairs 'with derision, as he knows only too well the weakness of the government here'. While Châteauneuf belittled the English as 'poor folk who can do neither good nor harm', fuelling the ambassador's contempt was, Soranzo suspected, 'some amount of secret satisfaction in him, as if this comparison only made the glories of France the more resplendent'.[20]

The Anglo-French diplomatic rapprochement coincided with growing confidence in the security of the Stuart–Bourbon marriage of Charles and Henrietta Maria, whose marital relations became noticeably closer after Buckingham's assassination. Amid reports that the queen was pregnant, Roe warned the Venetian envoy in The Hague that the Electress Elizabeth would not welcome such news, having 'lived in great hopes of that succession' as heir presumptive while her brother remained childless. Although Elizabeth had borne seven sons and four daughters by December 1628, tragedy struck the Palatine family the following month when the couple's eldest son, fifteen-year-old Frederick Henry, drowned in a nocturnal collision between boats on an inland lake near Haarlem, while travelling with his father to view a captured Spanish treasure fleet in Amsterdam. Although the baby son born to Henrietta Maria in May survived for only a few hours, the safe delivery of another son – the future Charles II – twelve months later on 29 May 1630 significantly enhanced the dynasty's security. Widely seen as confirmation of God's divine favours, Henrietta Maria's fecundity would produce another two sons and five daughters between 1631 and 1644, provoking fears among Puritan critics that Charles's interest in his own heirs inevitably diluted his zeal for addressing the plight of his sister's Palatine family. In a verse collection produced by Fellows of Oxford University to celebrate the birth of Charles's second son, and third surviving child, James, duke of York, the Bodleian Librarian, Thomas Lockey, observed that, by 1633, Charles I had fathered more children than Henry VIII had sired by six wives, while another contributor anticipated the possibility that one of Charles's children might become a future king or queen of France.[21]

Having concluded peace with France, Charles's ministers also sought to cut their losses by ending hostilities with Spain. In Madrid, the mood was concessive: France was no longer distracted by a war with England, while the Habsburgs had also suffered troubling losses throughout their global empire from military reverses in northern Europe to Dutch assaults on Spanish settlements in Brazil. Dispatched to London to test the diplomatic waters, Rubens acknowledged to Olivares in August 1629 that the idea of an Anglo-Spanish peace was 'of such consequence that it seems to me the connecting knot in the chain of all the confederations in Europe', with even its prospect focusing minds in different states. Rubens was also 'sure in my heart' that Charles would, personally, prefer 'a simple friendship with Spain a thousand times more than all the offers of France', suspecting that the English king 'curses the day when the Palatinate came to his attention'.[22]

While in London, Rubens presented Charles with a painting entitled *Peace and War*, or *Minerva protects Pax from Mars* (1629–30), offering allegorical acclamation of the English king as a virtuous *rex pacificus* in the model of his father. In January 1630, Don Carlos Coloma, marquis of Espinar, returned to London as an ambassador extraordinary, despite objecting so hotly to Middleton's *A Game at Chess* seven years earlier. Meanwhile, Charles had dispatched his Chancellor and experienced diplomat, Cottington, to Madrid where it was agreed that the Anglo-Dutch alliance agreed at the Treaty of Southampton (1625) would be abandoned in order to encourage a permanent end to Dutch hostilities with Spain. Although English undertakings were intended to match parallel commitments by Spain to promote restitution of the Palatine family's Electoral dignities and territories, the Treaty of Madrid signed in November 1630 contained no reference to Palatine affairs. Confirming the terms of the Treaty of London (1604), the Madrid agreement did not prevent English military assistance to the Dutch and reinstated access to West Indian waters for English ships. In much the same way as English concerns for the rights of French Huguenots had been airbrushed from the Treaty of Susa the previous year, the new Anglo-Spanish peace did not mention any measures to improve the condition of English Catholics.[23]

In January, Cottington signed another secret Anglo-Spanish accord that revived a – frankly flabbergasting – idea, first mooted by James VI & I in the 1620s, for Anglo-Spanish partition of the Netherlands. If Spain could not agree a viable settlement with the Dutch, a joint Anglo-Spanish force could be deployed to conquer the United Provinces, with certain (unspecified) territories ceded to England notwithstanding Elizabeth I's military and financial support that had helped the Dutch to overthrow Spanish rule less than half a century earlier. Although the secret treaty's provisions were never formally ratified, they revealed the trust that Charles was evidently willing to place in the Spanish court at Dutch expense.

In London, news of the Treaty of Madrid's conclusion reignited popular Hispanophobia, while Soranzo observed the outrage of the Dutch ambassador Albert Joachimi, but admitted that 'some monster was always expected from this pestiferous parturition'. For his part, Soranzo dismissed any threat posed by Anglo-Spanish amity, advising his Venetian diplomatic masters to 'consider this kingdom [England] as a cipher at the present time', predicting that 'this nullity will continue for a long time'.[24] Published in Amsterdam, the anonymously authored *Practise of Princes* (1630) warned that Jesuitical, Spanish influence had so enfeebled the English body politic that it had become 'half-dead' and was 'unable to do any service effectually, as our men were at the Palatinate, Calais, Ré, Rochelle and in the Parliament House'.[25] In Madrid, Sir Arthur Hopton had remained in post as Charles's permanent representative after Cottington's return to England, and now became increasingly pessimistic regarding Spain's broader commitment to promote the Palatinate's restitution at the imperial court. Confronting Philip IV's chief minister with his doubts in late 1631, Hopton reported that Olivares had candidly retorted, 'what would you have us to do, for if we restore it, you cannot keep it without help, and it were a shame for us to restore it to you, and keep it for you, and have nothing in recompense'.[26]

Meanwhile, Charles's personal promotion of Protestantism was displaced into architectural edification. Having appointed commissioners in 1631 to raise funds to repair St Paul's Cathedral, the king paid for an immense portico – designed by Inigo Jones and larger than any church portico north of the Alps – to adorn the building's west door. Amid persistent calls for England to combat Catholicism on the battlefield, the court poet Edmund Waller suggested that 'Glad, though amazed, are our neighbour kings / To see such power employed in peaceful things'.[27] Charles's connoisseurial preoccupations were also a source of frustration to Dorchester who wrote to the Electress Elizabeth in December, describing a recent meeting with her brother at which he had tried to persuade Charles to reconsider taking decisive military action on the Palatine family's behalf, ideally in conjunction with Gustavus Adolphus, following the Swedish king's recent victory over Habsburg forces at Breitenfeld, near Leipzig. Bearing a bundle of correspondence from the Palatine court, Dorchester had entered Whitehall's Picture Gallery and found the English king 'in the midst of his antique pictures, no less seriously employed . . . placing and removing his Emperors' heads and putting them in right order'. Thereafter he had suggested to Charles that, 'now he had done disposing his emperors, he would think of supporting of kings', namely his brother-in-law Frederick and Gustavus

Adolphus, 'whose interests began to be joined with each other, and both with his Majesty'.[28]

Caroline pacifism and English penury contrasted starkly with the puissant Protestantism embodied by the Swedish 'Lion of the North' from whom, long ago, an offer of marriage to Elizabeth had been rejected by James VI & I, whose Danish Oldenburg in-laws were long-standing adversaries of the Swedish House of Vasa. By 1632, militant Protestants regarded Gustavus Adolphus as the only individual capable of defeating the Catholic Habsburg Antichrist after Swedish forces secured lightning victories across northern Germany. Auspicious Protestant portents were proclaimed as Catholic forces crumbled before the great 'Sued' – which spelled 'Deus' backwards. Seeing the Swedish king supplying soldiers and funds on the scale that was continually being requested by the English court, in January 1632 Frederick and Elizabeth christened their thirteenth child Gustavus Adolphus and named the Swedish king as one of the infant's godparents. Optimistically anticipating their imminent return to Heidelberg, the Palatine couple also had medals struck bearing their profiles and the motto *Sol Occidens Renascitur*: 'the setting sun rises again'.[29]

As Gustavus Adolphus's forces attacked Bavaria during the spring of 1632, observers acknowledged that promoting the Palatine family's interests offered the Swedish king a legitimate defence against charges of opportunistic expansionism. According to one English report, 'always it is good, the two kings should be together, for as Bohemia is protected by Sweden, so Sweden is justified by Bohemia'.[30] On the ground, the Scots soldier Robert Monro, who served as a lieutenant colonel in the Swedish army, confirmed his elation at being able to combine service for the legendary Gustavus Adolphus with service for the erstwhile Elector Palatine and the king's sister, Elizabeth, recounting how he had 'crossed the Rhine, fighting for the Queen of Soldiers, being led by the King of Captains, and Captain of Kings'.[31] Nearly two centuries later, Monro would serve as a model for Sir Walter Scott's depiction of the mercenary soldier Dugald Dalgetty in *A Legend of Montrose* (1819).

While Gustavus Adolphus shrewdly questioned Frederick's military capacity to retain territories to which he might be restored, Anglo-Swedish negotiations were abandoned following Frederick's refusal to accede to an arrangement whereby, after his restitution, his former Electoral lands would be retained by the Swedish king as surety against

Charles defaulting on agreed financial subsidies. 'With tears in his eyes', Frederick had bewailed to Sir Henry Vane and the marquess of Hamilton that such an agreement would place the Palatinate 'into an eternal subjection to be slaves to the crown and king of Sweden'.[32] Having relocated to Mainz, Frederick continued discussions with the Swedish king's representatives before developing a fatal fever from which he died on 29 November 1632. Elizabeth was devastated by her loss, later recounting to Roe how news of her husband's death had been 'the first time that ever I was frightened, for it struck me as cold as ice'. Elizabeth had found herself unable to cry, sleep, eat or drink for several days, although she had tried to put on 'a good show in company'.[33]

News of the former Elector Palatine's death was, however, eclipsed by the shock of Gustavus Adolphus being slain on the battlefield at Lützen, in Saxony, a fortnight earlier. The Swedish king's unexpected demise unleashed a flurry of encomiastic elegies in the English press and confirmed his status as a national hero in the popular imagination, despite being a foreign monarch who had never visited Britain and had no dynastic relationship to the Stuarts. Poetic appreciations of Gustavus – itself an anagram of Augustus, with Roman imperial echoes – were published by anonymous pens and recognized authors alike, including Alexander Gil, James Howell, Philip Massinger, Francis Quarles, George Tooke and Aurelian Townshend. Effusive acclaim for the Swedish king's martial achievements inevitably risked implicit criticism of Charles's inaction and risked echoing the unfavourable comparisons previously drawn between the king's father, James VI & I, and his Danish uncle, Christian IV. In an epic account of the battles at Leipzig and Lützen, published in 1634, the Cambridge poet John Russell acknowledged that 'happy England' seemed 'drunk with security', but wondered

> Are you become like to the Sybarite,
> Whose softened spirit, sottish appetite
> Could no harsh sound endure, nor that shrill sound,
> That doth from hammered steel and brass redound?[34]

The erstwhile Elector Palatine, Frederick, became, as one contributor to *The Swedish Intelligencer* newsletter put it, 'the Prince for whom Gustavus fell'.[35] In a sermon preached at the German church in The Hague and translated into English, Frederick Schloer confessed his disbelief that 'those two Christian kings, should follow one another in less than a fortnight', having been 'snatched from among us by such immature death, in the summer of their age, in the midst of their victories, in the entrance to greater hopes'. Albeit flattering Frederick's meagre contribution, Schloer had been convinced that 'they were the men by whom God would ruin the throne of Antichrist, and save his Israel'. Suddenly bereft of both kings, Schloer looked to their posterity for inspiration, and urged his congregation to transfer their loyalties to Gustavus Adolphus's five-year-old daughter, now Queen Christina of Sweden, as well as to Frederick's heirs.[36] Other commentators reckoned the Palatine cause was rendered more straightforward by Frederick's demise. Unlike his father, Elizabeth's eldest surviving son, Charles Louis, was not tainted by the crime of having rebelled against the Holy Roman Emperor. To the mind of the newsletter-writer John Pory, Frederick's removal ensured that 'our king and state are obliged to do more for a nephew than for a brother-in-law, and more likewise for a widow than for a wife'.[37]

II

A passive foreign policy that failed to defend Palatine interests potentially betokened an alarming confessional indifference at the Caroline court. Indeed, while Protestant and Catholic armies fought one another across innumerable Continental battlefields, diplomatic relations between England and Rome were restarted for the first time since the Reformation, following approval of a 'mutual exchange' of agents between the papacy and Queen Henrietta Maria's court, now constituted as a separate channel of international influence. In December 1634, an Italian Oratorian priest, Gregorio Panzani, was sent to London as Pope Urban VIII's representative, succeeded eighteen months later by the Aberdeenshire-born Franciscan George Conn. In 1624, Conn had published a hagiographic life of Mary, Queen of Scots, *Vita Mariae Stuartae Reginae*, which formed the basis for Lope Félix de Vega Carpio's epic biographical chronicle of Mary's life, *La Corona Trágica* (1627), published in Madrid. Amid residual papal hopes that Charles might yet convert to Catholicism, in pious emulation of his martyred grandmother, Conn arrived in London bearing artistic treasures for the connoisseur English king, later denounced by the Puritan polemicist William Prynne as 'gifts of pictures, antique idols and suchlike trumperies brought from Rome'.[38]

Prynne personified the penalties risked by criticizing Caroline court culture. Several years earlier, he had attacked all theatrical performances as dangerous instances of diabolic immorality in a work entitled *Histrio-mastix, or the Players' Scourge* (1632) that ran to more than a thousand pages and was dedicated to Prynne's fellow barristers at Lincoln's Inn. Insisting of those who 'serve the Devil in plays and playhouses, it's impossible for them to serve the Lord sincerely in prayers and churches', Prynne had also drawn a contemporary parallel with 'Nero, that vicious Roman Emperor, who was so much besotted with stage-plays, as sometimes to play the actor'. Alongside vituperative condemnation of commercial theatre's iniquities, Prynne had execrated theatre-loving princes, asserting that 'an emperor dancing, or acting a part in plays or masques even in his own private palace, is infamous and his resort to playhouses more abominable'. Given the regular and enthusiastic involvement of both Charles and Henrietta Maria in elaborate theatrical productions, Prynne only added further combustion by describing female players as 'all notorious impudent, prostituted strumpets'.[39]

Prynne was charged with sedition in a case that started in the Star Chamber on 7 February 1634, four days after the four Inns of Court had collaborated to perform a masque before the king and queen at Whitehall, amassing production costs of over £21,000. Scripted by James Shirley and performed on a set designed by Inigo Jones, *The Triumph of Peace* not only attempted to atone for Prynne's insults, but also endorsed Caroline foreign policy by celebrating the virtuous benefits of peace with an anti-masque that depicted battles, war and dissension. Before the performance, the play's costumed performers had paraded through London's streets from Holborn to Whitehall, with the Hispanic influence of Cervantes's *Don Quixote* apparent in the inclusion of an ambulatory windmill, 'a fantastic knight' and 'his squire armed', as Shirley's script explained that 'the fantastic adventurer, with his lance makes attempts upon the windmill'.[40] While 3,000 copies of *The Triumph of Peace*'s script were printed to extend the masque's message beyond its invited audience of courtiers and ambassadors, the masque was also performed at the Merchant Taylors' Hall in the City. Prynne, meanwhile, was convicted of 'seditious, libellous railing', fined £5,000 and sentenced to life imprisonment and the removal of both ears. Three months later, a mutilated Prynne appeared in a Cheapside pillory where he was forced to watch *Histrio-mastix* become the first book in England to be publicly burned by the common hangman.[41]

As sectarian warfare continued to rage across Continental Europe, a compelling case could be made – as equally on diplomatic as theatrical stages – for Charles to continue his father's pacific policy. With Swedish troops occupying the late Elector Frederick's former lands in the spring of 1634, a Swedish envoy, Henry Oxenstierna, arrived in London and unsuccessfully tried to persuade Charles to join an anti-Habsburg alliance. Having received repeated rebuffs, Oxenstierna declined a present of silver gilt vessels, explaining that ambassadorial gifts should only be proffered and received as 'a testimony of both their satisfactions, which he, for his part' could not pretend, 'having not dispatched his business'.[42] Following Oxenstierna's departure from Gravesend in July, the new Venetian resident in London, Francesco Zonca, reported that the Swedish envoy had been disgusted, both by the extent to which English foreign policy seemed intent on 'preserving a general neutrality and a firm determination to avoid complications of every sort', and by the 'execrable and rotten' degree to which it had become infected by Hispanic influence. Parallel pleas by the long-serving Dutch ambassador in London, Joachimi, that English military involvement would greatly assist in securing a permanent Continental peace likewise fell on deaf ears. By October, Zonca reported that Joachimi despaired 'of making any impression on the ministry here, grown drowsy, as he says, in the delights and commodities of the country and in the charms of peace'.[43]

Even individuals who had previously recommended military intervention became more cautious. When France declared war against Spain in May 1635, Roe conveyed to the Electress Elizabeth a view prevailing in London that her brother's best option might indeed be to let 'England with happiness look on a while' and let 'those elephants waste their strength'. If England could remain neutral while maintaining a substantial naval presence, the warring parties would seek to retain Charles's amity and, 'when both sides are out of breath', Roe believed that England could 'sway the end and reap the benefit of the war'.[44] That summer, Anzolo Correr identified a new, third faction at the Caroline court that was neither Hispanophile nor Francophile. Rather, its members admired 'how useful and opportune it is to stand and look on at the tragedy of others as spectators and enjoy peacefully that blessedness which God has chosen to grant to these realms, amid such universal calamities'.[45]

At the same time, popular resentment at Charles's reliance on prerogative fiscal levies left the English king with little option aside from pacific diplomacy. Having deemed the dissolution of Parliament in March 1629 to be the blackest day in English history for five centuries, the Puritan diarist Sir Simonds D'Ewes denounced writs issued by the king in October 1634 for the prerogative levy of 'Ship Money', ostensibly to support the Navy, in similarly apocalyptic terms. According to D'Ewes, by imposing such exactions, 'the liberty of the subjects of England received the most deadly and fatal blow it had been sensible of in five hundred years'. Despite Charles's 'pretext and colour to provide ships for the defence of the kingdom', D'Ewes denied additional revenue was needed since England was 'now at peace with all the world, and the royal fleet was never stronger or in better case'.[46]

Suspicions persisted that English neutrality more accurately denoted court support for the Spanish Habsburgs. In the autumn of 1634, the Venetian envoy in Madrid, Francesco Cornaro, reported that Philip IV's ministers 'assert here more than ever that they have England favourable' and in 'playhouses they applaud the English nation as one allied' with Spain. Closer to home, Philip's younger brother, the Cardinal Infante Ferdinand, became Governor General of the Spanish Netherlands after Archduchess Isabella's death in December 1633. When Ferdinand assumed office the following autumn, Cornaro's counterpart in The Hague, Francesco Michiel, described the lavish hospitality organized by the English envoy in Brussels, Sir Balthasar Gerbier. The large images of St George displayed and 'a great quantity of wine' drunk led Michiel to infer that such 'excessive demonstrations confirm the impression of the leanings of England towards the crown of Spain'.[47] But Charles's ambassador in Madrid, Hopton, remained equivocal; he had admitted to Windebank earlier that year that he 'could never find reason to affirm, that their hearts are right towards us, in the matter of the Palatinate'.[48] Hopton advised against over-estimating Spain's capacity to effect restitution, since Emperor Ferdinand's sense of his imperial responsibilities might well be trumped by loyalty to his own Habsburg relations. Having already assigned Frederick's former territories and dignities to Maximilian I of Bavaria as a reward for suppressing the Bohemian rebels, Ferdinand seemed unlikely to incur Bavarian hostility by returning strategically situated lands and an Electoral title to Protestant heretics whose exiled court was housed and supported by Spain's long-standing enemy, the Dutch Republic. Hopton advised Windebank in July 1635 that Charles should prioritize amassing a powerful and independent Navy, since England was 'compassed about by warlike nations, strong by land and sea, whose countries are all fortified, which makes them higher-minded than is fit'. In Madrid, 'the action of 1588 is still in men's minds; and ought chiefly to be in ours'.[49]

Residual fears of Spanish perfidy deepened when news arrived in London of a settlement known as the Peace of Prague, initially concluded in May 1635 between Emperor Ferdinand and the Lutheran Elector, John George of Saxony, and later extended to other warring parties in an attempt to end nearly two decades of fighting between Catholic and Protestant states. Dubbed a '*monstrum pacis*' ('monstrous peace') by disappointed parties, its terms included confirmation of the permanent transfer of the Palatinate's Electoral rights and privileges to the duke of Bavaria.[50] The Electress Elizabeth – now vindicated in her scepticism regarding Charles's reliance on pacific diplomacy – expressed to Roe her hope that such a blatant betrayal of earlier undertakings might now 'open their eyes on your side [of] the seas if they be not shot out with pistols'.[51] The Palatine family's alarm only increased when it became known that Maximilian of Bavaria, who was in his sixties and childless, had recently married his own niece – the Emperor's daughter – who was nearly forty years her husband's junior. The duke's marriage inevitably raised the prospect of future heirs being born to secure Bavaria's succession to the Palatine Electorate around the same time as Elizabeth's oldest surviving son, Charles Louis, was due to achieve his legal majority in January 1636 – which, by imperial law, theoretically enabled him to govern his estates and to petition the Emperor for a formal investiture.

To defend her family's interests, Elizabeth dispatched Charles Louis to England, where he survived an overly enthusiastic welcome at Dover, in which stray bullets from a volley of greeting shots killed five men aboard his ship. Charles Louis's presence at Charles's court from November 1635 to July 1637 stoked bellicose hopes that the English king might finally reverse his Hispanophile inclinations and promote the Palatine family's cause through alliances with anti-Habsburg powers, including France. Initially, however, the Palatine prince's arrival presented difficulties for Louis's ambassador Jean d'Angennes, marquis of Pougny, who declined to address Charles Louis with his Electoral title on account of the alliance concluded between France and Bavaria at the Treaty of Fontainebleau (1631) by which Duke Maximilian had received French protection for his newly acquired Palatine territories. As Windebank observed to Hopton, despite having 'built castles in the air upon the straight intelligence they intended to hold with him', the French envoys were consequently rebuffed by Charles Louis.[52] By contrast, Spain's representatives freely used his Electoral title, although Correr suspected that they did so only in order to mock Charles by 'showing his nephew, to mortify him the more, the shadow of that body of which they themselves have taken away the substance'. Meanwhile, Pougny's frustrated French delegation was left objecting that, 'under the honey of their words and behind the vanity of titles', the Spanish sought to 'hide the poison of everlasting procrastination' and 'gently waft the Palatine's affairs to final perdition'.[53]

Disappointed by the Peace of Prague's terms, Charles dispatched more envoys to Continental courts to insist that English efforts to bring about the Palatine family's restitution to its former lands and dignities had been in earnest. Sir Walter Aston returned to Spain in August 1635 as an ambassador extraordinary – having been attached to the English embassy in Madrid during Prince Charles's visit more than a decade earlier – and was directed to make clear that 'we sent our said ambassadors to treat, and not to exasperate' foreign courts. But 'finding all passages to the Emperor's mercy shut up, and all the world wondering at our patience', England was now ready to engage in hostilities.[54] That autumn, Charles also instructed his resident ambassador in Paris, Scudamore, to suggest to Louis's court a settlement whereby Emperor Ferdinand might agree to effect restitution of the Palatinate's territories and privileges in exchange for France returning the duchy of Lorraine to Habsburg control. Disregarding predictable French reluctance to relinquish their own strategic gains for Palatine ends, Charles then sent Robert Sidney, earl of Leicester, as an ambassador extraordinary to Paris to pursue this initiative the following summer. Leicester took an instant dislike to Scudamore, privately objecting that he 'speaks French, as if he had learned it in Herefordshire' and 'thinks he never has respect enough, and yet endeavours not at all to deserve any'.[55] Regarding an Anglo-French military initiative against the Habsburgs as more likely to succeed than eternal diplomatic negotiations, Leicester believed 'the diseases of Christendom are not to be cured like the King's Evil with touching, but with striking'.[56]

Further afield, Charles had also sent a Catholic envoy, John Taylor, to test the diplomatic waters at the imperial court in September 1635. Travelling through central Europe, Taylor had been dismayed by the ubiquitous devastation, deprivation and disease left in the wake of war. Writing to Windebank, he lamented that 'Germany, the greatest and whilom [formerly] the fairest country of Europe, is now the most miserable, and looks hideous to the eye'. Germany appeared a dying corpse with 'diverse mortal wounds . . . and gasps for life like a body whose veins are quite exhausted of blood'. Once in Vienna, Taylor remained mindful of the need to promote Charles Louis's claims to his Electoral dignities and titles as quickly as possible, having heard that the territories' current occupant, Maximilian of Bavaria, 'since this marriage feeds of nothing, but on capons and chicken, fed with flesh of vipers'. While Taylor mused as to what sort of offspring Maximilian might 'beget to infect the world', his naïvely optimistic accounts of the Emperor Ferdinand's apparent willingness to resolve the Palatine matter encouraged Charles to confer plenipotentiary powers on the earl of Arundel to negotiate further.[57] Travelling to join Taylor in Vienna, Arundel was accompanied by the Bohemian artist Wenceslaus Hollar, whose skilful engravings provided visual confirmation of the scale of German devastation, while a *True Relation* of Arundel's embassy conveyed in prose 'a sense of quotidian horror through its repetitive catalogue of burnt, plundered, depopulated, famished towns and villages'.[58] In Bacharach, on the Rhine, Crowne encountered such dearth that 'the poor people are found dead with grass in their mouths', while at Hradčany Castle in Prague, he viewed 'one room furnished with English pictures of our nobility', where Frederick and Elizabeth had briefly held sway as rulers of Bohemia.[59]

III

While Charles's envoys solicited on his behalf overseas, the Prince Palatine's presence in London – where he had been joined by his younger brother, Rupert – encouraged the king's domestic critics to demand Parliament's recall in order to vote sufficient funds to promote Charles Louis's forcible restoration in an anti-Habsburg military alliance with the French and Dutch. As support for an extensive land war gathered momentum in early 1636, Correr observed how such 'ideas are occasionally maintained before the king, and are constantly dinned into the Palatine's ears', although 'the less impression they make on His Majesty, the more they increase the distress and discontent of the poor prince'.[60] While Charles's ministers procrastinated, Charles Louis participated in the Inns of Courts' Shrovetide revels, which included election of a festive 'Prince d'Amour' and performance of a masque. Discussing seating arrangements for the masque, John Finet, Charles's Master of Ceremonies, warned the law students that, since the Palatine Prince had already made clear 'that he would not be a prince, in jest, as the other was', Charles Louis should be seated centrally with his brother Rupert on his right and the 'Prince d'Amour' (played by a Cornish law student, Richard Vivian) on his left.[61] Several days earlier, the 'Prince d'Amour' had presided over his temporary court, having been given pretended powers for thirty days to receive ambassadors, appoint councillors, arraign criminals and enact legislation. Skating on thin political ice, the 'Prince d'Amour' had been invited to consider 'queries of state', including whether or not it was more honourable for 'subjects of an elect prince to replenish his coffers' through parliamentary supply or, by denying funds, oblige such a prince to resort to prerogative levies.[62] As political theatre filled a vacuum of decisive action, Henrietta Maria also took Charles Louis to Blackfriars Theatre to watch a revived Elizabethan tragedy, *Alphonsus, Emperor of Germany*, which dramatized a power struggle between the eponymous 'Spanish tyrant', Alphonsus, and Prince Edward of England and Earl Richard of Cornwall, in which the martial resistance of the two Englishmen revived nostalgic echoes of Elizabethan heroism.

But theatrical diversions remained a poor alternative to military intervention. In late 1636, Elizabeth was dismayed when Charles refused permission for his nephew to recruit English troops to join the Landgrave of Hesse-Cassel's forces in action against the Habsburgs; instead, the English king offered a monthly subsidy and would only sanction Charles Louis serving as a volunteer. Frustrated at seeing her son 'stay idly in England whilst all the world was in action' fighting on his behalf, the Electress Elizabeth responded indignantly to Roe that serving as a volunteer would so dilute the prince's royal dignity that 'he were better be in his grave than do it'. Earlier that year, one of Charles Louis's entourage, Colonel Thomas Ferencz, had written to Elizabeth from her former childhood home in Warwickshire, Coombe Abbey, complaining that although her sons had now spent nine months in England, the business of Palatinate restitution was 'going nowhere; one feels shamefully duped, so one prepares oneself to achieve nothing effective or essential'. Ferencz detected parallel disappointment among envoys sent by other Protestant powers, such as Sweden and Denmark, who found 'nothing coming from England except fine words in the mouth of some courtier ambassador' which did 'nothing except broadcast further our humiliation'. Not only did Charles's administration lack any means to take action, but his ministers seemed uninterested in trying to raise funds or discuss strategy. Rather, Ferencz ventured that the Caroline court preferred 'looking for excuses to let time pass, and not to trouble the calm of the meal and the course of present delights!'[63]

Protestant anxieties were only exacerbated by the high-profile conversions to Catholicism of courtiers including Tobie Matthew, son of Archbishop Tobias Matthew of York, and Walter Montagu, as well as courtiers' spouses, such as the erstwhile Puritan Anne Blount, Lady Newport. In Newport's case, her outraged husband, Mountjoy Blount, earl of Newport, was 'so fierce in complaining for his wife being made a Papist' by suasion from associates of Henrietta Maria and Conn that the matter was formally debated in the Privy Council where the Archbishop of Canterbury, William Laud, recorded 'a great noise about the perverting of the Lady Newport'.[64] On the diplomatic front, Charles remained optimistically hopeful that papal intervention might offer another route to securing the Palatinate's restitution, since Pope Urban VIII was trying to end Continental hostilities through a peace conference in Cologne.

In London, Pope Urban's envoy, Conn, held Mass up to eight times a day in his Long Acre chapel, where the cosmopolitan, ostentatious and proselytizing spirit of court Catholicism contrasted with the characteristic quiescence of most gentry recusants in England's rural shires. While a distrustful Laud speculated aloud as to whether Conn was really an 'ambassador, agent or spy',[65] Correr was also disconcerted by the English king's readiness to take the papal agent into his political confidence. In May 1637, Correr expressed his amazement that 'it is certainly a wonderful thing to see in England a dependant of the Holy See not only living at liberty, but frequenting the court at all hours with so much confidence, and having such familiar access to the king's ear, as if he was one of his most intimate servants'.[66] But further afield, the likely local impact of closer Anglo-papal relations prompted the Irish Lord Deputy, Thomas Wentworth, to write to Conn that same month, describing the large numbers of expatriate Irish that 'wander abroad', bearing 'an unjust, yet habitual hatred to the English government . . . stirring and inciting all they can to blood and rebellion'. As Wentworth warned Windebank later that year, as well as constant appeals for papal assistance, some Irish peers were so confident of popular support that 'they desire nothing of Spain, but to furnish them with arms for 12,000 men – all the rest they will be able to do for themselves'.[67]

The Caroline court's propensity to indulge in escapist fantasy was epitomized in plans, discussed in early 1637, to dispatch the younger Palatine Prince Rupert to Madagascar to establish a new English settlement and thereby to disrupt Dutch trade routes to the East Indies. The Madagascan project was promoted by Hispanophile courtiers, who had secured royal approval to raise funds for a project that potentially offered colonial compensation to a prince whose family had been deprived of its ancestral inheritance by aggressive Spanish expansionism. Regarding the idea as an irresponsible dereliction of the Palatine family's central European responsibilities, an exasperated Electress Elizabeth decried the 'romance some would put into Rupert's head of conquering Madagascar' together with the diplomat and connoisseur Endymion Porter, whom 'they say is to be his squire, when he shall Don Quixote-like conquer that famous island'. While Elizabeth directed Roe to 'put such windmills out of his head', Roe had already written to Elizabeth, reassuring her that 'the plot is absurd, impossible, and of no use' in advancing Palatine interests and had 'little relation to Europe'; rather, it seemed more likely to imperil Rupert 'in a most desperate, dangerous, unwholesome, fruitless action'.[68]

Although the expeditionary scheme was soon aborted, it received literary realization in William Davenant's poem *Madagascar* (1638). Dedicated to Rupert, Davenant's epic described a dream in which the prince successfully led a seaborne invasion and conquest of the island, where his rule was warmly welcomed by entranced – and implausibly pacific – Malagasy natives who 'with jealous optics trace / Lines of thy mother's beauty in thy face'. Having repulsed a hostile Portuguese incursion, Rupert's peaceful dominion of the island was assured:

Here in a calm began thy regal sway;
Which with such cheerful hearts, all did obey,
As if no Law, were juster than thy word;
Thy Sceptre still were safe, without a Sword.
And here Chronologers pronounce thy style;
The first true Monarch of the 'Golden Isle':
An Isle, so seated for predominance,
Where naval strength, its power can so advance,
That it may tribute take, of what the East
Shall ever send in traffic to the West.[69]

Back at Charles's court in London, however, Charles Louis and Rupert saw little point remaining in England and returned to the Continent in July 1637. On their departure, the king urged his eldest nephew to persist in seeking his family's restoration to its former Palatine lands and privileges in the Rhineland. Reassuring Charles Louis that 'he was not the first great prince of Christendom to experience rude storms', the English king was evidently confident that, 'with prudence and good counsel, he would emerge happily'.[70] According to a newsletter report, after bestowing annual pensions on his German nephews, Charles I further reassured them that, aside from the Palatine 'business, he was the happiest king or prince in all Christendom'.[71]

In an engraving entitled *Den Coninckllijcken Morgen-Wecker* (1636) ('The Royal Alarm Clock'), the Dutchman Crispijn van de Passe captured the Janus-faced character of Caroline foreign policy by showing Charles asleep in a chair while, to his left, the Spanish ambassador played soporific melodies on a flute, having placed a toy basket and treasure chest at the English king's feet (Plate 12). On Charles's other side, Louis XIII of France was dressed for battle and trying to rouse the English king, assisted by the Palatine Princes Charles Louis and Rupert, while, through a window, the English fleet was finally being prepared for action. In the accompanying text, Louis beseeches Charles to realize that his Palatine relations 'never more shall repossess their land / By peace, as you do dream, but by strong hand'. But a pro-Spanish courtier (probably Cottington) retorts that it is better to

Dance, be merry, jovial still
With Spanish *pistolets* our purses fill,
Better with pictures gay to feed our sight
Than naked corpses gored with blood in fight.[72]

Speculation was nevertheless mounting that Charles might finally be willing to assemble a significant naval force which, unlike a large-scale deployment of land forces, would not require parliamentary funding. If nothing else, Charles's colossal new flagship, *The Sovereign of the Seas*, launched in the autumn of 1637, betokened a reinvigoration of English naval power. The vessel's construction had cost over £65,000 – which was £50,000 more than the original estimate – and had been funded by the unpopular Ship Money levy. Sourcing the necessary timber had entailed the felling of 2,500 mature oak trees before the warship was loaded with over a hundred cannon. Awed by the ship's sheer size, the poet Thomas Carew likened *The Sovereign of the Seas* to the Colossus of Rhodes and Egyptian pyramids, marvelling that 'we that have heard of seven, now see the eighth / Wonder at home, of naval art the height'.[73] Responsible for much of the warship's elaborate ornamentation, the playwright and set designer Thomas Heywood focused attention on the ship's figurehead that featured an equestrian carving of the tenth-century English king Edgar trampling seven Scottish and Welsh kings underfoot. Heywood described Edgar as not only 'the first that could truly write himself an absolute monarch of this island', but also 'Lord of the Four Seas' around Britain, and acclaimed Charles as Edgar's 'true and undoubted successor'. Launch of the king's triple-decked warship in 1637 suggested that England might yet make a belated entry into Continental hostilities. As Carew had also hoped, this 'triumphant ark, with Edgar's fame, / To Charles's sceptre, add [a] trident's claim'.[74]

The strategic objective would be the same as that attempted through diplomatic channels for nearly two decades: securing restitution of the Palatine territories and Electoral privileges to the family of Charles's sister, Elizabeth. But when Charles did, at last, assemble an army two years later, it would be deployed against his own Protestant subjects and in his own native land of Scotland. Moreover, rather than imitating Edgar by trampling the Scots underfoot, Charles's inability to suppress his Scottish critics on the battlefield would oblige him, reluctantly, to end more than a decade of 'Personal Rule' by summoning an English parliament.

10
Allowing Hannibal to Enter, 1637–1641

In July 1637, a fracas occurred in St Giles's Cathedral in Edinburgh when the congregation violently rejected what a Fife minister, John Row, execrated as a 'Popish-English-Scottish-Mass-Service-Book'.[1] Following the contentious imposition of revised church canons, the new Prayer Book was intended to provide a uniform liturgy throughout the country, but was popularly distrusted on the grounds that its content had been approved by neither the Church of Scotland's General Assembly nor the Scottish Parliament. Its content also denoted an unwelcome Anglicizing promotion of liturgical and ceremonial elements in Scottish worship. Opposition to royal ecclesiastical reforms swelled into a broader supplication movement, formalized by a 'National Covenant' that was signed at Edinburgh's Greyfriars Kirk in February 1638. Eventually attracting over 300,000 signatures, the National Covenant bound its signatories to defend Protestant worship as defined by the 'Negative Confession' (1581) and justified resistance to any innovations that risked 'the re-establishing of the popish religion and tyranny, and to the subversion and ruin of the true Reformed religion, and of our liberties, laws and estates'.[2]

In Whitehall, a dilatory and misjudged royal response to the Prayer Book's rejection saw popular riot steadily escalate from a nationwide supplication movement to constitutional revolution and armed hostilities as peaceful signatories were transformed into armed 'Covenanters'. Belatedly, Charles I sent James, marquess of Hamilton, to Scotland in May 1638, from where Hamilton engaged in shuttle diplomacy between Edinburgh and London, trying to persuade Charles to abandon his insistence that the Covenant must be abjured before negotiations could start. Since most Scots did not regard the Covenant's commitments as incompatible with either Scots law or royal government, Hamilton warned that the king's determination that the document must be surrendered and royal policy obeyed potentially entailed 'the hazarding of your three crowns'.[3] But 'so long as this Covenant is in force', Charles insisted, 'I have no more power than as a Duke of Venice: which I will rather die than suffer'.[4]

Charles's refusal to discuss the disturbances in Scotland with his English Privy Councillors also meant that 'the members of the government wash their hands of any disaster that may ensue', as observed by the resident Venetian secretary in London, Francesco Zonca.[5] Among Charles's ambassadors overseas, Robert Sidney, earl of Leicester, protested from Paris that he could not comment on 'the business of Scotland whereof I am as ignorant, as if I lived in Tartary'.[6] Pressure placed on Pope Urban VIII's agent, George Conn, to leave London was nevertheless interpreted as an attempt to assuage Scots fears and 'leave these people no vestige for believing he [Charles] is nearly a Roman Catholic, which is the point on which they lay stress'.[7] In an intercepted letter written in French in June 1638, apparently to his ecclesiastical superiors, 'a Jesuit' identified as 'G. T.' complained that he had 'never been in a country where things go so slowly or stupidly . . . I seem to be in the middle of Spain'. Claiming that the Scots, 'under the mask of religion' were 'setting up an anarchy', 'G. T.' criticized Charles's response as feebly inadequate and described England as 'one little kingdom, which seems to be in profound peace and flourishing, but *latet anguis in herba* [a snake hides in the grass]'.[8] In Scotland, after failed attempts at a negotiated settlement, a General Assembly met in Glasgow in November, only for Hamilton – as the king's commissioner – to attempt its dissolution after a week. Disregarding Hamilton's instructions, the Assembly's members remained in session and voted to abolish not only the controversial Articles of Perth approved in 1618, but also the ecclesiastical office of episcopacy, which led to the deposition of all fourteen Church of Scotland archbishops and bishops the following month. Despite complaining to Charles that 'next [to] Hell, I hate this place', Hamilton reassured his king that he would 'not weary till the government be again set right; and then I will forswear this country'.[9]

Concerted opposition to royal religious policy in Scotland eventually led to more than a decade of civil wars as Charles's authority collapsed across the British Isles. Encountering increasingly stubborn resistance to the imposition of religious reform and the levying of prerogative taxes,

Charles instinctively looked to exploit military and financial resources from across England, Scotland and Ireland as a means of imposing his will on opponents while also appealing for foreign assistance. Meanwhile, critics of Caroline rule proved equally ready to make common cause with discontented factions elsewhere in the British Isles and to seek international support in resisting royal authority.

After more than a decade of 'Personal Rule', Charles eventually summoned an English parliament in April 1640, seeking money and troops to suppress his Scottish opponents. Although MPs had – for two decades – been agitating for armed intervention to promote Protestant interests in Continental Europe, they were now confronted with an ambiguous dilemma. Was the English king seeking funds and forces to quell a domestic revolt in his realms, in which case MPs' support should be axiomatic and any moves to withhold assistance could be potentially treasonous? Or was Charles, instead, seeking to raise an army to forestall 'foreign' Scottish adversaries invading England, in which case careful thought should be given to the ethics of taking up arms against his own Protestant subjects? And if Charles failed to secure resources from the English Parliament, would he be justified in deploying international mercenary forces largely comprising Catholic troops from countries such as Ireland or Spain?

I

Domestic disturbances inevitably undermined the capacity for Charles's ministers to undertake Continental commitments. Frustrated by delays in finalizing the long-anticipated Anglo-French alliance, Louis XIII's ambassador extraordinary, Henri de Saint-Nectaire, marquis de La Ferté-Nabert, left London in July 1638 and was not replaced. The Venetian envoy Anzolo Correr, who had been redeployed from London to Paris, reported a conversation earlier that year in which Louis's chief adviser, Cardinal Richelieu, had 'stated emphatically that, at present, England might be called the country where they talk of everything and conclude nothing' as 'for three years the ambassadors have grown old in disputes'.[10]

In Germany, Sir Thomas Roe was dismayed by the damaging international repercussions of the unrest in Scotland. In the course of representing England's interests at a conference of anti-Habsburg powers in Hamburg that included France, Denmark, Sweden and the United Provinces, Roe suspected that those allies who had already committed extensive resources to the seemingly interminable Continental war were likely to demand a higher financial contribution from England, which had hitherto remained neutral, if English demands regarding the Palatinate's restitution were included in any coalition peace proposals. But as Roe told Charles's Secretary of State, Sir John Coke, widespread knowledge of the English king's difficulties in Scotland 'hath a very ill odour and makes our friends despair of us', especially with regard to financial undertakings. The Swedish representative, Johan Adler Salvius, had made it clear that 'they could not expect performance from us, if we should bind ourselves to give contribution, for he was advised that we had no money'. More generally, in a vast and protracted conflict that had seen up to a quarter of a million combatants fighting across the Holy Roman Empire and neighbouring states in a single year, the Stuarts' sole objective of securing restitution of the Palatinate's territories and dignities to one branch of its family inevitably risked being eclipsed among a complex host of rival territorial and confessional agendas. In trying to align English interests with initiatives simultaneously being discussed by French, imperial, Dutch, Danish and Swedish envoys in 1638, Roe admitted to Coke that 'if there be another world in the moon, certainly we live in it'.[11]

Roe's attempts to promote the Palatinate's restitution were further undermined by rumours regarding Charles's parallel interest in reviving an Anglo-Habsburg axis of influence, even if Spanish observers remained pessimistic about the impact of the unresolved Scottish crisis on English capabilities. In Brussels, Charles's envoy, Sir Balthasar Gerbier, reported discussions between the pro-Habsburg Henriette of Lorraine, Princess of Pfalzburg, and a Spanish Jesuit in which the priest had admitted that Philip IV and Louis XIII had both been forced 'to open their eyes' by the formation of Charles's impressive 'Ship Money fleet'. But the fact that the English warships remained unmanned and in harbour meant that '*esta flota no ha dado niedo sino a los pescados*, which is to say but that fleet gave fear but to the fish'.[12]

Habsburg forces gained a valuable diplomatic bargaining chip when the Palatine Prince Rupert was captured by imperial forces after the Battle of Vlotho in October 1638. While Rupert had been in London the previous year, both his elder brother, Charles Louis, and his mother, the Electress Elizabeth, had been alarmed by the contacts Rupert had formed with the papal agent, George Conn, and several aristocratic Catholic converts. Fearing Rupert's susceptibilities to suasion were greater now that he was detained by Catholic troops, Elizabeth admitted despairingly to Roe, 'I confess in my passion, I did rather wish him killed'.[13] At the same time, Louis's ministers were becoming frustrated by the extent to which Charles's court in London attracted prominent French exiles whose attempts to undermine Richelieu's administration usually involved promotion of Spanish interests. These exiles included the inveterate conspirator Marie de Rohan, duchess de Chevreuse, who had arrived in England in April and, as one of Henrietta Maria's ladies-in-waiting, had been accorded the coveted right to sit on the 'tabouret' (an upholstered stool) in the queen's presence. Since the same ceremonial privilege was not extended to the wife of the resident French ambassador in London, Pomponne de Bellièvre, objections arose regarding the diplomatic preference accorded to a subject – who was a declared enemy of the French state – over Louis's personal representative. When reciprocal tabouret rights at Louis's court were then denied to the wife of Charles's ambassador in Paris, Leicester wearily recalled the classical struggle between Herakles and Apollo at Delphi when he admitted to Secretary of State Sir Francis Windebank that 'there was not more ado in old time, for the Tripod, than there is now for the Tabouret'.[14]

In October 1638, Chevreuse was joined in London by Louis's estranged mother, Marie de'Médicis, whose dynastic influence extended via her well-connected daughters: Queen Henrietta Maria of England, Queen Elisabeth of Spain and Christine, duchess of Savoy. On her arrival in England, Marie de'Médicis was acclaimed by the court poet Edmund Waller as the 'Great Queen of Europe! Where thy offspring wears / All the chief crowns' and accorded an elaborate ceremonial entry into the English capital, despite torrential downpours and storms that were nicknamed 'queen mother's weather' by a mistrustful London populace.[15] With growing numbers of pro-Hispanic courtiers and potential agents provocateurs at Whitehall, Leicester warned Charles of reports circulating in Paris in February 1639 about 'some very dangerous conspiracy' that involved the papacy and French, Spanish and Hungarian kings each raising and funding 6,000 soldiers to be landed in England. Although Leicester was unsure if this combined army of

'24,000 men should be employed for your Majesty or against you', he feared a new 'Catholic League' and recalled that, during France's recent religious wars in which both Henri III and Henri IV had been assassinated, 'the pretext [was] religion, but the true design was the subversion of the state, and the destruction of the kings thereof'. As Leicester feared, 'the contrivers of this practice are your mortal enemies; and I fear have their spies and agents in your court'.[16]

The option of raising foreign troops to enforce cooperation among his subjects was nevertheless already being considered by Charles's administration. Before Hamilton's arrival in Scotland the previous summer, the Ayrshire divine Robert Baillie could scarcely believe that Charles could even contemplate deploying Catholic mercenaries to crush the protests of Scots Protestants. Writing to his friend William Spang (minister to the Scottish staple port at Veere in the United Provinces), Baillie worried that the Scots were 'threatened with a bloody onset by the Navy on the east coast, by an Irish army on the west' and, from the south, a combined force of Scots and northern English Catholics mustered on Charles's behalf.[17] In Sussex, members of the Gage family of recusants suggested to Windebank in the spring of 1639 that, in return for 20,000 new recruits raised for Spanish service in Ireland, 10,000 veterans might be redeployed from the Habsburg army of Flanders to Scotland, jointly funded by papal subsidies and voluntary contributions from English Catholics. In Ulster, the Catholic marquess of Antrim, Randal MacDonnell, devised an alternative scheme that envisaged raising 10,000 Royalist troops to be transported to Scotland, primarily comprising Irish Catholic recruits and commanded by expatriate officers returning from Spanish service. Having probed Antrim about the plan's logistics, Charles's Lord Deputy in Dublin, Sir Thomas Wentworth, was nevertheless appalled by the idea of subcontracting responsibility for enforcing religious reform in Scotland to Catholic families such as the O'Neills, O'Haras, Macguires and MacDonnells – in short, 'as many Oe's and Mac's as would startle a whole Council Board'. Warning Windebank against arming 'so great a number of the native Irish, children of habituated rebels' with 'ourselves left naked', Wentworth suspected that Antrim 'shuffles the pack dextrously enough', seeking to raise soldiers at Charles's expense to attack Scotland's western isles 'to recover for himself those great seignories belonging unto his ancestors'.[18] That Charles could have envisaged deploying Catholic troops on the mainland of Protestant Britain, after decades of intense sectarian warfare across Continental Europe, confirmed a capacity to devise strategies that were deeply provocative and practically ineffectual in equal measure.

For their part, Charles's critics in Scotland were equally ready to explore opportunities to secure military manpower, financial backing and diplomatic support from abroad. The previous summer, Hamilton had observed that the Covenanters were 'sending for more arms and ammunition not only from Holland, but likewise from Hamburg, Bremen, Lübeck, Danzig and Sweden, that if one part should fail, they may be supplied from another'.[19] In terms of encouraging the Scots to defy directions from London, the sixteenth-century Dutch Revolt offered a model of a Protestant success and, in their subsequent war of words with the English government, the Covenanters made extensive use of Dutch publishing houses, including the evocatively named 'Richt Right Press' in Amsterdam. Further north, Sweden was another country that owed its sixteenth-century independence to an uprising against the foreign rule of Denmark-Norway, explaining why Swedish ministers instinctively distrusted the dynastic links between the Stuarts and the Danish royal house of Oldenburg. Indeed, the Covenanters' success in militarizing so quickly against Charles derived partly from imitating Swedish models of troop quotas, formation of a centralized committee of war and appeals to local landowners for regional support. Strategic command of the Covenanting army was entrusted to Field Marshal Alexander Leslie, who had amassed three decades' worth of distinguished service in the Swedish army before returning to Scotland on leave from his governorship of the Swedish-controlled town of Stralsund in Pomerania.

On both sides, paper bullets were fired to justify mobilization on the ground. In February 1639, the Scots Covenanters issued *An Information to all Good Christians in the Kingdom of England*, protesting that 'we had never the least intention to cast off our dutiful obedience unto his Majesty's most lawful authority', but warning 'of the dangerous plots set afoot, and entertained by the churchmen of greatest power in England, for introducing innovations in religion, by corrupting the doctrine, changing the discipline' and 'daily innovating the external worship of God'.[20] That same month, the king ordered a print-run of 10,000 copies of a *Proclamation and Declaration* to be read aloud in every

English parish. The *Proclamation* insisted that the Scottish rebellion had been fomented by 'factious spirits, and those traitorously affected' under 'pretences of religion, the common cloak for all disobedience'. Dismissing his adversaries as suffering from 'brainsick distempers', Charles was adamant that loyal subjects in his other kingdoms should 'not be infected with their false, wicked, specious, but most seditious informations'. For Charles, the crux of the matter was not religious reform, but royal authority: 'The question is not now, whether a service book [is] to be received or not, nor whether episcopal government shall be continued, or Presbyterian admitted, but whether we are their king or not.'[21]

In further retaliation to royal edicts, the Church of Scotland's General Assembly published a *Remonstrance* in March – in both English and Dutch – regretting that 'princes, who ought to be common parents' had, in this case, become partisan. Attributing blame for the disturbances to a discredited episcopate, the *Remonstrance* depicted Charles as the misguided victim of malevolent counsel and claimed dismay that royal credence attached to 'so many absurd and incredible false calumnies against a whole nation, his own native country and kingdom'. The *Remonstrance*'s authors beseeched English readers to demand that their own Parliament be summoned to investigate the 'prime agents' of this 'craft and treachery, in joining both kingdoms in a bloody war that, by weakening both, Rome may be built in the midst of us, and the Pope in end set over all'.[22] Meanwhile, Charles left London and arrived in York at the end of March. With no standing army, he was obliged to rely on troop levies, the mustering of trained bands in northern Ireland and the revival of a medieval precedent whereby members of the northern nobility were summoned to attend Charles in person at York, each with a troop of armed horsemen. Overall strategic command was entrusted to the Catholic peer Thomas Howard, earl of Arundel, who had no direct military experience, but three years earlier had witnessed at first-hand the desolation wrought by confessional warfare during his unsuccessful diplomatic mission to the imperial court at Vienna.

After a decade of domestic peace and 'Personal Rule', there was little enthusiasm for the king's expedition against his Scots subjects. Among the vocal critics of Charles's preparations was the staunch Puritan William Fiennes, Viscount Saye and Sele, who travelled to York, but declined to swear the new 'military oath' that had been framed as an alternative to the difficulties involved in levying the Jacobean oath of allegiance on Catholic officers. Although Saye acknowledged an obligation to undertake military service on the crown's behalf to protect England's borders from invasion, 'to go and kill a man in Scotland, he was not satisfied of the lawfulness thereof'.[23]

As both sides mobilized, a satirical account, penned in 1639 and printed three years later, purportedly offered a Scottish account of English preparations. 'D. L.' had sailed from Scotland to Dover, claiming to have infiltrated Royalist forces, and there he had observed the preparation of 'men and arms to send into Scotland'. Informed by Kentish locals that 'it was an ill example for other ages, and an old 1588', the author added that the English soldiers seemed to 'think it a won game'. Fuelling a conspiracy theory that Anglo-Scottish tensions had been instigated by Continental Catholics to sow dissension, 'D. L.' claimed that a fellow scout had visited Westminster Abbey, where, among the tombs of Charles's royal predecessors, could be heard the ghosts of 'King James and Queen Elizabeth conferring about the troubles in Scotland' which they knew had been 'plotted in Spain, ratified at Rome, and agitated by the Jesuits in England, to be acted in a tragic procession in Scotland'. Seeing current events through the lens of Cervantes's fictional characters, 'D. L.' described the rendezvous of Charles's northern army as a 'regiment of giants sent out of Yorkshire, under the command of Don Quixote'. Having 'carbonaded the Scots like so many capons', the misguided knight would then direct his page, Sancho Panza, to 'cut off their heads, and carry them to the prelates for a present', but 'D. L.' warned that 'the enterprise will prove worse, than the windmills'.[24]

The scale, speed and efficiency of the Covenanters' mobilization certainly surprised the English. While Edinburgh Castle and key fortresses in Aberdeen and Dumbarton quickly came under Covenanting control, low morale was palpable among English officers encamped by the Anglo-Scottish border in May 1639. Sir Edmund Verney, the Knight Marshal, admitted to his son Ralph, 'our army is but weak, our purse weaker, and if we fight with these forces . . . we shall have our throats cut'. In short, 'there was never so raw, so unskilful, and so unwilling an army brought to fight'. Verney was dismayed by the Covenanters' success in fomenting common sympathies among Charles's critics north and south of the border, observing how 'the poorest scab in Scotland will tell us to our faces that two parts of England are on their side, and truly they behave themselves as if all England were so'.[25] In early June, English troops retreated from a Scottish encampment near Kelso after realizing they were significantly outnumbered, prompting negotiations between Charles and leading Covenanters. Although Charles refused to ratify the outcome of the General Assembly in Glasgow the previous year, in the Pacification of Berwick on 19 June he agreed that the General Assembly could reconvene in Edinburgh, to be followed by a meeting of the Scottish Parliament, while both sides undertook to disarm.

The shocking prospect of fighting fellow subjects could also prompt flights of literary bdelygmia. Once hostilities had been averted, the notorious diatribe penned by Captain Thomas Windebank (son of Charles's Secretary of State) was prefaced by the soldier's acknowledgement that he was self-consciously striving for rhetorical effect to describe simmering Anglo-Scottish ethnic tensions. Writing from Berwick to his cousin Robert Read, Windebank admitted that 'we have had a most cold, wet and long time of living in the field', but the troops had

> ... kept ourselves warm with the hopes of rubbing, fubbing and scrubbing those scurvy, filthy, dirty, nasty, lousy, itchy, scabby, shitten, stinking, slovenly, snotty-nosed, logger-headed, foolish, insolent, proud, beggarly, impertinent, absurd, grout-headed, villainous, barbarous, bestial, false, lying, roguish, devilish, long-eared, short-haired, damnable, atheistical, puritanical crew of the Scotch Covenant.[26]

Moreover, even if Continental conspirators were not directly liable for the crisis of Stuart authority, the resulting instability only encouraged further plotting. In September 1639, Charles's ambassador in Madrid, Sir Arthur Hopton, learned that Philip IV's chief minister, the count-duke Olivares, and Irish Catholic envoys had discussed proposals to raise a multinational army of nearly 100,000 soldiers from Spain, Ireland, England and Scotland in order to rid Ireland of English rule. Envisaging the creation of an independent Irish republic to be governed by a 'Council of State', the plan was evidently supported by Olivares, although, as Hopton ventured to Windebank, 'methinks the plot hath not *capriccio* enough to be his'. Hopton was nevertheless concerned by the visibility of Irish visitors to Philip's court, as well as reports that Colonel John O'Neill – son and heir to the fugitive Hugh O'Neill – was addressed as 'Prince of Ulster' in diplomatic correspondence from Madrid.[27] In London, matters were not helped by Charles's refusal to discuss the Scottish crisis with anyone other than Hamilton and Archbishop Laud. Even after what became known as the first 'Bishops' War' had petered out, the Lord High Admiral, Algernon Percy, earl of Northumberland, complained that the king 'communicates nothing of the affairs in Scotland, so that we are as great strangers to all those proceedings as if we lived at Constantinople'.[28]

As Lord High Admiral, Northumberland's attention remained focused on Continental threats, especially after Philip dispatched the largest seaborne armada into the English Channel since 1588 to lift a Dutch blockade of Dunkirk in order to supply the Habsburg army of Flanders. After coming under Dutch attack, the fleet of over sixty Spanish vessels and over 20,000 soldiers was forced to shelter in a large anchorage, known as 'The Downs', between Dover and Deal. Seeking to extract diplomatic advantage from the fleet's vulnerability, Charles demanded a protection fee of £150,000 as well as Spanish support in securing the Palatinate's restitution. Although Windebank described the sum as 'little enough for the saving of Flanders', when he confirmed that £50,000 must be paid instantly, the Spanish Resident in London, Alonso de Cárdenas, 'fell to crossing himself, and told me I demanded impossibilities'.[29] At the same time, Charles approached French representatives to see if the prospect of sacrificing Philip's fleet to France's Dutch allies could yield attractive terms for England. As both sides prevaricated, the Venetian envoy in The Hague, Gieronimo Giustinian, confirmed that the Dutch States General scornfully saw the Spanish fleet's protracted shelter as 'an indication rather of imbecility than of magnanimous resolution'.[30] Disregarding English neutrality, Admiral Maarten Harpertszoon Tromp then attacked the sitting armada in October and sank forty Spanish vessels in English waters and in full view of Dover, Deal and Walmer Castles. England's impotence was humiliatingly confirmed and Charles's instinct for inept double-dealing was noted.

II

Although the first 'Bishops' War' had ended with a mutual disarmament, if Charles intended to resume hostilities against the Covenanters he needed to reconvene the English Parliament. Having thereby resolved to end eleven years of 'Personal Rule', 'the day before the decision was communicated to the Council, Charles was reported to have started practising his dance steps' for what would prove the final masque performed at the Caroline court and the only occasion on which Charles and Henrietta Maria acted together.[31] Written by William Davenant and performed in January 1640, *Salmacida Spolia* emphasized the superiority of conflict resolution achieved by peaceful persuasion rather than by force and included suggestive allusions to Charles's tribulations with the Covenanters. The masque's title referred to the Salmacian spring near the Greek colony of Halicarnassus which attracted local barbarian tribes who became civilized and peaceable after drinking from the spring. In a conscious reference to Scottish Kirk intransigence, Inigo Jones's set design included a proscenium arch with three cherubs representing 'intellectual light' consorting with 'doctrine' and 'discipline'. While Charles appeared as 'Philogenes' – a 'lover of the people' – a visibly pregnant Queen Henrietta Maria was cast as Amazonia, partly in homage to her mother, Marie de'Médicis, before whom the masque was performed and who had once been painted in Amazonian costume by Peter Paul Rubens. Despite the Stuart dynasty's Scottish roots, and Charles himself having been born in Dunfermline Palace, the artistic message was clear: the Scots were now a barbarian tribe.

Meanwhile, Anglo-French diplomatic relations had further soured after Richelieu's ministers had arrested Charles's Palatine nephew, Charles Louis, in October 1639, using the pretext of the prince's travelling without a passport to prevent him seizing unauthorized control of troops formerly commanded by the recently deceased Duke Bernard of Saxe-Weimar. While the Palatine Prince Rupert remained in Habsburg custody at Linz, his elder brother was now being detained by the French. Suspicions that Charles's Scottish opponents might be receiving covert assistance from members of Louis XIII's court were confirmed when English ministers intercepted the draft of a letter to the French king, signed by seven Covenanters, including Leslie and five nobles, appealing for assistance and asking Louis to grant an audience to an emissary, William Colville, who would confirm their specific requirements. Acclaiming Louis as 'the refuge and sanctuary of afflicted princes and states', the Covenanters wanted 'our actions and proceedings, [and] our intentions' to be 'engraven and written to the whole world, with the beams of the sun, as well as to your Majesty'.[32] Charles evidently felt likewise, indicating to Leicester that he intended to publish the Covenanters' letter 'so the world may be no longer abused by their artifices, and pretences of conscience: but that they may appear in their own natural colours, to be incendiaries'. In France, Leicester could offer little reassurance regarding the extent of the Covenanters' contact with Louis's court, admitting that Scottish visitors to Paris 'take me, I think, to be the Ambassador of the King of England only'. Ironically, the person serving 'as ambassador for Scotland, in their opinion' was Richelieu's Scottish Jesuit almoner, Thomas Chambers.[33]

As the first meeting of the English Parliament for more than a decade approached, Charles's ministers hoped for prompt and dutiful compliance, after subsidies amounting to around £180,000 had already been approved by the Irish Parliament in March 1640 under the efficient management of Wentworth, now earl of Strafford. Opening the Westminster Parliament on 13 April, the newly appointed Lord Keeper, John, Lord Finch, sought to excite patriotic support for Charles by reading aloud, in English and French, the Covenanters' appeal to Louis. Since the letter bore the superscription 'au Roi' – 'to the king' – Finch insisted that the Covenanters had already renounced Charles's sovereignty over them. As Finch warned, English national security was also threatened by the Scots' appeal to a foreign force, since 'they may, as in the former times, find out a postern gate'.[34] That same month, Charles cited the Covenanters' letter in another printed *Declaration*, objecting to their 'malignity to us, their natural sovereign, in that they had rather prostitute themselves to a foreign government, and that such as is different in religion, than yield conformity to ours'.[35] Fearing that similar appeals were being made to other powers, Sir Francis Cottington warned a parliamentary committee that the Covenanters could yet 'draw in the Goths and Vandals and other great armies; and when the Swedes are quiet, for aught I know, they may offer them the crown of England'.[36]

But publicizing the Covenanters' Francophile treachery did not generate the nationalistic backlash for which Charles had hoped. English MPs still insisted that redress of grievances, such as the disputed legality of Ship Money and controversial religious reforms, must be debated before any financial supply could be agreed. Scottish publications directed at English MPs in April 1640 included Robert Baillie's anonymous *Ladensium Autokatakrisis, the Canterburians Self-Conviction*

(1640), which warned that Archbishop Laud and his associates were seeking 'to set up the Latin Mass in place of the Bible' and to substitute 'for your Magna Carta and acts of Parliament, the laws of Castile'. Embroidering his Hispanic theme, Baillie predicted that, in the conspiracy's final realization, Englishmen would be dispatched on Philip IV's behalf 'to work in fetters in his mines of Peru, [and] others in chains to row all their days in his galleys in the Mediterranean'. Such would be the lurid fallout if elected parliamentary representatives, long accustomed to articulating anxieties and seeking redress for grievances, were censured as 'traitors and rebels' who 'ought to have lost their heads and lands for their presumption to defend their liberties'.[37]

As mutual mistrust prevailed, the crown and MPs quickly reached a stalemate, prompting Charles's dissolution of the 'Short Parliament' on 5 May, after only three weeks in session. The day after the dissolution, the Lord High Admiral, Northumberland, wrote to his brother-in-law, Leicester, in Paris, dismayed that the king was apparently intending to maintain an army of 30,000 soldiers with no idea 'by what means we are certain to get one shilling, towards the defraying this great expense'. Northumberland wondered 'what will the world judge of us abroad, to see us enter into such an action as this is, not knowing how to maintain it for one month?'[38] In London, the dissolution prompted riots and an attack on Lambeth Palace as incensed crowds demanded 'the death of many leading ministers, reputed enemies of the commonweal', directing particular ire towards Laud, Hamilton and Wentworth.[39] The opposition initially levelled towards individuals central to Charles's government was a harbinger of the seismic difficulties that the king had largely created for himself. Meanwhile, the Covenanters sought to dispel suspicions of collusion with France by pointing out that their letter to Louis had not only been composed before the Berwick truce, but also that simply petitioning for support from another country was not tantamount to treason. In what purported to be *A True Representation* of events in Scotland, the rhetorical question was posed as to whether, by appealing to 'Denmark, Holland, Sweden, Poland, or other nations for help, are we therefore inviting them all to sovereignty over us?'[40]

The answer was, presumably, negative, for immediately after the Short Parliament's dissolution, it was Charles – rather than his adversaries – who authorized his Privy Councillors to negotiate with Spanish representatives to request the financial assistance denied by Parliament. In Madrid,

Philip's ministers had been infuriated by England's inability to protect the Spanish fleet in the Downs the previous autumn, but were even more alarmed by prescient fears that the Stuart monarchy might yet suffer a military coup and be replaced by an English republic. The fragility of Charles's position and reputation was already evident to external commentators. Two ambassadors extraordinary were sent to join Cárdenas in London: Don Antonio Sancho Dávila de Toledo, marquis of Velada, arrived from Flanders in April 1640 with an entourage of over a hundred, and was followed by the Marquis Virgilio Malvezzi. As Philip confirmed to Malvezzi in June, it was imperative for Spanish interests 'that we do not lose that king for, should that country become a republic, I have no doubts that I will lose my province of Flanders'.[41] Olivares also warned the Spanish Council of State that a future English republic, allied to the Dutch, would form 'a union of neighbour republics from which can be feared an irresistible invasion of all Europe'.[42] Even before the Short Parliament met, Olivares had suggested that a new Anglo-Spanish alliance could effect 'a breach between England and Holland, totally restore our fortunes in relation to France, and simultaneously restore the King of England's fortunes in Scotland, without his having to call parliament or break with the French'.[43]

But Anglo-Spanish negotiations proved abortive. Despite the tempting offer of a loan of around £300,000 to fight the Scots, Charles's ministers would not agree an offensive-defensive alliance that entailed immediately declaring war on the Dutch once the Scots had been defeated. Spain's capacity to dictate terms was also undermined by the outbreak of serious rebellions in Portugal and Catalonia. Regarding the latter, Olivares had complained to a colleague in February 1640 that 'no king in the world has a province like Catalonia . . . we always have to look and see if a constitution says this or that'. Following the Catalans' seizure of Barcelona in June, Hopton doubted if order could be restored 'without discomposing the king's authority, which might have been prevented if the business had been undertaken in time' – in much the same way as Olivares had 'once told me in the matter of Scotland'.[44]

In Scotland, a parliament assembled without royal approval on 2 June 1640 and, in eight days, passed thirty-nine statutes comprising a constitutional revolution that mandated triennial parliaments, abolished the clerical estate in Parliament, guaranteed parliamentary debate of all grievances, enabled committees to sit between parliamentary sessions and imposed a national tax to finance the war. For the Royalist antiquarian Sir James Balfour of Denmiln and Kinnaird the session produced 'the real greatest change at one blow that ever happened to this church and state these 600 years bypast; for in effect it overturned not only the ancient state government, but fettered monarchy with chains'.[45] On 20 August, a hostile Scottish military force set foot on English soil for the first time in nearly a century, when Leslie's army of 18,000 crossed the River Tweed. Bypassing English fortifications at Berwick, the army defeated Charles's forces at Newburn a week later, before proceeding to occupy Newcastle and Durham. At Newcastle, the Covenanters seized an arsenal of weaponry and food supplies intended for the king's troops, secured control of the city's lucrative coal trade and ensured safe access for trade and supplies.

As had been the case a year earlier, English readiness to confront their invaders remained far from universal. Amid frantic efforts to mobilize Yorkshire's trained bands, the vice president of the Council of the North, Sir Edward Osborne, objected that, unless troop payments were assured, 'I am persuaded if Hannibal were at our gates, some had rather open them than keep him out'.[46] Remaining in York, Charles spent his time, when not in the field with his troops or consulting councillors, playing chess with John Paulet, marquess of Winchester. In one game, as courtiers observed Charles pondering how to play a bishop, 'Winchester blurted out, "See, Sir, how troublesome these bishops are in jest and earnestly!" The king replied nothing but looked very grim.'[47] In October 1640, an interim ceasefire was agreed by the Treaty of Ripon which left the Covenanter army in Newcastle and receiving a daily subsidy of £850 sterling, since its leaders insisted that any formal settlement would require approval and ratification by the English Parliament.

News of the English king's military difficulties had quickly reached Continental courts. In Paris, Louis affected indifference to Charles's negotiations with Habsburg Spain and postponed sending a permanent ambassador to London. As Leicester feared, 'they begin to talk here already, as if England were half-lost, and that the English nation dares not, or will not, look the Scots in the face'.[48] The Venetian envoy in Paris, Correr, reported that Richelieu had deemed it 'clear that the King of Great Britain, a prince of peculiar ideas' was unlikely to 'extend his vision outside his own kingdom'. Hence the cardinal was confident 'that the king of Spain, whether he sends three or even ten ambassadors, will not conclude any agreement with him'. Admitting that Richelieu 'always speaks of it with derision', Correr confirmed the French court's view that 'England today has become a nation useless to all the rest of the world and consequently of no consideration'.[49]

In Zeeland, the Royalist Conservator of the Scots staple port at Veere was suspended by the Covenanting leadership amid rumours that Charles was 'already deposed and the Queen of Bohemia put in his place'.[50] Meanwhile, after Christian IV of Denmark's intervention had been sought by a Covenanting envoy, two Danes, Korfits Ulfeldt and Gregers Krabbe, had arrived in London in September 1640, ostensibly to negotiate a compromise between Charles and his Covenanting adversaries, but carrying secret instructions to discuss conditions by which the king might cede all territorial claims to the Orkney and Shetland isles to Denmark in return for military assistance. Charles's attempt to pawn the islands for 50,000 gold guilders was rebuffed by Christian, who regarded the sum as excessive and, in any event, doubted the reality of royal control of the islands themselves.[51]

III

On 3 November 1640, Charles opened what would later become known as the 'Long Parliament' and requested English MPs' help in 'the chastising out of the rebels' from northern England. Two days later, the king hastily clarified that, while the Scots were indeed also 'my subjects', their designation as rebels was justified 'so long as they have an army that do invade us'.[52] With a delegation of Scots commissioners now in London, the new Venetian ambassador, Giovanni Giustinian, predicted that the Westminster Parliament's deliberations would not be rushed, observing 'the English conspiring tacitly at the sojourn of a hostile force in their country'. Following announcement of a state-sponsored day of fasting, 'ministers of the churches delivered from their pulpits seditious sermons', as Giustinian admitted bafflement at the enthusiasm with which English clerics were 'exalting to the skies the generosity of the Scots', who were acclaimed as 'angels sent from God to deliver the kingdom from idolatry and tyranny'.[53]

Having been frustrated by the Short Parliament's precipitate dissolution in April 1640, English MPs again insisted that redress of grievances must precede approval of any financial supply requested by a now desperate crown. Keen to secure goodwill, Charles approved publication of the extensive constitutional measures enacted by the Scottish Parliament that had met in June. Encouraged by the king's concessive mood, English MPs moved to declare Ship Money illegal, condemned new Church of England canons and persuaded Charles to approve legislation instituting triennial English parliaments in January 1641. Keen to end the Scottish crisis as quickly as possible, government ministers also effectively caved in during negotiations with the Covenanters' representatives. Having been chastened by a superior military force of his own Protestant subjects, Charles agreed to the Anglo-Scottish Treaty of London in August 1641, which ratified the General Assembly's abolition of episcopacy, allowed the Covenanting leadership to retain royal castles at Edinburgh and Dumbarton for defensive purposes, undertook that no Scot should be prosecuted for signing the Covenant or fomenting disturbances, and agreed that the English Parliament would pay a sum of £300,000 sterling to the Scots as 'recompense' for the wars.

Charles's startling capitulation to the Covenanters' demands – beyond anything anticipated by resistance to the new Prayer Book four years earlier – sent a clear message to critics of royal policy elsewhere in the British Isles. At the same time, English MPs started pursuing individuals suspected of supplying 'evil counsel' during the long period of Charles's 'Personal Rule': most conspicuously the earl of Strafford, who was arrested and imprisoned in November 1640 as articles of impeachment were framed, and Archbishop Laud, who was impeached for high treason a month later. In a circulating manuscript tract entitled 'De Cive', Thomas Hobbes defended royal sovereignty and stridently denied that kingship and tyranny were 'different conditions of government'; they were, rather, subjective reflections of 'men's feelings' about particular rulers.[54] But seeing how 'words that tended to advance the prerogative of kings began to be examined in Parliament', Hobbes hurriedly relocated to France in November and was soon followed by Charles's Secretary of State, Windebank.[55] The next month, Lord Keeper Finch – who, as Commons Speaker more than a decade earlier, had been forcibly restrained during the tumultuous parliamentary dissolution of 1629 – fled to The Hague to avoid framing Strafford's response to impeachment articles.[56]

In London, the trio of Spanish ambassadors was still hoping to assist the beleaguered English king by concluding a new Anglo-Spanish alliance, but became frustrated by Charles's increasingly fragile grip on power. As Cárdenas acknowledged to the Habsburg minister for war in Brussels, Miguel de Salamanca, by November 1640 the king's erstwhile Hispanophile advisers were 'so terrified of the rigour with which the Parliament proceeds' that they 'excuse themselves from seeing us, leaving us without anyone with whom to treat'. In February 1641, Cárdenas, Velada and Malvezzi wrote to Philip IV's nephew and governor of the Spanish Netherlands, Cardinal-Infante Ferdinand, complaining that 'the mind of the king cannot be measured because each day he changes'. Having first negotiated with the Scots at Berwick, Charles had then taken up arms against the Scots before appearing to 'agree with the Parliament, only to turn against them in a sort of fever for which there is no cure, that leaves him discredited with everyone'.[57] Anglo-Spanish relations were also threatened by the arrival in Plymouth of two envoys from Lisbon – Tristan de Mendoza Furtado and Antonio d'Almayda – who had been sent by the duke of Braganza, newly installed as King John IV of Portugal after Spanish rule had been overthrown during a brief rebellion the previous December. As Philip's ambassadors tried unsuccessfully to persuade Charles's court to refuse an audience with the Portuguese envoys, counter-arguments were adduced, pointing out that, in the previous century, 'Philip II received those of Ireland, which rebelled against Queen Elizabeth'. More recently, the duke of Bavaria's representative had been received 'to the disparagement of the declaration and interests' of those hoping to restore the Palatine territories and Electoral privileges from Bavarian, Catholic control to the family of Charles's sister, the Electress Elizabeth.[58]

Anglo-Spanish tensions were further stoked by announcement of a dynastic match between Charles's nine-year-old daughter, Princess Mary, and William, the sixteen-year-old only son of the Dutch chief magistrate, known as 'Stadtholder', Frederick Henry, and his wife Amalia of Solms-Braunfels. Whereas marriage between a Stuart princess and a prominent Protestant would once have prompted enthusiastic celebrations, when the nuptial arrangement was announced in December 1640, Dutch republican distrust was provoked on account of the Stadtholder's likely ambitions for his Orangist dynasty as a member of the House of Orange-Nassau. Meanwhile, Charles's English critics entertained suspicions (albeit groundless) that the marriage alliance must include secret provision for Dutch funds and military assistance to remove the Scots army from England, vitiating any need for an English parliament.

From Brussels, the Cardinal-Infante Ferdinand hastily tried to derail the union by instructing Cárdenas to offer Philip's only son, Balthasar Carlos, as a more prestigious consort for Charles's eldest daughter.[59] Equally unimpressed by his family's exclusion from the marriage discussions was Charles's Palatine nephew, Charles Louis, who – mindful that William's mother had once been merely one of his own mother's ladies-in-waiting – declared of the Orange-Nassau family that it was 'a great sauciness in them to demand the breeding of so great a king's daughter'.[60] Returning unexpectedly to England in March 1641, Charles Louis unsuccessfully tried to dictate terms to the Dutch envoys to ensure that any nuptial contract included a mutually binding commitment to promote restoration of his family's rights and territories with provision for arms, cannon, horses and, ideally, a Dutch frontier town as a base for military operations. Rebuffed by the Dutch ambassadors who denied any competence to act on the Palatine family's behalf, Charles Louis declined to attend the festivities organized for William and Mary's marriage at Whitehall Palace on 2 May 1641. Even after the wedding, there were residual suspicions – shared 'in the opinion of the world' – that the English might yet renege on the union. Hugo Grotius's brother-in-law Nicolaes van Reigersberch distrusted the punctiliousness with which the nine-year-old English 'princess had been kept intactam' and her family's insistence that she remain in London after the wedding. While Van Reigersberch vicariously reported the royal couple publicly lying down after the marriage ceremony, with the princess wearing 'a double shirt, sown fast below and above, between two sheets, over which two more were spread in which the prince was lying', the resident French secretary, Jean de Montereul, also reassured Louis XIII's court that 'the bed curtains remained open throughout' the encounter.[61]

Ten days after Princess Mary's marriage, Strafford was executed before a crowd of at least 100,000 spectators at Tower Hill. When the earl's treason trial had started in March, Giustinian had feared that the popular fury against Strafford was such that he would inevitably be 'sacrificed at the altar of the public satisfaction, though he is possibly innocent'.[62] Meticulously defending his conduct, Strafford had denied that any of the specific acts with which he was charged could constitute treason, repeatedly asking if 'a thousand misdemeanours will not make one felony, shall twenty-eight misdemeanours heighten it to treason?'[63] As the prosecution struggled to prove that Strafford – in his capacity as a state official who conspicuously retained the king's steadfast support – had indeed acted against the crown's interests, MPs resorted instead to a bill of attainder that invoked public safety and necessity as sufficient grounds for securing a conviction. After the bill had passed the Commons, Oliver St John, as prosecution counsel, addressed the Lords, invoking vindictive metaphors of pest control to justify Strafford's destruction. As St John explained, although clear rules attached to the hunting of hares and deer in the English countryside, foxes and wolves were routinely destroyed without allegations of 'cruelty or foul play', while 'the warrener sets traps for polecats and other vermin, for preservation of the warren'.[64]

With the political temperature rising – and peers' attendance in the Lords melting away – Strafford was eventually convicted, by twenty-six votes to nineteen, of crimes that included seeking 'to introduce an arbitrary and tyrannical government against law' in England and Ireland, having reassured Charles that 'he had an army in Ireland which he might employ to reduce this kingdom' (taken to mean England) and having 'been an incendiary of the wars between the two kingdoms of England and Scotland'.[65] As royal control of the press disintegrated, over a hundred pamphlets printed in 1641 focused on Strafford's trial while the Prague-born artist Wenceslaus Hollar produced a vivid engraving entitled *The True Manner of the Execution of Thomas, Earl of Strafford, 1641* which depicted the spectators gathered at Tower Hill, sitting on walls and rooftops as temporary stands collapsed from overcrowding. Later interpreted as prefiguring the execution of Charles himself in 1649, Strafford's execution inspired the Dutch playwright Jan Vos to imagine the character of 'Britain' motivating an army of vengeance from Continental Europe. In *Brittanje aan Euroope* (1650) ('Britain to Europe'), those soldiers would be exhorted to 'stretch Lord Strafford's skin / About his skull with tendons', 'use his shins to strike the fearful drum' and 'blow the hollow bones as you march on'.[66]

Although Charles never forgave himself for being pressurized into giving royal assent to the Act confirming Strafford's attainder, the Palatine prince Charles Louis praised his uncle's sacrifice of Strafford, venturing to his mother, the Electress Elizabeth, that Charles had thereby 'showed himself a good master, and a good Christian, and at last a good king'.[67] The Palatine prince's apparent receptiveness to parliamentary populism was nevertheless precisely why Giustinian suspected that, when Charles Louis unexpectedly arrived in England, although 'they dissimulated their first feelings and received their nephew with the usual displays of affection and esteem', the court presumably wished to 'get rid of him as soon as possible'. Given mounting political tensions, the king was unlikely to relish the presence 'of a prince so near to the succession, the son of a mother acclaimed by the people' and for whom Charles's subjects 'have always displayed the greatest affection'.[68] Seeking military support for his Palatine relations nevertheless provided Charles with a plausible pretext for ignoring MPs' calls to disband the English Army, once peace had been concluded with the Scots. In his *Manifestation, Concerning the Palatine Cause*, Charles reminded readers that both he and his father 'during these twenty years past' had attempted numerous negotiations that had 'been delayed or deluded . . . and our patience and piety thereby abused'.[69] Among MPs calling for a Continental offensive, the Puritan MP Sir Simonds D'Ewes believed that Palatine restitution remained 'the most sublime, and most difficult business of the Christian world abroad' while emphasizing that Charles Louis was 'not causally guilty of any part of that ocean of blood, that hath been since spilt in Germany'.[70]

When the king indicated he intended to travel to Edinburgh to oversee the Scottish Parliament's ratification of the Treaty of London, the Palatine prince's reversionary potential was reinforced as Giustinian reported in August 1641 that some MPs had 'suggested a demonstration to parliament by 20,000 working men, who should boldly protest by their shouts that the king must not go'. Other MPs 'even went so far as to suggest depriving him [Charles] of the crown and giving it to the prince or the Palatine, or else to set up a democratic government'.[71] To avert a dynastic coup in his absence, Charles insisted that his nephew accompany him to Edinburgh. There, the Scottish Parliament's commissioners patriotically acclaimed the Stuart dynasty as the most ancient monarchy in the world, and endorsed Charles's pro-Palatine manifesto to support 'his royal sister, and nephews, who are descended of that royal stem, which by the succession of a hundred and eight kings, hath swayed the sceptre over this kingdom'.[72]

Appointed as Scottish Chancellor shortly afterwards, John Campbell, earl of Loudoun, the leading Covenanter, reflected that although God had recently suffered the English and Scots 'armies to meet in the field one against the other', they were now 'miraculously united' and joined in such an 'honourable enterprise' on Charles Louis's behalf.[73] While the Scottish Parliament undertook to provide 10,000 infantry troops for Palatine service, news of Prince Rupert's release from Habsburg detention in Linz led Charles Louis to congratulate the English envoy, Sir Thomas Roe, insisting that 'your obtaining it is a masterpiece, and makes me conceive the more hope' that other Palatine demands would be met.[74]

Having remained in London during the king's Scottish sojourn, Giustinian recognized the rashness of any 'prediction under so inconstant a sky, where their principles and resolutions are changed every day'. The Venetian ambassador nevertheless remained sceptical that Charles's Palatine nephew would now 'proceed to Germany with a powerful army', not least because 'he lacks money, not to speak of strength, good counsel and ability'.[75] Yet in the next four years, it would prove to be Charles I who conspicuously lacked money, strength, good counsel and strategic ability and suffered successive defeats by 'a powerful army' – which, most ominously of all, was composed of his own British subjects.

11

Earthquakes of State, 1641–1644

In a tract entitled *Den Britannischen Blixem* (1643) ('The British Lightning'), the Dutch theologian Gisbertus Voetius recalled how an earthquake that had struck the northern regions of Africa in 1640 had been followed by a 'revolt of Catalonia, the falling-off of Portugal, the stirs in Scotland; the rebellion of the Irish' and 'those civil (uncivil) wars, great alterations, [and] unexpected tumults in England'.[1] At Philip IV's court in Madrid, the anonymous author of *El Nicandro o Defensa del Conde-Duque de Olivares* (1643) sought to defend Gaspar de Guzmán, count-duke of Olivares – accused of mismanaging Spain's economy and mishandling disturbances in Catalonia and Portugal – by observing the same combustible combinations in which, across the world, 'every nation is turned upside down'. With 'England, Ireland and Scotland aflame with civil war', disturbances were disrupting Constantinople, China, Ethiopia and India, while other regions were simultaneously suffering 'earthquakes, plague and famine'.[2] Across the globe, unusual climatic adversity was experienced during the 1640s as northern Europe endured markedly colder temperatures, harvest failures and rising prices. In England, a meteorological analogy was invoked by one writer, 'H. G.', who ventured that civil disorders usually 'fall like hailstones, one no sooner drops, but a whole storm do follow', as he watched 'Germany leading this dance of death', which was soon joined by multiple conflicts and rebellions across Europe.[3] With around 1.8 million military personnel killed during the Thirty Years War, the total number of war-related deaths in the Holy Roman Empire may eventually have reached 5 million, representing a fifth of the region's pre-war population.[4]

As the 'Englishman' in Voetius's *British Lightning* lamented to his Dutch friend, by 1643 it was 'a civil war that scourges us' in the British

Isles: the 'most miserable' form of war that pitted 'the one kingdom against the other, the father against the son, one citizen against the other'.[5] During the 1640s, men took up arms either for or against Charles I's authority in nearly every part of the British Isles, leading to around 200,000 military and civilian deaths in a greater loss of life – as a proportion of the population – than both twentieth-century world wars combined. With alliterative inventiveness, one pamphleteer writing in October 1642 bemoaned that 'each hour is a herald of homicides, each day a messenger of mischiefs, each week a diurnal of dangers, each month a motto of misery' with 'no language now amongst us but war'.[6] In February 1643, Sir Benjamin Rudyerd urged his fellow MPs to agree an interim cessation of hostilities, warning that, unlike Germany, England was not a 'great, large, vast continent'. He feared that, instead, the country would be compelled 'to fight as in a cockpit . . . surrounded with the sea', and that 'the whole kingdom will suddenly be but one flame'.[7]

Fought brutally and at close range across England, Scotland and Ireland, the civil wars bred bitterness and confusion in equal measure. Recalling his own Royalist service during the wars, the diplomat Richard Bulstrode later admitted the inevitably partial and partisan character of all eyewitness accounts. With 'such a hurry and smoke' on the battlefield, 'no man [can] give a clear account of particular passages', given that 'the next man can hardly make a true relation of the actions of him that is next to him'.[8] On both sides, military mobilization was also justified defensively, as in so many civil wars, as the means of last resort by which a satisfactory peace settlement could be secured. Even as late as September 1645, the Parliamentarian general Sir Thomas Fairfax was still protesting to Charles's German nephew Prince Rupert that 'the crown of England is and will be where it ought to be, we fight to maintain it there'. As Fairfax explained, the heavy defeat recently suffered by Royalist forces at the Battle of Naseby had been inflicted by those seeking to promote both the king's 'safety, and his people's interest', after Charles had been 'misled by evil counsellors or through a seduced heart, hath left his Parliament and his people'.[9]

Aside from a minority of Catholics seeking Ireland's secession from the Stuart monarch, neither Charles nor his adversaries pledged allegiance to an alternative power outside the British Isles. The civil wars' participants were, nevertheless, haunted by continual fears of foreign instigation, interference and involvement, whether by seeing events as part of an international popish plot to extirpate Protestantism or by appealing to other states for money, munitions and men. While the devastation of central Europe by rival armies of outsiders pointed to the likelihood of external intervention, in terms of the Stuarts' dynastic connections the foreign powers that initially seemed most likely to support the English king against his own subjects included Charles I's brother-in-law, Louis XIII of France, his uncle, Christian IV of Denmark and, after 1641, his daughter's new father-in-law, the Dutch Stadtholder, Frederick Henry. In practice, however, the limited amount of foreign support secured by Royalist forces paled in comparison with exaggerated rumours of imminent invasion, fuelled by a burgeoning print culture. In a fictional dialogue published in 1643 by the Welsh Royalist James Howell, the character 'Patricius' objected that 'palpable and horrid lies were daily printed', supplying a 'superfetation of lies, which continues to this day'. Printed reports had warned that 'the King of Denmark was coming over from the Sound', 'the King of France had a huge army about Calais designed for England', there was 'an army of Irish rebels coming over' and 'subterranean invisible troops mustered underground in Wales, and thousands of Papists armed in Lancashire'.[10]

I

In February 1641, the English ambassador in Madrid, Sir Arthur Hopton, had warned Secretary of State Sir Henry Vane that 'at this instant, among the Irish friars, there is nothing as much spoken of as of a rebellion in Ireland'.[11] That autumn, members of the Old English and Gaelic Irish communities combined to launch a pre-emptive Catholic attack on Protestant settlers in Ulster that resulted in the deaths of around 3,000 individuals, although sensationalist newsletter reports in England alleged likely Protestant death tolls closer to 20,000. News of the Irish Rebellion that started on 23 October 1641 reached Charles in Edinburgh, where he was temporarily resident while overseeing ratification of the Anglo-Scottish peace agreed in the Treaty of London. In the king's absence, MPs at Westminster coordinated an emergency disaster response, approving defensive measures for the capital and key ports, requesting an urgent loan of £50,000 from the City of London and imposing restrictions on Catholics across England, including Queen Henrietta Maria's royal household.

As news of the Irish Rebellion coincided with annual commemorations of the Gunpowder Plot's discovery on 5 November, it was quickly assimilated within a providentialist framework of serial popish plotting. Preaching before the House of Commons at Westminster on 5 November 1641, a Somerset Presbyterian named Cornelius Burges fitted events in Ireland into an eschatological chronology that included the Spanish Armada of 1588, Tyrone's Rebellion and the Gunpowder Plot. Burges compared the crudeness of Fawkes's failed conspiracy with the sophistication of recent Catholic plots, likening all popish intrigues to vomit produced by 'foul stomachs', but warning that 'the best that comes up into the basin, is but filthy stuff, but that which is behind, and comes last, is far more loathsome and bitter'.[12]

In Edinburgh, Charles informed the Scottish Parliament of the Irish Rebellion's outbreak on 28 October, confident that the revolt could be contained. External support for the rebellious Catholics was unlikely to be offered by Charles's ally, France, while Spain currently had 'so much to do' fighting the French, Dutch and Portuguese and suppressing internal revolts in Catalonia, Aragon and Castile itself. If the Irish rebels were to seek assistance from English Catholics, Charles admitted that this would render 'the business of a greater consequence, and of a more transcendent nature'.[13] The Irish Rebellion's prompt suppression was nevertheless frustrated by mutual Anglo-Scottish suspicions, since the Scots regarded Irish governance as an English responsibility and did not wish to incur the costs of deploying an expeditionary force. At Westminster, MPs seeking redress from the crown were not only instinctively loath to raise an army under royal control, but were also concerned that the Scots might exploit the rising to assert rights of future influence over Irish affairs and, potentially, even claim disputed plantation territories in Ulster as payment for any intervention.

More alarmingly, fears that the Stuart court might itself be involved in this latest manifestation of an international popish conspiracy were seemingly confirmed at Newry on 4 November when one of the Rebellion's leaders, Sir Phelim O'Neill, produced a 'commission', purportedly from Charles, that authorized Irish Catholics to take up arms against their Protestant neighbours. Although the 'commission' was forged, the king's belated denial of royal involvement in the rising failed to convince sceptical minds. Amid a swirl of conspiracy theories, Irish Catholics had also been worried by the English Parliament's recent refusal to permit the Spanish and French recruitment of Irish levies of soldiers disbanded from the late earl of Strafford's forces. Although Charles's German nephew Charles Louis was in Edinburgh with his uncle, false rumours were circulating that militantly Protestant interests had already engineered a pro-Palatine dynastic coup that augured ill for Irish Catholics in the longer term. In County Meath, one landowner, Thomas Ashe, reported claims that 'the king was deposed, the Palsgrave [Palatine prince] crowned, and that the king had given the Catholics in Ireland direction to rebel, least they should assist the Puritans in England'.[14]

As the rising's violence extended throughout Ireland, an influx of Protestant refugees to England brought gruesome tales of murder, sectarian savagery and forced evictions, feeding an expanding print market that detailed disturbing, lurid and often pornographic tales of Catholic atrocity and massacre. The undeniable horror of events in Ireland was quickly overlaid with monstrous fantasy. In March 1642, the Protestant Dean Henry Jones of Kilmore and several colleagues supplied the English Parliament with witness statements from deponents, recounting innumerable atrocities committed by Catholic rebels, described as 'inhumane blood-sucking tigers'. Published as *A Remonstrance of Diverse Remarkable Passages*, Jones's anthology included accounts of Protestant men, women and children beaten, stripped and perishing, while others had been hacked to death or forcibly drowned. One woman was reported to have been 'delivered of a child while she was hanging' while Catholic crowds cheered 'dogs tearing children out of the womb' and watched a child 'boiled alive in a cauldron'. The Protestant ministers feared 'a general extirpation, even to the last and least drop of English blood', predicting that 'what the sword cannot, for the present, effect, an Inquisition, like that of Spain, for finding out the Jewish and Moorish blood, shall in time thoroughly accomplish'.[15] Although English MPs ordered the immediate publication of Jones's *Remonstrance*, the extent to which misinformation thrived in such a frenzied atmosphere was confirmed by a group of Irish Protestant gentry, now in England, who petitioned Parliament 'against the common abuse of publishing false and feigned news from Ireland', insisting that 'no news be printed' unless its veracity had been officially confirmed.[16] In November 1641, the Commons had ordered a London printer, John Greensmith, to be imprisoned indefinitely after he admitted paying two Cambridge undergraduates to pen fictitious tales of Irish atrocities, including *Bloody*

Battle, or the Rebels' Overthrow and the Protestants' Victory (1641) and *Happiest News from Ireland* (1641).[17]

In The Hague, the Electress Elizabeth suspected that the Irish Rebellion had been instigated by pro-Habsburg interests to hinder any English military intervention on the Continent. Writing of 'the business in Ireland' to Sir Thomas Roe – who was attending another Imperial Diet in Regensburg trying to promote Palatine interests – Elizabeth confirmed, 'I verily believe that it proceeds from Vienna and Madrid to hinder my brother's help to us'.[18] In his tract *British Lightning*, Voetius had warned that, notwithstanding all the wars currently convulsing Continental Europe, none was 'more fearful and dangerous to us, than the rebellion of Ireland'. Fomented by the Dutch Republic's Catholic enemies, the rising had been 'seconded by our deadly enemy, the King of Spain, plotted by the Jesuits, [and] executed by the barbarous Irish, who are already grown so proficient in the school of those murdering Jesuits'.[19]

Meanwhile, in a rival confessional context, events in Ireland quickly featured as *Noues Extraordinaries* ('Extraordinary News') in a Catalan pamphlet published in Barcelona in mid-November 1641, which bore an image of a feather quill to confirm that the report came 'from our own correspondent'. Like the Catalans, the Portuguese were also engaged in a struggle to overthrow Castilian authority and the *Gazeta do mes de Junho de 1642*, summarizing international events in June 1642, cited materials from Jones's *Remonstrance* to assert a meritorious Counter-Reformation success. In 'claiming that over a 100,000 heretics had already been killed', the Lisbon gazette 'accepted English Protestant propaganda as it made the success even more glorious to Catholic eyes'.[20] A later Portuguese tract pursued parallels between events in Ireland and the expulsion of the Moriscos (descendants of forcibly converted Muslims) from Spain between 1609 and 1614, blaming Philip III for expelling – rather than exterminating – the Moriscos who 'now infest many Catholic kingdoms as pirates'. Accordingly, the author reasoned, 'it would be a mistake to expel the heretics from Ireland alive'.[21]

II

In a determined initiative to repair relations between Charles and his English critics, the Lord Mayor of London, Sir Richard Gurney, invested

£4,000 in a lavish ceremony to celebrate the king's return from Scotland and formal entry into London on 25 November 1641. An effusive printed account of events related how the king and his Palatine nephew Charles Louis were greeted at Moorgate by Henrietta Maria and Prince Charles and welcomed into the City by spectators of 'all degrees, sexes, ages and sizes' as London's 'banks, hedges, highways, streets, stalls and windows were all embroidered with millions of people, of all sorts and fashions'.[22] In a posthumous biographical account of Charles, the republican John Milton recalled how, on this occasion, Charles had sedulously acknowledged his subjects' welcome by repeatedly removing his hat, cynically suspecting this to be a new 'favour which till then neither himself or his father before him had never bestowed upon the vulgar'.[23]

Three days before the festive royal return to London, however, the House of Commons had narrowly approved a 'Grand Remonstrance' demanding parliamentary approval of the king's appointment of his domestic and foreign ministers, increased religious 'discipline' and a significant reduction in episcopal power. After the Remonstrance's unauthorized publication, Charles formally rejected its demands on 23 December. Moves were made to prevent bishops from sitting in the House of Lords before twelve bishops were charged with high treason and imprisoned for challenging the legitimacy of parliamentary business conducted in their absence. Writing from London in late December, a naval officer, Sir Robert Slingsby, admitted to Admiral Sir John Pennington that 'I cannot say we have had a merry Christmas, but the maddest one that ever I saw'. Having commanded a ship supplying English forces in Edinburgh during the Second Bishops' War, Slingsby feared the escalation of tensions: 'both factions talk very big, and it is a wonder there is no more blood yet spilt, seeing how earnest both sides are'. Unless Charles acquiesced in MPs' demands, Slingsby warned that 'a sudden civil war must ensue, which every day we see approaches nearer'.[24] While an angry crowd of around 200 gathered on New Year's Eve in front of Whitehall Palace, the new French ambassador, Jacques d'Éstampes, marquis of La Ferté-Imbault, ventured that, were he in any other nation but England, the repeated clashes between crown and Parliament would have seen London 'on fire and in bloodshed within twenty-four hours'.[25]

The most dramatic confrontation between Charles and his Parliamentarian critics occurred on 4 January 1642, when the king tried to arrest five MPs and one peer, accusing them of treason in encouraging a foreign power (Scotland) to invade England and in raising tumults against royal authority. Having entered the Commons with an entourage that included his German nephew Charles Louis the king was surprised to find 'all the birds flown'.[26] (Today, the annual theatre of state that occurs when 'Black Rod' – as the senior official in the House of Lords – formally seeks permission from MPs for the sovereign to enter the Commons chamber at the start of each new parliamentary session is there to recall the controversy provoked by Charles's uninvited entrance.) Foreign meddling was confirmed by La Ferté-Imbault's later admission that he had instructed a French contact to warn 'my friends' in the Commons, only fifteen minutes before the king's arrival.[27] Since MPs required royal authority to adjourn and meet elsewhere, members of the Commons reconstituted themselves as a parliamentary committee and relocated to the City of London where Charles suffered a second humiliation when the City's Common Council refused to surrender the five MPs. In a *Declaration* issued from the Guildhall, MPs confirmed their anger at the manner of the king's intrusion into the Commons 'with a great multitude of men, armed in warlike manner, with halberds, swords and pistols . . . to the great terror and disturbance of the Members'. Although the arrest of John Hampden, Sir Arthur Haselrig, Denzil Holles, John Pym and William Strode had been demanded by royal proclamation, MPs warned that anyone adhering to the king's request would be 'guilty of the breach of the liberties of the subject, and of the privilege of Parliament, and a public enemy to the Commonwealth'.[28]

On 7 January, a City tailor recounted to the Northamptonshire peer Edward, Lord Montagu, how 'the king had the worst day in London yesterday that ever he had, the people crying "privilege of parliament"' in their thousands as shopkeepers closed stores and stood 'at their doors, with swords and halberds'.[29] Any show of popular affection that had greeted Charles on his return from Scotland had entirely evaporated. With the king now fearing for his own safety, the royal family fled to Hampton Court on 10 January, while the following day, over 2,000 members of the City's trained bands accompanied MPs on a triumphal return to Westminster, where MPs 'reacted, like any burgled householder, by ordering a new lock for their door'.[30] But when MPs also sought to prevent ordnance and weaponry stored in the Tower of London being claimed by the king, the Lieutenant of the Tower, Sir John

Byron, indicated that he only obeyed royal orders, 'whereat the mustard got into the noses of the saintly Parliamentarians', as described by Hugh Bourke, Franciscan Vicar General of the Irish regiments in Flanders. Writing from Brussels to Luke Wadding, the Jesuit guardian of St Isidore's College in Rome, Bourke ventured that 'as to Charles, the general opinion is that he will never again be King unless he draws the sword for it, and they say that he is not so much pacific as cowardly'.[31]

In the event, Charles would not return to London again until January 1649, less than a fortnight before his execution. In the intervening seven years, London became a byword for Parliamentarian resistance. As the self-styled 'Mercurius Civicus' claimed in 1643, 'in all England, there is but one rebel, and that is London'. Regretting his former 'credulity to be deceived, and fooled by the empty name of a Parliament', the author admired Charles's restraint in not emulating his wife's grandfather, Henri III of France – 'though well he might', having been 'fouly provoked in like manner'. When Henri had been forced by Catholic Leaguers to flee Paris on the 'Day of the Barricades' in May 1588, 'Mercurius Civicus' recalled how the French king had stopped at the Palais de Chaillot to curse the 'disloyal and ungrateful city' that he had 'always honoured with my continual abode'.[32]

Leaving behind her two youngest children, Prince Henry and Princess Elizabeth, Henrietta Maria sailed from Dover in February 1642, using the pretext of escorting Princess Mary to The Hague as a means of seeking Continental support and supplies for her husband. Meanwhile, Charles avoided a threatened custody battle with MPs over his eldest son, the Prince of Wales, admitting to his adviser Edward Hyde that 'now I have gotten Charles, I care not what answer' was made regarding MPs' further demands.[33] In March, however, Parliament had issued a Militia Ordinance, assuming control of the armed forces, revoking royal authority over lord lieutenants and county trained bands, and obliging the king to resort to medieval precedent by issuing Commissions for Array to raise troops that could be deployed anywhere in England.

After Charles, his two older sons and a reduced royal court relocated to York, further humiliation ensued when the king travelled to Hull in April, intending to secure the city's large arsenal of weaponry and strategic port access to the Continent. While extending a civil welcome to the Prince Palatine, Charles Louis, and the king's eight-year-old son, the duke of York, the newly appointed Governor of the city's garrison, Sir

John Hotham, refused entry to Charles on the grounds that he had been directed only to admit individuals approved by MPs at Westminster. In June, the English Parliament sent 'Nineteen Propositions' to Charles's court at York, including demands for parliamentary approval of all state officers, confirmation of the Triennial Act passed the previous year to mandate Parliament's summoning at least every three years, parliamentary control of the nation's ordnance and tighter controls on the conditions permitting troop deployment. Reporting events from London, the horrified Venetian ambassador Giovanni Giustinian warned that Parliament's proposals would curtail the English monarchy's power so severely as to 'lay the foundations of a government resembling that of the States of Holland'.[34]

In an eloquent defence of monarchical moderation, Charles's *Answer to the Nineteen Propositions* rejected MPs' demands as a 'new utopia of religion and government' that would only see England's 'splendid and excellently distinguished form of government end in a dark equal chaos of confusion'. By forbidding any army to be raised except 'in case of actual rebellion or invasion', the king pointed out that numerous cherished English victories abroad could never have been won and 'nor could our blessed predecessor, Queen Elizabeth, have so defended herself in 1588'.[35] As printed declarations and proclamations were serially exchanged between Charles's court in York and the Westminster Parliament, the MP for Berkshire, Henry Marten, feared that, soon, 'we should be as famous for declarations as a certain king for sending ambassadors'.[36] Observing a bewildered English populace deluged by printed appeals and counter-appeals, Giustinian pitied 'these unhappy people attacked by the frequent appearance of these numerous documents, so mutually contradictory'.[37] The lawyer and MP for Marlow, Bulstrode Whitelocke, identified a clear chain of causation between the proliferation of printed attacks and the outbreak of musket fire, deeming it 'strange to note how we have insensibly slid into this beginning of a civil war, by one unexpected accident after another, as waves of the sea which have brought us this far'. Almost as if sleepwalking, 'from paper combats, by declarations, remonstrance, protestations, votes, messages, answers and replies, we are now come to the question of raising forces and naming a general and officers of the army'.[38]

When one of Charles's commanders travelled from York and was refused entry to Manchester by its citizens in early July, a two-day exchange of musket fire broke out. Describing the stand-off, a London newsletter defined the Manchester skirmish as 'the beginning of civil war, being the first stroke that hath been struck, and the first bullet that hath been shot, but God knows when the ending will be'. Despite pleading for hostilities to be averted, the author feared that 'many thousands' would lose their lives before peace returned to England, while many a 'child will be left fatherless, and many a poor wife husbandless'.[39] In London, MPs approved recruitment of a Parliamentarian army of 10,000 volunteers, largely from London musters, and appointed Robert Devereux, earl of Essex, as its general. On 22 August 1642, Charles raised the royal standard at Nottingham Castle and insisted that, unless his opponents laid down their arms, they would be declared rebels. But, as the poet and historian Thomas May recalled five years later, when Essex had left London with Parliament's forces in September to confront the king, he had appeared 'as much an Englishman, and as true a patriot, as if he had gone against a foreign enemy'.[40]

III

Domestic divisions distracted attention from Ireland. In May 1642, a Catholic league, known as the 'Confederation of Kilkenny', had been established with the aim of converting the Rebellion's tactical successes into permanent political and religious gains. The Confederation's executive power was vested in a Supreme Council, comprising twenty-four members from the four Irish provinces, with other members elected by regular General Assemblies. The Confederation's motto – *Pro Deo, Rege et Patria: Hiberni Unanimes* ('Irish united for God, king and country') – emphasized a natural correlation between adhering to the Catholic faith and remaining loyal to the Stuart monarchy. Promulgated in Ireland in variant forms, the Confederate oath committed its swearers to 'bear true faith and allegiance to my sovereign lord Charles, by the grace of God, king of Great Britain, France and Ireland', before undertaking to secure the free exercise of religion for Catholics and obeying decrees issued by the Confederation's Supreme Council.[41] Shifting the emphasis of priorities, the version of the Confederate oath published in French, Spanish and Latin presented the Irish Rebellion as a war of religion with oath-takers confirming that they would 'seek, in the first instance, freedom of conscience and the public exercise of our religion'.[42] When news of the Rebellion had reached the French court the previous November, the English ambassador, Sir Richard Browne, had heard numerous endorsements of Irish aspirations on the streets of Paris. While the Rebellion's adherents in France seemed 'like so many hydras that he could do little to suppress them', Browne hastily reassured Charles's Secretary of State, Vane, that he sought only 'to converse freely but not to cabalize with them'.[43]

The Irish Confederates self-consciously sought to emulate the Scottish Covenanters' success in extracting significant concessions from Charles: as one insurgent had confirmed, 'the Scots have taught us our ABC'.[44] Published in Madrid, the *Manifiesto de Católicos Confederados de Irlanda* (1642) attested that the Confederates sought 'the same conditions and articles' as 'his Majesty's Scottish subjects' had secured by 'their recent invasion of England'.[45] In another Madrid publication entitled *Relacion Verdadera de la Insigne Vitoria* (1642), the Irish Rebellion was compared to the successful thirteenth-century revolt known as the Sicilian Vespers.[46] Despite extolling the virtues of Irish resistance, the pamphlet's anonymous author conveniently failed to mention the recent Catalan Revolt where, rather than leading the insurgency, the Irish commander John O'Neill, earl of Tyrone, had (ironically) been killed at the Battle of Montjuïc in January 1641 in a failed attempt by the Spanish army to recapture Barcelona from Catalan rebels. From Brussels, Bourke reported that 'all the gazettes of Italy, France and Holland are full of what is being mooted in the consistories for the succour of the Catholics of Ireland'. Accordingly, immediate action was required, urging 'for the love of God, let not the Court of Rome miss this greatest opportunity that has presented itself in Europe from time immemorial'. As Charles's domestic troubles multiplied, Bourke could scarcely contain his optimistic excitement, reassuring Wadding that 'with this civil war afoot our affairs will go with the wind in the poop'. And if the idea of Catholic rebels emulating Calvinist heretics seemed ironic, Bourke reassured Wadding that the Irish struggle remained 'superior to the Scots, who by insurrection have won from the king absolute liberty of conscience, such as their conscience is'.[47]

When the Confederation of Kilkenny instructed several envoys to undertake Continental diplomatic missions with dignity and 'not to dishonour the nation . . . by way of craving or begging', this denoted the first and only time – before the creation of the Irish Free State in 1922 – that Catholic Ireland pursued a foreign policy entirely independent of England. When Confederate troops received fresh artillery and mortar supplies in mid-1643, Spanish ensigns were hung in Wexford amid popular shouts of 'God bless the king of Spain: For but for him, we should all be slain!'[48] Hopes that Charles might, however, be induced to grant full religious toleration remained optimistic. When Bourke had visited Henrietta Maria in The Hague in mid-1642, the queen had confirmed her husband's firm attachment to the Church of England and his insistence that the Irish Catholics were unlawful rebels, advising Bourke that Confederate envoys should humbly petition the king for greater religious liberties, but not the 'entire and public restoration of the Catholic religion'. Bourke retorted that 'it seemed now somewhat late in the day to counsel Catholics to content themselves with secret' freedom to worship, since they had already 'tasted the sweetness of public liberty of conscience'. Given that Charles was likely to 'hazard the loss of a realm', Bourke privately believed that, just as Henrietta Maria's father, Henri IV of France, had 'said that the kingdom of France was well worth a Mass, so the kingdom of Ireland was worth the concession of a franchise so legitimate and well founded'.[49] Meanwhile, any discussions with Catholic Royalists played disastrously with the king's Protestant critics who feared eventual popish subversion by a monarch in thrall to Rome.

In England, Henrietta Maria's sojourn at The Hague was regarded with apprehension by Charles's critics. From intercepted correspondence between the king in York and his wife, Parliamentarian pamphleteers alleged wildly exaggerated amounts of Continental support for the Royalist cause, claiming that 'papists in Holland and Friesland had lent the king £200,000', while ships left Dutch ports bound for England and 'laden with powder, muskets and other ammunition'.[50] As mobilization proceeded apace, the Prince Palatine, Charles Louis, left London and returned to The Hague in August 1642, from where he sent a printed manifesto to the Westminster Parliament confirming that 'contrary affections and intents' were now dividing his own family. That same month, his younger brothers, Princes Rupert and Maurice, had sailed across the North Sea in the reverse direction to England, where Rupert took command of the Royalist cavalry and Maurice became a colonel and sat on the Royalist Council of War. Fearing that his younger brothers' actions were only likely 'to increase the division between the king and parliament', Charles Louis reassured MPs that his mother, the Electress Elizabeth, disapproved of their actions.[51] With Charles I likely to approach Spain or the Holy Roman Empire for financial and military assistance, Elizabeth and her eldest son evidently regarded Palatine interests as better served by the English Parliament and, indeed, MPs acceded to Charles Louis's entreaty by maintaining the king's monthly subsidies to his family.

By contrast, Prince Rupert was described by Giustinian as 'brimful of zeal for his uncle's service' when he arrived in England and fought in the first major battle of the civil wars in England at Edgehill in Warwickshire in October 1642.[52] Although the battle's outcome was inconclusive, a 'well-wisher' to Charles was alarmed by the speed with which Rupert 'won the hearts of so many thousand soldiers of fortune', notwithstanding 'his German manner of plundering'. Counselling caution, the anonymous author warned Charles that his critics could potentially 'prefer another to the crown, who is no stranger in blood, and much more deserving by the sword, this whole war being managed by his skill, labour and industry'.[53] Indeed, Rupert's cavalry successes soon epitomized the imported, swaggering arrogance of Spanish 'Caballeros' after whom Charles's Royalist supporters incurred the derogatory nickname of 'Cavaliers'. For his part, Rupert wrote to the Parliamentarian general, Essex – who had previously fought against Habsburg forces in attempts to reclaim Palatine territories for his family – denying that it should seem 'strange that a foreigner should take footing upon your English shore with intention to draw the sword'. Rather, Rupert's actions conformed to the 'laws of God and man, in the defence of true religion, a king's prerogative, and uncle's right'.[54] Opposition to the Palatine prince's 'foreignness' nevertheless persisted as Rupert was regularly accused of contravening domestic codes of military conduct and of 'injurious innovation' in levying fines on rebellious towns. While Charles elevated his German nephew to the English peerage in 1644, creating him earl of Holderness and duke of Cumberland, and later appointed him as Captain General of all Royalist forces in England and Wales, Parliamentarian pamphleteers savaged Rupert as 'Prince Robber, duke of Plunderland'.

Seeking to construct an alternative axis of international support, the English Parliament dispatched its own envoy, Walter Strickland, to The

Hague in September 1642, hoping that the States General would see similarities between events in Britain and the sixteenth-century Dutch Revolt that had protected Protestantism and rejected Habsburg rule. Keen Dutch interest in the British civil wars was evidenced by the fact that, in 1643, half of all publications in the Dutch Republic were Dutch translations of original English titles.[55] Particularly in the maritime provinces of Holland and Zeeland, popular opinion was pro-Parliamentarian, creating an inauspicious environment for Henrietta Maria to seek supplies of arms, munitions and troops. Enduring a steady diet of gleeful – if fictitious – claims of Stuart disasters, the queen admitted to Charles in November that not only had sundry reports 'made you dead, and Prince Charles a Prisoner', but of 'Prince Rupert, there are men here who have seen and touched his dead body, and that of Prince Maurice', while 'there is not a day in the week in which you do not lose' a battle against Parliament.[56]

In an imagined dialogue between an 'Englishman' and a 'Netherlander' in Voetius's *British Lightning*, the 'Englishman' was dismayed by Henrietta Maria's influence, wailing that 'we are now so careless, knowing nothing but of devilish masquing, ungodly and wanton ballads, and dances, superfluous meals, wherewith we daily pamper ourselves as on a feast day', while 'the queen of England with our great ones . . . make themselves merry . . . as if this misery concerned them not'.[57] Returning to England from The Hague in February 1643, Henrietta Maria initially stayed in York, before styling herself a 'She-Majesty-Generalissima' when travelling with 3,000 soldiers and 2,000 cavalry to rejoin her husband at Stratford-on-Avon in July.[58]

Inevitably, the attempt of the Dutch States General to stay neutral pleased no one. English MPs were disappointed by the lukewarm reception accorded to Strickland's visit and outraged by Dutch disregard for Henrietta Maria's shipments of supplies. Attacking the States General's stance, one pamphleteer was incredulous that, although 'France and Spain stand still, you do show yourselves earnest to promote our ruin', contrary to MPs' expectations of their Protestant, republican allies.[59] For his part, Charles protested at the States General's decision even to receive Strickland, recalling the extensive assistance provided by previous English monarchs to the Dutch in their independence struggle against Spain. Anglo-Dutch amity would be nullified if the Dutch now tried 'to countenance such a commixture of government, as one while to treat with us, another while with our subjects; or, as you do now, both together'.[60]

By contrast, the French court initially appeared more supportive of the English Parliament's position, despite Henrietta Maria's Bourbon ancestry. Before leaving London for a new posting at the imperial court in Vienna in late 1642, Giustinian had been surprised by the overt manner in which La Ferté-Imbault held 'long conferences with the Parliamentarians who have promoted the present troubles and with the Scottish commissioners', observing that the French envoy 'professes to care nothing for the indignation' of Charles.[61] After returning to Paris, La Ferté-Imbault's partisanship continued, prompting complaint from the English ambassador, Browne, that he remained both 'a vehement stickler for the Scots' and the Parliamentarians and 'in all his discourse he raises their reputation to what height he can, and depresses his Majesty's causelessly, dishonestly and maliciously'.[62] Following the deaths of Cardinal Richelieu in December 1642, and of Louis XIII the following May, control of French foreign policy passed to a regency government presided over by the queen mother and Cardinal Jules Mazarin on behalf of the four-year-old Louis XIV. Although a new envoy, Henri de Lorraine, count of Harcourt, was sent to London in October 1643, French attempts to mediate soon stalled, primarily over a 'very ticklish point' of etiquette, namely, Harcourt's refusal to recognize the Commons and Lords as a legitimate English Parliament.[63]

IV

Ultimately, foreign intervention did prove decisive in turning the military tide in favour of the English Parliament, albeit in the form of another invasion by the Scottish Covenanters. In an account of the British civil wars penned in 1655, Philip IV's ambassador, Alonso de Cárdenas, recalled that 'in the pulpits, in the streets, and in private houses nothing was preached or talked about but the wisdom and necessity of uniting with the Scots'.[64] Parliamentarian leaders, most prominently John Pym, had been alarmed by a string of Royalist victories across England during 1643 that had included battles at Braddock Down in Cornwall, Roundway Down in Wiltshire, and Adwalton Moor in Yorkshire in addition to Prince Rupert's celebrated capture of Bristol in July. Having opened negotiations with Scots commissioners, a formal Anglo-Scottish alliance known as the 'Solemn League and Covenant' was ratified by the Edinburgh and Westminster legislatures in August and September 1643. In return for dispatching a sizeable army, funded by the English Parliament, to northern England, the Covenanters secured a commitment that the Church of England would be reformed along Presbyterian lines. Envisaged as a new covenant with God himself, its Scottish signatories accorded the Solemn League and Covenant a hallowed significance that differed from the Parliamentarians' immediate objective of simply obliging Charles to fight a British war on two fronts.

Among English peers, the idea of seeking Scottish involvement remained contentious. As the Ayrshire divine Robert Baillie recalled, several nobles had warned that if Parliament 'did begin to employ strangers, that hereby the king should be excused to fetch in Irish, French, and Danes'.[65] Indeed, in a proclamation issued in December 1643, Charles accused the Covenanters of breaching the recent pacification by 'not so much as pretending the least provocation or violation' by England and having no other agenda 'than a design of conquest'. Equally treasonous was the conduct of English MPs willing 'to invite and join with a foreign nation to ruin and extinguish their own'.[66] Writing from Edinburgh the previous month, a French envoy, Monsieur de Boisivon, reported to Louis XIV's Secretary of State, Henri-Auguste de Loménie, count of Brienne, that the Covenanters' military leader, General Alexander Leslie, earl of Leven, had demanded 30,000 men in order to 'be in a position to lay down the law to all Europe'. Hoping to emulate the victories of the late Swedish King Gustavus Adolphus, Leven had publicly invited Scots nobles to consider 'what a glorious thing it would be' if Scottish forces could 'drive the Catholics out of England', join forces with French Huguenots 'and thence, go to Rome, drive out Antichrist, and burn the town that disseminates superstition'. As Boisivon warned Brienne, the Scots' 'plans are so vast, [and] their presumption so great that there is no hope of obtaining anything from them'.[67]

On 19 January 1644, a Covenanter army of around 21,000 soldiers crossed the frozen River Tweed and entered Northumberland as the largest single fighting force yet raised for service in the British Isles. Three days later, Charles opened a rival Royalist parliament in Oxford, that attracted around 120 MPs and forty peers, which was equivalent to around a quarter of the Long Parliament's membership in the Commons and less than half of its membership in the Lords. While God had not yet 'put a short end to this great storm', Charles denounced his English adversaries as 'wicked' men: rather than 'removing and reconciling these bloody distractions, and restoring peace to this languishing country, they have invited a foreign power to invade this kingdom, and that in your names'.[68] Although the 'Oxford parliament' sat for two sessions from January to April 1644, and again from October 1644 to March 1645, Charles was soon frustrated by its members' keenness to negotiate with their colleagues at Westminster and, in a letter to Henrietta Maria, dismissed it as a 'mongrel parliament' of dubious loyalty.[69]

In February 1644, a disillusioned Harcourt returned to Paris, indicating that he intended to advise the French court to revive the ancient 'Auld Alliance' and 'address themselves to Scotland . . . since the direction of affairs will rest in their hands'.[70] A similar surmise was reached in Howell's fictional dialogue entitled *The True Informer* (1643) in which the character 'Peregrin' regretted that endemic chaos 'hath made the English lose much ground in point of esteem abroad', incurring 'the scorn of other people' as England's neighbours were insisting 'that the saying was never truer than now, *Rex Anglorum*, *Rex Diabolorum* (King of England, King of Devils)'. Fearing that 'the English have seen their best days', 'Peregrin' admitted that 'they say abroad, 'tis the Scots turn now to be a great nation'.[71]

Securing fewer strategic gains – but attracting intense hostility – were Irish soldiers recruited by Charles to join the Royalist army. Following a one-year truce agreed between James Butler, marquess of Ormond, and the Confederation of Kilkenny in September 1643, around 18,000 soldiers were dispatched to England from Ireland over the next nine months. But significant numbers of desertions occurred when the troops that were raised in Ireland, many of whom were English- or Welsh-born, refused to fight alongside Catholics in England. In the Parliamentarian press, moreover, the arrival of Irish Catholic troops to fight Charles's Protestant subjects was denounced as a means of extirpating the entire English nation. In November, the *Kingdom's Weekly Post* had warned its readers not to expect that 'the Irish rebels will be more merciful to you, your wives and children, than they were to the Protestants in Ireland'.[72] Specific atrocities in England also re-enacted, with chilling resonance, the very worst forms of sectarian violence that had occurred in Ulster. Following a major Royalist victory at Lostwithiel in Cornwall in September 1644, for example, the Royalists' readiness to beat, strip and drown Parliamentarians fleeing across Lostwithiel Bridge vividly revived traumatic memories of the deliberate drowning of around a hundred Protestant men, women and children who, three years earlier, had been stripped naked and forced into the River Bann from Portadown Bridge.[73]

The victory at Lostwithiel nevertheless followed a heavy Royalist defeat at the Battle of Marston Moor outside York on 2 July 1644, where a total of around 46,000 soldiers had confronted one another in one of the bloodiest encounters ever fought on English soil. As Leven's Scottish army joined with English Parliamentarian forces commanded by Ferdinando, Lord Fairfax, and Edward Montagu, earl of Manchester, Royalist forces were overwhelmed, leading to loss of royal control in York and much of northern England. Defeat at Marston Moor ended Prince Rupert's reputation as a seemingly invincible commander on his uncle's behalf and also saw the death of Rupert's talismanic dog named 'Boy', which the prince had acquired while detained by the Habsburgs in Linz.

More broadly, although Marston Moor clearly vindicated the strategic sense of the Parliamentarians' alliance with the Covenanters, Anglo-Scottish relations thereafter deteriorated. Within the English Parliament, divisions were emerging between a 'War party', later known as Independents – which favoured an outright military defeat of the king – and a 'Peace party', which was predominantly Presbyterian, and favoured seeking a negotiated settlement, albeit one that had been complicated by the Anglo-Scottish alliance which gave the Scots a justified stake in any English settlement. For Royalists, the Parliamentarian victory at Marston Moor only stoked resentment of Scottish dominance. As the editor of the Royalist gazette *Mercurius Aulicus* complained in August, Scots soldiers were 'ranging through every county to find the fattest earth for their new plantation' and clearly 'mean to take up quarters in England' permanently.[74] Other critics warned that such extensive intra-Protestant bloodshed only served to further Irish Catholic, English recusant, Spanish Habsburg and papal interests. In *The Earl of Strafford's Ghost* (1644), the spirit of Charles's erstwhile Irish Lord Deputy bewailed seeing how 'poor Ireland's desolate, England's desperate, and Scotland's in danger'. The sectarian killings of Protestants by Catholics and vice versa in Ireland were to be expected, but Strafford's ghost was aghast to see English and Scottish Protestants ensnared in a plot 'first contrived in the Devil's fencing-school' and ensuring that 'what the Irish rebels, English papists, and the bishops cannot do, to promote Popery, must be done by the Protestant himself'.[75]

After the Royalists' defeat at Marston Moor, hopes that dynastic solidarity with the Stuarts might encourage military assistance – at least in the French case – proved futile. Like most foreign powers, the French court welcomed England's enforced distraction from overseas entanglements. Moreover, as Charles's ambassador in Paris, George, Lord Goring, had complained to Secretary of State Sir Edward Nicholas in June, 'so high an opinion' was 'entertained on the Continent of the rebels' forces and of our weakness', it seemed unlikely that any foreign power would 'dare declare for us, for fear lest the burden of our war might solely rest upon their soldiers'.[76] Attempts to secure assistance nevertheless intensified after Henrietta Maria installed her exiled court at the Louvre and, in correspondence intercepted by Parliament in October, she reported an offer from the French noble, Bernard de Nogaret de La Valette, duke of Épernon, to provide 12,000 funded volunteers to strengthen Royalist forces. As the Venetian Secretary Gerolamo Agostini feared, even 'if such succour should come, there would be danger of the king's own party deserting him, as the English cannot stand foreigners, and the French in particular'. In the event, it was unexpected Scottish succour to Charles that ensured, as Agostini observed, that 'his Majesty is grown strong, and is determined to conquer or die'.[77] Civil war now also divided the Scottish populace. While the Covenanters were assisting Parliamentarian victories in northern England, a remarkable Royalist resurgence in northern Scotland, which had started in September 1644, saw James Graham, marquess of Montrose, win six successive victories over Covenanting forces at Tippermuir, Aberdeen, Inverlochy, Auldearn, Alford and Kilsyth.

In London, Charles I's Palatine nephew Charles Louis destabilized Stuart family loyalties further by returning to England in September 1644 at the invitation of prominent Parliamentarians. Presenting his *Motives and Reasons* for returning to Parliament, Charles Louis admitted the 'unspeakable grief' he felt at 'the public actions of some of the nearest of his blood' – i.e. his younger brothers, Princes Rupert and Maurice – but protested that he could not 'regulate what is out of his power'. Insisting that the civil wars across Britain 'originally derived from the same popish principles, hammered upon the same Jesuitical anvil' as those that had devastated Germany, Charles Louis remained 'confident, that the Parliaments, and people of God in these kingdoms' would yet 'prevail against whatever Spain, Rome or the Gates of Hell could do or devise to the contrary'.[78] Knowing that Charles Louis had sworn the Solemn League and Covenant and was living in his uncle's palace at Whitehall, Agostini inferred that the prince was, however, being cynically manipulated as a means of preserving 'the shadow of monarchy' that, in reality, consigned the prince to 'a position of dependency rather than command'. The Venetian resented Charles Louis's 'obsequiousness and reverence to parliament', lamenting that 'there is no hypocrisy that he does not practise', including feigning zealous overtures to Puritan clerics. But when Charles Louis's presence failed to attract the enthusiastic support originally envisaged, Agostini predicted his ignominious return to The Hague 'with the stigma of an ambition more reprehensible than his father's since it involves disloyalty to his uncle'.[79]

Amid growing divisions between warmongers and peacemakers, a widely reported clash of views occurred at a Council of War in November 1644 between the Parliamentarian commander, Edward Montagu, earl of Manchester, and his second-in-command: the forty-five-year-old MP for Cambridge and rising military mastermind, Oliver Cromwell. While Cromwell was frustrated by the army's failure to capitalize on victories at Marston Moor and Newbury, Manchester was reported to have reassured colleagues that they 'need not fear the coming in of the French, I know there is no such thing'. For Manchester, the priority remained seeking a permanent peace, rather than simply amassing military victories in the field. As he warned colleagues, even 'if we beat the king ninety-and-nine times, yet he is king still, and so will his posterity be after him; but if the king beat us once, we shall all be hanged, and our posterity be made slaves'.[80]

Reflecting close Anglo-Scottish cooperation in their formulation, peace proposals were presented to Charles in November 1644, demanding that the king swear the Solemn League and Covenant and impose the oath on all his subjects. Charles was also required to abolish Episcopalianism in England and Ireland while the joint consent of both the English and Scottish Parliaments would henceforth be needed before any monarch could declare war or make peace with foreign states. In addition to extending bilateral parliamentary oversight to the education of the monarch's children, the peace proposals included the required surrender to the English Parliament of fifty-eight named Royalists, including Princes Rupert and Maurice. Royalist and Parliamentarian commissioners were appointed as peace negotiations started at Uxbridge on 29 January 1645 and followed a cyclical timetable with three days spent discussing a future religious settlement; three days on future militia arrangements and another three days on Irish affairs, before returning to religion. Yet deadlock quickly ensued, as Charles had made clear his commitment to retaining episcopacy in England, and the talks ended without agreement on 22 February. A fortnight earlier, Charles had tellingly directed his commissioners that, in 'private discourses' at the negotiations, they should remind the Parliamentarian delegation 'that they were arrant rebels and that their end must be damnation, ruin and infamy, except they repented and found some way to free themselves from the damnable way they are in'. Writing 'not as your master, but your friend', Charles advised his representatives that 'the more of you that speak in this dialect, the better'.[81]

12

The Mediation of Strangers, 1644–1648

In a poem entitled 'The Rebel Scot' (1645), the Royalist satirist John Cleveland lamented how 'Pym's disease' had resulted in England 'By Scotch invasion to be made a prey / To such pig-wiggin myrmidons' as were currently occupying his country's northern counties. Contemplating England's destiny, Cleveland wondered, 'shall our Nation be in bondage thus / Unto a land that truckles under us'? Denouncing the Scots as 'a nation epidemical' that virulently spread contagion, Cleveland bitterly regretted that 'Sure England hath the haemorrhoids' which 'On the north postern of the patient seize / Like leeches'.[1] Since 1639, Scots Covenanting forces had indeed invaded England's northern border on three separate occasions and, having established garrisons, seemed in little rush to hasten south and assist their Parliamentarian allies. While MPs at Westminster set about 'new modelling' Parliament's armed force, in May 1645 the delegation of Scots commissioners in London warned their colleagues who were based with the Covenanting army in northern England that the Scots' repeated failures to march south was generating resentment that 'your army was going backwards, when they should advance'.[2]

If the Scots seemed in no hurry to proceed south, other foreign powers were visibly keen to act as mediators between Charles I and his warring subjects. At the start of 1644, Philip IV's ambassador, Alonso de Cárdenas, had been unable to present his court's traditional New Year's gifts to Charles I so instead bestowed them on members of the House of Commons and Lords, as well as 'officers of the militia, the Navy and the City of London', reasoning that Spain's interests would suffer if diplomatic courtesies were not maintained with those wielding effective power.[3] Surprising other foreign envoys by being 'the first to recognise them', Cárdenas attended meetings of the Anglo-Scottish 'Committee of Both Kingdoms'. Philip's ambassador also hoped to influence Parliamentarian foreign policy by seeking English assistance in resisting French attacks on the Spanish-held port of Gravelines, fifteen miles southwest of Dunkirk.[4]

As the anonymous *Discourse of a True Englishman* (1644) warned, England's national security could be promoted not by avoiding any action that might 'provoke France, which is sufficiently stirred up by her own ambition, and her desire to devour this kingdom', but 'by taking away from France means and power to hurt her'.[5] To counter Spanish influence, a unofficial French envoy, Melchior, sieur de Sabran, arrived in London in April 1644, but had little room for diplomatic manoeuvre, having been instructed not to recognize the English Parliament's authority as legitimate. Trying to effect a compromise settlement between Charles and his Parliament were three Dutch envoys, Willem Boreel, Albert Joachimi and Johan van Reede, who had arrived at Gravesend in January on a diplomatic mission that cost the Dutch nearly £150,000, but yielded few results. After visiting Charles in Oxford, and receiving a House of Commons audience, the Dutch envoys reported to the States General in June that, unless peace was soon concluded, both king and Parliament would continue denuding each other 'in strength, resources and manpower until these once powerful kingdoms become the subject of an invasion by a foreign nation'.[6] Dutch predictions that, after rival English armies had fatally weakened each other, the way would be cleared for a French, Spanish or Dutch military solution to the mid-century civil wars were to prove incorrect. But lurking at the back of English minds were fears of a successful new armada intent on invasion and images of the sort of massive fleet that, a generation later, would set sail from Dutch shores in November 1688.

If Scots Covenanting forces seemed reluctant to venture south, the rhetoric surrounding Parliamentarian attempts to reach a durable political settlement increasingly evinced an English exclusivity and distrust of all external involvement. Detecting a nationalist agenda animating Parliamentarian discourse, the Scots Commissioners in London warned the Covenanting leadership in Edinburgh in March 1644 that English MPs had recently approved a paper intended to initiate peace discussions that would 'prevent the mediation of strangers' – including the Scots.[7] Charles's opponents had indeed long mistrusted the Royalists' readiness to seek external support to uphold royal authority, if not to promote an international popish conspiracy.

In a new insult to royal dignity, the House of Lords had received articles of impeachment against Henrietta Maria in January 1644 that had been framed by MPs and accused the queen of having incited Presbyterian rebellion in Scotland, fomented the Irish Rebellion and having 'wickedly and traitorously endeavoured, practised, and conspired with diverse popish priests, Jesuits' and others to promote Catholic interests. Thereafter MPs charged that the queen had travelled overseas and returned to England in 1643 with 'great numbers of forces, commanders, and officers of divers nations as English, French, Walloons, Irish rebels, and other strangers and papists, and also great quantities of arms, munition, money, and other provision of war'.[8] While the Lords referred the impeachment articles to a committee, Henrietta Maria left England for France in July 1644, shortly after giving birth to a daughter, called Henrietta Anne, who remained in England. By November, Henrietta Maria had settled in the Louvre Palace in Paris, where she received a generous financial allowance and where she was eventually joined by Henrietta Anne in 1646. But Henrietta Maria would never see her husband again.

I

Further military hostilities between Charles and Parliamentarian forces seemed inevitable following the collapse of peace negotiations at Uxbridge in early 1645. While Royalists mocked the 'New Noddle' force reshaped by the English Parliament as the New Model Army, they underestimated the strategic impact of creating a single, centralized national army, directed by the joint Committee of Both Kingdoms. The New Model Army's creation had been facilitated by passing of a 'Self-denying Ordinance' by the Commons and Lords in April 1645 which had required most peers and MPs who also held military or naval office to resign those positions and seek reappointment. In what became the decisive battle of the civil wars, a Parliamentarian force of around 17,000 soldiers defeated a Royalist army of around 9,000 at the Battle of Naseby in Northamptonshire on 14 June 1645. While the Parliamentarians were under the overall command of Sir Thomas Fairfax, the cavalry was commanded by the recently appointed Lieutenant General of the Horse, Oliver Cromwell. The Royalist army suffered the capture of around 4,000 veteran foot soldiers, as well as the damaging seizure of the royal baggage-train which contained the king's political papers and private correspondence. In a Parliamentarian propaganda coup orchestrated by members of both the Commons and the Lords, *The King's Cabinet Opened* (1645) was published a month after the Naseby encounter, reproducing thirty-nine of Charles's letters and fourteen pages of annotation. Considerable trouble was taken to confirm the letters' authenticity, with the originals displayed at Westminster and named authenticators cited at the end of each letter.

Offering repeated instances of royal duplicity and deception, Charles's correspondence amply illustrated the king's persistent contempt for his Parliamentarian adversaries, adherence to his wife's counsel and his determination to strengthen Royalist forces with support from foreign powers. *The King's Cabinet Opened* provided clear confirmation that Charles and Henrietta Maria had serially sought to deploy French and Irish troops into England, had offered the Orkney and Shetland islands in return for Danish assistance, and had also sought arms and money from the duke of Lorraine and the Prince of Orange. As the editorial annotations confirmed, Charles's queen was discharging 'the offices of a Resident in France, to procure embargoes of our ships, [and] to raise foreign forces against us'. Even more perniciously, in an attempt to maximize Henrietta Maria's bargaining power, Charles had explicitly given his wife 'power to promise in my name' to whomsoever she wished 'that I will take away all the penal laws against the Roman Catholics in England as soon as God shall enable me to do it'. No longer was it possible to allege that Charles was the innocent victim of evil counsel and nor was it plausible to deny claims that the king was willing to sanction deployment of Irish Catholic soldiers against his Protestant subjects in England and Scotland. In a contravention of contemporary codes of patriarchy, it was clear (as the editorial apparatus insisted) that 'the King's counsels are wholly governed by the Queen; though she be of the weaker sex, born an alien, [and] bred up in a contrary religion'. Before publication, the king's letters had also required decipherment, as the encrypted correspondence between authoritarian monarch and exiled wife presented a synecdoche for the coded and closed world of 'Personal Rule' that Charles had pursued since 1629. The editorial preface to *The King's Cabinet Opened* acknowledged that, although MPs had never accorded monarchs 'infallibility to the seat of a king in parliament' in the way that Catholics revered the Pope, 'no English king did ever from that place speak destruction to his people' until now.[9] Among English Royalists, one sympathizer was nevertheless horrified by the way in which the king's letters were 'openly read, and copied out a thousand ways, printed ten thousand ways, dispersed a hundred thousand ways, and believed by millions of people'.[10]

The king and queen's use of foreign ambassadors as a clandestine conduit for their letters generated further offence as a cynical exploitation of the privileged respect that conventionally rendered diplomatic correspondence immune from interception. Particularly helpful to the royal couple in this regard had been the Portuguese ambassador, António de Sousa Macedo, who also used his posting to London to publish a vindication of Portuguese independence entitled *Lusitania Liberated from the Castilian Yoke* (1645). Parliamentarian concern to deter further diplomatic assistance being extended to Charles and his wife prompted the ransacking of the London residence occupied by the Holy Roman Emperor's representative, Franz Paul Freiherr von Lisola, while Lisola was abroad. Ironically, however, it was Cardinal Mazarin's unofficial envoy Sabran who became increasingly trusted by English MPs, precisely because publication of the king's letters had revealed Charles's suspicion that 'either he [Sabran] or his instructions are not right' for the Royalist cause.[11]

From Paris, the Scots Commissioners in London relayed reports from parliamentary agents that Charles's 'cause is given for lost' in France, following the Royalist defeat at Naseby and 'the printing of his letters, whereof the most part thereof are there translated'. Trying to counter such hopeless accounts, Henrietta Maria and her advisers had been insisting 'that the King hath great intelligence and correspondence with the Scots, so as all will be enough yet if foreign states send timely assistance'. But in September 1645, Scottish Royalist forces under James Graham, marquess of Montrose, were defeated by a Covenanting army at the Battle of Philiphaugh, in the Scottish Borders. Desperate to prevent any future Anglo-Scottish Royalist cooperation, the Commissioners in London beseeched the Covenanting leadership in Edinburgh to write a letter 'framed in such a friendly way of expostulation' to reassure their English allies 'that the kingdom of Scotland is resolved to live and die with them in prosecution of the ends expressed in the Covenant against all whomsoever'.[12]

The Scots Commissioners' concerns were justified: in February 1646 Henrietta Maria's almoner, Jacques du Perron, addressed a general assembly of French clergy in Paris, appealing for financial support and explicitly alluding to Charles's assurances that, in return for military assistance, the king would revoke the penal laws against Catholics in his British kingdoms. As Du Perron admitted, following publication of the *King's Cabinet Opened*, 'there is now no danger to declare this promise, which hath been kept secret hitherto'. Praising Henrietta Maria's achievements in promoting Catholic interests in England, Du Perron explained that, before the civil wars broke out, Catholic Mass had been freely celebrated at the Queen's Chapel in London 'with as much solemnity and liberty, and I durst even say in proportion, with as great affluence of people, as in any Church in Paris'. The reception of successive papal nuncios in England had further indicated the likelihood that Henrietta Maria's 'sweet steps' might have 'walked fairly on toward the conversion of that kingdom'. Du Perron also invited pity for the younger members of the Stuart dynasty who remained, after all, the 'grandchildren, nephews and cousin-germans of our kings', but were now on the verge of being 'despoiled of three great kingdoms' and forced into exile 'to wander in strange countries as vagabonds' and 'even there to eat that bread, which they cannot eat in their own house, and amongst their own subjects and citizens'.[13]

Meanwhile, although Henrietta Maria was separated from her younger children in England, in Paris she played 'the most secret mediatrix' for a younger Palatine nephew, Edward, who provoked scandal in the summer of 1645 by clandestinely marrying Anna Marie de Gonzague, daughter of the duke of Mantua and sister of the Polish queen. As the Venetian agent in Paris, Giovan Battista Nani, reported, after Anne had suddenly decided to wed a penniless, Protestant exile, eight years her junior, 'the contract was signed, the marriage consummated and this scion of a House which has done so much harm to the faith, became a Catholic, all on the same day', much to the disapproval of the French court which ordered the couple's immediate expulsion.[14] In The Hague, Edward's older sister Elisabeth wrote to the (Catholic) philosopher René Descartes, venting her frustration that Edward's conversion was proof that he had 'fallen into the hands of a certain group of people who have more hatred for our house than affection for their religion'.

Denouncing Edward for having 'let himself be taken in by their traps', Elisabeth rued that he was now 'abandoned to the scorn of the world and the loss of his soul (according to my belief)'.[15]

In England, Edward's older brothers – Princes Rupert and Maurice – were more likely to render Palatine Royalist service synonymous with Continental plunder, brutality and debauchery. At the outset of the wars, one Parliamentarian officer reported in September 1642 'tidings that Prince Rupert, that diabolical Cavalier, had surrounded Leicester, and demanded £2000, or else threatened to plunder the town, whereupon our soldiery were even mad to be at them'.[16] In *The Bloody Prince* (1643), 'I. W.' vituperatively attacked Rupert's Cavalier forces for 'robbing, stealing, whoring, and above all, killing the people of God when your devilish paws can fasten upon them', making 'yourselves drunk with blood as with sweet wine'.[17] Setting aside Parliamentarian obloquy, Rupert admitted in late 1644 that even within the Royalist command 'great factions are breeding', with some detractors identifying him as 'the only cause of war in this kingdom'.[18]

After Charles's defeat at Naseby, Rupert tried to retain Royalist control of Bristol, where Fairfax, as commander-in-chief of the New Model Army, challenged the prince's grounds for assuming that Palatine interests were best promoted by supporting Charles. Admitting that his approach was unorthodox, Fairfax sought in September 1645 to 'a little expostulate' with Rupert, insisting that his prompt surrender of the city would restore him to 'the endeared affection of the Parliament and people of England – the truest friends to your family it hath in the world'. While Rupert's forces attacked England by 'burning of its towns, ruining its cities, and destroying its people', Fairfax reminded the prince that the militant Calvinism historically espoused by the Palatine branch of the Stuart dynasty had always attracted 'the prayers, tears, purses and blood of its Parliament and people', while efforts to intervene on the Palatine family's behalf had been persistently 'hindered or made fruitless by the same party about his Majesty, whose counsels you act, and whose interests you pursue in this unnatural war'.[19] Certainly, the peace propositions tendered by Parliament to Charles at York in June 1642, and at Oxford the following February, had demanded that England form alliances with the United Provinces and other Protestant states, both to promote Palatine restitution and to withstand Catholic aggression in general.

Although Rupert resisted Fairfax's blandishments to surrender voluntarily, within a week the New Model Army had gained control of Bristol, compounding a series of Royalist losses at Devizes, Winchester, Basing House, Berkeley Castle and Chepstow. Moreover, the speed of Bristol's surrender provided further ammunition for Rupert's Royalist critics. In early 1645, the Venetian agent in Paris, Nani, learned that Charles was starting to mistrust the fidelity of his Palatine nephews, Rupert and Maurice, suspecting 'that they aspire to the crown and kingdom and are plotting secretly for his ruin with Parliament, in concert with their eldest brother [the titular Elector], who is living in London'.[20] After ordering that Rupert be arrested and compelled to leave England within a fortnight, Charles wrote to Maurice, regretting that his brother's loyalties had been 'seduced by some rotten-hearted villain' and admitting that Rupert's 'great error' in surrendering Bristol too hastily had 'given me more grief than any misfortune since this damnable rebellion' had started.[21] While Rupert successfully cleared his name in a court martial at Newark, bitter internecine divisions within the Royalist command continued, eventually prompting both Rupert and Maurice to return to the Continent in July 1646. Before the brothers' departure, their older sibling, Charles Louis – who had sided with the Parliamentarians – petitioned the Commons Speaker, William Lenthall, hoping that 'it may stand with the liking of the parliament' for him to meet Rupert and Maurice, explaining that he would need 'the consent of all my brothers' if any resolution regarding the Palatinate's restoration was achieved at peace conferences currently taking place in Münster and Osnabrück.[22] On 1 July, the brothers met at Guildford and, four days later, Rupert left Dover and sailed to Calais, while Maurice returned to Holland. Since his arrival in England four years earlier, Rupert's journal recorded that he had ridden around 5,750 miles, campaigning for his beleaguered uncle's cause.[23]

In Parliamentarian newsbooks, increasingly audacious attacks were directed towards Charles as an itinerant monarch who was seemingly determined to ignore Parliament's attempts to make peace, preferring to abandon his people and encourage foreign Catholic powers to invade England. While Marchamont Nedham, as editor of *Mercurius Britanicus*, had suggested to readers in the autumn of 1644 that 'never did any great tennis-ball of passion and fortune roll about more than he has done', such criticism only intensified after the collapse of peace negotiations at Uxbridge. By the following January, Nedham's newspaper was suggesting that the king must have died, deeming it 'as sure as can be, King Charles is dead, and yet we never heard of it' and wondering why 'we have not his funeral sermon in print here, and the young prince sent up to London'.[24]

In Paris, the Venetian agent Nani was shocked to receive reports during the summer of 1645 that Parliamentarian newsletter-writers had 'thrown all respect to the winds' by sending publications abroad, ostensibly seeking information from 'anyone who finds a king, obstinate, a traitor to his promises, perfidious in his words, who has now absented himself from the parliament for four years, to bathe his hands in the blood of his subjects'. Reminding readers of the king's speech defect, Charles was described as easily identifiable, since 'anyone who gets him to speak will see that he is a stammerer, that he cannot speak the truth or talk plainly'.[25] That same month, readers of *Mercurius Britanicus* in England were confronted by a remarkable opening passage that simply asked 'Where is King Charles? What's become of him?' As speculation mounted, the newsbook cited reports that 'he ran away out of his own kingdom very majestically', with some sources suggesting that 'he ran away to his dearly beloved Ireland' while 'others will have him erecting a new monarchy in the Isle of Anglesey'.[26]

Foreign envoys adapted to the royal vacuum that had subsisted in London since 1642. When a Scots envoy to Sweden, Hugh Mowat, approached Parliament seeking agreements to hire ships and raise levies for Swedish service in early 1645, the Venetian secretary, Gerolamo Agostini, observed how MPs made 'use of these offers to impress upon the people that they are as well provided with foreign friends as the king'.[27] In May, Cárdenas reported that the Committee of Both Kingdoms was intending to sell goods owned by the late duke of Buckingham, with a view to pursuing a similar policy regarding Charles's possessions. Intrigued, Philip IV instructed Cárdenas to purchase any paintings 'which might be originals by Titian, Paolo Veronese, or other old painting of distinction', but to avoid letting 'it be known that you are acquiring them for me'.[28]

In November 1645, a Russian embassy led by Gerasim Semenovich Dokhturov arrived in London, having been sent by Tsar Aleksei Mikhailovich to inform Charles of the death of his predecessor, Tsar Mikhail, and to gather information on the political situation in

England. With Charles no longer resident in his capital city, the Russian delegation was instead entertained by senior Parliamentarians during its seven-month stay in London. Visiting the shops and houses on London Bridge, the envoys were, however, alarmed by pikes onto which were affixed the heads of men who, they were told, had been executed for supporting Charles I. Unsurprisingly, 'this sight puzzled the Russians who expected people to be considered traitors for opposing rather than supporting their sovereign'.[29] The piecemeal disintegration of royal authority in practice only compounded the damage inflicted on Charles by Royalist defeats on the battlefield.

Having established his royal court in Oxford, Charles had become increasingly isolated by the autumn of 1645, especially after his main counsellor, George Digby, was defeated in battle at Sherburn in Yorkshire and fled to Ireland. Suffering a similar fate to that of his king's, Digby's correspondence had been captured at Sherburn and was also published, on Parliamentary orders, as proof of persistent Royalist attempts to seek foreign assistance. As the Parliamentarian editor explained, letters from Charles I, Digby, Jermyn and others clearly showed the Royalists' 'restless endeavours to bring in foreign aids from Holland, [the Baltic duchy of] Courland, Denmark, Portugal, Ireland, France and from Rome itself, of shipping, arms, ammunition, men, money, horse and foot'. Setting aside their practical failure to secure meaningful assistance, the Royalists' strategy presented a paradoxical and 'strange conjuncture': 'the king and Pope to defend the Protestant religion, Denmark and Lorraine to maintain laws and liberties, [and] bloody rebels in Ireland to uphold the privileges of Parliament in England'.[30]

It was, moreover, from Ireland that depressingly familiar evidence of royal duplicity and diplomatic ineptitude resurfaced, after Charles commissioned a Catholic Royalist, Edward Herbert, to pursue secret talks with the Confederate Assembly of Kilkenny as a covert alternative to negotiations started by his Lord Deputy, James Butler, marquess of Ormond. Herbert – known as the 'earl of Glamorgan', a title that Charles had apparently promised to confer if the negotiations succeeded – agreed a secret treaty in August 1645 which secured 10,000 Confederate soldiers for use anywhere in the British Isles, in return for all penal laws being abolished in Ireland and toleration for Catholics to worship freely without interference. But, shortly afterwards, Herbert's negotiations were disrupted by the arrival in Kilkenny of Pope Innocent X's nuncio, Giovanni Battista Rinuccini, who sought to secure a permanent transformation in the lives of Irish Catholics. Rinuccini distrusted not only Herbert's authority to negotiate, but also Charles's commitment to abide by treaty commitments once he had received the troops. To offer reassurance, Herbert showed Rinuccini a letter – of doubtful authenticity – pre-addressed by Charles to the nuncio, emphasizing 'how important it is, that the affair should be kept secret', given the momentous religious concessions at stake. Despite being 'the first letter which we have ever wrote immediately to any minister of state of the Pope', its author hoped 'that it will not be the last'.[31] Rinuccini nevertheless insisted on additional terms, resulting in a second secret agreement in December that committed Charles to appointing a Catholic Lord Deputy, allowing Catholic bishops to sit in the Irish House of Lords and establishing a Catholic university in Ireland. But after details of the treaty were leaked and published by an incandescent Parliamentarian press, an outraged Ormond accused Herbert of treason and imprisoned him in Dublin, while Charles blithely disavowed knowledge of any treaty or separate commission.

Although Charles failed to secure the immediate manpower he desperately needed, in early 1646 his son and heir, Prince Charles, was evacuated from Cornwall to the Scilly Isles aboard armed frigates obtained by an Irish Catholic peer, Randal MacDonnell, marquess of Antrim, from the Governor of the Spanish Netherlands, Don Manuel de Moura y Corte Real, marquis of Castel Rodrigo. A year earlier, the king had given the fourteen-year-old prince nominal command of the Royalist war effort in the West Country, but after the prince left Oxford for Bristol in March 1645 he never saw his father again. As south-western towns such as Bath, Bridgwater and Sherborne had steadily fallen to the Parliamentarians, the prince had retreated to Pendennis Castle in Cornwall. In return for securing ships to retrieve the king's heir, Antrim had promised to raise levies of Irish and Scots recruits for Habsburg service, but had not been required to provide collateral for the ships on account – as Spanish observers noted – of 'his high quality and the zeal he has for the service of His Majesty [Philip IV]'.[32] Ironically, around the same time, two Parliamentarian envoys were dispatched from Westminster to Philip's court, which the Venetian ambassador in Madrid, Girolamo Giustinian, interpreted as a move intended to counter Henrietta Maria's

Royalist negotiations in Paris. But Philip only listened 'with half an ear, not from any real inclination, but from a feeling of pique', recalling the insult to Spanish interests when Charles had recognized a Portuguese envoy in England in 1641.[33]

II

The 'mediation of strangers' in the British civil wars was motivated by different, and often entirely antithetical, rationales. On the military front, France and Spain remained keen to raise levies of soldiers, usually from Ireland and Scotland, to serve in Continental armies. On the confessional front, although the Spanish court had long seemed the most likely external means of re-establishing Catholicism in Ireland, the priorities of Philip IV's administration in the mid-1640s lay in defeating anti-Habsburg forces in Continental Europe and suppressing revolts in Catalonia and Portugal. Among the Catholic 'Old English', religious commitments subsisted alongside a dynastic loyalty to Charles I, who was married to a French Bourbon, Henrietta Maria. On opposing sides of the Royalist–Parliamentarian chasm were Charles's Palatine nephews Charles Louis, Rupert and Maurice, whose ancestral territories and privileges were being discussed, in their absence, at the large Continental peace conferences in Westphalia that continued throughout the 1640s. An entirely separate set of priorities animated Pope Innocent X's nuncio, Rinuccini, who hoped to make the Confederation of Kilkenny a counter-Reformation vehicle to enable full reform of the Irish Church. Meanwhile, at the Louvre, Charles's increasingly calamitous situation had sufficiently alarmed Cardinal Mazarin's administration for the French to try to bolster a regime that was monarchical, financially needy and friendly to Catholics, as opposed to the prospect of a militarily powerful, Puritan and republican alternative.

Aware that Louis's court was intending to appoint an ambassador to England, the French chargé d'affaires in London, Jean de Montereul, doubted the feasibility of supplying significant assistance to Charles, protesting to Mazarin in early 1646 that any 'forces coming from abroad would only serve to unite his enemies against him, in order to repel conjointly the foreign force'. Moreover, Montereul begged Mazarin not to dismiss his scepticism as 'an opinion in which I have been indoctrinated here, but one which my small knowledge of this country leads me to consider very correct'. Having met the Covenanting leadership in Scotland, and visited the king and his advisers in Oxford, Montereul reported that Charles had 'complained of the rigour of the Scots', claiming that they 'wished him to lose his soul, as well as his kingdom' by insisting not only that he swear the Covenant, but also establish Presbyterian church government.[34] Despite his Catholic wife's inclination to regard Presbyterianism and Episcopacy as equally heretical, but therefore interchangeable, forms of church government, Charles protested that, for his part, he would regard as equally antithetical the options of either 'setting up the Presbyterian government, or submitting to the Church of Rome'. Entreating Henrietta Maria to 'make the case thine own', Charles encouraged his wife to imagine how resolutely she would resist anyone 'who should persuade thee, for worldly respects, to leave the communion of the Roman church for any other'. For 'indeed, sweetheart, this is my case'. More optimistically, Charles had been cheered by divisions among his enemies as he observed 'the unquestionable garinosity [animosity]' that subsisted at Westminster between pro-Scottish Presbyterian factions and their 'Independent' rivals who were no more enamoured of Scots Presbyterianism than of the Laudian Anglicanism upheld by their Royalist adversaries.[35] At the same time, differences persisted between the Scots Covenanters and their English Parliamentarian allies regarding the acceptability of any eventual peace settlement.

As Parliamentarian forces closed in on Oxford, Charles sent a covert appeal to the prominent Independent Sir Henry Vane in March 1646, suggesting that, if he were allowed to return to London, a workable settlement might be devised, based on their shared distrust of English and Scottish Presbyterian demands, vouching to Vane that he could 'trust to me for the performance of it . . . again rely upon me'. For if – as seemed likely to Charles – a Franco-Spanish peace was soon agreed, the king warned that the French were already making 'great preparations to join with the Scots', knowing that the Covenanters' alliance with the English Parliamentarians had become brittle, 'whilst Spain labours to be Protector of Ireland, and will undoubtedly carry it'.[36]

While Charles's (doubtless disingenuous) overture fell on deaf ears, the French court was intent on dissuading the king from reaching an English peace settlement with the Independents. Believing that the Scots, at least, remained committed to a monarchical settlement to end the wars, Montereul had several promising preliminary discussions to see if Charles might join the Covenanting army that was currently besieging Newark. When initial undertakings concerning the king's Royalist supporters were later retracted, Montereul was obliged to report changes to agreed conditions by which the army had consented to receive its beleaguered king. As Charles wrote to Henrietta Maria, 'in short, the Scots are abominable, relapsed rogues', observing that 'Montereul now dissuades me as much as he did before persuade' him to surrender. Fearing imminent capture by approaching Parliamentarian forces, Charles admitted, the following day, that his only means of avoiding imprisonment seemed to be requesting safe passage from his opponents to enable him to travel to King's Lynn, from where he could sail to Scotland – assuming Montrose was able to summon Royalist support to receive him – 'otherwise I mean to make for Ireland, France or Denmark'. Still unsure where to go, Charles wrote to Henrietta Maria, hoping 'to have thy judgement before I put to sea, to direct my course by'.[37]

In the end, Charles disguised himself as a servant and escaped from Oxford in the early hours of 27 April 1646. While the Scots commissioners in London reported that the king was variously rumoured to be in London, Ireland, Scotland or with the Scottish army, Charles surrendered to the besieging Covenanting army at Southwell, near Newark on 5 May. That same day, the army's commissioners confirmed to its English Parliamentarian allies that 'the king's coming into our army this morning' had 'overtaken us unexpectedly, hath filled us with amazement, and made us like men that dream'. Optimistically, the commissioners could not credit that Charles would have 'been so unadvised in his resolution, [as] to have cast himself upon us without a real intention to give full satisfaction to both kingdoms in all their just and reasonable demands'.[38] Surrender orders were issued to the Royalist troops holding Newark, among whom was the author of 'The Rebel Scot', John Cleveland. In 'The King's Disguise' (1647), Cleveland's Royalist sympathies had become more ambivalent, describing the king as 'so coffined in this vile disguise'. As Charles placed himself ignominiously in the Scottish army's custody, Cleveland only hoped 'May thy strange journey contradictions twist, / And force fair weather from a Scottish mist'.[39]

With the siege at Newark ended and the king in its custody, the Scottish army returned north to its camp at Newcastle. Although English

Independent MPs feared that the Covenanters and their English Presbyterian allies now seemed likely to dominate any future peace settlement, a motion proposing that 'there is no further use for the Scots Army' passed a House of Commons vote in May 1646, before being rejected by the Lords.[40] In reality, however, Scottish chances of concluding peace were continually frustrated by Charles's refusal to swear the Covenant. Admitting that he 'never knew what it was to be barbarously baited before', Charles confirmed to Henrietta Maria that 'nothing must serve, but my signing the Covenant'.[41] But Montereul, who had accompanied the king to Newcastle, remained wary of the Scots' loyalty to their king and reminded Mazarin, 'I am in a country where people's promises and their performances of them are somewhat different'.[42] For his part, Charles identified four factions among his Scottish hosts: Montrose's Royalist supporters; a faction attached to James, marquess of Hamilton; supporters of Archibald Campbell, marquess of Argyll; and 'neutrals', accurately observing that 'none of them trusts one another'. In June, the king pessimistically warned his wife that he could only 'expect the worst of events, unless the gathering of a storm from abroad make them alter their minds'.[43]

At Louis XIV's court, it was hoped that a Royalist coalition of Scots, English Presbyterians and Irish Catholics might prove sufficiently strong to prevent the Independent faction abolishing the monarchy entirely and establishing a republic. Newly appointed as ambassador to England, Pomponne de Bellièvre – whose namesake and grandfather had served as ambassador to Elizabeth I – received instructions in June 1646, recommending that Charles 'ought not to be too scrupulous' in negotiating with his enemies as 'the only hope that now remains to save himself from the shipwreck he has made'.[44] Bellièvre was also directed to impress on Charles the urgent need to avoid exacerbating 'the bad example which the subjects of other princes receive from the revolts of the English and the Scots against their king'.[45]

In Paris, Henrietta Maria and her advisers supported peace proposals submitted by the English Parliament in July 1646, known as the 'Newcastle Propositions', which, unlike the 'Uxbridge Propositions', had not been framed in collaboration with Parliament's Scots allies and were concerned only to secure an English settlement. By the 'Newcastle Propositions', Charles was required to confirm all parliamentary ordinances, become a Presbyterian, abolish Episcopacy in England and surrender command of the militia for twenty years, while several named Royalists remained exempt from pardon. In successive responses returned between August 1646 and September 1647, Charles evinced a willingness to negotiate over militia control and was even prepared to allow a temporary establishment of Presbyterian government, but resolutely refused to swear the Covenant. Indeed, the king's repeated refusals to swear the Covenant made it increasingly difficult for the Covenanters to justify either retaining control of the king's person or their continued military presence in England to their Parliamentarian allies. While neither Argyll nor Hamilton were prepared to return to Scotland with an uncovenanted king, Charles himself protested to Henrietta Maria in July, 'I would sooner choose the farthest part of the world than go into Scotland where I can never expect to see thee.'[46]

Once in Newcastle, Bellièvre repeatedly tried to persuade Charles and the Covenanters to conclude peace with one another, reassuring Louis's Secretary of State for Foreign Affairs, Henri-Auguste de Loménie, count of Brienne, that 'I omit neither prayers nor threats – always conveyed with the necessary temper – nor anything that I think can induce the Scots to oppose the ruin of their king and take upon themselves the glory of his re-establishment.' Sharing Montereul's distaste for the Scots, Bellièvre confirmed 'the little sincerity I have remarked in their behaviour' and 'the small affection and respect they have for their king'.[47] Repeated accounts of the English king's pertinacity provoked exasperation in Brienne. Having learned that Charles wanted to go to London – believing that he could prevail in person over his Parliamentarian adversaries – Brienne admitted bitterly to Bellièvre that the tactics of both Henrietta Maria and Charles made it 'necessary to prevent oneself from giving them advice because they are incapable of using it in a reasonable manner'.[48]

At the French court, Mazarin had concluded by November 1646 that only divine intervention could bring Charles to reason, 'for in vain do good doctors hope to restore health to a patient if he rejects all the remedies which can give it to him'.[49] Attempting to keep Louis's court apprised of the English king's intentions, Bellièvre reported, later the same month, that Charles had been contemplating the idea of abdicating his thrones to his eldest teenage son, although the ambassador conceded that he did 'not pretend to prove to you that this proposition is very intelligible, or that it may not even convey some contradiction'.

Unable to persuade the Covenanters to promote Charles's cause effectively, Bellièvre – erstwhile President of the Paris law courts – hoped that Brienne would not judge his failure too severely, bearing in mind he had been negotiating 'with people whose affairs are desperate and their minds agitated'. 'Fickle by nature', the Scots 'change their maxims each hour according to their interests, however small these may be', and were also 'puffed up with the success they have obtained' and 'all, without exception, jealous of France'. Furthermore, Bellièvre felt frustrated at having been dealing with 'a king who does not tell to me all his affairs' and 'in essential matters pays little deference to my counsels', and who repeatedly concluded underhand agreements with different parties.[50]

With a settlement between the Covenanting leadership and the king appearing increasingly unlikely, the grounds for Charles's continued detention in Newcastle were questioned. In October 1646, the Scots Commissioners in London reported objections from English MPs that the Scottish army had taken Charles to Newcastle without even informing the Committee of Both Kingdoms, which was the Covenanting army's nominal commander and paymaster. In response, the Covenanters had defended their action by insisting that Charles was 'king of both kingdoms, and his person indivisible'. Accordingly, they insisted that 'he could not be disposed of by any one of the kingdoms', irrespective of location, 'without the other, but ought to be disposed of by both for the good of both'.[51] English MPs responded with a firm rebuttal, maintaining that 'although the person of the king be not divisible, yet his relations are divisible both in their nature and their exercise; the King of England and the King of Scotland are one man, but they are not one thing'. Denying that the Scots would have any joint interest in the king's fate if he came to Westminster, MPs confirmed that 'neither should we claim any, if he were duly at Edinburgh'.[52] The Independent, Sir John Evelyn, recalled the fate of Charles's grandmother, Mary, Queen of Scots, bluntly reminding the Scots Commissioners 'of the power the English could wield over a Scottish royal "prisoner"'.[53]

Appalled by the irreverence of Commons debates, a Royalist pamphleteer condemned such a 'saucy dispute about the disposing of the sacred person of the King, as if he were a child, a ward, or an idiot'. Although Charles had already conceded triennial parliaments, the author observed that now MPs 'must needs have an everlasting parliament', and also attacked the Palatine Prince Charles Louis for ignoring his uncle's predicament, preferring the company of Westminster Assembly divines and displaying a 'princely faculty of snuffing up the back-breath of the Reverend Synod, and in a blind devotion takes it for incense'.[54] Meanwhile, in Newcastle the embattled king shared the Independents' distaste for overweening Scottish influence and warned Henrietta Maria in December that if she was ever told that 'any alteration can make the Covenant passable', her advisers were 'either fool or knave; for this damned Covenant is the child of rebellion, and breathes nothing but treason'.[55] Even if the Covenant bound its signatories to introduce Episcopacy, Charles insisted that he would still refuse to sign as to do so would fundamentally breach the integrity of royal power.

By this stage, Bellièvre was wearily beseeching Brienne to secure his recall to Paris, grimly apprehending that, since Charles's fate seemed hopeless, 'the last doctors called in receive the blame', even if difficulties were largely due to 'the errors of their predecessors or the bad conduct of the patient have rendered the malady incurable'. Trying to gauge the English king's medium-term intentions, the ambassador gloomily admitted on Christmas Eve 1646, 'I always fear it may be that of going to France', despite Bellièvre's advice that if Charles left his kingdoms, 'it may be very difficult for him to return again'.[56] But matters had moved ahead of the king's musings. The English Parliament agreed to pay the Scottish Estates the immense sum of £400,000 as retrospective recompense for their army's assistance in the war against Charles, the surrender of the king and the army's return to Scotland. As parliamentary representatives arrived in Newcastle to take custody of Charles in January 1647, one of the Scots Commissioners in London, John Maitland, earl of Lauderdale, feared that delivery of the king to the English would result in the Scots being 'hissed at by all nations; yea, the dogs in the street would piss upon them', while Montereul later confirmed popular denunciations of the Scots as 'people who had sold their king, and their honour'.[57]

To foreign observers, Charles was clearly now a prisoner of the English Parliament. In the Dutch Republic, Joost van den Vondel published a play entitled *Maria Stuart of Gemartelde Majesteit* (1646) ('Mary Stuart, or Martyred Majesty') which was evidently not performed but went through five printed editions in two years. Reimagining the final day in the life of Charles's grandmother, Mary, Queen of Scots, Vondel's anonymous play invoked divine parallels by recreating the queen's 'final supper' with her Catholic ladies-in-waiting in 1587 and was dedicated to Mary's great-grandson, the Palatine Prince Edward, whose clandestine marriage in France had prompted the prince's recent conversion to Catholicism. With the play's emotional weight now freighted by contemporary dilemmas in England, rather than events under Elizabeth I, Vondel's text emphasized the brutality of a country that could order the murder of a divinely ordained monarch. Since 'this realm has witnessed more than once its monarch die', 'Mary' asked:

> What wonder is it then, if yet another mob
> Increases with my corpse the count of slaughtered Kings
> Of English blood. Is't not the English custom
> To hold the blood of Kings of very little worth?[58]

III

With Charles detained in Parliamentarian custody at Holdenby House in Northamptonshire, opportunities for foreign involvement were necessarily limited. Having returned to London after the king's departure from Newcastle, Bellièvre confided to Brienne that, 'in doing nothing, he risks everything'. Had Charles 'done the little we wished of him, he would have re-established himself', but Bellièvre feared that 'it is very difficult to save him against his will'.[59] As Independent factions in both the English Parliament and New Model Army gained ascendancy over their Presbyterian, pro-Scottish rivals, Charles was forcibly seized by a junior military officer, George Joyce, and transferred from Holdenby House to the Army's headquarters at Newmarket in early June 1647, before being moved to Hampton Court Palace, nearer London, in August. A new set of markedly moderate peace terms was framed by the Army's General Council and presented to the king as the *Heads of the Proposals* in July. The proposals envisaged biennial parliaments; entrusting control of England's armed forces and foreign policy to a Council of State for ten years; preserving Episcopacy (albeit without any authority) in the Church of England; avoiding enforcement of either the Covenant or Book of Common Prayer; and limiting the number of named Royalists to be exempted from pardon to single figures. But to Henrietta Maria's dismay, Charles summarily rejected the *Heads of the Proposals* as too restrictive. According to a London newsletter received by the Venetian ambassador in Paris, 'the one thing certain is that nothing is certain, as confusion has reached such a pitch that the most essential decrees do not ordinarily last more than a day'.[60]

While Charles was at Hampton Court, he was regularly visited by foreign envoys, as well as by family, including his Palatine nephew Charles Louis. Writing to his mother, the Electress Elizabeth, in November, Charles Louis described a difficult meeting with his uncle, in which the king had rejected Charles Louis's protests of financial necessity, telling him 'that I should rather have lived on bread and water, than to have complied with his Parliament'. To the king's mind, Charles Louis had cynically sought to have 'one more chicken in my dish', evidently believing 'it a design more worthy [of] his nephew, if I had gone about to have taken the crown from his head'.[61] The day after this tense exchange between uncle and nephew, the king donned a disguise for the second time in two years to effect a nocturnal escape from Hampton Court. As one attendant described, after finding the king had disappeared 'in his shoes and stockings, it was supposed he might be in the garden, [or] down the backstairs', before speculating that he may instead be heading 'some think for Scotland, others for London, some for Jersey: others (which is more probable) to the Isle of Wight'.[62] Having indeed fled to Carisbrooke Castle on the Isle of Wight, Charles again found himself detained as a Parliamentarian prisoner. Although always foiled in the attempt, he plotted a creative range of escapes that variously included 'breaking through to the roof of the room above his bedroom, crawling through a window and descending on a rope, filing through the bars or dissolving them with acid, bribing his guards, starting a fire in the castle and exiting amidst the confusion, leaving disguised in a porter's frock, [or] switching clothes with a visitor' and thereafter sailing to Gosport, Jersey or Holland.[63]

In Ireland, interminable delays incurred in achieving peace between Charles's administration in Dublin and the Confederate Assembly of Kilkenny had deprived the Royalists of potential military support, while also delivering serial propaganda coups to the Parliamentarians. In July 1646, Ormond had eventually concluded a peace that raised a Royalist army and agreed extensive political and economic concessions to Catholic landowners but avoided significant religious commitments. Ormond's peace was, however, denounced by the papal nuncio, Rinuccini, who excommunicated any Assembly member who accepted its terms and, assuming control of the Assembly's Supreme Council, declared the peace to be void. But in Paris, the 'Ormond Peace' had been warmly received by Henrietta Maria's circle and Digby wrote to Mazarin, acclaiming 'the so effective involvement of France' in its achievement.[64] After Royalist troops had unsuccessfully tried to attack Dublin, a delegation from the English Parliament arrived in the Irish capital and Ormond eventually surrendered both the city and his office to Colonel Michael Jones in July 1647.

As the eighth Confederate General Assembly gathered at Kilkenny in November, Ormond admitted to Mazarin that it seemed 'impossible that Ireland can subsist [alone] but must immediately submit to England, and so considerably increase the power thereof; or else give herself to the pope or the king of Spain'.[65] Debates lasting over a month considered the relative merits of seeking unofficial French military assistance via Henrietta Maria and Prince Charles, or formally inviting foreign intervention from either Pope Innocent X, Louis XIV or Philip IV, before resolving to send envoys to Rome, Paris and Madrid to establish the likely terms of any intervention. But by 1647, Spain was trying to suppress rebellion in Naples and Sicily, as well as in Catalonia and Portugal. Accordingly, when the prospect of Spain assuming the Protectorship of Ireland was mooted, Philip had responded that 'we are not in a time of conquering new kingdoms, but of recovering those we have lost and of holding onto those we have'.[66] For its part, the Confederate Assembly resolved to invite the Prince of Wales to install himself as Protector of Ireland or, alternatively, to ask the prince to nominate a Catholic Lord Deputy. Meanwhile, the anti-Spanish uprisings simultaneously taking place in southern Europe provided direct encouragement to more radical 'Leveller' civilians and factions within the New Model Army that were agitating for extensive constitutional and social reform. Admiring the republican impetus gaining ground in Italy, one attendee at a Leveller rally in London in November 1647 observed, 'the same business we are upon is perfected in Naples; for if any persons stand up for monarchy there, he is immediately hanged at his door'.[67]

Resisting Leveller radicalism, Parliamentarian leaders instead determined to test Charles's resolution to seek peace by presenting a minimalist framework for a settlement, termed the 'Four Bills', to the king at Carisbrooke Castle on Christmas Eve 1647. Based on the

Newcastle Propositions offered the previous year, the 'Four Bills' accorded Parliament control of the army in England, Wales and Ireland for twenty years and recognized Parliament's right to adjourn itself to any location it wished. Charles was uninterested, however, in agreeing to peace proposals, having succeeded in negotiating, while at Carisbrooke, with three Scottish envoys – the earls of Lanark, Loudoun and Lauderdale – in a new Royalist alliance. In the process he warned the Scots that, without their support, he might have no option but to conclude a peace with the English Independents that could lead to the English conquest of Ireland and also, potentially, of Scotland. In an 'Engagement' concluded with the Scots on 26 December, terms were agreed for a future settlement whereby, apart from the royal household, Presbyterianism would be established throughout England for three years before an assembly of divines agreed a permanent religious settlement. Charles also agreed to ensure that one third of his state officers and Privy Councillors were Scots, and to 'endeavour a complete union' of England and Scotland. If the Westminster Parliament refused to accept these new terms, a Scottish army would be dispatched to invade England for a fourth time.

Cheered by securing the 'Engagement', Charles was convinced that he was now heading a new, triangulated pan-archipelagic Royalist coalition and rejected the 'Four Bills' on 28 December. As news of Charles's new Scottish alliance became known, his Parliamentarian adversaries reacted with predictably apoplectic rage. On 3 January 1648, a 'Vote of No Addresses' passed the Commons, precluding any further negotiations with the king and barring both Houses of Parliament from receiving future representations from Charles. The following month, the Commons published a *Declaration*, proclaiming MPs' attempts to reach a peaceful settlement to have been continually frustrated and protesting that, since 'we have no less than seven times made such applications to the king', it was Charles who should be held accountable for 'the blood of many hundred thousand freeborn subjects in three great kingdoms'. As well as the king's persistent attempts to 'enslave' England through the use of 'German, Spanish, French, Lorraine, Irish, Danish and other forces', MPs also added, for good measure, the old accusation that Charles and the late marquess of Buckingham had been complicit in James VI & I's death in 1625. After calls in the parliament of 1626 for an investigation of the circumstances surrounding

James's death had gone unheeded, MPs now warned, 'we leave the world now to judge where the guilt of this remains'.[68] Deeming Charles's most recent duplicity 'a more prodigious treason than any that had been perfected before', an outraged Oliver Cromwell acknowledged that earlier hostilities had arisen over whether 'Englishmen might rule over one another', but Charles's new alliance with the Scots denoted a clear attempt 'to vassalise us to a foreign nation'.[69] The stage was set for renewed civil war.

13
England shall become Hell, 1648–1650

In February 1649, a shocked Venetian envoy, Alvise Contarini, reported to the Doge and Senate from Munster that, following the English Parliament's decision to place its king on trial for treason, a capital sentence had been passed and Charles I had been executed on 30 January 1649 'like a common criminal, in London, before all the people . . . history affords no example of the like'.[1] An anonymous *Advertisement* to kings and princes, published in Paris, denounced the horror as scarcely credible: 'to see a hereditary monarch die in the infamy of a public execution, it is, to speak truly, a monster'.[2] But, as another French pamphleteer confirmed of England's political elite, this was not, of course, 'the first time that they have exercised their cruelty on the sacred person of their kings'.[3] Recalling the fate of an erstwhile queen of France, another commentator reminded French readers that, despite having 'covered her scaffolds with Mary Stuart's blood', the English had now plunged their 'sacrilegious hands into the blood of this queen's grandson'.[4] Posterity would nevertheless find it difficult to credit that the English had dispatched a British-born Protestant king, whose accession to the English throne had been uncontested, and who had legitimate heirs and powerful foreign relations and allies.

In London, the Royalist newsbook *The Man in the Moon* dubbed the first anniversary of Charles's execution 'Saint Regicide's Day' and demanded that 'every 30 of January may be printed in red letters in the Devil's Calendar' as 'the highest holy-day' in the diabolical year.[5] In 1650, the German playwright Andreas Gryphius started composing a tragedy entitled *Carolus Stuardus*, published seven years later, which blasted the regicide as abhorrent and despicably blasphemous. Gryphius's drama concluded with a chorus of 'the assassinated kings of

England' appealing to the character 'Revenge' who proleptically warned *Aus Engelland wird helle werden* – 'England shall become Hell'.[6]

I

The likelihood of such a radical outcome to the civil wars had, however, only recently seemed remote. Indeed, in the first half of 1648, it had been popular Royalist risings that had erupted across Kent, Essex, the Home Counties, northern England and the Welsh Marcher counties, as well as across north and south Wales, amid calls for royal authority to be restored and the New Model Army disbanded. Parliamentarian nervousness was especially acute in regard to disturbances in Kent, given the county's attractiveness as a potential landing-point for foreign forces as well as its capacity to disrupt London's trade routes. As the Westminster authorities ordered publication of intercepted letters that indicated an imminent invasion by combined Franco-Danish-Dutch forces, a Kentish commander warned the Parliamentarian Lord General, Sir Thomas Fairfax, that local insurgents hoped to 'possess themselves of all the castles and strongholds and thereby secure landing for the Irish, French or Danes, of whose coming they fondly flatter themselves'.[7]

In May 1648, a naval mutiny saw the crews of twelve Parliamentarian warships defect to the Royalist cause, including the Parliamentarian flagship, the *Constant Reformation*. Although the switch of allegiance proved temporary for the crews of the *Greyhound* and *Antelope* in the North Sea squadron, further unrest left the fleet's Lord Admiral, Robert Rich, earl of Warwick, with fewer scattered ships than his Royalist adversaries.[8] That same month, Charles's second son, James, duke of York, disguised himself as a young woman and escaped Parliamentarian custody, later arriving at the court of his sister Mary in The Hague, where he joined his Palatine cousins Princes Rupert and Maurice, together with the Prince of Wales, who had left the French court in July to assume command of an expanded Royalist naval force at Helvoetsluys. Accompanying the naval mutinies and military resurgence in the localities was an efflorescence of Royalist newsletters, including the satirical *Mercurius Insanus, Insanissimus*, which chronicled 'these mad times' and pitied the English people being oppressed by a deluded Parliament that imposed mounting taxes and tried 'to stop their mouths' with invented reports of 'plots, conspiracies, fears, and jealousies, from Scotland, France, Spain, Rome, Ireland, Wales, Holland, Dover and Dunbar, Utopia, The Devil's Arse a peak'.[9] Earlier that year, *Mercurius Aulicus* had likewise rejected Parliamentarian calls for religious 'reformation' as a 'stalking horse' that had thrown 'our English world quite off the wheels'.[10]

More sceptical voices cautioned that further Royalist ventures in England and Wales would only succeed if coordinated with support promised by Charles's recent 'Engagement' with the Scots. Recalled from Continental exile, the Royalist army officer John, Lord Byron, identified the anticipated Scots' invasion as 'the *primum mobile* from whence these orbs here must receive their motion', warning that 'nothing can be so prejudicial to this design as delay'.[11] But internal divisions within the Scottish Parliament meant that the 'Engager' army of around 10,000 soldiers commanded by James, duke of Hamilton, and James Livingston, earl of Callendar, did not cross the Cumbrian border into England until early July, by which time most of the popular uprisings in Wales and southern England had been quelled. Despite reinforcements of another 10,000 English troops, Hamilton's army was comprehensively defeated by Parliamentarian forces, commanded by Lieutenant General Oliver Cromwell, at the Battle of Preston in mid-August. Meanwhile, although Prince Charles's fleet had sailed with around twenty ships and 2,000 men to Yarmouth in July, the ships were refused permission to land, prompting a retreat to the Downs in east Kent. While the fleet lay at the Downs, a Scot, William Lauderdale, had arrived with a message from the king requesting his rescue from the Isle of Wight, but 'it was no more listened to, nor regarded, than if a dog had been sent to them'.[12] After opting instead for ill-advised forays into privateering that only antagonized local merchants, the prince's fleet returned to Holland in late August, having achieved nothing.

At Westminster, moderate Parliamentarians lent their support to a House of Commons decision to reverse the 'Vote of No Further Addresses' in late August. The following month, peace talks were restarted with the king at Newport on the Isle of Wight and, by late November, Charles had agreed to cede to Parliament control of the militia, the appointment of state officers and direction of Irish affairs for twenty years, together with establishment of Presbyterianism in England for three years and a ban on further negotiations with the Irish

Confederate Assembly. Setting aside the question of Charles's likely fidelity to such terms, had they been formally translated into a peace agreement, the Treaty of Newport would have denoted a clear capitulation. As the Royalist James Howell had warned in September, any monarch that surrendered control of his army would 'render himself such a ridiculous king' as to become 'a king of clouts, or as the Spaniard hath it, Rey de Havas, a Bean-King': a stock-figure of Twelfth Night revelry. Such terms not only invalidated a king's claim to be 'Defender of the Faith', but Howell also doubted that any 'foreign prince or state will send either Ambassador, Resident or Agent to him, when they understand his sword is taken from him'. Disarming a monarch meant that 'the whole kingdom is under an eclipse' and trying to conclude a settlement on such terms was 'as absurd' as trying 'to set a watch by the gnomon' on a sundial 'when the sun is in a cloud'.[13]

Echoing Howell's solar imagery, the anti-Independent Somerset MP, Clement Walker, observed how Parliamentarian newsbook writers were increasingly 'taught to speak no language but Cromwell and his party', invoking Cervantes to infer that 'all other men must be eclipsed' to render Oliver Cromwell as 'the Knight of the Sun and Don Quixote of the Independents'.[14] Cromwell's meteoric rise from successful soldier to Parliamentarian powerbroker had only been spurred by masterminding the recent victory at Preston, against overwhelming numerical odds, which Cromwell had insisted was due to 'nothing [but] the hand of God'.[15] Yet in a later account of the British civil wars, Philip IV's ambassador, Alonso de Cárdenas, recalled being appalled by Cromwell's inclination to present his determination to exclude Charles from any lasting settlement as the result of 'long consultations with God', with the English populace 'tricked by Cromwell into believing these ramblings, which he sold to the people as divine revelations'.[16]

While Royalists were disgusted by the demeaning scope of the Treaty of Newport's terms, the New Model Army's leaders were equally furious that MPs could even countenance agreeing a settlement with a monarch they regarded as irremediably perfidious. In November 1648, the Army directed a *Remonstrance* to the House of Commons that identified Charles as 'that capital and grand author of our troubles' and demanded that 'exemplary justice be done in capital punishment upon the principal author and some prime instruments of our late wars, and thereby the blood thereof expiated'.[17] Time-limited provision was extended to the Prince of Wales and duke of York to agree terms with Parliament or face permanent banishment and exclusion from future royal office. For his part, when Charles wrote to his eldest son in late November, he acknowledged that 'this may be the last time we may speak to you, or the world publicly'. He beseeched the prince to 'censure us not for having parted with so much of our own right' and insisted that peace remained his priority, being convinced that 'the English nation are a sober people, however at present infatuated'.[18] When MPs ignored the Army's *Remonstrance* and voted in favour of the Newport terms as a basis for future negotiations, the Army took unilateral action in the form of 'Pride's Purge' on 6 December. Troops led by Colonel Thomas Pride arrested forty-five MPs and secluded another 186, while a further eighty-six members withdrew in protest, leaving a 'Rump' Parliament of around 150 MPs willing to approve the Army's proposals. Facilitated by a military coup d'état, Parliamentarian moves towards regicide could now be realized.

An Army escort moved the king from Carisbrooke Castle, first across the Solent to Hurst Castle and then to Windsor Castle on 23 December. Having been a victim of Pride's Purge, the Puritan pamphleteer and imprisoned MP William Prynne published a spirited assault on the 'Rump' Parliament's proceedings on 1 January 1649, warning that 'no Protestant kingdom or state, ever yet defiled their hands' or compromised their faith's purity, by deposing a Protestant prince. To do so would fatally vitiate decades of stringent Protestant opposition to papal deposition theories and present 'such an unparalleled scandal to the Protestant religion' that it would 'give the greatest occasion, advantage and encouragement to the Jesuits, papists, and all licentious persons'. Moreover, Prynne warned that killing Charles would not only 'make parliaments forever hereafter execrable and detestable' to monarchs and subjects alike, it would also disregard the fact that Scotland and Ireland were 'tenants in common with us in the king's person' and that custody of Charles had been surrendered by the Scots at Newcastle in 1647 on the explicit understanding that the king's person would remain unharmed. Failing to secure assent for regicide from the Scots and Irish would 'engage both kingdoms to make a just war against you' that would reignite English Royalism and attract foreign support. As Prynne reminded MPs, 'you have neither law nor direct precedent for what you are going about'.[19]

Prynne's horror was shared by members of Louis XIV's court in Paris which issued a *Declaration* condemning the intentions of 'a small handful of the basest of people, crept into the Lower House of Parliament, but being not the tenth part thereof'. Alarmed at English MPs' treatment of 'our neighbouring king and uncle', Louis's ministers called on all neighbouring nations – whether allies or foes of France – to bury their differences and 'revenge the hypocrisy of enraged villains' who claimed to be acting in God's name. Assuring other states of French assistance 'if the like madness took any of their armies', the *Declaration* called on other Continental powers to present a united front so that, when 'chased out of their native country', those involved in proceedings against Charles would be denied refuge and find themselves obliged to 'wander like vagabonds in heathen places with the odious brand of regicides upon them'.[20]

On 6 January, the Scottish Parliament's resident Commissioners in London – William Kerr, earl of Lothian, Sir John Chiesley and William Glendinning – echoed Prynne's alarm and protested to the Commons Speaker, William Lenthall, that English MPs' actions would 'greatly weaken and divide us amongst ourselves, invite foreign enemies against us, advance the Popish interest, lose Ireland' and undermine both Protestantism and any prospect of peace in Britain.[21] That same day, however, creation of a High Court of Justice was approved which undertook not to hear the king's case before a common law jury, but to be constituted as a judicial body, comprising 135 nominated judges. Although only fifty-three of the nominated judges presented themselves for the court's first session two days later, those appointed as prosecution counsel included a Dutch-born historian and diplomat, Isaac Dorislaus, a Congregationalist solicitor, John Cook and a barrister, John Bradshaw.

Charles's trial started in Westminster Hall on 20 January and was watched by fee-paying members of the public. The king faced charges that included being 'the occasioner, author and continuer of the said unnatural, cruel and bloody wars, and therein guilty of all the treasons, murders, rapines, burnings, spoils, desolations, damages and mischiefs to this nation' that had ensued. Dismayed that Charles had now been 'brought before this new extraordinary Court', the Scots Commissioners issued another plea on the day that the king's trial started, insisting that Parliament's proceedings were 'so far contrary to the declared intentions of the kingdom of Scotland' and in breach of earlier undertakings by their English allies.[22] Judicial proceedings were, however, frustrated by Charles's insistence that the assembled court lacked competent authority to try him. Placed on trial for treason by the English state, Charles adopted a different course to that chosen by his grandmother Mary, Queen of Scots, by refusing even to enter a plea of guilty or non-guilty on the grounds that it was 'as great a sin to withstand lawful authority, as it is to submit to a tyrannical, or any other ways unlawful authority'. When Bradshaw insisted that he was answerable to 'the people of England, of which you are elected king', Charles retorted simply that 'England was never an elective kingdom, but a hereditary kingdom for near these thousand years'.[23]

After several hearings and adjournments, the king was again summoned before the court on 27 January and informed that 'Charles Stuart, as a tyrant, traitor, murderer, and public enemy to the good people of this nation, shall be put to death by the severing of his head from his body'.[24] Two days later, fifty-nine of the 135 members of the High Court of Justice put their names as signatories to the king's death warrant. That same day, the king bid farewell to his two children who remained in Parliamentarian custody – Princess Elizabeth, aged thirteen, and eight-year-old Henry, duke of Gloucester – and enjoined the latter to refuse any overtures from the authorities to be crowned in succession to his father. Aware that Henry's coronation as a puppet monarch would render hollow the grounds on which he had refused to acknowledge the court's authority, Charles warned Henry that 'they will cut off your brothers' heads (when they can catch them) and cut off thy head too at last'.[25]

On 30 January 1649, the king walked through the Banqueting Hall at Whitehall – under the baroque frescoed ceiling that he had commissioned from Peter Paul Rubens to honour his father, James VI & I – onto a temporary scaffold outside. To avoid appearing to tremble from fear, the king had donned two thick shirts to brave the January cold and, on the scaffold, insisted to soldiers enclosing the area 'that I am an innocent man' and denied that he had ever sought to 'begin a war with the two Houses of Parliament'. He did, however, acknowledge culpability for the earl of Strafford's death, nearly eight years earlier, expressing remorse that 'an unjust sentence' that he had allowed to stand 'is punished now by an unjust sentence upon me'. Regarding his subjects, Charles maintained that he sought 'their liberty and freedom as much as anybody', but denied that their interests would be promoted by a Parliamentarian regime that based its illegal claims to authority solely on military conquest. As the king insisted from the scaffold, 'I am the martyr of the people'.[26]

II

Whereas his grandmother's execution at the hands of the English state had occurred behind closed doors in rural Northamptonshire in 1587, the avowedly public character of Charles's trial and execution in England's capital city invited public judgement and debate. Only three days after the regicide, the dazed Spanish ambassador, Cárdenas, wrote to Philip IV's secretary, Geronimo de la Torre, lamenting that 'we are here in utter chaos, living without religion, king or law, subject entirely to the power of the sword'. Observing a small faction establishing itself as 'the conqueror of the realm', Cárdenas feared 'many novelties will spring'.[27]

On 4 February – five days after the regicide and five days before the dead king's burial at St George's Chapel, Windsor – Bishop John Warner preached a sermon entitled *The Devilish Conspiracy, Hellish Treason, Heathenish Condemnation, and Damnable Murder* (1649). Drawing an extended parallel between Christ's Passion and Charles's execution, Warner attacked 'the soldiers, who did vomit out their excrementitious froth upon him' and 'the scum of the people' who had the temerity to 'slaughter him, the Anointed of the Lord'. In the sermon's printed version, Warner referred interchangeably to 'Ch: the King' who had died 'for our laws and liberties, and so is become, by his death, your martyr, your sacrifice and your saviour'.[28] In The Hague on the same day, Charles's eighteen-year-old son and heir received the devastating news of his father's public execution in London. No longer the Prince of Wales, the young king was immediately addressed as 'Your Majesty'.

When news of the regicide reached Edinburgh on 5 February, the Scottish Parliament instantly proclaimed Charles II king not only of Scotland, but also of England, Ireland and (notionally) France, in succession to his father. The following day, the English House of Commons voted to abolish the House of Lords as 'useless and dangerous', before voting on 7 February to abolish the monarchy as 'unnecessary, burdensome and dangerous to the liberty, safety and public interest' of the people, although legislation confirming these votes was not enacted until mid-March. The Scots Commissioners in London formally objected to such sweeping constitutional changes, urged MPs to accept Charles II's monarchical authority and fled to Gravesend, hoping to sail to The Hague. But as their ship was about to depart, the Scots were intercepted and detained in Gravesend by the Parliamentarian army officer Edward Sexby, who politely offered that 'if they liked to take any house in the town it should be prepared for them, which they kindly accepted' and, after further liaison with Westminster, secured the Commissioners' return to Scotland, rather than to the exiled Royalist court.[29]

Queen Henrietta Maria received news of her husband's death on 9 February at the Louvre Palace in Paris where, a month earlier, she had been left isolated after Louis XIV's court had withdrawn to St Germain-en-Laye and ordered a blockade of Paris to try to suppress the popular uprising known as 'the Fronde'. In Madrid, the Venetian ambassador Pietro Basadonna bemoaned 'a fresh cause of expense' when full mourning dress for foreign envoys was ordered to honour the death of a king acclaimed by Philip IV as a brother-in-law, on account of Philip's Bourbon queen, Elisabeth, being Henrietta Maria's older sister.[30] In the United Provinces, the former Grand Pensionary of Holland, Adriaen Pauw van Heemstede, addressed the States General and admitted that his last-minute journey to London had been a futile attempt to dissuade English Parliamentarian leaders from executing their king. Pauw conceded that he and the resident Dutch ambassador in London, Albert Joachimi, had been received 'with every civility', but their Parliamentarian hosts had nevertheless treated the Dutch envoys in the same manner as the Scots Commissioners by insisting 'substantially that neither the one nor the others, nor any foreigner soever, understood the affairs of England better than the English themselves'. Although, after the regicide, members of the Rump Parliament had evidently considered 'sending ambassadors to all the princes of Europe, to notify what they had done and to justify their proceedings', Pauw added that the new regime's leaders seemed indifferent to overseas reaction, 'feeling perfectly confident that they could defend themselves effectively'.[31]

Confidence among the Rump's leaders derived partly from knowing that the likelihood of French intervention was diluted by the country's internal distractions. Observing the Paris *Parlement* levying troops against Louis's regency government in February 1649, the Royalist exile Sir Edward Nicholas feared that the French were 'here as eager upon rebellion against their governor and government as ever our wretched English were'. Two days after the regicide in London, Nicholas insisted from Caen in Normandy that just as the 'contrivers of the present rebellion in England' had consciously followed in the footsteps of sixteenth-century Catholic Leaguers, so too did Fronde leaders 'trace our Covenanters in all their acts and proceedings'.[32] The Frondeurs could, moreover, quickly learn of events in England as a result of the Rump Parliament's speedy decision to publish detailed accounts of proceedings in the High Court of Justice. For Francophone readers, a full *Narration des Procédures de la Haute Court de Justice en l'Examen du Roy Charles* (1649) was printed in London, while the translator of a *Relation Générale et Veritable* admitted that the king's trial and execution were 'incredible and one of the most strange catastrophes'.[33] In Paris, although the government-sponsored *Gazette de France* reported the regicide three weeks after the event, fears that news from England might exacerbate domestic tensions prevented any further reporting until a truce had been agreed between the Frondeurs and the French court at the end of March. As Cardinal Mazarin's librarian, Gabriel Naudé, objected to the *Gazette*'s editor, Théophraste Renaudot, foreign news only made French readers 'too aware of their conditions, of their business, and this awareness also applies to the affairs of neighbouring peoples'. As matters stood, 'the common people do not know much about these new novelties, and it serves no purpose to inform them minutely about the revolts of Naples, the sedition of Turkey and the horrific attack in England'.[34]

In Brussels, the English resident, Sir Henry de Vic, approached the Governor of the Spanish Netherlands, Archduke Leopold Wilhelm of Austria, to request that formal condolences be sent to Charles I's son in The Hague. De Vic claimed that although envoys from the Dutch States General had visited the young king, they had addressed him as 'Sire in French', before styling him '"Your Majesty", but pronounced the word indistinctly and decline to put in writing what they had said verbally'. De Vic also asked Leopold to obtain confirmation of Charles II's royal title from his nephew Emperor Ferdinand III and from Philip IV, since 'all Europe is in suspense regarding the resolution which the two greatest sovereigns in the world are likely to adopt on this matter'. When a senior Spanish diplomat, Don Gaspar de Bracamonte y Guzman, count of Peñaranda, visited Brussels and coincided with De Vic in July, he knew that the English Parliament would resent any show of diplomatic courtesy to Charles's representative. As Peñaranda wrote to a colleague, he was also mindful that Louis XIV 'has not yet written a single letter of condolence to this poor devil [Charles II], nor has made the slightest manifestation, for six months, that his father's head has been struck off'.[35]

Powerful propaganda success was nevertheless secured for the Royalists by the posthumous publication, a few days after Charles's execution, of the *Eikon Basilike: The Portraiture of His Sacred Majesty in his Solitudes and Sufferings* (1649). Ostensibly presenting the deceased king's direct words to his bereft subjects through a collection of personal meditations assembled shortly before his trial and execution, the *Eikon Basilike* was later recognized as a work of collaborative authorship between the king and the Essex cleric John Gauden. Extending perceived parallels between Christ's Passion and Charles's execution, the *Eikon Basilike* proved immensely popular and appeared in thirty-five English editions in 1649 alone. In March, the royal printer William Dugard produced an expanded edition that included prayers attributed to Charles, a narrative of the king's final farewell to his young children and epitaphs on his death. The work was venerated almost as an appendix to Holy Scripture and speedily resurrected the dead king's reputation. An emotive engraving by William Marshall appeared as the frontispiece, showing Charles holding a crown of thorns, as his earthly crown lay on the floor. Combining political memoir, spiritual reflection and devotional meditation, the *Eikon Basilike* entrenched the image of Charles suffering *in imitatio Christi* and included numerous instances of the late king extending mercy to his adversaries, beseeching God, 'forgive them! Oh my Father, for they know not what they do'. The work presented Charles as flawed but forgiving, and offered readers comfort with its suggestion that the 'most part of my subjects fought against my supposed errors, not my person; and intended to mend me, not to end me'.[36]

The *Eikon Basilike* also attracted an influential international readership, with three Latin and seven Dutch editions being produced in 1649. Retitled the *Konincklick Memoriael* ('Royal Memorial'), the first Dutch translations appeared weeks after the regicide, while Johan Dullaerts created a dramatized version in a play entitled *Karel Stuart of Rampzalige*

Majesteyt ('Charles Stuart or Disastrous Majesty') that was written in 1649 and published three years later. In France, English copies of *Eikon Basilike* appeared within months of the regicide, intended for Royalist exiles, before the first French translation was published at Rouen in June by a Huguenot, Jean-Baptiste Porée.

From the opposite end of the polemical spectrum, the English republican John Milton defended the regicide in *The Tenure of Kings and Magistrates*, published in February 1649, which vituperatively attacked the Scots for claiming to be outraged by the king's execution, given that their resistance to royal policy had been the original trigger of civil wars in Britain. Echoing language deployed in Shakespeare's 'Scottish play', *Macbeth* (1606), Milton reminded readers that it had been Scots Presbyterians who had 'juggled and paltered with the world, bandied and borne arms against their king, divested him, disanointed him, nay cursed him all over in their pulpits and their pamphlets'. But after the king's trial, Charles's erstwhile Scots enemies had resurfaced, 'with a riddling Covenant in their mouths, seeming to swear counter almost in the same breath allegiance, and no allegiance' and in 'cloven tongues of falsehood and dissension' now sought to foment new divisions by appearing to acquit Charles of his alleged crimes and proclaiming his son as immediate successor to all his father's former thrones.[37]

Milton had been appointed by the republican Council of State as the new regime's Secretary for Foreign Tongues, and attacked *Eikon Basilike* directly in his *Eikonoklastes*, published in October 1649, disparaging those 'fools and silly gazers' who had been seduced by the king's fabricated rehabilitation, as newly pious homage to a saintly dead king threatened to rewrite a practical legacy of misrule, division and bloodshed. To this end, Milton lambasted the fawning readiness of Englishmen to 'fall flat and give adoration to the image and memory of this man' who had done more 'to undermine our liberties and put tyranny into an art, than any British king before him'. Rejecting Charles's objections to having been judged and convicted by his political adversaries, Milton retorted that 'they of the Powder-plot against his father might as well have pleaded the same'. Rather than invoking divine images of the suffering Christ, Milton insisted that Charles had resembled 'not our Saviour, but his grandmother Mary, Queen of Scots, as also in the most of his other scruples, exceptions and evasions'. Attempting to counter the *Eikon Basilike*'s propagandistic success, Milton warned that Charles 'seems to have learned, as it were by heart' a script of performative tragedy from his executed grandmother, by appearing 'most martyr-like both of his words and speeches here, and of his answers and behaviour at his trial'. Dismissing Charles's vaunted compassion merely as a device calculated to distract attention, Milton warned that just as 'he glories much in the forgiveness of his enemies; so did his grandmother at her death'.[38]

In the United Provinces, Charles's trial and execution prompted so many partisan responses that the Venetian envoy, Contarini, reported in early March that the Dutch authorities had issued a blanket ban on such publications after 'the people began to take sides for one or the other of the parties and with such fervour that in many places they came to blows'.[39] The keen interest of the country's clerics in unsuccessful Presbyterian attempts to prevent the king's death was evidenced in three different editions of the *Serious and Faithful Representation* – prepared in Amsterdam, Dordrecht and The Hague – that had been made to General Fairfax by a delegation of London Presbyterian ministers, headed by Thomas Gataker. Elsewhere, a Dutch poem entitled '*Op de koning-dooders*' (1649) ('On the regicides') – compared Charles's executioners to Christ-killing Jews, Anabaptists and regicidal popes, as well as (correctly) predicting that the king's death would result in the readmission of Jews into England. Denouncing the dominant influence of religious Independents among the regicides, the anonymous author objected:

> You cut off heads as only Popes have done.
> You've crossed a Rubicon uncrossed by anyone
> Red with Holy Blood spilled from the King's veins
> Freely readmit the Jews; you over-knave their ancestors
> To be Independent, is to be Anabaptist
> Wilier than Jewry, eviller than Popery.[40]

Speedier retribution of sorts was forthcoming when the Rump Parliament sent one of the leading prosecution counsels in the king's trial, Isaac Dorislaus, to The Hague as its envoy in April 1649. As Charles II's presence in The Hague had rendered the city 'a hornet's nest of outraged Royalist exiles', Dorislaus stayed at the Witte Zwaan Inn in Scheveningen before presenting his credentials to the States General.[41] In early May, a Scots military officer (and son of the bishop of Dunblane),

Colonel Walter Whitford, asked the English confessor to the Portuguese ambassador, Don Francesco de Sousa Coutinho, 'whether, in the eyes of God, he had the right to kill the murderer of his king'. Although the confessor's response remains unknown, later that day Whitford and eleven accomplices entered the Witte Zwaan Inn and assassinated Dorislaus before returning to the Portuguese embassy for sanctuary – and diplomatic immunity – from where they made their subsequent escape. Dutch public opinion inclined to support the fugitive murderers, and printed reactions to the assassination included one tract envisaging Dorislaus drowning 'in an abyss of hellish horror, his decaying body oozing forth cancers and pests, capable of scaring off bats, owls and other creatures of the night'.[42] Republican fellow-feeling was also in scarce supply from the Venetian Contarini, who described Dorislaus's murder as 'the well-merited punishment of his temerity': having framed the charges by which Charles I had been tried, Dorislaus had 'the audacity to betake himself to Holland where the king's son was'.[43]

While the Dutch authorities defended themselves against suspicions of negligence in apprehending the assassins, the envoy's body was returned to London where it lay in state at Worcester House before being buried at Westminster Abbey in June. Dorislaus's funeral was attended by all members of the House of Commons, the Lord Mayor and aldermen of London and Chief Justices. Unimpressed by this spectacle of republican piety, an anonymous broadside entitled *A Salt Tear, or the Weeping Onion* objected:

> O how damned Bradshaw quivers as he comes!
> And Fairfax groans! And Cromwell bites his thumbs!
>
> . . . Now pray observe the pomp, the persons, state
> That did attend this alien reprobate.
> Here went Lieutenant General Crocodile,
> And cubs, bred of the slime of our rich Nile
> Who weep before they kill, and whose false tears
> Trickle from blood-shed eyes of murderers.[44]

In the Dutch Republic, Royalist pamphlets promoting the young king's cause included *De Geest van Karolus Stuart verscheenen aan de Nederlanden* (1649) ('The Ghost of Charles Stuart appearing to the Netherlands') in which the ghost of the decapitated king appeared as a bloody corpse, carrying its severed head and beseeching his son-in-law William II of

Orange to intervene in English affairs and seek vengeance on Charles's behalf.[45]

Later that same year, an émigré French Huguenot professor at the University of Leiden, Claude de Saumaise, issued a *Defensio Regia, pro Carolo I*, seeking to unite the forces of international Calvinism with Royalist sympathizers in France and the United Provinces. Execrating the regicide as a sacrilegious parricide undertaken by common rebels, Saumaise denied that the new English Commonwealth promoted popular freedom: rather its 'soldatesque' (military) character denoted an 'odd republic, where it is permitted neither to think what one wants nor to say what one thinks'. To encourage republican revolt overseas, the 'devilish products' intended, Saumaise warned, to kill a further six crowned heads including the French, Spanish, Swedish, Danish and Polish monarchs, before turning their murderous fury on either the Holy Roman Emperor or the Turkish Sultan.[46] Instructed by the English Council to respond publicly, Milton contumeliously attacked the *Defensio Regia* and disparaged Saumaise as a 'French good-for-nothing quack' and meddling 'foreigner who are a complete stranger to our affairs'. By contrast, Milton maintained that he sought to defend the regicide as both 'an eye-witness and a native'. To puncture international sympathy for Charles I's plight, Milton's *Pro Populo Anglicano Defensio* (1651) supplied a Latin rebuttal of Saumaise's claims, deploring the Frenchman's folly in seeking 'to plunge himself gratuitously into our affairs' and judging it unlikely that 'the very English nation should take any public notice of you, you worm'.[47]

III

After the regicide, different Stuart courts-in-exile offered refuge to rival Royalist factions. From 1644, Charles I's widow Henrietta Maria primarily resided at the Louvre Palace in Paris, while her second son, James, duke of York, maintained a separate retinue, initially in Paris, and later entered military service in French and Spanish Habsburg forces. Charles I's eighteen-year-old heir remained at his sister's court at The Hague, trying to discern whether his best chance of recovering his British thrones lay in leading an Irish Royalist counter-attack after a 'Second Ormond Peace' had been reached in January 1649 between

James Butler, marquess of Ormond, and the Confederate Assembly of Kilkenny. The precarious peace had agreed that, pending a Royalist restoration and free parliamentary elections, Irish Catholics would be able to practise their religion freely. Within weeks of the regicide, Charles II's Palatine cousin Prince Rupert had landed near Kinsale, in southern Ireland, with a small fleet of warships, determined to harry the Parliamentarian fleet.

At the same time, an alternative route to regaining his crowns was offered to Charles by a delegation of Scots Commissioners that arrived at The Hague in March 1649. But clear strings attached to any Scottish support: Charles would need to confirm his monarchical authority by swearing the Solemn League and Covenant that his father had so persistently declined. Viewing the prospect of Charles's 'going into Scotland' as 'the worst advice [that] can be given', the king's nominal Chancellor, Sir Edward Hyde, resented the appearance of Scots Commissioners acting 'as if they had rescued his Majesty from destruction, not sold his father to those who murdered him'.[48] Living in exile in Brussels, John Bramhall, the English-born Church of Ireland bishop of Derry, was likewise intent on saving Charles from falling into the Scots' snare and, in *A Fair Warning, to take Heed of the Scottish Discipline* (1649), declared that it was 'time to let the world see' that Scottish Presbyterianism represented 'a greater tyranny than ever Rome brought forth'. Were Charles to return to Scotland as a Covenanted king, Bramhall warned that he would soon see how Kirk control 'makes a monster' of the political commonwealth, turning it into 'an amphisbaena, or a serpent with two heads, one at either end', leaving 'kings but half-kings' with 'no more legislative power in ecclesiastical causes, than a cobbler'.[49] One of the Scots Commissioners at The Hague, Robert Baillie, was horrified when Bramhall then presented his treatise to Charles's Dutch brother-in-law, William, and to several Dutch universities, while also threatening to translate the *Fair Warning* into 'Dutch, French, and Latin' to ensure 'that in the whole neighbouring world, the reputation of the Scots might thereby be wounded, killed and buried'. Baillie's *Review of the Seditious Pamphlet* (1649), published in Delft, discharged an impassioned counter-attack on 'Dr Bramhell' – also styled 'Dr Bramble' – in which Baillie defended Scots' Presbyterian loyalty to the Stuart dynasty and insisted, of the young Charles II, that 'all that comes near may see him as lovely, hopeful and promising a prince for all natural endowments as this day breathes in Europe, or for a long time has swayed a sceptre in Britain'.[50]

Were Charles to return to Scotland as a crowned king and sway his sceptre in Britain, such recognition could, indeed, encourage foreign powers to provide financial and military assistance in his bid to recover all three of his British thrones. In May, Charles sent Hyde, together with Francis, Lord Cottington, on an embassy to Madrid. While the elderly Hispanophile Cottington would be returning to a country in which he had already undertaken three diplomatic postings from 1605 onwards, Hyde suspected that his dispatch offered a means for Charles 'to be rid of him' in order to pursue diplomatic options of which Hyde disapproved, namely, negotiations with the Scots.[51] Once in Spain, ambivalence underpinning the appropriate reception of the exiled king's envoys resulted in repeated postponements of a private audience with Philip IV. When an audience was finally secured in December 1649, Cottington and Hyde reported that the Spanish king had 'asked us very many questions concerning your Majesty's person, of your age, your stature, your complexion, and colour of your hair', as well as the location of his exiled court, 'the extent and strength of it, of the number of the people, and whether the place were secure from surprise or sudden invasion'. Franco-Spanish rivalries nevertheless ensured that Philip's ministers were keen to avoid provoking the republican regime in London: as Hyde admitted to Ormond, he detected 'a wariness how they too boldly provoke those powerful devils, lest France should reap the benefit of it'. More generally, Hyde despaired of the labyrinthine complexities that characterized Spanish court culture as repeated professions of goodwill towards Charles failed to generate any practical assistance. As Hyde complained to Secretary of State Edward Nicholas the following March, 'this court is as void of justice, wisdom, or any virtue which can make it subsist long, as any I ever saw; and the whole people incline to all that mutiny and madness our nation was possessed of before our ruin'. Predicting that Spain would soon follow the same rebellious path as England, Hyde admitted 'I hope to be gone first'.[52]

In a different direction, the playwright Thomas Killigrew was dispatched on a Royalist mission to Venice in a journey that included visits to the Turin court of Charles II's maternal aunt Christine, duchess of Savoy, before stays at Genoa, Livorno, Pisa and Florence. When Killigrew finally arrived in Venice in early 1650, he presented a detailed account of the British civil wars to the Doge and Senate which attributed 'the decadence of our English nation' to the alliance formed between English Parliamentarians and the Scottish Covenanters. Censuring the betrayal of Charles I by the Covenanting army, Killigrew lamented how the late king's life had been 'exposed to the highest bidder, and like a lamb he is sold for 1,200,000 crowns'. Indeed, Killigrew maintained that Charles's adversaries had not 'been able to supply a horrified world with any plausible reason why they involved their king in such miseries or ruined their country with a war in which there were forty pitched battles and at least 300,000 persons slain in the three kingdoms'. Although the dead king's son was now seeking to avenge his father's murder, Killigrew admitted that 'the weapon must be supplied by foreign princes'. If overseas allies failed to help, Killigrew feared that future rebels would only be encouraged 'when they see how easy it is to reduce the best of kings, and see the sudden fall of an empire so firmly founded'. The English Parliament's summary abolition of the monarchy had resulted in the annihilation of an institution that had 'endured nearly 2,000 years and remained firm in spite of the numerous and considerable changes throughout the world'. Somewhat fancifully, Killigrew insisted that, only 'a few years ago, the monarch of Great Britain could lay down the law to all the world, being a prince entirely without enemies and united by marriage and by blood to almost all the Christian princes of Europe'.[53] But although the Venetian authorities made sympathetic noises, again no practical assistance was forthcoming.

More successful was the outcome of Lord Colepeper's mission to Moscow in May 1650. Making his ceremonial entrance, Colepeper had apologized to Tsar Aleksei Mikhailovich and 'excused the King's not sending a present to his Majesty', but secured in return from the Tsar a loan of 20,000 roubles (around £50,000) in furs and corn.[54] Royalist propagandists also took advantage of outraged foreign reaction to the regicide to pen purported 'declarations' in the name of foreign rulers. A printed *Declaration* ostensibly issued by Tsar Aleksei appeared in London in 1650 and justified the recent expulsion of English merchants from Moscow by insisting that 'the rebellion of England, as a universal contagion being become epidemical' had 'poisoned and infected most parts of Christendom'. The fictitious *Declaration* attacked Parliamentarian agents operating 'in all kingdoms and territories of Europe; whose restless industry is to crack the bonds of allegiance and fealty between subjects and their sovereigns'. Events in England had revealed a shockingly 'new method of treason, so miraculously proditorious [perfidious], that the whole council of Devils could give them no direction in, nor the records of Hell afford a pattern' so hazardous. Claiming to echo Louis XIV's call that 'ancient and private quarrels' should be forgotten, the 'Tsar' invited all Christian princes to a conference in Antwerp in April 1650 in order to raise a coalition army to fight 'this second holy war, wherewith we will invade that kingdom both by sea and land'.[55]

However plausible the prospect of a Russian Tsar spearheading an international holy war against an illegal republican regime might seem, envoys sent to foreign courts found their freedom for manoeuvre constrained by an inescapable pessimism attaching to the Stuart cause. In England, the Council of State had prioritized the re-conquest of Ireland and Parliamentarian forces under Cromwell had secured a major battlefield victory at the Battle of Rathmines in August 1649, followed by bloody sieges at Drogheda and Wexford that autumn. As Royalist plans to undertake a major Irish counter-offensive had to be abandoned, Charles's exiled court relocated to Jersey between September 1649 and February 1650 where the king's ministers quarrelled over different strategic options. Writing to Hyde in December, the Royalist officer Sir John Berkeley admitted his frustration with 'those paragons now at Jersey', whose unrealistic punctilios ensured that Charles's party was continually 'losing what we might have had, because we could not obtain what we wished to have'. In Berkeley's view, 'we ought to give one hand to the Catholic Roman, and the other to the Presbyterian, and join with them both to the destruction of our common enemy'.[56] Following Charles's decision to leave Jersey and return via France to Breda, an English republican spy trailing the exiled court observed the deleterious effect of divided counsel, predicting that the king's advisers were more likely 'to lose him ten kingdoms (if he had them) than to recover him one'.[57]

Although Ireland had been comprehensively and violently subjugated by Cromwell's troops, Charles knew that Scotland remained divided between the Covenanting regime in power and Royalist forces loyal to James Graham, marquess of Montrose, who was currently attempting an invasion of Scotland, with Scandinavian funds, via the Orkney Islands. Directly after his father's death, Charles had written to Frederick III of Denmark, reminding his cousin of the dynastic

Oldenburg–Stuart alliance and soliciting support to reclaim his father's thrones, 'by the laws of nature, as a son; by the reasons and interests of state, as a prince; and by the rule of piety as a Christian'.[58] A year later, in February 1650, a newsletter from Stockholm relayed reports that Montrose's fleet bore taffeta flags 'with a man's head in the middle, bleeding as if new cut off', while Queen Christina of Sweden informed her country's *Riksråd* that 'it was of concern to all potentates to see Charles II reinstalled in his kingdoms'.[59]

As uncertainty surrounded the outcome of Montrose's mission, Charles embarked on new negotiations with a second delegation of Scots Commissioners who had arrived in Breda in March, albeit to the amusement of the English spy who confirmed the extent of their mutual antipathy. Of Charles, it was 'evident still that he perfectly hates them, and neither of them can so dissemble it, but each other knows it'. As the spy perceived, the Scots' main aim in courting Charles was to encourage another advance on England: 'if the King please them and sign the Covenant, and satisfy the Kirk, they are ready, the whole nation as one man, to invade England'. Meanwhile, the young king 'strokes them till he can get into the saddle, and then he will make them feel his spurs for all their old jades' tricks they have played his father'. Alarmed by Charles's apparent readiness to conclude terms, his anti-Scottish advisers 'tell him he is a dead man if ever he gives himself up to the Scots, for they will sell him to the scaffold, as they sold his father'.[60]

Further afield, rumours that Charles might make concessions to the Scots Presbyterians undermined the efforts of envoys seeking assistance from Catholic powers. From Rome, Sir Robert Meynell admitted to Cottington in April that, despite professions of support for the Royalist cause, concerns about a potential agreement between Charles and the Scots was 'where the shoe pinches'. Following the failed attempts of the papal nuncio Giovanni Battista Rinuccini to transform Catholic interests in Ireland, Pope Innocent X now demanded concrete assurances that practical assistance would translate into specific guarantees. As Meynell explained, papal support was only likely if Charles's ministers, under the new king's seal, should confirm that 'we will do this for Catholics, if you will do this for us . . . in positive instructions'.[61] At home, prominent members of the English republican regime nevertheless anticipated large-scale military desertions to Charles's cause if the young king were to lead an army of invasion from Scotland into England. In

May 1650, an intercepted Royalist report described a dinner attended by the Yorkshire judge (and lapsed Parliamentarian) Francis Thorpe who had feigned loyalty to his fellow diners so as 'not to make himself suspected'. Believing himself to be among allies, Councillor of State Sir Henry Vane had bewailed that 'they were in a far worse estate than ever they had yet been' and 'that all the world was, and would be, their enemies'. As the New Model Army's pay arrears mounted, Vane worried that the regime's 'own army and generals were not to be trusted' and that 'the whole kingdom would rise and cut their throats upon the first good occasion'. Nor could Vane imagine 'any place to go to be safe'.[62]

The following month, Madrid proved anything but safe when a newly arrived Parliamentarian envoy, Anthony Ascham, was assassinated by Royalists. In the preceding weeks, Charles's representatives, Cottington and Hyde, had appealed to the Spanish court not to receive Ascham and had emphasized the stridently republican content of his published works. Although Philip's ministers had countered such appeals by citing Charles I's willingness to receive John of Braganza's Portuguese representative in 1641, Hyde and Cottington pointed out that Ascham had cited 'examples from the Spanish monarchy and especially from the causes of the Neapolitan insurrection' of 1647–8 to argue that all forms of monarchical government were contrary to the laws of nations and usually degenerated into tyranny. But before he could be accorded any form of public reception, Ascham was murdered by six English, Scots and Irish soldiers, in Spanish service, at a guest-house in Madrid's Caballero de Gracia. All but one of the fleeing attackers had found sanctuary in a nearby religious hospital, having been denied asylum by the Venetian ambassador Pietro Basadonna who had, however, facilitated the discreet escape of the single Protestant attacker, after appeals from Cottington and Hyde. As Basadonna acknowledged to the Doge and Senate, he had thereby had 'the good fortune to receive simultaneously the thanks of the king for declining to receive the murderers of the republican envoy, and those of the Royalist ambassadors for saving their steward'.[63] While the ambassador's comments implied collusion, Basadonna believed that the English envoys lacked sufficient funds to have organized Ascham's murder, while an officially sanctioned assassination would presumably also have made better plans for the attackers' escape.

For their part, Hyde and Cottington were determined to prevent

Ascham's assassination from being treated as the outrageous murder of an accredited public minister of a legitimate regime. Following the Spanish authorities' decision to detain the attackers, Hyde composed a Latin treatise, the Spanish translation of which appeared as *Consideraciones Dignas de Atencion, y Peso, sobre el Caso de los Cavalleros Ingeles* (1650) ('Important and Weighty Considerations in the Case of the English soldiers').[64] As Hyde reminded Philip's ministers, following Isaac Dorislaus's death in The Hague the Dutch authorities had not pursued matters further and the known suspects had 'walked freely in those streets', even though Dorislaus had been Dutch-born. Hyde knew that the Spanish court was anxious not to antagonize the Parliamentarian regime, partly from concern for the personal safety of their representative in London, Cárdenas, who had been denied diplomatic immunity and protection on the grounds that he had not yet officially recognized the republican regime as legitimate and sovereign. Hyde warned that the English Parliament was nevertheless also making 'specious overtures to France and Portugal, thereby hoping to keep all the world in suspense, till they can by degrees kindle domestic troubles and distractions in the several dominions'.[65] Philip's ministers refused to be cowed by Royalist or republican pressures into expediting the judicial process and Ascham's attackers remained in custody until 1653.

Having failed to secure Spanish assistance for Charles's cause, Hyde and Cottington took their leave of Philip IV's court in March 1651, with Cottington opting to reside permanently thereafter in Valladolid, following his conversion to Catholicism, while Hyde headed for Antwerp. By that time, Charles had long since concluded terms with the Scots Commissioners in Breda and had left the United Provinces. On 1 January 1651, Charles became the last British monarch to be crowned in Scotland, thereby recovering the first of his father's lost thrones. A Dutch print of Charles's coronation at Scone Palace by Hugo Allard the Elder depicted the young king with a plumed helmet and formal deed containing his royal titles. In Allard's print, 'Ireland' knelt by the king and adjusted his armour, while 'Scotland' gave Charles a pistol marked *Getergde Wraak*: 'Provoked Vengeance'.[66]

14

'Here *was* ye King's Head', 1650–1654

In 1652, the resident Spanish ambassador in London, Alonso de Cárdenas, acquired Peter Paul Rubens's masterpiece *Minerva Protects Pax from Mars* – known as the *Allegory of War and Peace* – from the erstwhile King's embroiderer, Edmund Harrison, for the knock-down price of £77. Now owned by the National Gallery, Rubens's large canvas, extending three metres wide and two metres high, depicts a naked 'Pax' succouring an infant amid a vivid cornucopia of plenty; in the background, Minerva, as the goddess of wisdom and the arts, firmly restrains Mars, the god of war. Rubens had presented the painting to Charles I in 1630, having been sent to London on a diplomatic mission by Philip IV's court the previous year. Hoping to lay the groundwork for a permanent Anglo-Spanish peace to be agreed through a formal exchange of ambassadors, Rubens promoted the benefits of a *Pax Hispanica* by presenting 'Pax' herself, draped in 'Habsburg red' with a burst pomegranate providing a symbolic allusion to the Habsburg dynasty's fecundity. The figures revelling in Pax's bounty were modelled on the young children of Balthasar Gerbier, the Dutch-born diplomat and connoisseur who had hosted Rubens during his ten-month stay in London.[1] By 1652, however, Mars's bellicose forces of war had dominated the British Isles for over a decade, Charles had been executed and Rubens had died in Antwerp in 1640.

The extent to which the world had been turned upside down was reflected in Parliamentary requisitioning of the Stuart dynasty's palaces, alongside the hasty liquidation of its material assets. The Nottinghamshire regicide Colonel John Hutchinson became 'the largest cash-buyer of paintings from the dead king's collection', justifying purchases of Catholic, baroque and 'idolatrous' artworks by the large profits derived from their lucrative resale to Continental collectors, including Cárdenas.[2] For his part, Gerbier – who had once served as Charles I's Master of Ceremonies – had also operated as a double-agent, supplying Stuart secrets to the Habsburg court of Archduchess Isabella of the Spanish Netherlands. After the regicide, Gerbier, together with two Netherlands painters, George Geldorp and Peter Lely, proposed an (ultimately abortive) interior decoration scheme for Inigo Jones's Banqueting House and other state apartments in Whitehall which would have comprised a series of vast oil paintings depicting 'all the most remarkable battles and the most considerable sieges of towns' that had occurred in England, Scotland and Ireland during the recent civil wars, accompanied by portraits of the Parliamentarian generals and commanders that had 'fought the said battles and gained the said towns'.[3] Inspired by the series of tapestries commemorating England's defeat of the Spanish Armada in 1588 then hanging in the Palace of Westminster, such a conspicuous celebration of republican military might and parliamentary rule was intended to offer emulative stimulus for the Commonwealth's leaders. But by the summer of 1651, reports of a Royalist resurgence prompted Cárdenas to fear that a reconstituted army, under Charles II's command, might soon leave Scotland to enter northern England. Accordingly, Cárdenas warned his diplomatic masters in Madrid 'of the possibility that fate might bring him [Charles] to London, thus making it impossible to ship the paintings' so eagerly purchased for the Spanish court.[4] Observers would need to wait and see if England's new republic could now establish itself as a permanent and internationally recognized alternative to Stuart monarchy and set aside its pariah status as an interim regime of army-backed usurpers.

I

Charles II's Scottish sojourn had been anything but straightforward. Before concluding terms with the Scots Commissioners sent to Breda in March 1650, Charles had declined to swear the Solemn League and Covenant on the grounds that he could not commit himself to particular forms of ecclesiastical government in England and Ireland without summoning free parliaments in those realms. But after he had left the United Provinces to return to Britain, it became clear that Charles would not be allowed to set foot on Scottish soil as an 'uncovenanted' king. Thus he swore both the National Covenant and the Solemn League and Covenant while his ship moored off Garmouth, east of Inverness, in June 1650. In later years, one of the Commissioners present, Alexander Jaffray, admitted how 'that poor young prince' had been obliged by the Scots delegation to swear an oath 'which we knew, from clear and demonstrable reasons, that he hated in his heart', concluding that '*our* sin was more than *his*'.[5] That autumn, published correspondence confirming Charles's parallel attempts to solicit assistance from the papal court in Rome cast further doubt on the king's likely adherence to Covenanting strictures. A Parliamentarian pamphleteer reminded readers that Charles's maternal grandfather, Henri IV of France, had conveniently converted to Catholicism in the belief that 'the crown of France was worth little, if it were not worth a Mass or two'. Charles might well have made a similar calculation, 'though he publicly begins on the other side, by swallowing a Covenant or two, which if his father could have done, he might have undone us all'.[6]

Charles's physical presence in Scotland nevertheless posed a serious security threat to the Commonwealth regime and obliged Oliver Cromwell to embark on a reluctant war of re-conquest in Scotland. Although Ireland's military subjugation had been brutally effected, advocating war against a fellow Protestant nation was problematic, especially since the Covenanters had, after all, been Parliament's allies against the king. When the New Model Army's Lord General, Sir Thomas Fairfax, became a prominent conscientious objector and refused to lead an invading army, he was replaced by Cromwell whose troops crossed into Scotland in July. Having reached Musselburgh, outside Edinburgh, Cromwell appealed to the Church of Scotland's General Assembly to question the rectitude of the Scots' alliance with Charles Stuart, writing 'I beseech you, in the bowels of Christ, think it possible you may be mistaken'; indeed, 'there may be a Covenant made with Death and Hell!'[7] While the Covenanting leadership set about purging its army of suspected 'malignants', Charles was pressurized into repenting publicly for his own sins and those of his discredited family.

With around 15,000 English soldiers camped at Dunbar, a member of the Kirk Party's 'Committee of War', Archibald Johnston of Wariston, recorded how he and colleagues had 'used great freedom of expression' in admonishing the young king that his misguided loyalty to his family's errors only 'continued God's absence, impeded His influence, forslowed our action, encouraged enemies, [and] discouraged His people'. When the Covenanters came to face Cromwell on the battlefield, Charles was warned that, 'if beaten, the blame would lie on him'.[8] A week later, the king issued a *Declaration* from Dunfermline Palace which claimed that, by allying with the Covenanters, he had been 'recovered out of the snare of evil counsel' that had afflicted his father and wrought bloodshed across Britain. Moreover, 'the idolatry of his mother' and its toleration at court could likewise only have been 'a high provocation against Him, who is a jealous God, visiting the sins of the fathers upon the children'.[9] But on 3 September, Cromwell's forces heavily defeated the Scots at the Battle of Dunbar, notwithstanding Charles's public repentance and the fact that Cromwell's army was only half the size of its Scottish opposition. Around 10,000 Scots soldiers were taken prisoner, many of whom were later sent as indentured labour to North America and the Caribbean.

In English republican newsbooks, satirical attacks on the Scots' deluded obsession with monarchical loyalty continued, as Marchamont Nedham's *Mercurius Politicus* derided commissioners in the Scottish Parliament who 'promised the baby, a bell, a bib and a rattle' when planning Charles's coronation.[10] Chafing against restrictions imposed by his Covenanter hosts, the young king even attempted a desperate escape, fleeing from Perth to spend several nights sleeping rough in Glen Clova. In an attempt to repair relations, a coronation was arranged at Scone Palace in Perthshire on 1 January 1651, at which Charles was presented with the ancient 'Honours of Scotland' – crown, sceptre and sword of state – that had been smuggled out of Edinburgh Castle as Cromwell's forces approached and, after the ceremony, were unceremoniously wrapped in seaweed and buried in Kinneff Church in Kincardineshire to avoid seizure by the English. In his coronation sermon, Robert Douglas left the newly crowned king in little doubt as to the precarious nature of royal power. Since 'the sins of former kings, have made this a tottering crown', if Charles followed in his family's sinful footsteps 'all the well-wishers to a king in the three kingdoms, will not be able to hold on the crown, and keep it from tottering, yea from falling'. As a Covenanted king, Charles could be 'controlled and opposed'; indeed, should he try to disregard 'the very fundamentals of this contract and covenant', his subjects 'may and ought to resist by arms' (see Plate 15).[11] Meanwhile, the English military conquest continued: a week before Charles's coronation at Scone, Edinburgh Castle had been subjected to the heaviest bombardment in its history before its Governor, Walter Dundas, had surrendered to Cromwellian forces on Christmas Eve 1650.

News of the English regime's remarkable military triumphs reverberated overseas. In France, Louis XIV's chief adviser Cardinal Jules Mazarin received reports that, after Dunbar, Cromwell had advised his followers that, with the Irish and Scots now conquered, they should focus on converting all monarchies into republics.[12] Impressed by Cromwell's victory at Dunbar, and fearing diplomatic reprisals for the recent murder in Madrid of the Parliamentarian envoy Anthony Ascham, Philip IV dispatched formal ambassadorial credentials to Cárdenas, addressed to the 'Parliamento Reipublico Angliae'. On grounds of realpolitik, Spain thereby became the first major Continental power to acknowledge the Commonwealth regime, earning a dazzling display of republican pomp and circumstance which accompanied Cárdenas's parliamentary audience on 26 December 1650. With around a thousand soldiers massed before Parliament, the ambassador was escorted to Westminster by the regime's leaders and twenty state coaches, each pulled by six horses, eclipsing the traditional pair of state coaches normally laid on by the regime's monarchical predecessors.[13] During his audience, Cárdenas addressed MPs in Spanish and confirmed Philip's readiness, as 'the greatest and first king of Christendom' to become 'the first, who should make this acknowledgement, by me his ambassador'.[14] Cárdenas also reiterated Philip's condemnation of Ascham's murder and insisted that efforts 'to bring the delinquents to justice' were proceeding with as much urgency as 'if the dead person were a prince, heir to the crown of Spain'.[15]

But the new English republic's leadership remained unpredictable. Two months after Cárdenas's audience, Philip's court was disturbed by widespread reporting of the boast made in the town square of Cadiz by the Parliamentarian naval commander Admiral Robert Blake that, following England's example, 'all kingdoms will annihilate tyranny and become republics'.[16] In London, the English Council of State complained to Cárdenas that, further east along the Spanish coast at Malaga, the local governor had ceremoniously welcomed a fleet commanded by Blake's defeated adversary, Prince Rupert, into the town's harbour, while locals had directed 'odious names and vile reproaches of rebels, traitors, and parliament dogs' at English merchants and ship-owners, to the Commonwealth's 'slighting, disrespect and great dishonour'.[17] Although Charles's Royalist envoys had recently left Madrid, the Venetian ambassador in the city, Pietro Basadonna, ventriloquized their views to the Doge and Senate when he reported in June that, in England, all authority had been usurped by a House of Commons 'composed for the most part of mechanics, unadorned by distinguished birth, and the majority equally devoid of intelligence'. Since the Council of State 'governs rather by impulse than by knowledge and true political science', Basadonna predicted that personal avarice and instinctive suspicion would doubtless 'sway the minds of men unused to command'.[18]

Accreditation of Cárdenas's role contrasted with the ambiguous status of other foreign envoys in London. The previous December, John IV of Portugal had sent a lawyer, João de Guimarães, to England as escalating Anglo-Portuguese tensions had seen Blake's Parliamentarian fleet blockade access to Lisbon harbour, where shelter had been granted to Prince Rupert's Royalist ships. On arriving in England, however, Guimarães had been placed under armed guard in Southampton and refused permission to travel to London until confirmation was received that his status was indeed that of an accredited ambassador, agent or envoy.[19] As the president of the new Commission of Trade, Henry Vane, affirmed to Cromwell, then in Edinburgh, the regime's awareness that the Portuguese king's representative 'stands knocking at the door for audience' had stiffened their resolve to 'pause upon it a little, that he may be sensible of his error in so rashly engaging against us'. To another colleague also in Edinburgh, Vane predicted that 'the French and Dutch will not sit sullen long, but either fall out with us downright' or pragmatically judge it in their interests to follow Spain's example.[20]

Indeed, the day before Cárdenas's audience, the Council of State had expelled the secretary to the French embassy, the sieur de Croullé, ordering his prompt departure from England, after raiding and searching his residence. In France, Mazarin was alarmed by the destabilizing influence of English revolutionary rhetoric, which coincided with the series of popular uprisings, known as the Fronde, that had begun in 1648. Trying to deflect attacks on his own influence over the young Louis XIV, Mazarin rashly likened the Parisian *Parlement* to the English House of Commons and equated prominent Frondeurs, such as the city's Coadjutor (assistant to its diocesan bishop), Jean François Paul de Gondi, later cardinal of Retz, to the English Parliamentarian leaders, Fairfax and Cromwell. Uproar ensued when Louis's uncle Gaston, duke of Orléans, let Mazarin's analogies become known within the *Parlement*, prompting its president, Jacques Le Coigneaux, to insist that such incendiary allegations deserved the death penalty.[21] After Mazarin went into voluntary exile near Cologne, he denounced Retz's policy of sponsoring published accounts of revolutionary events in England for French readers. The Scots-born Catholic convert Robert Mentet de Salmonet dedicated his *Histoire des Troubles de la Grande Bretagne* (1649) ('History of the British Troubles') to Retz and described events to 1646, while a later sequel continued the narrative to 1650. Deeming the tumultuous times he lived in to be 'an iron age', Salmonet ventured that, 'of all the revolutions that have happened in this age, that of Great Britain is the most remarkable, the most surprising and the most fatal in all of its circumstances'.[22] As Anglo-French skirmishes broke out in the English Channel, Bay of Biscay and Mediterranean during the summer of 1651, Basadonna was struck by the Commonwealth's contemptuous attitude towards the French when visited in Madrid by George Fisher, the former secretary of the murdered Parliamentarian envoy Ascham. Having insisted 'that no friendship exists between that country and the English, who set no store by it', Fisher had added, 'laughing, by God's grace, we have rid London of the French, who made us as mad as themselves'.[23]

By conspicuous contrast, the Commonwealth regime aspired to a closer alliance with the Dutch and sent two prominent MPs, Walter Strickland and Oliver St John, as ambassadors to The Hague in March 1651, accompanied by an entourage of nearly 250 attendants. Following Charles II's agreement with the Scots at Breda the previous spring, the United Provinces had initially seemed likely to offer the Stuarts crucial support in seeking to regain their British thrones, but Royalist hopes had been reversed when the country's Stadtholder (and Charles's brother-in-law), William II, had died unexpectedly in November 1650. When the Dutch States General then declined to appoint William's son (born just a week after his father's death) as the country's Stadtholder, republican momentum gathered pace. Moreover, Charles's nineteen-year-old sister Mary was obliged to share custody of her infant son – later William III – with her ambitious mother-in-law, Amalia of

Solms-Braunfels, who feared that the House of Orange's interests might be jeopardized by Mary's young age and her dynastic links to the ejected Stuart king. In January 1651, the child's christening service had been delayed for several hours while mother and grandmother argued over his agreed name, with Mary refusing to attend when her choice – Charles – was rejected in favour of William.

To English Commonwealth leaders, the likelihood of securing a Dutch alliance appeared auspicious as, shortly before his death, William II had tried to wrest greater control from his republican adversaries in Amsterdam by attempting a military coup. John Milton's *Defence of the People of England* (1651), which was published to coincide with the arrival of Strickland and St John in The Hague, warned the Dutch that 'slavery and a new master had been made ready for you': their hard-won liberty would have been 'nearly obliterated' but for the providential delivery of 'the most timely death recently of a rash young man', the Stadtholder.[24] In a Latin poem on the diplomatic mission, Andrew Marvell drew attention to the ways in which Oliver St John's name symbolized the choice faced by the Dutch. While an olive branch traditionally signified peace and St John was the herald of war, St John also shared a forename with his bellicose cousin and friend Cromwell.[25]

Although details of any closer union envisaged between the English and Dutch republics remained secret, hopes of a speedy outcome to talks were complicated by the need to consult representatives in provinces with pro-Orangist political inclinations, such as Friesland and Gelderland. Moreover, suspicion arose in relation to an apparent Dutch reluctance to align themselves wholeheartedly with their republican counterparts in England. As one editorial in *Mercurius Pragmaticus* opined, the Dutch were acting 'like cunning foxes', evidently 'gazing after the negotiations in Scotland' before deciding whether or not to accede to the Commonwealth's overtures.[26] In The Hague, Strickland and St John were particularly frustrated by Dutch refusals to commit to denying shelter to Royalists fleeing the Commonwealth. Directly blaming the Dutch for Charles's current activities in Scotland, one member of the delegation, John Thurloe, objected that the Dutch seemed 'to be perfectly of the Scots mould', having learned from the Scots and French 'the art of making huge professions' so plausibly 'that men are almost necessitated to believe them', despite intending 'to perform no more of them than apparently stands with their own advantage'.[27]

The Hague was also home to the exiled court of Charles II's aunt, the Electress Elizabeth, and her family. In the city, Strickland and St John often encountered 'a general disgust in the people in whose minds the blood of the late king was fresh', with embassy personnel decried as 'rogues and murderers of their king, as they passed through the streets'. On one occasion, the Palatine Prince Edward confronted the envoys' ambassadorial coach and, as *Mercurius Politicus* reported, 'made monkey-like mouths at them; and with a squeaking voice called them dogs, rogues, traitors'. On another occasion, a repetition of Dorislaus's fate was only narrowly averted when St John escaped a direct assassination attempt by a Cavalier, Colonel James Apsley.[28] Strickland and St John also declined to consider a request for financial assistance from the exiled Palatine court, referred to them by the States General, advising that such entreaties should instead be sent to the English Parliament. The envoys nevertheless cavilled at the way the States General now styled Elizabeth's brother 'Charles the first, which implies that there is a second Charles king of England', notwithstanding the Commonwealth's clear declarations that there was 'no person whatsoever having any right or title to be king of England'.[29] In 1651, the Dutch statesman and poet Constantijn Huygens composed a country-house poem, *Hofwyck*, that was published two years later and described Charles I's regicide in terms of a game of bowls, recalling 'kings undone amidst assembled crowds' in an act that served to

> Strike down three crowns at once with unheard claps
> Make bowling grave, and bowls a Parliament.[30]

Huygens's metaphor of a bowling game echoed the expostulation of the French Royalist Claude de Saumaise at the outrageous ways in which the English had historically treated their kings. Rejecting Saumaise's censure, Milton had denied that 'we treat kings' heads' like 'balls; play with crowns like hoops; care no more for imperial sceptres than fools' staffs topped with heads'.[31]

Having failed to agree an Anglo-Dutch alliance, Strickland and St John returned to England in July 1651, by which time the Commonwealth regime's leaders were anxiously fearing imminent invasion from Scotland under forces led by Charles II. Despite his defeat at Dunbar the previous September, Stuart sympathies remained strong in Scotland and offered the young king a base from which he hoped to enter England

and attract Royalist support. Among republican propagandists resentful of repeated external interference in English politics, a stream of xenophobic invective blasted the Scots as 'poor, rude, savage, ragged, shagged and jagged', as evidenced by proverbial allusions to 'the treacherous Scot, the beggarly Scot, the proud Scot, the daring Scot, the pilfering Scot, the sly Scot, the lazy Scot and the lousy Scot'. Everything the Scots had ever acquired was 'by stealth, from England, France, Holland and other countries'.[32] In August 1651, the English Council of State wrote to the Isle of Wight's Governor, requesting that the island's militia be summoned and placed on a defensive footing, lest the same 'Scots army, that could by no means be provoked to fight in Scotland' during the civil wars, once again entered English territory. As the instructions added, intelligence suggested that 'the Scots themselves have no great opinion' of their strategy, but 'have no other game to play'.[33]

II

The likelihood of a Royalist resurgence across Britain ended when the New Model Army, led by Cromwell, decisively defeated Charles II's force at the Battle of Worcester on 3 September 1651, a year to the day after Cromwell's victory at Dunbar. Having finally ended his Scottish sojourn to cross into northern England in August with 12,000 Scottish troops, Charles had failed to attract extensive Royalist recruits. At Worcester – which had been the first city to declare for his father during the civil wars – Charles's force was routed by a Commonwealth army of 28,000 soldiers in a long day of street-to-street combat.

Fleeing from the city, the twenty-one-year-old king took shelter in a former Cistercian priory, Whiteladies, near Boscobel House, owned by the Catholic Penderel family. It was at Boscobel that Charles and a fellow commander, William Carlis, spent the day of 6 September hiding among the branches of a large oak tree in an escapade that subsequently gained legendary status and explains why the Royal Oak remains the second most common pub name in England, after the Red Lion.[34] Fronting many of the several hundred pubs bearing this name are colourful signs depicting the young, dark-haired king, peeping out from his quercine refuge amid a garland of dense and distinctive oak leaves. But what this rustic pictorial vignette omits is what Charles himself acutely remembered in later years: 'soldiers going up and down in the thickest [part] of the wood, searching for persons escaped, we seeing them now and then, peeping out'.[35] Thereafter, the king sought sanctuary in a series of Royalist 'safe houses' in the Midlands, before disguising himself as a manservant of a Royalist officer's sister called 'William Jackson' as the small party embarked on a 100-mile journey through Bromsgrove, Stratford-upon-Avon, Cirencester, Chipping Sodbury and Abbots Leigh, near Bristol, before moving on to the Somerset home of another Royalist colonel at Trent. From there, the king altered his disguise to appear part of a runaway elopement and headed for the Dorset port of Charmouth, hoping to reach the Continent. After passing through Bridport, and moving to Heale House, near Amesbury, Charles travelled to Brighton and finally secured passage on a ship named the *Surprise* that left Shoreham on 15 October and arrived at Fécamp, on the Normandy coast, the following morning.

Charles spent most of his flight from Worcester either alone, or in the company of Henry, Viscount Wilmot, who had fought for Charles I in the civil wars and, at thirty-eight, was seventeen years the king's senior. During their forty-three days on the run, Charles and Wilmot relied on the repeated loyalty, courage and discretion of subjects who found themselves unexpectedly responsible for sheltering a fugitive king, as rewards for his capture – and penalties for his concealment – steadily escalated. Six days after the battle at Worcester, the first proclamation had been issued, demanding the king's apprehension before an official reward of £1,000 was offered to anyone who successfully detained 'such a malicious and dangerous traitor'.[36]

Retrospectively dictated to the diarist Samuel Pepys in 1680, Charles's own account of his escape was wryly self-deprecating in embellishing picaresque incidents. The king recalled, for instance, that, when travelling to Abbots Leigh, his assumed role of manservant had meant overseeing the unexpected shoeing of a horse. When a Bromsgrove blacksmith had reported 'the good news of the beating of the rogues, the Scots' and admitted that he did not know if 'that rogue, Charles Stuart' had also been captured. In response, Charles had ventured that 'if that rogue were taken, he deserved to be hanged more than all the rest for bringing in the Scots'; to which the blacksmith had averred 'that I spoke like an honest man, and so we parted'. At Abbots Leigh, the king also remembered encountering a servant who had served in his own regiment at Worcester, prompting Charles nervously to enquire what 'kind of man' the servant's commander had been. After 'describing exactly both my clothes and my horse', the former soldier, 'looking upon me', had obliviously replied that 'the king was at least three fingers taller than I'.[37] For six weeks during 1651, life had indeed imitated art as Charles's escape corresponded to older folk traditions of an incognito ruler passing undetected within his realm, asking unsuspecting subjects about their political opinions and sharing their daily lives and discomforts. Unsurprisingly, by the time Charles finally reached Paris in November, the Venetian ambassador, Michiel Morosini, reported that 'his dress was calculated to move laughter than respect, and his aspect is so changed that those who were nearest believed him to be one of the lower servants'.[38] Charles's trust in support from his Scottish subjects had also been entirely liquidated. Asked by Louis XIV's uncle Gaston, duke of Orléans, about rumours that he intended to return to Scotland, Charles reportedly replied, 'I had rather have been hanged first' – and, indeed, he never again set foot on Scottish soil.[39]

Victory at Worcester markedly increased the English Commonwealth's confidence in its foreign relations. Preaching on the anniversary of the Gunpowder Plot in 1651, Cromwell's chaplain, Peter Sterry, insisted that subjection to the Scots would have entailed a worse fate than that envisaged by Guy Fawkes in 1605. Identifying England's twin enemies as 'the Romish-Papacy' and 'the Scotch-Presbytery', Sterry maintained that the latter's 'Zeal-Plot' had sought 'the ruin of governors, government, people and all, by an army of Highlanders, who never knew Christianity or civility' and whose triumph would 'have torn in pieces all before it with a greater fury, than that of gunpowder'.[40] Across the British Isles, the last vestige of Royalist resistance was extinguished when the loyalist garrison at Castle Cornet on Guernsey surrendered, after a siege that had started in 1642 and had lasted for 3,190 days.[41]

Parliamentarian retribution was also directed towards the Dutch Republic via a Navigation Act, passed in October 1651, which aimed to redress England's balance of payments deficit by prohibiting the import of any goods into England, Ireland or its colonies, except in English or colonial ships, or in ships of the countries from which the goods had been grown or manufactured. Accordingly, none of the most common fish catches could be landed in England unless caught in English boats, and similar restrictions applied to fish-curing. While the States General expanded its naval fleet to retaliate if needed, a Dutch embassy, headed by three ambassadors extraordinary, Jacob Cats, Gerard Schaep and Paulus van der Perre, arrived in London in December to try to induce the Commonwealth to reverse its policy. Included in the entourage was the twenty-year-old son of Constantijn Huygens, Lodewijck, whose journal recorded the fragile veneer of republicanism that hastily overlay Stuart monarchical culture. In April 1652, Huygens travelled west out of London to visit Brentford, which he described as 'a rather nice village with a great number of inns, some with signs such as "Here *was* ye King's Head" or "Here *was* ye King's Arms"'. The previous month, Huygens and an English friend, William Brereton, had visited the Tower of London, where a guide had shown them 'a beautiful lion, called Prince Charles'. Citing an anecdote 'told in The Hague . . . that had spread all over England', Huygens asked if it had indeed been the case that 'when a handkerchief dipped in the blood' of the executed Charles I 'had been thrown to this lion, he had shown peculiar signs of recognition and affection towards it', before noting that 'they denied it'.[42]

Despite the Commonwealth's controverted legitimacy, foreign states remained keen to maintain a diplomatic presence in London. In February 1652, the Venetian ambassador in France, Morosini, was directed to send his embassy secretary, Lorenzo Paulucci, to England on the pretence of seeking to hire ships and negotiate levies to support the Venetian Republic's long-running war against the Ottoman Empire. After arriving in London in May, Paulucci consulted the Master of Ceremonies, Sir Oliver Fleming (Cromwell's cousin), who delivered short shrift to the secretary for arriving without formal credentials, warning him that the 'Council of State will be even more amazed than I am at your coming in this way'. Reminding Paulucci that, like Croullé, another unofficial French agent, the sieur de Gentillot, had presumed that he might be free 'to see the lay of the land, to investigate and observe', but he had been 'arrested as a suspect, and though sick or feigning' had been 'forcibly expelled from the country' in March 1651. While the English Commonwealth appreciated the punctilious, if protracted, character of Venetian foreign relations, the republic's failure to recognize the new regime in London was resented, given that Venice 'puts up with a subaltern agent of Charles Stuart' who had been making risible attempts to secure assistance for the exiled king. Following this unpropitious start, Paulucci suggested to Morosini in Paris that, 'although in their hearts the English perhaps desire foreign alliances', he remained pessimistic, denying that 'the loftiest conceptions or the wisest reasoning will alter the dominant tone here, which is umbrageous, suspicious and self-sufficient in the extreme'.[43]

Meanwhile, amid deepening domestic tensions in France, placards posted in Paris during the summer of 1652 exhorted the city's inhabitants 'to get rid of the King and of the *Parlement* and to establish a republic like that of England', as observed by one of Louis XIV's agents, Père Berthod.[44] But it was not until December that another French representative and president of the Grand Conseil, Antoine de Bordeaux-Neufville, was accorded an audience in the English Parliament at which he presented a letter from Louis that finally recognized the Commonwealth. Insisting that alliances between states should not depend on individual governmental forms, the French king acknowledged that England 'has been able to change from a monarchy to a republic, but geographical facts remain unaltered'. Somewhat spuriously, international treaties were deemed 'of less import to their sovereigns than to their peoples', given that subjects were directly affected by commercial and trading restrictions.[45] But until Bordeaux received full diplomatic credentials from the French court in early 1654, he remained relegated to the fringes of Commonwealth ceremonial.

On the Anglo-Dutch front, despite simultaneous attempts to engage in negotiations, tensions erupted into armed hostilities at sea. To English minds, the Dutch were inherently ungrateful: having relied on English support to secure independence from Spanish Habsburg rule in the 1580s, they were now willing to attack their former ally. In *Brandy-Wine, in the Hollanders Ingratitude* (1652), for example, an English soldier unleashed 'a serious expostulation', reminding the Dutch of former favours and warning that, despite their republican constitution, they seemed now 'so fascinated with Machiavelli's policies' and 'foolishly charmed with the magical spells of monarchy' that they risked subverting their own self-interest and hard-won liberties. Recalling English assistance supplied during the Dutch Revolt, the tract's author, 'J. W.', described how English heroes had confronted the over-mighty Spaniard who

... with Mustachios starched, he looked as big
As Don Quixote, and valued not a Fig,
Thy [Johan Van Olden] Barneveldt, (had not our gallant [Sir Horace] Vere,
And most renowned [Sir Philip] Sidney, still been there
With thousands more brave English). We still stood
Firm to thy Quarrel, sealing with our Blood
Thy vindication, when thou were so low,
In power and strength, that thou dost chiefly owe
Thy State and fortunes, to those valiant hands,
That made thee Master of the Netherlands.[46]

A year later, a republican spy in The Hague echoed such views, denouncing 'this unthankful people, whose walls have been cemented with English blood'.[47] In *A Brief Character of the Low-Countries under the States* (1652), Owen Felltham described the Dutch Republic as 'a general sea-land' with no clearly defined geographical borders: the country was 'the great bog of Europe', 'a universal quagmire epitomised' and 'an equilibrium of mud and water', while its soil served as 'the buttock of the world, full of veins and blood, but no bones in it'. Its inhabitants were 'like frogs' who 'live both on land and water'.[48]

But if the Dutch were depicted as frogs in English publications, Dutch writers and artists equally enthusiastically presented the English as vicious wild dogs. In a print entitled '*De Dappere Leeuw*' (1652) ('The Valiant Lion'), a sailor was shown wielding the same axe that had been used to kill Charles I to dock the tails of English dogs, thereby combining an envisaged emasculation of English power with denunciation of the regicide, with a deliberate reference to the longstanding insult that implied all Englishmen had diabolical tails.[49] A rival English image, *Dr Dorislaus's Ghost, Presented by Time to unmask the Vizards of the Holland* (1652), showed 'Time's' presentation of his nude daughter 'Truth' to the spectre of the recently murdered Commonwealth envoy Dorislaus, whose spectral presence confirmed a long history of Dutch cruelty and duplicity that included the Amboyna massacre in the 1620s, while a Dutch retort, *De Geest van Dr Dooreslaer*, was published several months later in The Hague.[50]

While printed polemical insults and satirical caricatures were exchanged in London, Amsterdam and The Hague, ships sailing in the Channel under the Dutch commander-in-chief, Admiral Maarten Harpertszoon Tromp, prominently displayed allegiance to the Orange dynasty and refused to accept that traditional English claims to sovereignty of the seas had automatically transferred to the new Commonwealth. A hostile, if inconclusive, naval encounter near Dover between Admiral Blake and Tromp signalled the start of hostilities in May while A *Declaration of the Parliament of the Commonwealth of England* (1652), which purportedly reviewed recent Anglo-Dutch relations, served as an effective declaration of war and was translated into Latin, French and Dutch, as well as German, Italian and Danish. Hoping to turn Anglo-Dutch animosity to Stuart advantage, Charles II sent two agents, John, Lord Colepeper, and John Middleton, from Paris to The Hague to explore ways in which financial and military attacks on England might be coordinated. In August 1652, the Council of State relayed intelligence 'that the Dutch have some design upon the Isle of Wight, for the surprise thereof' to the island's Governor.[51] Despite the island's strong defences, the Commonwealth resolved to move Charles I's third son, Henry, duke of Gloucester, from his protracted incarceration at Carisbrooke Castle, where his elder sister, Princess Elizabeth, had died of pneumonia in September 1650. In the event, Dutch forces might well have welcomed a coordinated Stuart distraction, rather than bearing the brunt of naval defeats in the Battle of the Kentish Knock in September 1652, followed by skirmishes at Portland Bill and Beachy Head the following February, and at Gabbard Bank in June.

Hoping to reverse apparent international indifference to his plight, Charles also dispatched a small delegation to central Europe – headed by his co-fugitive from Worcester, Henry Wilmot – to the Imperial Diet convened at Regensburg in the summer of 1653 to celebrate the coronation of the Holy Roman Emperor's son Ferdinand IV as the new 'King of the Romans', or recognized imperial heir. The previous year, the exiled court in Paris had received reports of the enthusiastic reception accorded to an impostor who had posed as Charles's younger brother James, duke of York, at the imperial court in Vienna. As Edward Hyde reported, the duke had been 'wonderfully delighted with the civility and respects which have been paid to his counterfeit in those parts', inferring strong potential support for the Stuart cause in central Europe.[52] But in a letter intercepted by the Commonwealth, one of Wilmot's party at Regensburg admitted in May 1653 that no firm offers of assistance had been secured, but only 'fair words at random, so that when we talk to ourselves (which we are very apt to do)', dreams of sizeable sums of money and troop supplies could optimistically be envisaged. Indeed, 'the boggling state of affairs here startles us much' as Stuart appeals for support faced competition from representatives of the Polish king, John II Casimir, who was seeking imperial assistance to defeat the Ukrainian Cossacks. Moreover, since most Catholic imperial princes were predictably reluctant to support a heretic exile, the Royalist envoy admitted that 'we cast many a false dice, to win the game' by insisting 'that our king will be a Catholic, when he shall be in power'.[53]

That same month, at The Hague, opportunities for dynastic diplomacy arose when the secretary of Charles's widowed sister Mary met a representative of the Polish Prince Bogusław Radziwiłł to discuss Mary's possible remarriage. Although the Polish envoy believed that Radziwiłł's claim to succeed the childless John Casimir would be strengthened by closer connections to the Stuart, Orange and Hohenzollern dynasties, the idea proved abortive. As one Leiden citizen observed, the Stuarts' priority remained recovery of Charles's British thrones and any prospective suitor hoping to 'be the hero' that effected his restoration needed 'not only valour and influence, but wealth'.[54]

III

In addition to finding itself at war with the United Provinces, the English Commonwealth's internal instabilities deterred foreign powers from closer diplomatic alliance. In the spring of 1653, the first general parliamentary elections held since 1640 were announced, but Cromwell's opposition to proposed franchise terms and voting restrictions prompted his dissolution of the 'Rump' Parliament in April. An interim Council of State, known as the 'Committee of Thirteen', was appointed, primarily comprising army officers. In a letter intercepted by the republic's authorities, a frustrated Royalist denounced the passivity of London's 'foolish, senseless, stupid citizens' in not mounting stiffer resistance to Cromwell's unilateral action. Only a decade ago, 'the challenging of five members' by Charles I had been 'cried out upon for an unheard-of breach of privilege of parliament', but now an entire assembly had been summarily ejected.[55] A satirical Dutch print entitled *On the Destruction of the so-called English Parliament, by their General, Oliver Cromwell* (1653) likewise presented a tailed Cromwell as Hercules, smashing a barrel filled with Parliament's treasure, illegally acquired from a suffering populace.[56] Another Dutch pamphlet derided the humble social origins of English Commonwealth politicians, its author incensed by 'the ambitions of these avaricious, all devouring English devils, these shoe-makers, cheap tailors, kettle-menders, rag-pedlars, rat-catchers, dog-butchers, manure-sweepers, cutpurses, privy-cleaners [and] animal-castraters'.[57]

In June, a new Dutch delegation, headed by Jerome Beverning together with Allart Pieter van Jongestal and Willem Nieupoort, arrived in London in a renewed attempt to negotiate an end to hostilities. As Beverning acknowledged to the republican Pensionary of Holland, John de Witt, 'all the world doth take notice of our treaty, and how we walk', aware that Dutch naval defeats by the new republican regime in London had been noted across Europe. From the Imperial Diet at Regensburg, an English spy reassured the Commonwealth regime that 'Cromwell [was] cried up for the most gallant man in the world by the princes here at their feasting and drinking' and even his 'very enemies acknowledge it'.[58] But in London, the Dutch deputies were dismayed when the Committee of Thirteen simply resuscitated older proposals advocating a narrow, formalized Anglo-Dutch union. As Van der Perre reported, both republics were envisaged as constituting 'one supreme power' in which English and Dutch would 'enjoy the like privileges and freedoms in respect of habitations, possessions, trade, ports, fishing, and all other advantages whatsoever in each other's countries, as natives without any difference or distinction'.[59] While the Dutch envoys rejected the union proposals as constitutionally impossible, implying 'every kind of novelty, confusion, [and] absurdity', the 'Committee of Thirteen' was, in any event, replaced by a 'Nominated Assembly' in July, known as the 'Barebones' or 'Little Parliament', which created a new Council of State.[60]

From Paris, the Dutch ambassador to France (and Stuart sympathizer), Willem Boreel, confirmed to his counterparts in London that he was, 'as it were, enraged to hear of a nearer union and coalition of government' proposed by the English. Such a union would entail 'a giving up and yielding or submitting of the state of the United Provinces to the English with the loss of their dear bought liberties'. Having served in a diplomatic mission to England in the mid-1640s, Boreel added that he had 'long and often had to do and conversed with that nation', warning that the English were likely 'to drill your lordships on with further arguments of unheard-of business'. After returning to The Hague, Nieupoort likewise protested that only 'when we have lost all our fortunes, estates and country (as the Irish and Scots)' would the Dutch be considered 'good enough to be admitted into this coalition'.[61] Indeed, as one London critic recognized in a letter intercepted by the authorities, Cromwell had essentially offered 'these drunken, pickled, stuff . . . a cheap silent conquest' on 'the same terms Ireland and Scotland had of us'.[62] Dutch disillusionment had deepened when, despite lifting an English blockade of its coast, their fleet was heavily defeated by General George Monck's Parliamentarian ships at the Battle of Scheveningen later that summer in an encounter that also saw the great Admiral Tromp killed.

With regard to Scotland, military conquest had yet to translate into formal union after an original Bill of Union, considered by the House of Commons in April 1652, had expired with Parliament's dissolution a year later, while a similar fate befell a second bill of Union presented to the 'Barebones' Parliament in October 1653. Two months later, the authority of the 'Barebones' Parliament was replaced by the Council of State's proclamation of a Protectorate on 16 December 1653 to be called 'the Commonwealth of England, Scotland and Ireland'. Yet in Scotland, significant military resistance to English control was coordinated by William Cunningham, earl of Glencairn, who mustered a force of around 7,000 soldiers and issued a declaration in June that attacked the English regime for having 'reared up a monstrous republic, built with the bones and cemented with the blood of their dread sovereign'. Trusting that divine protection would continue to shelter Charles II 'from the paws of these murderers', Glencairn sought to secure Scotland's 'deliverance from servile bondage' under the English and to thwart 'their deep and devilish design'. His manifesto conjured up 'the call of Scottish hearts struggling within our breasts to be rid of thraldom', reminding readers of 'the many bloody battles in defence of Scotland's right against Picts, Danes and Britons, Saxons, Irish, English, and the conquering Romans'. Recalling the heroism of 'King Robert the Bruce of famous memory, Sir William Wallace and many others', the declaration insisted that the Scots had repelled all previous attempts at foreign conquest and had proudly transmitted their independent crown, 'always under the government of one race of kings' (the Stuarts) to the present generation, now taking up arms against their regicidal English enemies.[63] But by the time Cromwell approved a formal Ordinance of Anglo-Scottish Union in April 1654, Monck had suppressed Royalist resistance, subsequently offering an amnesty and pardon to any Scot who laid down their arms within twenty days, only seeking the arrest of named leaders in Glencairn's rebellion.

Domestic political stability had also been enhanced through the creation of the Protectorate when Major General John Lambert had written an 'Instrument of Government' which became England's first written constitution. After the Instrument was presented to the Council of Officers on 13 December 1653, a ceremonial inauguration was held three days later at Westminster Hall at which Cromwell swore an oath to govern England, Scotland and Ireland according to law, in his new capacity as Lord Protector. A printed account of the inauguration ceremony insisted that, by the Protectorate's creation, 'this Commonwealth is become the wonder and emulation of Europe; nay, of the whole world', and attacked 'the bird-witted opiniators of this age, who already begin to breathe forth a disowning and dislike of this great and unparalleled change'.[64] In an intercepted letter sent from London in late December 1653, one commentator described Cromwell as 'the craziest man of all Christendom' who had 'made himself the greatest prince of the world', but remained 'a man without desert, and of no quality'.[65] Observing the constitutional revolution from Paris, the Venetian ambassador Giovanni Sagredo admitted that 'there is no doubt that the English government is powerful. It shows no sign of its tottering or fall.' Even Louis XIV's minister Bordeaux-Neufville 'calls Cromwell one of the cleverest men of the century; that he set up two defective parliaments in order to discredit them and exalt himself in their dismissal'.[66]

The rapid succession of different constitutional arrangements nevertheless placed the Commonwealth's own envoys in a precarious position, since they were often unaware of regime changes that potentially undermined their diplomatic credentials. In November 1653, the Puritan lawyer Bulstrode Whitelocke had left England for Sweden, instructed by Cromwell to negotiate a treaty that could unite Anglo-Swedish forces against the Danes and the Dutch and facilitate the reopening of the Danish Sound to English ships. Travelling through Köping, Whitelocke's entourage were denied lodgings by a local magistrate whose 'ill language of the Parliament' objected 'that they had killed their king, and were a company of tailors and cobblers'. In his journal, Whitelocke recorded how he had remonstrated with the magistrate's superior consul, but had been reassured that – although such derogatory claims were common in Dutch gazettes – the consul himself admired the English Parliament's actions and had not only read John Milton's *Defence of the People of England* but had 'liked it, and had it at home'.[67]

Whitelocke also recorded his first private audience with Queen Christina, who had acclaimed Cromwell as 'one of the gallantest men in the world' who 'hath done the greatest things of any man in the world' and, several days earlier, predicted that he 'will be king of England in conclusion'. Unaware of Cromwell's recent elevation as Lord Protector, Whitelocke had insisted that such an outcome 'cannot be, because England is resolved into a commonwealth; and my General hath already sufficient power and greatness'. In ensuing audiences, the Swedish queen had remained curious as to Cromwell's monarchical aspirations, especially after news arrived of the Protectorate's creation. When Christina had observed that since Cromwell's 'power is the same with that of king and why should not his title have been the same?', Whitelocke had evasively replied that 'it is the power which makes the title, and not the title the power'. Queen Christina's Chancellor, Axel Oxenstierna, also questioned Whitelocke about political arrangements, observing of Charles I that, while 'other nations have sometimes caused their kings to be made away secretly, or have expelled them', the English had instead, 'in the face of all princes, and of the whole world, proceeded against him as a common criminory person', thereby breaching human and divine law.[68]

Away from the royal court, Whitelocke's entourage attracted anti-English abuse from Uppsala locals as the ambassador later recalled how a drunken crowd had surrounded his private residence in February 1654, 'with naked swords in their hands, making a loud noise, and crying "Come out ye English dogs, ye King-Killers, base rogues!" and the like compliments'. Two days later, vivid displays of the Northern Lights had prompted Whitelocke to apprehend providentially arranged sky armies and military prophecies: describing chromatic transformations during one storm, he watched how lightning flashes and thundery clouds 'divided themselves as into bodies of pikes and musketeers' as the Swedish 'sky appeared sometimes all of blood-colour, afterwards green, yellow and grey, then all black, and as it were a new battle from the north to the south'. In April, Whitelocke agreed the Anglo-Swedish Treaty of Uppsala, by which time Sweden was, however, undergoing its own constitutional revolution when Christina voluntarily abdicated in favour of her cousin who became Charles X Gustav. For Whitelocke, the abdication ceremony at the end of May confirmed the queen's disconcerting determination: several days later, she left Sweden, disguised as a man, to seek refuge in the Spanish Netherlands where she converted to Catholicism.[69]

Back in London, the Protectorate agreed an end to Anglo-Dutch hostilities via the Treaty of Westminster concluded in April 1654. But to most Dutch commentators, Cromwell epitomized neither Protestant piety nor republican virtue, but only illegal usurpation and diabolical hypocrisy. In the first of ten allegorical tableaux created for Amsterdam's official celebration of the peace, the city's poet, Jan Vos, alluded to England by presenting Pluto, sitting in Hell and surrounded by furies, while a circulating poem entitled '*Protecteur Weerwolf*' ('Protector Werewolf') warned that, when Cromwell 'starts to speak from his Bible / One hears the Passion preached by the Devil'.[70] At Cromwell's insistence, the Treaty of Westminster also included a secret, controversial clause, known as the 'Act of Seclusion', that permanently barred the former Stadtholder's posthumously-born three-year-old son (also Charles II's nephew) from holding political or military office. Although the Act of Seclusion was approved by the States General, internal dissensions ensured, as an intelligence report from The Hague in June warned, that it 'doth and will engender many fables and fancies'.[71] The Treaty also forbade the prince's mother, Mary Stuart, from offering sanctuary to Charles II whose position in France was becoming uncomfortable as Louis's ministers seemed likely to follow the Dutch example by seeking an Anglo-French alliance. Preferring voluntary departure to forced expulsion, Charles left his mother's court in Paris in July 1654 and relocated to Germany, having been encouraged by support articulated for his position at the Imperial Diet of Regensburg the previous year. As the Venetian diplomat Sagredo reported, the young king departed 'with the sympathy of all France' as observers acknowledged 'that the ties of blood are sacrificed to policy'. Despite Charles's dynastic links to the Bourbons, he was now compelled 'to wander as an outcast for the sake of flattering Cromwell, whom the French admire for his good fortune more than they love him for the despotic violence with which he keeps his seat'.[72]

15
Castles in the Air, 1654–1658

In *The Embassador and his Functions*, first published in French in 1681, the Dutch-born diplomat Abraham de Wicquefort ventured that 'if ever there appeared in any state, a chief who was at the same time both tyrant and usurper', it had been Oliver Cromwell in England; indeed, 'never was there a usurper so solemnly acknowledged'. As Wicquefort related, immediately after Charles I's execution, the Spanish monarchy's ambassador had 'legitimised this bastard republic' and no sooner had Cromwell become England's Lord Protector in December 1653 than 'all the kings of this earth prostrated themselves before this idol'.[1] Certainly, contemporaries in London observed the conspicuous presence of foreign diplomatic delegations spouting sycophantic encomia: as one exasperated Royalist exclaimed in March 1654, 'Good God! What damned lick-arses are here!'[2]

In Madrid, the Venetian ambassador, Giacomo Quirini, reported in June that Philip IV's Secretary of State, Don Luis Méndez de Haro y Guzmán, had 'frankly' conceded that, 'at the present moment, the court of London has rendered itself conspicuous by the number of its negotiations with foreign powers'. Still envisaging the English state in monarchical terms, Haro had admired how 'that crown had made itself the third power in Europe' (after Spain and France) and had predicted that 'we shall soon be seeing them take a leading hand in affairs'.[3] A year later, Quirini's counterpart in Paris, Giovanni Sagredo, was dismayed when informed by the Venetian Doge and Senate that his next posting would be to London, protesting that 'the court of England, by sheer force, has made itself the most dreaded and the most conspicuous in the world'. By 1655, the Protectorate regime was hosting permanent embassies from six Continental monarchies, alongside delegations from smaller ducal states and republics and 'pomp has reached such a pitch' that recently arrived Genoese envoys had brought an entourage of eighty attendants. Setting aside the flattering obsequies in which consular communications were conventionally couched, Sagredo begged his diplomatic masters to change their minds. To embark on a mission to England without ample funds was, Sagredo protested, 'so monstrous a suggestion that I would rather risk my life in battle than venture my reputation by bearing such a burden'.[4]

Sagredo's appeal fell on deaf ears, but his posting to London lasted less than a year. Before returning to Venice in 1656, he described Cromwell as 'a man whom fortune and industry have rendered the most famous of the present age'. Sagredo also surmised that England's republican leaders 'think the less of foreign powers since these have competed with each other in the most open way to show their esteem for the present ruler'.[5] On the Continent, Louis XIV's estranged cousin, Louis II de Bourbon, Prince of Condé, was known to have openly drunk Cromwell's health at Antwerp in 1653, acclaiming the English Lord Protector as 'the wisest, ablest, and greatest commander in Europe', while newsletter reports from Regensburg described how German princes, at ceremonial feasts, 'cried up' Cromwell as 'the most gallant man in the world'.[6] In May 1654, a republican spy had confirmed that 'France fears very much England and the Protector's person' – so much so that Louis's chief minister, Cardinal Mazarin, had Cromwell's 'picture in his chamber, being sent from London'. French frustration was stoked by Cromwell's audacious pursuit of parallel alliances with rival Continental states. In July 1655, another spy reported a satirical cartoon being sold in Paris that showed the English Lord Protector seated 'at his business' on a portable toilet, with 'the King of Spain on the one side and the King of France on the other, offering him paper to wipe his breech'.[7]

In retrospective accounts of the 1650s, Cromwell's capacity to impress and irritate foreign powers in equal measure was relished by chroniclers. According to an early eighteenth-century history, 'it was said that Cardinal Mazarin would change countenance' whenever Cromwell's name was mentioned, 'so that it passed into a proverb in France', that Mazarin 'was not so much afraid of the Devil, as of Oliver Cromwell'.[8] There were compelling reasons for foreign admiration. Between 1651 and 1654, the Commonwealth and Protectorate administrations had built, in tonnage, as many new warships as Tudor and Stuart monarchs had achieved in more than half a century from the Spanish Armada's defeat in 1588 to the outbreak of civil war in England in 1642. Travelling to Woolwich Dockyard in April 1655 to see the eighty-gun warship, the *Naseby*, 'newly built by the Usurper, Oliver', the diarist John Evelyn described how the ship's carved prow depicted 'Oliver on horseback trampling six nations under foot: a Scot, Irishman, Dutch, French, Spaniard and English as was easily made out by their several habits'.[9] As the poet Andrew Marvell observed of Cromwell that same year:

He seems a King by long Succession born,
And yet the same to be a King does scorn.
Abroad a King he seems, and something more,
At Home a Subject on the equal Floor.[10]

I

The ostentatious displays of diplomatic ceremonial, flattering rhetoric and ambassadorial audiences that characterized the Protectorate's foreign policy ambitions contrasted starkly with the impotence of Charles II's itinerant entourage which had, effectively, been expelled from France and was forbidden from entering Dutch territory. Having relocated to Spa in the Habsburg-controlled Spanish Netherlands, Charles was joined in the summer of 1654 by his widowed sister, Mary. Describing the twenty-two-year-old princess as 'only too well for a woman of her age, deserving more to be married than a widow', one spy reported to the republican regime that Mary's visit to Spa was 'undoubtedly more for her pleasure and divertisement, than want of health'. In September, the Stuart siblings visited Aachen where they viewed the relics of the former Holy Roman Emperor Charlemagne. As another English spy noted, while Mary 'kissed the skull and hand of great Charlemagne', her brother 'drew out Charlemagne's sword, and kissed it, and measured it with his own'.[11]

After Mary returned to The Hague, Charles established his exiled court in Cologne, but prospects for a Stuart restoration were undermined that autumn by fractured family loyalties, following Henrietta

Maria's attempt to secure the conversion to Catholicism of the siblings' younger brother Henry, duke of Gloucester. Having been taken into Parliamentarian custody as a toddler when civil war broke out in England in 1642, Henry had eventually been permitted to leave Carisbrooke Castle on the Isle of Wight to rejoin his family on the Continent in 1653. After Charles had left the French court the following year, Henry had remained in Paris, financially dependent on Henrietta Maria, whose youngest daughter, Henrietta Anne, had been raised as a Catholic. To Henrietta Maria's mind, Henry's conversion might well attract support for the Stuart cause from Catholic states, such as France, Spain or the papacy. The queen's project generated enthusiasm at the Louvre, prompting one exiled Royalist to advise that 'the Papists are already busy with their old prophecy that Henry IX must repair what Henry VIII ruined'.[12]

But from Cologne, a choleric Charles warned Henrietta Maria's confidant Henry Jermyn that he was 'so full of passion that I cannot express myself', and protested to his mother that her actions implied that she did not 'either believe or wish my return into England'. Knowing that Henry's conversion would prompt revulsion among British and Continental Protestants, Charles explained to his mother that, although it would represent 'the greatest misfortune that ever befell me in all my life', there would be nothing 'that I can say or do' to 'make my Protestant subjects believe but it is done with my consent'.[13] Writing directly to Henry that same day, Charles insisted that his conversion would not only be 'the cause of ruining a brother, that loves you so well, but also of your king and country'. Were Henry to convert, Charles frankly added that 'this shall be the last time' he would make contact.[14]

The public battle for the Stuart teenager's soul – which was widely reported in London and Continental cities – only succeeded in discouraging Catholic observers from supporting an exiled king who remained so steadfast in his heretical errors, while simultaneously reigniting Protestant anxieties regarding the Stuarts' recurrent proclivities towards popery. Before Charles had left his mother's court in Paris, a Calvinist-turned-Catholic theologian, Théophile Brachet de la Militière, had appealed to the exiled young king to abandon Protestantism, insisting that the 'sacrilegious parricide' of Charles I had been 'the grand work of man's malice and the Devil's stratagem', unleashed by a false, pretended and 'preposterous Reformation'. While de la Militière had advised

Charles that conversion to Catholicism offered 'the indubitable way of re-establishing you in your throne', the exiled Archbishop John Bramhall of Derry had angrily rejected such counsel, warning that the king's conversion to Catholicism would, rather, be 'the readiest way to ruin his hopes, by the alienation of his friends, by the confirmation of his foes, and in some sort the justification of their former feigned fears'. As Bramhall had added, neither Mary, Queen of Scots's 'constancy in the Roman Catholic faith, nor Henri IV's change to the Roman Catholic faith, could save them from a bloody end'.[15]

Charles's departure from the French court in 1654 did not immediately facilitate closer relations between the English republic and Louis XIII's administration. Anticipating an imminent peace being reached between England and the Dutch Republic in early 1654, Louis dispatched an additional envoy to London, Paul, baron de Baas, to join his resident ambassador, Antoine de Bordeaux-Neufville. In ensuing negotiations, the French offered military assistance to the Protectorate if English forces agreed to besiege the Spanish-held Channel port of Dunkirk. At the same time, English control of Dunkirk was also suggested by Philip IV's representatives, the resident Spanish ambassador, Don Alonso de Cárdenas, and the Prince of Condé's agent, Monsieur Barrière, if a commitment to undertake Anglo-Spanish operations in Flanders could be secured.

Unsurprisingly, Cromwell's attempt to conduct parallel negotiations with warring powers did not go unnoticed. In June, a French Anabaptist interrogated by the Protectorate authorities alleged that, since de Baas no longer believed an Anglo-French alliance was likely, he had sought out dissident elements in London with 'a design to trouble the affairs of England, and to make divisions in the army'.[16] Summoned before an inquiry comprising Cromwell, Secretary of State John Thurloe and other Councillors of State, de Baas audaciously defended his actions by citing previous English attempts to destabilize domestic affairs in France by courting Huguenot factions and sending envoys to Bordeaux during the Fronde. Writing to Louis XIV, Cromwell explained that de Baas had been given three days to leave England, justifying the diplomat's expulsion on the grounds that he had been 'fomenting evil designs' with 'turbulent and perverse men', having become 'mixed up in their criminal machinations to cause disturbance in this Commonwealth, in order to overthrow the present constitution, and to plunge us again in murder and bloodshed'. But Cromwell reassured Louis that he was satisfied de

Baas had acted 'on his own authority only', rather than on official instructions.[17] From Paris, Sagredo described Mazarin's irate denials of royal sanction for de Baas's actions, implying, instead, that Cromwell had concocted 'the plot himself in order to have a pretext for marching with a guard, like royalty'. Sagredo characterized events as 'an affair of pot and kettle' with Mazarin and Cromwell both 'trying to best each other, but it may generate bad blood'.[18]

Another hasty consular departure occurred in July 1654 when the Portuguese ambassador, Dom João Rodriguez de Sá e Menezes, count of Peneguião, left London on the same day that his younger brother, Dom Pataleone de Sá e Menezes, was publicly executed at Tower Hill for involvement in the murder of an innocent English bystander in a case of mistaken identity the previous autumn. Sá's case had provoked extensive debate as to whether an ambassador's brother could claim diplomatic immunity from prosecution and a commission of 'oyer and terminer' had been convened to determine the matter with a jury comprising equal numbers of Englishmen and foreigners. Chief Justice Henry Rolle argued that a sibling relationship did not entitle an individual to ambassadorial privilege, and envisaged the country being left in 'a frightful condition . . . if the doctrine were laid down that all who are in the employment of a foreign ambassador in England may rob, ravish and murder with impunity!'[19] Following Sá's prosecution and conviction, hopes that the capital sentence might be commuted proved futile. A disgusted Wicquefort commented on the incident in his survey of ambassadorial functions, conceding that, since Cromwell had already 'committed a parricide' by sanctioning Charles I's execution, 'he did not scruple the committing a sacrilege' and violating the law of nations when he approved the public hanging of an ambassador's brother.[20] Despite Peneguião's anguish at his brother's plight, a formal Anglo-Portuguese alliance was nevertheless agreed on the morning of Sá's execution, guaranteeing English trading privileges in Portugal in return for English assistance in Portugal's war with Spain.

Meanwhile Cromwell continued to consider parallel overtures from France and Spain. Frustrated by the Protectorate's reluctance to commit to an anti-Spanish alliance, the French ambassador, Bordeaux, feared in October that 'if this government doth continue to proceed as slowly in my negotiation, as it doth at present, it may be measured with the siege of Troy' – which had lasted a decade. Several months later, the French ambassador at The Hague, Pierre Chanut, sympathized with Bordeaux's predicament, doubting that 'Cicero, as eloquent as he was, could change any expression so many ways as you have been forced to invent' through repeated reassurances to Louis's court 'that your negotiation is still in the same condition'.[21] Anglo-French relations were further strained in April 1655 when Louis's ally (and Henrietta Maria's nephew) Duke Charles Emmanuel II of Savoy sanctioned an attack on members of a long-established community of Waldensian Protestants in Piedmont. The fact that the Savoyard forces included Irish regiments only intensified Protestant revulsion at the ensuing massacre and revived traumatic memories of Protestants killed during the Irish Rebellion in 1641. To Willem Nieupoort, the Dutch ambassador in London, Cromwell had explained that 'the example of Ireland was still in fresh memory, where he told me, that above two hundred thousand souls were massacred'.[22] In addition to organizing monetary collections to support the Waldensians, Cromwell orchestrated international protest at the Savoyard action, writing to the 'Evangelical Cities of Switzerland' in protest that the Vaudois Protestants had been given three days to convert to Catholicism before troops 'turned their dwellings into slaughter-houses'. Others had fled, 'naked and afflicted', as 'ready to perish through hunger and cold, they miserably wander through desert mountains and depths of snow, together with their wives and children'.[23]

By August, international pressure led to the Treaty of Pignerol between Charles Emmanuel and the Vaudois community, which guaranteed freedom of Protestant worship in Piedmont and consequently enabled Anglo-French negotiations to resume in London. Although Secretary of State John Thurloe complained to Cromwell's son Henry that Bordeaux's approach to diplomacy 'was more like a wrangling lawyer than an ambassador', a defensive Treaty of Westminster was eventually concluded between England and France in October 1655 that bound both states not to assist rebels of the other state and confirmed the cessation and retrospective adjudication of commercial disputes. Secret clauses also guaranteed the expulsion of prominent dissidents from both countries, including Charles II's younger brothers, the dukes of York and Gloucester, from France, together with other Royalists including Edward Hyde and James Butler, marquess of Ormond, while the Protectorate regime likewise agreed to order the expulsion of Barrière and other named opponents of Louis's administration.

In England, a Royalist rising led by Colonel John Penruddock had started in Wiltshire in March 1655 but was suppressed by military force and the Protectorate's sophisticated intelligence networks. Still in Cologne, Charles was mocked in Parliamentarian newsbooks for 'having the wit to keep out of harm's way, loving to sleep in a whole skin, whilst his friends adventure and lose their lives for his sake'.[24] In his defence, Charles rejected criticism for failing to support every rising undertaken on his behalf in the British Isles. As he wrote to a correspondent in June, those 'who will not believe anything to be reasonably designed, except it be successfully executed, had need of a less difficult game to play than mine is'.[25] Nevertheless, as Charles admitted to fellow Royalist exile Henry Bennet, 'I cannot hinder myself from building castles in the air'.[26]

As members of Charles's court conceded, the Protectorate's military prowess presented a more powerful attraction to international allies than promoting Stuart legitimism. In December 1655, a Protectorate spy reported from Paris that, while Philip IV of Spain 'trembles within himself for fear of the English fleet', scant attention was paid to 'the poor king of Scotland, who lies lurking behind the hangings, having no part to act upon the theatre of the world'. Continental European geopolitics were also changing quickly. While Savoyard troops had attacked the Waldensians that summer, Sweden's new Protestant king, Charles X Gustavus, had simultaneously secured a string of military victories against the Catholic John II Casimir of Poland, as Swedish troops entered Prussia and also occupied the cities of Warsaw and Kracow. Reporting from Poland that summer, Cromwell's relation Edward Rolt reassured the Lord Protector that a projected marriage between the Swedish king's brother Adolphus and Charles II's Palatine cousin Sophia had been aborted. Charles X Gustavus had opposed his brother forming a dynastic union 'with those that were enemies to his Highness', the English Lord Protector. The Swedish king had further indicated that 'a more close and firmer league of amity and alliance' with England was 'a thing he more desired than with all the princes of Europe'.[27]

As sister to the Palatine Princes Rupert and Maurice – notorious scourges of the Parliamentarian army during the civil wars – Sophia and her family connections proved anathema during the Protectorate, but half a century later, succession to the English throne would be vested in Sophia's Hanoverian line via the Act of Settlement in 1701, with Sophia herself only failing to become queen of Great Britain by predeceasing Queen Anne by two months in 1714. But during the 1650s, internal family tensions among the Stuarts persisted on account of the Parliamentarian loyalties of the siblings' eldest brother, Charles Louis, who had finally been restored to his family's Electoral lands and privileges in the Palatinate by the Peace of Westphalia in 1648, almost three decades after Frederick V's ejection from power. Accordingly, when Charles and his sister had visited the Frankfurt Fair in August 1655, the exiled king's determination to avoid contact with his estranged cousin had been observed by a Protectorate spy who confirmed that, despite the Elector's approaches, Charles and Mary 'had no mind nor desire either to see or salute him' which 'everybody took notice of and marvelled at his [Charles's] unnatural strangeness'.[28]

II

Cromwell's strategy of pursuing mutually contradictory diplomatic negotiations became increasingly difficult to sustain. After peace had been agreed between England and the Dutch Republic in 1654, interest was directed towards the likely future target of the Protectorate's impressive naval and military capability. As early as August 1653, the Venetian envoy Lorenzo Paulucci had warned that, since England's political leaders were 'compelled to keep their forces employed', they would 'turn their thoughts to some gigantic undertaking, of great advantage to themselves, and detrimental to all monarchies, which they will always do their utmost to humble'.[29] Fuelling traditional Hispanophobia, in 1654 an Oxford chaplain, Edmund Chilmead, produced the first English translation of Tommaso Campanella's *Discourse touching the Spanish Monarchy*, which had first appeared in 1600 as counsel to Spain's hegemonic monarchs on acquiring and retaining a world empire. As Campanella had suggested, 'if the King of Spain could but once make himself Master of England, and the Low Countries, he would quickly get to be sole monarch of all Europe, and of the greatest part of the New World'. In 1600, Campanella had advised Philip III to exploit tensions arising from the unsettled succession to Elizabeth I by sowing as much confusion as possible, since everyone knew 'what horrid civil wars, and what strange alterations and turns have happened several times in England'.[30]

Half a century later, England had indeed just emerged from a decade of 'horrid civil wars' and it was unclear that the nation's interests would be promoted through alliance with Spain. Among vociferous opponents of any Spanish overture was the former Parliamentarian officer Edward Sexby, who had been sent to south-western France by Cromwell in 1652 to assess whether the Commonwealth regime might make common cause with domestic opponents to Louis XIV's administration, known as the Frondeurs. Sexby had presented local republicans with a manifesto entitled *L'Accord du Peuple* – a French version of the radical Levellers' *Agreement of the People* from 1647 – but returned to England once the Frondeurs' rebellion had been suppressed. Advising the Council of State on foreign policy in 1654, Sexby denied the logic of acceding to entreaties from Cárdenas and Condé to coordinate a joint offensive against France, believing, rather, that the benefits of Spain and France remaining at war, without involving England on either side, were 'so obvious to the weakest wit and dimmest sight'.[31]

In December 1654, a Protectorate fleet of nearly forty warships and transport vessels, together with 9,000 soldiers, left Portsmouth for an unknown destination; as one newsletter writer confirmed, the fleet's 'design is secret, known to the designer only, who says, if he thought his shirt knew it, he would burn it'.[32] Meanwhile, in Madrid, frustration at the Protectorate's depredations of Spanish ships had been prompting Philip IV's administration to consider retaliatory action against the English. As Quirini reported in February 1655, although 'the duke of Medina Celi would like to command this force', this proposal was unpopular, given 'the misfortunes of his grandfather [the duke of Medina Sidonia] in the English Channel in the time of Philip II'. By July, it was also known that Cárdenas was seeking a formal recall from London, objecting that it demeaned Philip's dignity for the English to 'be reinforcing the fleet for America under his very nose', while 'everyone is slandering the name of Spain freely'.[33] Having arrived in London to oversee English ratification of the Treaty of Uppsala, the Swedish envoy Christer Bonde reported to Charles X Gustavus in October a recent conversation with Cárdenas in which the Spanish ambassador had admitted that it was 'vain and childish to suppose that one can be on terms of amity in Europe and wage war in America'.[34] In his own memoirs, Cárdenas bitterly regretted that, although he had managed 'to work out what was going on in the Protector's mind', his councillors 'pretended not to understand what was happening'.[35]

English intentions were finally made explicit when, two days after concluding the Anglo-French Treaty of Westminster, the Protectorate issued a *Declaration* of hostilities against Spain on 26 October 1655. First published in Latin, the *Declaration* was translated into English, Dutch, German, Spanish and French, and specifically recalled events in 1588 when Philip II had sought 'to attempt a total conquest of this nation', memories of which 'lie close by Englishmen's hearts' and were not 'easily out of their minds'. Despite Anglo-Spanish amity in Europe, the *Declaration* insisted that a state of perpetual warfare persisted in the West Indies where retribution was now sought for repeated 'enslaving, hanging, drowning and cruelly torturing to death, our countrymen, spoiling their ships and goods, and destroying their colonies in the times of greatest peace, without any just cause or provocation at all'.[36]

More accurately, the *Declaration* was a retrospective attempt to justify an audacious innovation in English colonial policy: the gaining of new territory by seizing an established settlement. Commanded by William Penn senior (while Cromwell's erstwhile deputy in the Irish campaign, Robert Venables, headed its army), the Protectorate fleet arrived in Barbados in January 1655 and launched an amphibious assault on the island of Hispaniola on 14 April, attacking the town of San Domingo ten days later. Now comprising modern-day Haiti and the Dominican Republic and stretching over 29,000 square miles, Hispaniola's size dwarfed the small English-held island of Barbados. Penn's fleet was also treading in Elizabethan footsteps after Sir Francis Drake had attacked San Domingo in 1586, which had led to a month-long occupation of the town, during which Drake had razed buildings and fortifications and extracted a substantial ransom from the Spanish authorities before leaving.

A new edition of *Sir Francis Drake Revived* had appeared in 1653, reminding English readers of Drake's exploits and exhorting 'this dull and effeminate age, to follow his noble steps for gold and silver'.[37] But landing a significantly larger force and intending a permanent conquest brought cumbersome logistical challenges for Penn and Venables whose forces were quickly overwhelmed by the small Spanish garrison. Having lost 2,000 to 3,000 men, the English force left Hispaniola on 3 May and reached Jamaica ten days later. With its eventual permanent settlement, Jamaica became the first English colony acquired through military seizure; it extended 4,200 square miles with a resident population of 2,000 to 2,500 Spanish, Portuguese, Africans and Indians. To contemporary minds, however, Jamaica was viewed as a consolation conquest.

Indeed, when news of events on Hispaniola reached England in July 1655, it marked Cromwell's first experience of military defeat. As Paulucci put it, 'the English are certainly puzzled and humbled and have undoubtedly been worsted'.[38] Writing from The Hague, the English Royalist Joseph Jane savoured the fact that Cromwell 'hath never felt a loss till now, and all agree it's very sharp'. Writing to Charles I's former Secretary of State Sir Edward Nicholas, Jane ventured that news of the Hispaniola defeat 'strikes him [Cromwell] in point of reputation with the vulgar in England who believed him invincible, and the soldiery in regard of former success thought themselves too'.[39] On their return from the West Indies, both Penn and Venables were initially detained in the Tower of London, which they ominously entered, as the Swedish ambassador noted, via the Traitors' Gate.[40] From Cologne, Charles II described to Henry Bennet how his exiled court sought to 'pass our time as well as people can do that have no more money, for we dance and play as if we have taken the Plate Fleet' returning imperial treasure to Spain. They could at least comfort themselves that 'our losses are not so great as Cromwell's is, who for certain has received a very considerable one at Hispaniola'.[41]

Ironically, Cromwell's interpretation of the defeat as a providential sign of divine disfavour echoed Philip II's reaction to the Armada's failure to conquer England, nearly seven decades earlier. In October, Cromwell wrote to Venables's successor as commander-in chief in Jamaica, Major General Richard Fortescue, reminding him of the need for godly discipline. As Cromwell admitted, his administration had 'to be humbled for the reproof God gave us' on account of the 'extreme avarice, pride and confidence, disorders and debauchedness; profaneness and wickedness, commonly practised in that Army'.[42] Poignantly, Fortescue could not have received this counsel as he died that same month, amid the desperate conditions that Protectorate troops encountered in Jamaica. As the Spanish naval captain Julian de Castilla recalled, the arriving English forces had demanded vast amounts of food and 'did not spare any of the dogs, cats, colts or donkeys which their bullets reached, so exceedingly hungry were they when they landed'. In a tropical variant of the Alpine miseries endured by persecuted Protestants in Piedmont, Castilla confirmed the high mortality rate among English invaders and locals alike, as all suffered from 'cold pains and fevers, frenzies or madness, carbuncles, swellings (in such manner that men and women puffed up like hogsheads, of this malady), and almost none escaped dysentery'.[43]

Closer to home, the Anglo-French Treaty of Westminster concluded in November 1655 offered an ironic reckoning of the Protectorate's diplomatic achievements. Despite having articulated a bellicose rhetoric that envisaged creating a powerful league of Continental Protestant states, Cromwell's main alliance was concluded with Catholic France. Trying to draw England into closer alliance with Protestant Sweden, Charles X Gustavus had, earlier that year, dispatched Christer Bonde as a special ambassador to London at the same time as Nieupoort tried to promote a closer Anglo-Dutch league that could involve other Protestant powers, such as Denmark and Brandenburg. Three months earlier, amid sumptuous ceremonial, Bonde had a public audience with Cromwell in the Banqueting House at Whitehall – the venue for Charles I's public execution. Reflecting on the regicide, Bonde described to Charles X Gustavus how, under Rubens's famous painted ceiling of James VI & I, the Banqueting House was not only 'hung with the most costly tapestries' from the royal collection, but was 'now the scene of the splendid triumph of one who (to put it *mitissime*) had been a main agent in that deed'. For Bonde, it was impossible to 'look on it without emotion and compassion for the mutabilities of this world'. Subsequent negotiations with the Protectorate administration also proved tricky: as Bonde complained in November, 'those who sit in the government have never dealt with affairs before, and particularly not with foreign affairs'. Consequently, 'they blunder through ignorance' and were 'not helped by the fact they are much puffed up' and overly confident of 'their advantageous situation and great power at sea'.[44]

While considering proposals for a Protestant league, the Protectorate regime was still concerned to foster Anglo-French initiatives to reduce the likelihood of any Franco-Spanish peace. Fearing that momentum might be lost by Bordeaux's return to France after the Treaty of Westminster's conclusion, Cromwell contemplated sending his own envoy to Louis's court. In a letter intercepted by Thurloe's intelligence network in early 1656, Bordeaux asserted 'with great passion' to a female correspondent, his hope of returning to London soon, reassuring her that 'neither the business private or public, nor the sight of my wife, do make any change in my inclination'. But from Paris, an English spy warned Thurloe to beware excessive French influence, predicting that Bordeaux 'would fain prove a Gondomar, and by report owns as much power on his Highness [Cromwell], as Gondomar had over King James'.[45]

In France, the pro-English aspect of Louis's foreign policy was also denounced in a remonstrance submitted by senior ecclesiastics who opposed their country's alliance with a heretic nation and offered large financial subsidies as an inducement to reorientate French foreign policy in a pro-Catholic direction. Fearing that a Protectorate envoy might suffer a similar fate to Isaac Dorislaus and Anthony Ascham, in April Mazarin urged Bordeaux, who had returned to London, to petition Whitehall 'not to send an ambassador to this court'. Given the large numbers of English and Irish Royalists in Paris, Mazarin worried that 'there may be some desperate fellows amongst them, that may attempt to do him a mischief'.[46] But before this advice reached London, the Council of State had appointed Colonel William Lockhart (who was married to one of Cromwell's nieces) as an additional ambassador to explore 'a nearer union, and more intimate alliance' than the Westminster treaty's terms. Lockhart was also directed by Cromwell to assure Mazarin, in confidence, 'that there is no person in Europe who will be a more certain and constant friend to him and the affairs of France than myself'.[47] But as Lockhart soon discovered, Mazarin was an adept double-dealer who had recently sent the Secretary of State Hugues de Lionne to Madrid to explore terms for a possible Franco-Spanish peace. While Mazarin reassured Lockhart that Lionne's mission would certainly fail, Henri-Auguste de Loménie, count of Brienne, exhorted Bordeaux – in another missive read by Thurloe's intelligence officers in August – to flatter Cromwell and constantly convince him of French amity: 'as much as you can, let him know, he is very much respected and considered in this court'.[48]

Closer Anglo-French cooperation also rendered the duke of York's continued employment in the French army untenable. Indeed, an awkward encounter arose when, after finally taking his leave of the French court, York's coach stopped at the same Clermont post-house at which, coincidentally, the Protectorate's envoy, Lockhart, was staying in September 1656. As York later recalled, Lockhart had quickly armed himself and the ambassador and duke directly exchanged glances with one another. As local townspeople gathered, York believed that, had he given 'the least word or intimation', he 'verily believed they would have fallen upon the ambassador', given 'what hatred and aversion they had to the English of Lockhart's party'.[49]

At the French court, Mazarin continued to assure Lockhart of French support for the Protectorate on the grounds that, paradoxically, Louis XIV would prefer Philip IV to conquer England directly than that he should re-establish Charles II as a puppet king. A simple conquest that placed the English under Catholic Habsburg rule would inevitably provoke rebellion and prove short-lived. By contrast, if Charles Stuart was restored, Mazarin feared that 'England would in a little time reunite under him, and forget their late differences' and Charles would be 'charmed into an implicit belief' of Spanish favour, resulting in 'very dangerous enterprises against France'. Hence if Cromwell had ever doubted 'the reality of his kindness upon the account of his affection', Mazarin admitted that his professed amity to England's new rulers was also predicated on a strategic calculation of French interests.[50]

III

For Charles's exiled court at Cologne, closer cooperation between France and the Protectorate brought a silver lining in terms of encouraging Spanish support, despite the Stuarts' dynastic links with the French Bourbons and York's military service in French campaigns against Spain. After Cromwell's attack on Hispaniola, the Spanish ambassador at The Hague, Antoine Brun, on being asked whether he was 'for the king or parliament or Cromwell', acknowledged that it had been unwisely premature for Spain to recognize the Commonwealth and publicly drank 'a health to the King of England, which with great readiness went about the table'.[51]

In January 1656, Charles had sent James Butler, marquess of Ormond, to Brussels to discuss the likelihood of securing support from Habsburg ministers and had requested a New Testament in Spanish, hoping that he would soon have 'much need of that language'. Three months later, the Treaty of Brussels was agreed between Philip IV and Charles, and subsequently ratified in Madrid, renewing the Anglo-Spanish alliance concluded with Charles I in 1630 and offering the exiled court 4,000 infantry and 2,000 cavalry, equipped with ammunition, transport ships and maintenance funds, once a suitable English port had been secured to disembark an army of reconquest. On his side, Charles undertook – once restored to his British thrones – to return recently acquired territories in the West Indies to Spanish rule and to offer religious concessions to his Catholic subjects. Having resolved to relocate to Bruges, Charles beseeched his nominal Chancellor, Edward Hyde, to join him, with 'as much haste as your gouty feet will give you leave' and requested a list of 'inscriptions, subscriptions, and superscriptions' to ensure that correct epistolary etiquette was observed in approaches to Philip's natural son Don Juan José of Austria, who had been appointed Governor of the Spanish Netherlands.[52] Prospects for a Spanish-backed restoration of the Stuarts were further boosted in July 1656 when Don Juan secured a rare military victory over the formidable French commander – and the duke of York's revered mentor – Marshal Henri de La Tour d'Auvergne, viscount of Turenne, at the Battle of Valenciennes in the Spanish Netherlands.

Negotiations between Spanish ministers and the exiled Stuart court provoked predictable alarm in London. In May, John Thurloe had admitted to Henry Cromwell that 'the Spaniard, Cavalier, Papists and Levellers, are all come into a confederacy'. Although unclear as to 'what monstrous birth this womb will bring forth', Thurloe worried that the Protectorate's enemies 'threaten hard, but I perceive they are not quite ready'.[53] Rumoured and actual assassination plots were pervasive and variously directed against Cromwell, Charles or their diplomatic representatives. In May 1656, the Protectorate's envoy to Lisbon, Philip Meadows, had successfully concluded an Anglo-Portuguese alliance but, later that day, was injured in a failed assassination attempt assumed to be retaliation for Dom Pataleone de Sá e Menezes's execution in London two years earlier. Writing to Thurloe from aboard the *Naseby* warship, General Edward Montagu reported that 'it is almost in the mouth of every Portuguese in Lisbon, that it was Don Pantaleon himself, and his brother, the conde de Torre, that acted that base part' in orchestrating revenge for their sibling. That autumn, an English spy relayed rumours from Brussels that Spain's former ambassador in London, Cárdenas, had strongly urged Cromwell's removal. Although Charles's advisers remained sceptical as to the feasibility of an assassination plot, Cárdenas's secretary had claimed that the Lord Protector 'may be watched, as he walks in the garden, and keys may be easily had to the gates'. In November 1656, the Protectorate administration received further intelligence of an assassination plot against Cromwell 'to be done by powder, and in the night', prompting a thorough search of chimneys at Whitehall Palace. The informant alleged the conspirators to be 'either Presbyterians, or Levellers, or a mixture of all sorts' who hoped that Cromwell's removal would facilitate a general uprising in which 'they intend to cry out liberty, religion, and taking away of taxes', while 'Kent is named as well for the landing of Charles Stuart' or a port near King's Lynn, with the exiled king's arrival expected within weeks.[54]

Rumoured plots translated into a narrow miss when, two months later, the resident secretary at the Venetian embassy in London, Francesco Giavarina, reported the detection, in the Whitehall Palace chapel, of 'a long train lighted at both ends with a quantity of gunpowder to be fired in the middle of the night', clearly designed to 'blow up a great part of the palace, if not the whole'.[55] Just as James VI & I had personally interrogated Guy Fawkes after the Gunpowder Plot's discovery in 1605, Cromwell learned at first hand from a former lifeguard, John Toop, that motivation for his involvement in the conspiracy had been Toop's belief 'that it was better to have Charles Stuart to reign here, than this tyrant'.[56] Even customary exchanges of diplomatic gifts became objects of paranoid suspicion. In May 1657, Giavarina described the presentation by the long-serving Tuscan Resident in London, Amerigo Salvetti, of various wines, 'fancy foodstuffs, oils and essences' to a mistrustful Lord Protector. As one of his physicians admitted, Cromwell 'has not the courage to put such liquors to his lips ... being fearful of his own shadow, so to speak, and living in constant apprehension of everything, for he trusts no-one'.[57]

Pressure to regularize future succession to the Protectoral office also reflected a growing recognition of Cromwell's physical vulnerabilities. Meeting Cromwell for the first time after he had recovered from illness during the autumn of 1655, Sagredo had observed clear 'signs that his health is not stable and perfect'. Despite being 'robust, of martial presence', the Venetian noticed that 'as he stood uncovered, the hand holding his hat trembled'.[58] Illness aside, ever since the Protectorate's creation persistent speculation had encouraged popular expectations that it was only a matter of when – rather than if – Cromwell would be vested with monarchical authority. *An Admonition to my Lord Protector and his Council, of their Present Danger* (1654), attributed to James Heath, had suggested that Cromwell should consider 'a treaty with Charles Stuart, if he will accept of the Crown after your decease' to rule upon the same terms as the Lord Protector, in conjunction with a Council of State and Parliament with clear limits thereby attaching to monarchical power. As the author surmised, Charles would presumably prefer to 'expect quietly the decease of an old man (as your Highness is) than run an improbable hazard of all his fortunes' by trying to regain his thrones by force.[59]

While politicians who supported Cromwell's elevation to the crown were satirically derided as 'kinglings', foreign envoys were prone to over-emphasize the apparent inevitability of a Cromwellian coronation as a means of reassuring their own monarchs that England's revolutionary regime would yet revert to traditional constitutional forms. Shortly after arriving in England in July 1655, Christer Bonde had reassured Charles X Gustavus that it was 'no longer a question whether they shall have a king, but who the king shall be, and so the former difference between the House of Stuart and all the inhabitants of this land is converted into a difference between the Houses of Stuart and Cromwell'.[60] Indeed, following Cromwell's elevation as Lord Protector, his contemplation of a subsequent coronation had appalled exiled Royalists. From Paris, Sir Edward Nicholas had judged it 'the saddest change that could be to have that bloody rebel so enthroned'.[61]

A fully fledged 'kingship crisis' emerged in early 1657, prompted by the presentation to Parliament of constitutional proposals by a former Mayor of London, Sir Christopher Packe, the first of which requested that Cromwell assume the 'name, style, title and dignity of king'. Known as the *Humble Petition and Advice*, the proposals also made provision for a second parliamentary house to be revived in the form of a nominated assembly of life peers.[62] While the *Humble Petition* was opposed by republicans and army officers, divisions over kingly office were also complicated by the extent to which the monarchical title was regarded as separate from calls for a regulated succession. While welcoming the monarchy's abolition in England, for example, a *Letter written to an Officer of the Army* (1657) demanded a regulated succession to the Protectorate to avoid civil disorder and constitutional confusion. The *Letter*'s anonymous author advised against waiting until after Cromwell had died to nominate a successor, recalling that late-sixteenth-century advisers had warned Elizabeth I 'how great a storm of calamities would hang over England, if she should put off her mortality, designing no certain successor'. Moreover, since Charles I's execution, subjects had been 'levelled all to the order of Commons' and lacked a nobility empowered to adjudicate among potential competitors, while 'being also an island' England remained 'so much in danger of foreign surprise and invasion' ready to exploit internal divisions.[63] Settling the Protectorate's succession would avoid such dangers and would also remove the premium currently placed on Cromwell's assassination as the only means of achieving regime change.

Notwithstanding such arguments, Cromwell declined the offer of the crown in April and explained to a parliamentary committee that 'the providence of God has laid this title aside'. In England, monarchy was '*de facto* . . . blotted out, it is a thing cast out by Act of Parliament, it's a thing [that] has been kept out to this day'. Refusing 'to set up that [which] providence hath destroyed and laid in the dust', Cromwell invoked the scriptural book of Joshua to confirm that he 'would not build Jericho again'. To the whole House of Commons gathered in the Banqueting House, Cromwell reiterated in early May, 'I cannot undertake this government with that title of king. And that is my answer to this great weighty business'.[64]

That same month, a tract appeared in London entitled *Killing No Murder* (1657) that sought to avert an imminent Cromwellian coronation by calling for the Lord Protector's immediate assassination. Described by the diplomat and intelligence specialist Samuel Morland as 'the most dangerous pamphlet lately thrown about the streets that ever has been printed in these times', the tract had been published in Holland and pseudonymously authored by two former opponents of Charles I, Edward Sexby and Silius Titus. While Morland objected that, in terms of 'rancour, malice and wickedness . . . the Devil himself could not have shown more', the pamphlet demanded Cromwell's removal by insisting that, 'whilst this monster lives, we are not members of a commonwealth, but only his living tools and instruments'. Skilfully echoing Charles I's warning in *Eikon Basilike* against misled subjects who unwittingly 'let in the wild boar and subtle foxes, to waste and destroy thy vineyard', *Killing No Murder*'s authors emphasized the urgent necessity 'of saving the vineyard of the Commonwealth if possible, by destroying the wild boar that has broken into it'.[65] Although around 1,400 illegally imported copies were seized by the Protectorate authorities, *Killing No Murder* later went through at least twenty-one English editions and five French editions, inspiring eighteenth-century Jacobites in Britain, French revolutionaries and domestic opponents of Napoleon Bonaparte and Louis Napoleon.[66]

Although the anticipated coronation did not take place, a second investiture ceremony to confirm Cromwell's authority as Lord Protector was held on 26 June 1657, shortly before Parliament's prorogation. As one newsletter-writer reported, Cromwell was presented 'with a robe, a Bible, sceptre, and sword; but the crown was wanting'.[67] The national mood was further bolstered by news that Admiral Robert Blake's fleet had secured a major victory over Philip IV's ships at the Battle of Santa Cruz in Tenerife in April. Having found the Spanish fleet sitting in harbour, Blake's surprise attack had sunk sixteen galleons laden with silver and treasures. Giavarina acknowledged this victory to be 'considered the greatest which they have won against the Spaniards since that of 1588', although Blake himself died aboard his flagship, the *George*, on his fleet's return to Plymouth that autumn.[68] Chances of launching a successful attack on Spain with land forces were further promoted by a second Anglo-French treaty signed in Paris in March 1657. Binding for a year, the treaty committed Louis XIV to providing an army of 20,000 men for a new campaign against Spanish possessions in Flanders, with England contributing 6,000 troops, supported by the Protectorate fleet. The Spanish-held coastal fortresses of Dunkirk, Mardyke and Gravelines would be targeted, the first two of which, if captured, would be ceded to England. In September, Spanish forces mounted little resistance when the fortress at Mardyke was captured by an Anglo-French force that was commanded by Turenne and purged of any Scottish and Irish regiments for fear of those soldiers' residual loyalties to the Stuarts.

The prospect of English forces gaining a foothold on the coast of northern Europe prompted foreign interest. Watching 'bombs, gunpowder and every sort of material required for a siege' being sent from the Tower of London to Flanders in October, Giavarina confirmed that the Dutch would not welcome the English having 'positions that side of the water'. Once English forces occupied 'a coast town they will never be driven out; they will have an open way into France, Flanders and the territory of the States; they will hold the sea as if it were their home' and would soon exact heavy tolls and threaten shipping.[69] While members of the English garrison set about improving fortifications at Mardyke, the fortress's new Protectorate governor, Sir John Reynolds, remained sensitive to the local presence of the exiled Stuarts. According to the duke of York's memoirs, Reynolds contrived a meeting in no man's land where he asked York 'not to look on him as one sent over by Cromwell, but as one serving the king of France' and provoked suspicion by ordering his troops to desist from firing if either Charles or York were in the vicinity and also by dispatching gifts of wine to the royal brothers.[70]

Fears of a foreign-backed Stuart restoration always haunted the Protectorate. When the prorogued Parliament reconvened in January 1658, Nathaniel Fiennes warned fellow MPs of the dangerous 'conjunction of our late inbred enemy [the Stuarts] with that old enemy of our nation and religion [Spain]'. Unless increased sums of money were devoted to national security, Fiennes feared that 'the poor lambs of Christ' would be devoured if Charles was 'brought in upon the wings of that double-headed black eagle, or rather vulture': the House of Habsburg.[71] Newly appointed as the Protectorate's ambassador to The Hague in November 1657, George Downing was disconcerted to find prayers still being offered for Charles in the city's English churches. Objecting that such public practices had 'made this place a mere nursery of Cavalierism', Downing feared for his personal safety. As well as hearing of 'a report at London, that I was stabbed', he warned Thurloe the following summer that there were individuals 'now in this country, who are come with design and order to kill me', including a 'Major Whitefield' who was widely suspected of involvement in Isaac Dorislaus's murder in the same city, shortly after Charles I's execution.[72]

Suspicions of the Stuart dynasty's inherently popish inclinations had not been allayed by the exiled court's alliance with Catholic Spain and were only reinforced when Charles's Palatine cousin Princess Louise Hollandine fled from The Hague in December 1657. A skilled artist, who had trained with the Dutch painter Gerard van Honthorst, the princess sought refuge in an English Carmelite convent in Antwerp and converted to Catholicism, delighting Jesuit observers who celebrated 'the brilliance of her pedigree' as the niece of the murdered Charles I and the Palatine Elector's sister (see Plate 19).[73] That same month, Charles's own reputation was damaged by a bungled attempt to remove his eight-year-old natural son James – later duke of Monmouth – from his mother, Lucy Walter. After being detained with her son in the Tower of London the previous summer, Walter had been deported from England, prompting censorious observations in *Mercurius Politicus* that

Royalists hoping for Charles's restoration 'may see they are furnished already with an heir apparent' as the young king sought funds for 'the maintenance of his concubines and royal issue'.[74] Eighteen months later, rumours that the child's abduction had been ordered by Charles led to the intervention of Don Juan of Austria, as Governor of the Spanish Netherlands, as well as the town council of Brabant and the former Spanish ambassador to London Alonso de Cárdenas, whose secretary described to the marquess of Ormond 'the clamour of the people, who found this action most barbarous, abominable and most unnatural'. In response, Ormond explained that Charles had intended 'in a quiet, and silent way, if it could be, to get the child out of the mother's hands', but not 'with that noise and scandal that hath happened'. Although Charles was warned by the Royalist officer with whom Walter was lodging, that 'if your Majesty does not send her pension, she would post up all your Majesty's letters to her', a second attempt to take the child into the king's custody succeeded in March 1658, while Walter died six months later.[75]

At Whitehall, Cromwell's keenness to target Spanish–Stuart interests in Flanders ensured that renewal of the Anglo-French alliance in March 1658 had contained a prioritized commitment to capture Dunkirk, which, if victory was secured, would become a Protectorate possession. At the epochal Battle of the Dunes in June, three Stuart brothers – Charles, James, duke of York, and Henry, duke of Gloucester – fought for the Spanish Habsburgs against the French, who had been joined by an expeditionary force of 6,000 Protectorate veterans. In a posthumously published account of the battle, the Protectorate commander, General Thomas Morgan, recalled how, as his redcoat soldiers approached their Royalist adversaries, both sides 'fell into great friendship, one asking, is such an officer in your army; another, is such a soldier in yours', before Morgan warned 'that for anything they knew, they would be cutting one another's throats, within a minute of an hour'.[76] The battle lasted only two hours, and the Spanish forces, together with their English Royalist and French Fronde allies, were overwhelmed by a joint Franco-Protectorate assault along the Spanish perimeter.

Following the Franco-Protectorate victory, Mazarin came under domestic pressure not to cede Dunkirk to a heretic power with royal advisers 'mad to see themselves part with that they call *un si bon morceau* (such a good part)'. French commander Turenne, however, surrendered the fortress immediately and Louis XIV then travelled to Dunkirk to hand over the town's keys to Colonel William Lockhart, who, as well as serving as the Protectorate's ambassador in France, had assumed a military command at the Dunes and now became Dunkirk's governor and undertook to respect the rights of the town's Catholic population. Reassuring Cromwell of his respectful conduct, Lockhart confirmed that he had 'not hindered the departure of any bourgeois' to other French towns, but had 'upon the contrary given them leave to transport their goods . . . as peaceably as if they had removed from one street in London to another'.[77]

Meanwhile, outraged by the liquidation of French and Catholic interests, Mazarin's adversary Cardinal de Retz penned a *Most Humble and Important Remonstrance* (1658), lambasting Louis for abasing the French monarchy into one that 'humbles itself at the least signal of a pirate' and 'the bark of a tyrant, the murderer of your uncle'. Ceding Dunkirk would only 'feed the greedy eyes of Cromwell towards the beginning of the next campaign' as 'this false prophet beholds from the top of the Tower of London all those combats' that brought new acquisitions. Although Dunkirk had been retrieved from the Spanish 'at the price of our [French] blood, of our goods, of our honour, and of our consciences', it would become 'in a short time the magazines and arsenals, that shall furnish out the ammunition destined to batter down ours'. A century earlier, England had lost its last Continental possession with the fall of Calais in 1558. Bewailing the sight of the St George's Cross 'triumphing upon Catholic ramparts' in 1658, de Retz feared the imminent surrender to Cromwell of Calais and Boulogne and concluded, despairingly, 'Sir, we feel in our hearts a combat of religion against the state, and of the state against itself'.[78]

16

Now in Another World, 1658–1660

On 3 September 1658, Oliver Cromwell died at Whitehall Palace at the age of fifty-nine, the date of his death coinciding with the seventh and eighth anniversaries of his military victories at the Battles of Dunbar and Worcester. Physicians declared the Lord Protector had died of a 'bastard tertian ague', now assumed to have been a recurrence of a latent malarial infection. In the days preceding his death, pervasive uncertainty had prevailed. On 30 August, Secretary of State John Thurloe admitted to the Irish Lord Deputy, Henry Cromwell, his fear that 'great stirrings' would ensue if the Lord Protector 'should not settle and fix his successor before he dies, which truly I believe he hath not yet done'. Insisting that anxieties about the succession be kept 'an absolute secret', Thurloe informed Henry that his father was believed to have confirmed the name of his chosen successor in a sealed envelope in his study, but no such document could be found 'though it hath been very narrowly looked for'. Replying from Dublin on 8 September – unaware that his father had now died – Henry worried that, even if he 'would declare his successor, where is that person of wisdom, courage, conduct and (which is equivalent to all) reputation at home and abroad' so critical 'to preserve our peace'? Although Henry had evidently not considered his elder brother Richard an obvious candidate, it was quickly announced that the Lord Protector had indeed nominated his eldest son as his successor. Writing again to Henry on 4 September, Thurloe hastily recast recent events, insisting that the Lord Protector had been 'pleased before his death to declare my lord Richard successor', adding that 'he did it upon Monday' (30 August), despite the fact that Thurloe had not mentioned any such nomination to Henry in another letter sent on 31 August.[1]

Reports that the Council of State had thereafter voted unanimously in favour of confirming Richard Cromwell's succession also appeared to contradict the Instrument of Government's stipulation that the Lord Protector retained the right to nominate his successor. Writing to the exiled Charles II, one Royalist cleric described the Lord Protector's nomination of his successor as having been managed 'so sleightly, as some doubt whether he did it at all'.[2] In Edinburgh, the Army's Governor, General George Monck, heard how a millenarian 'Fifth Monarchist' preacher in London, Christopher Feake, had preached against Richard's succession, venturing that 'if they had brought a Devil out of Whitehall in the shape of a man they would have made publication for him'.[3] Yet familial preferment had been a notable feature of Cromwellian rule. At the time of Oliver's death, his son Henry was Irish Lord Deputy, while his son-in-law Thomas Belasyse, Earl Fauconberg, served as an ambassador extraordinary for the Protectorate at Louis XIV's court, alongside the resident ambassador to France and Governor of the Dunkirk garrison, William Lockhart, who was married to Oliver's niece. Another son-in-law and Parliamentarian soldier, Charles Fleetwood, had been widely tipped as a potential successor to Oliver as Lord Protector, having served as a major general in 1655, as had Oliver's brother-in-law, John Desborough. Ironically, Cromwell himself had insisted that, if the Instrument of Government had vested the Protectorate office 'in my family hereditarily, I would have rejected it'.[4]

Richard Cromwell was thirty-one at the time of his father's death, and despite attracting posthumous scorn as hapless 'Tumbledown Dick', contemporary assessments were more equivocal. In the view of the poet and memorialist Lucy Hutchinson, Richard was 'so flexible to good counsels, that there was nothing desirable in a prince which might not have been hoped in him, but a great spirit and a just title'. He was 'pleasant in his nature, yet gentle and virtuous, but became not greatness'.[5] But greatness – rather than hereditary right – was essential to secure stability and its absence was soon evident. In the twenty months after Cromwell's death in September 1658, England experienced a bewildering array of regime changes, interspersed with army coups, before the Convention Parliament voted in May 1660 to restore the monarchy under Charles II.

I

On the day of Oliver Cromwell's death, the exiled Charles II was travelling to Amsterdam to meet the Friesian Stadtholder, Count William

Frederick of Nassau-Dietz. The king's first response to the altered political situation was to propose marriage to Henriette Catherine, the Protestant daughter of Mary Stuart's ambitious mother-in-law and dowager princess consort of Orange, Amalia of Solms-Braunfels. Writing to Amalia, Charles did not mention his alliance with Habsburg Spain, but instead claimed that the United Provinces remained the most likely source of support in regaining his British thrones, despite 'the mistrust that may have been infused to them of me by my enemies, or such as know me not'. Insisting that he would prefer to be 'restored rather by them than by any other people, but my own', he would thereby have every reason to promote Dutch interests once restored as king.[6] From Amsterdam, the Royalist John, Lord Colepeper, described the Dutch people as 'mad with joy' at the news of Cromwell's death: while 'the young fry dance in the streets' and '"the Devil is dead" is the language at every turn', even 'the graver sort' wanted 'to contemplate the happy days now approaching'. Writing to Charles's nominal Chancellor, Edward Hyde, Colepeper nevertheless advised the exiled court not to act rashly, but to bide its time and only make discreet approaches to those 'most discontented with Cromwell's partiality in setting this young man [Richard Cromwell] over their heads'.[7]

From The Hague, the Protectorate's ambassador George Downing admitted to Thurloe that news of Richard Cromwell's peaceful succession 'doth most wonderfully amaze all that hear of it, who expected nothing but confusion in England, after his late Highness's death, and thereby a wide door opened for Charles Stuart'. In London, any likelihood that Oliver Cromwell's death might instantly precipitate a Royalist rising evaporated: as Thurloe reassured Henry Cromwell, stability prevailed and 'there is not a dog that wags his tongue, so great a calm we are in'.[8] With no alteration to the Stuart court's impoverished exile looking likely, Amalia of Solms-Braunfels hastily withdrew her initial consent for Charles to marry her daughter Henriette Catherine in favour of a more promising match to John George, Prince of Anhalt-Dessau. From Madrid, Charles II's representative Sir Henry Bennet wondered if the exiled court's enthusiasm for sponsoring new diplomatic overtures was waning; as he sarcastically suggested to Hyde in December 1658, perhaps 'you have so good hopes from home as to make you neglect all succour abroad'. Bennet judged such a scenario unlikely, 'after all the king's disappointments, so many winters and wants, [and] so many summers' waiting for an opportune moment to act.[9]

But if Charles's envoys were frustrated by the seemingly minimal fall-out from Cromwell's death, a sombre mood also prevailed at Louis XIV's court regarding the uncertain direction of English affairs. Writing to the French ambassador in London, Cardinal Mazarin, Louis's chief minister, admitted that the news of Cromwell's death 'causes me the utmost affliction, not only for reasons of public interest . . . but on account of the friendship which I well know his Highness felt for us'.[10] Having been reassured by the Protectorate's quasi-monarchical apparatus and its anti-Spanish stance, Louis's ministers wanted to provide covert support to maintain Richard Cromwell's Protectorate as an alternative to a resurgent English republicanism. Indeed, the Protectorate's own French-language newspaper, the *Nouvelles Ordinaires de Londres*, republished fifty loyalist addresses sent by English towns and corporations to Whitehall as evidence of the new regime's provincial popularity.[11] As pressure mounted for a new Protectorate parliament, Louis's ambassador, Antoine de Bordeaux-Neufville, acknowledged to Henri-Auguste de Loménie, count of Brienne, that, even if Richard Cromwell succeeded in securing the loyalty of all new MPs, 'a body composed of five hundred persons cannot fail to be very difficult to govern'.[12] French anxieties were realized when the third Protectorate parliament convened in late January 1659; as well as attracting too many members for all to find seats, it included a significant phalanx of committed republicans.

Scepticism regarding the legitimacy of Richard Cromwell's pseudo-monarchical succession was quickly evident as well as trenchant criticism of Oliver Cromwell's foreign policy. In early February, the republican MP for Leicester, Sir Arthur Haselrig, denounced the 'Western Design' on Hispaniola as a disastrous failure and criticized the peace terms concluded with the Dutch in 1654, prompting the courtier-lawyer John Maynard to cavil sarcastically that 'if you go on at this rate, to have a speech a day, the Dutch will give you £2000 a day to do so'.[13] An attempt to introduce a 'Bill of Recognition' confirming Richard Cromwell's authority as Lord Protector provoked so many objections that it was jettisoned. Major General William Packer was one critic who challenged the validity of Richard's 'nomination' on the grounds that the procedure 'brings in hereditary government by a side wind'. Nor was Packer persuaded by the numerous professions of civic loyalism received at Whitehall, venturing that 'if the King of Scots had landed at Dover, and had a force, he might have had as many addresses . . . such are easily obtained. The people are like a flock of sheep.'[14]

Factious, prolix and heated debates at Westminster reflected fundamental ambiguities attaching to Richard Cromwell's Protectoral authority over the Council, Parliament and the Army, which was presumed to be predicated on provisions set out in the conservative *Humble Petition and Advice* (1657): constitutional proposals originally framed in confident expectation that Oliver Cromwell would assume the kingship. Two years later, sensitive matters that remained unresolved included the future status of the militia, mechanisms for raising non-parliamentary revenue through the excise, potential reconstitution of a second chamber or 'Other House', as well as the legitimacy and extent of Scots and Irish representation. In one conspicuous anomaly, English MPs sitting in Richard Cromwell's parliament had been returned via traditional constituency writs, whereas Scots and Irish members had been elected according to the *Humble Petition and Advice*'s terms. Writing to Hyde in March, the Royalist Allan Broderick described the new Lord Protector as 'a person of great affability' who seemed 'to decline the acrimony of the dispute, and with all gentleness to treat whoever addresses'. By contrast, 'the Commonwealthmen' were 'industrious, popular, plausible, eloquent in the language of the times, cunning in the rules of the House, and thereby ready to entrap or discountenance all opposers less dextrous than themselves', creating unstable alliances among 'the giddier sort of members who fall into no classes', 'counterfeit Commonwealthsmen', court lawyers and army officers.[15]

Within the Army's leadership, frustration at Parliament's apparent reluctance to pay army arrears fused with fears that MPs wanted to restrict the right of the Army's General Council to meet independently. Richard Cromwell's brother-in-law Fleetwood then instigated another military coup as troops sought to control access to a locked Commons chamber and senior army officers demanded the dissolution of Parliament, which occurred on 22 April. In May, 'a Rump of a Rump' convened, comprising around fifty survivors of the seventy members of the original Rump Parliament that had met in 1648, who were invited by the Army to promote republican ideals, catchily nicknamed 'the Good Old Cause'. Further measures were promised, namely the creation of a new Senate to replace the Protectorate Council, which would include army personnel and allow freedom of worship and law reform, and, after the Rump's dissolution, fresh elections for a new Parliament.

Aware of competing demands from republicans, religious sectaries and agitated soldiers, Bordeaux reiterated to Thurloe that Louis XIV would 'spare neither money nor troops in order to re-establish the Protector, if there were any likelihood of success'. As Bordeaux informed Mazarin, he had also advised Thurloe that it was always 'expedient, in an affair of this nature, to act in concert with perfect confidence, to open one's heart and discover the evil as well as the good' if Richard Cromwell's supporters wanted Louis 'to make every effort of which France was capable'.[16] French meddling was, however, frustrated when the restored Rump refused to recognize the Protectorate's legitimacy and demanded Richard's resignation, which was tendered on 25 May. A week earlier, Richard had written to his younger brother Henry, warning him to 'have a care who you trust, the world is false', lamenting how 'those that were my father's friends' were 'pretended ones only' and had 'tripped up my heels before I knew them', while others were family 'relations, yet they forsook me'.[17]

In Paris, there was concern that republican critics of the Protectorate's pro-French inclinations already knew that secret Franco-Spanish peace talks had started in Madrid, initiated by Hugues de Lionne, that not only breached the terms of France's alliance with England, but could yet produce a Franco-Spanish peace that would leave both crowns free to attack the English republic and sponsor a foreign-backed Stuart restoration. Accordingly, it seemed prudent to embrace peace rather than pursue war. In *Considerations and Proposals ... Touching the not Warring with Spain* (1659), 'F. B.' opposed dispatching warships and soldiers to the West Indies from where they would be unable to return 'home again upon necessity, England being surrounded with so many considerable potentates'.[18] Conditions also seemed favourable for English envoys seeking to derail French diplomacy by negotiating a separate peace with Spain that would equally benefit English merchants and Spain's government. In an intelligence report supplied to Thurloe from Madrid the previous December, the penurious state of Habsburg crown finances had been clear. As Thurloe's informant had averred, 'the efficacious certainty of their adage – *con todo el mundo guerra, y paz con Inglaterra* [war with all the world and peace with England]' had 'never been so apparent unto them, as now, and would make any notion of treaty most welcome to them'.[19]

The Protectorate's collapse thus signalled an end to a bellicose foreign policy. After meeting the prominent republican spokesman Sir Henry Vane, Bordeaux reported to Brienne in July 1659 that Vane had 'made no mystery about it, but told me plainly that the government had no desire but to live on good terms with all neighbouring states', being 'convinced that it will never be respected abroad' until domestic peace and order could be assured.[20] The previous month, the governing Council of State had appointed a delegation to broker an end to Sweden's long-running war against Denmark in order to restore lucrative trade networks and deter Charles X Gustavus from over-running Copenhagen. The delegation, which included Vane and another committed republican, Algernon Sidney, arrived in Elsinore having already agreed a set of Anglo-Dutch proposals that threatened a joint naval attack against Sweden or Denmark if either power should refuse to conclude peace terms.

Pressed by Sidney to accept the Anglo-Dutch proposals at a public audience, an irate Charles Gustavus declared himself insulted by the diplomats' temerity, 'laying his hand on his sword', and refused 'to be persuaded to any alliance by anyone, no matter whom'. The Venetian ambassador in Pressburg, Alvise Molin, reported that the Swedish king had added that 'the English lords would always be his friends, if they confined themselves to the limits of friendship, but the Dutch he considered his enemies'.[21] As the regicide Colonel Edmund Ludlow later reflected, Charles Gustavus's reaction signalled his outrage that 'two Commonwealths should form conditions to be imposed on crowned heads'.[22] For his part, Sidney found himself fêted by admiring Danes for his stance against Swedish aggression and penned his famous inscription in the University of Copenhagen's visitor book: '*manus hanc inimical tyrannis / einse petit placidam cum libertate quietem*' ('this hand, always an enemy to tyrants, seeks a little peace under liberty'). Although the Commonwealth's attempt at gunboat diplomacy visibly failed, when its fleet of forty ships, commanded by Edward Montagu, left the Sound to return to England, Sidney's hubristic vaunt later became the official motto of the American state of Massachusetts: *ense petit placidam sub libertate quiete* ('by the sword we seek peace, but peace only under liberty').

While Vane and Sidney tried to end hostilities in the Baltic, the Commonwealth's ambassador to the French court, William Lockhart, travelled to the Pyrenean border town of Hondarribia in the summer of 1659. Aware that Charles II also intended to promote Stuart interests among the assembled powers, Lockhart needed to maintain an English presence at the Franco-Spanish peace negotiations. Initially, Philip IV's Council of State had advised the chief minister, Don Luis Méndez de Haro y Guzmán, against receiving the representative of 'a tyrannical republic, which by a most disgraceful public execution, had removed their monarch's head and crown'.[23] But in a letter intercepted by Charles's court in August, Lockhart reported to the Council of State that he had secured an audience with Haro at the conference location: Pheasant Island, in the Bidasoa river. By the ensuing Treaty of the Pyrenees, this island on the border became a Franco-Spanish condominium that remains, to this day, administered by Spain from 1 February to 31 July each year and by France between 1 August and 31 January. To Haro, Lockhart had insisted that the English Commonwealth was now seeking friendship with Spain on account of a principled 'love to peace in general, and to justify to all the world the maxims whereby they intend to walk, of beginning or prosecuting no war without just provocations, and of preserving and maintaining amities and confederations with all freedom, faith and sincerity', to which Haro had evidently answered 'much to the same purpose only changing names, and varying the phrase'. Encountering numerous Royalists in the Pyrenees, Lockhart especially objected to the activities of an Irish agent, Richard Talbot, complaining to Fleetwood and Vane that 'this man hath made it his business to bespatter me with as much dirt as is possible', trying 'to render me the most insignificant, unfaithful, and untrusted creature that can be'.[24]

Certainly, the prospect of imminent peace between France and Spain augured well for the likelihood of either state agreeing to intervene in English affairs to restore the Stuarts. Following Charles's unexpected arrival in Hondarribia in October, Daniel O'Neill, an Irish Royalist, reported to Hyde that the king 'hath behaved himself here as if he had been bred more years in Spain than in France', while the French envoys were equally 'well satisfied with their reception'.[25] In England, a pamphlet entitled *Certamen Britannicum, Gallico Hispanicum* (1659) purportedly recounted a conversation that had taken place at the negotiations wherein Mazarin had advised Charles that, were he to convert to Catholicism, 'all difficulties will so easily be removed' and he could speedily 'have men, monies, ammunition, ships, and what not'. When Charles had insisted that he would 'sooner choose to die an exile' than abandon the Church of England, Mazarin had perceived in Charles II a similar stubborn obstinacy to his father, objecting 'what is your religion, but a new fangle, a thing never thought of till Luther's time?'[26] Meanwhile, the following spring Philip IV's administration made a remarkable offer to Charles's brother, James, duke of York, when they appointed him to the highest office in the Spanish admiralty as Principe de la Mare. Although the position was largely honorific and normally held by a member of the Spanish royal house or close relation, it remained an unusual privilege to confer on a Stuart foreigner and Protestant heretic.

Both Charles and James had hoped to return to England, but they had been dissuaded by the speedy suppression of Sir George Booth's Royalist uprising in Cheshire in August 1659. In the wake of the rebellion's failure, a Royalist correspondent wrote to Hyde from London, admitting that 'all our hopes now are from abroad', although he inclined to pessimism, 'considering how the Spaniard uses you, the French betray you, and the Dutch [are] already declared against you'. From Paris, James Butler, marquess of Ormond, also wrote to Hyde in August, admitting that, without substantive evidence of Royalist success in England, it was difficult to persuade foreign powers to promote Charles's cause. Yet Mazarin remained a pragmatist and, after the French had failed to prop up the Protectorate, Henrietta Maria's chaplain, Walter Montagu, suspected that the Stuarts appeared more likely French allies than Protestant republicans. Accordingly, Montagu had advised Ormond that 'if our [English Royalist] friends could stand on their own legs' and convince Mazarin 'that he could turn the balance, and have the principal honour of doing it', French assistance might be forthcoming, although Mazarin would require prior assurance regarding the near 'infallibility of the success' of any such venture.[27]

But a deep aversion to foreign aid persisted among Royalists. Writing to Hyde from Antwerp in June, Lord Thomas Wentworth admitted he was 'so much an Englishman' that he hoped 'the king may owe his restoration only to his own countrymen'.[28] Such views were echoed that autumn by John, Viscount Mordaunt, who reassured York that he would fight for his brother 'in any invasion, though by the Turks, yet I had rather have it done by the English, though I suffered in it'. Drafting a letter for Mordaunt's use, Charles likewise confirmed in December that he was 'looking upon my restoration as most happy if effected by my own subjects with as little foreign assistance as may be'.[29]

II

In England, while the Army successfully suppressed local Royalist insurgencies, its political influence was resisted by the Rump Parliament, with the Army's leadership seeing little evidence of promised reforms or the Rump's anticipated dissolution. Domestic security remained on a knife-edge: with almost 25,000 soldiers still employed in the English Army, the London barber and diarist Thomas Rugg recorded how 'Parliament soldiers watched as a cat would watch for a mouse, expecting that there would have been a general rising'.[30] In October 1659, troops commanded by General John Lambert encircled Parliament, blocked access by road and river and refused MPs entry to the Commons. Having voted to dissolve itself, the Council of State was replaced by a twenty-three-member 'Committee of Safety' directed by Lambert, as an interim administration. As John Evelyn observed, there was 'now no government in the nation, all in confusion; no magistrate either owned or pretended, but the soldiers' who were internally divided into different factions.[31] From the Venetian embassy, Francesco Giavarina reported that, whichever way political power was reconfigured, it was now 'the sword that governs and directs everything'. Nevertheless, Giavarina marvelled that, despite endless constitutional tergiversations, 'never a drop of blood is shed', which he ventured 'could hardly happen in any other part of the world, and is solely due to the great phlegm of this people'.[32]

The armed forces were divided up. In November, Lambert marched north with around 12,000 troops to Newcastle, prepared to confront the Army's general in Scotland, George Monck, who had confirmed his support for the dissolved parliament. Published after the restoration, Thomas Flatman's mock-romance *Don Juan Lamberto* (1661) offered a 'comical history' of events, depicting Lambert constructing a huge defensive 'wall in the land of Northumbria, which in breadth should reach from sea to sea, and in height up unto the clouds' in order to prevent 'the Loyal Knight' (Monck) from invading.[33] In Kent, the Channel fleet under Vice Admiral John Lawson sailed to Gravesend and threatened to blockade London if Parliament's authority was not respected. Writing a despairing diary entry for Christmas Eve 1659, the Scottish Covenanter and erstwhile Councillor of State, Archibald Johnston of Wariston, denied that there had ever been 'a pack of men' more 'emptied of wit, sense, reason, common honesty and moral trustiness', having taken on 'government whereof they have twice in one year given a demonstration of their incapacity to wield or manage'. As Johnston feared, 'posterity will hardly believe the story of these giddy heads and reeling times in matters of religion and government'.[34] After the Committee of Safety voted to dissolve itself, the Rump Parliament resumed its sittings two days later.

Constitutional confusion inevitably stimulated nostalgic memories of Stuart rule alongside a sense of unfinished business. Oliver Cromwell's quiet demise, behind closed doors, had prevented contemporaries from reading any final utterance or scaffold speech, but his legacy was clearly precarious after the serial collapse of his son's Protectorate, the re-establishment of the Commonwealth, the recall of the Rump Parliament, and creation and dissolution of the Committee of Safety. In June 1659 the Council of State had ominously ordered the dismantling of Cromwell's elaborate funeral vault at Westminster which had been finished only a few months earlier to house the remains of a new Protectorate dynasty in Henry VII's Chapel.

In printed tracts, a veritable fright of ventriloquizing ghosts offered subjects the opportunity to overhear 'the conversant dead' in imagined dialogues between the two former heads of state. In *The Court Career: Death Shadowed to Life* (1659), Cromwell's ghost ruefully conceded to Charles I's spirit that 'your private unpolished vault accrued more to your honour, than all my costly £40,000 funeral structure'. Deferentially addressing Charles's ghost as 'Sir', Cromwell's spectre confessed to being disturbed at Hampton Court and Windsor 'where your incensed and unrevenged ghost oft-times affrighted me', acknowledging that he had 'never walked so irrationally as to make my cross-grained progeny heirs to your family'.[35] In another dialogue, a penitent version of Cromwell's ghost admitted that his tenure as Lord Protector 'was (as all usurpers must be) more like to a Hell than a Heaven'. Turning one way, 'methought I see you without a head bleeding afresh', while turning the other, 'I see your sons and friends all with their swords drawn . . . to take vengeance on me'.[36] Richard Perrinchief's *A Messenger from the Dead* (1658) provided an inventive twist by imagining the spectre of Henry VIII berating the king's spirit for its timidity as king and likening Charles's demise to that of his grandmother (and Henry's niece), Mary, Queen of Scots, in 1587. Believing that the most dangerous risk for any monarch was 'the loss of his people's love', Henry's spirit feared that the sins of royal ancestors were often visited on their successors. Musing on Mary's execution, 'the two ghosts remember an event that neither would have experienced in the corporeal world', given that Henry had already been dead for forty years at the time of the queen's death, while Charles would not be born for another thirteen.[37]

While Charles I's vengeful ghost stalked the pages of printed pamphlets, his son and heir remained a viable king-in-waiting, watching the political turmoil. Writing from London in June 1659, one Royalist had admitted to Hyde that 'the confusions here are so great' that 'chaos was a perfection in comparison of our order and government', describing how different 'parties are like so many floating islands, sometimes joining and appearing like a continent' before 'the next flood or ebb separates them'. At the time of Oliver Cromwell's death, Colepeper had confided to Hyde that, regarding domestic prospects for a Stuart restoration, 'the person that my eye is chiefly on, as able alone to restore the king, and not absolutely averse to it' was General Monck. Although 'a sullen man', Colepeper had suspected that Monck knew 'that his knowledge and reputation in arms fits him for the title of Highness and the office of Protector, better than Mr Richard Cromwell's skill in horse-races and husbandry'. Accordingly, Colepeper had advised the Stuart court to approach Monck covertly, offering reassurances with regard to the soldier's past actions and evincing a disinclination 'to boggle at any way he shall propose in the declaring himself, let it at the first be Presbyterian, be King and Parliament, be a Third Party, or what he will', confident that, if Monck's support for Charles's restoration could be secured, 'you may mould him into what form you please' thereafter.[38]

Another distinguished soldier and former MP, Roger Boyle, Lord Broghill, had also warned the Protectorate's ministers that memories of older constitutional forms were nostalgically attractive following repeated failures to secure republican aspirations or religious visions of a godly state. Writing to Thurloe in December 1658, Broghill had contrasted the relative quiet that he and Monck enjoyed in Ireland and

Scotland respectively, believing 'we are sober enough to think you half-mad in England'. Internal divisions risked alienating subjects' loyalties and provoking unforeseen consequences. As a soldier, Broghill had cautioned that 'when we sow wheat, we know we shall reap wheat; but you statesmen, when you sow one sort of fruit, often reap another: nay, I hear some amongst you are like to reap fruit, whose seed you never sowed, neither will any own the sowing of it'.[39] A year later, Giavarina speculated that a majority of army officers were 'disposed to give the king his own back again' and take the political initiative, fearing that 'if they do not put the sceptre in his hands, it will be restored to him by foreign forces, of which these people have an unspeakable dread'.[40]

Predicting the next constitutional configuration was impossible. In December, one of Hyde's correspondents complained that, for 'too many years has our government been tossed up and down like a tennis ball'. The following month, Hyde himself wrote to Henry Bennet in Madrid, admitting the 'difficulty in continuing my journal of the affairs of England', venturing that were he to 'receive twenty letters from London of the same date', he would find as many 'opinions of the state of affairs there, according to the constitutions of the persons who write'. Weeks later, another Royalist echoed similar bewilderment to Hyde, feeling as though he was 'violently carried away by a swift and rapid torrent, quite losing my sight, unable either to inform myself, or instruct others', and wondering 'what pen, nay whose imagination, can keep pace with the precipitate motion of these times?'[41]

Meanwhile, demands for a full and free English Parliament were gaining ground, with calls that no additional limits should be placed on the franchise and a new elected assembly should meet in open, formal sessions with all elected members able to attend. At the Rump Parliament's invitation, Monck marched south from Coldstream in the Scottish Borders on 1 January 1660. By bringing his troops into England, Monck was paradoxically flexing his own military muscle in order to challenge the Army's attempts to dominate domestic politics, being opposed to 'that intolerable slavery of a sword government' which he knew 'England cannot, nay, will not endure'.[42] When Monck arrived in London in early February, Giavarina observed how he 'listens to all and receives all but answers only in generalities . . . he unbosoms himself to no-one and keeps his opinions to himself'.[43]

In London, the Lord Mayor and Council received a petition from the

City's householders and freemen, urging that no taxes should be paid unless approved by a full parliament. In response, the Rump ordered the Army's commissioners, led by Monck, to enter the City on 9 February with a force of 6,000 soldiers to occupy its Corporation, dismantle the City's gates, remove street chains and arrest several aldermen and councillors. After incurring criticism for acquiescing to the Rump's instructions, Monck was warned by his brother-in-law that 'if London should be made a village' in this way, 'all the cities and towns would be alarmed', fearing their traditional privileges and freedoms were threatened.[44] Having moved the remainder of his forces to Finsbury's fields, Monck then switched sides, relocated to the Guildhall, joined the City of London's opposition to the Rump and, on 21 February, secured the return of surviving 'secluded members' expelled from the Commons by Pride's Purge in 1648. In Brussels, Hyde received news of Monck's transformation from 'a triumphant conqueror, trampling upon the liberties of this great City, and prostituting her nakedness to the open view, contempt and scorn of all beholders', but the following day suddenly 'courting her as his mistress, and throwing himself into her arms for protection'. Warming to his theme, Hyde's correspondent described how London had seemed, after Monck's initial actions, 'like a disconsolate widow, all in mourning, or rather like a deflowered virgin, with eyes full of anger and of tears, weeping over her lost virginity, hanging down her head, and covering her face, for the very shame of the disgraceful rape committed upon her the day before'. But following Monck's volte-face, 'you would have seen the same City all in mirth and jollity, like a brisk and sprightly bride in the hand of her beloved, hastening to the place of her espousals'.[45]

The newly reunited and enlarged Long Parliament – which had technically been in existence since 1640 – now acceded to popular calls for the first fresh elections for two decades and dissolved itself on 16 March 1660. With a majority of MPs favouring Charles's restoration likely to be elected to a new Convention Parliament, one Royalist marvelled that 'we are now in another world'.[46] A week before the dissolution, Ormond was advised by a correspondent in London that the exiled court should make its 'preparatives as vigorously as you can, and make them sound as loud as you can', emphasizing the 'firmness to the Protestant religion' in both Charles's case and that of his brothers, York and Gloucester, and being sure to 'stifle all reports of any foreign match' through controversial dynastic marriages.[47] In April, Charles's court effected a surreptitious move from the capital of the Catholic Spanish Netherlands, Brussels, to the town of Breda, in the Protestant Dutch Republic.

Ahead of any official communications from the exiled court, polemical pamphlets and feigned proclamations presented rival impressions of the king-in-waiting. In his anonymous *News from Brussels* (1660), Marchamont Nedham, the republican editor of *Mercurius Politicus*, posed as a well-positioned courtier to warn readers of the tyranny likely to be unleashed by a vengeful restored monarch. Ridiculing the idea that Charles might 'come in on terms', the author recalled 'that blessed line I marked in Machiavelli: he's an oaf that thinks an oath ... can tame a prince beyond his pleasure'.[48] In response, outraged Royalist rejoinders published in Charles's defence included John Evelyn's anonymous *Late News or Message from Brussels Unmasked* (1660), which called, rather, for compassion towards 'that innocent prince ... hunted like a partridge upon the mountains from place to place, from one nation to another people' and 'enforced to live (as it were) upon the alms and charity of his neighbour princes'. Denouncing Nedham's attack as 'the filthy foam of a black and hellish mouth, arising from a viperous and venomous heart', Evelyn reassured readers that Charles and his court were 'so far from any thoughts of rancour, malice and revenge'.[49]

On 4 April 1660, Charles issued a strategically worded 'Declaration of Breda', committing himself to settling his subjects' rights through a 'free parliament', extending 'a free and general pardon' to everyone 'excepting only such persons as shall hereafter be excepted by Parliament', offering a 'liberty to tender consciences' in religious matters and guaranteeing the settlement of all army pay arrears.[50] Unlike the sensational and fictitious communications recently issued in his name, the language of the Breda Declaration was succinct and forthright. By delegating responsibility for a new political and religious settlement to Parliament, the exiled court not only appeared to be supporting public opinion, but could also defer responsibility for inevitably difficult decisions. Meanwhile, an urgent need to familiarize subjects with their new king's physical appearance presented itself, since Charles had last lived in England as a teenager, while displaying images of the 'King of Scots' had been a criminal offence during the Commonwealth and

Protectorate. Describing popular anticipation in London, one correspondent recounted to Hyde how Charles's 'picture is hung up in many places in the streets', but when a passer-by, who had recently seen the king in person, had suggested that 'he was not so handsome as that picture ... the people were so angry that they fell upon the man and beat him soundly'.[51] To disseminate his image as widely as possible, depictions of Charles appeared in numerous prints, dishes, mugs, tankards, wine bottles, tiles and jewellery. Acquiring items bearing the new king's image offered a quick means of affirming loyalty to the new regime, although the Royalist Roger L'Estrange scorned such ostentation as patent opportunism. As he observed of Charles's newfound supporters, 'out comes the spruce tobacco-box, with the king's picture at it, which he wears, and kisses ... as for a hint, and introduction, to his politics, now at hand'.[52]

While Royalist fervour gathered pace in England, Louis XIV's court remained wary. As Bordeaux warned Mazarin in April 1660, Charles's entourage at Breda were 'straining every nerve to prevent us from having any part in the accommodation'. Rumours were circulating that Louis was seeking to restore the Stuarts with a French army; that the king's French mother, Henrietta Maria, was demanding liberty of conscience for Catholics in Britain; and that Mazarin was seeking to effect a marriage between Charles and his twelve-year-old niece, Hortense Manzini.[53] The Irish priest Peter Talbot nevertheless insisted to Ormond that it was 'incredible how earnest and real' was Mazarin's private support for Charles's restoration, having advised Talbot that 'the English are mad, if they impose any Covenant or unhandsome things upon him; because the French armies, Spanish coin, and the king's friends will be able to trouble England, if need be'.[54] When the new Convention Parliament opened in London on 25 April, Giavarina reported that all foreign envoys in London enthusiastically lit bonfires and sponsored lavish celebrations, 'except France, who, to the general astonishment, showed so much reserve' that no festivities were staged.[55]

After versions of Charles's Declaration had been warmly received by the Houses of Commons and Lords, General Monck, Admiral Sir Edward Montagu and by the Mayor, aldermen and Common Council of the City, the Convention Parliament voted on 8 May that Charles II had, in fact, been king of England since the moment of his father's death. Included in the official party dispatched to the Dutch Republic to escort the king home, the young naval administrator Samuel Pepys recorded 'what a sad, poor condition for clothes and money the king was, and all his attendants'. When Sir John Grenville had arrived with 'some money', Charles had been 'so joyful, that he called the Princess Royal and Duke of York to look upon it as it lay in the portmanteau before it was taken out'.[56] Having been invited by the Dutch States General to move from Breda to The Hague, Charles received congratulatory visits from envoys sent by states including France, Spain, Sweden, Denmark, Brandenburg and Hesse. On Charles's thirtieth birthday by the Gregorian calendar – 29 May in The Hague and 19 May in London – he was joined by his brothers, sister and aunt, the Electress Elizabeth, at a 'most splendid and stately' private banquet given by the Spanish ambassador in The Hague, Don Esteban de Gamarra, comprising 'two great services of fish, or rather of sea-monsters'. The dramatist Sir William Lower recorded Charles as being 'in the best humour that ever he was seen to be; he had not even been disconcerted by the surprise appearance, around midnight, of the Protectorate's erstwhile ambassador, George Downing. Knighting the ambassador soon afterwards, the exiled court insisted that Downing's activities against royal interests had 'proceeded not from any evil intention, but only from a deep dissimulation' by which Downing had been 'constrained to cover his true sentiments'.[57] Charles also accepted an official invitation to visit the States General, accompanied by Count William of Nassau-Dietz, choosing to disregard his earlier failure to persuade that assembly to intervene on his father's behalf in 1649 and overlooking measures taken by the States General against the Stuarts during the 1650s.

Having left the Dutch shoreline at Schevening 'covered black with people', Charles sailed for England aboard the refitted *Naseby* warship – hastily renamed the *Royal Charles* – while the accompanying vessels *Richard*, *Speaker* and *Dunbar* likewise received Stuart rechristenings as the *James*, *Mary* and *Henry*.[58] En route, Pepys recorded that one of the king's favourite dogs 'shit in the boat, which made us laugh', prompting the twenty-seven-year-old diarist to realize 'that a king, and all that belong to him, are but just as others are'.[59] On the royal party's landing at Dover, one observer noticed that 'while all the rest were shouting "God save the King!", Charles's brother, Gloucester enthusiastically 'threw up his hat and cried "God bless General Monck"'. In London, bonfires were built 'three or four storeys high' with 'the Protector's effigy and the States' arms being placed at the top, to be burned'.[60] For his part, Charles wrote to his sister Henrietta Anne in Paris, admitting that 'my head is so dreadfully stunned with the acclamation of the people, and the vast amount of business, that I know not whether I am writing sense or nonsense'.[61] Amid a mood of optimistic euphoria, Charles entered London on his thirtieth birthday, 29 May, this time according to the Julian calendar. Evelyn marvelled that the king's return had been effected 'without one drop of blood and by that very army which rebelled against him'.[62] Before the king's return, the Convention Parliament had approved legislation to make 29 May an annual holiday, implying that a national resurrection had occurred whereby Charles's kingdoms were 'all in a great measure newborn and raised from the dead on this most joyful day'.[63]

III

The king's restoration was accompanied by a deliberate decision to erase public memory of recent events. Charles II's reign was declared to have started on 30 January 1649 – the day of Charles I's execution – and events that had occurred in the intervening years were physically deleted from official records in a concerted attempt at national amnesia. In England, an 'Act of Free and General Pardon, Indemnity and Oblivion' had been introduced into the Convention Parliament in early May 1660 and received royal assent in August. Without attributing culpability for the civil wars to any party, the legislation confirmed the premium henceforth to be placed on reconciliation by pardoning all involved in the wars of any crimes, except thirty-three named regicides. But as the Act's title suggested, tensions inevitably subsisted between a desire for 'oblivion' – an intentional disregard of previous actions – and 'pardon' which necessitated intentional remembrance, accompanied by forgiveness. When the legislation was considered by the first Restoration parliament in July 1661, Charles exhorted its members: 'Let us look forward, and not backward, and never think of what is past, except men put us in mind of it, by repeating faults we had forgot.'[64] Speaking after the king, Hyde (now earl of Clarendon) also drew attention to the Act's clauses that made malicious reminders of previous actions a criminal offence. Clarendon counselled England's political leaders to 'teach your neighbours and your friends . . . how to learn this excellent art of forgetfulness' and avoid finding new labels of division to ensure that 'the old reproaches of Cavalier, and Roundhead, and Malignant, be committed to the grave'.[65]

Official injunctions to forgetfulness notwithstanding, the early Restoration state's attitude towards recent history could be contradictory. On 30 January 1661, being the twelfth anniversary of Charles I's execution, Oliver Cromwell's elaborate vault in Westminster Abbey was ordered to be opened and his body exhumed, together with that of his son-in-law and fellow regicide, Henry Ireton. Lying in their opened coffins and joined by the exhumed corpse of John Bradshaw (who had presided over the court that had tried Charles I), the bodies were dragged by sledge to the public gallows at Tyburn, where they hung for around six hours before being cut down and the heads severed from the bodies. While the bodies were thrown into a nearby pit, the heads were stuck on 'traitor's poles' and placed on the roof of Westminster Hall as a gruesome deterrent to future anti-monarchical agitators.

In pamphlets, Cromwell was scourged as *The English Devil* (1660): 'that Hellish monster, and damnable Machiavellian' who had the temerity 'to aspire from a brew-house to the throne'. At the same time, Cromwell had 'represented the real tragedy of a king and no king' for despite 'washing his accursed hands in the blood of his royal sovereign' and having 'made a football of a crown', he had refused the offer of kingship, seeking rather to extirpate monarchy altogether.[66] It was, indeed, difficult to celebrate the country's newfound peace without recalling recent traumas. Invoking the well-worn ship of state metaphor, another author described how 'the vexed government of frantic England' had been 'bandied from wave to wave, from rock to sand / A prey to pirates from a foreign land'. The anonymous writer hoped, however, that 'our distracted England be a warning-piece to all nations, that they never attempt to try and judge their king'. Acclaiming Charles as 'our rising sun', the author admired how 'the rays of his sacred majesty shine throughout the world'.[67] In the punning panegyric that accompanied his restoration, Charles could thus be dually acclaimed as both a worthy 'son' and heir to his executed father as well as an allegorical 'sun' to his subjects.

Erasing republican currency was both a material and symbolic priority in order to render monarchical authority visible. With Commonwealth coins displaying the shield of St George on both their obverse and reverse, the 1650s had been a time when, as the Royalist poet Alexander Brome recalled, 'I cannot see my king, / Neither in his person or his coin', although the republican regime could not make him forget the monarch 'whom I do wear engraven on my heart'. Concerned to put the king's image back into his subjects' pockets, the Royal Mint ceased production of the Commonwealth's coinage the day after Charles II entered London, and the following year a royal proclamation ordered its formal recall, declaring that it had been issued and 'intended by the late usurpers as a high contempt of us, our crown and dignity'.[68] In a more curious celebration of the Stuart monarchy's restoration, a painting now in Gripsholm Castle in Sweden presents an anamorphic image of a death's head (Plate 14). When a cylindrical mirror is placed over the head, the distorted image is corrected to reveal a portrait of Charles I, wearing his Garter badge and dressed in black, with an elaborate lace collar. On the reverse side of the painting is an image of an orb of sovereignty which, when likewise viewed via a cylindrical mirror, shows Charles II wearing ermine and scarlet, confirming his royal status. Etymologically derived from the Greek meaning 'to shape again', anamorphosis affected all the restored king's subjects who inescapably found themselves viewing the monarchy's re-established authority through the harrowing prism of recent memories.[69]

In 1660, the English welcomed the restoration not only of Charles as king, but also of the Stuart royal family, including the king's mother Henrietta Maria and his four siblings: his two brothers, York and Gloucester, and his widowed sister, Mary of Orange, and younger sister, Henrietta Anne. Predictably, the Stuarts' restoration signalled a revival of interest in dynastic diplomacy, both as a means of securing foreign alliances and the monarchy's assured succession. But in the autumn of 1660, Clarendon was shocked to learn that his daughter Anne was expecting York's child and had been secretly married to the duke that September. Protesting that he would 'turn her out of his house, as a strumpet, to shift for herself', the Chancellor called for Charles to order Anne to be 'sent to the Tower . . . to be cast into a dungeon' while 'an Act of Parliament should be immediately passed for the cutting off her head'.[70] For her part, Anne steadfastly insisted that she and the duke had been lawfully married when questioned about the child's paternity by Church of England bishops before giving birth to a son, Charles, in

October 1660. By that time, York's status as next-in-line to the British thrones had moved into the spotlight after his younger brother, Gloucester, had unexpectedly died from smallpox. Unsurprisingly, the Yorks' marriage was bitterly opposed by Henrietta Maria, whose 'Louvrian' faction in Paris had resented Clarendon's influence over Charles during the 1650s. Meanwhile, Charles's sister Mary had arrived in London from the United Provinces, followed by Henrietta Maria and the youngest Stuart princess, Henrietta Anne, who had left England as a toddler in 1646. But when Mary also succumbed to smallpox and died on Christmas Eve, Henrietta Maria sought a speedy return to France, having secured permission for Henrietta Anne to marry Louis XIV's brother, Philippe, duke of Orléans. As Giavarina reported, the king's mother was 'counting the moments and only longing for the time' for winter storms to abate, and 'declares roundly that if she stays in England she will soon end her days'.[71]

Regarding the king's own marriage prospects, speedy initiative was taken by the Portuguese envoy Don Francisco de Melo who had arrived in London in July 1660. Four years earlier, King John IV's death had prompted the succession of John's disabled son, Afonso VI, whose mother, Luisa Maria de Guzmán, acted as the country's regent. With Portugal urgently seeking a powerful ally to preserve its recent independence from Spain and also to repulse Dutch incursions overseas, De Melo was instructed to offer Afonso's sister Catarina to Charles with an estimated dowry of around 2 million escudos (around £300,000), the territories of Tangier and Bombay, and trading rights with Brazil and the Portuguese East Indies.

Such a move naturally provoked alarm in Madrid where the Venetian ambassador Giacomo Quirini reported objections made by Philip's chief minister, Haro, to Charles's representative, Bennet, regarding England's evident willingness to countenance an Anglo-Portuguese alliance, despite the assistance that Spain had so recently supplied to the exiled Stuart court. For his part, Bennet ventured 'that the late revolutions had ruined and upset all the good maxims of the English ministers' and, while 'he was sorry to speak in disparagement of his own nation ... in London at present the only thing they cared about was gold'. Bennet had also defended the English court's reception of De Melo by pointing out that the previous year Haro had accorded the Commonwealth's envoy, William Lockhart, a public audience at Hondarribia 'under the very nose of

King Charles'. Further alarmed by Charles's seeming reluctance to return the Cromwellian acquisitions of Dunkirk and Jamaica to Spain, Philip's ambassador, Charles, baron de Watteville de Joux, arrived in London in September to promote the claims of an alternative bride for Charles: Eleonora Gonzaga, widow of the late Holy Roman Emperor, Ferdinand III. Although Watteville set about mendaciously 'disparaging the Portuguese [princess] as much as possible, calling her hunchbacked and lame', Quirini reported that Charles seemed unmoved, 'hinting gently that the [Habsburg] empress was poor in money, but rich in years' – despite Eleonora being six months younger than Charles himself.[72] In late 1660, De Melo returned to Lisbon, encouraged by his reception in England and bearing a letter from the king to the queen mother containing what Charles himself described as 'the worst Spanish that ever was writ'. Having resolved to marry Catarina – henceforth known as Catherine – Charles acknowledged the likely unpopularity of a Catholic bride, but warned English MPs the following summer that, had he waited to find a spouse likely to command universal approval, 'you would live to see me an old bachelor, which I think you do not desire to do'.[73]

The dynamics of Continental geopolitics were also shifting rapidly with the natural deaths, in quick succession, of Oliver Cromwell in September 1658, Charles X Gustavus in November 1660, Mazarin in March 1661 and Haro the following November. From Paris, the Venetian ambassador Alvise Grimani reported that, before his death, Mazarin had admitted that 'although Cromwell was a great Hell-cat', his foreign policy had served French interests well, while in England, contemporary satirists could not resist imagining the classical leader of the underworld, Pluto, confronted with the boisterous arrival in Hell of Cromwell, Charles X and Mazarin, rowdily claiming precedence over one another for iniquities accomplished on earth.[74]

Having spent over a decade in Continental exile, Charles now intended to reverse the traditional disinclinations of English monarchs to travel by putting his cosmopolitan experiences to use in directing Restoration foreign affairs. Execrable written Spanish aside, when Giavarina had met the king at Canterbury in May, he had been impressed that Charles, and his brothers York and Gloucester had all conversed with him in Italian. When Giavarina informed the king in August that Angelo Correr and Michiel Morosini had been appointed as ambassadors to England, Charles confirmed that 'he well remembered Correr' who had been envoy to London 'in his father's time, over twenty years ago', while York 'spoke highly of Morosini' whom he had met at the French court.[75] Acclaiming Charles's foreign expertise in a panegyric, Edmund Waller welcomed a monarch who, unusually, brought

> No small advantage to your present reign;
> For, having viewed the persons and the things,
> The councils, state and strength of Europe's kings,
> You know your work; ambition to restrain,
> And set them bounds, as Heaven does the main.
> We have you now with ruling wisdom fraught,
> Not such as books, but such as practice, taught.[76]

Another English dramatist and poet, Richard Flecknoe, likewise confirmed of Charles that

> So as each Nation's Wisdom he does know,
> And each one's Language to express it too.
> Whence he compared with other Princes, sit
> Dully at home, and nothing know but it,
> Seems just like some huge Galleon does come
> From farthest Indies, richly laden home.[77]

Yet England's restored monarch now needed a cool head, adequate funds and domestic security. After Correr and Morosini's arrival in London, Charles regretted that he could not offer troops or finances to support Venice in its war against the Ottoman Empire, given that his own authority in Britain remained insecure. Indeed, when Charles had openly admitted 'I am not yet well re-established', the Venetians had respected 'such confidence, expressed so frankly, which touched a point perhaps only too true'. Although English MPs voted the king an unprecedented annual subsidy of £1.2 million in December 1661, Giavarina remained far from confident that Charles's regime could yet 'secure permanent tranquillity in this inconstant and chimerical island'.[78]

17
Hell, France, Rome or Amsterdam, 1661–1667

Charles II's coronation on 23 April 1661 was the most magnificent ceremonial occasion of his reign. No previous monarch had been crowned on St George's Day and, by choosing this date, the king ensured that the two events would thereafter be celebrated together. At his Scottish coronation a decade earlier, Charles had been humiliatingly obliged to acknowledge his family's sins and seek public forgiveness, but in the coronation sermon preached at Westminster Abbey, Bishop George Morley of Worcester drew parallels between Charles and Christ as each had sought to build kingdoms after sojourns in the wilderness. The inclusion of sacral elements confirmed Charles's status as especially chosen by God to rule; he was anointed with holy oil and invested with the royal robes and regalia. Charles had also insisted that the organizing committee consult archival records to ensure that his coronation conformed to ancient practice to reinforce the legitimacy of his accession.

After witnessing the lavish outdoor spectacle that had preceded the coronation service, funded by the City of London's livery companies, an exhausted Samuel Pepys concluded in his diary that he could 'now shut my eyes against any other objects' and avoid future displays of 'state and show', being 'sure never to see the like again in this world', before waking the next day with a painful hangover.[1] The spectacle's ceremonial theme had been devised by a Scottish impresario, John Ogilby, who drew on Virgilian epics to acclaim Charles in heroic vein as both Aeneas founding Rome after the fall of Troy and the Emperor Augustus, who had presided over the Roman Empire's most sustained era of peace and prosperity after republican turmoil. Whereas a formal state portrait had hitherto accompanied every new English monarch's accession since Henry VIII, no official coronation portrait was commissioned in 1661, reflecting the precarity still surrounding the restoration of monarchical authority.

Rivalling the coronation's projections of majesty were lavish ambassadorial receptions that welcomed the foreign envoys who flocked to London to congratulate the restored monarch. Arriving in London in September 1660 as Philip IV of Spain's representative, Claude Lamoral, Prince of Ligne, was the first ambassador sent by a major power and both his disembarkation at the Tower of London and ceremonial reception at the Banqueting House were memorialized in paintings by Flemish artists François Duchatel and Gillis van Tilborch, while a narrative account in French recounting Ligne's 'magnificent entrance' was published in London.[2] The Habsburg delegation's sumptuous silks and colourful apparel contrasted, however, with the sombre mourning dress worn by Charles and his courtiers, following the duke of Gloucester's death from smallpox only days earlier. Consequently Ligne brought forward his return to the Spanish Netherlands, being – as one newsletter-writer put it – 'sorry for the fatal necessity that debars him from appearing to his greatest advantage of splendour'.[3] The delegation that arrived from the Protestant Netherlands in November brought a 'Dutch Gift' that had cost the States General, city of Amsterdam and provincial assembly of Holland around 600,000 guilders (at a time when an average monthly wage was around twenty-five guilders). Presented in the Banqueting House by Louis of Nassau, Lord of De Lek and Beverweerd, and three colleagues, the gift carried both considerable symbolic freight as well as monetary value, since it restored to royal ownership twenty-eight mostly Italian Renaissance paintings and twelve statues formerly owned by Charles I but sold by the Commonwealth, together with the marital bed purchased for Charles's sister Mary by William II, underscoring the familial connections between the Houses of Stuart and Orange.[4]

For foreign powers, Charles's restoration as king demanded material recognition as well as diplomatic congratulation. Two Venetian ambassadors, Angelo Correr and Michiel Morosini, arriving in London in July 1661, were disconcerted by the extent to which Charles's ministers seemed intent 'to impose on foreigners'. Although the Master of Ceremonies, Sir Charles Cotterell, had 'artfully contrived to show us the list of the presents' gifted to Charles by their French and Spanish counterparts – 'which, if true, are intolerably exorbitant' – the Venetians had 'pretended not to see them and gently intimated' that they would be guided by their predecessors' precedents.[5] But later that year, Charles prevailed on the Venetian embassy's resident secretary, Francesco Giavarina, to request two gondolas, with gondoliers, to be sent to England and also made hopeful noises about acquiring distinctive fishing vessels, known as *fisolere*. In late 1662, three Russian ambassadors arrived in London – Prince Peter Prozorovsky, Ivan Afonas'evich Zhelyabuzhsky and Ivan Stepanovich Davydov – sent by Tsar Aleksei Mikhailovich to request reimbursement for loans made during Charles's exile and to seek assistance for Russia in its war against Poland. Watching an audience that lasted over five hours, Pepys endured 'long waiting and fear of the falling of the gallery' as overcrowding threatened the collapse of the Banqueting House's public galleries.[6] During the ceremony, Charles received gifts including 'two Persian horses, a quantity of sables, black fox, ermine and other precious furs, teeth of sea-horses, rich carpets, cloth of gold of Persia, some pelicans and other live animals', presented by a retinue of 165 Russians 'in superb raiment, covered with jewels, pearls and other precious ornaments'.[7] Awaiting collection by English merchants from the northern Russian port of Archangel were also 150 tonnes of hemp, vital for naval supplies. Pending restoration of Anglo-Russian commercial relations, the hemp was intended to encourage Charles to assist the Tsar and signal a conducive basis for future trade negotiations.[8]

Reinstating court etiquette inevitably reignited longstanding disputes over diplomatic precedence that could prove fatal. During the public entry of the Swedish ambassador Count Nils Nillsson Brahe in September 1661, a violent clash occurred during which the coach of the resident Spanish representative, Charles, baron of Watteville de Joux, forced its way in front of the coach belonging to the new French ambassador, Godefroy d'Estrades. When the Spanish delegation opened fire, several Frenchmen and horses were killed, their coach damaged and the French delegation prevented from participating in the procession. Observing popular cheering and bell-ringing in response to the perceived Spanish triumph, Pepys admitted that 'indeed we do naturally all love the Spanish and hate the French'. While Pepys – who had a French father-in-law – later took pleasure in vexing his wife by 'pleading for the Spaniard against the French', when Louis XIV heard of the incident in London, he regarded the diplomatic insult as potential grounds to declare a new war on his Spanish father-in-law, Philip IV.[9] As D'Estrades complained, 'in the course of eight days, I was twice in danger of being assassinated and a musket ball went through my hat; soldiers and a mob have come to attack me in my own house'.[10]

I

Fireworks and pageantry also accompanied the ceremonial departure of Catherine of Braganza from Lisbon harbour, as she set off to London for a new life as a Stuart queen consort. Staged on 23 April 1662, according to the Gregorian calendar, the date of Catherine's departure deliberately celebrated St George as dual patron saint of Portugal and England, with hopes that the Stuart–Braganza union would preserve Portuguese independence from Spanish aggression and provide heirs for the Stuart monarchy in Britain. Since Portuguese independence from Spain had not, as yet, been recognized by the papacy, no papal dispensation was sought, nor proxy marriage conducted. Despite difficulties securing the extensive dowry promised by the marriage contract, Charles's representative, the Cromwellian naval general, Edward Montagu, earl of Sandwich, reluctantly acceded to Portuguese pressure to facilitate Catherine's departure, aware that her arrival at Charles's court was eagerly anticipated and reassured by knowing that English forces had already taken possession of the Portuguese fortress of Tangier. As Sandwich recorded, the twenty-three-year-old princess had 'very earnestly' beseeched him to disregard concerns about the dowry, admitting that the Portuguese court was in financial straits on account of Spanish depredations, and insisting that she 'had overcome almost impossibilities to hasten her voyage'.[11] On her arrival at Portsmouth on 14 May, Catherine was welcomed by her future brother-in-law, the duke of York, before the king arrived several days later.

Delaying the king's departure to Portsmouth had been the English Parliament's passage of a stringent Act of Uniformity that required all Church of England ministers to accept the Book of Common Prayer and renounce the Solemn League and Covenant by the following August. In his capacity as the Church of England's 'Supreme Governor', Charles had been reminded by his Lord Chancellor, Edward Hyde, earl of Clarendon, that, by the terms of the Anglo-Portuguese nuptial treaty, 'you must have a Bishop with you, and he must marry you before you go to bed . . . you cannot be married by a Roman priest'.[12] But on 21 May, Charles and Catherine were secretly married in the queen's bedchamber in Portsmouth by her Chief Almoner and the king's distant relative, Ludovic Stewart, seigneur d'Aubigny. Later that day – and unaware that his service was now denuded of any religious worth – Bishop Gilbert Sheldon of London conducted another marriage, in the Governor's House, attended by courtiers and Catherine's retinue. Since Catherine did not speak English, the newlyweds conversed in Spanish and, four days later, the king ventured to Clarendon, 'I cannot easily tell you how happy I think myself . . . I am confident never two humours were better fitted together than ours are.'[13] On the newlyweds' return to Hampton Court Palace, Giavarina was delighted to report that the king and queen were amusing themselves by taking rides in the Venetian gondolas that had arrived safely and were now afloat on the Thames.

The Thames also provided the venue for a sumptuous pageant staged in August to introduce Catherine to her subjects. Although the diarist John Evelyn had flinched at the foreign queen's arrival with a train of 'Portuguese ladies in their monstrous farthingales' and 'complexions olivaster', he deemed the aquatic display 'the most magnificent triumph that certainly ever floated on the Thames', being far superior to 'all the Venetian Bucentaurs' on Ascension Day when the Doge famously married the republic of Venice to the sea.[14] Somewhat fancifully, Pepys estimated that the flotilla accompanying the state procession comprised '10,000 barges and boats, I think, for we could see no water for them', although his personal highlight of the day was ogling the king's mistress, Barbara Villiers, countess of Castlemaine, as he 'glutted myself with looking on her'.[15]

Funded by the City of London, the pageant of August 1662 was the largest staged on the Thames until the Diamond Jubilee celebrations for Elizabeth II in 2012. In the pageant's script, entitled *Aqua Triumphalis*, John Tatham celebrated British and Portuguese global ambitions, voyages of exploration and commercial prosperity, as the allegorical character of 'Tham[es]' sat atop a floating island between Vauxhall and Lambeth to emphasize Britain's insular boundaries. Despite acclaiming Charles as 'England's Charlemagne', 'Tham' referred several times to recent history, recalling the king's recent 'return to make our hopes complete', having 'declared that all was clear, the sky serene, / And ships in safety rode where the storm had been'. A Thames 'Waterman' likewise greeted 'King Charles, and thy good woman there', before audaciously alluding to Charles's romantic entanglements while in exile, observing 'thou hast had a merry time of it . . . I need say no more, a word to the wise, thou understands me'. Wishing Charles and Catherine well, the 'Waterman' concluded that just 'as sands and fish are thought numberless, / So may your joys be pregnant, and increase'.[16]

The fictitious waterman's predictions were to prove poignant as Catherine thereafter struggled to become pregnant, while Castlemaine produced her second child by the king, Henry, on 18 June 1662, only weeks after Catherine's arrival in England. Following strenuous objections by the queen to Charles's insistence that Castlemaine be appointed as one of her ladies-in-waiting, the king warned Clarendon that if anyone should 'endeavour to hinder this resolution of mine . . . I will be his enemy to the last moment of my life'.[17] Threatened with expulsion of all her Portuguese retinue, Catherine eventually yielded and, later that summer, also met her mother-in-law Henrietta Maria and Charles's eldest natural son James Scott, now aged thirteen, who was created duke of Monmouth in November. In 1663, Catherine embarked on the first of serial summer visits to the newly fashionable spa waters in Tunbridge Wells and Bath, prompting the French ambassador, Gaston Jean-Baptiste, count of Cominges, to realize that 'nothing will be left unattempted to give an heir to the British crown'.[18]

While the court hoped for a royal heir, Catherine's dowry brought significant cash to the English Treasury – despite recurrent defaults and delays in payment – as well as the imperial acquisitions of Tangier and Bombay. But by 1663, the English crown appeared to reverse its interest in territorial expansion by deciding to sell off the fortified town and garrison of Dunkirk that Protectorate forces had acquired from Spain in 1658. Aware that Philip IV was in his late fifties and ailing, with a young epileptic son as his heir, Clarendon had covertly invited Louis XIV's former ambassador to England, Godefroy d'Estrades, to London in 1662 to suggest 'of what great use it [Dunkirk] might be', should Louis 'ever have any design of extending [his] conquests in Flanders' to include provinces still governed by Spain. Despite Clarendon's initial suggestion that Dunkirk's delivery was worth 12 million livres, a sum of 5 million was agreed and, although Louis privately regretted that 'I have paid a price beyond the worth of it', the French were reassured by

Charles's agreement to spend these funds supporting Portuguese resistance against Spain.[19]

News of Dunkirk's sale to the French was nevertheless deeply unpopular, as London merchants feared an inevitable increase in attacks by Flemish corsairs. As D'Estrades reported, particular vitriol was directed towards Clarendon, who was accused of betraying national interests by deciding 'to sacrifice a place, which was more to the reputation of England in the eyes of foreigners, and more considerable than the whole kingdom of Ireland'. To mollify matters, D'Estrades admitted that the sale treaty's preamble misleadingly implied that Louis had initially suggested the sale, 'whereas, in truth, it was offered to your Majesty first by them'. But D'Estrades had drawn the line at a request for French armed assistance should the popular outcry spread, politely informing English courtiers that 'a seller's demanding indemnity from a purchaser, for the things sold, was never heard of' – 'so uncivil' a notion was unthinkable.[20]

Charles II's readiness to reach a deal with his French cousin also prompted outrage in Madrid where the Venetian ambassador Giovanni Cornaro reported that Philip's ministers 'cannot contain themselves in their denunciation of the dissimulation of France, for bargaining about what does not belong to her, and England, which is trading to others what rightfully belongs to Spain'. In London, Giavarina agreed that 'Dunkirk is indeed a plum which the possessor will not readily part with, especially as it cost so much money.'[21] Indeed, explaining Dunkirk's abandonment demanded creative justification since the English envoy at The Hague, Sir George Downing, had argued in early 1662 that England had only become 'considerable' by having 'a footing on this side [of] the water'. As Downing had warned, 'if this footing be lost, I doubt whether the youngest that is now alive will ever see England have any other'.[22]

The previous year, James Howell had produced a 'short discourse of the late foreign acquests', following his appointment as the country's inaugural Historiographer Royal. Howell's tract, which remained unpublished, provided 'clear political reasons' for retaining Bombay, Dunkirk, Jamaica and Tangier in order to promote England's 'honour, security, and advantage'. As well as supplying symbolic confirmation of English monarchs' longstanding claims to be sovereign over 'the narrow seas' of the Channel, Dunkirk's strategic location had several practical advantages: attracting foreign allies seeking territorial gains in France and Flanders; curbing Dutch aggression; providing a trained garrison to suppress domestic insurgencies; and bringing welcome relief from the former depredations of piratical 'Dunkirkers'.[23] But by late 1662, Howell had revised his reflections in a *Discourse of Dunkirk*, which was published two years later and in which the advantages of retaining Dunkirk were canvassed, but refuted point by point, with emphasis now placed on the port's financial unsustainability and its ownership increasing the likelihood of England becoming entangled in unwelcome and irrelevant territorial disputes with Spain, France and the Dutch Republic. Howell further counselled against appearing to 'continue the fame of an infamous rebel' since 'the world held Dunkirk to be an acquest' of Cromwell.[24] A relatively rare example of British territorial alienation, Charles's sale of Dunkirk later prompted the translation and publication of D'Estrades's correspondence in 1728, specifically to urge that Gibraltar – captured from the Spanish in 1704 and confirmed in British ownership by the Treaty of Utrecht in 1713 – should not suffer a similar fate but instead be protected 'against all Covenant-breakers and aggressors whatsoever'.[25]

II

Dunkirk's sale exacerbated a growing disappointment with government actions, as the initial optimism that had greeted the Restoration soon waned. Instead, Charles's ministers parried rumours of anti-government plots, often involving disbanded ex-soldiers or adherents of the numerous Presbyterian and Puritan clerics ejected from their parochial livings for failing to comply with the Act of Uniformity. Investigating one rumoured plot in March 1663, Secretary of State Henry Bennet received intelligence regarding the activities of a 'Captain Gregory', who had formerly served under Major General John Lambert. Information supplied by Gregory's wife indicated that 'they had 500 men ready who had vowed to kill the king, and as to the false villain Monk' (now duke of Albemarle), the plotters intended that he 'be starved in an iron cage', set 'upon St Paul's Church'.[26]

Terrified by fears of imminent insurgency at home, Charles's ministers feared the meddling of foreign powers. Still smarting from the

Anglo-Portuguese marriage, the Council of State in Madrid formally resolved, in the spring of 1662, to promote Spanish interests by seeking 'to stir up trouble, within the kingdom [England], which will make impossible any adventures outside it', recommending that covert contact be made with the fugitive regicide Colonel Edmund Ludlow – referred to by the Spaniards as 'General Dodololo' – to foment rebellion in England, Ireland and the Dutch Republic.[27] Given such threats, English ministers were especially frustrated by the Dutch Republic's willingness to shelter regicides such as Ludlow as well as anti-government rebels. Behind the façade of Royalist enthusiasm on show when Charles had returned from Schevening in May 1660, prominent Dutch republican rulers, such as Holland's Grand Pensionary, John De Witt, and Hieronymus van Beverningh, were determined to resist any moves by England's restored monarch to promote monarchical Orangist interests on behalf of his orphaned teenage nephew William. In December 1660, Clarendon had ventured to Charles that 'nothing is of more importance' than the prompt dispatch of a trusted diplomat 'into Holland, both in respect of your nephew, and your own affairs, to watch De Witt and Beverningh, who play the Devil at present'.[28] Exploiting republican readiness to form any alliance that could resist Orangist expansion – and retaining an acquisitive eye on the Spanish Netherlands – Louis XIV concluded a defensive alliance with the United Provinces in the spring of 1662, airily guaranteeing Dutch fishing rights in the North Sea in the process.

At the same time, Louis also instructed his ambassador in London, Cominges, to capitalize on Dunkirk's sale and explore potentially closer Anglo-French relations. But Cominges advised the French king to be patient, observing that 'men here scarcely know themselves; they have almost no form of government' and 'the evils they have suffered are yet so recent that all their efforts aim at preventing the return of the same'. Charles's ministers were 'cold, slow, phlegmatic . . . motionless, frozen'. Moreover, Cominges was astounded by the outspokenness of government critics such as George Digby, earl of Bristol (son of Charles I's ambassador to Madrid and a Catholic convert), who openly accused Clarendon of treason in the House of Lords in July 1663. Insisting that 'nothing can be more astonishing and extraordinary', Cominges insisted that, for historical parallels, Louis would need to 'go back in your mind to the times that saw the violence of Sulla, the outbursts of the Gracchi, and the accusation of Caesar (then a private citizen) against Dolabella'. A bewildered Cominges could not credit that Clarendon should endure such censure, given his status as Chancellor and the fact that his daughter, the duchess of York, had just given birth to another son, James, who was second-in-line to the English throne after his father, following the death of his seven-month-old brother, Charles. Observing how Bristol 'walks about town as if nothing were the matter', Cominges confessed to Louis, 'I am at my wits' end . . . it seems to me as if I were transported beyond the sphere of the moon'.[29] Bristol's derogatory attacks on Clarendon were also observed by another Frenchman, the physician Samuel de Sorbière whose published travelogues described the English populace as being 'as much upon the politics' as Italians, spending 'all the while exercising their talents about the government'. While seemingly 'fond enough' of monarchical government as a means of promoting national honour, the English – in Sorbière's account – remained instinctively suspicious of government ministers, deeming it 'not reasonable some Court bloodsuckers should gorge themselves alone' on state business.[30]

While English ministers were particularly keen to re-establish foreign alliances with trading benefits, they also hoped to foster warmer diplomatic relations with Moscow, following the Russian delegation's visit to London in 1662. The following July, Charles Howard, earl of Carlisle, undertook a reciprocal mission, hoping that trading privileges for London's Muscovy Company which had been terminated by the regicide in 1649 could now be restored. Accompanied by an entourage of around eighty individuals, including his wife and son, Carlisle employed the poet and skilled Latinist Andrew Marvell as his secretary in a mission that was bedevilled by mutual misunderstandings and breaches of diplomatic etiquette. Despite rhetorical reassurances of longstanding Anglo-Russian amity, terms for future trading relations could not be agreed amid recurrent disputes over ceremonial courtesies and ensuring appropriately respectful translations of English, Russian and Latin forms of salutation. Aware of international interest in the Moscow negotiations, a frustrated Carlisle hotly objected to Bennet that little should 'be expected in a country where all other beasts change their colours twice a year, but the rational beasts change their souls thrice a day'.[31]

Another member of the ambassadorial retinue, Guy Miège, later produced a lively, if distorted, account of serial diplomatic derailments.

Following Russian refusal to accede to English proposals to restore customs freedoms, for instance, Miège described how Carlisle had protested to the Tsar that 'had Heaven fallen, as the windows of the Council-chamber broke in twice at the recital, it could scarce have been more strange or miraculous to me'. At the conclusion of the embassy, having taken formal leave of the Russian court, Carlisle had confirmed his mission's failure by declining the customary farewell gifts from one of the Tsar's secretaries, Loukian Golozof. 'Extremely amazed', Golozof had 'immediately swelled up with rage' and 'leapt down the stairs by half-dozens, as if he had been mad, and clapping his breast, cried out with a loud voice, that such a thing had not been heard of, nor ever happened before in the whole empire of Russia'. As Miège added, Golozof 'was in such a rage, that one would have sworn, he would have caused us all to be banished into Siberia'.[32] While the onward journey of Carlisle's entourage to the Swedish and Danish courts proved more harmonious, it was similarly inconclusive in terms of cementing political alliances.

Closer to home, Sir Richard Fanshawe was sent to Madrid in January 1664 to explore the possibility of concluding an Anglo-Spanish commercial treaty as well as to assess the likelihood of peace being negotiated between Spain and England's ally, Portugal. In Madrid, Fanshawe was accommodated in the residence traditionally used by ambassadors of the Stuarts, the Casa de las Siete Chimeneas, albeit only after displacing the Venetian representative, Cornaro, who complained that it was 'the strangest and most capricious thing imaginable to take the house of one ambassador in order to give it to another'.[33] While Fanshawe returned pessimistic reports regarding the likelihood of an Anglo-Spanish alliance, Bennet insisted that he must appear confident and 'keep up all public appearance' of amity at Philip's court since 'the very noise of it will do us good at Amsterdam, and elsewhere'. Appearances certainly alarmed Louis's representative in Madrid, Georges d'Aubusson de La Feuillade, Archbishop of Embrun, who had appeared 'in great choler to expostulate' publicly with Philip and ask 'why all this to an English ambassador? . . . what need had Spain of any friend but France?', his wrath convincing Fanshawe that the French intended 'something of menace to this court'. As the Spaniards stalled indecisively, Fanshawe was reassured by another courtier, Sir Philip Warwick, that, in addition to the notorious 'dilatory genius' of Castilian diplomacy, clearly 'Portugal, Tangier and Jamaica, are too great pills for the squeamish throat of a Spaniard glibly to swallow'; further time and patience were required.[34]

Meanwhile, escalating tensions between England and the United Provinces reflected the two countries' colonial competition overseas, commercial rivalry, political divisions and simmering resentments from the Treaty of Westminster agreed in 1654. After the Restoration, the English envoy in The Hague, Downing, observed how De Witt and his republican allies 'make it their study' to belittle Charles II, warning ministers in London in May 1662 that 'they do already look upon his Majesty through a diminishing glass and themselves through a multiplying glass'.[35] Two years later, a parliamentary investigation at Westminster into domestic trade difficulties prompted a House of Commons resolution that cited 'the several, and respective wrongs, dishonours, and indignities' inflicted by Dutch subjects on Charles 'by invading his rights in India, Africa and elsewhere', together with 'the damages, affronts and injuries done by them to our merchants' as intense competition between members of the rival Dutch and English East India Companies extended across the globe.[36] Reasserting those rights in Africa, Captain Robert Holmes launched a series of aggressive attacks on Guinea that spring, which resulted in the English seizure of several Dutch fortresses and capture of numerous vessels. On the other side of the Atlantic, the Royal Navy's *Guinea* 32-gun warship was one of four frigates that approached the Dutch colony of the New Netherlands in August 1664, after Charles had granted deeds covering territories from Delaware Bay to Maine to his brother, the duke of York. The colony's Dutch governor, Peter Stuyvesant, with no substantial forces of his own, very reluctantly agreed articles of surrender and the port of New Amsterdam was renamed New York.

Aware that the Franco-Dutch defensive treaty would require deployment of French forces if the Dutch were attacked, Louis XIV was anxious to avoid Anglo-Dutch antagonism escalating into open war, especially after news of New Amsterdam's surrender to the English reached the Continent in October. Writing to his representative at The Hague, D'Estrades, in late 1664, Louis was obliged to 'confess to you, I'm a little embarrassed' by the situation in which he found himself, since supporting the Dutch in a war against England would do 'a great prejudice to my principal interest, and that for a people from whom I shall have no assistance'. Referring to his 'principal interest' – extending

French influence in Spanish Flanders – Louis boasted that England was offering him 'a carte blanche for everything I can desire as to the Netherlands, without pretending to an inch of ground for herself'.[37] After Charles's ambassador in Paris, Denzil Holles, first Baron Holles, had opined that 'peace or war depended on what happened in Guinea', Louis was outraged that 'a war should be kindled in Europe' on such an account, denying that his obligations extended to any Dutch 'accessory and dependencies'.[38]

Having been voted £2.5 million by the English parliament that convened in December 1664, Charles formally declared war against the United Provinces two months later. In a tract entitled *Europae Modernae Speculum* (1665), an anonymous author aligned English grievances with a rhetoric condemning overweening Dutch ambition and warned that the Dutch were so intent on achieving 'a universal sovereignty' that 'in a few years, if uninterrupted, they will gain all the wealth of the world into their hands; which is what they drive at'.[39] In his *Belgica Caracteristica* (1665), the Royalist poet John Crouch likewise protested in that

> You think the Narrow Seas for us too much
> Yet the whole globe too little for the Dutch
> . . . while fair liberty you give, and crave
> You would be free, to make the world a slave.[40]

But despite rising Hollandophobia in the printed press, not all government servants were convinced that Stuart England was ready to wage war. Trying to coordinate the Royal Navy's victualling and supply, Samuel Pepys was nonplussed by the hapless responses he received to funding requests submitted the following April 1665 to Clarendon, Albemarle and the Lord Treasurer, Thomas Wriothesley, earl of Southampton. As Pepys recorded, it was 'strange, to see how they held up their hands, crying, "what shall we do?"', while Southampton asked '"why, what means all this, Mr Pepys? This is true you say, but what would you have me to do? . . . Why will not people lend their money? Why will they not trust the king as well as Oliver?"'[41]

That same month, a new Spanish ambassador, Antonio Francesco Mesia, count of Molina, arrived in London, hoping that Anglo-Dutch hostilities might helpfully distract English and French attention away from Iberia. Meanwhile, Louis renewed French efforts to avert hostilities by appointing two more envoys to join Cominges in London: the natural son of Henri IV, Henri de Bourbon, duke of Verneuil, and Honoré Courtin, a friend of Secretary of State Hugues de Lionne's with legal expertise. But as Cominges admitted to Louis in April, although Charles had patiently listened to the ambassadors' entreaties, he had pointed out that the English fleet was 'out of the harbour even now, and I cannot call it back with honour', adding that the Frenchmen should 'remember my people are in a rage against the Dutch'.[42]

Initially, the second Anglo-Dutch war went well for the English. As Lord High Admiral, the duke of York shared overall command of the English Navy with his Palatine cousin Prince Rupert and Sandwich. On 3 June 1665, the two fleets encountered one another off Lowestoft, where Dutch strategy was hampered by the decision to divide their fleet into seven squadrons, each commanded by a different admiral from each of the seven provinces. Fierce fighting ensued: in The Hague, the English ambassador, Sir George Downing, heard 'a continued terrible thunder' all day, while in London the poet John Dryden later recalled how 'the noise of the cannon from both navies reached our ears' as the city's inhabitants variously 'took towards the park, some cross the river, others down it; all seeking the noise in the depth of silence'.[43] When a stray shot from the *Royal Charles* hit the *Eendracht*'s magazine, the Dutch flagship was destroyed and the enemy line divided. With the English victorious, the Dutch had lost seventeen ships with another nine captured, while three of their seven admirals had died and around 5,000 to 6,000 sailors killed, wounded or taken prisoner. Writing from aboard the *Royal Charles* as one of the court's naval commissioners, an exhausted Sir William Coventry reported to Bennet (now earl of Arlington) that, although Charles's brother 'the Duke is safe', several senior officers had been lost, including York's close friend Charles Berkeley, earl of Falmouth. As Coventry described, York had been 'so near the noble persons killed . . . that his clothes were besmeared with their blood'.[44]

Celebrating the victory in his poem *The Dutch Armado, a Meer Bravado* (1665), John Crouch recalled the legendary encounter between the Holy Roman and Ottoman empires in 1571, venturing that 'Lepanto's force, compared to this dread sight, / Was a faint skirmish, or a painted fight.' Nearly a century later, 'the astonished sea in horror stood, / Discoloured with two tinctures: flames and blood'.[45] Edmund Waller invoked an equally hubristic register when drawing on a Venetian genre to expand an earlier version of a poem supplying instructions to an artist regarding the most appropriate commemoration of a victory. Endowing the Lowestoft victory with heroic precedents, Waller's *Instructions to a Painter* (1666) envisaged the conflict between the Dutch and English fleets echoing the classical encounter between the combined forces of Mark Anthony and Cleopatra against Octavian at the battle of Actium in 31 BC to determine domination of the Roman world.

The English victory near Lowestoft prompted popular rejoicing and a parliamentary vote of thanks for the duke of York's bravery, as well as additional financial subsidies. Still hoping to appear as neutral mediators, the French envoys in London abstained from lighting celebratory bonfires, which only prompted attacks on their residences by a hostile mob. As Courtin wrote to Lionne, while there were 'a dozen glass panes broken' in the room occupied by Lionne's son, 'if we had not kept our temper well, you would have heard of a fine grilling of ambassadors, for the streets were full of ready burning coals'. Although Cominges protested that he had readily supplied firewood to those preparing bonfires, suspicions of French evasiveness remained. With a major outbreak of plague engulfing London, Cominges reported that the mob had 'marked all the entrances to my house with a number of white crosses and inscriptions . . . as if the plague were in it, and its inhabitants had been destroyed'.[46]

The 'Great Plague' that broke out in London and surrounding English counties in 1665 inflicted higher mortality levels than any previous epidemic since the Black Death. Of nearly 100,000 deaths recorded in London that year, over 68,000 were formally attributed to the plague. Revived Elizabethan and Jacobean 'Plague Orders' required the houses of infected persons to be shut up and marked with a painted cross to forbid all access during quarantine periods of between twenty-eight and forty days. Additional public health measures in the city included more frequent street-cleaning, the destruction of stray cats and dogs, the closure of playhouses and the imposition of an evening curfew on tavern-drinkers.[47]

While the royal court relocated from Whitehall to Hampton Court, and subsequently to Salisbury and Oxford, Pepys and other civil servants remained in London. Walking to Greenwich in August 1665, he lamented that 'this disease [is] making us more cruel to one another than we are to dogs' as he observed an unburied coffin being watched to prevent approaches from relatives. With over 7,000 deaths recorded in a single week in September, Pepys nervously navigated the Royal Exchange, trying 'to talk with as few as I could', knowing that, despite quarantine requirements, 'we do converse and meet with people that have the plague upon them'.[48] Pamphlet debates raged over the epidemiological wisdom of imposing isolation on all infected households. As one anonymous author objected, the 'infection may have killed thousands, but shutting up hath killed its ten [of] thousands' by confining sick and healthy alike to fetid environments without access to paid employment, medical advice, fresh air and human company. Were physicians able to 'converse freely with the patient as men do in Holland', the author insisted that treatment could be improved.[49] Other medical practitioners, however, adhered to a theodicy of plague in which sinful readers needed to be reminded that risking God's wrath was significantly more serious than 'the lack of trade, or separation of friends'. Appealing to 'the undaunted valour of the invincible English nation', William Kemp denied that there was any comparison to be made between 'the shivering of a cold fit to the gnashing of teeth' and 'a burning fever to the flames of Hell-fire', insisting that 'the worm of conscience [was] more painful than a carbuncle'. Compared to the minor inconvenience of being 'shut up for a month in your own habitation', Kemp conjured readers to imagine being 'imprisoned and tormented with the Devil and his Angels in the lake of fire and brimstone for evermore'.[50]

III

Under the restored Stuart king and his swashbuckling brother, English foreign policy could appear, in mid-1665 at least, to have continued Cromwellian foreign policy success: the Dutch had been defeated at sea and Dutch possessions captured in North America and Africa, while French, Spanish, Portuguese, Russian and other powers sought an English alliance. To the mind of the Venetian ambassador in Paris, Alvise Sagredo, 'the movements of England have today become the principal phenomenon of the affairs of Europe'. But mounting Francophobia in England reflected fears that Louis XIV intended to enter the war on the Dutch side. Meeting Courtin in Salisbury, Charles had reportedly warned that, 'speaking as a private English gentleman', while Londoners had loaned him £100,000 'to continue the war with the United Provinces', they would offer him 'four times as much' if he were to declare war against France.[51]

Flushed with success at sea, Charles's brother James, duke of York, refused to contemplate the idea of peace talks. In October, he confirmed to Louis's ambassadors that he would meet them 'with pleasure, but as for changing his opinion, *that* he would not; being as he said, an Englishman, and therefore stubbornness itself'. When the envoys had objected that York was, in fact, half-French on his mother's side, the duke had admitted 'it is true', but since 'the English are obstinate when they are in the right', if they were 'in the wrong, then the French have all reason to be obstinate too'.[52] Following concerns about the risks suffered by Charles's heir presumptive during the recent battle, York reluctantly withdrew from further active service at sea, although he remained as Lord High Admiral. In Paris, renewed attempts were made to deflect Dutch demands for French involvement as Louis's ministers became incensed by the attention focused on the spice island of Run, then known as 'Poleron' – one of the smallest of the Banda Islands in modern Indonesia – which the English were demanding should be vacated by the Dutch in compliance with the Treaty of Westminster of 1654 and an Anglo-Dutch commercial agreement of 1662. As Lionne warned the States General's representative in Paris, Conrad van Beuningen, the Dutch should beware seeking to 'set all Christendom in a flame'. Although 'their fingers itch to be fighting', since the Dutch had 'no difference with England, as to anything within Europe', Louis did not want to be 'drawn into a war, so little necessary, for the isle of Poleron', which measured less than two miles by half a mile and which the Dutch 'set at no price, having grubbed up the trees'.[53]

In January 1666, however, Louis finally declared war on England, much to the despair of Henrietta Maria, who had long sought to dissuade her English son and French nephew from waging war against one another. The following month, the United Provinces also formed an alliance with Denmark that closed the Sound to English vessels. Describing Britain as 'surrounded by an impenetrable hedge of cliffs and precipices', the new Venetian ambassador in Paris, Marc'Antonio Giustinian, described how Louis's ministers 'studied and examined the map and the layout of the island, the ports, the gulfs, the shores and the sandbanks', but could not agree a strategy, being 'dismayed by the difficulties of the enterprise'.[54] Another violent engagement between the English and Dutch fleets occurred near the Thames estuary in June, with the outcome of the 'Four Days' Battle' initially unclear, but later recognized as a Dutch victory.

From The Hague, D'Estrades warned Lionne that De Witt was more ambitious and bellicose than ever, insisting that 'now would be the time to attempt something of importance'. Indeed, De Witt had recommended that if Louis were to 'attack the Isle of Wight, he might easily take it and keep it', while Frederick III of Denmark could 'at the same time attack the Orkneys and Shetland' and the Dutch fleet's blockade of the Channel and the Thames would eventually result in an allied conquest of the British Isles.[55] The English fleet nevertheless proved victorious in the 'St James's Day Fight' near North Foreland in July before Holmes, who had triumphed in Guinea, attacked the Dutch island of Terschelling and set fire to around 160 merchant ships at harbour in the Vlie channel. In a verse celebration of *Sir Robert Holmes his Bonfire: or, The Dutch Doomsday* (1666), one poet taunted the Dutch fleet as appearing

> Like Quixote's windmills, swiftly tacking round.
> Soon as they saw the English made up? They
> Progressed like crabs the clean contrary way.
> Who then has cause to boast, the World may see,
> They are our shadows, follow, and they flee?

On the Vlie, Holmes had succeeded in 'imitating the flames of Troy / And making bonfires of their towns for joy', as the English 'fought their Admirals with fisher-boats'.[56]

With the numeral '666' denoting the sign of the Beast in the biblical Book of Revelation, the year's apocalyptic and combustible resonances only intensified with the Great Fire of London in September. The five-day conflagration, now known to have started accidentally in a local bakery, destroyed over 13,000 homes, laid waste 400 acres of land in the City and caused damage to property and goods estimated at around £3 million. With popular opinion initially attributing the Fire's outbreak to a foreign conspiracy, one London-based Dutchman wrote to friends in The Hague, five days after the Fire had ended, admitting that he remained housebound, too scared to venture outdoors in case he became the target of a random violent attack. As he feared, 'it will be a long time before the people of London forget their wild rage against foreigners'.[57] Elsewhere in London, a schoolboy, William Taswell, described how 'the ignorant and deluded mob' unleashed 'their rage against the Roman Catholics and Frenchmen, imagining those incendiaries (as they thought) had thrown red hot balls into the houses', while his brother 'saw a Frenchman almost dismembered' in Moorfields, suspected of carrying 'balls of fire . . . when in truth they were only tennis balls'.[58] In Rotterdam, a tract entitled *Londens Puyn-hoop, Godts Rechvaerdige Strasse* (1666) ('London's Rubbish Heap, God's Righteous Punishment') acclaimed the calamity as divine retribution for Holmes's attack on the Vlie estuary the previous month. But as *A Poem on the Burning of London* conceded the following year, it was 'still unknown from whence our ruin came / Whether from Hell, France, Rome or Amsterdam'.[59]

In a newsletter sent to Paris describing the devastation, Giustinian read 'of the terrible sights of persons burned to death and calcined limbs, making it easy to believe the terror, though it cannot be exactly described'. More worryingly for the government, 'cries are now heard on every hand, that since the House of Stuart came to the throne, England has never enjoyed felicity but has suffered from incessant miseries'.[60] But in London, the personal involvement of both Charles and his brother in coordinating the disaster response had attracted admiration, with John Evelyn judging 'extraordinary the vigilance and activity of the king and duke . . . labouring in person, and being present, to command, order, reward and encourage workmen by which he showed his affection to his people and gained theirs'.[61] Addressing displaced Londoners directly, Charles insisted that the Fire's cause had been the 'hand of God', exacerbated by 'the terrible wind', thereby blaming divine displeasure, rather than a Dutch, French or general Catholic plot.[62]

When he first learned of the Fire, Sir William Temple – who had recently been appointed as Charles's resident ambassador in Brussels – had difficulty believing 'that what I read was more than a dream'. But to the Governor of the Spanish Netherlands, Francisco de Moura y Cortereal, marquis of Castel Rodrigo, Temple confidently predicted the stylish reconstruction of London with a new riverside quay, elegant gardens and broad thoroughfares, quoting Horace's admiration for the Emperor Augustus who had famously transformed Rome from a city of brick into one of marble.[63] In Madrid, Sandwich informed his Venetian counterpart, Marin Zorzi, that reports of 'the damage done had been exaggerated by the malignant'. Having been sent to Spain to offer condolences for Philip IV's death the previous September and to replace Fanshawe as English ambassador, Sandwich defensively insisted to Ramiro Núñez de Guzmán, count of Medina de las Torres, that Charles had already ordered London's rebuilding 'in a more beautiful and stately form', predicting that 'there would soon arise buildings at once conspicuous and luxurious, changing the compassion of their friends into admiration and leaving their enemies confounded'.[64]

Diplomatic braggadocio in Brussels and Madrid notwithstanding, national confidence was shattered and English public opinion quickly turned against continuing the Dutch war as wasteful of lives and money and economically detrimental. As one East India Company merchant grumbled from the Gujarati port of Surat in November, international trade 'was never more interrupted from the beginning of the world by those unnatural wars now in Europe, where the several princes seem to play at nine pins to tip down one another'.[65] In Paris, Louis continued to complain about Dutch demands, reminding D'Estrades that he had 'entered into a war with a king my near relation, and my friend [Charles], for their interest only', when it was not even 'very evident that the said king was the aggressor'.[66] In The Hague, the pro-war republican leader De Witt joined with D'Estrades in encouraging anti-English sentiments in Charles's teenage nephew Prince William of Orange, who had been formally declared 'a child of state' by the States General. In the spring of 1666, D'Estrades had resisted tearful appeals from William, following the removal of the Orangist governor of his household, Frederick Nassau de Zuylestein, with D'Estrades confidently assuring the prince that it 'was not for his interest to fall in with the King of England, who owes him three millions and pays him not a sol'.[67] Having taken William to visit the States General's fleet at Texel in order to rally Dutch sailors in their war against his English uncle, De Witt encouraged the prince to accept that 'if he cannot be the head himself' of the country's armed forces, as his late father had been, 'he may at least be the shoulders to support it and have the honour of peace with us'.[68]

The French, meanwhile, still had designs on Spanish-controlled Flanders. Exploiting the instability that prevailed in Spain during the regency of the ailing Carlos II, Louis was sponsoring publications which claimed that obligations placed on his Habsburg wife, Maria Theresa, to renounce her dynastic rights by the Treaty of the Pyrenees in 1659 had been unjustified. Rather, Louis argued that, as the issue of Philip IV's first marriage, Maria Theresa – not her half-brother Carlos – was rightful heir to the Spanish Netherlands according to Brabant customs of 'devolution' whereby inheritance rights, in the event of a second marriage, devolved upon heirs of a first union. In the autumn of 1666, a Burgundian Jesuit envoy, Baron François-Paul de Lisola, arrived in London to promote the interests of the Holy Roman Emperor, Leopold I, who had recently married another of Philip IV's daughters, Margaret Theresa, who was Carlos II's full sister. In *The Buckler of State and Justice against the Design manifestly discovered of the Universal Monarchy* (1667), Lisola vigorously warned that, although Louis's court deployed clever pretexts 'to disguise the vast designs' being prepared, they were 'false colours to mask the true spring which gives the motion to this machine'. Determined to expose French attempts to render naked ambitions towards 'universal monarchy pass under the veil of justice', Lisola sought to correct 'malicious artifices', 'so many hyperbolical exaggerations to cast dust in the eyes of neighbouring princes' and 'so many pernicious maxims'. Blaming Anglo-Dutch hostilities on French meddling, Lisola insisted that, despite trying 'to lull us asleep with the assurances of peace', the French were instead ensuring that the war was 'prolonged by a thousand artifices' in order to give the French 'elbow room to invade the Low Countries', confident that England and the Dutch 'should be drowned in blood to their reciprocal ruin'.[69]

Charles's former ambassador to Madrid, Arlington, made a similar case when he sponsored the anonymous *Free Conference Touching the Present State of England* (1668), somewhat preposterously framed as the account of a private ministerial conversation which the author chanced to overhear while hiding in a royal bedroom where he had passed out during a raucous dinner. Despite holding that the English were not naturally 'knights-errant' who involved themselves in other states' quarrels, the ministers had agreed that neutrality was not an option, since it would only incur scorn 'for having insipidly abandoned our proper reason of state' and risk England suffering 'the oblivion of Europe, that nobody will scarce remember there is such a nation in the world, excepting only those who have a mind to conquer us'. Contending that 'France offers roses unto us; Spain nothing but thorns', the advantages of allying with Louis's expansionist agenda were promoted by one courtier who envisaged 'a communion of conquests with the French' whereby 'the subduing of Flanders will serve us as ladders to arrive at other projects' of mutual Anglo-French profit. Such reasoning was, however, rejected by the other discussants who inverted the metaphor to warn that the English would thereby only facilitate French 'ambition, and be made use of like a pair of stairs, on which they do mean to tread in order to their obtaining the universal monarchy'.[70]

During the 1660s, Charles's ministers, whether at the negotiating table or in imagined pamphlet debates, pursued chaotically different diplomatic agendas, reminiscent of the sundry improvised expedients adopted during the exiled court's decade of itinerant exile. In Paris, Henrietta Maria's English adviser Henry Jermyn, earl of St Albans, promoted French interests by securing a secret undertaking from Charles to desist from taking any action if Louis invaded Flanders. In May 1667, French troops duly did so, rapidly seizing Flemish cities and strongholds including Ath, Bergues, Charleroi, Courtrai, Douai, Lille, Oudenaarde and Tournai. In Madrid, alarm at the vulnerability of Spanish-controlled territories in Flanders ensured that the protracted attempts of Fanshawe and Sandwich to conclude an Anglo-Spanish alliance finally bore fruit in the Treaty of Madrid, signed in May 1667. By this accord, England received 'most favoured nation' status, equalling the Dutch in securing access to Spanish trade in Europe, while English ships could now bring colonial goods from Atlantic and Indian markets to Spain.

Meanwhile, French fears that the English might quickly conclude peace with the Dutch and form a new pan-Protestant coalition against Louis's expansionism seemed unlikely. In late May, negotiations between Charles's ambassadors and the Dutch States General opened at Breda Castle with three Swedish diplomats acting as mediators since Charles XI Gustavus had remained neutral throughout the conflict. But while the negotiations were taking place, the Dutch battle fleet, commanded by John De Witt's brother Cornelis, took possession of the fort at Sheerness in Kent, before discovering the English fleet laid up and poorly protected at Chatham. On 12 June 1667, Dutch ships audaciously rode an incoming tide and surged up the River Medway, broke a defensive iron chain, captured the Royal Navy's flagship, the *Royal Charles*, and burned other vessels including the *Loyal London*, the *Royal Oak* and the *Royal James*.

Fearing imminent foreign invasion, Evelyn recorded how news of the Dutch attack 'put both country and city into a panic, fear and consternation . . . everybody were flying, none knew why or whither'.[71] By the following day, the popular mood was one of dejection. As Pepys recorded, City pundits 'look on us as lost' and, noting that Louis XIV had moved to Dunkirk with an army, assumed 'it is to invade us – and that we shall be invaded'. A month later, Pepys was still struggling to keep abreast of panicked rumour, recording that 'news came the other day so fast, of the Dutch fleets being in so many places' around the English coast that the Surveyor of the Navy, Sir William Batten, burst out, '"By God", says he, "I think the Devil shits Dutchmen".'[72] When news of the Dutch attack on the Medway had reached the peace talks in the United Provinces, the Swedish mediators had initially struggled to keep the warring parties at the negotiating table. But on 31 July 1667 the Treaty of Breda was agreed with remarkably generous terms for the English that retained the New Netherlands in North America, but accorded the Dutch a global monopoly on nutmeg by renouncing all claims to the tiny Indonesian island of Run.

18

Tributary to the French, 1667–1677

On 16 September 1667, Anne, duchess of York, gave birth to a son named Edgar, who became second-in-line to the English throne after his father, following the early deaths of the infant's older brothers. Having expected the new arrival to be named James, Charles or Henry, like most Stuart progeny, one of Edgar's godparents, Henry Somerset, marquess of Worcester, attributed the choice to the baby's father 'fancying that name': King Edgar, who had ruled England from 959 to 975 and 'was the first king that had the dominion of the seas, which he went upon about the kingdom every year with a thousand ships'.[1] Only months after the English Navy had suffered the humiliation of seeing its flagship, the *Royal Charles*, triumphantly towed away by a Dutch flotilla, its Lord High Admiral confidently named his son and heir after the first monarch to assert English sovereignty over the 'four seas', namely the North Sea, English Channel, Irish Sea and St George's Channel.

By 1667, the Stuarts' dynastic future appeared to lie with the duke of York's young family, which included Prince Edgar's older sisters, Mary and Anne. While one *Royal Charles* lay in ignominious Dutch custody, the real royal Charles had conspicuously failed to produce an heir to the throne by Queen Catherine, despite having fathered at least nine illegitimate children by four other women. Charles's eldest son, James, duke of Monmouth, had been born to Lucy Walter in 1649, followed by a daughter, Charlotte, to Elizabeth Killligrew, viscountess of Shannon. By the daughter of a Derbyshire Royalist, Catherine Pegge, Charles had fathered a son and daughter, Charles and Catherine, in 1657 and 1658. After the Restoration, Charles had five children by Barbara Villiers, countess of Castlemaine: three sons, Charles, Henry and George, and two daughters, Anne and Charlotte, of whom the youngest, George, had been born in 1665.

Amid an increasingly apprehensive public mood, Charles's personal foibles became conflated with national failings. Walking together in April 1667, John Evelyn and Samuel Pepys found themselves 'talking of the badness of the government, where nothing but wickedness, and wicked men and women command the king' and blaming Charles for being too lackadaisical to 'gainsay anything that relates to his pleasures'.[2] Finding ironical inspiration in Edmund Waller's poem *Instruction to a Painter* that had celebrated the English naval victory off Lowestoft in 1665, the poet and MP for Hull, Andrew Marvell, penned a series of satirical rejoinders, caustically cataloguing an ensuing litany of military incompetence, political hypocrisy and national disgrace. Marvell's *Last Instructions to a Painter* (1667) dissected Charles's failings as a monarch and, extending to nearly a thousand lines, concluded with a scene in which a sleeping Charles awakes to find a vision of a bound, gagged, humiliated and tearful virgin. Aroused by her distress, the king attempts rape, but is rebuffed by the apparition which he then recognizes as the elusive 'England or the Peace' before it evaporates. Entangling punning references to coins, medals, prostitutes ('pieces') and politics, Marvell's *Last Instructions* underlined Charles's perceived inability to distinguish erotic fantasy from state affairs, while additional resonance derived from the fact that the king's *desirée* Frances Stuart had posed as 'Britannia' for a medal designed by the Antwerp-born engraver John Roettier and adapted as a commemorative accompaniment to the Peace of Breda. This image of Frances Stuart reappeared on the Royal Mint's fifty-pence coins between 1969 and 2008 and on two-pound coins from 2015 – long outlasting the Stuart dynasty she was intended to celebrate.

Popular dissatisfaction with a dissolute king was, to some extent, deflected as subjects' fury turned on Prince Edgar's maternal grandfather, Edward Hyde, earl of Clarendon, who was accused of knowingly marrying Charles to an infertile queen to promote his own family's dynastic interests, steering a Francophile foreign policy that involved selling Dunkirk while pocketing secret French payments and mismanaging the recent war effort. When the Dutch fleet had set fire to English warships in the Medway that summer, Pepys reported that a hostile mob had gathered outside Clarendon's palatial new residence opposite

St James's Palace – satirically known as 'New Dunkirk' – and smashed windows, uprooted trees and daubed on its gates, 'Three Sights to be Seen: Dunkirk, Tangier and a Barren Queen'.[3] After being dismissed from office and facing impeachment proceedings in Parliament, Clarendon fled to France in November, mindful that, in 1641, Charles I's sacrifice of his chief minister, Thomas Wentworth, earl of Strafford, had ended in Strafford's execution. While Clarendon protested that he had never acted against the national interest, the Venetian ambassador to the French court, Marc'Antonio Giustinian, reported that the former Chancellor's arrival in Paris obliged Louis XIV 'to steer between dangerous rocks' in potentially offending the duke of York by banishing his father-in-law from the country or 'getting into the bad books of the [English] parliament by offering him a safe asylum'.[4]

I

Standing in puissant contrast to Charles's plight was his younger French cousin Louis, whose forces had audaciously seized a significant number of Flemish towns in the Spanish Netherlands during the summer of 1667. Half-Spanish through his mother Anne of Austria and married to a Spanish queen, Maria Theresa, Louis evinced a territorial cupidity that was fuelled by the precarious future of Spain's monarchy under its sickly six-year-old king, Carlos II. In covert talks held in January 1668, Louis's representative, Jacques Bretel de Grémonville, concluded an astonishingly ambitious bilateral compact in Vienna with Johann Weikhard, Prince of Auersperg, an envoy of the Holy Roman Emperor Leopold I, who was married to Carlos's elder sister, Margaret Theresa. By the treaty, if the male Spanish Habsburg line expired with Carlos, an envisaged partition of the Spanish monarchy would give Louis the Spanish Netherlands, Navarre, Sicily, the Philippines and Spain's North African conquests, while the Austrian Habsburgs would retain control of the Spanish mainland and all other overseas possessions.[5]

Although the Grémonville treaty remained unknown until the nineteenth century, a parallel attempt to arrest French expansionism underpinned the 'Triple Alliance' simultaneously concluded between England, the United Provinces and Sweden in January 1668, which threatened a joint attack in the event of further French aggression and relied on Spanish subsidies to finance deployment of Swedish troops. But given that France had only recently supported the United Provinces against England in the Second Anglo-Dutch War, the Dutch diplomat Abraham de Wicquefort deemed the new alliance 'so bizarre and mysterious that it is difficult to make sense of it'.[6] As Louis later recalled of the English alliance in his *Mémoires* of the Dutch war, 'their insolence struck me to the quick' and momentarily tempted him to risk his recent conquests in Flanders by 'turning my arms against this haughty and ungrateful nation'.[7]

Having been appointed as Charles's special ambassador to the United Provinces, Sir William Temple was coldly informed in The Hague by the French diplomat Godefroy d'Estrades that even if the English or Dutch should presume 'to prescribe him [Louis] laws, and force him to compliance, by leagues between ourselves, or with Spain, though Sweden and the German princes should join with us', the French king's ambitions in Flanders would remain undeterred. With disconcertingly accurate insight, D'Estrades ventured 'that it would come to a war of forty years' – and, indeed, French hostilities against England and the Dutch Republic only ended with the Peace of Utrecht in 1713.[8] For the moment, however, French resolve was outwardly reflected in generous terms confirmed by the peace treaty signed in May 1668 at Aix-la-Chapelle (now Aachen) by which Louis returned Franche-Comté to Spain, but retained a dozen fortified towns in Flanders and avoided entering into any commitment to abstain from future aggrandizement. Temporarily checked by the Triple Alliance, Louis later admitted in his *Mémoires* that 'peace would allow me every day to improve my finances, my Navy, my contacts and whatever else' needed to secure his strategic ambitions.[9]

Distrusting the Dutch, Louis wanted to observe English intentions closely and dispatched a new ambassador to London in August 1668: Charles Colbert, marquis of Croissy, and brother of the powerful Controller-General of Finances, Jean-Baptiste Colbert. In London, Croissy attracted suspicion through his sedulous attentions to the English court, where he regularly dined and played tennis with Charles. Within months of his brother's arrival in London, Jean-Baptiste Colbert confirmed that he would be 'very happy to see the memoir that you are writing about the English Navy', given French hopes to 'profit from their great experience in this type of war'. Accordingly, Colbert indicated that 'if you could get the plans for the battles they have had at sea, you would please me greatly', albeit acknowledging 'that this is a delicate matter'.[10] In London, the Venetian ambassador Pietro Mocenigo complained that Croissy's lavish entertainment of the royal family meant that 'the burden of embassies is ever being rendered more intolerable by such exorbitant and constant examples', while Giustinian had earlier confirmed that, in Paris, 'every industry is being employed' at Louis's court 'to undo the knot of the Triple Alliance'.[11]

In The Hague, the republican Pensionary of Holland, John De Witt, warned Temple 'as a friend, not as a minister' of rumours regarding Charles II's pro-French inclinations. Writing to the Lord Keeper, Sir Orlando Bridgeman, Temple described how De Witt had enquired further, 'with a very equal countenance; though I found he had observed mine very narrowly, all the while he was talking, as well as when he ended'. Temple had insisted that he knew of no reason why Charles would wish to undermine the Triple Alliance while Temple himself would never 'have any part in destroying what I had the honour of building'. From London, Charles's Secretary of State, Henry Bennet, earl of Arlington, warned Temple that popular opinion suspected Temple of being unduly influenced by De Witt's counsel. Vigorously rebutting the charge of being overly deferential to Dutch designs, Temple denied that he could not prevent political adversaries 'thinking me so weak a man as to be governed by De Witt's lead to what he pleases', but countered that such criticism instead reflected frustration at 'my not leading him to all they pleased, so that my fault is not his governing me, but my not governing him'. Again, Temple insisted that England's interests were best served by seeking 'to balance the affairs of Europe, to hinder the exorbitant growing power of France, to defend Flanders' and, by upholding the Triple Alliance, allowing Charles to 'head all the affairs of Christendom on one side as France will do on the other'.[12]

In England, popular Francophobia evoked fears of Gallic absolutism and the eclipse of parliamentary scrutiny and public debate. Following the Westminster Parliament's prorogation in May 1668, the new Danish envoy in London, Christopher Lindenov, reported 'a bitter dispute in the king's council' in December, 'concerning the proroguing of parliament, for the reason that no precedent is to be found for one prorogation after the other', especially when 'there are so many matters which parliament alone can resolve'.[13] Increasingly critical of 'Court' policies was an identifiable faction of 'Country' MPs that included the MP for Stockbridge, Sir Robert Howard, whose play *The Country Gentleman* had been scheduled to première in spring 1669, but was suppressed after the unflattering character of 'Sir Cautious Trouble-all' was recognized as Sir William Coventry who had recently been dismissed as a Privy Councillor and then imprisoned after challenging George Villiers, duke of Buckingham, to a duel. In Howard's play, 'Sir Cautious' explained how statesmen retained up-to-date knowledge 'of the several interests of foreign potentates, how they stand in amity or animosity towards us, and with one another' by showing off two rotating circular tables, with holes in the middle, representing domestic affairs and foreign policy, giving their owners 'the whole world at their fingertips'. Indeed, 'Sir Cautious' boasted that he needed never to 'trouble myself with reading newsbooks or gazettes' but could instead 'go into my chamber, look upon my table, and snap – presently I'll tell you how the whole world is disposed', although he admitted to occasionally losing 'a town or two' by mistake. In contrast to the foppish Francophilia evinced by other characters in Howard's play, 'Sir Richard Plainbred' was dismayed to arrive in London from the country to find food prepared 'according to the *mode*' such as 'soup, côtelettes, ragouts, fricassés, omelettes, desserts', leaving Plainbred to conclude that 'they eat no English meat here, but send into France for victuals and cooks'.[14]

A fear of Francophile political maxims ran alongside suspicions of effeminate fashions, outlandish cuisine and Gallic culture. In Paris, Charles's ambassador Ralph Montagu was disconcerted to discover that, on Croissy's recommendation, Louis XIV had approved a gift worth around £1,000 for Charles's mistress, the countess of Castlemaine, although Charles let Croissy know that the only woman who influenced his actions as king was his younger sister, Henrietta Anne, duchess of Orléans.[15] The previous October, Henrietta had indeed advised her brother on foreign policy, acknowledging that 'the majority of people who do not know the inside of things' would counsel prudence in avoiding any anti-Dutch engagement. But, as Henrietta was aware, 'the matter takes on a different aspect, firstly because you have need of France to ensure the success of the design about R'. Grateful for his sister's advice, Charles thereafter provided Henrietta with a cipher for future correspondence, reassuring her of his intention to 'set my affairs in that posture as there will not be so many miscarriages to be hunted after' by prying parliamentarians.[16] Henrietta's discreet reference to 'R' denoted 'religion': more specifically, Charles's private desire to declare his religious conversion to Catholicism. In his later memoirs, the siblings' brother, the duke of York, claimed that, at a private meeting at Whitehall on 25 January 1669 – the anniversary of St Paul's conversion to Christianity – Charles, 'with great earnestness, and even with tears in his eyes', had confirmed 'how uneasy it was to him not to profess the faith he believed'. After Charles had confided to York, Arlington, Lord Arundel of Wardour and Sir Thomas Clifford his wish to make a public declaration of his conversion to Catholicism, the ministers had agreed that French military assistance might well be required at such a juncture.[17]

French esteem for the Catholic piety of other members of Britain's ruling house was further evidenced after Queen Henrietta Maria – a figure from a former era – died in Paris in September 1669. Mourning a devout 'daughter of France', the renowned court preacher Jacques-Bénigne Bossuet delivered a funeral sermon warning that the English populace had become so 'factious, rebellious and opinionated' and 'incapable of constancy' that, after the mid-century civil wars, nothing but 'appalling precipices' could be anticipated.[18] After Henrietta Maria's interment at the Basilica of Saint-Denis alongside other members of French royalty, a member of the English embassy in Paris, William Perwich, warned Arlington's colleague, Sir Joseph Williamson, to 'believe not anything of the sermon preached' by Bossuet at the queen's funeral, claiming that the eulogy had 'set her forth for an Amazon riding at the head of an army to relieve her husband at Oxon'.[19]

Nevertheless, it had been Charles II who, more than a decade earlier, had angrily forestalled his mother from entering his younger brother, Henry, into a Jesuit College on the grounds that the Stuart dynasty's chances of regaining its British thrones would be fatally ruined by any move that undermined its perceived attachment to Protestantism. But by the late 1660s, Charles had recovered his thrones and married a Catholic queen, while his favourite mistress, Castlemaine, had converted to Catholicism in 1663. The king's sister-in-law, the duchess of York, was another Catholic convert, whose husband (and Charles's heir) was increasingly suspected of Catholic inclinations, especially after the unexpected and dramatic conversion in October 1668 of York's

French mentor, Henri de La Tour d'Auvergne, viscount of Turenne.[20] Across northern Europe, the conversions to Catholicism of other northern European leaders, including Queen Christina of Sweden and Duke John Frederick of Brunswick-Lüneburg, during the 1650s had reduced the number of major Protestant powers clearly positioned to resist Louis XIV's expansionism a decade later.

Charles II's apparent readiness to consider publicly declaring his conversion to Catholicism reflected both a personal shift and one that resonated with the aspirations of key advisers such as Clifford, who envisaged a potential means of achieving Christian reunion through a Gallican-style national church that retained clerical marriage, a vernacular liturgy and regal powers of appointment. Politically, such a church was clearly closer to the established religion of the 'Most Christian' king, Louis XIV, than to the 'Most Catholic' king of Spain or the papacy.[21] Ideas of Christian reunion also appealed to commentators alarmed by the reality of western European powers waging war against each other while the Turkish Ottoman Empire's territorial ambitions expanded. Since 1648, Venetian forces had been repelling Ottoman attacks in the siege of Candia, in modern-day Heraklion, on Crete. Tasked with raising funds and levying British troops to support his country's resistance, the Venetian ambassador in London, Mocenigo, was frustrated by the Stuart court's repeated retreats to Hampton Court and other country estates. As Mocenigo complained in September 1668, he was forced 'to wait for the king's return, while burning not to waste a moment. While Candia is suffering from the delay, every day seems a year.'[22] The Venetians' surrender the following August ended what remains the second-longest siege in history. To the mind of the disillusioned Mocenigo, Charles's ministers had seemed more concerned to avoid antagonizing Levantine trading interests than defending Christendom from Muslim attack.

II

Suspicions that the French and English courts were engaged in covert negotiations were fuelled by the arrival in London, during the summer of 1669, of a member of Henrietta Maria's former household, Henry Jermyn, earl of St Albans, 'whom everyone calls the English ambassador of France in England', in the words of the Florentine commentator Lorenzo Magalotti.[23] While terms for an Anglo-French commercial compact were ostensibly under discussion, a more ambitious agenda was alleged. Assuming 'that the division of the Spanish Netherlands between these two kingdoms would be easy', Mocenigo reported rumours 'that St Albans has authority to offer money to the king here to pay all his debts provided he detaches himself from the Triple Alliance'.[24] In reality, St Albans was laying the groundwork for an offensive alliance to be secretly agreed between Charles and his Paris-based sister Henrietta Anne when the latter visited England the following year. The visit was publicly promoted as a rare family reunion for the Stuart siblings and Lindenov informed Christian V of Denmark that Henrietta Anne had assured Charles that 'she was in no ways coming to concern herself with any affairs of state, as the queen, her mother, had usually done'.[25]

Notwithstanding such pledges, the terms of the secret Anglo-French Treaty of Dover were finalized during Henrietta Anne's brief stay on the English south coast and signed in June 1670, on Louis XIV's behalf by Ambassador Croissy and, for Charles, by Arlington, Clifford, Arundel and another Catholic courtier, Sir Richard Bellings. To secure English support for his territorial claims in Spanish Flanders and in any future war against the Dutch Republic, Louis undertook to pay the English king £1 million in advance and a yearly subsidy of £600,000 for the war's duration, with an additional £200,000 subsidy when Charles publicly declared his conversion to Catholicism. If popular unrest broke out after such an announcement, Louis also agreed to supply a force of 6,000 soldiers to be maintained at French expense. Meanwhile, in return for Louis's use of the Royal Navy's warships, England was promised the Dutch islands of Walcheren and Cadzand in the Scheldt estuary, as well as the port of Sluys. Securing English support for his territorial ambitions was particularly important for Louis after Carlos II of Spain had suffered another serious illness earlier that year. Perwich received reports of Carlos's recovery in May 1670 and informed Williamson from Paris that the eight-year-old king was 'better, though at the same time, it's rumoured about the city that he cannot live much longer (or, to say the truth, the French would not have him do so)'.[26]

But in late June 1670, the close conduit established between the English and French courts was abruptly terminated when Henrietta Anne died unexpectedly, less than a month after returning to Paris from meeting Charles at Dover. Since the duchess had become violently ill after drinking iced chicory water, fears that she might have been poisoned prompted Louis to order a thorough post-mortem involving French medical experts as well as representatives and doctors from the English embassy in Paris. Perwich reported to Williamson that, once the autopsy had started, 'all the house was filled with the most horrible stench that anybody ever smelled' on account of the duchess being 'stuffed up with bile'. While the physicians 'wondered not why she died then, but that she [had] lived so long', the risk of deliberate poisoning could nevertheless be discounted and the duchess's death was later attributed to acute peritonitis following perforation of a duodenal ulcer.[27] Delivering a funeral sermon in the duchess's honour at Saint-Denis, Bossuet described Henrietta Anne as the 'worthy link' between 'the two greatest kings in the world'.[28]

To facilitate payment of French subsidies in the event of an allied war against the Dutch, Charles dispatched the unwitting George Villiers, second duke of Buckingham, to negotiate a *traité simulé* ('simulated treaty'), agreeing an Anglo-French alliance and French funds but omitting any mention of a royal conversion to Catholicism. For Buckingham at least, such a mission proved remarkably easy to accomplish. While foreign envoys were surprised by the fulsome honours bestowed on Buckingham by Louis's court at Versailles, in The Hague, Temple detected in De Witt 'a coldness in all our negotiations of that kind'. As Temple reported, De Witt remained sceptical that Buckingham had travelled to Paris '*pour voir le pays ou apprendre la langue*' ('to see the country or learn the language').[29]

Diplomatic tensions had only increased after Louis had audaciously invaded the duchy of Lorraine in August 1670, having first tried to abduct its anti-French ruler, Charles IV, while insisting that he was not annexing the territory, but merely taking it under French protection. As Lindenov admitted to Christian IV, even Charles II had become concerned by the French ministerial practice 'of executing their plans first and publishing their reasons for what has happened later'.[30] Visiting England, Temple described the alarm exhibited by the Dutch envoys in London, John Boreel and Conrad van Beuningen, who were 'in such a state of apprehension' over Louis's actions 'that in a panic of perpetual fear, they have lost control of their reason' and were convinced 'that everything is tending to their hurt'.[31] Back in The Hague, republican factions associated with De Witt were further discomfited by the twenty-year-old Prince of Orange's decision to visit his English uncle, Charles II, that autumn amid shifting dynastic and international alliances. Dutch fears were confirmed at the end of 1670 when the Anglo-French agreement ostensibly negotiated by Buckingham was ratified in London by Clifford and Arlington, who, together with Anthony Ashley Cooper, Lord Ashley, John Maitland, earl of Lauderdale, and Buckingham himself, became signatories to a treaty that now promised two additional islands in the tally of Charles's promised acquisitions in the event of a Dutch defeat.

A different type of geopolitical union was simultaneously envisaged within the British Isles after new sessions of both the English and Scottish Parliaments had opened on 19 October 1669: the only occasion in the seventeenth century that both legislatures started new parliamentary sessions on the same day. In their opening speeches at Westminster, Charles and Lord Keeper Bridgeman recalled James VI & I's unfulfilled ambitions for closer British integration after the regal union of 1603 and suggested that such an aspiration was ripe for resuscitation, after the English and Scots had lived under the same monarch now 'for near threescore and seven years, having begotten the same common friends, and common enemies to both nations'.[32] More pressingly, unpopular disruption to Scottish trading networks incurred during the Second Anglo-Dutch War had prompted negotiations for closer Anglo-Scottish commercial union in 1668 that had proved abortive. Although ministers were keen to recruit commissioners to consider broader forms of political and legal union, as well as new economic arrangements, Anglo-Scottish union had still not been debated at Westminster by the time the Scottish parliamentary session ended in December 1669.

In Edinburgh, the advocate and writer Sir George Mackenzie of Rosehaugh later recalled that proposals for closer Anglo-Scottish union could not 'have been less acceptable to the people at any time, than at this, in which the remembrance of their oppression from the Usurper [Oliver Cromwell] was yet fresh with them'.[33] Such pessimism was shared by Charles's parliamentary commissioner, Lauderdale, who warned the English court of popular hostility to ideas of British union, detecting among his fellow Scots a pervasive dread 'to have made us slaves by garrisons' while anxieties about the likely economic impact of union 'frights all ranks of men from having to do with England'.[34]

Indeed, when the Scottish royal regalia had been returned to Edinburgh Castle after the parliamentary session had ended, Lauderdale had wryly 'desired the wives of Edinburgh might take notice, that he had not sold the Crown to the English, as was informed'.[35] When Anglo-Scottish relations were finally discussed at Westminster in March 1670, Lindenov reported to the Danish Chancery that English MPs were seemingly 'finding this matter of the union so delicate', with 'a constant fear that there is something behind it all, more than they are able now to see'.[36] Although fourteen English and seventeen Scots commissioners started bilateral talks in mid-September 1670 at Westminster, they failed to find common ground on key matters including parliamentary representation and judicial appeals. While the union discussions were adjourned and never restarted in the king's lifetime, negotiations leading to Anglo-Scottish political union were concluded during the reign of Charles's niece Queen Anne in 1707.

While the English and Scottish crowns remained separate, attention focused on the identity of Charles's likely successor as king in both nations. Following several rumoured and failed pregnancies, Catherine of Braganza had suffered another miscarriage in June 1669, after a pet fox reportedly jumped on to her bed and startled the queen. As hopes receded that Charles would produce an heir by Catherine, informal pressure mounted on the king to follow Henry VIII's precedent and divorce his wife in order to remarry, defying diplomatic repercussions with Portugal. In 1670, aristocratic divorce became especially prominent after John Manners, Baron Roos, introduced private legislation into the House of Lords, seeking a divorce in order to remarry and sire an heir, having unexpectedly succeeded to the earldom of Rutland. Roos's bill was promoted by Bishop John Wilkins of Chester, who argued that divorces might be granted both for adultery and for 'immundicity of the womb, which is given forth to be the queen's condition'.[37] Having attracted attention by attending the Lords debates in person, Charles enthusiastically acclaimed parliamentary proceedings as 'better than going to a play' and his known support for Roos's case aided the bill's narrow victory. As Marvell reported, Charles had also publicly claimed 'he knew not why a woman might not be divorced for barrenness, as a man for impotency'.[38]

Equally committed to denying Roos's right to divorce his wife had been Charles's brother and heir, James, duke of York, although Mocenigo perceived 'nothing whatever behind this [opposition] as it is due solely to private considerations'.[39] Nevertheless, so long as the childless Catherine of Braganza remained alive and Charles seemed disinclined to consider divorce, the duke's family attracted public interest, which only increased when the duchess of York died of cancer in March 1671 and, three months later, was followed to the grave by the couple's only surviving son, Edgar, duke of Cambridge. The resident Venetian secretary Girolamo Alberti alleged that the duchess of York had not even been 'buried when negotiations were begun for a fresh marriage', with the most likely bride identified as the Habsburg archduchess Claudia Felicitas of Innsbruck. The perceived fragility of the Stuart dynasty's future was further underlined by a diplomatic dilemma that arose in autumn 1671 as to whether Charles should formally receive the Portuguese ambassador, Dom Francisco de Melo, after Catherine of Braganza's youngest brother, Pedro, had removed their disabled brother, Afonso VI, to the Azores to assume de facto authority as sovereign. As Alberti reported, several Privy Councillors warned Charles to beware the usurping potential of younger brothers, for even if 'the legitimate king of Portugal had no children, that was not a crime deserving imprisonment at the Terceiras'. With Charles's subjects 'having barely emerged from the civil wars, it was dangerous to countenance such an example, when England was in precisely the same case, the king not yet having legitimate heirs and the duke being inclined to supply the deficiency'.[40]

On the diplomatic front, Charles also needed to deflect suspicions of manufacturing hostilities against the Dutch in order to justify a closer alliance with France. He reran history a third time by concluding another Anglo-French treaty that was publicly signed in February 1672 by the same commissioners that had agreed the simulated treaty in December 1670. Although the Venetian ambassador in Paris, Francesco Michiel, acknowledged that Anglo-French amity was now 'known to the whole world', intelligence at Louis's court knew that 'the voyage to Dover of the late duchess of Orléans was arranged for this purpose' to perfect a proposal that had previously 'received no more than the first tints or rough sketch at the hands of ministers'.[41] Moreover, in 1670, Henrietta Anne had been accompanied on her journey to Dover by a young Breton noblewoman, Louise Renée de Penancoët de Kéroualle, who returned to Whitehall as a lady-in-waiting to Queen Catherine after Henrietta's death (Plate 20). Becoming Charles's mistress in the autumn of 1671, Kéroualle bore the king a son named Charles in July 1672; the French ambassador Croissy recognized the attendant potential to advance French interests, suggesting to the French Secretary of State for War that if Kéroualle 'makes enough progress in her friendship with the king to be useful in the service of his Majesty [Louis XIV], she will do her duty'.[42]

At Whitehall, a new French mistress and a new French alliance also encouraged a return to French court dress. To counter mounting Francophobia in 1666, Charles had symbolically abandoned French couture by donning new outfits that comprised a 'vest', or long waistcoat made from English wool (rather than French silk), with a knee-length coat and long shirt. As the king's confidant George Savile, marquess of Halifax, later recalled, the sartorial shift had been intended 'that we might look more like a distinct people, and not be under the servility of imitation'. Speculating that one purpose of Henrietta Anne's visit in 1670 had been 'to laugh us out of these vests', Halifax believed that Charles's reversion thereafter to doublet and hose 'gave a critical advantage to France, since it looked like an evidence of our returning to their interests as well as to their fashion'.[43]

To finance his imminent war against the Dutch, Charles ordered a 'Stop on the Exchequer' that postponed repayment of all royal debts from 2 January to 31 December 1672 and assured creditors that future repayments would benefit from generous rates of compound interest. To promote domestic unity, Charles also promulgated a prerogative Declaration of Indulgence in March that suspended all penal laws against Protestant nonconformists and Catholics. Two days earlier, a failed attempt by English ships near the Isle of Wight to capture a Dutch fleet returning from Smyrna, finally proved, as one Dutch pamphleteer insisted, that England was 'an open enemy, instead of a feigned friend', while De Witt privately confirmed that 'England had finally taken down its mask'.[44] Observing a government intent on fabricating a rupture with its former Dutch allies, Evelyn denounced the tensions as 'a quarrel slenderly grounded and not becoming Christian neighbours'.[45] Meanwhile Marcus Gjøe Falcksen, having arrived in London as Lindenov's replacement, observed the frantic press-ganging of seamen for the English fleet, admitting to Christian V that he 'would not have believed it', had he not been obliged to extend diplomatic protection to merchants and 'my own domestics, to assure their liberty when they accompany me'.[46]

III

In late March 1672, Louis declared war against the Dutch Republic. Several days later, Charles did likewise, issuing a declaration of war that claimed a range of insults including Dutch vessels failing to render the flag salute to English ships at sea and objecting that, even when formerly allied to England, there was 'scarce a town within their territories that is not filled with abusive pictures, and false historical medals and pillars; some of which have been exposed to the public view by command of the States themselves'.[47] Hired to defend the government's decision, the former Parliamentarian Henry Stubbe published *A Justification of the Present War Against the United Netherlands* (1672) that deplored Dutch malice in 'rendering the English cheap and ridiculous by their lying pictures, and libelling pamphlets'. As Stubbe warned, Dutch prints depicting Charles as a lion with cropped ears or a dog with a docked tail 'take much with the barbarous people, when nobody is present to contradict them'.[48] Although the anonymous author of *Consideratien over den Tegenwoordigen Toestant van het Vereenigde Nederland* (1672) ('Considerations concerning the present state of the United Netherlands') mockingly warned that 'the world should be afraid of a king who wants to go to war and shed blood over a painting', hubristic glorifications of Stuart weakness could backfire.[49] In May, an incensed mob broke into Dordrecht's City Hall, intent on destroying the 'expensive painting of Chatham . . . which had cost thousands, made for the glory of Mr Cornelis De Witt' and had been specifically cited as a *casus belli* in Charles's declaration of war. The painting of the Dutch raid on the Medway was 'ripped into a thousand pieces' and a depiction of De Witt's head was nailed to a scaffold, as pro-Orangist factions blamed the renewed outbreak of a costly war on their bellicose republican adversaries.[50]

While the Third Anglo-Dutch war proved militarily inconclusive for England, the lightning success of Louis XIV's land attacks rendered 1672 the 'Year of Disaster' for the Dutch. Within forty days, a French force of around 120,000 soldiers, reinforced by troops from Münster and Cologne, virtually overran the Dutch Republic, conquering the provinces of Gelderland, Overijssel and Utrecht and capturing nearly fifty fortified towns (see map on p. xiv). Following the seizure of

Utrecht in June, the former French ambassador in The Hague, D'Estrades – who now held a military command in the invading force – suggested that the entire Dutch Republic could be 'abolished' if Louis wished.[51] Weeks later, the French symbolically celebrated Catholic Mass in the former Calvinist bastion of Utrecht's Domkerk, while the province of Holland was only protected by the deliberate flooding of the country's sixteenth-century water defences. In Dordrecht, Cornelis De Witt was arrested in July and accused of plotting to assassinate Charles's nephew, the Prince of Orange, although even the application of torture by the Dutch authorities failed to elicit a confession. When John De Witt visited Cornelis the following month, rioters stormed The Hague's Gevangenpoort prison and brutally lynched both brothers, before dismembering their bodies and hanging their mutilated and naked corpses for public display. While horrified Dutch pamphleteers drew parallels between the brothers' murderers and the English regicides in 1649, Charles's nephew William became the beneficiary of events when the anti-Orangist Act of Seclusion and Perpetual Edict (passed in 1654 and 1667 respectively) were rescinded and the prince was restored to his ancestors' civil and military offices.

Having declared war without Parliament's approval the previous year, Charles opened a new parliamentary session at Westminster in February 1673, hoping that financial subsidies would be forthcoming. The Chancellor, Anthony Ashley Cooper, recently elevated as the earl of Shaftesbury, compared England to Rome and the Dutch Republic to ancient Carthage, flattering his listeners by invoking Cato and agreeing that 'you judged aright, that at any rate *delenda est Carthago* [Carthage is destroyed]'. With the conflict ostensibly undertaken to prevent Dutch domination, Shaftesbury maintained, 'the king may well say to you, this is your war'.[52] During the ensuing debate for financial aid to pay for the war, MPs then 'sat full four hours by one candle till there was not one inch of it left', before adjourning. Reflecting increasingly partisan divisions, a speech made by the Lincoln MP Sir Thomas Meres was censured for implying 'a distinction in the House between the country gentlemen and the courtiers' with increased use of 'the words "of this side of the House, and that side", which were not parliamentary', but would shortly become a permanent feature of English politics.[53]

While Parliament continued in session, an anonymous pamphlet circulated among MPs entitled *England's Appeal from the Private Cabal at Whitehall to the Great Council of the Nation* (1673). Later attributed to the naturalized French Huguenot Pierre Du Moulin, *England's Appeal* was sceptical of French intentions, warning that, if German princes and Spanish forces proved unwilling or unable to arrest French expansionism, 'what will become of poor England': might Charles become a 'tenant at will?' Du Moulin demanded that Charles's pro-war advisers should 'now pull their vizard off . . . and tell us plainly whether they are paid for making the French King the universal monarch' and whether, therefore, 'England must at least be made tributary to the French'. While acknowledging Anglo-Dutch tensions, 'twenty silly stories against Holland cannot make it advisable for us to join with the French king against the greatest part of Europe'. Suspicious of Croissy's familiarity with Charles's courtiers, which ironically echoed criticism of Temple's closeness to John De Witt, Du Moulin objected that intimacy 'between foreign ambassadors and first ministers of state, continual treatings and frequent goings to country houses, there to stay several days and weeks, is a new thing in the world'.[54]

Charles, meanwhile, realized that he could only secure parliamentary funds to continue the war if he withdrew the Declaration of Indulgence issued in 1672 which had been seen by Catholics as an auspicious move towards a broader religious toleration. By contrast, appalled Protestants were determined that the Declaration be ditched, given, as one anonymous pamphleteer put it, 'how many Popish emissaries are come from the See of Rome into this nation, like the salmon into fresh rivers, to beget a new spawn and fry of Catholics among us'.[55] Hence, as well as withdrawing the Declaration, Charles also approved a new Test Act that required all civil and military office-holders to swear the oaths of Supremacy and Allegiance, repudiate the Catholic doctrine of transubstantiation, and provide proof of recent receipt of communion in the established Church; his reward was a parliamentary subsidy of £1.26 million. That Easter, the king's brother and heir, James, duke of York, confirmed his private conversion to Catholicism by failing to take the Anglican communion and, by the new Test Act's provisions, resigned as Lord High Admiral.

More broadly, the secret subsidies sent from Louis XIV's court provided significant, but erratic, financial support to Charles's court. Between 1671 and 1677, a total of around £700,000 was received, with a further £322,500 between 1681 and 1685. Discreetly deposited with

London bankers and made payable to Charles's trusted Page of the Backstairs, William Chiffinch, the subsidies were a risky liability. Nevertheless, compared to the size of potential parliamentary subsidies sought from Westminster and the expansion of ordinary crown revenue from flourishing customs and excise receipts, hearth tax income, rents from crown lands and wine licences during the 1670s, the total value of French subsidies never exceeded a single year's ordinary revenue, bearing 'more the appearance of pin-money than of a serious contribution to the royal finances'.[56]

As pressure mounted on Louis to open negotiations with the Dutch, Sir Joseph Williamson and Sir Leoline Jenkins were dispatched to represent English interests at peace talks convened in Cologne in the spring of 1673. On arrival, Williamson recorded advice from their French counterpart, Honoré Courtin, that the main Dutch negotiator, Hieronymus van Beverningh, had 'a Republican complexion' and was 'a little hot, especially upon wine, ergo to be dealt with in the morning only', though advantage could be obtained when the Dutchman was thus 'a little fuddled, [and] apt to talk and even to drop his own senses'.[57] Fearing that the Dutch Republic faced evisceration by French conquest, the Middelburg-based nonconformist divine and lexicographer Joseph Hill urged the Dutch to make peace with England in *The Interest of these United Provinces* (1673). Warning that 'France's design is absolutely to conquer us: whereas England seeks only (to use their expression) their own security', Hill reminded English readers of Elizabethan support for Dutch independence and the mutual benefits that would accrue from peacetime trade. To Hill's mind, 'England had better lose Scotland or Ireland, than let the French have these provinces'.[58] Immediate prospects for peace with England were, however, effectively nullified by the Quadruple Alliance agreed in August 1673 in which Spain, the Holy Roman Emperor Leopold I and the exiled Duke Charles IV of Lorraine joined the United Provinces in an attempt to prevent Dutch obliteration. Having arrived in London the previous spring, the Spanish ambassador Pedro Fernández de Velasco y Tovar, marquis of Fresno, was observed by Venetian secretary Alberti loudly objecting that, as matters stood, 'England was the only power in the world that did not oppose the violence of France' as Charles's ministers took 'all that the Ambassador Colbert says for gospel'. As Alberti added, Fresno 'spoke in a tone implying that he had orders from Spain to make himself heard all over London'.[59]

When the English Parliament reconvened in October 1673, a palpable escalation in anti-French rhetoric was evident, fuelled by reports that a proxy marriage had been agreed between James, duke of York, and an Italian princess, Mary of Modena, after the duke's original choice, the archduchess Claudia Felicitas of Innsbruck, had married Emperor Leopold I. A proxy marriage had, in fact, taken place in September in Rome at which Henry Mordaunt, earl of Peterborough, had deputized for York. In a Commons address requesting that his brother's marriage to the 'Princess of Modena should be not consummated' when the fifteen-year-old bride arrived in England, MPs made clear to Charles that they were more concerned by Mary of Modena's close connections to the French court than by her Catholicism, which had not been regarded as an insuperable obstacle in relation to the archduchess.[60] Sir William Coventry starkly warned that 'France is too big' and England's duty was to preserve a Continental balance of power. Waiting 'till all Flanders be gone' would be to follow the regrettable precedent of Charles's grandfather James VI & I 'in the Palatinate War' when the king had sought only to 'treat, and treat, till all was gone, and nobody to treat with him'.[61] Indeed, at the opening of Parliament, a disillusioned lawyer, John Ayloffe, had entered the Commons chamber and thrown an object under the Speaker's chair. An attendant, 'imagining it had been a fireball, cried out "Treason!" Treason!"' The symbolic object was a *sabot* – a French wooden shoe – with the arms of Louis XIV carved on one side and those of Charles II on the other, and a motto *utrum horum mavis accipe* ('take whichever of these you prefer') and a Catholic rosary attached to the shoe's heel.[62]

To persuade Charles to conclude peace with the Dutch, the Spanish ambassador Fresno sponsored the dissemination of copies of likely peace terms among MPs and peers. Writing to the Irish Lord Lieutenant, Arthur Capel, earl of Essex, on Christmas Day, Temple rued that 'our present story seems to be that the Court will upon no terms fall out with the French alliance, and the nation will upon no terms fall in with it'. In William Temple's view, the court's refusal to change course reflected not only the duke of York's influence, but also 'the dread of having all that has passed between them and France published if they anger France, and how this will be remedied, God of Heaven knows'.[63]

By the time Parliament reconvened in January 1674, Charles resorted to outright lies in trying to defend the indefensible, protesting that his relations with Louis's court had 'been very strangely misrepresented to you, as if there were certain secret articles of dangerous consequence'. Referring only to the sanitized version of the Dover treaty publicly agreed in December 1670, Charles mendaciously sought to 'assure you there is no other treaty with France, either before or since, not already printed, which shall not be made known'.[64] Although the king's speech ran to just over a hundred words in length – and could only have taken around a minute to read aloud – one peer who observed Charles's demeanour informed Essex in Dublin that despite representing 'the consultation of many days and nights', the king had 'fumbled in delivering it, and made it worse than in the print', rendering his claims simply 'incoherent'.[65]

A manuscript memorandum circulating among MPs and peers declared it 'high time' to address the question of Charles's successor to 'secure us and our posterities from those bloody massacres and inhuman Smithfield butcheries' that would be 'the certain consequences of a Popish government'. Arranging for York's eldest daughter Mary to marry her Protestant Dutch cousin William of Orange would ensure that 'all future disputes about the crown will be quieted'.[66] Amid reports that York had counselled his brother to avoid public criticism by refusing to reconvene Parliament, Charles believed, as Alberti put it, that 'it would be fatal for the kings of England' to appear to act repressively against their subjects. Wistfully deploying imagery familiar to Newmarket's horse-racing turf, Charles had, rather, 'determined to give the people an open field in order to curb them the better when they were tired with their gallop', especially since opposition MPs 'had not yet meddled with any of the royal prerogatives'.[67] Realizing that further French gallops would be futile and aware that Dutch peace terms seemed generous, Charles sanctioned negotiations that produced, remarkably quickly, the Treaty of Westminster signed in February 1674. Largely confirming the Treaty of Breda's provisions from 1667, the treaty's conclusion also allowed a prompt prorogation of the rambunctious English Parliament.

As peace with the Dutch prompted civic rejoicing, popular Francophobia intensified. In an anonymous poem, 'Britannia and Rawleigh', probably written in early 1674, the character of 'Britannia' bitterly explained that 'A colony of French Possess the Court', surrounding Charles and in his 'sacred ear Tyrannical Arts they Croak, / Pervert his mind, his good Intentions Choke'. While the French, 'Thus Fairy-like the King they steal away, / And in his place a Louis Changeling lay', the desperate hope of Sir Walter Ralegh's ghost that Charles might be reclaimed if reminded of his father's fate was dismissed by 'Britannia', who regretted that 'too long in vain, I've tried / The Stuart from the Tyrant to divide'.[68] At the opening of the new Drury Lane Theatre in March 1674, England's first Poet Laureate, John Dryden, even imagined a second Norman conquest in his public denunciation of French influence in drama and culture, fearing that 'Old English authors vanish, and give place / To these new conquerors of the Norman race'.[69] In his comedy *Marriage A-la-Mode*, first performed in 1673, Dryden had articulated similar fears of national eclipse, when the character Leonidas was asked, 'what French invasion have you found to fear?' Without denying military conquest or Catholic conversion, the play's characters seemed equally worried about likely linguistic and cultural erosion as Rhodophil claimed that an Englishwoman's fascination with foreign neologisms rendered her 'the very mint of the nation; and as fast as any bullion comes out of France, [she] coins it immediately into our language'. Dryden's play also implied that Gallic influences were of deceptively thin veneer as another character disparaged French poetry as the 'very leaf-gold of wit, the very wafers and whipped cream of sense, for which a man opens his mouth and gapes, to swallow nothing'.[70]

Following peace with the Dutch, the royal court turned to visual propaganda, as Charles commissioned a series of ten Mortlake tapestries for Windsor Castle, known as *The Sea-Fights*, which echoed tapestries commissioned by James VI & I to celebrate the Spanish Armada's defeat. Each measuring thirty-six by twenty-four feet and designed by the Dutch draughtsmen Willem van de Velde the Elder and the Younger, five of the new tapestries depicted the Battle of Lowestoft (1665) and five commemorated the Battle of Solebay (1672).[71] To reinforce the Treaty of Westminster's confirmation of England's maritime dominance, Antonio Verrio's enormous baroque painting *The Sea Triumph of Charles II* (1674) presented Charles as a Roman emperor, attended by his Navy and driven through the waves by Neptune and four sea horses (Plate 18).

With England now a neutral observer of Franco-Dutch hostilities, when Parliament reconvened between April and June 1675, pressure mounted for the government to recall all of Charles's subjects still serving in Louis's forces amid fears that overseas regiments might yet be retained for deployment in England. As party rivalries intensified, Viscount Conway described a Commons division tied at 135 votes for and against the forces' recall, whereupon 'both parties thinking themselves wronged in the reckoning called one another all the opprobrious names imaginable, spit in one another's faces, pulled off one another's periwigs, and were drawing their swords' before the Speaker restored order.[72] For the anti-French coalition still fighting, England's withdrawal from the conflict seemingly made little difference, as French troops overran the Spanish province of Franche-Comté in 1676 and Dutch troops failed to recapture the strategic stronghold of Maastricht.

Dynastic diplomacy and military strategy thereafter converged, as Charles sought to present himself as a suitable mediator, simultaneously able to promote Franco-Dutch peace terms alongside private discussions regarding the potential marriage of his Dutch nephew William of Orange, who was fourth-in-line to the British thrones, to his first cousin, the duke of York's eldest daughter, Mary, who was second-in-line. Having accepted another diplomatic posting to The Hague in 1675, Temple became a trusted conduit for Anglo-Dutch negotiations and described a stony audience with the prince in January 1677. After William 'began with telling me I had spoiled his dinner', Temple recalled the prince's objections to his uncle's suggested peace terms – which would have confirmed a number of key French conquests, including Franche-Comté – on the grounds that 'if Flanders must be lost, it had better be so by a war than by peace'. The prince also resented being patronized by Secretary Williamson, claiming that peace proposals were framed 'in a style as if he thought him a child, or to be fed with whipped cream'. Since the proposals had been approved by Charles's Foreign Committee, William alleged of the French ambassador in London, Henri de Massue, marquis of Ruvigny, that the terms were his, and 'a great deal worse than they could have [been] directly from France'. But by the summer of 1676, the Dutch had suffered further territorial losses, while the possibility that the duchess of York's latest pregnancy might produce a Catholic male heir to supplant Mary's hereditary claim alarmed the English populace. When the Dutch prince visited London that autumn, he insisted that peace terms be negotiated separately from his marriage. Boasting of his physiognomic skills, Charles was moved to declare 'if I am not deceived in the Prince's face, he is the honestest man in the world, and I will trust him, and he shall have his wife'.[73]

On 4 November 1677, William of Orange married his fifteen-year-old cousin, Princess Mary. With hopes rekindled for a future Protestant succession, Charles reportedly closed the curtains of the couple's bridal bed with the exhortation, 'Now, nephew, to your work! Hey! St George for England'![74] The following month, hopes for a Protestant succession were further boosted by the death of the duke of York's new son, Charles, who had been born three days after William and Mary's wedding but died from smallpox on 12 December, just over a week after being visited by his Protestant half-sister Princess Anne, who had been in quarantine with the disease.[75] Although the infant's early death was not regarded as suspicious, the combination of William and Mary's wedding preparations with an announcement that Parliament would be adjourned until 1678 generated other conspiracy theories. Doubts were raised that the Prince of Orange's vaunted Protestantism could yet cloak papist 'shape-shifting'. In October, a Catholic barrister, Richard Langhorne, had observed 'how coldly our malcontents look upon, and how maliciously they speak' of William, believing 'that he is a papist and will certainly declare himself to be so whenever the French king shall give him directions'.[76]

Shortly after the royal marriage, pope-burnings were held to commemorate Elizabeth I's accession, which reflecting an increasingly entrenched and pervasive popular anti-Catholicism, included an effigy of a pope with a string of Dutch oranges around its neck, holding a paper peace treaty reading 'France helps me above all'. Inscribed on to the citrus rosary was the slogan 'What the great duke of Alva could not do will be done by the skirts of a woman', recalling the attempted eradication of Protestantism from the Spanish Netherlands in the 1560s and 1570s by the provinces' former Governor Fernando Álvarez de Toledo, third duke of Alba. That William of Orange could appear in the guise of a papal effigy would doubtless surprise today's Orangemen in Northern Ireland, accustomed to civil murals celebrating the Dutch prince's legendary status as Protestant victor in the Battle of the Boyne in 1690.

19
Devils who intend my ruin, 1678–1683

On the eve of the anniversary of Charles I's execution, nearly thirty years earlier, MPs in the House of Commons passed a vote of thanks on 29 January 1678 for Charles II's 'great care of the Protestant religion' in marrying his niece Princess Mary to her Dutch Calvinist cousin William of Orange. A further motion was approved, proposing 'a more decent and solemn interment' of William and Mary's shared grandfather, Charles I, whose hasty burial in a makeshift grave in St George's Chapel at Windsor contrasted uncomfortably with the elaborate marble canopy tomb erected by James VI & I in Westminster Abbey for the reburial of his executed mother and Charles I's grandmother Mary, Queen of Scots. As Surveyor of the King's Works, Sir Christopher Wren produced plans for a magnificent double-storeyed, domed rotunda tomb, stylistically echoing Inigo Jones's catafalque for James VI & I with a projected cost of over £43,000. Despite parliamentary wrangling over Charles II's requests for financial subsidies, poet and MP for Hastings Edmund Waller acclaimed plans for Charles I's reburial as a project that was also conducive to 'bury all the jealousies between the king and us'.[1]

Deteriorating relations between crown and Parliament nevertheless frustrated passage of the required Subsidy Bill and left Wren's projected mausoleum sadly unbuilt. As Charles relied instead on his secret payments from Louis XIV to remain solvent, anxieties attaching to the crown's Francophile foreign policy fuelled panic as allegations were uncovered, in the late summer of 1678, of a 'Popish Plot' to assassinate the king and install his Catholic brother and heir, James, duke of York, on the throne. Fallout from the Popish Plot escalated into a full-blown succession crisis and a bill demanding York's removal from the royal line of succession passed its second reading in the Commons in May

1679. That same month, the loss of government control over the press unleashed a torrent of critical comment, following the unanticipated expiry of the Licensing Act which had prohibited all materials from being printed without pre-publication approval. A growth in popular punditry saw 'little citizens become (in their own opinion) statesmen, and instead of minding their shops and businesses' turn to devising 'fit instruments to be set up to carry on their little policies against the established government and laws'.[2]

As arguments were marshalled to preclude a Catholic from succeeding as king of England, historical memories stretched beyond Charles I's execution to the late sixteenth-century Elizabethan succession crisis. In 1584, the Dutch Stadtholder William of Orange – also known as 'William the Silent' – had been murdered by a Catholic assassin, in the same year as discovery of the Throckmorton Plot in England had become the latest popish conspiracy to envisage killing Elizabeth and replacing her as queen with her Catholic cousin Mary Stuart. Elizabeth's councillors had suggested a Bond of Association that was comprehended within the Act for the Queen's Safety (1584), which prescribed penalties for individuals convicted of plotting against the monarch. Addressing the Commons in 1680, the Welsh MP Edward Vaughan warned that he did not wish 'to speak in masquerade. The case is now with the king, as it was betwixt Queen Elizabeth and Mary, Queen of Scots' and 'we ought not to hazard the king's life under such a temptation'.[3] The poet John Dryden denied that there had ever been a 'plainer parallel than of the troubles of France, and of Great Britain', perceiving that '1584 and 1684 have but a century and a sea between them, to be the same'.[4] In the French case, since the Catholic League's determination to prevent the Protestant Henri of Navarre from succeeding as king of France had been solved by Henri's subsequent conversion to Catholicism, hopes remained that York might yet be persuaded to reconvert to Protestantism. Other scenarios included appointing a Protestant regent to exercise monarchical power in York's place with the duke's daughter Mary, his Dutch Stadtholder son-in-law William of Orange, and Charles's eldest natural son James, duke of Monmouth, the most likely candidates.

As Elizabethan polemic was repurposed for a Restoration audience, *A Conference About the Next Succession to the Crown of England*, first published in 1594 by the English Jesuit Robert Persons, was reprinted verbatim in 1681. Without mentioning York's name, John Somers's

Brief History of the Succession (1681) drew on Persons's constitutional history to declare it 'the constant opinion of all ages that the Parliament of England had an unquestionable power to limit, restrain and qualify the succession as they pleased, and that in all ages they have put their power in practice'.[5] If public debate about the royal succession had been successfully silenced under Elizabeth, by Charles II's reign it had become a damaging cacophony.

I

In 1677, Charles had hoped that Princess Mary's marriage to William of Orange would foster improved relations with his English Parliament. In the United Provinces, the marriage served to resuscitate internal divisions between Orangist and republican factions, as William envisaged his marriage bringing increased military resources to fight France, while his republican 'Louvenstein' opponents sought to curb Orangist power by supporting the peace negotiations that had started at Nijmegen in 1676. English and papal representatives were designated as official mediators at Nijmegen, despite English forces having fired the opening shots against the Dutch in 1672. By the spring of 1677, Charles's ambitious ambassador in Paris, Ralph Montagu, was doubting the wisdom of the English king 'being styled the mediator' and suggested to Lord Treasurer Thomas Osborne, earl of Danby, that Charles should instead be 'sole arbiter of the peace' and demanded that 'all the parties concerned send their ambassadors and treat at London, or else fight dog, fight bear'. Montagu also predicted that, at Nijmegen, the French negotiators would be confident in 'the partiality they think the king has for them', while the Dutch 'will be fools enough to think they shall find theirs by the partiality of the people' in England.[6]

French confidence in the English king's 'partiality' had nevertheless been shaken by Charles's decision to marry his niece Mary to Louis XIV's inveterate enemy, William of Orange. Before the wedding, the new French ambassador to London, Paul Barillon d'Amoncourt, marquis of Branges, reported that Charles had defended the match as a means of deflecting anti-French criticism. For whereas in 1667 the English people had regarded 'all the conquests that were made in Flanders with indifference, and cared little about them', after the duke of York's conversion to Catholicism became public knowledge, 'all England has been in motion, and apprehensive that I have other designs' to undermine the country's Protestant establishment.[7]

To this end, Charles sought to devise peace terms that would not jeopardize the continuation of the secret French subsidies while also proving acceptable to the Dutch. But after Montagu had suggested that France surrender Condé-sur-l'Escaut, Valenciennes and Tournai, Secretary of State for War François Michel Le Tellier, marquis of Louvois, informed him in December 1677 that Louis 'would make war [for] a hundred years rather than part with them'. Determined that Charles should not recall the bellicose English Parliament, Louvois had confirmed that, if the problem remained 'your Majesty's great want of money, there was no sum you could desire' that would not be found. Confident that 'you could stop their [MPs'] mouths with a general truce for a year', Louvois had admitted that a massive payment 'would be hard to return, but it should be put into wedges of gold, and so put into bales of silk and sent over in a yacht'.[8] The following month, Charles's Breton mistress, Louise de Kéroualle (now duchess of Portsmouth) tried a different tack by suggesting to Barillon that the southern Netherlands town of Ypres might be yielded to France, if Tournai, Valenciennes and Condé were returned to Spain. Although Barillon doubted Ypres's strategic value, he reported to the French court that Portsmouth had persisted and 'smiling, she told me: we have looked at the map, the King of England and I' and although she had 'argued for a long time against him . . . finally he convinced me that Ypres was as considerable as Tournai'. Asking whether he should thereby infer that Charles approved of this proposal, Barillon was reassured by Portsmouth that 'she would not wish for anything in the world that it was thought she interfered in politics'.[9]

Frustrated by repeated French attempts to prolong the Nijmegen negotiations, both Houses of Parliament issued a joint declaration in March 1678 insisting that England should re-enter the conflict, but this time by declaring war on France and allying with the Dutch. Suspecting that MPs' fervour might not be matched by sufficient funds, the Dutch ambassador in London, Conrad van Beuningen, had audaciously informed Charles that 'since the parliament had so boldly addressed against all his ministers', he no longer knew whether further appeals should be made 'to him or them', but, as a courtier observed, 'the jest was not well pleasing' to the king.[10] Although Charles agreed further secret subsidies with Barillon in May, he simultaneously directed Sir William Temple to conclude an Anglo-Dutch agreement in July that bound England to declare war on France if treaty terms were not forthcoming. Admitting to Irish Lord Deputy James Butler, duke of Ormond, that negotiating this new Anglo-Dutch alliance had been 'the hardest pinch of business that ever befell me in my life', Temple acknowledged 'a strange change of style in the world' whereby Charles was 'once more at the head of affairs in Christendom'. In a remarkable year that would see three solar and two lunar eclipses, Temple conceded that predicting the upshot of 'this conjuncture is in the stars'.[11] Ultimately, both sides simply ignored Charles's attempted mediation. Louis concluded separate agreements with the Dutch and their Confederate allies as part of the Treaty of Nijmegen which significantly expanded French territory along the country's north-eastern border, prompting a disillusioned Temple to concede that he had never known 'any negotiation managed, with greater address and skill, than this had been by the French in the whole course of the affair'.[12] Unsurprisingly, neither Temple nor any other English mediator featured in Henri Gascard's triumphal painting, *The Signing of the Peace between France and Spain* (*c.*1678), commissioned by Louis and now displayed at Nijmegen's Museum Het Valkhof.

In England, fears of French domination and Catholic encirclement were exacerbated by discovery of another 'Popish Plot'. In August 1678, a clerical informer, Israel Tonge, and a renegade priest, Titus Oates, presented the monarch with 'revelations', claiming to have infiltrated a Jesuit plot to assassinate Charles and replace him as king with his brother to ensure England's return to Catholicism (Plate 21). Although Charles himself coolly assured Parliament that he would 'leave the matter to the law', critics of the court's Francophile inclinations made capital from the rumours and quickly convinced themselves of the Plot's veracity.[13] Circumstantial details added credibility to the Plot, especially after the magistrate to whom Oates had sworn a deposition, Sir Edmund Berry Godfrey, was found murdered in October. In a funeral sermon for Godfrey, the dean of Bangor, William Lloyd, blamed the Jesuits and offered thanks that, at least this time, the king remained unharmed, trusting that God who 'saved us in Eighty-Eight [1588]' and 'saved us from the Gunpowder Plot ... will deliver us from this cursed conspiracy'.[14] While this new Popish Plot easily fitted into a narrative of previous Catholic attempts, including Philip II's Armada, Guy Fawkes's Gunpowder Plot and the Great Fire of London, concerns about the royal court's possible involvement were prompted by discovery of incriminating letters sent from York's former secretary Edward Coleman to influential Continental contacts, including Louis XIV's confessors, Jean Ferrier and François de la Chaise, seeking financial subsidies to promote Catholic interests.

As popular hysteria escalated, Catholics were banned from London and searches for priests conducted across England. The Oxford cleric Charles Allestree recalled how 'all of us' were 'possessed with a dreadful expectation of having our throats cut by papists in a sudden insurrection, which was to be made and assisted with an invasion of the French'.[15] A Dorset barrister, William Lawrence, observed his neighbours professing 'great courage and resolution to fight the enemy' that was reported to have landed in December, but local disorganization had left them 'in such a confusion, they knew not who was to command, or who to obey' as he regretted seeing 'so many stout men so unarmed, undisciplined and unprovided as they were'.[16] That same month, a Yorkshire magistrate, Henry Layton, wrote to Secretary of State Sir Joseph Williamson confirming that, with news 'of the great Popish Plot, the crack and noise filled us with great visions and the apparitions of armed men assembled and riding by night'. Although searches had established 'that all such rumours were vain and false', Layton reported persistent claims 'that Spaniards are landed in Ireland and 5,000 of them got over into Wales, that French are landed in Scotland and more ready to be transported into England from Dunkirk', with foreign invasion enabled since 'all the big ships at Chatham or elsewhere are to be burnt'.[17]

In 1679, a new edition of Samuel Clarke's *England's Remembrancer*, first published in 1657, reminded readers of England's narrow escape from Philip II's Armada in 1588. Clarke described gigantic Spanish galleons, 'like floating towers and castles, so that the swelling waves of the sea could hardly be seen; and the flags, streamers and ensigns so spread in the wind, that they seemed even to darken the sun'.[18] Publication of Oates's allegations in April 1679 also detailed plans for Ireland's subjugation to the 'tyranny of the Pope and French' with foreign funds and arms facilitating 'a general rebellion and massacre of the Protestants as formerly', reigniting traumatic memories of the Ulster Rebellion in 1641.[19] Depending on the partisan lens adopted, the Popish Plot was either the latest manifestation of an international Catholic conspiracy or a fabricated fiction conducive to cynical manipulation. In Dublin, Ormond resisted alarmist pressure from the Lord President of Munster, Roger Boyle, earl of Orrery, to impose extensive security measures throughout Ireland, dismissing Orrery's anxieties as 'but a storm in a cream bowl'.[20] In London, Chief Justice Sir Francis North observed the Plot's traction with scepticism, compiling directions to Charles's government 'for undeceiving the people about the late Popish Plot'. As North observed, it was in opponents' interests to foment public anxiety: 'to make the name more odious, the Plot must be magnified, and the posts and chains set up in the City, and the trained bands up every night, to the citizens' immense charge, who were in so real (though senseless) a fright that they bore it very patiently'.[21]

Fears that the official version of England's foreign policy commitments was a sham were, however, dramatically stoked when in December 1678 Charles's erstwhile – but now embittered – ambassador to Paris, Montagu, read aloud in the House of Commons two letters he had received from Lord Treasurer Danby earlier that year. In the second letter, dated 25 March – only days after Parliament had approved funds to fight a war *against* the French – Danby had confirmed that, if English peace proposals were accepted by Louis, Charles 'expects to have six millions of livres a year, for three years . . . because it will probably be two or three years before the Parliament will be in the humour to give him any supplies, after the making any peace with France'. But if Louis declined the proposals, Montagu was 'not to mention the money at all'; indeed, 'all possible care must be taken to have this whole negotiation as private as is possible'.[22] Charles had already been alerted to the ambassador's questionable loyalty by his former mistress Barbara Villiers, countess of Castlemaine, whose recent affair with Montagu had soured after the ambassador had also seduced Castlemaine's teenage daughter by the king, Anne, countess of Sussex. Having warned Charles that their daughter's notoriety was the focus of Parisian gossip, Castlemaine added that Montagu 'despised you and your brother' and 'wished with all his heart the parliament would send you both to travel, for you were a dull, governable fool and the duke a wilful fool'.[23]

It was, moreover, not only Charles and his ministers who were in receipt of covert foreign subsidies as Montagu had himself been promised a French pension if he successfully engineered the anti-French Danby's removal as Lord Treasurer. Forewarned of Montagu's intention to embarrass Charles, Barillon had written to the French king acknowledging that 'although no-one can ever be sure of anything in this country', Louis had, after all, 'commanded me to do everything that is possible to raise troubles to the king of England'.[24] To this end, the French government sanctioned subsidies to Charles's court while simultaneously bribing republican factions, in both London and Amsterdam, that sought to curb royal power of either Stuart or Orange hue. In October 1678, Barillon had confided to Louis that 'just at the moment, my most intimate liaison is with Mr Algernon Sidney', identifying the staunch republican as 'the man in England who seems to me to have the greatest understanding of affairs'.[25] The anonymous author of *A Letter from Amsterdam to a Friend in England* (1678) described Britain as 'either the floating island, or founded upon quicksilver' in terms of its mutable foreign attachments, suspecting that the 'charging of *pistoles* [gold coins] by a French hand, may sometimes do more than all their cannon'. Having reassured Barillon that Charles sought French subsidies as a means to increase the crown's financial independence from Parliament, and not to restart hostilities against France, Sidney received 500 guineas from Barillon between December 1678 and March 1679, and a similar amount a year later.[26]

Meanwhile, for those not privy to inside intelligence or lucrative bribes, Montagu's revelations in the Commons had provoked outrage. The Bristol MP Sir John Knight demanded Danby's impeachment, rueing that hundreds of thousands of pounds had been voted for a war against France 'and yet we had no war! Money given to disband the army, and that not done! The Popish Plot discovered at that time! And all runs parallel.'[27] To prevent further damaging revelations emerging in an impeachment process against Danby, Charles dissolved Parliament and called a General Election for the first time since 1661. As the Essex clergyman and diarist Ralph Josselin reported, popular anti-government animus seemed so pervasive that even the king had reportedly ventured that 'the country would choose a dog if he stood against a courtier'.[28] Recalled from The Hague in February 1679, Temple was informed by William of Orange that Charles 'was in his heart a Roman Catholic, though he durst not profess it'. Unsure what to believe, Temple feared, on returning to England, that 'from such contrary winds and tides, such a storm must rise, as would tear the ship [of state] to pieces, whatever hand was at the helm'.[29] Meanwhile, James, duke of York, found himself sailing in the opposite direction towards a temporary exile in the Spanish Netherlands, as growing numbers of government critics insisted that the nation's Protestant establishment simply could not withstand the accession of a Catholic monarch.

II

Opening the new English Parliament at Westminster on 6 March 1679, Charles confirmed that he had ordered his brother's relocation to Brussels to avoid malicious accusations of acceding to 'popish counsels'. Rather, Charles hoped that the fresh assembly of MPs would prove a 'healing Parliament', while insisting that 'I will, with my life, defend both the Protestant religion, and the laws of this kingdom'. Repeatedly intoning that 'this is the time', Sir Heneage Finch, the Lord Chancellor, directed MPs to focus on securing Protestant interests, maintaining monarchical authority, desisting from factional division and fostering domestic unity.[30] Finch's rhetoric lent itself to irresistible imitation and was reworked in manuscript rejoinders that asked

Would you send Kate to Portugal,
Great James to be a cardinal,
And make Prince Rupert admiral?
This is the time.

With Charles's Palatine cousin Prince Rupert associated with the 'Country opposition' and pressure on Charles to divorce 'Queen Kate' in order to marry a Protestant, the verses ran on

Would you bless our English nation,
By changing of Queen Kate's vocation
And find one fit for procreation?
This is the time.[31]

Notwithstanding entreaties to MPs to be compliant, differences ran deep. George Savile, marquess of Halifax, wrote to his brother Henry, who was serving as an English envoy in Paris, describing himself 'engaged in an active and angry world'.[32] During a Commons debate on the safety of Protestantism under a Catholic monarch, Sir John Knight declared the prospect 'as inconsistent as light and darkness' and predicted that 'if the Pope gets his great toe into England, all his body will follow'. For the Cornish MP Hugh Boscawen, a Catholic king of England would ensure that 'the whole Protestant religion in Europe is struck at'. Deeming England's Protestant future precarious, Boscawen admitted that 'Popery and French government are almost checkmate with us'. MPs were aware that depriving York of his hereditary right might also encourage him to seek foreign military assistance to claim his crown by force and recognized that their legislative remit only applied to England. Accordingly, as Secretary of State Henry Coventry warned, if the Scots 'set him up for king, whom you acknowledge not', the Scots would become 'such a thorn in your sides, by the help of France, that you will never be able to get it out'.[33] At a visibly well-attended session on 21 May 1679, a bill denying York's right to succeed his brother as king passed its second reading by 207 votes to 128, stipulating that, on Charles's death, the English crown would pass to the next-in-line of succession as if York were dead: Mary of Orange. But the bill's legislative progress was thereafter halted when, six days later, Charles prorogued, and subsequently dissolved, Parliament.

Fretting in his Brussels exile, York was naturally alarmed and wrote to his son-in-law and nephew William of Orange that events in England risked taking such an extreme course that, unless Charles acceded to MPs' demands and effectively became 'less than a duke of Venice, it is my opinion they will fly out into an open rebellion'. Hoping that his brother would 'take courage and at last be a king', York suspected that, otherwise, MPs who 'pretend to lay aside one [royal heir] for his religion, may as well lay aside another for some fancy or another'. Unaware that Parliament had been dissolved, York reiterated his anxieties ten days later, hoping that, if nothing else, events had ensured that 'not only his Majesty's eyes, but all the honest men's eyes are opened' to 'see that a commonwealth is what is driven at' by those who claimed only to be protecting Protestantism.[34]

In Scotland, sectarian violence erupted after Presbyterian Covenanters brutally murdered the head of the established church, Archbishop James Sharp of St Andrews, on 3 May 1679. The following month, government forces, led by Charles's natural son James Scott, duke of Monmouth, suppressed the Covenanters' rebellion at the Battle of

Bothwell Bridge in Lanarkshire in June. In London, Charles impressed on Barillon that Louis XIV needed to decide 'whether he wanted a republic or a monarchy in England': without further French subsidies, there seemed little to 'prevent parliament taking over control of foreign affairs and everything else'.[35]

An actual succession crisis then became imminent when Charles contracted a malarial-type fever in August 1679, prompting York to leave Brussels and return to London. Faced with the prospect of the king's death at such an uncertain juncture, Henry Savile wrote from Paris to the English ambassador in The Hague, Henry Sidney, admitting 'Good God, what a change would such an accident make! The very thought of it frights me out of my wits.' But within days, Sidney – whose loyalism starkly contrasted with the republicanism of his older brother Algernon – had received reassurance from Windsor that Charles was recovering, having 'exchanged water-gruels and potions for muttons and partridges, on which he feeds frequently and heartily'. The dynastic alarm had nevertheless clearly sounded. Visiting England that autumn, Sidney's nephew Robert Spencer, earl of Sunderland, confirmed that, had the king died, it had been feared that Monmouth 'would have made great troubles, either setting up for himself, or for a commonwealth'.[36] To stem the traction attaching to his son as a popular Protestant alternative to his Catholic uncle, Charles ordered Monmouth to leave England for Utrecht, while York returned to Brussels, before being sent to Edinburgh later that year.

Often identified as the predicament that created Britain's two-party political system, the Restoration succession crisis pitted Tory loyalists against Whig opponents, both parties incurring monikers originally intended as terms of abuse: a 'Tory' denoting an outlawed Irish robber and a 'Whig' a rebellious Scots Presbyterian Covenanter. A second General Election held in October 1679 returned a majority of MPs known to favour York's exclusion, but serial prorogations ensured that the assembly did not meet for another twelve months. Meanwhile, partisan politics moved to the streets as elaborate pope-burning processions were organized to mark the November anniversaries of the Gunpowder Plot's discovery and Elizabeth I's accession. Papal effigies were paraded through London's streets by citizens dressed up as devils or Catholic priests, with newspaper reports claiming that 200,000 spectators witnessed the effigy's burning at Temple Bar.[37] Attributed to the Whig freethinker Charles Blount, *An Appeal from the Country to the City* (1679) was only one of several tracts that perpetuated Popish Plot panic by inviting readers to envisage the violent persecution of Protestants that would accompany a Catholic succession: 'troops of papists, ravishing your wives and your daughters, dashing your little children's brains out against the walls, plundering your houses and cutting your own throats, by the name of heretic dogs'. As a Protestant alternative, Blount insisted that 'no person is fitter' than the king's son Monmouth, whose 'life and fortune depends upon the same bottom' as the people; indeed, 'he who hath the worst title, ever makes the best king'.[38]

Whig hostility was also directed towards Charles's Catholic mistress, Portsmouth, who had effectively become a Whitehall equivalent of the French court's position of *maîtresse-en-titre*, controlling courtiers' access to the king and presiding over patronage appointments while providing the French ambassador with regular intelligence and access to Charles. By January 1680, articles of intended impeachment had been framed against Portsmouth, echoing accusations once levelled against Charles I's unpopular favourite, George Villiers, duke of Buckingham, in the 1620s. Presented by the Whig leader, Anthony Ashley Cooper, earl of Shaftesbury, before a Middlesex Grand Jury during the summer of 1681, the articles included charges that Portsmouth 'intermeddled and advised in matters of the highest moment and importance in government, as peace and war; several dissolutions and prorogations of parliament'. Moreover, the duchess's energetic promotion of Anglo-French amity rendered 'ineffectual those frequent addresses in parliament for a war with the French king', while Portsmouth herself commanded 'absolute dominion and power over the king's heart' and had regular 'opportunity to draw from him the secrets of his government'.[39] Shaftesbury's attempt to impeach the duchess for treasonable conduct was forestalled by Lord Chief Justice Sir William Scroggs's rejection of the indictment, but Portsmouth's compliance was secured through her subsequent decision to support exclusion.

To appease his Whig critics, Charles also sought to end England's diplomatic isolation and form foreign alliances aimed at curtailing French expansionism. Aware that Charles was dispatching envoys to German states and other territories, Barillon was unsure how much of the king's activity was intended solely as a means of assuaging public opinion, admitting to Louis in March 1680 that 'it would be very difficult to explain to Your Majesty what is the real design of the king of England and his ministers'.[40] In the Dutch Republic, an English agent known as 'Mr Freeman' prepared a memorandum calling for an international coalition, warning that disarmament after the Nijmegen peace treaty potentially let France 'insult over the world, by a peace more tyrannical than the war of a gallant enemy'. Through covert financial subsidies, Louis had secured 'the supine negligence of England', giving the French repeated English parliamentary 'prorogations there for their money, till they have eaten up the rest of Europe as they eat bread'. 'Freeman' exhorted England and the Dutch to join forces 'not only to preserve the rest of the Spanish Netherlands from falling into the hands of France, but to make him vomit up what he has already swallowed of them'.[41]

Following the arrival in London of a new Spanish ambassador, Don Pedro Ronquillo, an Anglo-Spanish alliance was concluded in June 1680 that committed both powers to assisting one another if requested, as the administration in Madrid feared renewed French attacks on the Spanish Netherlands. The day after its signing, Sir Leoline Jenkins, who had assumed office as Secretary of State in April, emphasized the agreement's defensive character and instructed Charles's envoy in Vienna, Bevil Skelton, 'not to make any boast or flourish of this treaty' to ensure that 'no jealousy nor umbrage to any neighbour prince' might arise.[42] But in The Hague, representatives from Amsterdam refused to sanction the Dutch States General joining the new Anglo-Spanish alliance, deeming England's domestic political situation too unstable. Writing to Sidney in July, Jenkins objected to foreign newsletters asserting 'that we are represented there as if we were already in a flame'. While English affairs were 'as still and peaceable as ever they were', Jenkins was frustrated that 'we are pelted at with impudent, horrid libels'.[43] Sir Robert Southwell, the English envoy in Berlin, likewise complained three times that summer to Elector Frederick William of Brandenburg that the local gazette was reporting that the new English Parliament had been dissolved, whereas in reality it had not even sat.[44]

When the Westminster Parliament eventually met in October 1680, the king's opening speech warned that 'all Europe have their eyes upon this assembly, and think their own happiness or misery, as well as ours, will depend upon it'. Charles reiterated his readiness to approve any measures designed to protect Protestantism that did not divert the line of hereditary succession. If divisions ensued, Charles insisted that 'the world will see it was no fault of mine; for I have done all that was possible for me to do, to keep you in peace while I live, and to leave you so when I die'.[45] Only five days later, however, the Tewkesbury MP Sir Henry Capel denounced foreign interference in England's domestic affairs. Capel resented Barillon's visibility at court, objecting that he 'seemed rather one of the family and king's household, than a foreign ambassador'. Enjoying constant 'egress and regress' to the king, Barillon appeared 'rather a prime minister of state of this kingdom, than a councillor to another prince'.[46]

Defying the royal injunction to leave the line of succession intact, a second 'Exclusion' bill was presented to the Commons in November. Opposing the motion, the earl of Clarendon's son Laurence Hyde admitted to hoping that Charles might outlive his brother, but recognized that – since any legislation aimed at excluding James, duke of York, would be rejected by both the House of Lords and the king – 'the short question will be, "whether a civil war is more dangerous than a popish successor?"' Moreover, as any legislation framed at Westminster did not apply to Scotland, the Carlisle MP Christopher Musgrave also feared that exclusion 'may endanger a civil war' and admitted he would 'be glad to have the Borders secured, for my own concern, for I live near them'. As Secretary of State, Jenkins denounced the bill as 'founded upon the same principle and practice of the papists', citing the Catholic League's attempts to debar Henri of Navarre from succeeding as King Henri IV of France. In that instance, French Catholics had, in fact, submitted to Henri's authority, knowing 'they should be in less danger with a heretic prince, than by a civil war if the thing was contended'.[47] Although the bill received Commons approval, it was defeated by sixty-three votes to thirty in the House of Lords, following debates attended in person by Charles. When the duke of Monmouth cited concern for his father's personal safety as the reason for voting in favour of his uncle's exclusion, Charles was heard sourly to observe, 'it is a Judas kiss which he gives me'.[48]

Although Charles was often a pragmatic royal operator, defending hereditary succession to the crown became a key principle over which he refused to compromise, having been deprived of his own British thrones for more than a decade after his father's execution. He refused to accede to repeated entreaties to divorce Queen Catherine, remarry a Protestant queen and produce a legitimate heir. The king also resisted calls to legitimate his eldest natural son, Monmouth, as persistent rumours of a clandestine youthful marriage between Charles and the duke's mother, Lucy Walter, forced him to issue three separate declarations publicly confirming that 'I never was married nor gave any contract to any woman whatsoever but to my wife, Queen Catherine, to whom I am now married.'[49] More radically, in *The Right of Primogeniture, in Succession to the Kingdoms of England, Scotland and Ireland* (1681), the Whig barrister William Lawrence upheld Monmouth's right to succeed on the simple grounds of his being the king's eldest son. Like Elizabeth I, Monmouth's illegitimacy was only defined as such by marriage laws framed by Catholic theologians which served, in practice, to disqualify a Protestant son from succeeding to his father's throne and shifted that right to the son's unpopular, Catholic uncle.[50]

During the summer of 1680, Monmouth himself undertook a series of quasi-royal progresses around southern and western England, visiting Chichester, Bath, Dorset, Wiltshire, Somerset and Devon. Describing the crowds of enthusiastic well-wishers that had flocked to greet Charles's son, one printed account acclaimed Monmouth as 'an example to all the gentry for his loyalty to his king, and love to his country, for being an orthodox Protestant, and a true hospitable lover of our dear true Protestant Englishmen'.[51] While he was on tour, London press reports claimed that Monmouth had also 'touched for the king's evil', presenting his capacity to heal sufferers of the glandular condition scrofula as a means of further promoting his authentically royal lineage and rival claim to succeed his father as king.

Resenting repeated foreign interventions in domestic debates, Charles dispatched two envoys, William Carr and Thomas Plott, to the United Provinces to try to exert greater influence over foreign news reporting. In November 1680, Plott delivered 'a very sharp reprimand' to the *Rotterdam Gazette* for claiming that English affairs were 'in such confusion that a revolt was daily expected'.[52] In The Hague, exchanges between deputies of the Dutch States General and Sidney, the English ambassador, were reproduced in pamphlets to illustrate how Charles's resolute opposition to his brother's exclusion undermined England's credentials as a Protestant bulwark. To Dutch minds, repeated dissolutions of the English Parliament were unsettling for Charles's subjects and, referring to Louis XIV, also served 'to animate foreign powers so strongly armed, to execute their projects'. Accordingly, the Dutch deputies sought to register 'their own unhappiness, that a business so uncertain as is that of a future succession . . . should occasion their entire ruin: and that the interests of Europe, principally of all Protestant princes, and of this state, should be sacrificed for so uncertain a matter'.[53]

Making a similar point, in 1681 the Whig publisher Francis Smith printed *The Last Memorial of the Spanish Ambassador*, which confirmed Ronquillo's alarm at calamitous French depredations on the Continent and his belief that, 'at present, nothing is capable to suppress these evils, but the power of England – at this time, the only in Europe that can restrain the torrent of France'. But as Ronquillo had lamented, so long as domestic divisions persisted in England, there was nothing to inhibit French forces from undertaking 'the conquest of the Low Countries, which is the master-key of the universal monarchy, and the first door which he will open with it, shall be that of England'.[54] Moreover, Ronquillo despaired of being able to match the French payments distributed to pliant courtiers and opposition politicians alike, describing the English as 'the most mercenary people in the world'.[55]

Following defeat of the second Exclusion bill in November 1680, another bill that avoided formal exclusion, but prescribed extensive limitations on a Catholic successor, passed two readings in the Lords. It included a provision to treat James, duke of York, as a minor on his succession, denying him powers of ministerial and military appointment without parliamentary approval, vesting control over foreign policy and Irish affairs in an enlarged Privy Council and, on pain of treason, banning York and his supporters from coming within 500 miles of the British Isles during Charles's life. As York recalled in his posthumously published memoirs, he let his brother know that 'this limitation project [was] worse, if possible, than the bill of exclusion, and would give a greater shock to the monarchy' and 'drop the government more gently into a commonwealth'. To York's mind, 'matters were come to such a head that the monarchy must be either more absolute or quite abolished, that France would be sorry to see England a commonwealth, that Spain desired it, and Holland would not be displeased at it'.[56]

But if republicans in Holland might not mind, the Dutch Stadtholder certainly did. As William warned Secretary of State Jenkins, despite Whig claims that such limitations would only apply to Catholic successors, 'it must not be imagined, that if they had once taken away from the crown such considerable prerogatives as are talked of, that they would ever return again'.[57] Meanwhile, Charles remained aware that pressure was being placed on William to increase his visibility as an alternative successor. Amid the Gunpowder Plot commemorations in November 1680, Anne Spencer, countess of Sunderland, wrote to her brother Henry Sidney in The Hague, exhorting William to visit London, concerned that 'if there be nothing to fix on, 'tis certain the duke of Monmouth must do the thing'. The countess despaired that William evidently 'thinks it not worth going over a threshold for three kingdoms', insisting that there was no longer time for 'more ifs and ands' and wishing 'the prince would not be such an ass'.[58]

In January 1681, Charles terminated the legislative passage of the bill prescribing limitations on a Catholic successor by once again dissolving Parliament and calling fresh elections. Having decided to move parliamentary sessions away from London's febrile and partisan milieu, Charles verbally concluded another secret agreement with Barillon, undertaking to ensure that no English parliament adopted measures against French interests, while Barillon confirmed Louis's willingness to desist from further attacks in the Spanish Netherlands. On 21 March 1681, Charles opened a new parliament in Oxford University's Convocation House and reiterated his readiness to approve measures to uphold Protestantism and monarchical authority. Insisting that 'I, who will never use arbitrary government myself, am resolved not to suffer it in others', the king hoped, instead, that crown and Parliament 'be united at home, that we may recover the esteem and consideration we used to have abroad'.[59] The scope of likely limitations on a Catholic successor nevertheless remained uncertain and it was clear that York would reject any regency arrangement. When a new bill of exclusion was introduced, Charles surprised MPs by dissolving the parliament within a week of its opening. A young courtier, Thomas Bruce, found himself 'witness of the dreadful faces of the members, and the loud sighs' among those present, but was reassured by Charles – bearing 'a most pleasing and cheerful countenance' – that Bruce was much better off than he had been a quarter of an hour earlier, having now 'one king [rather] than five hundred'.[60]

III

Correctly judging that public opinion feared a return to civil war more than a Catholic successor, Charles seized the initiative to direct charges of irresponsible recklessness against his Whig critics. *His Majesty's Declaration to all his Loving Subjects* was published in April 1681 and defended the Oxford Parliament's dissolution on the grounds that the king's willingness to assent to any necessary security measures aside from exclusion had been ignored. Charging that MPs' actions had risked plunging England into chaos, Charles's *Declaration* attacked 'the restless malice of ill men who are labouring to poison our people, some out of fondness for their old beloved Commonwealth principles' and others from private jealousies and resentments.[61] The Tory poet John Dryden was relieved that 'the king has learned from the unhappy example of his father, not to perpetuate a parliament' and mocked the Whigs' naïve courting of Monmouth, who Dryden predicted would not tolerate very long being 'confined in the narrow compass of a curtailed, mongrel monarchy, half-commonwealth'.[62] Another pamphleteer rejected rumours that MPs bribed by Barillon had encouraged Charles to dissolve Parliament, adapting an Elizabethan maxim to admit that 'I have often heard say, that a parliament can turn a man into a woman; and now I see, they can make a man into a pensioner of France, though he be none.'[63]

In July 1681, a Scottish Parliament was convened in Edinburgh over which James, duke of York, presided as High Commissioner. Having stated their intent 'to let your other kingdoms and all the world see' the illegality of exclusion, parliamentary commissioners passed an 'Act Anent the Succession' (1681), confirming that monarchical succession was solely determined by proximity of blood and was unalterable by parliamentary statute.[64] In Amsterdam, William Carr oversaw the Scottish Act's translation and publication into Dutch and French, and provided the city's magistrates with copies to disprove claims spread by 'our fanatics, the English merchants, that the Scottish Parliament was dissolved and very much displeased with the duke' for obtaining dispensation from taking the Protestant oaths normally required to hold political office.[65] Meanwhile, William of Orange visited London in July, ostensibly seeking English assistance against renewed French attacks. Before William left The Hague, however, Henry Sidney had advised the Stadtholder that his uncle's advisers, Halifax and Hyde, 'do both complain of your letters being too high and too sharp, and say that if you had written in a more gentle style, it would have had a better effect with the king'.[66] At Windsor, William and the Dutch ambassador met with the Spanish representative, Ronquillo, who 'made a chart of all the French conquests and pretensions', but William left London in August, dissatisfied after failing to secure further support from Charles.[67]

Haunting English readers during the Popish Plot and succession crisis were literary ghosts advancing conspiracy theories, alleging miscarriages of justice and complaining about the partisan reporting of events. One of the most opinionated and loquacious spectres was, predictably, that of Oliver Cromwell, who was frankly appalled to see the 'king tugging one way, and Parliament tugging another: whilst the sly Papist leaves no stone unturned to destroy both together'. Now 'the Popish Irish, the fantastical French, and the worst part of the Scots have every one an eye upon England's ruin'. By contrast, as Cromwell's ghost recalled, Catholic ambitions had been visibly humbled during the 1650s and 'the French were as calm as the Thames in the midst of summer!'[68] In another imagined dialogue, parliaments were likened to skittles that were frequently set up only to be knocked down, with Charles's ministers characterized as 'a sort of English Frenchmen and Protestant Papists'. Despite claiming to promote 'the Protestant religion, and the lessening of France . . . all they do is for the growth of popery, and the French power'.[69]

England's failure to frustrate French expansionism was also vigorously denounced in Jean-Paul de Cerdan's *Europe a Slave, Unless England Break her Chains* (1681). First published in French four years earlier, Cerdan had asked 'what can England say for itself, a nation, formerly of all Europe, most fierce and jealous of their liberty?' Through bribery and personal contacts, 'the Seine now triumphs over the maritime grandeur of England', as France 'has found a means to lull asleep the English Samson, that having cut off the locks of his hair, she may be able to make herself master of his honour and his puissance'. As 'French politics are already at work for the ruin and destruction of England', Cerdan identified 'the chiefest masterpiece of their craft and cunning' as being the success with which Louis XIV had effectively divorced Charles's interests from those of his English subjects.[70]

Yet as French forces threatened the Spanish-controlled fortress town of Luxembourg in late 1681, Barillon feared that popular pressure could still persuade the king to summon another parliament which, as he warned Hyde in November, might entail York's ruin. For Charles, this would prove 'a much greater loss than that of the town of Luxembourg'.

Having met Charles privately at Portsmouth's apartments, Barillon had advised the king that his best option remained abandoning the Spanish treaty and concluding an open alliance with France and insisted that Luxembourg's subjugation would be followed by a permanent peace. Despite offering such a strong steer, Barillon admitted to Louis that 'I have so often seen them take wrong steps here, that it would be very imprudent in me to flatter myself with being able to persuade the king of England'. Having obtained French agreement that, after Luxembourg had been conquered, its walls would be razed to ensure that the fortress bore no further strategic value, Charles secured the promise of a further subsidy and reassured Barillon that he had 'no intention to call a parliament; these are devils who intend my ruin'.[71]

No longer willing to court recalcitrant MPs, Charles thereafter oversaw a partisan 'Tory Reaction' that recast his critics as republican rebels and arrested and executed prominent Whig leaders, appointed Tories to political and judicial office, directed the partisan remodelling of civil authorities and tightened government control of the press. Additional political capital, supplying a helpful pretext for vengeful action, was derived by the discovery in June 1683 of interrelated intrigues, known as the 'Rye House Plot', that planned to ambush and kill both Charles and York as they passed Rye House in Hertfordshire on their return to London from Newmarket. Addressing his 'loving subjects' in another declaration, Charles attacked those who 'promote sedition by false news, libellous pamphlets and other wicked arts' including, most recently, 'that horrid and execrable plot of assassinating our royal person, and our dearest brother'.[72] Following his conviction for treasonable involvement in the Rye House Plot, the Whig peer William, Lord Russell, delivered a speech from his execution scaffold on 21 July 1683, denying that 'some discourses about making some stirs' which 'cannot be more than a bare misprision' constituted proof that he had ever designed to kill Charles II.[73]

On the same day as Russell's execution, the University of Oxford's Convocation condemned twenty-seven 'damnable doctrines' and ordered the public burning of books by authors whose incendiary works served to 'stir up seditions and tumults, overthrow states and kingdoms, and lead to rebellion, murder of princes, and atheism itself'.[74] One week later, Protestant interests strengthened when the duke of York's younger daughter Princess Anne married Christian V of Denmark's brother

George. While the duke of Ormond noted that court critics 'give out that it is a French match', on account of Denmark's military alliance with France, he emphasized George's Protestantism, military achievements and reputation as 'a brisk man, qualifications which possibly they do not like'.[75] Becoming a prince of the 'blood royal' that accorded him equal dynastic rank to a son of York, the Danish prince was instructed by Charles to 'walk with him, hunt with his brother, and do justice on his niece'.[76]

Further afield, dramatic events in central Europe offered Charles's supporters opportunities to discredit their Whig opponents by alleging pernicious similarities between radical Whiggery and Muslim expansionism. In 1682, Austrian Habsburg forces had failed to prevent an Ottoman-backed rebellion in Hungary that saw Imre Thököly crowned King of Upper Hungary, with Catholics, Protestants, Jews and Greek Orthodox communities granted toleration under Ottoman protection. The following summer, a massive Ottoman army, commanded by Grand Vizier Merzifonlu Kara Mustafa, attacked the Habsburg capital of Vienna which endured a two-month siege before being relieved by combined Protestant and Catholic forces under King Jan Sobieski III of Poland in September 1683. Turning to allegory to feed a febrile English readership, Tory propagandists insisted that Whig calls for liberty of conscience denoted a darker agenda of 'turning Turk' and agitating for rebellion. In a ballad entitled 'The Bloody Siege of Vienna', Hungarian rebels became 'German Whigs' who might 'pretend religion' in promoting nonconformist interests, but really aimed at their own tyranny:

> But Hungary, that Bloody Scene,
> Of which the German Whigs have been
> The provocation, and the Cause,
> 'Gainst God, the Emperor and their Laws,
> Yet still pretend Religion;
> At the same time brought in the Turk,
> They are all turned Mahometan,
> Like ours, against the Duke of York.

Another Tory writer likened the God-given victory of Christian forces over the Ottoman Antichrist at Vienna to Charles's suppression of the Whigs, rejoicing that 'Turkish Whigs be damned'. But as the author of 'No Protestant Plot, or the Whigs' Loyalty' (1683) warned, little room remained for complacency, since 'Hell's restless, factious agents still plot on, / And [16]83 smells rank of [16]41'.[77]

While consolidating his 'personal rule' at home, Charles also ordered the evacuation and destruction of the English colony at Tangier in north Africa, two decades after receiving it via Catherine of Braganza's marriage dowry. In 1662, the Genoese ambassador sent to congratulate Charles on his restoration, Giovanni Luca Durazzo, had acclaimed Tangier's potential to allow the English king to control the Strait of Gibraltar as an ambitious echo of Henry VIII's aspiration to 'open and close the ocean at the strait of Calais'. Samuel Pepys had likewise been confident that Tangier was 'likely to be the most considerable place that the king of England hath in the world'.[78] Whereas management of Bombay, which had also been part of Catherine's dowry, had been entrusted to the East India Company in 1667, Charles had retained Tangier as a crown colony, hoping that it would become a financially self-sustaining trading hub and a strategically located safe harbour. Yet despite £2 million spent on its fortifications, the colony had been repeatedly attacked by its Moroccan neighbours and in 1680 one of the king's natural sons, Charles, earl of Plymouth, had died of dysentery there, shortly after recapturing English forts taken by the Moors.

While accompanying George Legge, earl of Dartmouth, on the expedition to oversee Tangier's evacuation, Pepys choreographed a careful rationale for the colony's liquidation, soliciting from its leaders confirmation of their grateful relief at Dartmouth's 'recalling us from scarcity to plenty, from danger to security, from imprisonment to liberty, and from banishment to our own native country'.[79] The symbolic date chosen for the fortification's destruction – 5 November 1683 – further underscored the crown's public commitment to Protestantism. While Pepys remained mindful of the opprobrium that had followed Dunkirk's sale to the French over two decades earlier, on the return voyage to England Dartmouth warned him that, although both Charles and the duke of York were 'good at giving orders', they were 'never found stable enough to support officers in the performance of their orders', meaning that 'no man was safe in doing them service'.[80]

By the end of 1683, the Whigs might have argued that no man was safe, even in his thoughts. On 7 December, the duke of York wrote to William, noting with satisfaction that Algernon Sidney had been executed that day, having 'died very resolutely, and like a true rebel and republican'.[81] Having been convicted of treason on evidence that included an unfinished manuscript in his possession – the authorship of which remained unproven – Sidney made a speech on the scaffold that lamented: 'we live in an age that makes truth pass for treason'. Since 'nothing of particular application unto time, place or person could be found' in his manuscripts, 'all was supplied by innuendos'. While his own reflections on rulers, such as Tarquin, Nero, Caligula, Domitian or Hugh Capet, might have been subjected to scholarly scrutiny, Sidney objected that his fate had instead been decided by a jury 'composed of men utterly unable to understand them' as judicial prosecutors became partisan literary critics.[82] In his summing-up, however, Judge George Jeffreys had insisted that, in Charles II's England, '*scribere est agere*' – to write is to act.

20

A New Magna Carta, 1683–1687

After dissolving the assembly that had met in Oxford in March 1681, Charles II never summoned another English parliament and relied instead on lucrative customs revenues, French subsidies and support from Tory loyalists during his 'Personal Rule'. Courtiers nevertheless detected a certain apprehensiveness in the veteran monarch regarding the fitness of his Catholic brother, James, duke of York, to succeed him as king. The erstwhile English agent in Brussels, Sir Richard Bulstrode, recalled a conversation with the king in 1683 in which Charles had feared that 'when I am dead and gone, I know not what my brother will do'. Describing himself as 'weary of travelling' and 'resolved to go abroad no more', the king had ominously predicted that 'when my brother comes to the crown, he will be obliged again to leave his native soil'. Nor, when looking to the future, could Charles vest confidence in his eldest natural son, James Scott, duke of Monmouth, who had only narrowly avoided criminal prosecution for involvement in the Rye House Plot that had envisaged the assassination of both Charles and the duke of York. In November 1683, Monmouth had signed a declaration, confirming that both his father and uncle 'know how ingenuously I have owned the late conspiracy, and though I was not conscious of any design against your Majesty's life, yet I lament the having a great hand in the other part of the conspiracy' that had sought to foment a popular rebellion against the government.[1]

To avoid testifying against his Whig associates, Monmouth had gone into exile in Brussels and never saw his father again. Relieved at his popular rival's removal, York wrote to his Dutch son-in-law and nephew, William of Orange, deprecating Monmouth's 'extraordinary carriage' and feeling reassured that the disgraced duke was now overseas, 'for had he stayed and dissembled, he might have done much mischief'. Six months later, however, York warned his daughter Mary that 'it scandalises all loyal and monarchical people' in England to hear reports that Monmouth had been warmly welcomed by her husband William, as Dutch Stadtholder, at his court in The Hague. As York warned Mary, were Monmouth to outlive his father and uncle, William should realize that 'the Duke of Monmouth will do his part to have a push with him for the crown' that should otherwise pass to Mary on York's death.[2] Suspecting that William 'seemed to be glad of the opportunity of insulting' his English father-in-law, Louis XIV of France's ambassador in The Hague, Jean-Antoine de Mesmes, count d'Avaux, recalled that William had even encouraged Mary to share in Monmouth's enthusiasm for ice-skating, deeming it 'a very extraordinary thing, to see the Princess of Orange, with very short petticoats, and those tucked up half-way to her waist, and with iron pattins on her feet, learning to slide, sometimes on one foot, sometimes on the other'.[3]

In February 1685, Charles suddenly became ill, suffering either a stroke or the effects of chronic kidney disease. As the resident French ambassador in London, Paul Barillon d'Amoncourt, marquis of Branges, explained to Louis XIV, on hearing of the king's illness, he had immediately gone to the royal apartments at Whitehall where Charles's Breton mistress, the duchess of Portsmouth, had revealed 'the greatest secret in the world', admitting that 'my head would be in danger if it was known'. Insisting that 'the King of England at the bottom of his heart is a Catholic', Portsmouth had beseeched Barillon to enable Charles to be secretly, and speedily, received into the Catholic Church. By a curiously circuitous coincidence, Barillon and the duke of York then found, among the priests attached to Queen Catherine's household, John Huddleston, who, over three decades earlier, had courageously sheltered Charles during his dramatic escape after the Battle of Worcester in 1651. After Barillon and York had 'put a wig and gown on him to disguise him', Huddleston had given Charles absolution, communion and extreme unction and had also 'made the king formally promise to declare himself openly a Catholic, if he recovered his health'. Among the courtiers waiting outside the royal bedroom, Barillon recalled that 'nobody said anything but by their eyes and in whispers' and doubted that 'the secret can be long kept'.[4] But even without Charles II's conversion becoming more widely known, initial plans for his state funeral were set aside in favour of a scaled-down evening burial at Westminster Abbey that conveniently minimized the need for ostentatious Protestant obsequies.

I

Although the political nation nervously held its breath as James became the first openly Catholic monarch of England since the traumatic reign of Mary Tudor, his succession proved surprisingly peaceful. In *A Compendious View of the Late Tumults and Troubles in this Kingdom* (1685), James Wright welcomed tributes to Charles comprising 'statues of marble and triumphal arches', but suggested that a more fitting way for subjects to honour their former king would be through demonstrating their firm loyalty to his brother.[5] On the day after Charles's death, James met his Privy Councillors to whom he offered impromptu remarks that quickly appeared in print. Acknowledging that 'I have been reported to be a man for arbitrary power', James had reassured his Councillors that he intended 'to preserve this government both in church and state as it is now by law established', believing that 'the laws of England are sufficient to make the king as great a monarch as I can wish'.[6] According to his posthumously published memoirs, James had recognized that his 'candid declaration' to uphold the Anglican establishment had been to 'the unspeakable satisfaction of the nation', but admitted that, at the time, he had been 'in such a hurry' that he had approved publication of his words 'without reflection'. He had, rather, been 'impatient to assist at his devotions on so extraordinary an occasion' and, two days after Charles's death, had attended Mass at St James's Palace, leaving the chapel doors open so that 'all the world might see his present grandeur was as incapable of influencing him in matters relating to his duty to God, as his past sufferings had been'. Believing that 'plain and open dealing is for the most part the best policy', James later speculated that his Protestant subjects had been 'the more induced to rely upon the promise he then had made in favour of their religion, when they saw he would not dissemble in reference to his own'.[7]

Among contemporaries who admired the openness of James's religious devotions was the Spanish ambassador Don Pedro Ronquillo who remarked to the Governor of the Spanish Netherlands, Ottone Enrico del Caretto, marquis of Grana, that 'the glory of this action is double for not doing it in hiding, and the most consoling thing of it all is that the people were happy'.[8] Reinforcing the popular acclamation that accompanied James's accession, when William of Orange learned of Charles's death, he dutifully ejected the duke of Monmouth from his court, while over 360 loyal addresses from across England were received at Whitehall. As the Oxford antiquary Anthony Wood marvelled, only five years earlier James had been 'written against by every scribbler; vilified and abused and scandalised' but 'was now proclaimed generally throughout with great applause and settled in his throne without a bloody nose. Such is the world's career.'[9]

Shortly after his accession, James ordered new parliamentary elections, explaining to Barillon that, otherwise, 'malcontents would have formed cabals to demand a parliament'; as the king had insisted, 'I know the English: you must not show them any fear in the beginning.'[10] James also followed his brother's precedent in timing his coronation to coincide with St George's Day on 23 April 1685 in an order of service amended to omit the Anglican communion rite. In his coronation sermon, Bishop Francis Turner of Ely admitted that James had not been 'bred up at ease in the court of his father, but in the school of hardship and affliction', suggesting that 'no prince within the memory of man has come to a crown with so vast a stock of experience'. Described by Turner as 'incapable of dissimulation', James had succeeded as king, despite 'the madness of the people' and 'that abominable Excluding Bill'.[11] In terms of 'hardship and affliction', as duke of York, James had absconded from Parliamentarian custody and fled to the Continent disguised as a woman in 1648, had narrowly escaped being killed at the Battle of Lowestoft in 1665 and had survived shipwreck when, sailing to Scotland in 1682, his frigate HMS *Gloucester* had run aground off Great Yarmouth. Aged fifty-one at the time of his accession, James II – also James VII of Scotland – was a familiar Restoration figure, known for his military service, civic service during the Great Fire and for being the son of an executed father. Although his conversion to Catholicism was regarded as regrettable by most of his British subjects, James's legitimacy was unquestioned and being only three years younger than Charles II, with two Protestant daughters ready to succeed him, it was anticipated that James's reign would be relatively short.

The coronation service was followed by a magnificent feast,

comprising 1,445 separate dishes, and an impressive fireworks display on the River Thames at which, as one commentator noted admiringly, the pyrotechnics 'seemed to equal those natural prodigies of Etna and Vesuvius' without the devastation wrought by volcanic eruptions.[12] A coronation medal designed by the Flemish engraver Jan Roettier bore the motto *a militari ad regiam* ('from the military to the royal crown') in tribute to the king's extensive naval and military service in French, Spanish and English forces. In Edinburgh, a new parliament opened on the same day as James's coronation in England and, five days later, its members annexed all excise revenues to the crown in perpetuity. Insisting that Scotland had 'continued now upwards of 2,000 years in the unaltered form of our monarchical government under the uninterrupted line of 111 kings', the Parliament's Commissioners sought to 'declare to the world' their detestation of 'all principles and positions which are contrary or derogatory to the king's sacred, supreme, absolute power and authority'.[13] A Scottish coronation medal, designed by the Dutch engraver Jan Smeltzing, depicted a crouching lion grasping the regalia with the traditional Stuart motto, *nemo me impugne lacessit*: 'no one provokes me with impunity'.

By the time James addressed his new English parliament on 22 May 1685, he had received an unwelcome reminder of Scottish recalcitrance, having learned that the exiled Presbyterian peer Archibald Campbell, earl of Argyll, had landed in Kintyre, on the Scottish west coast, intent on raising a rebellion. Before alerting MPs to this news, James reiterated his commitment to preserving the Church of England, choosing 'the same words I used at my first coming to the crown' as proof 'that I spoke them not by chance'. While the Anglican establishment had been 'eminently loyal in the worst of times', James warned MPs against trying to engineer frequent parliamentary sessions 'by feeding me from time to time' serial instalments of financial supply, but should instead 'comply with me in what I have desired, and that you will do it speedily'.[14] Within a week, English MPs had approved, in perpetuity, the same annual revenues for the crown that had been granted to Charles II on a yearly basis, prompting a grateful king to assure Parliament that 'I have a true English heart' and – having previously risked his life for his country in military service – now hoped to 'carry the reputation of it yet higher in the world, than ever it has been in the time of any of my ancestors'.[15]

As evinced by news of Argyll's Rising, James's accession had provoked renewed plotting among the sizeable community of expatriate English and Scots Whigs living in Dutch exile. Shortly after Charles's death, Argyll had met Monmouth in Amsterdam to coordinate a surprise Anglo-Scottish invasion. Having attracted support from Scots serving in William of Orange's forces, Argyll's departure from Amsterdam in early May had been prompted by alarm that soldiers were inclined 'to tattle, that the matter began to be talked of as freely in Amsterdam and Rotterdam among the Dutchmen as any other news'.[16] Included in Argyll's party was a Scots law student, John Erskine of Carnock, who recorded in his journal that he was 'fully determined' to assist in 'the delivery of our native land from being again drowned in popish idolatry and slavery'. To Erskine's mind, 'the standing or falling of the Protestant interest in Europe depended in a great measure upon the event of this undertaking in Britain'.[17] While the recent Habsburg triumph at Vienna had denoted a victory for Christendom over Ottoman incursions, its achievement had been secured by a predominantly Catholic alliance. Protestantism's precarity had, once again, been underscored, as the British Isles, now ruled by a Catholic king, appeared a plausible counter-Reformation target.

Argyll's small flotilla – with 300 men in three ships – sailed around northern Scotland in May 1685, past the Orkney islands, before reaching the west coast where 2,500 supporters were recruited on Mull, Islay and Kintyre. Combining Presbyterian opposition to prelacy with a determination to recover his forfeited ancestral rights and properties, Argyll issued a printed *Declaration* that denounced the accession of 'a notorious apostate and bigot papist to the throne, notwithstanding his thrice being excluded by the Commons of England'. Denying that James could uphold Protestantism without being 'a hypocritical and damning cheat', Argyll described the new English parliament as 'packed, caballed and returned by all the arts and methods that either fraud or injustice could invent, to render it pliable to his intentions'.[18] The rebels landed on the Isle of Bute and then made for Loch Lomond, before Argyll became separated from his supporters who were then defeated in a skirmish near Lochwinnoch on 18 June. Meanwhile Argyll was captured and executed in Edinburgh on 30 June, having been convicted of treason in absentia, four years earlier.

Monmouth, meanwhile, had prepared his own *Declaration* of 'war against James, duke of York, as a murderer, and an assassin of innocent men; a popish usurper of the crown; a traitor to the nation, and tyrant over the people' whom he, somewhat wildly, held responsible for Charles II's death. Having left Texel in the Netherlands with eighty-three supporters and landed at Lyme Regis on 11 June, Monmouth stated his intention as not being 'to introduce anarchy and confusion' nor to assert his right to succeed as king, but to leave 'the determination thereof to the wisdom, justice, and authority of a Parliament, legally chosen and acting with freedom'.[19] Monmouth's *Declaration* was penned by the Scottish Presbyterian Robert Ferguson, and also published in French, Dutch and German translations. The *Declaration* confirmed the duke's notoriety on the Continent, where the Dutch authorities were suspected of having turned a blind eye to the British exiles' invasion preparations. In the view of James's Francophile ambassador in The Hague, Bevil Skelton, 'there are no greater villains upon earth' than Amsterdam's republican citizenry whom he believed were 'as inveterate enemies to his Majesty as either Argyll or Monmouth'.[20] In Dutch prints, images of Monmouth in 'a warlike posture' circulated alongside satirical depictions of a decapitated James VII & II, with the king's severed head between his legs and the Spanish Habsburg motto *non plus ultra* ('nothing further') over his neck stump.[21]

Despite his *Declaration*'s recommendation that the English Parliament should choose its monarch, a new 'King James' was proclaimed in Taunton on 20 June as Monmouth tried to dissociate himself from suspicions of republican extremism. Having served as Captain General of all the land forces in England, Wales and Berwick under Charles II, Monmouth hoped that his presence would prompt a patriotic, Protestant uprising against his unpopular Catholic uncle, but local gentry in south-west England did not rally in support. Instead, Monmouth's 'pitchfork army' was easily defeated at the Battle of Sedgemoor on 6 July by government forces that were commanded by the French-born Louis Duras, earl of Feversham, and included Monmouth's half-brother Henry Fitzroy, duke of Grafton. Around 200 of Monmouth's supporters died in what remains the last pitched battle to take place on English soil, with many more summarily killed in its unruly aftermath (see Plate 22). Monmouth himself was executed at Tower Hill on 15 July, having already been convicted of high treason by a bill of attainder the previous month.

In Somerset, the severity of judicial response became known as the 'Bloody Assizes' as around 250 of the duke's supporters were tried and executed and another 850 transported to the West Indies as indentured labour. Abhorred as a fanatical and regicidal sequel to earlier Whig conspiracies such as the Rye House Plot, Monmouth's rebellion was commemorated in a mocking bronze medal that depicted the abject duke falling headlong from a column topped with three crowns and the motto *improvidentia* confirming his improvident recklessness. On the day of thanksgiving appointed for the rebellion's defeat, Augustine Frezer preached to English merchants in Dordrecht, denying that, 'since the time of Pontius Pilate', there had ever been such a 'height of unaccountable madness against a prince' as that suffered by James VII & II. Charging Monmouth's Protestant adherents with popish designs of king-killing, Frezer reminded his congregation that an earlier plot of 'blowing up the King and Parliament upon a fifth of November was a design of religion' and quoted from Charles I's *Eikon Basilike* to recall that, if 'the breath of religion fills the sails' of rebellion, 'profit is the compass by which factious men steer their course'.[22] In Bilbao, an acrostic poem honouring 'Jacobo Stuardo' accompanied a printed *Relacion de las Fiestas* (1685) describing both the coronation of 'el muy Catholico' [*sic*] ('the most Catholic') James and his triumph over the arrogant and rebellious Monmouth.[23]

Suppressing the rebellions of Argyll and Monmouth also provided James with a pretext to recommend that a large, professional standing army be maintained during peacetime as a necessary alternative to unreliable local militias. James had inherited a force of around 9,000 troops on his accession and had steadily expanded his army to about 20,000 soldiers by December 1685, instigating annual summer camps at Hounslow Heath. When the English Parliament reconvened in November, the king insisted that it was only 'a good force of well-disciplined troops in constant pay, that can defend us from such as either at home or abroad are disposed to disturb us', provoking Sir Thomas Clarges to recall fears, articulated during exclusion debates, that 'we should, in case of a Popish successor, have a Popish army'.[24] MPs also expressed concern at the sizeable number of Catholic officers commissioned into the Army's ranks in breach of the Test Acts. In the House of Lords, Bishop Henry Compton of London vividly 'compared the Test Act and penal laws to the dykes of Holland: once breached, at any single point inundation would follow'.[25] Without waiting to hear more, James prorogued the

14. Anamorphic painting of Charles I at Castle Gripsholm after 1649, near Stockholm. Initially confronted by a distorted and unsettling image, the viewer is presented with a corrected appearance of Charles I, with lace collar and 'George medal' symbolizing the Knights of the Garter, when a cylindrical mirror is placed over an emblem of the skull.

15. The broadside illustration *The Scots Holding their Young King's Nose to the Grindstone* (1651) satirized the stringent conditions exacted from Charles II before his austere coronation at Scone Palace on 1 January 1650.

16. An anonymous Dutch engraving, *Den Afgrysselikken Start-Man* (*The Horrible Tail-Man*) (1652) shows a tailed Oliver Cromwell, being presented with the three Stuart crowns by Thomas, Lord Fairfax, while in the background a Scotsman attempts to sever the scaly tail.

17. Probably an imagined reconstruction of a banquet held in Charles's honour at The Hague, Hieronymus Janssens's *Charles II Dancing at a Ball at Court* (detail, *c.* 1660) was painted shortly before the king's return to England. Charles appears twice: dancing in the outer room with his sister Mary, Princess of Orange, and dining in the inner room, seated next to Mary.

18. Detail from Antonio Verrio's frothy *Sea Triumph of Charles II* (1674) presents the king in classical armour, being driven through the seas by Neptune, while three women represent England, Scotland and Ireland. A scroll held by 'Fame' reads *Imperium oceano famam qui terminet astris*: 'let the boundary of his empire be the ocean and the limits of his fame be the stars'.

19. Depicting herself holding a paintbrush in a self-portrait (*c.* 1650), Louise Hollandine was Elizabeth of Bohemia's seventh child and named after the country that hosted the exiled Palatine dynasty.

20. Nicknamed 'Fubs' by Charles II for her chubby cheeks, the king's mistress, Louise de Kéroualle, duchess of Portsmouth, is here depicted as Venus, with their son Charles as Cupid, *c.* 1673.

21. The King of Hearts from a pack of playing cards from 1679 narrating the Popish Plot in which 'Dr Oates discovers the Plot to the King and Council'.

22. The King of Spades from a pack of playing cards narrating the Monmouth Rebellion in 1685 in which two devils taunt the hapless duke, recalling satirical Whig images of James VII & II as a popish devil.

23. Produced by the Rotterdam-born printmaker Adriaen Schoonebeek, a bird's eye view of the massed Dutch fleet assembled for the invasion of England by William of Orange in November 1688. In the foreground, the Dutch army rescues 'religion' and drives away 'war' and the Catholic regime of William's English father-in-law and uncle, James VII & II. The cartouche bearing the print's title is decorated with orange branches.

24. John Savage's engraving *The Usurper's Habit* (1691) depicts Louis XIV of France in clothing displaying images of twenty-four towns and strongholds seized by his armies. Prominent among the French acquisitions are Sligo, Athlone, Galway and Limerick in Ireland, but the comment by the observer at the window – 'he begins to unrig' – suggests that momentum is starting to shift in favour of the Grand Alliance.

25. On display in Amsterdam's Rijksmuseum, the carved sternpiece of Charles II's 100-gun flagship the *Royal Charles* (originally named the *Naseby* when built in 1655). Seized by the Dutch fleet in its attack on the River Medway in June 1667, the *Royal Charles* was towed back to the Dutch Republic and broken up in 1673, but its stern decoration was preserved as a triumphant memento.

assembly, eleven days after its opening, foregoing the chance of additional financial supply.

To vindicate royal use of the dispensing power as a means of circumventing the statutory exclusion of Catholics from political and military office, a test case was contrived whereby the MP for Canterbury and a recent Catholic convert, Sir Edward Hales, was sued by his coachman Arthur Godden for the £500 to which Godden was entitled as an informer if it was found that Hales had acted illegally by accepting an army commission without taking the Test. Having been convicted at the Rochester Assizes, Hales appealed his conviction at the Court of King's Bench, citing letters patent issued by the king which allowed specific exceptions to the law and thereby permitted what would otherwise be illegal. Before the case was heard, however, several dissenting judges were dismissed, including the Chief Justice of the Common Pleas, Sir Thomas Jones. Jones warned James that, since he was demanding 'such a construction of the law from him, as he could not honestly give', he would soon discover that 'none but indigent, ignorant or ambitious people would give their judgements as he expected'.[26] When more pliant colleagues duly produced a majority ruling of 11:1 in the crown's favour in *Godden* v. *Hales* in June 1686, the king obtained legal sanction for his actions. Three months earlier, Barillon had reported to Louis XIV a ministerial conversation in which James had wagered that MPs would henceforth be 'more disposed to behave well, when they saw that without their assistance, so many matters of importance could be effectuated'; in short, 'his resolution was, not to reign precariously'.[27]

II

Recalling the Scottish Parliament's loyalty in passing a Succession Act in 1681, at the height of English Whig attempts to debar him from the throne, James initially looked north to secure legislative support for abolishing the Test Acts that excluded Presbyterian nonconformists and Catholics from civil and military office. Writing to the new session of the Scottish Parliament that opened in April 1686, James indicated that, together with a request to abrogate the penal laws and Test Acts, he had 'made the opening of a free trade with England our particular care', but the Commissioners' reply to the king only conceded a willingness, with respect to religious policy, to 'go as great lengths therein, as our conscience will allow'.[28] Amid torrential downpours that led to the assembly being dubbed 'the black rainy parliament', so many restrictions were attached to draft legislation intended to offer Catholics immunity from prosecution under the penal laws that James prorogued the Parliament on 15 June.[29] The previous month, prominent opponents of the king's legislative agenda, including the Lord Advocate Sir George Mackenzie of Rosehaugh, had been summarily dismissed from office. In London, the Puritan Whig diarist Roger Morrice deemed it 'most certain that this surprising and conspicuous miscarriage' in Edinburgh 'has clogged all their affairs elsewhere', correctly predicting that the court 'would make no further trial of that parliament'.[30]

In England, James had sought to curb criticism from the country's pulpits by issuing 'directions to preachers' in March 1686, warning that sermons should not be used 'to handle the deep points of God's eternal councils and decrees, or to meddle with the affairs of state and government, or to wrangle about forms and gestures, and other fruitless disputes and controversies'.[31] That summer, a Commission for Ecclesiastical Causes was created to oversee church affairs, with summary powers of suspension, deprivation and excommunication. Resented as 'a new court of inquisition', the Commission's remit revived disturbing memories of the notoriety that had attached to Charles I's Court of High Commission before the civil wars.[32] Morrice, meanwhile, looked further back and described the new body's responsibilities as echoing 'the form of the Commission given to the Lord [Thomas] Cromwell in Henry VIII's time'.[33] It was, indeed, ironic that the powers of the supreme governor of the Church of England, which had been specifically designed to exclude interference from external bodies such as the papacy, could – under a Catholic supreme governor – now facilitate censure of Church of England clergy and the extension of indulgences to Protestant nonconformists and Catholics.

One of the Commission's first actions was to suspend Henry Compton from his London bishopric for not taking stronger measures against anti-Catholic sermons preached in his diocese. Compton was also known to have encouraged London's Lord Mayor, Sir John Peake, to override royal authority and order workers to halt construction of a new Catholic chapel for the Elector Palatine in Lime Street, which was not located near other foreign embassy chapels but intended instead to attract Catholic merchants in the City. As rioting had disrupted the embassy chapel's opening in April 1686, the Spanish consul in London, Felipe de la Guerra, reported that the mayor's intervention had 'caused a sudden blaze', but believed that 'the diplomat should first have gone to live in the house and then thought about a chapel, but they have done it backwards and so things have happened in this way'.[34] It then transpired that since the Palatine Elector Philip William, duke of Neuburg, had not himself been consulted about the chapel's creation, he intended anyway to dissociate himself from its controversial installation.

Neuburg had acquired his Electoral title in May 1685 after succeeding Charles II of Simmern, who had been James VII & II's first-cousin-once-removed. Before becoming Elector, Charles had visited London incognito in 1680, arriving so discreetly that Charles II had only learned of his presence in England by reading the *London Gazette*, whereupon the Master of Ceremonies had been hurriedly directed to find the Palatine prince and transfer him to royal apartments at Windsor.[35] When Charles II of Simmern had died childless in 1685, Louis XIV had hoped that the Palatinate's Rhineland territories might pass to Charles's younger sister, Elisabeth Charlotte, who had married Louis's widowed brother, the duke of Orléans, after the death of the previous duchess of Orléans, Henrietta Anne (James VII & II's sister). But Louis had been outmanoeuvred by the Holy Roman Emperor Leopold I, who had installed his father-in-law, Neuburg, as Elector, prompting fears that the French king might forcibly claim the Palatinate's Rhineland territories for his sister-in-law – as he had threatened to do in the Spanish Netherlands on behalf of his Spanish wife in the 1670s.

French territorial aggrandizement was also feared on account of Louis's dramatic decision to revoke the Edict of Nantes in October 1685. Decreed in 1598 as a means of resolving the country's long-running sectarian wars, the Edict had guaranteed freedom of conscience and protected the civil rights of French Protestants, known as Huguenots. Increasingly intimidatory policies had been pursued against the Huguenots during the 1680s, including the billeting of military dragoons on Protestant households, before the Edict's Revocation simply outlawed Protestantism in France and demanded the destruction of all Protestant churches. In a House of Lords debate shortly after the Edict's Revocation, James's accession was identified as germane to events across the Channel as one peer posited that the 'French king would not have ventured to use his Protestant subjects so ill' without being reassured that 'the English had a popish king, who would not resent it'.[36]

At Whitehall, the court response to Louis's actions was ambiguous. Instinctively, James claimed to eschew persecution and, in advice to his infant son written in 1692, observed that Christ may have 'whipped people out of the Temple, but I never heard he commanded any should be forced into it'. As James insisted, ''tis by gentleness, instruction and good example, people are to be gained, and not frightened into it'.[37] From the outset of his reign, James had also articulated a clear wish to enact liberty of conscience and remove the requirement for religious qualifications from office-holding. During debates on penal law repeal in the Scottish Parliament in May 1686, one manuscript advice paper in favour of repeal had pointedly criticized those who insisted on the retention of penal laws while simultaneously condemning 'the French king's method in forcing men's consciences'. That 'persecuting prince', Louis XIV, might fairly upbraid Scots for violating the consciences of his co-religionists and threatening Catholic lives and livelihoods 'though they are quiet, loyal and peaceable'.[38]

Official reaction to the Revocation, however, seemed suspiciously muted. In early November, John Evelyn noted that the twice-weekly *London Gazette* 'informing us what was done all Europe over . . . never all this time, spoke one syllable' of the French Huguenots, rendering it 'very extraordinary in a Protestant country, that we should know nothing of what Protestants suffered'.[39] Having fled to The Hague, where he was granted a Dutch state pension, Jean Claude, the Protestant pastor of Charenton, penned *Les Plaintes des Protestants Cruellement Opprimez dans la Royaume de France* (1686) ('The Complaint of Protestants Cruelly Oppressed in the French Kingdom'), which was translated into English and warned that Huguenot sufferings remained 'matters known, not by gazettes, and newsletters, but by an infinite number of fugitives'. Through the 'tears and miseries' of fleeing refugees, Claude trusted that 'the world will surely open its eyes' as their testimonies attested, to Protestants and Catholics alike, the scale of violent iniquities being perpetrated. Although Claude thanked the English king for having 'received us into his countries, succoured and relieved us', French and English versions of Claude's tract were publicly burned, on James's orders, at the Royal Exchange in May 1686 while Evelyn attributed delays in organizing financial collections for Huguenot relief to 'the French ambassador and cruel papists obstructing it'.[40] In May, Louis's nephew Victor Amadeus, duke of Savoy, ordered the massacre of around 2,000 Protestant Waldensians in the Italian Alps, with the forced conversion, or escape into exile, of thousands of others whose plight was graphically observed and described by the Scots Whig Gilbert Burnet, in his *History of the Persecution of the Valleys of Piedmont* (1687).

Watching Protestant communities in Continental Europe face serial threats of extirpation only fuelled anxieties about the long-term intentions of Britain's Catholic king. In England, local populations heard first-hand tales of Catholic cruelty from Huguenot refugees who managed to avoid detention in convents or impressment as galley slaves and evade the coastal watches intended to prevent their escape. In April 1687, six children from a noble Huguenot family fled from La Rochelle, after paying 1,000 livres to a sea captain to accept them as stowaways. The eldest teenage daughter, Suzanne de Robillard, later recalled how she and her siblings had avoided detection by crouching among the ship's cargo and putting 'our heads directly under the beams so that when the inspectors, as was their lovely custom, thrust their swords through, they would not pierce our skulls'. Despite fearing that they would succumb to suffocation, the refugees emerged 'more dead than alive' from the hold and were deposited at Salcombe in Devon where they were hospitably received by the local populace with whom they conversed in Latin. Although the siblings were reunited with their mother a few months later, the family quickly relocated to Holland, feeling unsafe in an England in which James 'was beginning to take away the Protestants' privileges, which raised fear of persecution'.[41]

Critics attributed Louis's aggressive expansionism to territorial greed rather than a pious mission to eradicate heresy. As the Buckingham gentleman Edmund Verney lamented in May 1686, Louis 'never will have done demanding, claiming and destroying, and taking forcibly, until the Devil hath him'.[42] That September, the English ambassador in Paris, Sir William Trumbull, was relieved to be recalled from a tempestuous ten-month posting during which he had objected to Louis's depredations in William of Orange's lands in southern France and had repeatedly submitted hopeless appeals against the religious persecution of English and Scottish Protestant merchants living in France. As Trumbull later recalled, 'my soul abhorred the French court' with its 'little flattering courtiers' who 'came and bespattered me with their whipped cream'. Destined 'everlastingly to complain', Trumbull knew that 'it was useless to be angry without hopes of redress'. Thankful to have received a new posting to Constantinople and alarmed by Anglo-French amity, Trumbull anticipated imminent disaster in his own country, having 'seen too much of the friendship between the two kings cemented by the designs of promoting popery, and how we were pushing on at Whitehall, with incredible folly and invincible obstinacy, either to conquer Protestantism and the English liberties, or to perish in the attempt'.[43]

Contemporaries shared Trumbull's disquiet regarding the readiness with which James's policies appeared to align with the bombastic demands of his French cousin Louis. If James could instead demonstrate independence of mind, the anonymous author of *The Designs of France against England and Holland Discovered* (1686) argued that he would become 'the professed umpire of the universe, the sovereign mediator and decider of controversies, and the giver of peace to all Europe'. But to merit such a role, the English king would need to work productively with his parliaments and ally with the Dutch. Bemoaning James's feeble responses to French imperiousness, the pamphleteer insisted on the need to 'resist the Devil, and he will fly from you; but if you fear him, he will make you his slaves'. Although much had been expected from a martial monarch who had seen active service on Continental battlefields, James seemed concerned only 'to please the Jesuits, and to kindle a fire in his own kingdom, which probably he will never be able to quench' if 'he dares not convene a free Parliament'.[44]

James's Francophile inclinations and reliance on Jesuitical counsel also risked undermining international cooperation overseas. In September 1686, the Habsburg Holy Roman Emperor Leopold I recaptured the Hungarian capital, Buda, from the Ottomans after a three-month siege witnessed by James's teenage natural son James FitzJames, later duke of Berwick. Following Leopold's preservation of Vienna in 1683 and then Buda as Christian cities, prayers were ordered to be read in English churches, including the Chapel Royal at Windsor, supplicating 'all Christian kings, princes and governors' to 'wax valiant in battle, see their desires on their enemies, and put to flight the armies of the aliens'.[45] Military encounters were also restaged for popular audiences: the Siege of Buda was re-enacted at the Hounslow Heath camp in 1687, while Monmouth's defeat at the Battle of Sedgemoor had been restaged in Hyde Park a year earlier.[46]

But when James had voiced delight at Buda's capture in 1686, not 'all Christian kings' (or their diplomatic representatives) had concurred. As the Dutch ambassador Aernout van Citters reported, James's warm endorsement 'made the French ambassador and the minister of Denmark here turn their backs'.[47] With his forces conspicuously absent from the international coalition fighting the Ottomans at Vienna and Buda, Louis XIV was nicknamed 'the Christian Turk' by critics who denounced the French king's persecutory intolerance, perfidious diplomacy and suspicious willingness to exploit Ottoman activities as a means of distracting Habsburg attention away from French expansionism in the Rhineland. The London mob remained, however, less discriminating in its anti-popish animus. When the Spanish ambassador Don Pedro Ronquillo lit bonfires and approved celebration of Mass and a *Te Deum* to mark Buda's capture, the embassy was besieged by protestors. As the Florentine ambassador Francesco Terriesi reported, 'the common people publicly say that they would rather see Buda in the hands of the Devil than in those of the Catholics, and they feel for the Turkish defeat without thinking of its advantages'.[48]

The accession of England's first openly Catholic monarch since the mid-sixteenth century coincided with a period of deepening fissures within the Catholic Church itself as Louis XIV's insistence on his right to collect revenues from vacant bishoprics and to control certain ecclesiastical appointments had damaged Franco-papal relations. In July 1685, Barillon had reassured Louis of James's insistence that he 'had been brought up in France, and eaten of your Majesty's bread, and that his heart was French'.[49] Concomitant with James's Francophilia was his reliance on Jesuit advisers, including his confessor Father John Warner and Father Edward Petre, who became a Privy Councillor in November 1687. That April, Morrice had observed that Petre and Warner were 'the life and soul of the Jesuitical interest under the king of France here', but 'stand in direct opposition to the Pope's interest' that was promoted by James's Italian queen Mary, the papal envoy Ferdinando d'Adda and the Vicar Apostolic of England, Father John Leyburn.[50]

Notwithstanding these divisions, James's keenness to promote England's reintegration into the Continental Catholic fold was reflected in his appointment of Roger Palmer, earl of Castlemaine – whose wife, Barbara, had been mother to five of Charles II's illegitimate offspring – to become England's first post-Reformation ambassador to the papal see. Castlemaine's embassy to Rome required use of the dispensing power to circumvent the statutory prohibition on Anglo-papal relations imposed at the Reformation, and was the most expensive diplomatic mission undertaken by any Stuart monarch. As well as a one-off sum of £3,000, the earl received a weekly salary of £100 that was dwarfed by his weekly entertainment allowance of £1,000. Arriving in Rome in April 1686, Castlemaine's ambassadorial credentials were initially denied by Pope Innocent XI who objected that, irrespective of James VII & II's Catholicism, he could not receive the representative of a sovereign who remained the head of a heretical church. A compromise agreement was reached in January 1687, by which time the earl had, in a private capacity, already had nine papal audiences as well as meetings with senior cardinals and Jesuits.[51]

Although Castlemaine's mission failed in one of its aims (securing promotion for Father Petre to a titular bishopric or cardinalate), the published account of the embassy compiled by Castlemaine's artistic steward John Michael Wright celebrated instead the impressive cultural credit gained by the English delegation. Having directed the construction of over thirty elaborate coaches to convey Castlemaine to the Vatican for his official reception in January 1687, Wright described how the procession had ceremoniously passed through Rome's streets 'crowded with people, all shouting and crying out, *Viva Il grand Re d'Inghilterra*! Long live the King of England!' Coinciding with Twelfth Day celebrations in Rome, the coaches had passed gilded wooden tableaux, twenty-four feet high that not only joined the papal and Stuart coats of arms but also depicted Britannia and Heracles (James) triumphing over religious dissent, political rebellion and Ottoman incursion. A week later, Castlemaine hosted a banquet for eighty-four Catholic cardinals and prelates, presided over by a life-size portrait of James, with a vast dining table decorated with figures from classical history carved 'some almost half as big as the life' from 'a kind of sugar-paste, but modelled, to the utmost skill of a statuary'. After expending immense sums of money, Castlemaine concluded his mission by taking the English delegation to attend an operetta hosted by the former Queen Christina of Sweden. During the performance, an Italian prelate celebrated James's success in 'joining divided Britain, once more to the Continent', while a chorus of over a hundred singers rejoiced that as James was 'Great in Britain, even, / Let him be Great in Rome, and Great in Heaven!'[52]

III

In early 1687, an unnamed Jesuit penned an excitedly upbeat account of religious affairs in England to a colleague at the Jesuit College in Fribourg, citing James's reported insistence 'that he would either convert England, or die a martyr', adding that 'he had rather die the next day and convert it, than reign twenty years piously and happily and not affect it'. When it had been suggested that James's religious agenda might be pursued more gradually, the author alleged that the English king had disagreed and insisted on the need for haste, aware that he was 'growing old, and must take large steps' to safeguard the interests of his Catholic co-religionists before the crown passed to his Protestant daughter Mary. Confessional change was accompanied by visible military investment as the author reported 'a great preparation of war at London' where over a hundred warships were being fitted out; although the fleet's intended target was not known, 'the Dutch are under great apprehensions'.[53] While spoof Jesuitical missives were regularly penned as persuasive Protestant propaganda, this letter – which circulated in English, French and Latin – was regarded by contemporaries as authentic, while its content, albeit alarming to Protestant readers, was not demonstrably false.

Intent on expediting his religious agenda, James imposed toleration in Scotland by royal proclamation in February 1687. Issued on the king's 'sovereign authority, prerogative royal and absolute power, which all our subjects are to obey without reserve', the proclamation removed all constraints on freedom to worship and all religious qualifications in state oaths.[54] Extending benefits both to Presbyterian nonconformists and Catholics, the measure alarmed Episcopalians, including the Scots Whig exile Burnet, who warned that James's expectation of unqualified compliance was 'carrying obedience many sizes beyond what the [Ottoman] Grand Seigneur has ever yet claimed'. Not only would the proclamation's provisions exacerbate intra-Protestant divisions, but, given the onus placed on Catholics to extirpate heresy and recent events in France, James's injunction might imply 'that we are either to obey without reserve, or to be burned without reserve'.[55]

Two months after the proclamation's publication, a Scots peer, Patrick Hume, Lord Polwarth, supplied William of Orange with a 'memorial' written by lay and clerical Scots in response to James's imposition of toleration. Speaking on behalf of fellow exiles who were not 'the ranting, talking sort of men', Polwarth indicated that they 'look upon Your Highness as the great wheel which under God must give life and motion to any good project'. Describing James's religious zeal as 'like a strong twist in a clew' that determined all his actions, the memorial's authors knew that the timing of any intervention was delicate and 'the danger of precipitation is as great as of too slow progress'. Nevertheless, were the domestic sufferings of James's subjects to become so extreme as to require external involvement, William would either need to 'hazard himself for them and become their deliverer or else he will risk and hazard his interest in these kingdoms forever'. For as the Scottish authors warned William, should the English 'get deliverance by their own means or by any other', his prospects of becoming king of England would evaporate, since even the most fervent monarchists at Westminster 'carry to this hour a dislike of the race and branches of the Scots family, and if they could fix elsewhere, would certainly reject it'.[56]

A more circumspect Declaration of Indulgence was promulgated in England on 4 April 1687, suspending the penal laws, facilitating freedom of religious worship and enabling individuals to hold civil or military office without swearing the oaths of supremacy and allegiance. Reviewing successive policies that had sought to 'reduce this kingdom to an exact conformity in religion' under Elizabeth I, James VI & I, Charles I and Charles II, James VII & II believed that 'the success has not answered the design, and that the difficulty is invincible'. Although issued by prerogative, the king had 'no doubt of the concurrence of our two houses of parliament when we shall think it convenient for them to meet'.[57] In a tract published in English and Dutch, the Scots Presbyterian Robert Ferguson – who had drafted Monmouth's manifesto two years earlier – warned Protestant nonconformists against being seduced into trusting that James's indulgences and toleration would be welcomed at face value. For once James 'had abused their credulity into serving his ends as far' as was needed, dissenters would be 'made to drink deepest in the cup of fury and wrath that is mingling and preparing for all Protestants'.[58]

Before the English Declaration was issued, James's daughter Princess Anne had written to her elder sister Mary in The Hague, lamenting that 'things are come to that pass now that if they go on much longer, I believe, in a little while, no Protestant will be able to live here'. Despite continual entreaties from her father to convert to Catholicism, Anne reassured Mary that she was 'resolved to undergo anything rather than change my religion'; accordingly, 'if it should come to such extremities, I will choose to live on alms rather than change'. Aware that approaches were being made to William by concerned Tories and Whigs alike, Anne counselled her sister and brother-in-law against any well-intentioned visit to England, for although 'I should be very glad to see you, but really if you or the Prince shall come, I should be frightened out of my wits for fear any harm should happen to either of you.'[59]

In July 1687, James dissolved the English Parliament that had not sat since 1685 and sought to galvanize support for his religious policies before calling fresh elections. That summer he toured England, accompanied by the Quaker William Penn who had long called for legislation enacting religious toleration, which would be equivalent to achieving a new Magna Carta, and now addressed crowds of hundreds, sometimes thousands, in towns and cities including Bristol, Devizes, Newbury, Reading and Windsor. Meeting local gentry in Chester in August, James asked the assembled dignitaries to 'join with him in making a Magna Carta for conscience, as well as properties and other liberties'. Conjuring his listeners to imagine 'a law made that all black men should be imprisoned', such a statute would be axiomatically deemed 'unreasonable and we had as little reason to quarrel with other men for being of different opinions as for being of different complexions'. It was time to 'show ourselves Englishmen' and secure liberty of conscience since 'no Englishman could desire to see others persecuted for differences of opinion'.[60] Aside from the question of whether James's own conversion to Catholicism had been voluntary or involuntary, his subjects remained unsure as to whether the king's commitment to religious toleration denoted a permanent, transcendent right for all or a temporary and tactical necessity to attract Protestant nonconformists in order to facilitate a Catholic takeover of England's political, military and religious establishment.

One country that did experience such a transformation was Ireland, where the aftermath of the mid-century civil wars had resulted in one of the most seismic expropriations of land from Catholic to Protestant ownership in early modern Europe. Newly consecrated as the Church of Ireland bishop of Derry in 1691, William King later recalled publicly stated hopes at the time of James's accession that 'Ireland must be a Catholic country whatever it cost' and that reversing the controversial land settlement would render 'the English . . . as poor devils as when they came first into Ireland'.[61] By contrast, both in Ireland and at Whitehall, English interests insisted that preservation of the Restoration land settlement was 'the Magna Carta of Ireland' which, 'like the banks of Holland', were essential safeguards to keep popery and poverty at bay.[62] Moreover, as the (then Protestant) duke of York, James had ironically become one of the land settlement's greatest beneficiaries as nearly 170,000 acres of confiscated Irish land had been transferred into his ownership.

While James's Protestant brother-in-law, Henry Hyde, earl of Clarendon, defended English interests as the country's Lord Lieutenant, control of Irish affairs was increasingly vested in the Catholic courtier Richard Talbot, earl of Tyrconnell, who had served in the Royalist garrison at Drogheda when it had been stormed by Oliver Cromwell's forces in 1649 and had later been part of a conspiracy to assassinate Cromwell in 1655. Disquieted by Tyrconnell's ambitions, Clarendon wrote from Dublin Castle to his brother Laurence in February 1686, admitting that 'this is a very tattling town' and fearing that it would be 'a terrible thing to be whispered out of office'. But Clarendon was alarmed by Tyrconnell's arrogance and 'monstrous vanity': 'by his discourses, one would have thought that he had the absolute dominion to get the king to do whatever he proposed'. While Clarendon resolved 'to make myself a very pattern of patience', he was appalled by Tyrconnell's 'ranting, swaggering way' and his 'abominable, insolent language', fearing that if he remained 'in the temper he is, he will gain the reputation of a madman'.[63] Tyrconnell, meanwhile, set about rapidly restructuring the Irish army from a force in which all the officer corps and most soldiers had been Protestant at James's accession to one in which two-fifths of the officers and two-thirds of the rank and file were Catholic by the autumn of 1686.[64]

Accompanied by a parallel metamorphosis of Ireland's judiciary, central government and municipal corporations, Protestant panic was palpable. As Clarendon struggled to find a precedent whereby 'the sword and the administration of justice were put into the hands of a conquered people', he saw Dublin's investors hurriedly reinvesting assets in England and the Dutch Republic. In August, he wrote to James explaining that he was besieged by Protestants, denying their ability 'to forget the barbarous murders committed on us by their fathers' at a time when Irish Catholics were increasingly insisting 'that there was no rebellion in 1641'.[65] Discussing Ireland's destiny after James's death, Tyrconnell's erstwhile secretary Thomas Sheridan later recalled being shocked by the earl's insistence, in a conversation at Windsor in August 1686, that 'the Irish would be fools or madmen' if they readily became subjects of the Protestant William and Mary and remained 'slaves to England'. Rather, Tyrconnell hoped that the Irish had 'set up a king of their own, and put themselves under the protection of France, which he was sure would readily be granted'.[66] Meanwhile, in London, Clarendon's brother Rochester was frankly advised by French ambassador Barillon that 'if I did not become Catholic, I must quit' his position in James's government.[67] At the same time as his brother Rochester lost his post as Lord Treasurer in January 1687, Clarendon was recalled to England and Tyrconnell became the first Irish-born head of the Dublin administration, albeit with the lesser title of Lord Deputy.

Watching events from The Hague was William of Orange, who dispatched the experienced envoy Everaard van Weede, Lord of Dijkvelt, to England between February and June 1687. As James complained to the papal nuncio, d'Adda, he suspected Dijkvelt's main purpose was to put William 'on a good footing with me', albeit only if 'I shall act according to his will, not as is proper, he according to mine'.[68] But if James's intention was to secure William's support for the repeal of any religious qualifications for holding office, Dijkvelt's mission misfired. In June, William confirmed to his father-in-law that although 'there is no person in the world who has more aversion that I have for all sort of persecution on the score of religion', he 'cannot concur in what your Majesty asks of me' regarding Test Act repeal. In response, an embittered James blamed Dijkvelt for 'giving so much credit to some that do not wish me and the monarchy well' and 'creating fears and jealousies' among English politicians.[69]

One such politician was Charles II's former confidant George Savile, marquess of Halifax, whose anonymous *A Letter to a Dissenter* was published in September 1687 and went through six editions, attracted twenty-four printed replies and had a print run of around 20,000 copies. Determined to dispel dissenters' support for James's toleration crusade, Halifax warned that naïve enthusiasm for removal of the penal laws and religious tests could only serve Catholic interests in the long term. Following James's dissolution of Parliament in July, Halifax feared extensive electoral manipulation would contaminate any future assembly and warned dissenters that they were 'to be hugged now, only that you may be the better squeezed at another time'. Rather than 'silently receiving the benefit of this Indulgence', Protestant nonconformists had, by promoting James's policies, 'become voluntary aggressors, and look like counsel retained by the prerogative against your old friend Magna Carta'.[70] Halifax was also mindful of the international dimensions to domestic debates, both in terms of French support for James's pro-Catholic initiatives and dissenters' claims that James was simply seeking to emulate the celebrated religious diversity and toleration that prevailed in the United Provinces. As Halifax had admitted to William of Orange earlier that year, 'our affairs here depend so much upon what may be done abroad, that our thoughts, though never so reasonable, may be changed by what we may hear by the next post'.[71]

In November, the Grand Pensionary of Holland, Gaspar Fagel – whose office had once been synonymous with republican resistance to William's Orangist dynasticism – wrote publicly to the Scots Presbyterian lawyer James Stewart of Goodtrees to correct apparent misapprehensions regarding the admission of Catholics to civil and military office in the Netherlands. Fagel's *A Letter Writ By Mijn Heer Fagel, Pensioner of Holland, to Mr. James Stewart, Advocate* (1688), which was also translated into Dutch, Latin and French, confirmed that, notwithstanding William and Mary's support for toleration, they opposed the removal of measures 'by which the Roman Catholics are shut out of both Houses of Parliament, and out of all public employments, ecclesiastical, civil and military' and could not consent to repealing legislation that protected Protestantism 'against all the attempts of the Roman Catholics'.[72] Given Stewart's involvement in Whig conspiracies against Charles II and James, including the Rye House Plot and the rebellions of Argyll and Monmouth (and his subsequent appointment as Scottish Lord Advocate under William in the 1690s), his curious readiness to canvass in favour of James's religious policy perhaps denoted the lawyer's unprincipled opportunism. Alternatively, it was a sophisticated manoeuvre, designed to provoke wider opposition to James's authority by forcing public recognition of its pro-Catholic and absolutist underpinnings.

Although Stewart hotly protested against Fagel's exploitation of their private correspondence, Fagel's reiteration of his position in *Their Highness the Prince and Princess of Orange's Opinion about a General Liberty of Conscience* (1688) generated a print run of 50,000 copies. It was now clear that, under William and Mary, English subjects would enjoy freedom of conscience, but the Church of England's monopoly of office-holding and the country's political, religious, legal and military establishments would remain intact. As William Cavendish, earl of Devonshire, confirmed to William, 'people are in raptures to find the sentiments of your Highness and of the Princess in matters of religion, not only so equitable, but so agreeable to the interest, and to the taste of all the nation'.[73] By implication, James's alternative vision for England was not so agreeable. In 1688, the Dutch engraver Jan Smeltzing, who had produced a sturdy leonine image of James at his coronation three years earlier, now designed a medal entitled *The Religious State of England*. On one side, a Church of England mitre, a dove representing Protestant dissent and a Catholic chalice, wafer and rosary appeared in peaceful coexistence, together with a copy of Fagel's *Letter*. On the other, James VII & II was depicted removing the penal laws and Test Act, trampling on liberty of conscience and devouring his coronation oath.[74]

21

The Dutch Design Anatomized, 1687–1690

In August 1687, James VII & II visited St Winefride's Chapel and Holy Well in Flintshire, reputedly the oldest continually visited site of pilgrimage in Britain. On behalf of his Italian queen, Mary of Modena, James sought the saint's intercession in producing a son and heir. Over a century later, the Welsh antiquarian Thomas Pennant described how 'the prince who lost three kingdoms for a Mass' had received, from the shrine's Jesuit guardians, 'a present of the very shift in which his great-grandmother, Mary Stuart, lost her head'.[1] Acclaimed for supplying miraculous assistance to barren women, the seventh-century virgin martyr St Winefride had, like Mary, Queen of Scots, been decapitated for her steadfast adherence to the Catholic faith, having become a nun after rejecting the advances of a suitor, Caradog.

On James's accession it had been the fervent hope of Catholics – as expressed by an Irish priest, John Weldon – that God would 'grant a further increase' of progeny to the new king and queen, 'that the name of Stuart may rule over the lions, regulate the leopards, receive the fragrant scent of the lilies, and keep the harp in a pleasant tune to the world's end'.[2] Just over nine months after James's visit to the saint's healing spring, Mary of Modena gave birth to a son, James, on 10 June 1688. As duke of York, James had suffered the loss of several sons in infancy, so was overjoyed to have a new son and heir whose hereditary right trumped that of his Protestant daughters Mary and Anne and increased the likelihood of a perennial Catholic succession to the thrones of England, Scotland and Ireland. A service of thanksgiving for the prince's birth issued for use in churches across England and Wales included a prayer that acknowledged God's beneficence in preserving James VII & II 'from the dangers of war, from the rage of the sea, and from the madness of the people', and in granting 'his heart's desire': the arrival of a son and heir.[3]

When news of the prince's birth reached the French court at Versailles, the English ambassador Bevil Skelton reported that Louis XIV had insisted that, aside from the baby's father, 'no man had a greater joy than he, for the news of a prince being born', bearing 'a satisfaction in his face not to be expressed'.[4] In Vienna, James's envoy, Nicholas Taaffe, earl of Carlingford, ordered a celebratory Mass and *Te Deum* and hosted a sumptuous banquet. Having ensured that the city's fountains poured with wine, 'being the best in Vienna', until midnight, amid 'repeated huzzas and salvoes to the young prince's health', Carlingford had hoped 'to have had bonfires through all the streets' and a fireworks display, before learning that pyrotechnics were banned on account of the city's wooden houses.[5] Underlining the international significance attached to this new Stuart arrival, celebrations were also held in The Hague, Madrid, Venice, Hamburg, Copenhagen and Rome.[6] In Constantinople, an '*allegrezza*' – public rejoicing – was organized at the English embassy to which the French and Dutch ambassadors and their families were invited, as well as representatives from local Dominican, Capuchin, Franciscan and Jesuit orders. With the embassy building illuminated, an ornate triumphal arch erected in its garden glorified the Stuart dynasty.[7] Back in London, a lavish fireworks show costing over £25,000 was staged from barges on the River Thames, featuring a figure of Bacchus that toasted the new prince's birth with the Latin caption *Laetitia Populi* ('the joy of the people').[8]

It was, however, unclear that the prince's arrival was universally 'to the joy of the people'. When the English consul in Rotterdam, Daniel Petit, set off celebratory fireworks, a hostile crowd shouted insults about the English king and obliged Petit to submit a claim of 200 guilders to James's Irish-born ambassador in The Hague, Ignatius White, marquess d'Albeville, 'for damage sustained by the rabble who broke the windows of my house and of my neighbour's, for which I must pay'.[9] More generally, the prince's birth negated the rationale by which many of James's subjects had resigned themselves to enduring the king's pro-Catholic policies, believing that the majority of changes would be reversed when he was succeeded by either of his Protestant daughters, Mary or Anne, or by Mary's husband William of Orange who, after the new prince's arrival, was now fourth in line to succeed in his own right, as James's nephew.

Confronted by the very real prospect of an eternal Catholic succession, the king's confidence that his wife would certainly bear a son also seemed dubious in retrospect. In March 1688, Princess Anne had written to her sister Mary in The Hague, observing that the queen's 'great belly is a little suspicious'; indeed, their stepmother was 'so positive it will be a son' that Anne had feared 'there may be foul play intended'. A week after the prince's birth in June, Anne admitted to Mary that, since she had been away from London at the time, she would 'never now be satisfied, whether the child be true or false'. Anne conceded it was 'possible it may be her child; but where one believes it, a thousand do not', prompting Mary to return a list of over twenty questions to her sister, including whether the queen's reported breast milk 'was seen by many, or conducted in a mystery' and, regarding the new baby, 'is the queen fond of it?'[10]

Among disaffected English and Scots exiles attached to William and Mary's court in The Hague, the cleric Gilbert Burnet was regarded by D'Albeville as an especially subversive influence, warning that 'the devils in Hell could not invent more for the supposition of the Prince of Wales than he does'.[11] As rumours spread that the baby prince might be a commoner's child smuggled into the royal apartments in a warming-pan, other sceptics suspected an international popish plot that, however implausibly, attributed the infant's paternity to Pope Innocent XI's representative, Ferdinando d'Adda, whose name offered irresistible punning potential. In a parody of the Annunciation, one lampoon posited that James's Italian queen had hoped to 'give England a son in this critical point, / To put little Orange's nose out of joint'. The queen's prayers had been answered by the Holy Ghost who resolved to intervene 'in some shape or other, / Perhaps like Count Dada, and make her a mother'.[12] Congratulating James on his son's birth, the poet and playwright Aphra Behn anticipated the likely reaction of his son-in-law and nephew, William, with the lines

> Methinks I hear the Belgic lion roar,
> And lash his angry tail against the shore,
> Enraged to hear a Prince of Wales is born.[13]

But it was from English shores that William received an explicit invitation to intervene via a letter, written on 30 June 1688, bearing the ciphered endorsement of William Cavendish, earl of Devonshire,

Thomas Osborne, earl of Danby, Charles Talbot, earl of Shrewsbury, Richard, Viscount Lumley, Bishop Henry Compton of London, Admiral of the Fleet Edward Russell and the former ambassador to The Hague Henry Sidney. Assuring William that 'there are nineteen parts of twenty of the people throughout the kingdom who are desirous of a change', the letter's authors deemed it 'no less certain that much the greatest part of the nobility and gentry are as much dissatisfied' as themselves, adding that 'some of the most considerable of them would venture themselves with your Highness at your first landing'. At the same time, William was warned that congratulations he had sent to James following the Prince of Wales's birth 'hath done you some injury' in acclaiming the arrival of a child that 'not one in a thousand here believes to be the queen's'.[14] Articulating their disenchantment with James's regime, the authors dispatched their missive on the same day as popular rejoicing greeted the acquittal at the Court of King's Bench of Archbishop William Sancroft of Canterbury and six episcopal colleagues of a charge of seditious libel after the clerics had refused to accede to James's demand that his Declaration of Indulgence be read from all Church of England pulpits. One peer who had declined to add his cipher to the letter was Daniel Finch, earl of Nottingham, who later served as one of William's Secretaries of State. Describing his dilemma as 'the greatest difficulty that ever I was plunged into in my whole life', Nottingham admitted that he 'was indeed ashamed to quit the company who had admitted me into their secrets' but simply did 'not dare to proceed in an affair of which the next step would be high treason'.[15]

I

If Nottingham was too trepidatious to invite a foreign prince to intervene in English politics, William was intent on preventing history from repeating itself. He remained haunted by memories of events in 1672 – the *Rampjaar* or 'Year of Disaster' – when England and France had concluded the secret Treaty of Dover before jointly declaring war against the Dutch Republic in an offensive that had nearly resulted in his country's obliteration. Almost two decades later, while James's Francophile inclinations clearly threatened the Dutch, William also feared that an internal overthrow of James's authority as king could result in the creation of a new republic, and history lessons from the 1650s suggested that an English republican regime would be just as likely to declare war against the Dutch as commercial and colonial rivals. As William's favourite, Hans Willem Bentinck, wrote to one of the States General's envoys in July, it seemed all too likely that English politics 'would burst into extremities, in which case we cannot sit still, but have to do our best, or the Republic and religion is lost'.[16] Since William's priority remained constructing an international coalition against Louis XIV, he hoped that potential Catholic allies, such as Emperor Leopold I and Carlos II of Spain, had been reassured by *Their Highness the Prince & Princess of Orange's Opinion about a General Liberty of Conscience* (1688) which had confirmed that, should William or Mary succeed as monarchs of England, their Catholic subjects would not suffer persecution.

William was also worried by renewed instability in the Rhineland, following the death in June 1688 of the pro-French Archbishop-Elector of Cologne Maximilian Henry whose lands had been used to attack the Dutch Republic in 1672. While Louis strenuously insisted that the sixty-year-old William Egon, Cardinal of Fürstenburg, should succeed as Archbishop-Elector, Emperor Leopold promoted an alternative candidate: Joseph-Clément, the seventeen-year-old brother of Maximilian Emanuel, Elector of Bavaria. After Innocent XI decreed that Joseph-Clément should indeed succeed as Archbishop-Elector, French troops not only entered the Rhineland and attacked the imperial fortress at Philippsburg in September, but also invaded the papal city of Avignon in the same month. Traumatic memories of events in 1672 meant, however, that French diplomats could no longer dilute Dutch resistance by exploiting divisions between republicans and Orangists. In August, Louis's ambassador in The Hague, Jean-Antoine de Mesmes, count d'Avaux, relayed the resigned frustration of a prominent Amsterdam burgomaster that any compunction about Orangist bellicosity was now construed as unpatriotic. If invited by William to support a military initiative in Cologne, local leaders would 'be carried away willy-nilly by the torrent ... if they tried to open their mouths, they would be reproached with throwing the Republic into its present state' and accused of seeking 'an understanding with the enemy to see the annihilation of their religion and the destruction of their trade'.[17]

The French court – focused on an expansionist mission in the

Rhineland – was disturbed by rumours that, as one regent from Delft quipped, William of Orange 'may be planning to play the little Monmouth' by attempting to invade England.[18] In early September 1688, D'Avaux presented two memorials to the Dutch States General, the first warning the Dutch against meddling in the disputed succession in Cologne and the other confirming that Louis would interpret any 'act of hostility by your troops or by your ships against his Britannic Majesty, as an open fracture of the peace and as an act of war against his own crown', on account of 'the treaty of friendship and alliance' between himself and his English cousin James. Yet only the day before, D'Albeville had submitted a memorial to the States General denying the existence of any Anglo-French alliance and emphasizing James's desire to maintain harmonious Anglo-Dutch relations. The timing of the divergent assertions seemed too coincidental to be credible. As another pamphleteer, commenting on D'Albeville's speech, explained, the States General now 'understood, from the mouth of Count D'Avaux, that there was a great union of friendship and alliance' between Louis and James, 'which they had never made public and which they had concluded in secret'. While D'Albeville's denial of any alliance only twenty-four hours earlier seemed deliberately misleading, the royal cousins clearly 'confer together daily' and 'communicate together in a brotherly fashion over their memorials and designs', which thereby 'persuades us that Count D'Avaux has said the truth'.[19]

At the imperial court in Vienna, interest in English affairs had become such that, as an anxious Carlingford reported in September, there was 'nothing more talked of here than the quarrel between the Dutch and us, or rather the quarrel of the Prince of Orange against us'. Rumours alleged that William had 'resolved to invade England and to carry his princess along with him', that 'he has already a great faction in England formed and ready to receive him' and 'the inclinations of two parts in three are already with him'. D'Avaux's allusion to an Anglo-French alliance had prompted the imperial court to prioritize opposition to French aggrandizement over confessional solidarity with Louis and James. Despite Austrian Habsburg concern that James 'drives on too fast and his design to promote the Catholic religion lies too open' in England, there had hitherto been little appetite for involvement in the country's domestic affairs. But 'that forward and wretched step in the French policy broke all these measures', as Carlingford observed such alarm in imperial circles that 'now they wished well to the Protestant party which they imagined was a hearty enemy to France'.[20] The previous day, James's agent in Rome, Sir John Lytcott, had written to James's Secretary of State (and recent Catholic convert), Robert Spencer, earl of Sunderland, reporting that anti-French animus was similarly influencing the papacy, where rumours 'of the designs of Holland against England give great gusto to this court'.[21]

In late September, William addressed the Dutch States General, confirming his intention to launch an expedition to England. Five days later, James issued a proclamation from Whitehall, citing intelligence reports that 'a great and sudden invasion from Holland, with an armed force of foreigners and strangers, will speedily be made in a hostile manner upon this our kingdom'. While any attack would be speciously justified by 'false pretences relating to liberty, property and religion, contrived or worded with art and subtlety', James was dismayed at the involvement of disaffected English and Scots exiles who seemingly had 'no sense of former intestine distractions, the memory and misery whereof' should have served as a deterrent.[22] Hearing that a manifesto by the Prince of Orange would imminently be published, D'Albeville searched for an advance copy, promising that although 'the States' printer is not to be corrupted', he wanted 'to see if any of his servants can be' and would 'leave no stone unmoved'.[23] While D'Albeville's French counterpart, D'Avaux, successfully secured a stolen version from a printer's office, copies of William's *Declaration* had been intended to be dispersed only after the invasion fleet had set sail.[24]

Distributed to all foreign representatives in The Hague except D'Albeville and D'Avaux, around twenty different versions of William's *Declaration* were printed in The Hague, Amsterdam, Hamburg, Magdeburg, London and Edinburgh in English, Dutch, French, German and Latin with a cumulative print run of around 60,000 copies. The text had been compiled by the Grand Pensionary of Holland, Gaspar Fagel, assisted by Bentinck and a former envoy to England, Everaard van Weede, Lord of Dijkvelt, while the English translation had been undertaken by Burnet. The *Declaration* not only deemed intervention in English and Scottish affairs essential to uphold Protestantism and 'the laws and liberties of those kingdoms', but also confirmed that the Prince of Orange's involvement had been 'most earnestly solicited by a great many lords, both spiritual and temporal, and by many gentlemen and other subjects of all ranks'. Having explained that 'our expedition is intended for no other design, but to have a free and lawful parliament assembled as soon as is possible', the *Declaration* appealed to James's subjects over the head of their king and drew a parallel with events in 1672 when the English people's inclinations had been 'in opposition to those who were then in the government' of Charles II that had joined Louis XIV in declaring war on the Dutch. Reminding readers of William's own hereditary right to succeed James, as well as that of his wife, the *Declaration* also cited 'so many just and visible grounds of suspicion, that not only we ourselves, but all the good subjects of those kingdoms, do vehemently suspect, that the pretended Prince of Wales was not born by the Queen'.[25] A separate *Declaration* to James's Scottish subjects confirmed 'the true reasons of our present undertaking' as seeking to free the king's northern kingdom 'from all hazard of popery and arbitrary power' and to settle matters by summoning a new parliament in Edinburgh.[26]

A fortnight after William's *Declaration* was issued, the Dutch States General published its own *Resolution* citing the 'manifold representations' received by William from prominent members of the English political nation which evinced a 'reiterated and earnest desire' for his intervention. Accordingly, the Dutch deputies endorsed their Stadtholder's decision 'to go over into England, not with the least insight or intention to invade or subdue that kingdom, or to remove the king from the throne, much less to make himself master thereof'. Although the prince's expedition was 'only and solely to help that nation in re-establishing the laws and privileges that have been broken', the States General's deputies promoted England's rehabilitation as being 'to the common benefit of Christendom, and to the restoring and maintaining of peace and tranquillity in Europe'.[27]

Given the States General's long record of resisting Orangist initiatives, D'Albeville could only characterize their ready support for William's military enterprise as 'strange perfidy!', while rueing that 'there is not in hell a wickeder crew of men, than most of the English and Scots that go over' with the prince. Lamenting the lack of confessional solidarity from fellow Catholic powers, D'Albeville reported that the Spanish envoy in The Hague, Don Manuel Coloma, 'had prayers said in his chapel for the success of the Prince's design'.[28] At the imperial court, the Dutch States General's envoy, Cornelis Hop, observed that

James's representative Carlingford kept up 'such an intimate and familiar correspondence with the French ministers' in Vienna, promoting Louis's interests with 'an extraordinary heat'. Suspecting a covert Anglo-French alliance, imperial advisers inclined to support William's expedition as 'now the affection which this Court has had for England is quite lost'. As Hop noted several weeks later, when Carlingford presented a memorial 'conceived in very sharp terms', entreating Leopold 'to look upon the Prince of Orange's expedition to England as a religious war' and support James as a fellow Catholic sovereign, Leopold declined on the grounds that the English king 'kept so close a correspondence with France'.[29]

By the time it set sail, William had amassed an invasion force of around 400 ships, 15,000 soldiers and 3,000 to 4,000 horses. Although many of Louis's troops were occupied in the Rhineland, few observers believed that William would risk leaving the Netherlands unprotected to venture a hazardous invasion of England so late in the military season. Although William had secured the loan of around 14,000 troops from allies in Brandenburg, Celle, Hanover, Hesse-Cassel and Wolfenbüttel to protect Dutch borders during his absence, he could not control autumnal storms or prevailing westerly winds.[30] An English chaplain, John Whittel, recalled that, in the weeks before William's fleet departed, everyone in the Netherlands became fixated by wind direction. In all social interactions, 'concerning any manner of business, the very first question by all was, Sir, I pray, how is the wind today? Are we likely to get an easterly wind 'ere long? Pray God sent it, and such like.'[31] In London, the pamphleteer Edmund Bohun likewise remembered how 'for about almost three weeks together the wind stood perpetually west; during all which time, the common question was every morning, where is the wind today?' Watching the weathervane of the city's Bow Church in vexation, one sailor had been moved 'to curse the Dragon in the Cheapside, for turning his head where his tail should be'.[32]

With a westerly wind still blowing, William's ships left harbour but sailed into a storm off Zeeland that scattered the fleet and drowned up to a thousand horses. Thereafter, however, the wind shifted to an easterly direction and the regrouped fleet left Hellevoetsluis on 1 November and sailed north past the Thames estuary where James's navy was stationed at the Gunfleet, near Harwich, under the command of George Legge, Baron Dartmouth. Strong winds and the difficulty of identifying a suitable landing-place in north-east England then prompted William to turn the fleet around, retrace its steps and pass the English fleet again, now harbour-bound by the easterly wind. On reaching Dover, Whittel recalled how every soldier went on deck as 'the whole fleet was resolved to make a bravado' and 'bespangled the whole Channel with beautiful ships, and colours flying'. As shots were fired towards fortifications at Dover and Calais, spectators gathered on the shoreline 'were amazed at such a glorious sight', believing 'the whole seas were over-spread with ships, and how each ship was laden with soldiers'.[33] After celebrating his thirty-eighth birthday on 4 November (by the English calendar), the next day William anchored at Torbay in Devon, his arrival auspiciously coinciding with Protestant commemorations of the Gunpowder Plot's discovery on 5 November 1605. While the English and Scottish regiments of William's army were the first to disembark at Brixham, unloading the expedition's vast supplies took two days. By 6 November, the Governor of the Isle of Wight, Sir Robert Holmes – who had unleashed 'Holmes's Bonfire' that had burned the Dutch merchant fleet on the Vlie estuary in 1666 – was reporting that 'part of the militia is grown mutinous already and refuses to follow their commanders' orders'.[34] With a new south-westerly wind, Dartmouth's ships finally gave chase to the Prince of Orange, but in vain. At harbour off the Downs in Kent, Dartmouth wrote to James on 11 November, mournfully marvelling that ''tis strange that such mad proceedings should have had such success!'[35]

II

Mad or miraculous, William's armed expedition to England represented the first successful foreign invasion of England since the Norman Conquest in 1066. Describing himself as 'a true member of the Church of England', the anonymous author of *The Dutch Design Anatomized* (1688) denied that an army of 'Swedes, Brandenburgers and other Dutch and German soldiers, of Hesse-Cassel, and Lunenburg, come for any other end, than to steal and plunder, or burn and destroy whatever comes within their reach'. The author advised readers not 'to sell our birth-right for a mess of Dutch-excised herb-pottage', although he accepted that 'cross winds' had induced James VII & II 'to pursue some courses in the steerage of the vessel of the commonwealth, that appeared not so acceptable'. But 'now when his Majesty changes the point of the compass, and tacks about with a gentle gale', this was not 'a time to mutiny and murmur, as if never any pilot had mistaken the chart before'.[36] James had indeed put several controversial policies into speedy reverse by dissolving the Commission for Ecclesiastical Causes, restoring the City of London's municipal charter, annulling legal proceedings against borough charters, readmitting ejected Justices of the Peace and deputy lieutenants and reinstating the majority of the Fellowship of Magdalen College, Oxford, who had been expelled for refusing to accept the king's nomination of a Catholic Master in 1687.

After William's army landed at Brixham, James issued a counter *Declaration* on 6 November 1688, denouncing 'the many mischiefs and calamities which an army of foreigners and rebels must unavoidably bring upon our people'. The king rejected his son-in-law's intention to entrust Parliament with adjudicating domestic grievances on the grounds that 'nothing is more evident, than that a parliament cannot be free, so long as there is an army of foreigners in the heart of our kingdoms'.[37] In south-west England, William entered Exeter on 9 November. After the city's bishop, Thomas Lamplugh, had fled in loyalty to James, reports received in London indicated that 'Dr Burnet has taken possession of the cathedral' in Exeter to read aloud William's *Declaration*.[38] In a propagandist eyewitness account of the prince's entry into the city, William was described as riding 'a milk-white palfrey . . . all in bright armour, and forty-two footmen running by him'. Included in the cavalcade were '200 blacks brought from the plantations of the Netherlands in America' wearing 'embroidered caps lined with white fur, and plumes of white feathers', together with '200 Finlanders or Laplanders in bearskins taken from the wild beasts they had slain . . . with black armour, and broad flaming swords'.[39]

To confront the country's invaders, James and his Danish son-in-law Prince George left Windsor and arrived in Salisbury on 19 November with around 30,000 soldiers ordered to join the king's force, making James's army around double the size of his son-in-law's. But little action ensued as James suffered a series of incapacitating nosebleeds, while morale was sapped by serial desertions to William's army and news of a major pro-Orangist rising in Cheshire, led by Henry Booth, Lord Delamer. As the prospect of a military encounter between the armies of

James and William evaporated, the king ordered a retreat to London, having rejected the advice of Lieutenant General John Churchill to advance towards the enemy. When Churchill then defected to William's side, the Austrian Habsburg Resident in London lambasted Churchill's desertion as 'disloyal to an extent abhorrent even in a country used to such dreadful and monstrous goings-on'.[40] Churchill's defection was followed by that of Prince George who wrote to James in his capacity as one of 'the Protestant Princes of Christendom'. In a letter later published in English, Dutch and German, George regretted that he could 'no longer disguise my just concern' at the deleterious effects of his father-in-law's actions for Protestants in both 'your distracted kingdoms' and throughout Europe.[41] George Clarke, the former MP for Oxford University, was travelling with the physician John Radcliffe and joined James at Andover the morning after Prince George's defection, later recalling that he would 'never forget the confusion the court was in'. As Clarke observed, 'the king knew not whom to trust, and the fright was so great that they were apt to believe an impossible report just then brought in that the Prince of Orange was come with 12,000 men between Warminster and Salisbury'. Meanwhile 'everybody in this hurly-burly was thinking of himself, and nobody minded the king, who came up to Dr Radcliffe and asked him what was good for the bleeding of his nose'.[42]

On returning to London, James learned that Princess Anne had joined her husband in deserting to William's cause. After agreeing to summon a new English parliament in January, James appointed three peers as emissaries to meet William whose gradual progress towards the English capital had reached Hungerford in Berkshire. John Evelyn observed on 2 December that 'all the eminent nobility and persons of quality throughout England declare for the Protestant religion and laws, and go to meet the Prince; who every day sets forth new declarations against the papists'. Meanwhile, 'the papists in offices lay down their commissions and flee: universal consternation amongst them: it looks like a Revolution'.[43] With publication of *The Prince of Orange his Third Declaration* (1688) in December came assertions that 'great numbers of armed papists' were converging on London and Westminster in 'a wicked and barbarous design to make some desperate attempt upon the said cities, and their inhabitants by fire, or a sudden massacre, or both'. Warning that French troops were about to land, the *Third Declaration* insisted that James and Louis XIV sought 'the utter extirpation of the Protestant religion out of Europe'.[44] Although the *Third Declaration* was a spoof imitation later attributed to the radical Whig Hugh Speke, to readers it appeared as a clear injunction from William, exhorting Protestants to take pre-emptive action to avoid having their throats cut by papist swords.

As tensions rose, James became acutely concerned for his family's safety. Admitting that it was 'my son they aim at, and 'tis my son I must endeavour to preserve', he charged Dartmouth to secure a passage for the queen and prince to 'the first port they can get to in France, and that with as much secrecy as may be'.[45] Replying from the Spithead in the Solent in Hampshire, Dartmouth declined, insisting that 'sending away the Prince of Wales without the consent of the nation is at no time advisable'. Placing the heir to the throne in Louis's custody would result in 'a perpetual war upon your nation and posterity, and giving France always a temptation to molest, invade, nay hazard the conquest of England'. Advising James to make timely concessions instead, Dartmouth judged that 'men are hardly today and tomorrow in the same minds'; although he 'did not think seamen would have troubled themselves about parliaments', his crew aboard the *Resolution* had been reassured by James's agreement to summon Parliament.[46] For his part, William had returned a measured response to the king's emissaries at Hungerford, insisting that, if James wished to remain in London while Parliament met, 'that we may be there also, with an equal number of our guards'. Alternatively, if the king preferred to withdraw from the capital to 'whatever distance he thinks fit, that we may be at the same distance' from London with other measures also put in place 'for preventing the French or other foreign troops from landing'.[47] After arranging a passage to France for the queen and Prince of Wales on 9 December, James secretly fled Whitehall two nights later, accompanied by two Catholic courtiers.

Following the king's flight, a frenzy of rioting erupted across London. The Catholic chapel of the Palatine envoy, recently opened in 1686, was destroyed, together with a Carmelite convent in Cheapside and the royal printing-house at Blackfriars. The Spanish ambassador's official residence, Weld House, was attacked by a mob claiming 'they were coming not to the residence of the ambassador of Spain, but to the home of the Masses' and forcing the ambassador, Don Pedro Ronquillo, and his family to escape through their back garden and wander

London's streets seeking overnight shelter. Included among the silver, jewels, books and artefacts looted from Weld House were possessions of prominent Catholics who had entrusted their valuables to the ambassador for safe-keeping; Ronquillo initially estimated the cost of losses at £50,000, although he subsequently reduced his claim to the English Parliament to £20,000 to facilitate rebuilding of the embassy chapel.[48] Ironically, Ronquillo was a known supporter of William's intervention and had distributed copies of the prince's *Declaration*, having long complained that James was 'entirely devoted to the king of France, and had made a private league or contract with him, for the destruction of Germany, Flanders and Holland'.[49] Acknowledging Ronquillo as 'a great agent under his master for the Prince', the Puritan diarist Roger Morrice identified a more pragmatic reason for targeting the embassy. While Ronquillo 'contracts great debts and pays no man', the residence of the French ambassador – 'the great head of the opposite faction to that of the Prince' – had escaped relatively unscathed, since Barillon 'pays all tradesmen their bills immediately and owes not a penny'.[50]

To address the vacuum created by James's flight, the king's former brother-in-law, Laurence Hyde, earl of Rochester, and Bishop Francis Turner of Ely implemented an emergency plan for a provisional government by summoning all peers in London to the Guildhall to take measures to preserve civil order and, ideally, facilitate negotiations between James and William. As Turner explained, he believed that the absent king would have approved such a course of action 'since for his own sake he must needs be content to have a kingdom preserved for him'.[51] The country's febrile mood was dramatically demonstrated by the 'Irish Fright' that started on 13 December with rumours in London and Westminster of an imminent massacre of all Protestants by Irish and French Catholics. The following day, this 'universal terrible alarm was taken all over London' and extended to England's counties, as Chesterfield's mayor warned the earl of Danby that 7,000 Catholics and Irish had burned Birmingham and were heading towards Derby. As one Yorkshire diarist recorded, although the 'Irish Fright' rumour started in southern England, it swiftly moved north, prompting orders 'everywhere to get everyone in arms' to defend themselves, until 'the whole nation was in such a ferment that they sweat for fear!'[52] The author of the fake Williamite *Declaration*, Hugh Speke, later claimed responsibility for the popular panic that had gripped England in mid-December

1688. Careful observation of the country's postal networks had enabled Speke to 'set fire to the train, and it spread like wildfire in a moment through the whole kingdom of England to the great amazement and astonishment of all persons'.[53]

Meanwhile, England's fugitive king had only reached the Isle of Sheppey in Kent. James had fled with the Tower of London's former Governor, Sir Edward Hales, to Hales's estate at Elmley Ferry, near Sheerness, but their passage to France was forestalled when fishermen boarded their boat searching for Hales as a local papist. Although the king's identity was not immediately realized, James accompanied Hales to the nearby town of Faversham and, once his presence became known, the ad hoc 'Assembly of Peers' meeting in London ordered a military escort to be dispatched to return the king safely to London. Arriving in Faversham as part of that escort, Thomas Bruce, earl of Ailesbury, described seeing James 'sitting in a great chair, his hat on, and his beard much grown', uncannily resembling 'the picture of his royal father at the pretended High Court of Justice' in 1649.[54]

Despite the warm popular reception that greeted James on his return to London, the king later recalled that William's missives 'now began to take the air of commands rather than requests' as his son-in-law 'threw off the mask before the end of the first scene' and abandoned the pacific 'pretence of the expedition'.[55] Ordered by William to leave London, James travelled back to Kent, reached Rochester on 19 December and, four days later, covertly sailed for France, arriving at Louis XIV's court on Christmas Eve 1688. In the new year, James wrote to his Privy Councillors from Saint-Germain-en-Laye, regretting that it had been 'no longer safe for us to remain within our kingdom of England'. Poignantly, James recalled his father's warning 'in the like circumstances' that 'there is little distance between the prisons and the graves of princes', which 'proved too true in his case'.[56]

Hearing of James's flight, William hastened to London where he arrived on 18 December and established St James's Palace as his headquarters. As one observer noted, it was remarkable to see 'a foreign enemy in a hostile manner march through the metropolis of this kingdom with no other diversion than the repeated hurrahs and loud acclamations of the inhabitants'.[57] While the French ambassador Barillon was summarily given twenty-four hours to leave England, on the same day that James sailed for France, on 23 December, Gilbert Burnet preached before the Prince of Orange at St James's Palace, taking his text from Psalm 118: 'It is the Lord's doing, and it is marvellous in our eyes.' Interpreting events providentially, Burnet acknowledged that 'we have before us a work, that seems to ourselves a dream, and that will appear to posterity a fiction'. Reminding listeners that 'you all know what you both felt and feared' under James's rule, Burnet insisted that a godly reformation was required to secure William's revolution and to ensure 'that the name of an Englishman and a Protestant may have a sound all the world over, that may give terror as well as create esteem'. Denouncing 'the criminal excesses of the year 1660', Burnet recalled that Charles II's restoration had initially 'seemed to promise all that a nation that had been so long tossed with wars and changes of government could wish for', but had been accompanied by 'excesses of rioting and drunkenness' and an alarming 'spirit of atheism'.[58] Popular pamphlets likewise alluded to the chimerical quality of recent events: in one fictional dialogue, 'Dick' ventured that William's progress 'looks like a dream, but to posterity it must certainly appear a romance'. Compared to the speed with which 'all the politics of several years last past, should be unravelled in three months', 'Dick' ventured that the fictional 'histories of Don Quixote, or Gargantua, will seem the more authentic relations of the two'.[59]

Although the Prince of Orange's *Declaration* had disavowed any intention to supplant his father-in-law as king, it had not anticipated James's flight to France. The king's desertion significantly expanded William's scope for practical intervention in English politics, but rendered less plausible the prince's protests that he had only intended to oversee the meeting of a free parliament. As one balladeer rhymed, 'some people were glad at the monster's invasion . . . had the knave but stood to his declaration / But 'tis now too plain: he hath cheated the nation'.[60] Amid a rising chorus of Jacobite outrage, one pamphleteer bewailed James's fate in facing rebellions: first 'one of the nephew [Monmouth], and this of the son. Good God!' In another fictional dialogue, a Protestant character 'Frank' objected 'what a devil a foreign prince has to do with regulating our government here in England, I cannot imagine'. Invoking a contemporary slur deriving from the Dutch word *hoogmogenheiden*, meaning 'high mightiness', 'Frank' insisted that, notwithstanding the Prince's declarations, ''tis nothing but a reducing England under their Hogen-Mogen yoke, is the design'.[61]

III

Since an actual parliament could not be summoned without a monarch, a Convention opened at Westminster on 22 January 1689. Writing to the Convention's members, the Prince of Orange charged them with laying 'the foundations of a firm security for your religion, your laws and your liberties'. The representative for Cockermouth, Sir Henry Capel, was impressed to see 550 colleagues assembled in the Commons, observing that, although recent attendance had numbered around 160 MPs, 'now we have no king, we are a full House'. As debate got under way, John Somers – who had served as counsel for the seven bishops acquitted of sedition the previous year – insisted that the king's 'going to a foreign power, and casting himself into his hands, absolves the people from their allegiance'. James had withdrawn to a country 'which has always been against the interest of England' and could 'not come out of the French king's power without his consent'. Sir James Oxenden, having commanded a Kent militia involved in James's detention in Faversham the previous month, was similarly alarmed that the king had fled 'to stir up foreign princes to bring a foreign power to destroy us'.[62] Yet divisions soon emerged among the Convention's members when debating whether or not they were empowered to depose James for identified instances of misgovernment, whether the king's withdrawal to France denoted an effective abdication and whether the throne of England was currently vacant. As one pamphleteer observed, such constitutional dilemmas involved 'carrying men into such dark labyrinths of law and history etc., as very few know how to find their way out of again'.[63]

As debates at Westminster risked becoming dilatory, William convened confidential discussions with prominent peers, confirming his refusal simply to assume James's crown by conquest, but rejecting ideas of a possible regency or conferral of the crown solely on his wife Mary, as James's daughter. As Burnet later recalled, William refused to countenance Mary's sole rule, insisting that, irrespective of his esteem for his wife, 'he was so made, that he could not think of holding anything by apron-strings'. If the Convention's members preferred an outcome that William found unacceptable, rather than seizing the English throne by force he would simply 'go back to Holland, and meddle no more in their affairs'.[64] As France had now declared war on the United Provinces, William – as his country's Stadtholder and Captain General – was reluctant to prolong unnecessarily his absence overseas. Nor was he interested in abetting radical reform: as Ronquillo confirmed to a colleague, the prince made clear that while he had intervened 'to restore the religion, laws and liberties of the English people, he had not come to take away those of the crown'.[65]

In circumscribing the range of constitutional options regarding the English crown that he deemed acceptable, William was, moreover, supported by his wife, who explicitly refused to accept the crown in her sole capacity, and by Princess Anne, whose hereditary rights were accepted by William as superior to those of any future issue from a subsequent marriage if Mary predeceased him. On 12 February, Mary arrived from The Hague to join William in London and, that day, the Convention also agreed the final version of a 'Declaration of Rights' which articulated a framework of lawful government and resolved that William and Mary should jointly be declared king and queen of England, Ireland and (euphemistically) France. The following day, the crown was offered to England's new monarchs at a ceremony in the Banqueting House during which the Declaration of Rights was read aloud, intended as 'informative rather than contractual in purpose, and hortatory, not mandatory, in tone'.[66] Following the proclamation of William and Mary as king and queen on 14 February 1689, John Evelyn noted popular expectations that Mary 'would have showed some (seeming) reluctance at least, of assuming her father's crown' and regretted 'so extraordinary a proceeding' to substantiate the claim in her husband's *Declaration* that there had been 'no intention of deposing the king, but of succouring the nation'. But to Evelyn's surprise, 'nothing of all this appeared' as Mary 'came into Whitehall as to a wedding, riant and jolly'.[67]

Arriving at Westminster in the royal barge, and sitting on the throne with the royal regalia, William addressed the House of Lords for the first time on 18 February and, five days later, gave royal assent to legislation that converted the Convention into a parliament. International pressures demanded the speedy regularization of affairs. Representing Exeter, Sir Edward Seymour had warned that 'our condition is attended with many difficulties; Ireland is in ill condition, and we hear nothing from Scotland but uncertainty. The King of France has been the devil and walking ghost in every parliament.'[68] The imminent risk of seeing 'Ireland in French and popish hands' precluded punctilious adherence to parliamentary protocol and the time required to organize fresh elections. As Somers asked, 'what will the world say to what we have done in settling the King and Queen upon the throne if we agree ourselves to be such an irregular assembly that we cannot act?'[69] But Jacobite critics disagreed, alleging that Mary had been prevented from arriving in England until William had not only 'altered the fundamental constitution of the government' but had also, as king, set about 'transubstantiating (as it has been called)' the 'convention into a parliament, without writs or new elections'.[70]

In Edinburgh, the Convention of Estates that opened in mid-March 1689 concurred with its English counterpart in declaring the Scottish throne vacant on 4 April but adopted a more radical terminology, drawing on feudal Scots law, to insist that, by 'inverting all the ends of government', James had 'forefaulted the right to the crown' through illegal actions enumerated in a 'Claim of Right'. By denouncing the king as 'a professed papist' who had attempted to subvert Scotland's constitution 'from a legal limited monarchy to an arbitrary despotic power', the Convention's language echoed the terms on which James's Catholic great-grandmother had been deposed in 1567. As Sir James Montgomery of Skelmorlie reflected, James was forfaulted by the Convention's members 'upon the same grounds' as Mary, Queen of Scots had been 'forfaulted by the Protestant states of this kingdom (who were generally Presbyterians) for her practices and designs against religion and liberty'.[71] Having learned that William was taking action to protect Scots' safety by sending troops to northern England and by dispatching warships to protect the coast, the Convention's members offered the Scottish crown jointly to William and Mary on 11 April.

That same day, the new monarchs of England were crowned at Westminster Abbey. But with Dutch troops lining London's streets, one observer regretted that, for the first time 'since William the Conqueror's time . . . a king and queen of England should make their procession at the coronation through a treble rank of armed horse and foot, all foreigners'. Watching well-wishers 'rudely treated with stern countenances and Dutch curses', the writer lamented that William's subjects 'must suffer under these new Lord-Danes before the king can be so settled in this throne that he can dismiss his foreign force'.[72] Meanwhile Burnet, in a coronation sermon that was later translated into Dutch, French and German, confirmed to William and Mary that it was 'from you that we expect the glorious reverse of all cloudy days'. As well as bringing domestic peace and stability, he wished that the new monarchs' 'fleets be prosperous, and your armies victorious' and that they would succeed in 'securing the quiet of Europe'.[73]

Indeed, Europe's plight had never seemed greater on account of the calculated destruction wreaked by French troops on the Rhineland between the autumn of 1688 and summer of 1689. Louis XIV was determined to prevent hostile encroachment on France's western borders, and his troops now secured the surrender of key fortresses including Philippsburg, Mannheim and Frankenthal and razed over twenty major towns including Neustadt, Oppenheim, Worms, Alzey, Heidelberg, Heilbronn and Speyer. The brutal 'devastation of the Palatinate' was described in gruesome detail to an English public that retained sentimental attachment to the region, recalling Heidelberg as the former home of Elizabeth Stuart, and the towns of Oppenheim and Alzey as part of the Stuart princess's marital jointure in 1613. Invoking the eschatological call from the Book of Matthew, 'There shall not be left here one stone upon another, that shall not be thrown down', the French Secretary of State for War, François Michel Le Tellier, marquis of Louvois, had ordered the military to ensure the levelling of Mannheim 'so that there is not left one stone upon another that could tempt an elector'.[74] In May 1689, French troops plundered tombs of the Holy Roman Emperors in the Catholic cathedral of Speyer, while a printed account of a single week's depredations in Heidelberg – published in German in Augsburg and Nuremberg, and translated into English and Dutch – described how French soldiers had desecrated local graves and 'stabbed some dead bodies, and cut off the noses, and ears of others'.[75] Repulsed by scenes of unprecedented carnage, one pamphleteer alleged the French to have raged 'like living devils', while another spoke on behalf of displaced civilians who would 'serve for all eternity as witnesses of French brutality and to cry, to all Europe, where we have been driven into exile: Vengeance! Vengeance!'[76]

Accordingly, it was not until 6 May that William declared to the House of Commons that 'today is the first day of my kingship' after MPs supported his declaration of war against France.[77] Later that month, a formal alliance was concluded between the United Provinces and the Holy Roman Emperor Leopold, laying the foundations for a

'Grand Alliance' ratified in December involving England, the States General and the imperial court. William's audacious intervention in English domestic affairs had thereby not only prevented an Anglo-French attack on the Dutch Republic, but had also successfully mobilized England's military and naval resources within a powerful anti-French coalition. As Speaker of the House of Lords, George Savile, marquess of Halifax, had tendered the crown to England's new monarchs in the Banqueting House in February. By June, however, Halifax mused that William 'hath such a mind to [attack] France that it would incline one to think, he took England only in his way'.[78]

IV

A new front in William's Continental war against Louis XIV had meanwhile opened in Ireland where James had landed at Kinsale in County Cork with twenty-two French ships on 12 March 1689. The first English monarch to visit Ireland since Richard II in 1399, James was accompanied by his natural sons James, duke of Berwick, and Henry, and by the experienced French ambassador D'Avaux. Keen to distract William's attention from Flanders, French strategic interests rendered Ireland an attractive theatre for Louis to support James's attempts to regain his British thrones. Indeed, in 1687 – with a blatant disregard for Stuart royal authority – French diplomats had daringly discussed with the Irish Lord Deputy, Richard Talbot, earl of Tyrconnell, whether, after James's death, Louis might support Tyrconnell as governor of an independent Ireland, if William and Mary were to succeed to James's English and Scottish thrones. Although the Prince of Wales's birth in June 1688 had provided James with a Catholic heir and removed some of the rationale for Ireland's reconfiguration as a French protectorate, Louis still hoped that James could achieve 'favoured nation' status for France in Ireland, facilitating free trade and mutual naturalization between the two countries.[79]

James received a rapturous welcome as he travelled through Ireland, and was reassured in a loyalist address presented in Kilkenny that, whereas previous English monarchs only 'commanded our obedience; your Majesty sways our hearts'. Proclaiming 'the real sentiments of all Irish heads', the loyalists insisted that 'the sun has not seen us these

3,000 years so united as your Majesty's interest has at present knitted us'. While boasting that 'our barns are changed into armouries, [and] our shops are metamorphosed into magazines', Kilkenny's citizenry proclaimed themselves ready to attack 'your fanatic Bristol, your deserting Chester, your rebellious London' and to confront 'the source of treacherous Amsterdam, to surround the factious Hague, and seize the sinews of ungrateful Holland'.[80]

On his arrival in Dublin on 24 March, James issued writs for a new parliament, while printed pamphlets relayed local coffee-house confidence that the ejected king intended 'to regain his thrones by downright force of the arms of his Catholic subjects, and by assistance from France'.[81] With the country's mainly Catholic army having been expanded by Tyrconnell to around 45,000 soldiers, all of Ireland, except Enniskillen and Londonderry, was under Jacobite control by the late spring. When the first Irish Parliament to convene since 1666 opened on 7 May, only six of its 224 MPs were Protestant and the assembly's first act was to confirm James's title as king of Ireland. As Irish MPs insisted, the 'impudence and injustice' that had characterized the English Convention's offer of James's crown to William was only equalled by 'the barbarous murder of your royal father' by regicides 'from whom these late traitors have borrowed and revived their desperate antimonarchic principles'.[82]

In return for fervent loyalty and a monthly subsidy of £20,000, MPs in Dublin expected the first king of England and Ireland to attend an Irish Parliament to approve measures to secure the country's legislative independence and reverse the loathed land settlement that had seen a massive transfer of forfeited Catholic estates into Protestant ownership during the 1660s. Among those opposing amendment to the land settlement was the Church of Ireland's bishop of Meath, Anthony Dopping, who feared that the measure would destroy Ireland's economy and alienate support for James among English and Scottish Protestants; this was not a time 'for men to seek for vineyards and olive yards, when a civil war is raging in the nation', with 'invasions from abroad' expected imminently.[83] To this end, although James retained English parliamentary control over Irish affairs by refusing to sanction a repeal of Poynings' Law – the fifteenth-century statute that required all Irish parliamentary bills to receive prior scrutiny from the English Privy Council – his reluctance to repeal the land settlement effectively obliged

Irish Protestants to side with the Williamite opposition to retain their estates.

James also disappointed his French advisers by failing to secure a ban of Irish wool exports to England in favour of enhanced Franco-Irish trade. As D'Avaux reported to Louis XIV of James, 'he has a heart too English to take any step that could vex the English'.[84] But if D'Avaux deemed James 'too English', the Irish surgeon-general Charles Thompson relayed a diametrically different view of Protestants fleeing to England who reported that 'all things in Ireland were governed by the French ambassador, as if Ireland were the French king's, and King James under him'.[85] As the author of *King William or King Lewis* (1689) suspected, 'the French king uses King James in this juncture merely as a stalking-horse, over whose back he designs to render himself master of these kingdoms'. In Dublin, 'Monsieur d'Avaux gives all instructions' and 'King James has no more power in the matter, than the King of Bantam'.[86]

James had never envisaged landing in Ireland as more than a stepping-stone en route to mainland Britain and a French-backed campaign to regain his English and Scottish thrones. Fretting about French obtuseness in this regard, Tyrconnell (recently given a dukedom by James) wrote to Mary of Modena in November 1689, wondering why Louis XIV did not grant James use of 'their ships to waft him over into England at this time, when all men and things lie so well disposed to receive him?' Suspecting that Ireland offered Louis too valuable a means of diverting William's attention from the main theatre of war in Continental Europe, Tyrconnell feared that 'we are only destined to serve a present turn, and at last be a sacrifice to our enemies'. Still stuck in Dublin Castle the following spring, Tyrconnell watched 'great fleets of the enemy's pass by us, loaded with arms and ammunitions and provisions', heading for the north of Ireland, but reassured James's queen that, even if William arrived in Ireland, 'I am sure I could keep up the bustle here and give him work enough', if a French fleet could meanwhile escort James to England. Resenting the domination of James's affairs by D'Avaux, the irascible Tyrconnell grudgingly admitted the need to 'make as many friends and as few enemies as we can. It's a dissembling age.'[87]

For his part, William regarded events in Ireland to be equally as irritating a distraction as his father-in-law. An expeditionary force, commanded by the septuagenarian Huguenot Frederick Herman, duke of Schomberg, had landed at Belfast Lough in August 1689, but had only reached as far south as Dundalk before retreating to winter quarters in Ulster where the Williamite troops were decimated by dysentery and typhus. The following March, William wrote to the Bavarian Elector, Maximilian Emanuel, deeming it 'a terrible mortification to me' that he could not yet return to the Continental frontline. Rather, 'I am obliged to go to Ireland where I will be, as it were, cut off from the civilised world'.[88] In June, William landed at Carrickfergus on the Antrim coast, accompanied by a fleet of around 300 ships and 36,000 troops, comprising Dutch, Danish, German, French Huguenot, English and Scots soldiers. With the Jacobite army encamped by the River Boyne in County Meath, William was scouting the local terrain when his party came under enemy fire. As Jean Payen de la Fouleresse, envoy to Christian V of Denmark, reported, the cannonball 'almost overthrew the king', whose doublet, waistcoat and coat were burned 'and the skin grazed so closely that it bled'.[89] Admiring William's unperturbed reaction, one of his Dutch entourage, Constantijn Huygens, noted the king's terse comment of relief that the cannonball 'should not have been much closer'.[90]

The victory achieved by William's forces at the Battle of the Boyne on 1 July 1690 could be seen as a postponed proxy for the pitched battle between the two sides on Salisbury Plain that had been anticipated in November 1688, before James had retreated to London after becoming incapacitated by nosebleeds and beset by military desertions. The day after his forces suffered defeat at the Boyne, James hurriedly quit Ireland, leaving Dublin for France on 2 July and incurring the scornful sobriquet *Séamus an Chaca* ('James the Beshitten') for his cowardly flight. Back in Paris, the unimpressive figure cut by the fugitive king prompted the aristocratic letter-writer Marie de Rabutin-Chantal, marquise of Sévigné, to admit that 'when you listen to him, you immediately understand why he is here'. In stark contrast, Sévigné warmly admired James's Dutch son-in-law as a 'devil of a man', who 'alone puts all Europe in agitation. What a destiny!'[91]

Having entered Dublin on 6 July and attended a thanksgiving service in St Patrick's Cathedral, William then also left Ireland to return to England and a precarious military situation. The day before the Boyne encounter, the French Navy had defeated its Anglo-Dutch opponents at

Beachy Head, provoking panic in London. As John Evelyn recorded, 'the whole nation' was 'now exceedingly alarmed by the French fleet braving our coast even to the very Thames mouth'.[92] While the Dutch furiously alleged that the allied fleet's commander, Arthur Herbert, earl of Torrington, had abandoned Dutch squadrons during the encounter, England's new ambassador to Denmark, Robert Molesworth, warned that 'if some people's heads do not fly now, no foreign prince or state will believe there is a King or Queen in England'.[93] Weeks later, the Devon port of Teignmouth was burned by a French fleet containing fifteen galleys with enslaved crews made up of condemned criminals, French Huguenots and foreign Protestants whose miserable fate only intensified English revulsion towards French cruelty and tyranny.[94]

Back in Ireland, it took another fifteen months for William's forces, now commanded by the Dutch general Godert van Ginkel, to defeat a regrouped Jacobite army at the Battle of Aughrim in July 1691 and to break the Siege of Limerick in October. Reflecting popular suspicions that the wars in Ireland had always served primarily to promote French interests, an English engraving entitled *The Usurpers Habit* (1691) showed Louis XIV wearing clothing with designs depicting twenty-four towns and fortresses captured by French forces (Plate 24). While the accompanying motto – 'he begins to unrig' – implied that French forces were losing ground to the Grand Alliance, prominent among Louis's new acquisitions were the Irish towns of Limerick, Galway, Sligo and Athlone.[95]

Epilogue

A Heap of Conspiracies

Our story started with the unprecedented execution of one anointed queen, Mary Stuart, on the order of another: her Tudor cousin, Elizabeth I. It concludes with the accession to power of a different Mary Stuart as one half of another first in English history: a joint monarchy. Debating provisions to enable Mary to exercise executive power while William was fighting in Ireland, without thereby impairing her husband's authority, was – as veteran MP John Maynard admitted – 'like making a map of a country we have never seen'.[1] The octogenarian Maynard was well placed to comment on constitutional novelties, having first sat as an MP for Totnes in Charles I's Short Parliament in April 1640 and thereafter representing Devon constituencies in every subsequent Stuart parliament. Asserting Mary Stuart's hereditary right to succeed her father was central to defending the Revolution's legitimacy against charges of illegal invasion and Dutch conquest, but the refusal of James VII & II and his descendants to renounce their hereditary rights rendered Jacobitism an intrinsically destabilizing feature of English politics until the mid-eighteenth century.

In November 1688, only the most hubristic would have vested confidence in the eventual success of what was – by the eighteenth century – acclaimed as the 'Glorious Revolution'. Before leaving the port of Hellevoetsluis, William's Dutch secretary Constantijn Huygens had been assured by a military well-wisher that 'we were about to embark on a great and glorious enterprise', but Huygens had privately observed William to be 'very melancholy, because of his thoughts about the strange voyage, on which we embark in the winter, and the consequences it might have'.[2] For those willing William's enterprise to fail, the coincidence of the date was reassuring: as the Jacobite author of *The Dutch*

Design Anatomized (1688) had predicted, divine intervention 'will settle this storm' and 'render the invasion as ineffectual, and as fatal to the most unjust aggressors, as that was a hundred years since, Anno 1588'.[3] Even while William's forces were occupying London and James had fled to France, foreign observers knew that any regime change might well prove only temporary, given seventeenth-century England's maverick propensity to sudden and erratic upheaval. From Paris, the marquise of Sévigné wrote to her daughter in February 1689, reporting that, less than a week after receiving reports to the contrary, the English had, after all, offered the crown to William 'après des grandes contestations . . . mais, ce sont des Anglais' ('after major disagreements . . . but, these are the English').[4]

The foundations of William's regime remained fragile, however much instances of good fortune were reconfigured as providential or miraculous. In November 1690, William King delivered a thanksgiving sermon entitled *Europe's Delivery from France and Slavery*, offering frightening counter-factual speculations regarding William's Irish sojourn. Recalling how 'our danger came nearer, even within a hair's breadth', King asserted that 'all our lives in him were at the mercy of that one bullet'. Whatever had happened on the Boyne battlefield, Franco-Jacobite forces 'would have counted it a victory' if William had been killed. Given the simultaneous defeat of Anglo-Dutch naval forces at Beachy Head, King ventured that William's victory at the Boyne occurred 'at such a critical time, that the peace of England, nay, perhaps the fate of Europe, depended on it'. Had it been 'delayed one week, nobody knows what would have been the consequence'.[5]

To secure his *coup d'état*, William also needed to neutralize an invisible and unquantifiable threat in the British Isles. To maximize support, the oath of allegiance that had accompanied the Bill of Rights in February 1689 had only required his English subjects to swear to be 'faithful and bear true allegiance' to their new monarchs and to deny the right of foreign powers to wield authority in England. To salve the consciences of those willing to accept William and Mary's de facto authority without denying James VII & II's de jure right, the new oath had conspicuously omitted any reference to William and Mary as 'rightful and lawful' sovereigns. Before William left for Ireland in 1690, proposals for a new oath requiring subjects to abjure and renounce James's right to the crown were debated in the House of Commons but, as the

Abingdon MP, Simon Harcourt, warned, a new oath might imply that 'there is some defect in the government' requiring remedy. Since the key question – for William's supporters, as much as for James's – was 'can we gain more friends?', Harcourt advised that, if the government were to impose a new oath of abjuration, 'you will make no friends by it; you will make enemies'.[6]

Despite the oath of allegiance's minimal scope, significant numbers of 'non-jurors' refused its terms. A conspicuous absentee at William and Mary's coronation in February 1689 had been Archbishop William Sancroft of Canterbury who – despite having led the 'Seven Bishops' in their successful defence against royal charges of seditious libel in 1688 – refused to compromise his former oath of allegiance to James and was deprived of his post in February 1690, together with five other bishops and around 400 Church of England clergy. The previous month, Queen Mary's uncle Henry Hyde, earl of Clarendon, had entertained several senior Anglican clerics to dinner and had been shocked by the 'strange doctrine!' invoked by his guests to justify recognizing the new regime. When Bishop William Lloyd of St Asaph had ventured that 'he looked upon acquisition to beget a right' to royal authority, Clarendon recorded that 'I interrupted him in great heat, and said, if he preached such doctrine, he should not preach to me'. If senior churchmen could 'so vary in their practice from what themselves have formerly taught', Clarendon rued the implication that 'we were to change our principles as often as they change their humours'.[7]

Non-jurors were, at least, readily identifiable critics of the new regime. More alarming was reported disaffection among those tasked with ensuring its practical security. In September 1689, for instance, sworn depositions were received from local justices regarding the Governor of Upnor Castle, Robert Mynors, whose fortress overlooked the stretch of the River Medway that had been the site of the Dutch Navy's humiliating attack in 1667. Ostensibly responsible for protecting the vulnerable Kent coastline from Franco-Jacobite invasion, 'the Governor said that, rather than the Prince of Orange should have the castle, he would blow it up'. On another occasion, while 'the Governor drank confusion to the Prince of Orange and the Dutch fleet', an ensign from the castle 'drank damnation to the Prince of Orange' in a Rochester tavern and another associate 'said he would fight for none but King James' and, of those fighting for William, he 'hoped to wash his hands in their blood'.[8]

In June 1689, Sir Samuel Morland, veteran of the Cromwellian and Caroline intelligence services, had suggested to William's ministers that 'engines and utensils' be devised to open correspondence, counterfeit letters and seals and reproduce lengthy extracts from intercepted materials. Alarmed by the proposal, William had advised his Secretary of State, Charles Talbot, earl of Shrewsbury, to decline Morland's offer, believing that 'the secret ought to die with him, as too dangerous to be encouraged'.[9] Several years later, Morland privately expanded on his belief in the essential role for intelligence and espionage, believing that 'all sovereign princes and states ought, like cunning gamesters, to use all endeavours ... to know what cards are in their neighbours' hands' to 'play their own to the best advantage'. All governments – especially in England – should be just as suspicious of their own subjects as they were of foreign states. A notoriously fickle and unruly people, the English were 'untamed horses [who] have thrown their unskilful riders many times within these fifty years'.[10]

But as numerous equestrian portraits and sectarian murals vividly confirmed, William was a skilful rider who brooked no dilution of his monarchical authority. In March 1690, England's new king warned that although 'some wished to make him a Doge of Venice ... he had been called to the throne by God' and would 'maintain the authority reposed on him'.[11] Half a century earlier, when William's great-uncle Charles I had objected that the demands of the Scottish Covenanters would leave him 'no more power than as a Duke of Venice, which I will rather die than suffer', the prophecy eventually became self-fulfilling.[12] On another occasion, William made clear that 'he would not be dealt with as King Charles II', disdaining the paralysing penury that had obliged his uncle to adopt an erratic and ineffective foreign policy, dependent on French largesse. By contrast, England's new king refused to 'have bills of another nature tacked to money bills nor money bills delayed till other bills were signed by him'.[13]

The price for mutually constructive crown–Parliament relations was regular parliamentary sittings and the result was sizeable financial grants to sustain England's involvement in the Nine Years' War against France between 1689 and 1697. With an average of over 115,000 English soldiers deployed annually in Continental campaigns, military expenditure increased to a yearly average of around £5.5 million or 74 per cent of the national budget during William's reign.[14] The creation of the Bank of England in 1694 and new systems of fiscal levies and deficit financing facilitated the armed forces' recruitment, payment and supply. Royal penury, together with Royalist–Parliamentarian dysfunctionality had come to an end.

Yet although William was the first monarch in English history to summon parliamentary sessions in every year of his reign, sceptics questioned the extent to which Parliament's survival depended on its financial liberality. In *The Dear Bargain. Or, A True Representation of the State of the English Nation under the Dutch* (1690), the Tory Jacobite Nathaniel Johnston reminded readers that it had been 'the getting of more money' that had led William to dissolve his first English parliament in February 1690 after he 'found that no more milk could be got from that teat'.[15] Instead of focusing on restoring the English laws and liberties promised in his *Declaration*, William's obsession with ruinously expensive Continental wars led another critic, Sir James Montgomery of Skelmorlie, to rue how 'the true intent of parliaments is baffled, and the money business quickened and finished'. Indeed, Montgomery warned that 'this court may come at least to plead prescription against parliaments, as to any other business but money bills'.[16] In the event, annual sessions of Parliament were accompanied by fiercely partisan contests fought between Tories and Whigs in ten general elections that were held, on average, every two and a half years between 1690 and 1715. Such intensity of electoral activity remains unique in English and British history.

I

When the English acquired their first Stuart monarch in 1603, James VI & I, they obtained a foreign, Protestant king, with two sons and a daughter, two decades' experience as king of Scotland and a distinctly un-English vision of England being reconfigured as one part of a united Britain. In 1689, the English acquired a foreign, Protestant king with no children, nearly two decades' experience as Stadtholder in the United Provinces, minimal interest in notions of British union, but a distinctly un-English vision of England as a key player in a multi-confessional Grand Alliance with all the country's resources mobilized to operate in a European theatre of war. Moreover, whereas James's accession to the

English throne in 1603 had brought peace by quickly ending a long-running Anglo-Spanish war that had disrupted trade and exacerbated difficult economic conditions during the 1590s, William's accession in 1689 signalled England's participation in the Nine Years' War which directly brought about difficult economic conditions during the 1690s.

For his new British subjects, the fig-leaf of legitimist propriety that William had brought from the Dutch Republic was his English-born queen, but less than five years after their accession as joint monarchs Mary died from smallpox, aged thirty-two, in December 1694. Extensively mourned, Mary's memory was honoured in England through elegiac odes, medallic impressions and musical tributes as well as at least thirty-five sermons and seventy commemorative poems. Eulogistic tributes to Mary in Dutch, French and German were also published in cities including Amsterdam, Berlin, Bielefeld, Leipzig and Wittenberg.[17] From Mary's former home in The Hague, the English diplomat and poet Matthew Prior admitted that news of the queen's demise 'has struck us all here more than an earthquake', although he was soon irked by the 'volumes of bad poetry upon a blessed queen' that constituted 'a treasury of nonsense'.[18] The elaborate obsequies arranged for Mary at Westminster Abbey in March 1695 – now known mainly for the accompanying funeral music composed by Henry Purcell – cost well over £50,000 and, according to a French account published in Amsterdam, were conducted 'in a manner so solemn and so pompous that the noise of that could be transmitted to posterity'.[19] Uniquely in English history, members of both Houses of Parliament also attended the royal funeral, although Mary's grief-stricken widower stayed away.

Mary's death inevitably reignited interest in William's right to rule, and Jacobite resistance intensified, culminating in the discovery in February 1696 of a plot to assassinate the king in a narrow lane between Turnham Green and Brentford as William returned from a hunting trip. The diarist Narcissus Luttrell recorded that James VII & II and a French army were 'at Calais ready to embark for England so soon as the signal was given at Dover that the king was killed', while intelligence from Paris indicated that around 15,000–16,000 Jacobite troops had been assembled in Scotland.[20] On the same day that William presented details of the Assassination Plot to the House of Lords, MPs in the Commons drew up an oath of association, modelled on the 'Bond of Association' approved in 1586 as a means of reinforcing loyalty to Elizabeth

I. Formulation of the Elizabethan bond had been prompted by discovery of the 'Throckmorton Plot' in 1583, which had envisaged the French duke of Guise invading England to install his kinswoman Mary, Queen of Scots on the English throne. In April 1696, the new oath of association was tendered to the English public, requiring swearers to 'heartily, sincerely and solemnly profess, testify and declare that his present Majesty King William is rightful and lawful king of these realms'.[21] Although those who declined the new oath – including around one fifth of MPs – were not penalized, John Evelyn noted that its imposition was 'censured as a very entangling contrivance of the parliament', intended to divide the loyal from the disloyal.[22]

Seven years of continuous Continental warfare also generated significant trade disruption, rising prices, food scarcities and a chronic shortage of specie. Knowing that the Williamite state had been suspected of using spurious Jacobite conspiracies as a cynical pretext to frame suspected political enemies, one of John Locke's correspondents inferred in March 1696 that 'of all the sham plots you ever heard of, or read of, none was so serviceable to the persons that forged and laid them as this real one, so miraculously discovered, will prove to the government'.[23] The Catholic convert and erstwhile Fellow of Magdalen College, Oxford, Robert Charnock was executed in 1696 for treason on account of his involvement in the Assassination Plot, but defiantly defended his actions as serving the public interest. In Charnock's view, it was 'the duty of every loyal subject that has the courage and opportunity to do it, to rid the world of a public enemy who has kindled a war all over Europe, and sacrificed more lives of men to his insatiable ambition than all your Mariuses and Sullas, Caesars and Pompeys put together'.[24]

In 1697, a series of treaties known as the 'Peace of Ryswick' ended the Grand Alliance's nine-year war with France and included commitments by Louis XIV to recognize William as rightful king of England, Scotland and Ireland; not to support or assist William's Jacobite adversaries; and to withdraw French troops from William's ancestral enclave of Orange in Provence. But military victories and international treaties could not insure against dynastic disappointment. In January 1700, Princess Anne miscarried in her seventeenth (and final) pregnancy, six months before her only surviving son, William, duke of Gloucester, died from smallpox on 30 July. Accordingly, William turned to Parliament to insist on the need to preserve the Protestant succession by passing legislation that definitively vested succession to the English crown in the Hanoverian line attaching to Elizabeth of Bohemia's twelfth child, Sophia, and her descendants. In doing so, William earned admiration from pamphleteers who judged it much safer to 'have a successor declared, than confusion should make havoc of the state'.[25] For although the terms of the Revolution settlement in 1689 had barred Catholics from acceding as monarch of England, it had not formally identified the line of succession that would obtain if neither of James VII & II's Protestant daughters, Mary and Anne, left direct heirs. In that event, the English crown could potentially be claimed by sundry Stuart descendants – from James's other children to those of Sophia's many siblings – so long as they converted to Protestantism, however cynically or temporarily.

At the same time, another royal death in Madrid in the autumn of 1700 – that of the long ailing and childless Spanish king, Carlos II – left uncertain the future control of an enormous global empire. Earlier attempts to partition Carlos's vast inheritance had failed and although his two sisters (married to Louis XIV of France and the Holy Roman Emperor Leopold I) had renounced their rights to the Spanish crown at marriage, both had descendants on whose behalf vast territorial acquisitions could be claimed. In 1700, the English merchant and writer Daniel Defoe posed 'The Two Great Questions' – namely, how Louis XIV might seek to advance his family's interests on Carlos's death and how England should react. As Defoe feared, if the French crown were to secure Spain's global assets, the English would be 'beaten out of the field as to trade and . . . besieged in our own island'. At the same time, Defoe knew that England 'makes but a very mean figure abroad', although thankfully 'all the world does not yet see our weak side' since William's reputation 'makes us more formidable a great deal than we really are'.[26]

While the complex fallout from Carlos's death unleashed the cataclysmic War of the Spanish Succession (1702–13) between France and the Grand Alliance, the likelihood of a British war of succession increased when, on James VII & II's death in September 1701, Louis XIV breached the Peace of Ryswick's terms by publicly recognizing the exiled king's thirteen-year-old son as 'James VIII & III' and heir to his father's British crowns. Three months later, William forcefully impressed on peers and MPs the urgent need 'to consider what further effectual means may be used, for securing the succession of the crown in the Protestant line and extinguishing the hopes of all Pretenders'.[27] In response, the Act of Settlement (1701) legally and definitively vested the English and Irish lines of succession in the Electress Sophia of Hanover and her descendants and stipulated that no future monarch could be Catholic, or married to a Catholic. It was not until the Succession to the Crown Act was passed in 2013 that the Act's terms were amended to accord male and female heirs equal rights in the line of succession and no longer to disqualify claimants married to a Catholic spouse.

In March 1702, William died after sustaining injuries in a riding accident before contracting pulmonary fever. Unlike the state funeral organized for his wife, William received a private, nocturnal burial in Westminster Abbey. Although William had hoped that his cousin John William Friso, Stadtholder of Friesland and Gronigen, would inherit his Dutch offices, republican interests prevailed to leave vacant both the Stadtholderships in William's other provinces and his federal military roles. In London, William's sister-in-law, Queen Anne, announced to her first Westminster parliament on 11 March, 'I know my own heart to be entirely English' in an assertion that rang truer than similar claims attempted by her Stuart predecessors. Indeed, the new queen's subjects in Scotland had already been offended by the English Parliament's Act of Settlement with its unacceptably unilateral response to anxieties regarding the succession. In response, the Scottish Parliament's Act of Security (1704) reserved its right to choose an alternative successor to the Scottish crown unless Anglo-Scottish trade inequities were redressed. Retaliatory legislation by the English Parliament in March 1705 warned that, unless the Scots confirmed the Hanoverian succession, they would be declared aliens in England, and their coal, cattle and linen exports prohibited. Pending repeal of the so-called 'Aliens Act', the Scottish Parliament voted in the autumn of 1705 to invite Queen Anne to nominate commissioners to enter renewed negotiations for closer Anglo-Scottish union.

That November, John Ker, earl of Roxburghe, pithily predicted that Scots parliamentary support would be forthcoming: 'the motives will be, trade with most, Hanover with some, ease and security with others'.[28] Meanwhile, Defoe was sent to Edinburgh by Queen Anne's ministry to stir up Scottish support through pro-union publications. He emphasized the key need to ensure self-preservation when he reversed James VI & I's famous metaphor of suffering 'a divided and monstrous body' as joint ruler, or head, of both Scotland and England.[29] Instead, Defoe envisaged a pair of Siamese twins: 'two nations . . . already tied together in all the foundation-parts . . . inseparably joined in those parts which are the support and strength of the body', but 'divided in their upper parts, have two constitutions, two digestives, two wills, and too much opposite inclinations'. In a worst-case scenario, were one nation fatally to attack the other, Defoe warned that 'the mortality of the other would descend to the parts that were essential to them both' and 'the whole must die', rendering the aggressor guilty of suicide.[30]

In 1706, bilateral sets of commissioners agreed a Treaty of Union that created a single kingdom of 'Great Britain', vested the succession to the British crown in the Hanoverian line, created a single British Parliament at Westminster by expanding the membership of the Lords and Commons, established a British free trade area and accorded the Scots and English equal status in colonial trade. A separate Scottish legal system, Presbyterian national church and educational system were retained. Despite extensive popular opposition, the Treaty was approved by the Scottish Parliament in Edinburgh before being debated at Westminster. Describing himself as 'altogether against the union', Bishop George Hooper of Bath and Wells likened the prospect 'to the mixing of strong liquors, of a contrary nature, in one and the same vessel, which would go nigh to be burst asunder by their furious fermentation'.[31] Notwithstanding such predictions, the Treaty was ratified and its provisions took effect from 1 May 1707. The following March, Louis XIV equipped the nineteen-year-old James Stuart with more than 30 ships and 6,000 men to invade Edinburgh and start a Jacobite uprising, but the fleet failed to land in Scotland and the attempt was aborted. On 1 August 1714, Queen Anne died at the age of forty-nine, three months after the Electress Sophia had died at Herrenhausen in Hanover. Having survived quite enough Stuart charisma and grandiloquent aspirations, the English thereby acquired another foreign king in Sophia's eldest son – and Queen Anne's second cousin – who became George I. But although a staunch Protestant with two legitimate heirs, England's new Hanoverian ruler was 'initially accepted more as an idea and as a symbol than as a man or a monarch'.[32]

II

There are many competing national, international and global ways of writing our seventeenth-century island story, but this book's focus on the Stuart dynasty has determined its Continental European perspective and British remit. The events that took place in England in the century after 1588 were so climacteric that they permanently altered our country's destiny and fundamentally explain current constitutional arrangements within the British Isles as well as the nature of England's historical relations with its Continental neighbours. To foreigners, seventeenth-century England was infuriating to observe – its political infrastructure weak, its inhabitants capricious and its intentions impossible to fathom. Although Louis XIV's court at Versailles might now seem a remarkable regime in itself, in November 1680 a despairing French ambassador in London, Paul Barillon d'Amoncourt, marquis of Branges, warned Louis that 'what I write will appear to your Majesty without doubt very extraordinary, but England has no resemblance to other countries'.[33]

Within a couple of decades, the unintended consequences of inviting a Dutch Stadtholder to become king of England in 1689 were a massive expansion of the country's fiscal resources, military capacity, civil service and overseas empire to render England an eighteenth-century superpower with a *reputacíon* rivalling that of Philip II's Spain or Louis XIV's France. But unlike seventeenth-century France, Great Britain's transformation into a fiscal-military state with global ambitions was accompanied by intensely partisan political divisions and compulsive scrutiny of state activity, with MPs as keen as pamphleteers to detect alleged corruption, misgovernment, peculation and misappropriation. Within a generation, the miracle of parliamentary empire ensured that Hanoverian Britain epitomized endurance to the same extent as Stuart England had served as a synonym for instability.

Having moved to London from France in 1728, a former Benedictine monk, the Abbé Prévost, believed that the English were unfairly judged by foreigners 'on the basis of what was assumed about a violent history from the time of the Saxon invasions to the Civil War'. As Prévost pointed out, the English were, moreover, 'separated from the continent by a dangerous sea. Travellers rarely visit them, and they are too little known'.[34] *Devil-Land* has explored both the complex geopolitical entanglements and the anxious precarity of life under England's Stuart rulers, in order to make them better known. In Jonathan Swift's *Gulliver's Travels* (1726), Lemuel Gulliver attempted something similar when he recounted recent events in England to the king of Brobdingnag, after which the king pronounced himself 'perfectly astonished with the historical account I gave him of our affairs during the last century'. To the king's mind, 'it was only a heap of conspiracies, rebellions, murders, massacres, revolutions, banishments; the very worst effects that avarice, faction, hypocrisy, perfidiousness, cruelty, rage, madness, hatred, envy, lust, malice, and ambition could produce'.[35]

Notes

ABBREVIATIONS

Akkerman (ed.), *Correspondence 1* — *The Correspondence of Elizabeth Stuart, Queen of Bohemia. Volume 1: 1603–1631*, Nadine Akkerman (ed.) (Oxford, 2015).

Akkerman (ed.) *Correspondence 2* — *The Correspondence of Elizabeth Stuart, Queen of Bohemia. Volume 2: 1632–1642*, Nadine Akkerman (ed.) (Oxford, 2011).

Bruce (ed.), *Charles I* — *Charles I in 1646: Letters of King Charles the First to Queen Henrietta Maria*, John Bruce (ed.) (London, 1855).

Cárdenas, *Revolución Inglesa* — Alonso de Cárdenas, *La Revolución Inglesa (1638–1656) / The English Revolution (1638–1656)*, Ángel Alloza and Glyn Redworth (eds) (Madrid, 2011).

Carte (ed.), *Collection* — Thomas Carte (ed.), *Collection of Original Letters and Papers*, 2 vols (London, 1739).

Chamberlain, *Letters* — Norman E. McClure (ed.), *The Letters of John Chamberlain*, 2 vols (Philadelphia PA, 1939).

Clarendon, *State Papers* — *State Papers Collected by Edward, Earl of Clarendon, Commencing from the Year MDCXXI*, R. Scrope and T. Monkhouse (eds), 3 vols (Oxford, 1767–86).

Clarke (ed.), *Life of James the Second* — J. S. Clarke (ed.), *The Life of James the Second, King of England &c. Collected out of the Memoirs Writ of his own*

	Hand, Together with the King's Advice to his Son and his Majesty's Will, 2 vols (London, 1816).
Collins (ed.), *Letters and Memorials*	*Letters and Memorials of State, in the Reigns of Queen Mary, Queen Elizabeth, King James, King Charles the First, Part of the Reign of King Charles the Second, and Oliver's Usurpation*, Arthur Collins (ed.), 2 vols (London, 1746).
CSP Domestic	*Calendar of State Papers Domestic . . . Preserved in the Public Record Office* [Edward VI to Queen Anne], 90 vols (London, 1856–1964).
CSP Foreign	*Calendar of State Papers Foreign Series of the Reign of Elizabeth, Preserved in the Public Record Office*, 25 vols (London, 1863–1936).
CSP Ireland	*Calendar of the State Papers Relating to Ireland, Preserved in the Public Record Office*, 24 vols (London, 1860–1910).
CSP Scotland	*Calendar of the State Papers Relating to Scotland and Mary, Queen of Scots, 1547–1603 &c.*, 13 vols (Edinburgh/Glasgow/London, 1898–1969).
CSP Simancas	*Calendar of Letters and State Papers Preserved in, Or Originally Belonging to, the Archives of Simancas.* Volume IV, *Elizabeth, 1587–1603*, Martin A. S. Hume (ed.), (London, 1899).
CSP Venice	*Calendar of State Papers and Manuscripts, relating to English Affairs, existing in the Archives and Collections of Venice, and in other Libraries of Northern Italy*, 38 vols (London, 1864–1947).
Dalrymple, *Memoirs*	Sir John Dalrymple, *Memoirs of Great Britain and Ireland. From the Dissolution of the Last Parliament of Charles II until the Sea-Battle off La Hogue*, 2 vols (London, 1773).

D'Estrades, *Letters and Negotiations*	*Letters and Negotiations of the Count D'Estrades, Ambassador from Louis XIV to the States-General of the United Provinces of the Low Countries From the Year 1663 to the Year 1669 &c.*, 3 vols (London, 1711).
Evelyn, *Diary*	*The Diary of John Evelyn*, E. S. De Beer (ed.) (London, 1959).
Fotheringham (ed.), *Diplomatic Correspondence*	*The Diplomatic Correspondence of Jean de Montereul and the Brothers de Bellièvre, French Ambassadors in England and Scotland 1645–1648*, J. G. Fotheringham (ed.), 2 vols (Edinburgh, 1898).
Gardiner (ed.), *England and Germany*	Samuel Rawson Gardiner (ed.), *Letters and other Documents Illustrating the Relations between England and Germany at the Commencement of the Thirty Years War* (London, 1865).
Gardiner (ed.), *England and Germany . . . Second Series*	Samuel Rawson Gardiner (ed.), *Letters and other Documents Illustrating the Relations between England and Germany at the Commencement of the Thirty Years War. Second Series* (London, 1868).
Grey (ed.), *Debates*	Anchitell Grey (ed.), *Debates in the House of Commons from the Year 1667 to the Year 1694*, 10 vols (London, 1769).
Guizot, *Oliver Cromwell*	François Guizot, *History of Oliver Cromwell and the English Revolution from the Execution of Charles I to the Death of Cromwell*, translated by Andrew R. Scoble, 2 vols (London, 1854).
Guizot, *Richard Cromwell*	François Guizot, *History of Richard Cromwell and the Restoration of Charles II*, translated by Andrew R. Scoble, 2 vols (London, 1856).
Hardwicke, *State Papers*	Philip Yorke, second earl of Hardwicke (ed.), *Miscellaneous State Papers. From 1501 to 1726*, 2 vols (London, 1778).

Helmers, *Royalist Republic*	Helmer J. Helmers, *The Royalist Republic. Literature, Politics and Religion in the Anglo-Dutch Public Sphere, 1639–1660* (Cambridge, 2015).
HMC *Buccleuch*	Historical Manuscripts Commission, *Report on the Manuscripts of the Duke of Buccleuch and Queensberry, K.G., K.T., Preserved at Montagu House, Whitehall. Volume I*, R. E. G. Kirk (ed.) (London, 1899).
HMC *Downshire*	Historical Manuscripts Commission, *Report on the Manuscripts of the Marquis of Downshire, preserved at Easthampstead Park, Berkshire*, 6 vols (London, 1924–95).
HMC *Franciscan*	Historical Manuscripts Commission, *Report on Franciscan Manuscripts Preserved at the Convent, Merchants' Quay, Dublin*, G. D. Burtchaell and J. M. Rigg (eds) (Dublin, 1906).
HMC *Ormonde*	Historical Manuscripts Commission, *Calendar of the Manuscripts of the Marquis of Ormonde, K.P., Preserved at Kilkenny Castle. New Series*, 8 vols, C. Litton Falkiner (ed.) (London, 1902–20).
HMC *Salisbury*	Historical Manuscripts Commission, *Calendar of the Manuscripts of the Most Hon. The Marquis of Salisbury K. G. &c., Preserved at Hatfield House, Hertfordshire*, 21 vols (London, 1883–1970).
Jusserand, *French Ambassador*	J.-J. Jusserand, *A French Ambassador at the Court of Charles II. Le Comte de Cominges from his Unpublished Correspondence* (London, 1912).
Loomie, *Spain*	Albert J. Loomie (ed.), *Spain and the Jacobean Catholics*, 2 vols (London, 1973).
Meikle (ed.), *Correspondence*	Henry W. Meikle (ed.), *Correspondence of the Scots Commissioners in London 1644–1646* (Edinburgh, 1917).

Morrice, *Entring Book*	*The Entring Book of Roger Morrice, 1677–1691*, 7 vols, Mark Goldie et al. (eds) (Woodbridge, 2007–9).
Pepys, *Diary*	Robert Latham and William Matthews (eds), *The Diary of Samuel Pepys*, 10 vols (Berkeley, CA, 1971).
Pérez Tostado, *Irish Influence*	Igor Pérez Tostado, *Irish Influence at the Court of Spain in the Seventeenth Century* (Dublin, 2008).
Pincus, *Protestantism*	Steven C. Pincus, *Protestantism and Patriotism. Ideologies and the Making of English Foreign Policy, 1650–1688* (Cambridge, 1996).
Ralegh, *Works*	*The Works of Sir Walter Ralegh Kt., Now first Collected*, 8 vols (Oxford, 1829).
Senning, *Spain, Rumor*	Calvin F. Senning, *Spain, Rumor, and Anti-Catholicism in mid-Jacobean England. The Palatine Match, Cleves, and the Armada Scares of 1612–1613 and 1614* (London, 2019).
Stuart Royal Proclamations 1	*Stuart Royal Proclamations, Volume 1: Royal Proclamations of King James I, 1603–1625*, James F. Larkin and Paul L. Hughes (eds) (Oxford, 1973).
Stuart Royal Proclamations 2	*Stuart Royal Proclamations, Volume 2: Royal Proclamations of King Charles I, 1625–1646*, James F. Larkin (ed.) (Oxford, 1983).
Sully, *Memoirs*	Pierre Mathurin de L'Écluse des Loges (ed.), *Memoirs of the Duke of Sully: During his Residence at the English Court; to which he was sent Ambassador from Henry IV of France, Upon the Accession of King James the First* (Dublin, 1751).
Temple, *Works*	*The Works of Sir William Temple Bart. In Four Volumes. To which is Prefixed, The Life and Character of the Author*, 4 vols (Edinburgh, 1754).

Thurloe, *State Papers*	*A Collection of the State Papers of John Thurloe Esq.; Secretary, First to the Council of State, and Afterwards to the Two Protectors, Oliver and Richard Cromwell*, Thomas Birch (ed.), 7 vols (London, 1742).
Warner (ed.), *Nicholas Papers*	*The Nicholas Papers. Correspondence of Sir Edward Nicholas, Secretary of State*, George F. Warner (ed.), 4 vols (London, 1886).
Winwood, *Memorials*	*Memorials of Affairs of State in the Reigns of Q. Elizabeth and K. James I, Collected Chiefly from the Original Papers of the Right Honourable Sir Ralph Winwood Kt., Sometime one of the Principal Secretaries of State* [Edmund Sawyer (ed.)], 3 vols (London, 1725).

INTRODUCING DEVIL-LAND

1. Quoted by Helmers, *Royalist Republic*, p. 209.
2. Quoted by Tim Harris, 'Did the English have a Script for Revolution?' in Keith Michael Baker and Dan Edelstein (eds), *Scripting Revolution. A Historical Approach to the Comparative Study of Revolutions* (Stanford, CA, 2015), pp. 25, 363, n. 1.
3. Temple, *Works*, Vol. IV, p. 31 (27 March 1674).
4. *Essays, Critical and Miscellaneous by T. Babington Macaulay* (Philadelphia, PA, 1846), p. 346 ('Life and Writings of Sir William Temple').
5. Edmund Garrard, *The Country Gentleman Moderator. Collections of such Intermarriages as have been between the two Royal Lines of England and Spain, since the Conquest &c.* (London, 1624), sig. A4r.
6. Quoted by Rebecca Olson, *Arras Hanging: The Textile that Determined Early Modern Literature and Drama* (Newark, DE, 2013), p. 34.
7. 'Prologue' to *Midas* [1592] in John Lyly, *The Complete Works*, R. Warwick Bond (ed.), 3 vols (Oxford, 1902), Vol. III, p. 115.
8. The phrase recurs in a sentimental context in Pope's 'Elegy to the Memory of an Unfortunate Lady' at lines 51–4: 'By foreign hands thy dying eyes were closed, / By foreign hands thy decent limbs composed, / By foreign hands thy humble grave adorned, / By strangers honoured, and by strangers mourned!' (Pat Rogers (ed.), *Alexander Pope. The Major Works including The Rape of the Lock and The Dunciad* (Oxford, 1993), pp. 148–9).

9. 'A. Ar.', *The Practise of Princes* ([Amsterdam], 1630), p. 11.
10. *CSP Venice, Volume XXVIII: 1647–1652*, pp. 169–70 (8 February 1651).
11. Quoted by Charles-Édouard Levillain, 'London Besieged? The City's Vulnerability during the Glorious Revolution' in Jason McElligott (ed.), *Fear, Exclusion and Revolution: Roger Morrice and Britain in the 1680s* (Aldershot, 2006), p. 106.
12. Quoted by Geoffrey Parker, *Global Crisis: War, Climate Change and Catastrophe in the Seventeenth Century* (New Haven, CT, 2013), p. xxiii.
13. Thurloe, *State Papers*, Vol. III, p. 135 (11 February 1655).
14. *CSP Venice, Volume XXX: 1655–1656*, p. 129 (29 October 1655).
15. James Harrington, *The Commonwealth of Oceana* and *A System of Politics*, J. G. A. Pocock (ed.) (Cambridge, 1977), p. 144.
16. [Pierre Du Moulin], *England's Appeal from the Private Cabal at Whitehall to the Great Council of the Nation, the Lords and Commons in Parliament assembled. By a True Lover of his Country* ([London], 1673), p. 1.
17. J. P. Kenyon (ed.), *The Stuart Constitution 1603–1608. Documents and Commentary* (Cambridge, 1986), pp. 29, 32 (Form of Apology and Satisfaction, 20 June 1604).
18. Before Charles's accession as king, Rubens had acclaimed his sophisticated connoisseurship, describing him as 'the greatest amateur of paintings among the princes of the world' (quoted by Per Rumberg and Desmond Shawe-Taylor, *Charles I. King and Collector* (London, 2018), p. 17).
19. John Milton, 'Of Reformation touching Church Discipline' [1641] in C. A. Patrides (ed.), *John Milton, Selected Prose* (Columbia, MN, 1985), p. 96.
20. Oliver Cromwell to Robert Jenner and John Ashe, 20 November 1648, Knottingley; <http://www.olivercromwell.org/Letters_and_speeches/letters/Letter_83.pdf> (accessed 16 December 2020).
21. J. L. 'Philalethes', *Old Sayings and Predictions Verified and Fulfilled. Touching the young King of Scotland and his Good Subjects* (London, 1651), single-sheet folio.
22. J.-J. Jusserand (ed.), *Recueil des Instructions Données aux Ambassadeurs et Ministres de France. Volume XXV* (Paris, 1929), p. 271 ('qu'il faut que votre Majesté détermine si'il lui convient que Angleterre soit gouvernée par une republique ou par un roi').
23. Jonathan I. Israel, 'The Dutch Role in the Glorious Revolution' in Jonathan I. Israel (ed.), *The Anglo-Dutch Moment: Essays on the Glorious Revolution and its World Impact* (Cambridge, 1991), p. 128.
24. N. Japikse (ed.), *Correspondentie van Willem III en van Hans Willem Bentinck . . . Deel II* (The Hague, 1928) pp. 20–21.
25. Quoted by Charles-Édouard Levillain, 'Cromwell Redivivus? William III as Military Dictator: Myth and Reality' in Esther Mijers and David Onnekink (eds), *Redefining William III. The Impact of the King-Stadholder in International Context* (Aldershot, 2007), p. 163.

26. Roberta Armstrong, 'Appendix. Diplomatic Representatives from the Habsburg Monarchy to the Court of James VI and I' in Alexander Samson (ed.), *The Spanish Match. Prince Charles's Journey to Madrid, 1623* (Aldershot, 2006), p. 210.
27. Jusserand, *French Ambassador*, p. 131 (22 February 1663).
28. James Howell, *Proedria Vasilikē: A Discourse concerning the Precedency of Kings . . . whereunto is also adjoined a Distinct Treatise of Ambassadors* &c. (London, 1664), p. 182, sig. B2r, 183.
29. Sir Richard Fanshawe, *Original Letters of his Excellency Sir Richard Fanshaw, during his Embassies in Spain and Portugal &c.* (London, 1701), p. 284 (25 August 1664).
30. Guy Miège, *A Relation of Three Embassies from his Sacred Majesty, Charles II to the Great Duke of Muscovy, the King of Sweden and the King of Denmark* (London, 1669), p. 257.
31. Logan Pearsall Smith (ed.), *The Life and Letters of Sir Henry Wotton*, 2 vols (Oxford, 1907), Vol. I, p. 49.
32. James Howell, *Epistolæ Ho-Elianæ. Familiar Letters Domestic and Foreign. Divided into Sundry Sections Partly Historical, Political, Philosophical* (London, 1655), p. 97 (10 June 1622).
33. Abraham de Wicquefort, *The Embassador and his Functions: Written by Monsieur de Wicquefort, Privy-Counsellor to the Duke of Brunswick and Lunenburg, Zell &c.* (London, 1716), p. 296.
34. Quoted by Cedric C. Brown, *Friendship and its Discourses in the Seventeenth Century* (Oxford, 2016), p. 163; HMC *Buccleuch* (London, 1899), p. 432 (26 July 1669).
35. H. J. Chaytor (trans. and ed.), 'Embajada Española: An Anonymous Contemporary Spanish Guide to Diplomatic Procedure in the Last Quarter of the Seventeenth Century', *Camden Miscellany. Volume XIV* (London, 1926), pp. 31, 15, 17.
36. Quoted by Douglas Biow, *Doctors, Ambassadors, Secretaries: Humanism and Professions in Renaissance Italy* (Chicago, IL, 2002), p. 143.
37. See Ian Michael, 'King James VI & I and the Count of Gondomar: Two London Bibliophiles 1613–1618 and 1620–1622' in Edward H. Friedman and Harlan Sturm (eds), *Never-ending Adventure: Studies in Medieval and Early Modern Spanish Literature in Honor of Peter N. Dunn* (Newark, DE, 2002), pp. 421–36.
38. C. Litton Falkiner (ed.), HMC *Ormonde . . . Volume IV* (London, 1904), pp. 307, 308 (20 January 1679).
39. Quoted by Michael Questier, *Dynastic Politics and the British Reformations 1558–1630* (Oxford, 2019), p. 1.
40. Quoted by Margaret Shewring, 'Divergent Discourses: Multiple Voices in Festival Accounts of the Marriage of Charles I and Henrietta Maria' in Marie-Claude Canova Green and Sara J. Wolfson (eds), *The Wedding of*

Charles I and Henrietta Maria, 1625. Celebrations and Controversy (Turnhout, 2020), p. 157.

41. Akkerman (ed.), *Correspondence 1*, pp. 827, 824 (14 February and 12 January 1631); see also John Reeve, 'Sir Dudley Carleton and Sir Thomas Roe: English Servants of the Queen of Bohemia and the Protestant International during the Thirty Years War', *Parergon*, 32:3 (2015), pp. 151–81.
42. John Morrill, 'Dynasties, Realms, Peoples and State Formation, 1500–1720' in Robert von Friedeburg and John Morrill (eds), *Monarchy Transformed: Princes and their Elites in Early Modern Western Europe* (Cambridge, 2017), p. 39.
43. [John Taylor], *Religion's Enemies. With a Brief and Ingenious Relation, as by Anabaptists, Brownists, Papists, Familists, Atheists and Foolists, saucily presuming to toss Religion in a Blanket* (London, 1641), p. 5.
44. Jonathan Scott, *England's Troubles: England's Seventeenth-Century Political Instability in European Context* (Cambridge, 2000) pp. 29–30.
45. *CSP Venice, Volume XXXI: 1657–1659*, p. 197 (17 May 1658).
46. Jusserand, *French Ambassador*, p. 115 (13 September 1663).
47. Pepys, *Diary*, Vol. VIII, pp. 26, 27 (23 January 1667).
48. *At the Council-Chamber in Whitehall, Monday the 22 of October, 1688* ([London, 1688]), pp. 2, 9.
49. Nathan Johnstone, *The Devil and Demonism in Early Modern England* (Cambridge, 2006), p. 46.
50. James VI, *A Fruitful Meditation containing a Plain and Facile Exposition of the 7th, 8th, 9th and 10th verses of the 20th Chapter of the Revelation in the Form of a Sermon* (Edinburgh, 1588), sig. B2v.
51. Thomas Nashe, *Pierce Penniless, His Supplication to the Devil* (London, 1592), sig. G2r.
52. James VI, *Daemonologie in Form of a Dialogue, Divided into Three Books* (Edinburgh, 1597), pp. 54–5.
53. Quoted by Stephen Clucas and Rosalind Davies in 'Introduction' to Stephen Clucas and Rosalind Davies (eds), *The Crisis of 1614 and The Addled Parliament. Literary and Historical Perspectives* (Farnham, 2003), p. 3.
54. *CSP Venice, Volume XVIII: 1623–1625*, pp. 254, 343 (29 March and 14 June 1624).
55. *CSP Venice, Volume XXIV: 1636–1639*, p. 236 (9 July 1637).
56. Anthony Nixon, *Great Britain's General Joys, London's Glorious Triumphs, Dedicated to the Immortal Memory of the Joyful Marriage of the two Famous and Illustrious Princes, Frederick and Elizabeth* (London, 1613), sig. A4r.
57. Sully, *Memoirs*, pp. 107–8.
58. Quoted by Parker, *Global Crisis*, pp. 584–5.
59. James Howell, *A German Diet, or, The Balance of Europe wherein the Power and Weakness . . . of all the Kingdoms and States of Christendom are Impartially Poised &c.* (London, 1653), pp. 53–4.

60. Michael Roberts (trans. and ed.), *Swedish Diplomats at Cromwell's Court, 1655–1656. The Missions of Peter Julius Coyet and Christer Bonde* (London, 1988), pp. 273, 114 (4 April 1656 and 3 August 1655).
61. John Florio, *Florio his First Fruits which yield which Familiar Speech, Merry Proverbs, Witty Sentences, and Golden Sayings* (London, 1578), p. 50.
62. Chaytor (trans. and ed.), 'Embajada Española', p. 7.
63. Quoted by William James Roosen, 'The Ambassador's Craft: A Study of the Functioning of French Ambassadors under Louis XIV' (University of Southern California PhD thesis, 1967), p. 24 (12/22 January 1663).
64. Jusserand, *French Ambassador*, pp. 106, 100 (23 July 1663 and 4 February 1664); [Charles-Louis de Secondat, baron de Montesquieu], *Montesquieu: The Spirit of the Laws*, Anne M. Cohler, Basia Carolyn Miller and Harold Samuel Stone (trans. and eds) (Cambridge, 1989), p. 70.
65. Jusserand, *French Ambassador*, pp. 160–61, 129 (2 July 1665 and 17 April 1664).
66. W. E. Knowles Middleton (ed.), *Lorenzo Magalotti at the Court of Charles II. His Relazione d'Inghilterra of 1668* (Waterloo, ON, 1980), pp. 16–17.
67. Quoted by Paul Slack, 'Perceptions of the Metropolis in Seventeenth-century England' in Peter Burke, Brian Harrison and Paul Slack (eds), *Civil Histories: Essays Presented to Sir Keith Thomas* (Oxford, 2000), p. 163.
68. James VI & I, 'A Speech in the Star Chamber, the 20 of June Anno 1616' in Johann P. Sommerville (ed.), *King James VI and I. Political Writings* (Cambridge, 1994), pp. 226, 225.
69. Thomas Dekker, *A Rod for Runaways God's Tokens, of his Fearful Judgments, sundry ways pronounced upon this City, and on Several Persons, both Flying from it, and Staying in it &c.* (London, 1626), sigs D3r, A2r, Bv.
70. Anonymous, *A Letter from Mercurius Civicus to Mercurius Rusticus: or, London's Confession but not Repentance, showing that the beginning and the obstinate pursuance of this accursed horrid Rebellion is principally to be ascribed to that Rebellious City* ([London], 1643), p. 32.
71. [James Howell], *The True Informer, who in the following Discourse or Colloquy, discovers unto the World the chief causes of the sad Distempers in Great Britain and Ireland &c.* ([London, 1643]), p. 15.
72. Jusserand, *French Ambassador*, p. 144 (1 June 1665).
73. Based on an ability to write their own name, around 5 per cent of women and 15 per cent of men were deemed 'literate' in 1550; these proportions had risen to 30 per cent and 40 per cent by 1700. But since more people could read before they could write, formal literacy rates often underestimate the extent of functional literacy; see David Cressy, 'Literacy in Context: Meaning and Measurement in Early Modern England' in John Brewer and Roy Porter (eds), *Consumption and the World of Goods* (London, 1993), pp. 305–19.

74. Chamberlain, *Letters*, Vol. II, p. 423 (16 February 1622).
75. Quoted by Kevin Sharpe, *The Personal Rule of Charles I* (New Haven, CT, 1992), pp. 646–7.
76. Joad Raymond, *Pamphlets and Pamphleteering in Early Modern Britain* (Cambridge, 2003), p. 163.
77. Thurloe, *State Papers*, Vol. I, p. 454 (13 September 1653).
78. Quoted by Andrew Pettegree, *The Invention of News: How the World Came to Know About Itself* (New Haven, CT, 2014), p. 237.
79. Samuel de Sorbière, *A Voyage to England, containing many things relating to the State of Learning, Religion, and other Curiosities of that Kingdom &c.* (London, 1709), p. 50.
80. *CSP Venice, Volume XXXII: 1659–1661*, pp. 80–81 (24 October 1659).

1 SO STRANGE A PRECEDENT, 1587

1. HMC *Salisbury, Part I*, pp. 401, 400 (26 February 1569).
2. Sir Henry Ellis (ed.), *Holinshed's Chronicles of England, Scotland and Ireland*, 6 vols (London, 1808), Vol. IV, p. 917.
3. *CSP Scotland, Volume VIII: 1585–1586*, p. 701 (8 September 1586).
4. *CSP Scotland, Volume IX: 1586–1588*, pp. 60, 96–7, 100 ('Declaration of Mary, September 1586', 'Mary's First Answer' and 'Mary's Third Answer').
5. *CSP Foreign, Volume XXI, Part I: June 1586–June 1588* (London, 1927), p. 119 (1 November 1586).
6. Quoted by Kristie Macrakis, *Prisoners, Lovers, & Spies: The Story of Invisible Ink from Herodotus to al-Qaeda* (New Haven, CT, 2014), p. 32.
7. T. E. Hartley (ed.), *Proceedings in the Parliaments of Elizabeth I. Volume II: 1584–1589* (London, 1995), p. 229.
8. Hartley (ed.), *Proceedings . . . Volume II: 1584–1589*, pp. 264, 241–2.
9. Quoted by Jeff Rufo, '*La Tragédie Politique*: Antoine de Montchrestien's *La Reine d'Ecosse*, Reconsidered', *Modern Philology*, 111:3 (2014), p. 448n.
10. *Elizabeth I: Collected Works*, Leah S. Marcus, Janel Mueller and Mary Beth Rose (eds) (Chicago, IL, 2000), pp. 189, 187, 188 (Queen Elizabeth's first reply . . . 12 November 1586).
11. Elizabeth I, *Collected Works*, pp. 197, 204 (Queen Elizabeth's second reply . . . 24 November 1586).
12. *CSP Scotland, Volume IX: 1586–1588*, p. 163 (24 November 1586).
13. Quoted by Alexander S. Wilkinson, *Mary, Queen of Scots and French Public Opinion, 1542–1600* (Basingstoke, 2004), p. 128.
14. *By the Queen. A True Copy of the Proclamation lately published by the Queen's Majesty, under the Great Seal of England, for the Declaring of the Sentence, lately given against the Queen of Scots* (London, 1586), p. 2.

15. *CSP Scotland, Volume IX: 1586–1588*, p. 198 (19 December 1586).
16. James Emerson Phillips, *Images of a Queen. Mary Stuart in Sixteenth-Century Literature* (Los Angeles, CA, 1964), p. 277, n.4.
17. *CSP Foreign, Volume XXI, Part I: June 1586–June 1588* (London, 1927), pp. 169–70 (30 December 1586).
18. *CSP Venice, Volume VIII: 1581–1591*, p. 227 (15 December 1586).
19. Robert Bell (ed. and trans.), *Extract from the Despatches of M. de Courcelles, French Ambassador at the Court of Scotland, 1586–1587* (Edinburgh, 1828), pp. 4, 11, 18.
20. G. P. V. Akrigg (ed.), *Letters of King James VI & I* (Berkeley, CA, 1984), pp. 74–5 (*c.* 27 November 1586).
21. John Bruce (ed.), *Letters of Queen Elizabeth and King James of Scotland &c.* (London, 1849), pp. 43, 42.
22. Akrigg (ed.), *Letters of King James VI & I*, p. 82 (26 January 1587).
23. *CSP Foreign, Volume XXI, Part I: June 1586–June 1588* (London, 1927), p. 97 (29 September 1586).
24. *CSP Venice, Volume VIII: 1581–1591*, p. 222 (27 November 1586).
25. *CSP Scotland, Volume IX: 1586–1588*, p. 417 ('Proceedings of the French Ambassador in England'). As Jenny Wormald observed, Elizabeth's agonies over the prospect of Mary's unnatural death 'stands in stark and instructive contrast to Mary's cheerful willingness to countenance hers' (Jenny Wormald, *Mary, Queen of Scots. A Study in Failure* (London, 1988), p. 186).
26. Quoted by Alan G. R. Smith (ed.), *The Last Years of Mary, Queen of Scots. Documents from the Cecil Papers at Hatfield House* (London, 1990), p. 23.
27. *CSP Foreign, Volume XXI, Part I: June 1586–June 1588* (London, 1927), p. 241 (9 March 1587).
28. John Morris (ed.), *The Letter-Books of Sir Amias Poulet: Keeper of Mary Queen of Scots* (London, 1874), p. 362.
29. Rayne Allison, 'The Queen's Three Bodies: Gender, Criminality and Sovereignty in the Execution of Mary, Queen of Scots' in Megan Cassidy Welch and Peter Sherlock (eds), *Practices of Gender in Late Medieval and Early Modern Europe* (Turnhout, 2008), p. 100.
30. Robert Pitcairn (ed.), *Collections Relative to the Funerals of Mary, Queen of Scots* (Edinburgh, 1822), p. ix.
31. 'A Report of the Manner of the Execution of the Scottish Queen &c.' in Henry Ellis (ed.), *Original Letters, Illustrative of English History &c.*, Second Series, 4 vols (London, 1828), Vol. III, pp. 114, 113, 117.
32. *CSP Simancas*, p. 158 (24 October 1587).
33. Smith (ed.), *Last Years of Mary, Queen of Scots*, p. 75 (12 February 1587).
34. [George Puttenham], 'A Justification of Queen Elizabeth &c.' in Allan J. Crosby and John Bruce (eds), *Accounts and Papers Relating to Mary, Queen of Scots* (London, 1867), pp. 83–4.

35. *CSP Simancas*, pp. 35–6 (7 March 1587).
36. Quoted by Peter E. McCullough, 'Out of Egypt: Richard Fletcher's Sermon before Elizabeth I after the Execution of Mary Queen of Scots' in Julia M. Walker (ed.), *Dissing Elizabeth: Negative Representations of Gloriana* (Durham, NC, 1998), p. 138. Although the date of Fletcher's sermon is unknown, McCullough reasons that 'since outside Lent Elizabeth routinely heard sermons only on Sundays, 12 and 19 February, the Sundays immediately following the execution on Wednesday 8 February, seem the most likely dates' (p. 123).
37. Hartley (ed.), *Proceedings ... Volume II: 1584–1589*, pp. 280, 285. With English ministers sensitive about the reception of such anti-Stuart rhetoric in Scotland, the incendiary contents of this speech prompted Throckmorton's imprisonment in the Tower of London (Susan Doran, 'Revenge her Foul and Most Unnatural Murder? The Impact of Mary Stewart's Execution on Anglo-Scottish Relations', *History*, 85:280 (2000), p. 601).
38. Bell (ed. and trans.), *Despatches of M. de Courcelles*, p. 24.
39. Akrigg (ed.), *Letters of King James VI & I*, p. 82 (26 January 1587).
40. Sir Walter Scott (ed.), *Memoirs of Robert Cary, Earl of Monmouth, Written by Himself* (Edinburgh, 1808), p. 12.
41. *Elizabeth I: Collected Works*, p. 296 (14 February 1587).
42. *CSP Scotland, Volume IX: 1586–1588*, p. 330 (6 March 1587).
43. Quoted by Phillips, *Images of a Queen*, p. 129.
44. James Dennistoun (ed.), *Memoirs of the Affairs of Scotland, by David Moysie, M.D.LXXVII – M.DC.III* (Edinburgh, 1830), pp. 60–61.
45. Quoted by Wilkinson, *Mary, Queen of Scots and French Public Opinion*, p. 120.
46. Quoted by Phillips, *Images of a Queen*, p. 147.
47. *CSP Foreign, Volume XXI, Part I: June 1586–June 1588*, pp. 227, 236, 252 and 276 (22 February, 5 March and 24 March 1587).
48. Mitchell Leimon and Geoffrey Parker, 'Treason and Plot in Elizabethan Diplomacy: The "Fame of Sir Edward Stafford" Reconsidered', *English Historical Review*, 111:444 (1996), p. 1148.
49. *CSP Simancas*, p. 57 (31 March 1587).
50. Quoted by Allison, 'The Queen's Three Bodies', pp. 114–15.
51. *CSP Foreign, Volume XXI, Part II: April–December 1587*, p. 192 (23 July 1587).
52. *CSP Venice, Volume VIII: 1581–1591*, p. 260 (28 March 1587).
53. *CSP Simancas*, p. 31 (6 March 1587).
54. Quoted by Jesús M. Usunáriz, 'The Political Discourse on Elizabeth I in Sixteenth- and Seventeenth-Century Spain' in Eduardo Olid Guerrero and Esther Fernández (eds), *The Image of Elizabeth I in Early Modern Spain* (Lincoln, NE, 2019), p. 93.

55. *CSP Venice, Volume VIII: 1581–1591*, p. 256 (13 March 1587).
56. Quoted by Phillips, *Images of a Queen*, p. 129.
57. Quoted by Christopher Highley, 'Richard Verstegan's Book of Martyrs' in Christopher Highley and John N. King (eds), *John Foxe and his World* (Abingdon, 2002), p. 185.
58. *CSP Foreign, Volume XXI, Part I: June 1586–June 1588*, pp. 316, 455 (22 June 1587 and 23 December 1587/2 January 1588). The first dramatic recreation of Mary's execution was a Latin school play, *Maria Stuarta Tragoedia*, written by a French Jesuit, Jean de Bordes, while teaching in Milan in 1589 (Phillips, *Images of a Queen*, pp. 189–95).
59. Maria Jesus Perez-Jauregui, 'A Queen in a "Purple Robe": Henry Constable's Poetic Tribute to Mary, Queen of Scots', *Studies in Philology*, 113:3 (2016), pp. 587, 581.
60. James H. McDonald and Nancy Pollard Brown (eds), *The Poems of Robert Southwell, S. J.* (Oxford, 1967), pp. 47–8.
61. Perez-Jauregui, 'A Queen in a "Purple Robe"', p. 585.
62. James Steven Curl, 'After 1587: A Flemish Funerary Connection to Mary Queen of Scots', *Church Monuments. Journal of the Church Monuments Society*, 32 (2017), p. 89.
63. Wilkinson, *Mary, Queen of Scots and French Public Opinion*, pp. 110–11.
64. Bell (ed. and trans.), *Despatches of M. de Courcelles*, pp. 75–6.
65. Joseph Bain (ed.), *The Border Papers. Calendar of Letters and Papers relating to the Affairs of the Borders of England and Scotland, Preserved in her Majesty's Public Record Office, London. Volume 1: 1560–1594* (Edinburgh, 1894), pp. 308, 305 (23 and 17 January 1588).
66. *CSP Venice, Volume VIII: 1581–1591*, p. 306 (18 August 1587).
67. Quoted by De Lamar Jensen, 'The Phantom Will of Mary Queen of Scots', *Scotia*, 4 (1980), p. 1.
68. Quoted by Colin Martin and Geoffrey Parker, *The Spanish Armada* (Manchester, 1999), p. 111.
69. *CSP Simancas*, pp. 163, 167, 295 (Advices from London, November 1587 and General Orders by Medina Sidonia).

2 THE ENTERPRISE OF ENGLAND, 1588

1. Geoffrey Parker, 'David or Goliath? Philip II and his World in the 1580s' in Richard L. Kagan and Geoffrey Parker (eds), *Spain, Europe and the Atlantic. Essays in Honour of J. H. Elliott* (Cambridge, 2002), p. 246.
2. Quoted by Parker, 'David or Goliath?', p. 256.
3. Alexander Samson, 'Changing Places: The Marriage and Royal Entry of Philip, Prince of Austria, and Mary Tudor, July–August 1554', *The Sixteenth Century Journal*, 36:3 (2005), p. 766.

4. Quoted by Geoffrey Parker, 'The Place of Tudor England in the Messianic Vision of Philip II of Spain: The Prothero Lecture', *Transactions of the Royal Historical Society*, 12 (2002), p. 185.
5. Spencer J. Weinreich (ed.), *Pedro de Ribadeneyra's Ecclesiastical History of the Schism in the Kingdom of England. A Spanish Jesuit's History of the English Reformation* (Leiden, 2017), pp. 535, 533, 745, 751–2; Ribadeneyra had visited England during Mary Tudor's reign in the 1550s.
6. Aislinn Muller, *The Excommunication of Elizabeth I. Faith, Politics and Resistance in Post-Reformation England, 1570–1603* (Leiden, 2020), p. 42.
7. *CSP Venice, Volume VIII: 1581–1591*, p. 272 (6 May 1587).
8. Weinreich (ed.), *Pedro de Ribadeneyra's Ecclesiastical History*, pp. 747, 749.
9. John Knox Laughton (ed.), *State Papers Relating to the Defeat of the Spanish Armada*, 2 vols (London, 1895), Vol. I, pp. 48–9 (27 January 1587).
10. *CSP Foreign, Volume XXI, Part I: June 1586–June 1588*, pp. 451–2 (23 December 1587/2 January 1588).
11. *CSP Venice, Volume VIII: 1581–1591*, p. 223 (3 December 1586).
12. Quoted by Geoffrey Parker, *The Grand Strategy of Philip II* (New Haven, CT, 1998), pp. 211–12.
13. Quoted by Mitchell Leimon and Geoffrey Parker, 'Treason and Plot in Elizabethan Diplomacy: The "Fame of Sir Edward Stafford" Reconsidered', *English Historical Review*, 111:444 (1996), pp. 1151, 1154.
14. *CSP Foreign, Volume XXI, Part I: June 1586–June 1588* (London, 1927), p. 590 (12 April 1588).
15. Parker, *Grand Strategy*, pp. 217, 209–10.
16. Laughton (ed.), *State Papers ... Defeat of the Spanish Armada*, Vol. I, pp. 196, 213–14 (13 June and 20 June 1588).
17. Laughton (ed.), *State Papers ... Defeat of the Spanish Armada*, Vol. I, pp. 131–2 (6 April 1588).
18. *CSP Domestic ... Elizabeth, 1581–1590*, p. 503 (16 July 1588).
19. *A True Discourse of the Army which the King of Spain caused to be assembled in the Haven of Lisbon, in the Kingdom of Portugal in the year 1588, against England* (Daniel Archdeacon trans., introduced by 'E.B.') (London, 1588).
20. Laughton (ed.), *State Papers ... Defeat of the Spanish Armada*, Vol. I, pp. 122–3 (29 March 1588).
21. William Allen, *An Admonition to the Nobility and People of England and Ireland concerning the Present Wars made for the Execution of His Holiness's Sentence by the High and Mighty King Catholic of Spain* ([?Antwerp], 1588, pp. 31, 34.
22. Paul L. Hughes and James F. Larkin (eds), *Tudor Royal Proclamations, Volume III: The Later Tudors (1588–1603)* (London, 1969), pp. 15, 14 ('Ordering Martial Law against Possessors of Papal Bulls, Books, Pamphlets', 1 July 1588).

23. 'G. D.', *A Brief Discovery of Doctor Allen's Seditious Drifts, Contained in a Pamphlet written by him, Concerning the Yielding up of the Town of Deventer (in Overijssel) &c.* (London, 1588), pp. 82–3, 121.
24. George P. B. Naish (ed.), *Documents Illustrating the History of the Spanish Armada* in *The Naval Miscellany, Volume IV* (London, 1952), p. 60.
25. Edmond Harris, *A Sermon Preached at Brocket Hall, before . . . Gentlemen there assembled for the Training of Soldiers, January 2 and 3* (London, 1588), sig. C4r.
26. Thomas Tymme, *A Preparation against the Prognosticated Dangers of this Year, 1588* (London, 1588), sigs B1v, B7r.
27. Laughton (ed.), *State Papers . . . Defeat of the Spanish Armada*, Vol. I, p. 254 (12 July 1588).
28. *CSP Venice, Volume VIII: 1581–1591*, pp. 345, 349 (19 March and 8 April 1588).
29. *CSP Simancas*, pp. 239, 367, 385 (21 March, 8 and 19 August 1588).
30. *CSP Simancas*, pp. 199, 207, 208 (31 January and 16 February 1588).
31. *CSP Simancas*, pp. 236, 246, 250 (20 March, 1 April 1588 and secret instructions to Medina Sidonia).
32. *CSP Simancas*, p. 318 (24 June 1588).
33. *CSP Foreign, Volume XXII: July–December 1588*, p. 34 (12 July 1588).
34. Laughton (ed.), *State Papers . . . Defeat of the Spanish Armada*, Vol. I, p. 341 (29 July 1588).
35. P. Gallagher and D. W. Cruickshank (eds), *God's Obvious Design: Papers for the Spanish Armada Symposium, Sligo, 1988, with an Edition and Translation of the Account of Francisco de Cuéllar* (London, 1990), p. 230.
36. John J. McAleer, 'Ballads on the Spanish Armada', *Texas Studies in Literature and Language*, 4:4 (1963), pp. 604–5.
37. Quoted by Susan Frye, 'The Myth of Elizabeth at Tilbury', *Sixteenth Century Journal*, 23:1 (1992), pp. 98, 102.
38. John Bruce (ed.), *Letters of Queen Elizabeth and King James of Scotland &c.* (London, 1849), p. 53 (August 1588).
39. *CSP Scotland, Volume IX: 1586–1588*, p. 593 (10 August 1588). Heeding such advice, it has been calculated Elizabeth spent over £58,000 sterling on James's pension and maintaining a resident ambassador in Scotland between 1586 and 1603 (Cynthia Fry, 'Diplomacy and Deception: King James VI of Scotland's Foreign Relations with Europe (*c.*1584–1603)') (St Andrews University PhD thesis, 2014), p. 11n.
40. Laughton (ed.), *State Papers . . . Defeat of the Spanish Armada*, Vol. II, p. 96 (10 August 1588).
41. Quoted by Carol Z. Wiener, 'The Beleaguered Isle: A Study of Elizabethan and Early Jacobean Anti-Catholicism', *Past & Present*, 51:1 (1971), p. 52.
42. Laughton (ed.), *State Papers . . . Defeat of the Spanish Armada*, Vol. II, pp. 17–20, 25–9.

43. *CSP Simancas*, pp. 480–81 (5 November 1588).
44. Quoted by Arthur F. Marotti and Steven W. May, 'Two Lost Ballads of the Armada Thanksgiving Celebration', *English Literary Renaissance*, 41:1 (2011), p. 55, n. 32.
45. *The Diary of Mr. James Melville, 1556–1601* (Edinburgh, 1829), pp. 174–5.
46. Quoted by Concepción Saenz-Cambra, 'James VI's *Ius Suum Conservare*: His Intrigues with Spain, 1580–1603', *International Review of Scottish Studies*, 30 (2005), p. 95.
47. *CSP Scotland, Volume IX: 1586–1588*, p. 607 (1 September 1588).
48. Gallagher and Cruickshank (eds), *God's Obvious Design*, p. 245.
49. Weinreich (ed.), *Pedro de Ribadeneyra's Ecclesiastical History*, p. 747.
50. [William Cecil, Lord Burghley], *The Copy of a Letter sent out of England to Don Bernardin Mendoza, Ambassador in France for the King of Spain, Declaring the State of England &c.* (London, 1588), pp. 3, 2, 31.
51. *CSP Simancas*, p. 484 (9 November 1588); see Meaghan J. Brown, '"The Hearts of All Sorts of People Were Enflamed": Manipulating Readers of Spanish Armada News', *Book History*, 17 (2014), 94–116.
52. Quoted by Edward P. Cheyney, *A History of England. From the Defeat of the Armada to the Death of Elizabeth*, 2 vols (London, 1914), Vol. I, p. 153 (18 October 1588).
53. *CSP Venice, Volume VIII: 1581–1591*, pp. 409–10 (1 November 1588).
54. *CSP Simancas*, pp. 452, 476 (26 September and 2 November 1588).
55. Laughton (ed.), *State Papers ... Defeat of the Spanish Armada*, Vol. II, pp. 310, 311 (20 December 1588).
56. Quoted by Christopher Maginn, 'After the Armada: Thanksgiving in Ireland, 1589', *Historical Research*, 93:259 (2020), p. 34.
57. Robert Humpston, *A Sermon Preached at Reysham in the County of Norfolk, the 22 of September, 1588 &c.* (London, 1589), pp. [22], 24.
58. Oliver Pigge, 'To the Reader' in *Meditations Concerning Prayers to Almighty God, When the Spaniards were come into the Narrow Seas* (London, 1589), sig. A5v.
59. King James VI, *Ane Meditation upon the XXV, XXVI, XXVII, XXVIII and XXIX Verses of the XV Chapter of the First Book of the Chronicles of the Kings &c.* (Edinburgh, 1589), sig. B3v ('brangling' is a Scots term for 'shaking').
60. Quoted by A. E. B. Coldiron, 'The World on One Page: An Octolingual Armada Broadside' in A. E. B. Coldiron, *Printers Without Borders: Translation and Textuality in the Renaissance* (Cambridge, 2015), p. 207.
61. I. L., *The Birth, Purpose, and Mortal Wound of the Romish Holy League* (London, 1589), sig. A3r.
62. Anonymous, *Skeletonical Salutation, or Condign Gratulation, and Just Vexation of the Spanish Nation, that in a Bravado, Spent many a Crusado, in Setting Forth an Armado, England to Invado* (Oxford, 1589), sigs A5r, A6v.

63. M. J. Rodríguez-Salgado (ed.), *Armada: 1588–1988: An International Exhibition to commemorate the Spanish Armada. The Official Catalogue* (London, 1988), p. 276.
64. Quoted by Pauline Croft, '"The State of the World is Marvellously Changed": England, Spain and Europe, 1558–1604' in Susan Doran and Glenn Richardson (eds), *Tudor England and its Neighbours* (Basingstoke, 2005), p. 178.
65. *CSP Venice, Volume VIII: 1581–1591*, p. 459 (28 June 1589).
66. Quoted by Matthew Dimmock, 'Crusading Piracy? The Curious Case of the Spanish in the Channel, 1590–1595' in Claire Jowitt (ed.), *Pirates? The Politics of Plunder, 1550–1650* (Basingstoke, 2007), p. 74.
67. Anonymous, *A Fig for the Spaniard, or Spanish Spirits &c.* (London, 1591), sigs B3v, D1v.

3 AN INTERNATIONAL SUCCESSION DEBATE, 1589–1601

1. [Robert Persons], *News from Spain and Holland* ([Antwerp], 1593), pp. 21, 40, 38.
2. G. R. Elton, *The Tudor Constitution. Documents and Commentary* (Cambridge, 1982), p. 75.
3. [Peter Wentworth], *A Pithy Exhortation to Her Majesty for Establishing her Successor to the Crown &c.* ([Edinburgh], 1598), pp. 8, 5, 71.
4. [Richard Verstegan], *A Copy of a Letter, Lately written by a Spanish Gentleman to his Friend in England &c.* ([Antwerp], 1589), pp. 20–21, 5.
5. See Susan Doran and Paulina Kewes, 'The Earlier Elizabethan Succession Question Revisited' in Susan Doran and Paulina Kewes (eds), *Doubtful and Dangerous: The Question of Succession in Late Elizabethan England* (Manchester, 2014), pp. 20–44.
6. *Elizabeth I: Collected Works*, Leah S. Marcus, Janel Mueller and Mary Beth Rose (eds) (Chicago, IL, 2000), p. 65 ('Queen Elizabeth's Conversations with the Scottish Ambassador . . . September and October 1561').
7. David Calderwood, *The True History of the Church of Scotland. From the beginning of the Reformation, unto the end of the Reign of King James VI* ([?Edinburgh], 1704), p. 238.
8. Annie I. Cameron and Robert S. Rait (eds), *The Warrender Papers. Volume II* (Edinburgh, 1932), p. 103 (16 March 1589).
9. *CSP Scotland, Volume IX: 1586–1588*, p. 707 (8 March 1589).
10. See Ruth Grant, 'The Brig o'Dee Affair, the Sixth Earl of Huntly and the Politics of the Counter-Reformation' in Julian Goodare and Michael Lynch (eds), *The Reign of James VI* (Edinburgh, 2000), pp. 93–109.
11. HMC *Salisbury, Part III*, p. 439 (20 October 1589).

12. G. P. V. Akrigg (ed.), *Letters of King James VI & I* (Berkeley, CA, 1984), p. 98 (*c.* 22 October 1589).
13. A. Francis Steuart (ed.), *Memoirs of His Own Life by Sir James Melville of Halhill, M.D.XLIX–M.D.XCIII* (Edinburgh, 1827), p. 365.
14. Cameron and Rait (eds), *Warrender Papers. Volume II*, p. 68 (14 February 1588).
15. See Thomas Riis, *Should Auld Acquaintance be Forgot . . . Scottish–Danish Relations c.1450–1707*, 2 vols (Odense, 1988), Vol. I, p. 33.
16. *CSP Scotland, Volume X: 1589–1593*, p. 212 (4 December 1589).
17. 'The Danish Account of the Marriage of James VI and Anne of Denmark' (translated by Peter Graves) in David Stevenson, *Scotland's Last Royal Wedding. The Marriage of James VI and Anne of Denmark* (Edinburgh, 1997), p. 80.
18. Hugo Johannsen, 'Images of Hereditary Succession' in Krista Kodres and Anu Mänd (eds), *Images and Objects in Ritual Practices in Medieval and Early Modern Northern and Central Europe* (Newcastle, 2013), p. 171.
19. John Bruce (ed.), *Letters of Queen Elizabeth and King James of Scotland &c.* (London, 1849), p. 57 (*c.* March 1590).
20. T. G. Law, 'The Spanish Blanks and Catholic Earls, 1592–1594' in P. Hume Brown (ed.), *Collected Essays and Reviews of Thomas Graves Law* (Edinburgh, 1904), pp. 270, 271.
21. Cameron and Rait (eds), *Warrender Papers. Volume II*, p. 221 (*c.* January 1594).
22. Quoted by Albert J. Loomie, *The Spanish Elizabethans: The English Exiles at the Court of Philip II* (London, 1963), p. 147.
23. *CSP Venice, Volume IX: 1592–1603*, pp. 57–8, 143 (30 January 1592 and 17 August 1594).
24. Quoted by Maureen M. Meikle and Helen M. Payne, 'From Lutheranism to Catholicism: The Faith of Anna of Denmark (1574–1619)', *Journal of Ecclesiastical History*, 64:1 (2013), p. 59.
25. James Dennistoun (ed.), *Memoirs of the Affairs of Scotland, by David Moysie, M.D.LXXVII–M.DC.III* (Edinburgh, 1830), p. 113.
26. Ian Campbell and Aonghus MacKechnie, 'The "Great Temple of Solomon" at Stirling Castle', *Architectural History*, 54 (2011), pp. 91–118.
27. *CSP Venice, Volume IX: 1592–1603*, p. 143 (8 September 1594).
28. Richard Bruce Wernham (ed.), *List and Analysis of State Papers: Foreign Series, Elizabeth I, preserved in the Public Record Office. Volume V: July 1593–December 1594* (London, 1989), p. 216 (21 July 1594).
29. *CSP Scotland, Volume XI: 1593–1595*, p. 422 (31 August 1594).
30. William Fowler, *A True Reportarie of the most Triumphant, and Royal Accomplishment, of the Baptism of the Most Excellent, Right High and Mighty Prince Frederick Henry &c.* (Edinburgh, 1594), sigs B2r, Dv, C4r; see

Rick Bowers, 'James VI, Prince Henry and *A True Reportarie* of Baptism at Stirling, 1594', *Renaissance and Reformation / Renaissance et Réforme*, n.s. 29:4 (2005), pp. 3–22.

31. Andrew Melville, 'On the Birth of the Scoto-Britannic Prince' in Paul J. McGinnis and Arthur H. Williamson (eds and trans.), *George Buchanan: The Political Poetry* (Edinburgh, 1995), pp. 278, 280.
32. *CSP Scotland, Volume XI: 1593–1595*, p. 431 (8 September 1594).
33. Paulina Kewes, '"The Idol of State Innovators and Republicans": Robert Persons's *A Conference about the Next Succession* (1594/5) in Stuart England' in Paulina Kewes and Andrew McRae (eds), *Stuart Succession Literature. Moments and Transformations* (Oxford, 2019), p. 152.
34. [Robert Persons], *A Conference about the Next Succession to the Crown of England, divided into Two Parts &c.* ([Antwerp, 1595]), pp. 67, 262, 263, 118.
35. Christopher Highley, *Catholics Writing the Nation in Early Modern Britain and Ireland* (Oxford, 2008), p. 166.
36. Quoted by Victor Houliston, *Catholic Resistance in Elizabethan England. Robert Persons's Jesuit Polemic, 1580–1610* (Aldershot, 2007), p. 87.
37. *CSP Scotland, Volume XII: 1595–1597*, p. 67 (28 November 1595).
38. Joseph Bain (ed.), *The Border Papers: Calendar of Letters and Papers relating to the Affairs of the Borders of England and Scotland, preserved in her Majesty's Public Record Office, London ... Volume II* (Edinburgh, 1896), p. 103 (1 February 1596).
39. *CSP Scotland, Volume XII: 1595–1597*, p. 193 (18 April 1596).
40. *CSP Venice, Volume IX: 1592–1603*, pp. 236, 239 (2 November 1596).
41. Quoted by Robert Dickinson, 'The Spanish Raid on Mount's Bay in 1595', *Journal of the Royal Institution of Cornwall*, 10:1 (1986–7), p. 182.
42. Quoted by Anne J. Cruz, 'Vindicating the *Vulnerata*: Cádiz and the Circulation of Religious Imagery as Weapons of War' in Anne J. Cruz (ed.), *Material and Symbolic Circulation between Spain and England, 1554–1604* (Aldershot, 2008), p. 43; quoted by Stephen and Elizabeth Usherwood (eds), *The Counter-Armada 1596: The Journall of the 'Mary Rose'* (London, 1983), p. 94. English hopes of seizing New World gold were, however, pre-empted by the Spanish decision to explode several West Indian treasure ships, rather than suffer their capture.
43. HMC *Salisbury, Part V*, p. 274 (10 July 1595).
44. Albert J. Loomie, 'Philip II's Armada Proclamation of 1597', *Recusant History*, 12 (1974), p. 221; see also Edward Tenace, 'A Strategy of Reaction: The Armadas of 1596 and 1597 and the Spanish Struggle for European Hegemony', *English Historical Review*, 118:478 (2003), pp. 855–82.
45. *CSP Ireland, 1596, July–1597*, pp. 15, 17 (6 July 1596).
46. Enrique García Hernán (ed.), *The Battle of Kinsale. Study and Documents from the Spanish Archives* (Valencia, 2013), p. 15.

47. T. G. Law (ed.), 'Documents illustrating Catholic Policy in the Reign of James VI, 1596–1598', *Miscellany of the Scottish History Society*, 15 (Edinburgh, 1893), pp. 32, 34, 37.
48. *CSP Scotland, Volume XII: 1595–1597*, p. 118 (11 January 1596).
49. Law (ed.), 'Documents illustrating Catholic Policy', p. 36.
50. *CSP Scotland, Volume XIII, Part 1: 1597–1603*, pp. 133, 136 (16 and 9 December 1597).
51. *CSP Scotland, Volume XIII, Part 1: 1597–1603*, p. 209 (22 May 1598).
52. 'Mandate of James VI for his Ambassadors ... August 1598' in Cameron and Rait (eds), *Warrender Papers. Volume II*, pp. 359–61.
53. James VI & I, *The Trew Law of Free Monarchies* (1598) in Johann P. Sommerville (ed.), *King James VI and I. Political Writings* (Cambridge, 1994), pp. 82–3.
54. [Wentworth], *A Pithy Exhortation to Her Majesty*, pp. 76, 77.
55. *CSP Venice, Volume IX: 1592–1603*, p. 327 (11 June 1598).
56. Robert Devereux, Earl of Essex, *To Maister Anthony Bacon. An Apology of the Earl of Essex, Against those which Falsely and Maliciously tax him to be the only Hinderer of the Peace, and Quiet of his Country* ([?London, ?1600]), sigs A2r, C3v.
57. Chamberlain, *Letters*, Vol. I, p. 81 (9 August 1599).
58. HMC *Salisbury, Part X*, p. 363 (27 October 1600).
59. William Forbes-Leith, *Narratives of Scottish Catholics under Mary Stuart and James VI* (London, 1889), p. 270.
60. *CSP Domestic ... Elizabeth I, 1598–1601*, pp. 189, 413 (28 April/8 May 1599 and 24 April/3 May 1600).
61. Quoted by Christian Schneider, 'A Kingdom for a Catholic? Pope Clement VIII, King James VI/I, and the English Succession in International Diplomacy (1592–1605)', *International History Review*, 37:1 (2015), p. 126.
62. *CSP Scotland, Volume XIII, Part 2: 1597–1603*, p. 770 (10 February 1601).
63. Willy Maley (ed.), 'The Supplication of the Blood of the English most Lamentably Murdered in Ireland, Crying out of the Yearth for Revenge (1598)', *Analecta Hibernica*, 36 (1995), pp. 21, 52, 54. Although Maley putatively suggested the author to be the Puritan Thomas Cartwright (p. 10), Hiram Morgan has insisted that '"The supplication of the blood of the English" can only be by one man – Edmund Spenser' (Hiram Morgan, '"Tempt not God too long, O Queen": Elizabeth and the Irish Crisis of the 1590s' in Brendan Kane and Valerie McGowan-Doyle (eds), *Elizabeth I and Ireland* (Cambridge, 2014), p. 234).
64. Quoted by Leah S. Marcus, 'Elizabeth on Ireland' in Kane and McGowan-Doyle (eds), *Elizabeth I and Ireland*, p. 56.
65. J. S. Brewer and W. M. Bullen (eds), *Calendar of the Carew Manuscripts*, 6 vols (London, 1867–73), Vol. III, p. 326 (17 September 1599).

66. 'Articles intended to be stood upon by Tyrone' in *CSP Ireland, 1599, April–1600*, pp. 279–80; Helen Georgia Stafford, *James VI of Scotland and the Throne of England* (New York, 1940), p. 223 (25 December 1600).
67. Quoted by Hiram Morgan, 'Disaster at Kinsale' in Hiram Morgan (ed.), *The Battle of Kinsale* (Wicklow, 2004), pp. 114–15, 113.
68. *CSP Simancas*, p. 690 (10 December 1601).

4 UNITING THIS SEA-WALLED ISLE, 1601–1605

1. Sir Henry Wotton, *Reliquiæ Wottonianæ; or a Collection of Lives, Letters, Poems, with characters of Sundry Personages: and other incomparable pieces of Language and Art* (London, 1651), p. 170.
2. Alexander Courtney, 'The Scottish King and the English Court: The Secret Correspondence of James VI, 1601–1603' in Susan Doran and Paulina Kewes (eds), *Doubtful and Dangerous: The Question of Succession in late Elizabethan England* (Manchester, 2014), p. 139.
3. John Bruce (ed.), *Correspondence of King James VI of Scotland with Sir Robert Cecil and others in England, During the Reign of Queen Elizabeth, with an Appendix containing Papers Illustrative of Transactions between King James and Robert, Earl of Essex* (London, 1861), pp. 23, 57.
4. *Stuart Royal Proclamations 1*, pp. 1, 3.
5. *CSP Venice, Volume X: 1603–1607*, pp. 509, 510 ('Report on England').
6. George Lawson, *Politica Sacra et Civilis*, Conal Condren (ed.) (Cambridge, 1991), p. 100.
7. Thomas Dekker, *The Wonderful Year. 1603. Wherein is shown the Picture of London Lying Sick of the Plague* (London, 1603), sig. Cv.
8. John Bruce (ed.), *Diary of John Manningham, of the Middle Temple, and of Bradbourne, Kent, Barrister-at-Law, 1602–1603* (London, 1868), p. 147.
9. HMC *Salisbury, Part XV*, p. 8 (27 March 1603).
10. Robert Cross, '"The Onely Soveraigne Medecine": Religious Politics and Political Culture in the British-Spanish Match, 1596–1625' in Valentina Caldari and Sara J. Wolfson (eds), *Stuart Marriage Diplomacy. Dynastic Politics in their European Context, 1604–1630* (Woodbridge, 2018), p. 68, n.4.
11. *CSP Simancas*, p. 735 (Report of the Council of State . . . on the English succession, 2 March 1603); see A. J. Loomie, 'Philip III and the Stuart Succession in England, 1600–1603', *Revue Belge de Philologie et d'Histoire*, 43 (1965), pp. 492–514.
12. Quoted by Nick Myers, '*Hercule Gaulois*, Great Britain's Solomon – Myths of Persuasion, Styles of Authority' in Eveline Cruickshanks (ed.), *The Stuart Courts* (Stroud, 2000), p. 34.
13. *CSP Venice, Volume X: 1603–1607*, p. 15 (3 April 1603).

14. Maurice Lee Jr (ed.), *Dudley Carleton to John Chamberlain 1603–1624. Jacobean Letters* (New Brunswick, NJ, 1972), p. 29.
15. Quoted by Robert Cross, 'To Counterbalance the World: England, Spain, and Peace in the early 17th century' (PhD thesis, Princeton University, 2012), pp. 54, 60 (31 March/10 April 1603).
16. *CSP Venice, Volume X: 1603–1607*, pp. 37, 14 (24 and 1 May 1603).
17. Quoted by Cristina Borreguero Beltrán, 'Isabel Clara Eugenia: Daughter of the Spanish Empire' in Tonio Andrade and William Reger (eds), *The Limits of Empire: European Imperial Formations in Early Modern World History* (Farnham, 2012), pp. 262, 263; quoted by Cross, 'To Counterbalance the World', p. 53 (6/16 April 1603).
18. Henri Lonchay and Joseph Cuvelier (eds), *Correspondance de la Cour d'Espagne sur les Affaires des Pays-Bas au XVIIe Siècle*, 6 vols (Brussels, 1923–1937), Vol. I, p. 141 (Report of Nicholas Scorza).
19. *CSP Venice, Volume X: 1603–1607*, p. 20 (8 May 1603).
20. HMC *Salisbury, Part XV*, p. 39 (8 April 1603).
21. Sir Walter Ralegh, 'A Discourse touching a War with Spain, and of the Protecting of the Netherlands' in Ralegh, *Works*, Vol. VIII, pp. 304, 314.
22. HMC *Salisbury, Part XV*, p. 44 (12 April 1603).
23. *CSP Venice, Volume X: 1603–1607*, pp. 9, 10 (24 April 1603).
24. James VI & I, 'Basilikon Doron' in Johann P. Sommerville (ed.), *King James VI and I. Political Writings* (Cambridge, 1994), pp. 23, 8.
25. Quoted by Jason Scott-Warren, *Sir John Harington and the Book as Gift* (Oxford, 2001), p. 9.
26. Cross, 'To Counterbalance the World', p. 104, n. 92.
27. Sully, *Memoirs*, p. 116.
28. *CSP Venice, Volume X: 1603–1607*, pp. 81, 39 (13 August and 28 May 1603).
29. Sully, *Memoirs*, p. 110.
30. *CSP Venice, Volume X: 1603–1607*, p. 55 (26 June 1603).
31. Sully, *Memoirs*, pp. 148, 123, 53, 149, 162; for Sully's 'Grand Design', see Peter Schröder, *Trust in Early Modern International Political Thought, 1598–1713* (Cambridge, 2017), pp. 48–69.
32. Mark Brayshay, 'Long-Distance Royal Journeys. Anne of Denmark's Journey from Stirling to Windsor in 1603', *Journal of Transport History*, 25:1 (2004), p. 5.
33. Quoted by Mark Nicholls, 'Treason's Reward: The Punishment of Conspirators in the Bye Plot of 1603', *Historical Journal*, 38:4 (1995), p. 826. As Nicholls shows, 'the sinister reference to the king and his family was naturally seized upon by the prosecution, even though Brooke spent the rest of his life [before his execution on 5 December 1603] withdrawing these precise words'.

34. Sully, *Memoirs*, p. 132.
35. Quoted by Mark Nicholls, 'Two Winchester Trials: The Prosecution of Henry, Lord Cobham, and Thomas, Lord Grey of Wilton, 1603', *Historical Research*, 68: 165 (1995), p. 38. Nicholls drew attention to 'a possibility that the authorities had evidence against Aremburg which it was impolitic to produce early in the reign of a king set on peace with Spain' (p. 42).
36. Ralegh, *Works*, Vol. I, pp. 684, 674 ('The Trial of Sir Walter Ralegh').
37. Quoted by Cross, 'To Counterbalance the World', p. 209 (20/30 January 1604). Before their formal reception at Winchester, the Spanish delegation visited Canterbury, Sittingbourne, Rochester, Greenwich, Hampton Court, Maidenhead, Henley, Oxford and Southampton.
38. HMC *Salisbury*, *Part XV*, p. 243 (2 September 1603).
39. John Nichols, *The Progresses, Processions and Magnificent Festivities of King James the First &c.*, 4 vols (London, 1828), Vol. I, p. 301.
40. Lee Jr (ed.), *Dudley Carleton to John Chamberlain 1603–1624*, p. 53.
41. Quoted by Alvin Kernan, *Shakespeare, the King's Playwright: Theater in the Stuart Court, 1603–1613* (London, 1995), p. 46; see Berta Caño-Echevarría and Mark Hutchings, 'The Spanish Ambassador and Samuel Daniel's *Vision of the Twelve Goddesses*: A New Document' in *English Literary Renaissance*, 42:2 (2012), pp. 223–57.
42. James VI & I, 'A Speech to Both the Houses of Parliament . . . the Last Day of March 1607' in Sommerville (ed.), *King James VI and I. Political Writings*, p. 169.
43. *CSP Venice, Volume X: 1603–1607*, p. 5 (17 April 1603).
44. 'A Proclamation for the Uniting of England and Scotland' in *Stuart Royal Proclamations 1*, p. 19.
45. James Spedding, Robert Leslie Ellis and Douglas Denon Heath (eds), *The Works of Francis Bacon*, 14 vols (London, 1861), Vol. X, p. 77 (*c.* April 1603).
46. Sully, *Memoirs*, p. 139.
47. *CSP Venice, Volume X: 1603–1607*, pp. 44, 94 (4 June and 18 September 1603).
48. David Masson (ed.), *The Register of the Privy Council of Scotland. Volume VI: AD 1599–1604* (Edinburgh, 1884), p. 596 (12 January 1604).
49. Nichols, *Progresses, Processions and Magnificent Festivities*, Vol. I, p. 301.
50. Quoted by Mark Hutchings and Berta Caño-Echevarría, 'The Spanish Ambassador's Account of James I's Entry into London, 1604', *The Seventeenth Century*, 33:3 (2018), p. 267.
51. James VI & I, 'A Speech, as it was delivered in the Upper House of the Parliament . . . on Monday the 19 day of March &c.' in Sommerville (ed.), *King James VI and I. Political Writings*, pp. 133, 135, 136, 137, 136.
52. C. Sanford Terry (ed.), *De Unione Regnorum Britanniæ Tractatus by Sir Thomas Craig &c.* (Edinburgh, 1909), pp. 208, 258, 260, 391.

53. [Sir Francis Bacon], *A Brief Discourse Touching the Happy Union of the Kingdoms of England and Scotland. Dedicated in Private to His Majesty* (London, 1603), sig. B2v.
54. Spedding, Ellis and Heath (eds), *The Works of Francis Bacon*, Vol. X, p. 221 ('Certain Articles or Considerations').
55. James VI & I, 'Speech . . . Last Day of March 1607' in Sommerville (ed.), *King James VI and I. Political Writings*, p. 169.
56. Sir Henry Savile, 'Historicall Collections' in Bruce R. Galloway and Brian P. Levack (eds), *The Jacobean Union. Six Tracts of 1604* (Edinburgh, 1985), pp. 202–3.
57. Arthur Agard, 'Of the Diversity of Names of this Island' in Thomas Hearne (ed.), *A Collection of Curious Discourses written by Eminent Antiquaries upon Several Heads in our English Antiquities*, 2 vols (London, 1771), Vol. I, p. 97.
58. Chris R. Kyle, *Parliament, Politics and Elections, 1604–1648* (Cambridge, 2001), p. 30.
59. Sir Henry Spelman, 'Of the Union' in Galloway and Levack (eds), *The Jacobean Union*, pp. 163, 170.
60. Quoted by Sarah Waurechen, 'Imagined Polities, Failed Dreams, and the Beginnings of an Unacknowledged Britain: English Responses to James VI and I's Vision of Perfect Union', *Journal of British Studies*, 52:3 (2013), pp. 581, 580.
61. *CSP Venice, Volume X: 1603–1607*, p. 150 (12 May 1604).
62. 'A Proclamation concerning the King's Majesty's Style, of King of Great Britain &c.' in *Stuart Royal Proclamations 1*, pp. 96, 97.
63. Quoted by Bruce Galloway, *The Union of England and Scotland 1603–1608* (Edinburgh, 1986), p. 61.
64. Quoted by B. J. Cook, '"Stampt with your own Image": The Numismatic Dimension of Two Stuart Successions' in Paulina Kewes and Andrew McRae (eds), *Stuart Succession Literature. Moments and Transformations* (Oxford, 2019), p. 310.
65. John Gordon, *Enōtikon, or A Sermon of the Union of Great Britain, in Antiquity of Language, Name, Religion, and Kingdom &c.* (London, 1604), p. 29.
66. Anonymous, 'A Treatise about the Union of England and Scotland' in Galloway and Levack (eds), *The Jacobean Union*, p. 73.
67. HMC *Salisbury, Part XVI*, p. 367 (25 November 1604).
68. Quoted by Galloway, *Union of England and Scotland 1603–1608*, p. 58 ('pauvres et avares').
69. Quoted by Astrid J. Stilma, '"As Warriouris in Ane Camp": The Image of King James VI as a Protestant Crusader' in Kevin J. McGinley and Nicola Royan (eds), *The Apparelling of Truth: Literature and Literary Culture in the Reign of James VI* (Newcastle, 2010), p. 247.
70. Quoted by Cross, 'To Counterbalance the World', p. 185 (18/28 February 1604).

71. HMC *Salisbury, Part XVI*, p. 85 (3 May 1604). As Winwood added, while Antwerp 'jewellers found strange this demand', the Spaniard found 'it more strange that he was refused'.
72. *CSP Venice, Volume X: 1603–1607*, p. 155 (8 June 1604).
73. Robert Watson and William Thomson (eds), *The History of the Reign of Philip the Third, King of Spain* (London, 1839), p. 380 (Journal of the Conference').
74. Quoted by Cross, 'To Counterbalance the World', p. 324; the official version appeared as *Relación de la Jornada del Excelentissimo Condestable de Castilla, a las pazes entre España y Inglaterra, que se concluyeron y juraron en Londres por el mes de Agosto, Año 1604* (Valencia, 1604).
75. Quoted by Óscar Recio Morales, *Ireland and the Spanish Empire 1600–1825* (Dublin, 2010), pp. 86–7; given the fate of Jewish, gypsy and Morisco populations, questions of potential repatriation were especially sensitive.
76. William Brenchley Rye (ed.), *England as seen by Foreigners in the Days of Elizabeth and James the First* (London, 1865), pp. 121, 119–20 ('Banquet and Entertainment given by James I to the Constable of Castile').
77. *CSP Venice, Volume X: 1603–1607*, p. 179 (1 September 1604).
78. Loomie, *Spain*, Vol. I, p. 37 (22 November 1604).
79. Quoted by Paul C. Allen, *Philip III and Pax Hispanica, 1598–1621. The Failure of Grand Strategy* (New Haven, CT, 2000), p. 115.
80. Robert Treswell, *A Relation of such Things as were Observed to Happen in the Journey of the Right Honourable Charles, earl of Nottingham &c.* (London, 1605), p. 63.
81. Quoted by Cross, 'To Counterbalance the World', p. 367; see Berta Caño-Echevarría and Mark Hutchings, 'Valladolid 1605: A Theatre for the Peace' in J. R. Mulryne, Krista De Jonge, R. L. M. Morris and Pieter Martens (eds), *Occasions of State: Early Modern European Festivals and the Negotiation of Power* (London, 2018), pp. 93–108.
82. Quoted by Cross, 'To Counterbalance the World', p. 438 (3/13 June 1605).

5 GUNPOWDER, TREASON AND SCOTS, 1605–1610

1. *Stuart Royal Proclamations 1*, p. 125 (7 November 1605).
2. Winwood, *Memorials*, Vol. II, p. 173 (9 November 1605).
3. James VI & I, 'A Speech in the Parliament House' in Johann P. Sommerville (ed.), *King James VI and I. Political Writings* (Cambridge, 1994), pp. 148–9, 149, 151, 152.
4. William Barlow, *The Sermon Preached at Paul's Crosse, the Tenth Day of November, being the next Sunday after the Discovery of this Late Horrible Treason &c.* (London, 1606), sigs C2v, Dr, D3r.

5. Quoted by Victoria Jane Buckley, 'Patterns of Mischief: The Impact of the Gunpowder Plot on the Jacobean Stage, 1605–1616' (University of Sussex PhD thesis, 2012), pp. 59, 61; Buckley suggests that John Hynd was the poem's author (p. 58).
6. [T. W.], *The Arraignment and Execution of the late Traitors with a relation of the other Traitors, which were executed at Worcester, the 27 of January last past* (London, 1606), sigs C2r–C2v.
7. Francis Herring, 'Popish Piety or a brief poetical outline of that conspiracy &c.' [1606], translated by Estelle Haan, 'Milton's "In Quintum Novembris" and the Anglo-Latin Gunpowder Epic', *Humanistica Lovaniensia*, 41 (1992), pp. 263, 265, 275.
8. *His Majesty's Speech in this Last Session of Parliament . . . With a Discourse of the Manner of Discovery of this Late Intended Treason, Joined with the Examination of Some of the Prisoners* (London, 1605), sigs E3r–E3v.
9. G. P. V. Akrigg (ed.), *Letters of King James VI & I* (Berkeley, CA, 1984), p. 276 (11 November 1605).
10. *CSP Venice, Volume X: 1603–1607*, pp. 296–7 (23 November 1605).
11. Matthew Kellison, *A Survey of the New Religion detecting many Gross Absurdities which it Implies &c.* (Douai, 1603), 'Epistle to the King'.
12. Loomie, *Spain*, Vol. I, pp. 39, 41 (22 November 1604).
13. James VI & I, 'A Speech in the Parliament House' in Sommerville (ed.), *King James VI and I. Political Writings*, pp. 148, 157.
14. *CSP Venice, Volume X: 1603–1607*, p. 293 (21 November 1605).
15. [Thomas Birch (ed.)], *The Court and Times of James the First; Illustrated by Authentic and Confidential Letters, from Various Public and Private Collections*, 2 vols (London, 1848), Vol. I, p. 37 (19 November 1605).
16. *CSP Venice, Volume X: 1603–1607*, p. 303 (22 December 1605).
17. HMC *Salisbury, Part XVII*, p. 478 (5 November 1605).
18. Winwood, *Memorials*, Vol. II, pp. 173, 169 (*c.* November 1605).
19. *CSP Venice, Volume X: 1603–1607*, pp. 307, 316 (24 December 1605 and 30 January 1606).
20. Winwood, *Memorials*, Vol. II, pp. 183–4 (27 December 1605).
21. *CSP Venice, Volume X: 1603–1607*, pp. 303, 321, 333 (22 December 1605, 24 February and 6 April 1606); *Stuart Royal Proclamations 1*, pp. 134–5.
22. HMC *Salisbury, Part XVIII*, p. 71 (5 March 1606).
23. J. P. Kenyon (ed.), *The Stuart Constitution 1603–1608. Documents and Commentary* (Cambridge, 1986), p. 170 (Act for the better Discovering and Repressing of Popish Recusants, 1606).
24. Albert J. Loomie (ed.), *English Polemics at the Spanish Court: Joseph Creswell's Letter to the Ambassador from England. The English and Spanish Texts of 1606* (New York, 1993), pp. 14–15, 79, 84.
25. Winwood, *Memorials*, Vol. II, p. 230 ([June 1606]).

26. *CSP Venice, Volume X: 1603–1607*, p. 308 (6 January 1606).
27. Quoted by Daniel McReynolds, 'Lying Abroad for the Good of His Country: Sir Henry Wotton and Venice in the Age of the Interdict' in Deborah Howard and Henrietta McBurney (eds), *The Image of Venice: Fialetti's View and Sir Henry Wotton* (London, 2014), p. 118 (17 February 1606).
28. *CSP Venice, Volume X: 1603–1607*, p. 361 (14 June 1606).
29. John Ford, 'Honor Triumphant and the Monarches Meeting' in Gilles Monsarrat, Brian Vickers and R. J. C. Watt (eds), *The Collected Works of John Ford*, 3 vols (Oxford, 2012), Vol. I, p. 108; Ford continued, 'we are not subtle French, to fawn and flatter: / Nor Spaniards hot in show, yet cold in matter. / Trothless [i.e. perfidious] Italian, fleeting Irish wiles / (Whose trust when most protesting most beguiles) / We deem dishonour. German policies, / Or ever-changing Indian fopperies / We spurn' (Vol. I, p. 109).
30. *CSP Venice, Volume X: 1603–1607*, p. 391 (16 August 1606).
31. Maurice Lee Jr (ed.), *Dudley Carleton to John Chamberlain 1603–1624. Jacobean Letters* (New Brunswick, NJ, 1972), p. 87.
32. Antoine le Fèvre de la Boderie, *Ambassades de Monsieur de la Boderie en Angleterre sous le Regne d'Henri IV & la Minorité de Louis XIII depuis les années 1606 jusqu'en 1611*, 5 vols (Paris, 1750), Vol. I, pp. 310–11 ('s'il ne vouloit se modérer en cette façon de vivre, on lui empoissoneroit tous les chiens'; 'ce brave Roi de Dannemarck . . . qu'il s'adonnât aux exercises vraiment royaux & martiaux'; 'ce Parangon [*sic*] du Roi de Dannemarck'; 'que n'avons-nous un tel Roi').
33. Sir John Harington, *Nugæ Antiquæ: Being a Miscellaneous Collection of Original Papers, in prose and verse*, Thomas Park (ed.), 2 vols (London, 1804), Vol. I, pp. 350, 351, 352, 352.
34. See H. Neville Davis, 'The Limitations of Festival: Christian IV's State Visit to England in 1606' in J. R. Mulryne and Margaret Shewring (eds), *Italian Renaissance Festivals and their European Influence* (Lewiston, NY, 1992), pp. 311–35.
35. David Harris Willson (ed.), *The Parliamentary Diary of Robert Bowyer, 1606–1607* (New York, 1971), pp. 196, n. 1, 203, n. 3.
36. Simon Healy, 'Debates in the House of Commons, 1604–1607' in Chris R. Kyle, *Parliament, Politics and Elections, 1604–1648* (Cambridge, 2001), p. 129. Pigott later protested that he had only intended to refer to 'the Scots that would have killed the King and not of the nation in general', but he was imprisoned in the Tower of London and a new MP selected in his place (p. 131).
37. Quoted by Bruce Galloway, *The Union of England and Scotland 1603–1608* (Edinburgh, 1986), p. 113.
38. Willson (ed.), *Parliamentary Diary of Robert Bowyer*, p. 220.
39. Boderie, *Ambassades de Monsieur de la Boderie*, Vol. II, p. 129.
40. Willson (ed.), *Parliamentary Diary of Robert Bowyer*, pp. 238, n. 4, 273.

41. Loomie, *Spain*, Vol. I, p. 97 (15 March 1607).
42. James VI & I, 'Speech . . . Last Day of March, 1607' in Sommerville (ed.), *King James VI and I. Political Writings*, pp. 160, 173, 177, 164.
43. *CSP Venice, Volume X: 1603–1607*, p. 498 (16 May 1607).
44. K. M. Brown et al. (eds), *The Records of the Parliaments of Scotland to 1707* (St Andrews, 2007–2020), 1607/3/12. Date accessed: 19 March 2020.
45. David Masson (ed.), *The Register of the Privy Council of Scotland. Volume VII: A.D. 1604–1607* (Edinburgh, 1885), p. 498 (7 August 1606); see Nick Groom, *The Union Jack. The Story of the British Flag* (London, 2006), pp. 124–38.
46. HMC *Salisbury, Part XIX*, p. 275 (11 October 1607).
47. 'Part Seven of the *Reports*' in Steve Sheppard (ed.), *The Selected Writings and Speeches of Sir Edward Coke*, 3 vols (Indianapolis, IN, 2003), Vol. I, pp. 172, 172–3.
48. Quoted by David Finnegan and Éamonn Ó Ciardha, 'Introduction. "Cáit ar ghabhadar Gaoidhil?" Where have the Gaels gone?' in David Finnegan, Éamonn Ó Ciardha and Marie-Claire Peters (eds), *The Flight of the Earls. Imeacht na nIarlaí* (Derry, 2010), p. xv.
49. Quoted by John McCavitt, 'The Flight of the Earls, 1607', *Irish Historical Studies*, 29:114 (1994), pp. 167, 171.
50. *Stuart Royal Proclamations 1*, pp. 178–9.
51. *CSP Ireland . . . James I: 1606–1608*, p. 625 (14 October 1607).
52. *CSP Venice, Volume XI: 1607–1610*, p. 50 (24 October 1607).
53. Micheline Kerney Walsh, *'Destruction by Peace': Hugh O'Neill after Kinsale: Glanconcadhain 1602–Rome 1616* (Armagh, 1986), p. 201 (12 March 1608).
54. Loomie, *Spain*, Vol. I, p. 100 (30 April 1607).
55. Quoted by Stefania Tutino, *Law and Conscience: Catholicism in Early Modern England, 1570–1625* (Aldershot, 2007), pp. 141, 142.
56. HMC *Salisbury, Part XIX*, p. 375 (13 December 1607).
57. James VI & I, 'Triplici Nodo, Triplex Cuneus &c.' in Sommerville (ed.), *Political Writings*, pp. 116, 86, 92, 86. The title of James's tract echoed the woody metaphors of (im)perfect British union by providing a three-pronged polemical wedge to refute the triangular woody knot posed by the two papal breves and a letter to Blackwell from Bellarmine.
58. *CSP Venice, Volume XI: 1607–1610*, p. 97 (21 February 1608).
59. Loomie, *Spain*, Vol. I, pp. 120, 121 (9 July 1608).
60. Akrigg (ed.), *Letters of King James VI & I*, p. 302 (17 October 1608).
61. Pierre de L'Estoile, *Mémoires-Journaux de Pierre de L'Éstoile*, 11 vols (Paris, 1875–83), Vol. IX, p. 70 (28 April 1608) ('Je luy (a Périer) en ay paié demi quart d'escu: et n'y avoit pas deux heures qu'à l'instance du Nonce du Pape on leur avoit à tous fait défense d'en vendre: qui est un bon moien pour en avoir prompte expedition').
62. *CSP Venice, Volume XI: 1607–1610*, pp. 277, 299 (28 May and 14 July 1609).

63. L'Estoile, *Mémoires-Journaux*, Vol. X, p. 286 (10 July 1609) ('en Latin assez bon pour que un Roy' and 'en un siècle où il est aussi monstreux de voir un Roy docte, qu'il estoit, due temps de Rabelais, ung [*sic*] moine sçavant').
64. James VI & I, *The Works of the most High and Mighty Prince, James by the Grace of God, King of Great Britain, France and Ireland &c.* (London, 1616), sigs C4v, D2r. The scriptural allusion is to Psalm 22, v.12: 'Many bulls have compassed me: strong bulls of Bashan have beset me round.'
65. Quoted by Diane Roussel, '"Several Fanatics Who Talked Only of Killing Kings": Conspirators and Regicides before the *Parlement de Paris* in the Wake of the Assassination of Henri IV, 1610', *French History*, 30:4 (2016), p. 461.
66. Boderie, *Ambassades de Monsieur de la Boderie*, Vol. V, p. 268 (24 May 1610; 'qu'il devint plus blanc que la chemise'); *CSP Venice, Volume XI: 1607–1610*, p. 494 (26 May 1610).
67. Elizabeth Read Foster (ed.), *Proceedings in Parliament, 1610*, 2 vols (New Haven, CT, 1966), Vol. II, pp. 81, 109, 106.
68. Quoted by G. Dyfnallt Owen, 'Introduction' to HMC *Salisbury, Part XXI (1609–1612)*, pp. xvi, xvii.
69. *Stuart Royal Proclamations 1*, p. 246.
70. *CSP Venice, Volume XII: 1610–1613*, p. 47 ('Remonstrance of the University of Paris, September 1610').

6 DYNASTIC MARRIAGE, DEATH AND DEBTS, 1610–1618

1. John Nichols (ed.), *The Progresses, Processions and Magnificent Festivities of King James the First &c.*, 4 vols (London, 1828), Vol. II, pp. 275, 278, 270n. ('The Speeches at Prince Henry's Barriers').
2. See Pauline Croft, 'The Parliamentary Installation of Henry, Prince of Wales', *Historical Research*, 65:157 (1992), pp. 177–93.
3. Elizabeth Read Foster (ed.), *Proceedings in Parliament, 1610*, 2 vols (New Haven, CT, 1966), Vol. II, pp. 127, 128.
4. Winwood, *Memorials*, Vol. II, p. 367 (9 January 1608). Accorded a chamber 'with a good fire in it' and 'a perfect view of all that passed', Cornwallis was precluded, as a Protestant, from attending the special Mass in the monastery of San Jerónimo el Real in Madrid.
5. Pauline Croft (ed.), 'A Collection of Several Speeches and Treatises of the Late Lord Treasurer Cecil and of several Observations of the Lords of the Council, given to King James concerning his Estate and Revenue in the Years 1608, 1609 and 1610', *Camden Miscellany XXIX* (1987), p. 283.
6. Foster (ed.), *Proceedings in Parliament, 1610*, Vol. I, pp. 7, 5, 34.
7. James VI & I, 'Speech . . . the 21 March [1610]' in Johann P. Sommerville (ed.), *King James VI and I. Political Writings* (Cambridge, 1994), pp. 197, 179, 203.

8. Quoted by John Cramsie, *Kingship and Crown Finance under James VI and I, 1603–1625* (Woodbridge, 2002), p. 95.
9. Foster (ed.), *Proceedings in Parliament, 1610*, Vol. II, p. 137.
10. Antoine le Fèvre de la Boderie, *Ambassades de Monsieur de la Boderie en Angleterre sous le Regne d'Henri IV & la Minorité de Louis XIII depuis les années 1606 jusqu'en 1611*, 5 vols (Paris, 1750), Vol. V, p. 355 (19 July 1610; 'un assez mauvais visage'); quoted by Foster (ed.), *Proceedings in Parliament, 1610*, Vol. II, p. 273.
11. Quoted by Cramsie, *Kingship and Crown Finance*, p. 109.
12. HMC *Salisbury, Part XXI (1609–1612)*, p. 266 (7 December 1610).
13. Croft (ed.), 'A Collection of Several Speeches', pp. 312–13.
14. J. H. Elliott, 'The Political Context of the 1612–1615 Franco-Spanish Treaty' in Margaret M. McGowan (ed.), *Dynastic Marriages, 1612/1615. A Celebration of the Habsburg and Bourbon Unions* (Farnham, 2013), p. 12.
15. Desiderius Erasmus, *The Education of a Christian Prince*, Lisa Jardine (ed.) (Cambridge, 1997), pp. 98, 97.
16. Ralegh, *Works*, Vol. VIII, pp. 239, 247, 249 ('Discourse touching a Marriage').
17. Quoted by Nicolas Le Roux, 'A Time of Frenzy: Dreams of Union and Aristocratic Turmoil (1610–1615)' in McGowan (ed.), *Dynastic Marriages, 1612/1615*, p. 26.
18. Jemma Field, *Anna of Denmark. The Material and Visual Culture of the Stuart Courts, 1589–1619* (Manchester, 2020), p. 140.
19. Thomas Birch, *The Life of Henry Prince of Wales, Eldest Son of King James I* (London, 1760), p. 539 ([Sir John Digby], 'A Relation of the Carriage of the Marriages').
20. Quoted by François Guizot, 'Un Projet de Mariage Royal', *Revue des Deux Mondes*, 8th series, 40 (July to August 1862), pp. 271–2.
21. Historical Manuscripts Commission, *Tenth Report on the Manuscripts of the Earl of Eglinton, Sir J. Stirling Maxwell, Bart., C. S. H. Drummond Moray, Esq., C. F. Weston Underwood, Esq., and G. Wingfield Digby, Esq.* (London, 1885), pp. 556–7 (19 January 1612). To Trumbull in Brussels, Digby reiterated his frustration 'that this is purposely thrown about to delude the world' as a smokescreen for other schemes (HMC *Downshire, Volume III*, p. 232 (2 February 1612)).
22. Senning, *Spain, Rumor*, p. 38, n. 36. In June 1613, Don Baltasar de Zúñiga – formerly Spain's resident ambassador to England – arrived in London as Philip's ambassador extraordinary, but encountered such a suspicious reception at James's court that no further discussions of a Spanish match ensued.
23. Quoted by Thomas Vernon Thoroughman, 'Some Political Aspects of Anglo-French Relations, 1610–1619' (University of North Carolina at Chapel Hill, PhD thesis, 1968), p. 114 (30 March 1611). Wotton was instructed that James's preference was always to negotiate separate dynastic matches 'for

the better corroboration of our self and our posterity with many branches of alliance' (HMC *Salisbury, Part XXI (1609–1612)*, p. 344 ('Instructions for Sir Henry Wotton'); see Andrea Pennini, 'Marriage Proposals: Seventeenth-Century Stuart–Savoy Matrimonial Prospects and Politics' in Paola Bianchi and Karin Wolfe (eds), *Turin and the British in the Age of the Grand Tour* (Cambridge, 2017), pp. 41–55.

24. HMC *Downshire, Volume III*, p. 192 (27 November 1611).
25. HMC *Salisbury, Part XXI (1609–1612)*, p. 344 ('Instructions for Sir Henry Wotton'); Andrew Thrush, 'The French Marriage and the Origins of the 1614 Parliament' in Stephen Clucas and Rosalind Davies (eds), *The Crisis of 1614 and The Addled Parliament. Literary and Historical Perspectives* (Farnham, 2003), p. 26.
26. Ralegh, *Works*, Vol. VIII, p. 250 ('Discourse touching a Marriage').
27. *CSP Venice, Volume XII: 1610–1613*, p. 365 (31 May 1612); for the suggested dowry of a million crowns, see Thoroughman, 'Some Political Aspects', p. 161.
28. John Gutch (ed.), *Collectanea Curiosa, or Miscellaneous Tracts relating to the History and Antiquities of England and Ireland &c.*, 2 vols. (Oxford, 1781), Vol. I, p. 160 (Cornwallis, 'Discourse concerning the Marriage'); see Katherine Watson and Charles Avery, 'Medici and Stuart: A Grand Ducal Gift of "Giovanni Bologna" Bronzes for Henry, Prince of Wales (1612)', *The Burlington Magazine*, 115:845 (1973), pp. 495–507.
29. James VI & I, 'Basilikon Doron' in Sommerville (ed.), *King James VI and I. Political Writings*, pp. 40–41.
30. Jean Loiseau de Tourval, *The French Herald Summoning all True Christian Princes to a General Crusade, for a Holy War . . . Upon the Occasion of the Most Execrable Murder of Henry the Great* (London, 1611), pp. 37, 39, 41.
31. Thrush, 'The French Marriage' in Clucas and Davies (eds), *Crisis of 1614*, pp. 26–7.
32. *CSP Venice, Volume XII: 1610–1613*, pp. 409, 411 (19 August 1612).
33. HMC *Downshire, Volume III*, pp. 381, 386 (14 and 31 October 1612).
34. G. P. V. Akrigg (ed.), *Letters of King James VI & I* (Berkeley, CA, 1984), p. 326 (28 September 1612).
35. *CSP Domestic . . . James I, 1611–1618*, p. 152 (10 October 1612).
36. Peter Sherlock, 'The Monuments of Elizabeth Tudor and Mary Stuart: King James and the Manipulation of Memory', *Journal of British Studies*, 46:2 (2007), p. 273.
37. *CSP Venice, Volume XII: 1610–1613*, p. 448 (17 November 1612); quoted by Thoroughman, 'Some Political Aspects', p. 179 (23 November 1612).
38. Catharine MacLeod (ed.), *The Lost Prince. The Life & Death of Henry Stuart* (London, 2012), pp. 13, 117, 14, 15.
39. Kevin Chovanec, *Pan-Protestant Heroism in Early Modern Europe* (Basingstoke, 2020), p. 117.

40. *CSP Venice, Volume XII: 1610–1613*, p. 450 (23 November 1612).
41. Winwood, *Memorials*, Vol. III, p. 410n. (17 November 1612); Naunton added that Henry had interpreted his serious illness as 'a deserved punishment upon him, for having ever opened his ears to admit treaty of a Popish match'.
42. *CSP Venice, Volume XII: 1610–1613*, p. 452 (27 November 1612).
43. HMC *Downshire, Volume III*, p. 417 (26 November 1612).
44. *CSP Venice, Volume XII: 1610–1613*, p. 459 (8 December 1612).
45. Micheline Kerney Walsh, 'Memorial of Hugh O'Neill' in Walsh, *'Destruction by Peace': Hugh O'Neill after Kinsale: Glanconcadhain 1602–Rome 1616* (Armagh, 1986), pp. 298, 299.
46. Quoted by Senning, *Spain, Rumor*, at pp. 68–70 and pp. 78–9.
47. Quoted by Jennifer Woodward, *The Theatre of Death. The Ritual Management of Royal Funerals in Renaissance England 1570–1625* (Woodbridge, 1997), p. 149.
48. Quoted by Senning, *Spain, Rumor*, p. 67.
49. HMC *Downshire, Volume III*, p. 436 (12 December 1612).
50. *CSP Venice, Volume XII: 1610–1613*, p. 472 (5 January 1613).
51. Winwood, *Memorials*, Vol. III, p. 420 (5 January 1613).
52. *Stuart Royal Proclamations 1*, p. 284.
53. Quoted by Senning, *Spain, Rumor*, p. 84.
54. HMC *Downshire, Volume IV*, p. 28 (29 January 1613). Foscarini confirmed that 'the king is informed from various quarters that there are people here who are plotting his death; the Palatine has received a like warning. The king is very anxious and elaborate pains are taken for his safety' (*CSP Venice, Volume XII: 1610–1613*, p. 491 (8 February 1613).
55. George Webbe, *The Bride Royal, or The Spiritual Marriage between Christ and his Church Delivered by Way of Congratulation Upon the Happy and Hopeful Marriage Between the Two Incomparable Princes, The Palsgrave, and The Lady Elizabeth &c.* (London, 1613), pp. 2–3, 81.
56. Marie-Claude Canova-Green, '"Particularitez des Resjoyssances Publiques et Cérémonyes du Mariage de la Princesse": An Ambassadorial Account of the Palatine Wedding' in Sara Smart and Mara R. Wade (eds), *The Palatine Wedding of 1613: Protestant Alliance and Court Festival* (Wiesbaden, 2013), p. 355.
57. John Taylor, *Heaven's Blessing and Earth's Joy; or, a True Relation of the supposed Sea-Fight and Fireworks as were accomplished before the Royal Celebration of the all-beloved Marriage of the two Peerless Paragons of Christendom, Frederick and Elizabeth &c.* (London, 1613), sig. A4r.
58. W. G. Perrin (ed.), *The Autobiography of Phineas Pett* (London, 1918), p. 103.
59. Canova-Green, '"Particularitez des Resjoyssances"' in Smart and Wade (eds), *Palatine Wedding of 1613*, p. 361.

60. Thomas P. Campbell, 'Disruption and Diaspora: Tapestry Weaving in Northern Europe, 1570–1600' in Thomas P. Campbell, *Tapestry in the Baroque. Threads of Splendor* (New Haven, CT, 2007), p. 23.
61. Glyn Redworth (ed.), *The Letters of Luisa de Carvajal y Mendoza. Volume II* (London, 2012), p. 300 (29 March 1613).
62. See Mark Brayshay, 'The Choreography of Journeys of Magnificence: Arranging the Post-Nuptial Progress of Frederick, the Elector Palatine and Princess Elizabeth of England from London to Heidelberg in 1613', *Journal of Early Modern History*, 12:5 (2008), pp. 383–408.
63. Quoted by Christof Ginzel, *Poetry, Politics and Promises of Europe: Prophetic Rhetoric in the English and Neo-Latin Epithalamia on the Occasion of the Palatine Marriage in 1613* (Göttingen, 2009), p. 146.
64. Henry Peacham, *Prince Henry Revived. Or a Poem upon the Birth, and in Honour of the hopeful young Prince Henry Frederick, first son and heir apparent to the most excellent princes, Frederick Count Palatine of the Rhine, and the Mirror of Ladies, Princess Elizabeth, his wife, only daughter to our Sovereign James King of Great Britain, &c.* (London, 1615), sigs C1v, B3v-B4r.
65. Maija Jansson (ed.), *Proceedings in Parliament 1614 (House of Commons)* (Philadelphia, PA, 1988), pp. 15, 16 (King's Speech; 5 April 1614). The naturalization and succession bill passed both the Commons and Lords but did not receive royal assent; as the Venetian ambassador Foscarini commented, the king had 'declared that the son of the Palatine does not need any decree of parliament to render him capable of succeeding' (p. 443n.).
66. James VI & I, 'Speech . . . Last Day of March, 1607' in Sommerville (ed.), *King James VI and I. Political Writings*, p. 170.
67. Jansson (ed.), *Proceedings in Parliament 1614*, p. 8 (The Ambassador's Account).
68. Their oldest child, Henry Frederick, drowned in 1629, aged fifteen. Their ninth, and youngest child, Sophia, was born eight months after Charles II. Eventually, via the 1701 Act of Settlement and the 1707 Act of Union, Sophia was named successor to the thrones of England, Scotland and Ireland.
69. Jansson (ed.), *Proceedings in Parliament 1614*, pp. 14, 19, 17 (The King's Speech).
70. Jansson (ed.), *Proceedings in Parliament 1614*, pp. 138, 316 (Anonymous Diary; 4 and 21 May 1614).
71. Jansson (ed.), *Proceedings in Parliament 1614*, pp. 420, 427, 433–4 (Anonymous Diary, 3 and 6 June 1614). For Hoskins's speech, see Chamberlain, *Letters*, Vol. I, p. 583. In Parliament, an anonymous diarist recorded that Hoskins had recommended 'send[ing] all strangers home to their countries (and upon that he used the phrase of Sicilian Vesper (which I understood not)' (Jansson (ed.), *Proceedings in Parliament 1614*, p. 423; for the phrase 'Addled Parliament', see p. xxxiv).

72. Jansson (ed.), *Proceedings in Parliament 1614*, p. 9 (The Ambassador's Account).
73. Samuel Rawson Gardiner (trans. and ed.), *El Hecho de los Tratados del Matrimonio Pretendido por el Principe de Gales con la serenissima infante de Espana ... por F. Francisco de Jesus* [*Narrative of the Spanish Marriage Treaty*] (London, 1869), pp. 288, 289.
74. Jansson (ed.), *Proceedings in Parliament 1614*, p. 71 (9 April 1614); in 1612, the Irish Solicitor General, Sir Roger Wilbraham, had estimated the yearly costs of governing Ireland to be around £30,000 more than the crown's annual Irish revenue of £25,000 (Conrad Russell, *James VI and I and his English Parliaments* (Oxford, 2011), p. 97).
75. J. S. Brewer and W. M. Bullen (eds), *Calendar of the Carew Manuscripts*, 6 vols (London, 1867–73), Vol. V, pp. 291, 289, 290 [20 April 1614]). In forming separate committees before resolving the matter of the Speaker, James added that 'you did put the plough before the horse, so as it went on untowardly like your Irish ploughs' (Vol. V, p. 290).
76. Brewer and Bullen (eds), *Calendar of the Carew Manuscripts*, Vol. V, pp. 307, 309, 310, 308 (Carew, 'Discourse', 1614).
77. Quoted in 'Introduction' to Jansson (ed.), *Proceedings in Parliament 1614*, pp. xv, xvi.
78. HMC *Downshire, Volume IV*, pp. 475–6, 429, 458, 513 (29 July 1614; 17 June, 29 July and 31 August 1614).
79. Wesel's location explained its frequent occupation by invading armies; it was held by the Dutch from 1611 to 1614, before being acquired by Spain from 1614 to 1629, retaken by the Dutch between 1629 and 1672 and then held by France from 1672 to 1680.
80. Quoted by J. Michael Hayden, *France and the Estates General of 1614* (Cambridge, 1974), p. 131.
81. Quoted by Ronald G. Asch, *Sacral Kingship between Disenchantment and Re-enchantment: The French and English Monarchies, 1587–1688* (Oxford, 2014), p. 193n ('[le serment] est venu par mer et à nagé d'Angleterre').
82. *A Remonstrance of the Most Gracious King James I, King of Great Britain, France & Ireland ... for the Right of Kings and the Independence of their Crowns. Against an Oration of the most Illustrious Cardinal of Perron, pronounced in the Chamber of the Third Estate, January 15, 1615* (Cambridge, 1616), sigs A1r, A2r, pp. 211, 239.
83. Quoted by Thoroughman, 'Some Political Aspects', p. 297 (25 August 1615).
84. Quoted by G. Dyfnallt Owen in 'Introduction' to HMC *Downshire, Volume V*, p. ix (7 September 1615).
85. Quoted by Noah Millstone, *Manuscript Circulation and the Invention of Politics in Early Stuart England* (Cambridge, 2016), p. 67.
86. *Letters from and to Sir Dudley Carleton, Knight During his Embassy in Holland, from January 1615/16, to December 1620* (London, 1775), pp. 28–9 (23 May 1616).

87. HMC *Downshire, Volume V*, p. 556 (20/30 July 1616).
88. John Row, *The History of the Kirk of Scotland: From the Year 1558 to August 1637 ... With a Continuation to July 1639, by his Son, John Row* (Edinburgh, 1842), p. 307; see William A. McNeill and Peter G. B. McNeill, 'The Scottish Progress of James VI, 1617', *Scottish Historical Review*, 75:199 (1996), pp. 38–51.
89. Nichols (ed.), *Progresses, Processions and Magnificent Festivities of James the First*, Vol. III, p. 309.
90. *CSP Venice, Volume XIV: 1615–1617*, pp. 476, 549 (30 March and 16 July 1617).
91. Quoted by R. T. Spence, 'A Royal Progress in the North: James I at Carlisle Castle and the Feast of Brougham, August 1617', *Northern History*, 27:1 (1991), p. 65.
92. HMC *Downshire, Volume VI*, p. 219 (July 1617).
93. David Laing (ed.), *Original Letters relating to the Ecclesiastical Affairs of Scotland, 1603–1625*, 2 vols (Edinburgh, 1851), Vol. II, pp. 524, 569 (6 December 1617 and 10 July 1618).
94. *CSP Venice, Volume XV: 1617–1619*, p. 420 ('Relation', written in late 1618).

7 CRISIS IN THE PALATINATE, 1618–1623

1. Quoted by Daniel Jütte, 'Defenestration as Ritual Punishment: Windows, Power and Political Culture in Early Modern Europe', *Journal of Modern History*, 89:1 (2017), pp. 7, 34–5.
2. Gardiner (ed.), *England and Germany*, p. 13.
3. James VI & I, 'Basilikon Doron' in Johann P. Sommerville (ed.), *King James VI and I. Political Writings* (Cambridge, 1994), p. 32; Robert Zaller, *The Parliament of 1621. A Study in Constitutional Conflict* (Berkeley, CA, 1971), p. 9.
4. Gardiner (ed.), *England and Germany*, pp. 135, 138 (19/29 June 1629).
5. Giovan Battista Nani, *The History of the Affairs of Europe in the Present Age, but more particularly of the Republic of Venice*, translated by Robert Honywood (London, 1673), p. 125.
6. Anonymous, *The Reasons which Compelled the States of Bohemia to Reject the Archduke Ferdinand &c. and Enforced them to Elect a new King &c.* (Dort, [1619]), p. 28.
7. Akkerman (ed.), *Correspondence 1*, p. 203 (31 August 1619).
8. Gardiner (ed.), *England and Germany ... Second Series*, pp. 13, 57 (9/19 September and 29 September/9 October 1619).
9. Quoted by Brennan C. Pursell, *The Winter King. Frederick V of the Palatinate and the Coming of the Thirty Years' War* (Farnham, 2003), p. 80.

10. Gardiner (ed.), *England and Germany . . . Second Series*, pp. 67, 68 (6/16 October 1619).
11. Gardiner (ed.), *England and Germany . . . Second Series*, pp. 40, 41, 42 (23 September/3 October 1619).
12. [John Harrison], *A Short Relation of the Departure of the High and Mighty Prince Frederick, King-Elect of Bohemia: With His Royal & Virtuous Lady Elizabeth; And the Thrice Hopeful Young Prince Henry, From Heidelberg towards Prague &c.* (Dort, 1619), sigs A3v, B4v.
13. *CSP Venice, Volume XVI: 1619–1621*, pp. 76, 77 (20 December 1619).
14. James VI & I, 'A Meditation upon the 27th, 28th and 29th Verses of the 27th Chapter of Saint Matthew (1619)' in Sommerville (ed.), *King James VI and I. Political Writings*, pp. 231, 239, 240.
15. Gardiner (ed.), *England and Germany*, pp. 148 (20/30 January 1620).
16. *CSP Venice, Volume XVI: 1619–1621*, p. 177 (20 February 1620).
17. See Jemma Field, '"Orderinge Things Accordinge to His Majesties Comaundment": The Funeral of the Stuart Queen Consort Anna of Denmark', *Women's History Review* (published online October 2020).
18. Quoted by Jeri-Smith Cronin, 'The Apocalyptic Chivalry of Thomas Dekker's *The Whore of Babylon* and Anglo-Spanish Diplomacy', *Journal of Medieval and Early Modern Studies*, 50:3 (2020), p. 633.
19. *CSP Venice, Volume XVI: 1619–1621*, pp. 250, 275, 276 (8 May and 11 June 1620).
20. [Thomas Scott] *Vox Populi, or News from Spain, Translated according to the Spanish Copy. Which may Serve to Forewarn Both England and the United Provinces How Far to Trust to Spanish Pretences* ([London, 1620]), sigs B1v, Cv.
21. *CSP Venice, Volume XVI: 1619–1621*, p. 491 (4 December 1620).
22. Akkerman (ed.), *Correspondence 1*, p. 254 (25 September 1620).
23. *CSP Venice, Volume XVI: 1619–1621*, p. 417 (25 September 1620).
24. Quoted by Zaller, *Parliament of 1621*, p. 17 (5/15 October 1620).
25. *CSP Venice, Volume XVI: 1619–1621*, p. 423 (2 October 1620).
26. *CSP Venice, Volume XVI: 1619–1621*, p. 490 (4 December 1620).
27. *Stuart Royal Proclamations 1*, pp. 495–6, 496n.
28. Quoted by Jayne E. E. Boys, *London's News Press and the Thirty Years War* (Woodbridge, 2011), p. 68.
29. Quoted by Marc Jacobs, 'King for a Day. Games of Inversion, Representation, and Appropriation in Ancien Regime Europe' in Jeroen Deploige and Gita Deneckere (eds), *Mystifying the Monarch: Studies on Discourse, Power, and History* (Amsterdam, 2006), p. 127.
30. Wallace Notestein, Frances Helen Relf and Hartley Simpson (eds), *Commons Debates, 1621*, 7 vols (New Haven, CT, 1935), Vol. II, pp. 2, 12; the following week, Secretary of State George Calvert tried to reassure MPs that the recent royal proclamation against licentious speech had been directed

towards 'such as make ordinary table talk of state matters in taverns and alehouses, and not against parliament men' (Vol. II, p. 25).

31. Notestein, Relf and Simpson (eds), *Commons Debates, 1621*, Vol. II, p. 489.
32. Quoted by Zaller, *Parliament of 1621*, p. 185.
33. James VI & I, 'His Majesty's Declaration, touching his Proceedings in the late Assembly and Convention of Parliament' in Sommerville (ed.), *King James VI and I. Political Writings*, pp. 259, 257, 258.
34. Quoted by Thomas Cogswell, 'England and the Spanish Match' in Richard Cust and Ann Hughes (eds), *Conflict in Early Stuart England. Studies in Religion and Politics, 1603–1642* (Harlow, 1989), p. 115; see also Valentina Caldari, 'James I and the Dissolution of the 1621 Parliament through Spanish Eyes' in Valentina Caldari and Sara J. Wolfson (eds), *Stuart Marriage Diplomacy. Dynastic Politics in their European Context, 1604–1630* (Woodbridge, 2018), pp. 79–94.
35. *CSP Venice, Volume XVII: 1621–1623*, p. 519 (9 December 1622).
36. See Roberta Anderson, '*Appendix*: Diplomatic Representatives from the Hapsburg Monarchy to the Court of James VI and I' in Alexander Samson (ed.), *The Spanish Match. Prince Charles's Journey to Madrid, 1623* (Aldershot, 2006), pp. 209–25.
37. *CSP Venice, Volume XVII: 1621–1623*, pp. 305, 480 (29 April and 21 October 1622).
38. *Stuart Royal Proclamations 1*, pp. 561, 562n.
39. *CSP Venice, Volume XVII: 1621–1623*, pp. 443, 442 ('Relation'); *CSP Venice, Volume XVI: 1619–1621*, p. 587 (5 March 1621); *CSP Venice, Volume XVII: 1621–1623*, p. 468 (3 October 1622).
40. Quoted by Jesús López-Peláez Casellas, 'Anthony Sherley's Spanish Writings and the Global Early Modern', *Journal of World History*, 26:3 (2015), p. 575.
41. *CSP Venice, Volume XVII: 1621–1623*, pp. 414, 270 (10 September and 21 March 1622); having reported this rumour, Surian added that the English ambassador, Carleton, 'laughs at the latter idea'.
42. James Howell, *Epistolæ Ho-Elianæ. Familiar Letters Domestic and Foreign. Divided into Sundry Sections Partly Historical, Political, Philosophical* (London, 1655), p. 123 (23 February 1623).
43. *CSP Venice, Volume XVI: 1619—1621*, p. 433 (11 October 1620).
44. Sir Henry Wotton, *Reliquiæ Wottonianæ; or a Collection of Lives, Letters, Poems, with characters of Sundry Personages: and other incomparable pieces of Language and Art* (London, 1651), p. 214.
45. *CSP Venice, Volume XVII: 1621–1623*, pp. 581–2, 584 (10 March 1623).
46. Malcolm Smuts, 'Prince Henry and His World' in Catharine MacLeod (ed.), *The Lost Prince. The Life & Death of Henry Stuart* (London, 2012), p. 25.
47. Sidney L. Lee (ed.), *The Autobiography of Edward, Lord Herbert of Cherbury* (London, 1886), pp. 239–40.

48. *CSP Venice*, Volume *XVII: 1621–1623*, pp. 586, 589 (12 and 14 March 1623).
49. Quoted by Thomas Cogswell, *The Blessed Revolution: English Politics and the Coming of War, 1621–1624* (Cambridge, 1989), p. 37.
50. James Orchard Halliwell (ed.), *Letters of the Kings of England, Now first Collected from the Originals &c.*, 2 vols (London, 1846), Vol. II, p. 172.
51. Quoted by Alexander Samson, 'Introduction. The Spanish Match' in Samson (ed.), *The Spanish Match*, p. 3.
52. Quoted by Henry Ettinghausen, *Prince Charles and the King of Spain's Sister – What the Papers Said: An Inaugural Lecture Delivered on 28 February 1985* (Southampton, [1987]), p. 8.
53. Hardwicke, *State Papers*, Vol. I, p. 399 (February 1623).
54. Ambrose Philips, *The Life of John Williams, Lord Keeper of the Great Seal &c.* (Cambridge, 1700), pp. 113–14.
55. Howell, *Epistolæ Ho-Elianæ*, p. 128 (1 April 1623).
56. Quoted by Jeremy Robbins, 'The Spanish Literary Response to the Visit of Charles, Prince of Wales' in Samson (ed.), *The Spanish Match*, p. 110.
57. Lee (ed.), *Autobiography of Edward, Lord Herbert of Cherbury*, p. 243.
58. Samuel Rawson Gardiner (trans. and ed.), *El Hecho de los Tratados del Matrimonio Pretendido por el Principe de Gales con la serenissima infante de Espana ... por F. Francisco de Jesus* [*Narrative of the Spanish Marriage Treaty*] (London, 1869), pp. 207, 208.
59. *CSP Venice, Volume XVII: 1621–1623* (London, 1911), pp. 590, 614 (14 March and 4 April 1623).
60. Quoted by David Sánchez Cano, 'Entertainments in Madrid for the Prince of Wales: Political Functions of Festivals' in Samson (ed.), *The Spanish Match*, p. 68.
61. *CSP Venice, Volume XVIII: 1623–1625*, p. 5 (5 May 1623).
62. Quoted by Robbins, 'The Spanish Literary Response' in Samson (ed.), *The Spanish Match*, p. 113.
63. Hardwicke, *State Papers*, Vol. I, pp. 411–12 (25 March 1623).
64. *CSP Venice, Volume XVII: 1621–1623*, pp. 626, 627 ('Considerations upon which the English marriage may prove useful to the Catholic religion'). There was also a risk that, if the marriage negotiations failed at a late stage, despite having been discussed since 1604, English Catholics could end up suffering persecution simply out of revenge.
65. Edmund Garrard, *The Country Gentleman Moderator. Collections of such Intermarriages as have been between the two Royal Lines of England and Spain, since the Conquest &c.* (London, 1624), pp. 52, 64, 65.
66. Chamberlain, *Letters*, Vol. II, p. 495 (3 May 1623).
67. Howell, *Epistolæ Ho-Elianæ*, pp. 130, 131 (10 July 1623).
68. Sánchez Cano, 'Entertainments in Madrid' in Samson (ed.), *The Spanish Match*, p. 58.
69. *CSP Venice, Volume XVIII: 1623–1625*, p. 75 (21 July 1623).

70. *CSP Venice, Volume XVIII: 1623–1625*, p. 47 (24 June 1623).
71. Quoted by Jerry Brotton, 'Buying the Renaissance: Prince Charles's Art Purchases in Madrid, 1623' in Samson (ed.), *The Spanish Match*, p. 16.
72. See D. W. Cruickshank, 'Calderón's *Amor, Honor y Poder* and the Prince of Wales, 1623', *Bulletin of Hispanic Studies*, 77:1 (2000), pp. 75–99.
73. Howell, *Epistolæ Ho-Elianæ*, p. 131 (10 July 1623).
74. *CSP Venice, Volume XVII: 1621–1623*, p. 630 (14 April 1623).
75. Quoted by Gary Schneider, *The Culture of Epistolarity. Vernacular Letters and Letter-Writing in Early Modern England, 1500–1700* (Newark, DE, 2005), p. 22.
76. *CSP Venice, Volume XVIII: 1623–1625*, p. 34 (9 June 1623).
77. Quoted by David Coast, *News and Rumour in Jacobean England. Information, Court Politics and Diplomacy, 1618–1625* (Manchester, 2014), p. 154.
78. *CSP Venice, Volume XVII: 1621–1623*, pp. 622, 632 (10 and 15 April 1623). In July, the Venetian agent in Florence reported that Robert Rich, second earl of Warwick, had described domestic disaffection with Charles's prospective Spanish marriage as so universal that 'if the Princess Palatine should go there from Holland, the king would fly to Scotland and she would be left mistress in England' (*CSP Venice, Volume XVIII: 1623–1625*, p. 57 (8 July 1623)).
79. Paul Arblaster, *From Ghent to Aix: How They Brought the News in the Habsburg Netherlands, 1550–1700* (Leiden, 2014), pp. 139–40.
80. Quoted by Pursell, *The Winter King*, p. 198 (11 July 1623). Christian of Brunswick was a cousin of Charles and Elizabeth Stuart, being the brother of Sophia Hedwig, daughter of their maternal aunt, Elisabeth of Denmark.
81. Hardwicke, *State Papers*, Vol. I, pp. 420, 421 (6 and 14 June 1623).
82. Hardwicke, *State Papers*, Vol. I, p. 430 (23 July 1623).
83. *CSP Venice, Volume XVIII: 1623–1625*, p. 78 (28 July 1623).
84. Hardwicke, *State Papers*, Vol. I, pp. 428, 449, 450 (21 July and 29 August 1623).
85. *CSP Venice, Volume XVIII: 1623–1625*, p. 115 (20 September 1623).
86. Quoted by Glyn Redworth, *The Prince and the Infanta. The Cultural Politics of the Spanish Match* (London, 2003), p. 190.

8 ALL HELL AGAINST ENGLAND, 1623–1628

1. Quoted by David Cressy, *Bonfires and Bells. National Memory and the Protestant Calendar in Elizabethan and Stuart England* (Stroud, 2004), p. 94.
2. Cressy, *Bonfires and Bells*, p. 105.
3. *CSP Venice, Volume XVIII: 1623–1625*, p. 135 (20 October 1623).
4. Quoted by Alexandra Walsham, '"The Fatall Vesper": Providentialism and Anti-Popery in late Jacobean London', *Past and Present*, 144:1 (1994), pp. 82–3.

5. *CSP Venice, Volume XVIII: 1623–1625*, p. 119 (22 September 1623).
6. Clarendon, *State Papers*, Vol. I, Appendix, p. xix (21 September 1623).
7. *Scrinia Sacra; Secrets of Empire, in Letters of Illustrious Persons. A Supplement of the Cabala &c.* (London, 1654), p. 136 (8 October 1623).
8. Sir John Finet, *Finetti Philoxenis: Some Choice Observations of Sir John Finett Knight ... Touching the Reception, and Precedence, the Treatment and Audience, the Puntillios and Contests of Foreign Ambassadors in England* (London, 1656), p. 243.
9. *CSP Venice, Volume XVIII: 1623–1625*, p. 123 (29 September 1623).
10. Hardwicke, *State Papers*, Vol. I, pp. 484–5 (24 October 1623).
11. Chamberlain, *Letters*, Vol. II, p. 525 (15 November 1623).
12. *CSP Venice, Volume XVIII: 1623–1625*, pp. 156, 157 (1 December 1623).
13. *CSP Venice, Volume XVIII: 1623–1625*, p. 272 (17 April 1624).
14. Samuel Rawson Gardiner (ed.), *Prince Charles and the Spanish Marriage, 1617–1623. A Chapter of English History &c.*, 2 vols (London, 1869), Vol. I, p. 457.
15. *CSP Venice, Volume XVIII: 1623–1625*, p. 191 (12 January 1624).
16. *CSP Venice, Volume XVIII: 1623–1625*, p. 178 (29 December 1623).
17. '19th February 1624', in *Proceedings in Parliament 1624: The House of Commons*, Philip Baker (ed.) (2015–18); British History Online: <http://www.british-history.ac.uk/no-series/proceedings-1624-parl/feb-19> (accessed 7 May 2018).
18. '24th February 1624', in *Proceedings in Parliament 1624: The House of Commons*, Baker (ed.) (2015–18); British History Online: <http://www.british-history.ac.uk/no-series/proceedings-1624-parl/feb-19> (accessed 7 April 2020).
19. Quoted by Thomas Cogswell, *The Blessed Revolution: English Politics and the Coming of War, 1621–1624* (Cambridge, 1989), p. 143 (as quoted by Cogswell, 'tout demeure en suspens', the English agent in Mainz maintained, 'et ha les ieux fiches sur le Parlement de Grande Bretagne', of which God himself would be 'pour son sainct esprit le president et Directeur').
20. '19th March 1624', in *Proceedings in Parliament 1624: The House of Commons*, Baker (ed.) (2015–18); British History Online: <http://www.british-history.ac.uk/no-series/proceedings-1624-parl/feb-19> (accessed 7 April 2020).
21. '25th March 1624' and '1st April 1624' in *Proceedings in Parliament 1624: The House of Commons*, Baker (ed.) (2015–18); British History Online: <http://www.british-history.ac.uk/no-series/proceedings-1624-parl/feb-19> (accessed 7 April 2020).
22. *CSP Venice, Volume XVIII: 1623–1625*, p. 265 (12 April 1624).
23. Chamberlain, *Letters*, Vol. II, pp. 549–50 (20 March 1624). A melocoton is a peach grafted onto a quince rootstock. Although Charles publicly declined the gift, Valaresso deemed its 'impertinence' such that 'the whole city is gossiping on the subject'; *CSP Venice, Volume XVIII: 1623–1625*, p. 257 (29 March 1624).

24. [John Reynolds], *Vox Coeli, or News from Heaven of a Consultation there held by the High and Mighty Princes, King Henry VIII, King Edward VI, Prince Henry, Queen Mary, Queen Elizabeth, and Queen Anne &c.* ('Elysium', 1624), pp. 35–6, 40, 43, 45, 46.
25. [John Reynolds], *Votivae Angliae; Or, The Desires and Wishes of England Contained in a Pathetic Discourse, Presented to the King on New Year's Day Last &c.* (Utrecht, 1624), sigs D4v, C2r-v.
26. [Thomas Scott], *The Second Part of Vox Populi, or Gondomar appearing in the Likeness of Machiavelli in a Spanish Parliament Wherein are Discovered his Treacherous & Subtle Practises to the Ruin as well of England, as the Netherlands* (Goricum [Gornichem], 1624), pp. 15, 41. Responding to critics who had denounced *Vox Populi*'s first part for fictitiously satirizing diplomatic discussions, Scott protested that he had never denied his dialogues' invented character. Indeed, the dialogues' title – *Vox Populi* – had indicated that their content was only 'what every man thinks, and speaks in their ordinary discourse'. Since all ambassadors returning to Madrid would expect a debrief with the Council of State, Scott's account remained purely conjectural: 'perhaps thus it was: or worse: I pray God the success prove it a fiction, and not to be too true' ([Thomas Scott], *Vox Regis* ([Utrecht, 1624]), p. 11, 10).
27. Quoted by Ernesto E. Oyarbide Magaña, 'Between Love and Hate: Thomas Scott's Puritan Propaganda and his Interest in Spanish Culture' in Yolanda Rodríguez Pérez (ed.), *Literary Hispanophobia and Hispanophilia in Britain and the Low Countries (1550–1850)* (Amsterdam, 2020), p. 95.
28. *Cabala. Mysteries of State, in Letters of the Great Ministers of King James and King Charles* (London, 1654), pp. 90–91 (7 April 1624). Such a construction of James's situation was not, however, uniquely Spanish, for that August Valaresso reported that 'the prince and Buckingham still keep the king in sort of mild state of siege' (*CSP Venice, Volume XVIII: 1623–1625*, p. 405 (2 August 1624)).
29. Robert E. Ruigh, *The Parliament of 1624. Politics and Foreign Policy* (Harvard, MA, 1971), p. 279.
30. Akkerman (ed.), *Correspondence 1*, p. 470 (7 June 1624).
31. Valaresso claimed that the Spanish envoys had conveyed to James 'a book about the authority of parliament, containing something about the power of deposing kings, and another called Mercury, like the Gazeteer of Italy containing the news of the world, printed in Germany, stating that Buckingham had upset the prince's marriage with the object of marrying his own daughter to the Palatine's eldest son, such good use do they make of every opportunity, and perhaps the news was printed with them in view' (*CSP Venice, Volume XVIII: 1623–1625*, pp. 334–5 (7 June 1624)).
32. Quoted by Ruigh, *Parliament of 1624*, p. 294.

33. *CSP Venice, Volume XVIII: 1623–1625*, pp. 373–4, 383n., 383 (5 and 12 July 1624). From Madrid, the Venetian Lunardo Moro reported that, after being briefly isolated, Hinojosa's invitation to join the Spanish Council of State 'amounts to an open declaration of approval of his action' (p. 472; 28 October 1624).
34. Quoted by Thomas Cogswell, 'What Can Be Fuller of Wonder? Buckingham and the Revenge of the Hispanophiles in 1626' in Valentina Caldari and Sara J. Wolfson (eds), *Stuart Marriage Diplomacy. Dynastic Politics in their European Context, 1604–1630* (Woodbridge, 2018), p. 41.
35. Thomas Middleton, *A Game at Chess, As it was Acted Nine Days Together at the Globe on the Bankside* ([London, ?1625]), sigs. Fv, H2v, K3r.
36. Quoted by Paul Yachnin, 'Playing with Space: Making a Public in Middleton's Theatre' in Gary Taylor and Trish Thomas Henley (eds), *The Oxford Handbook of Thomas Middleton* (Oxford, 2012), p. 38.
37. Chamberlain, *Letters*, Vol. II, p. 578 (21 August 1624).
38. Quoted by Edward M. Wilson and Olga Turner, 'The Spanish Protest against *A Game at Chesse*', *Modern Language Review*, 44:4 (1949), pp. 480–1; for the figure of 30,000 spectators, see Thomas Cogswell, 'Thomas Middleton and the Court, 1624: *A Game at Chess* in Context', *Huntington Library Quarterly*, 47:4 (1984), p. 273.
39. Quoted by Brennan C. Pursell, *The Winter King. Frederick V of the Palatinate and the Coming of the Thirty Years' War* (Farnham, 2003), pp. 222, 226.
40. *CSP Venice, Volume XVIII: 1623–1625*, p. 293 (3 May 1624).
41. Quoted by Albert Henry Marshall, 'Sir Dudley Carleton and English Diplomacy in the United Provinces, 1616–1628' (Rutgers State University of New Jersey, PhD thesis, 1978), p. 257 (2 November 1624).
42. *CSP Venice, Volume XVIII: 1623–1625*, pp. 332–3 (7 June 1624).
43. Quoted by Karen Chancey, 'The Amboyna Massacre in English Politics, 1624–1628', *Albion: A Quarterly Journal Concerned with British Studies*, 30:4 (1998), p. 589.
44. William Sanderson, *Graphice. The Use of the Pen and Pensil. Or, the most excellent Art of Painting &c.* (London, 1658), p. 14; see Anthony Milton, 'Marketing a Massacre: Amboyna, the East India Company and the Public Sphere in Early Modern England' in Peter Lake and Steven Pincus (eds), *The Politics of the Public Sphere in Early Modern England* (Manchester, 2007), pp. 177–8.
45. Quoted by Cogswell, *Blessed Revolution*, p. 125; as quoted by Cogswell, the Stuarts were 'en misèrable estate … sans argent, sans amis et sans reputation, neantmoins leur gloire et leur vanite leur reste'. The French court might find it had 'non seulement appuyer une vieille maison mais en soustenir une tombante' as well.

46. Hardwicke, *State Papers*, Vol. I, p. 546 ('qui'il permettra à tous les sujets Catholiques Romains de jouir de plus de liberté & franchise, en ce qui regarde leur religion, qu'il n'eussent fait en vertu d'articles quelconques accordès par le traité de mariage fait avec l'Espagne'; 18 November 1624).
47. John Williams, *Great Britain's Salomon. A Sermon preached at the Magnificent Funeral, of the most High and Mighty King, James, the Late King of Great Britain, France, and Ireland &c.* (London, 1625), pp. 41, 57.
48. Akkerman (ed.), *Correspondence 1*, p. 542 (23 June 1625).
49. P. R. Seddon (ed.), *Letters of John Holles 1587–1637*, 3 vols (Nottingham, 1983), Vol. 2, p. 303 (10 April 1625).
50. F. Pouy (ed.), *Instruction de la Reine Marie de Médicis a la Reine d'Angleterre Henriette-Marie de France, Sa Fille* (Amiens, 1878), p. 9 ['Dieu vous a envoyée en ce pays pour eux, car c'est son people, et son people qui a souffert depuis tant d'années'].
51. John Fisher, *The Answer unto the Nine Points of Controversy, proposed by our late Soueraign (of Famous Memory) unto M. Fisher of the Society of Jesus &c.* (Saint Omer, 1626), sig. *4r.
52. Maija Jansson and William B. Bidwell (eds), *Proceedings in Parliament 1625* (New Haven, CT, 1987), p. 554 (9 August 1625); 'thrasonical' derives from references to the boastful and swaggering character Thraso in Terence's play *Eunuchus*.
53. John Glanville, *The Voyage to Cadiz in 1625. Being a Journal written by John Glanville, Secretary to the Lord Admiral of the Fleet* (London, 1883), p. 60; for the size of the expedition force, see Steve Murdoch, *The Terror of the Seas? Scottish Maritime Warfare 1513–1713* (Leiden, 2010), p. 164.
54. Quoted by Ronald Bedford, Lloyd Davis and Philippa Kelly, 'The Expedition to Cadiz, 1625' in *Early Modern English Lives. Autobiography and Self-Representation 1500–1660* (Aldershot, 2007), p. 138.
55. J. H. Elliott, *The Count-Duke of Olivares: The Statesman in an Age of Decline* (New Haven, CT, 1986), p. 249.
56. Quoted by William R. Blue, 'Versions of the Battle of Cádiz, 1625' in Bárbara Mujica (ed.), *Shakespeare and the Spanish Comedia. Translation, Interpretation, Performance. Essays in Honor of Susan L. Fischer* (Lewisburg, PA, 2013), p. 110.
57. Ruth Saunders Magurn (trans. and ed.), *The Letters of Peter Paul Rubens* (Cambridge, MA, 1955), p. 119 (28 November 1625).
58. Quoted by David Coast, '"Reformation" or "Ruin"? The Impeachment of the Duke of Buckingham and Early Stuart Politics', *Historical Research*, 90:250 (2017), p. 712.
59. Anonymous, *Lachrymae Londinenses: Or, London's Lamentations and Tears for God's Heavy Visitation of the Plague of Pestilence &c.* (London, 1626), sigs A3v, Br.

60. Anonymous, *The Runaways' Answer to a Book called A Rod for Runaways &c.* (London, 1625), sigs A3v-Br.
61. *CSP Venice, Volume XX: 1626–1628*, p. 366 (11 September 1627).
62. Quoted by Sara J. Wolfson, 'The Female Bedchamber of Queen Henrietta Maria: Politics, Familial Networks and Policy, 1626–1640' in Nadine Akkerman and Birgit Houben (eds), *The Politics of Female Households: Ladies-in-Waiting across Early Modern Europe* (Leiden, 2014), p. 314n.
63. Quoted by Thomas Cogswell, 'John Felton, Popular Culture, and the Assassination of the Duke of Buckingham', *Historical Journal*, 49:2 (2006), p. 364.
64. Quoted by Alastair Bellany and Thomas Cogswell, *The Murder of King James I* (New Haven, CT, 2015), p. 236.
65. John Rushworth, *Historical Collections of Private Passages of State, Weighty Measures in Law, Remarkable Proceedings in Five Parliaments &c.*, 8 vols (London, 1721–2), Vol. I, pp. 223, 222, 225 (29 March 1626).
66. J. V. Lyle (ed.), *Acts of the Privy Council of England, Volume XXXXI, 1626* (London, 1938), p. 47 (30 June 1626).
67. Quoted by Óscar Recio Morales, *Ireland and the Spanish Empire 1600–1825* (Dublin, 2010), p. 105.
68. *CSP Venice, Volume XIX: 1625–1626*, pp. 461, 468, 466 (3 and 10 July 1626).
69. Quoted by Coast, '"Reformation" or "Ruin"?' p. 713.
70. Quoted by Cogswell, *Blessed Revolution*, p. 145.
71. Noel Malcolm, *Reason of State, Propaganda, and the Thirty Years' War. An Unknown Translation by Thomas Hobbes* (Oxford, 2007), pp. 132, 138, 180, 188.
72. Quoted by Bellany and Cogswell, *Murder of King James I*, p. 265.
73. *CSP Venice, Volume XX: 1626–1628*, p. 199 (27 April 1627).
74. *CSP Venice, Volume XX: 1626–1628*, p. 205 (2 May 1627).
75. Magurn (trans. and ed.), *Letters of Peter Paul Rubens*, p. 208 (14 October 1627).
76. Quoted by Thomas Cogswell, '"Published by Authoritie": Newsbooks and the Duke of Buckingham's Expedition to the Île de Ré', *Huntington Library Quarterly*, 67:1 (2004), p. 6.
77. *CSP Venice, Volume XX: 1626–1628*, pp. 362–3, 268, 335 (8 September, 29 June and 23 August 1627).
78. Quoted by Elliott, *The Count-Duke of Olivares*, pp. 329, 282.
79. Robert C. Johnson, Mary Frear Keeler, Maija Jansson Cole and William B. Bidwell (eds), *Commons Debates 1628*, 6 vols (New Haven, CT, 1977), Vol. II, p. 58 (22 March 1628); Vol. III, p. 128 (28 April 1628).
80. J. P. Kenyon (ed.), *The Stuart Constitution 1603–1608. Documents and Commentary* (Cambridge, 1986), p. 70 (The Petition of Right, 1628).
81. Johnson, Keeler, Cole and Bidwell (eds), *Commons Debates 1628*, Vol. IV, p. 315 (14 June 1628).

82. Quoted by Cogswell, '"Published by Authoritie"', p. 23.
83. [John Russell], *The Spy. Discovering the Danger of Arminian Heresy and Spanish Treachery* ('Strasburgh' [Amsterdam], 1628), sigs E4r, Er.
84. *CSP Domestic . . . Charles I, 1628–1629*, p. 240 (*c.* July 1628).
85. *CSP Venice, Volume XXI: 1628–1629*, p. 262 (2 September 1628).
86. Quoted by Cogswell, 'John Felton, Popular Culture', p. 365.

9 BETWEEN DONS AND MONSIEURS, 1629–1637

1. Noah Millstone, 'Evil Counsel: The *Propositions to Bridle the Impertinency of Parliament* and the Critique of Caroline Government in the Late 1620s', *Journal of British Studies*, 50:4 (2011), pp. 814, 829–30.
2. *CSP Venice, Volume XXIII: 1632–1636*, p. 366 ('Relation', *c.*1635); *CSP Venice, Volume XXIV: 1636–1639*, p. 124 (16 January 1637).
3. *CSP Venice, Volume XXIII: 1632–1636*, p. 361 ('Relation', *c.*1635).
4. *CSP Domestic . . . Charles I, 1631–1633*, p. 350 (9 June 1632).
5. Akkerman (ed.), *Correspondence 1*, p. 819 (8 December 1630). Akkerman has speculated that 'The Devil of Milan' may refer to Robert Gomersall's *The Tragedy of Lodovick Sforza, Duke of Milan* (1628) in which Sforza is, at one point, called a devil.
6. Ruth Saunders Magurn (trans. and ed.), *The Letters of Peter Paul Rubens* (Cambridge, MA, 1955), p. 301 (June 1629).
7. *CSP Domestic . . . Charles I, 1633–1634*, p. 76 (31 May 1633).
8. Clarendon, *State Papers*, Vol. I, p. 309 (15 August 1635).
9. Quoted by G. Dyfnallt Owen, 'Introduction' to Historical Manuscripts Commission, *Report on the Manuscripts of the Right Honourable Viscount de L'Isle, V.C., preserved at Penshurst Place, Kent. Volume VI: Sidney Papers, 1626–1698* (London, 1966), p. xxii (23 August/2 September 1636).
10. Quoted by Ian Atherton, *Ambition and Failure in Stuart England. The Career of John, First Viscount Scudamore* (Manchester, 1999), p. 198.
11. *CSP Venice, Volume XXI: 1628–1629*, p. 503 (26 January 1629).
12. Charles I, *His Majesty's Declaration to all his Loving Subjects, of the Causes which moved him to Dissolve the last Parliament . . .* (London, 1629), pp. 16, 5; see John Reeve, 'The Arguments in King's Bench in 1629 concerning the Imprisonment of John Selden and Other Members of the House of Commons', *Journal of British Studies*, 25:3 (1986), pp. 264–87. While Holles escaped, but later paid the fine, Eliot remained unrepentant and died in prison in 1632, and Valentine remained in prison until 1640.
13. Charles I, *His Majesty's Declaration*, p. 4.
14. James Orchard Halliwell (ed.), *The Autobiography and Correspondence of Sir Simonds D'Ewes Baronet &c.*, 2 vols (London, 1845), Vol. I, pp. 402, 404, 402.

15. Quoted by Thomas Cogswell, 'The Lord Admiral, the Parliament-Men and the Narrow Seas, 1625–27' in Chris R. Kyle and Jason Peacey (eds), *Connecting Centre and Locality: Political Communication in Early Modern England* (Manchester, 2020), p. 61.
16. Quoted by L. J. Reeve, 'Sir Thomas Roe's Prophecy of 1629', *Bulletin of the Institute of Historical Research*, 56:133 (1983), pp. 120, 121.
17. *CSP Venice, Volume XXI: 1628–1629*, pp. 590, 592 (23 March 1629).
18. Ole Peter Grell, *Brethren in Christ. A Calvinist Network in Reformation Europe* (Cambridge, 2011), p. 111.
19. *CSP Venice, Volume XXI: 1628–1629*, pp. 506, 521 (26 January and 3 February 1629).
20. *CSP Venice, Volume XXII: 1629–1632*, p. 177 (7 September 1629).
21. Kevin Sharpe, *Image Wars. Promoting Kings and Commonwealths in England, 1603–1660* (New Haven, CT, 2010), p. 258. The children born to the Palatine couple comprised Frederick Henry (1614–29); Charles Louis (1617–80); Elisabeth (1618–80); Rupert (1619–82); Maurice (1620–52); Louise Hollandine (1622–1709); Louis (born and died 1624); Edward (1625–63); Henriette Marie (1626–51); John Philip Frederick (1627–50); Charlotte (1628–31); Sophia (1630–1714) and Gustavus Adolphus (1632–41).
22. Magurn (trans. and ed.), *Letters of Peter Paul Rubens*, pp. 329, 328 (August 1629).
23. See Albert J. Loomie, 'Olivares, the English Catholics and the Peace of 1630', *Revue Belge de Philologie et d'Histoire*, 47:4 (1969), pp. 1154–66.
24. *CSP Venice, Volume XXII: 1629–1632*, pp. 432, 463 (25 October 1630 and 24 January 1631).
25. 'A. Ar.', *The Practise of Princes* (Amsterdam, 1630), p. 12.
26. Quoted by Patrick Ignacio O'Neill, 'Charles I and the Spanish Plot: Anglo-Habsburg Relations and the Outbreak of the War of the Three Kingdoms, 1630–1641' (University of California Riverside PhD thesis, 2015), p. 245 (1 December 1631).
27. Alan Rudrum, Joseph Black, Holly Faith Nelson (eds), *The Broadview Anthology of Seventeenth-Century Verse and Prose* (Peterborough, ON, 2004), p. 500.
28. Akkerman (ed.), *Correspondence 1*, pp. 860–61 (12 December 1631).
29. Akkerman (ed.), *Correspondence 2*, p. 121n.
30. Quoted by Brennan C. Pursell, *The Winter King. Frederick V of the Palatinate and the Coming of the Thirty Years' War* (Farnham, 2003), p. 271 (28 April / 8 May 1632).
31. Robert Monro, *Monro, His Expedition with the Worthy Scots Regiment (called Mac-Keyes Regiment) Levied in August 1626 &c.* (London, 1637), p. 93.
32. Quoted by Pursell, *The Winter King*, p. 275.
33. Akkerman (ed.), *Correspondence 2*, p. 177 (22 April 1633).

34. John Russell, *The Two Famous Pitched Battles of Lypsich and Lutzen wherein the ever-renowned Prince Gustavus the Great Lived and Died a Conqueror &c.* ([Cambridge], 1634), pp. 31, 32; see Simon McKeown, 'The Reception of Gustavus Adolphus in English Literary Culture: The Case of George Tooke', *Renaissance Studies*, 23:2 (2009), pp. 200–220.
35. Quoted by Ethel Seaton, *Literary Relations of England and Scandinavia in the Seventeenth Century* (Oxford, 1935), p. 83.
36. Frederick Schloer, *The Death of the Two Renowned Kings of Sweden and Bohemia &c.* (London, 1633), p. 15.
37. [Thomas Birch (ed.)], *The Court and Times of Charles I, illustrated by Authentic and Confidential Letters, from Various Public and Private Collections &c.*, 2 vols (London, 1848), Vol. II, p. 206 (6 December 1632).
38. Quoted by Susan Maddocks Lister, '"Trumperies brought from Rome": Barberini Gifts to the Stuart Court in 1635' in Elizabeth Cropper (ed.), *The Diplomacy of Art: Artistic Creation and Politics in Seicento Italy* (Milan, 2000), p. 152.
39. William Prynne, *Histrio-Mastix. The Players' Scourge or Actors' Tragedy, Divided into Two Parts &c.* (London, 1633), pp. 528, 460, 856, 214; see Karin Beushausen, *Theatre and the English Public from Reformation to Revolution* (Cambridge, 2018), pp. 81–9.
40. James Shirley, *The Triumph of Peace. A Masque, presented by the Four Honourable Houses, or Inns of Court, before the King and Queens' Majesties, in the Banqueting House at Whitehall &c.* (London, 1634), p. 11; see Kevin Sharpe, *Criticism and Compliment. The Politics of Literature in the England of Charles I* (Cambridge, 1990), pp. 214–15.
41. Mark Kishlansky, 'A Whipper Whipped: The Sedition of William Prynne', *Historical Journal*, 56:3 (2013), p. 604.
42. Albert J. Loomie (ed.), *Ceremonies of Charles I. The Notebooks of John Finet 1628–1641* (New York, 1987), p. 159.
43. *CSP Venice, Volume XXIII: 1632–1636*, pp. 240, 287 (7 July and 13 October 1634).
44. Akkerman (ed.), *Correspondence* 2, pp. 332–3 (3 May 1635).
45. *CSP Venice, Volume XXIII: 1632–1636*, p. 444 (31 August 1635).
46. Halliwell (ed.), *Autobiography and Correspondence of Sir Simonds D'Ewes*, Vol. II, pp. 129–30.
47. *CSP Venice, Volume XXIII: 1632–1636*, p. 279, 297 (28 September and 16 November 1634).
48. Clarendon, *State Papers*, Vol. I, p. 83 (7 April 1634).
49. Clarendon, *State Papers*, Vol. I, pp. 296, 297 (19 July 1635).
50. Martin Espenhorst, 'The Peace of Prague – A Failed Settlement?' in Olaf Asbach and Peter Schröder (eds), *The Ashgate Companion to the Thirty Years' War* (London, 2014), p. 286.

51. Akkerman (ed.), *Correspondence* 2, p. 338 (12 July 1635).
52. Clarendon, *State Papers*, Vol. I, p. 392 (20 December 1635).
53. *CSP Venice, Volume XXIII: 1632–1636*, p. 490 (21 December 1635).
54. Clarendon, *State Papers*, Vol. I, p. 309 (August 1635).
55. Collins (ed.), *Letters and Memorials*, Vol. II, p. 387 (16 June 1636).
56. Quoted by Atherton, *Ambition and Failure in Stuart England*, p. 193; see Clarendon, *State Papers*, Vol. I, p. 392 (November 1635).
57. Clarendon, *State Papers*, Vol. I, pp. 372, 375 (15 December 1635).
58. Barbara Donagan, *War in England, 1642–1649* (Oxford, 2010), p. 29.
59. William Crowne, *A True Relation of all the Remarkable Places and Passages observed in the Travels of the Right Honourable Thomas Lord Howard, Earl of Arundel and Surrey &c.* (London, 1637), pp. 8, 27.
60. *CSP Venice, Volume XXIII: 1632–1636*, p. 500 (11 January 1636).
61. Loomie (ed.), *Ceremonies of Charles I*, p. 196.
62. Martin Butler, 'Entertaining the Palatine Prince: Plays on Foreign Affairs, 1635–1637', *English Literary Renaissance*, 13:3 (1983), p. 330.
63. Akkerman (ed.), *Correspondence* 2, pp. 553, 498–9 (28 November and 11 August 1636).
64. Quoted by Diana Barnes, '*The Secretary of Ladies* and Feminine Friendship at the Court of Henrietta Maria' in Erin Griffey (ed.), *Henrietta Maria. Piety, Politics and Patronage* (Farnham, 2008), p. 53.
65. Quoted by Caroline M. Hibbard, *Charles I and the Popish Plot* (Chapel Hill, NC, 1983), p. 64.
66. *CSP Venice, Volume XXIV: 1636–1639*, p. 218 (29 May 1637).
67. William Knowler (ed.), *The Earl of Strafforde's Letters and Dispatches: With an Essay Towards his Life by Sir George Radcliffe*, 2 vols (London, 1739), Vol. II, pp. 112 and 111 (15 May and 5 October 1637).
68. Akkerman (ed.), *Correspondence* 2, pp. 583, 579 (4 April and 27 March 1637).
69. W. Davenant, *Madagascar with Other Poems* (London, 1638), pp. 3, 16; see Marlin E. Blaine, 'Epic, Romance, and History in Davenant's "Madagascar"', *Studies in Philology*, 95:3 (1998), pp. 293–319.
70. *CSP Venice, Volume XXIV: 1636–1639*, p. 235 (3 July 1637).
71. *CSP Domestic . . . Charles I, 1637*, p. 287 (6 July 1637).
72. The engraving's text is reproduced in Butler, 'Entertaining the Palatine Prince', p. 324.
73. Quoted by C. L. Powell, 'New Material on Thomas Carew', *Modern Language Review*, 11:3 (1916), p. 295.
74. Thomas Heywood, *A True Description of His Majesty's Royal Ship, Built This Year 1637 at Woolwich in Kent. To the Great Glory of our English Nation, and not paralleled in the whole Christian World* (London, 1637), pp. 30, 33; quoted by Powell, 'New Material on Thomas Carew', p. 295.

10 ALLOWING HANNIBAL TO ENTER, 1637–1641

1. John Row, *The History of the Kirk of Scotland: From the Year 1558 to August 1637 . . . With a Continuation to July 1639, by his Son, John Row* (Edinburgh, 1842), p. 398.
2. Gordon Donaldson (ed.), *Scottish Historical Documents* (Glasgow, 1970), p. 200.
3. Quoted by John Scally, 'Counsel in Crisis: James, Third Marquis of Hamilton and the Bishops' Wars, 1638–1640' in John R. Young (ed.), *Celtic Dimensions of the British Civil Wars* (Edinburgh, 1997), p. 23.
4. Alexander Peterkin (ed.), *Records of the Kirk of Scotland: containing the Acts and Proceedings of the General Assemblies, from the year 1638 &c.* ([Edinburgh], 1838), p. 70 (25 June 1638).
5. *CSP Venice, Volume XXIV: 1636–1639*, p. 392 (2 April 1638).
6. Collins (ed.), *Letters and Memorials*, Vol. II, p. 562 (29 June / 6 July 1638).
7. *CSP Venice, Volume XXIV: 1636–1639*, p. 419 (4 June 1638).
8. *CSP Domestic . . . Charles I, 1637–1638*, pp. 533, 534, 535 (28 June 1638).
9. Hardwicke, *State Papers*, Vol. II, pp. 119, 120 (27 November 1638).
10. *CSP Venice, Volume XXIV: 1636–1639*, p. 375 (25 February 1638).
11. Quoted by E. A. Beller, 'The Mission of Sir Thomas Roe to the Conference at Hamburg, 1638–1640', *English Historical Review*, 41:161 (1926), pp. 72, 70.
12. Quoted by Patrick Ignacio O'Neill, 'Charles I and the Spanish Plot: Anglo-Habsburg Relations and the Outbreak of the War of the Three Kingdoms, 1630–1641' (University of California Riverside PhD thesis, 2015), p. 311 (July 1638).
13. Akkerman (ed.), *Correspondence* 2, p. 726 (16 November 1638).
14. Collins (ed.), *Letters and Memorials*, Vol. II, p. 561 (29 June/6 July 1638).
15. G. Thorn Dury (ed.), *The Poems of Edmund Waller* (London, 1893), p. 35 ('To the Queen Mother of France, Upon her Landing'); Caroline M. Hibbard, *Charles I and the Popish Plot* (Chapel Hill, NC, 1983), p. 87.
16. Collins (ed.), *Letters and Memorials*, Vol. II, p. 596 (15/25 February 1639).
17. Robert Aiken (ed.), *Letters and Journals: Containing An Impartial Account of Public Transactions . . . From the MSS of Robert Baillie D.D. &c.*, 2 vols (Edinburgh, 1775), Vol. I, p. 57.
18. William Knowler (ed.), *The Earl of Strafforde's Letters and Dispatches: With an Essay Towards his Life by Sir George Radcliffe*, 2 vols (London, 1739), Vol. II, pp. 300, 304 (20 March 1639); Wentworth later moved to London from September 1639 to March 1640 to assist Charles.
19. Samuel Rawson Gardiner (ed.), *The Hamilton Papers: Being Selections from Original Letters in the Possession of His Grace, The Duke of Hamilton and*

Brandon, Relating to the Years 1638–1650 (London, 1880), p. 17 (24 June 1638).

20. [General Assembly, Church of Scotland], *An Information to all Good Christians within the Kingdom of England, from the Noblemen, Barons, Burghs, Ministers, and Commons of the Kingdom of Scotland, for Vindicating their Intentions and Actions from the unjust Calumnies of their Enemies* (Edinburgh, 1639), pp. 5, 6.
21. *By the King. A Proclamation and Declaration to inform our Loving Subjects of our Kingdom of England of the Seditious Practices of some in Scotland, seeking to overthrow our Regal Power under False Pretences of Religion* (1639), [20 February 1639]; for the print run, see Cynthia Clegg, *Press Censorship in Caroline England* (Cambridge, 2008), p. 210; see also Sarah Waurechen, 'Covenanter Propaganda and Conceptualizations of the Public during the Bishops' Wars, 1638–1640', *Historical Journal*, 52:1 (2009), pp. 63–86.
22. [General Assembly], *The Remonstrance of the Nobility, Barons, Burgesses, Ministers and Commons within the Kingdom of Scotland &c.* (Edinburgh, 1639), sigs A4r, D1v, C1v.
23. Quoted by Marc L. Schwarz, 'Viscount Saye and Sele, Lord Brooke and Aristocratic Protest to the First Bishops' War', *Canadian Journal of History*, 7:1 (1972), p. 25.
24. D. L., *The Scots Scouts Discoveries: By their London Intelligencer. And presented to the Lords of the Covenant of Scotland, Anno Domini 1639* (London, 1642), pp. 3, 14, 44.
25. John Bruce (ed.), *Letters and Papers of the Verney Family Down to the End of the Year 1639* (London, 1853), pp. 228, 246 (1 May and 5 June 1639).
26. *CSP Domestic . . . Charles I, 1639*, pp. 341–2 (22 June 1639).
27. Clarendon, *State Papers*, Vol. II, pp. 70, 71 (3/13 and 7/17 September 1639); see Fabio Troncarelli and Igor Pérez Tostado, 'A Plot without *Capriccio*: Irish Utopia and Political Activity in Madrid, 1639–1640' in Declan M. Downey and Julio Crespo MacLennan (eds), *Spanish–Irish Relations Through the Ages* (Dublin, 2008), pp. 128–9.
28. Quoted by Conrad Russell, *The Fall of the British Monarchies 1637–1642* (Oxford, 1991), p. 91 (September 1639).
29. Clarendon, *State Papers*, Vol. II, p. 74 (29 September 1639).
30. *CSP Venice, Volume XXIV: 1636–1639*, p. 582 (14 October 1639).
31. Martin Butler, 'Politics and the Masque: *Salmacida Spolia*' in Thomas Healy and Jonathan Sawday (eds), *Literature and the English Civil War* (Cambridge, 1990), p. 65.
32. John Rushworth, *Historical Collections of Private Passages of State, Weighty Measures in Law, Remarkable Proceedings in Five Parliaments &c.*, 8 vols (London, 1721–2), Vol. III, p. 1120.
33. Collins (ed.), *Letters and Memorials*, Vol. II, pp. 645, 646 (11 April and 25 April/5 May 1640).

34. Esther S. Cope and Willson H. Coates (eds), *Proceedings of the Short Parliament of 1640* (London, 1977), pp. 122, 118 (15 April 1640).
35. Charles I/Windebank, *His Majesty's Declaration Concerning his Proceedings with his Subjects of Scotland since the Pacification of Berwick* (London, 1640), p. 56.
36. Cope and Coates (eds), *Proceedings of the Short Parliament*, p. 77 (24 April 1640).
37. [Robert Baillie], *Ladensium Autokatakrisis, the Canterburians Self-Conviction Or an evident Demonstration of the avowed Arminianism, Popery, and Tyranny of that Faction &c.* (London, 1640), 'Preface', sig. A4v.
38. Collins (ed.), *Letters and Memorials*, Vol. II, p. 652 (7 May 1640).
39. *CSP Venice, Volume XXV: 1640–1642*, p. 47 (25 May 1640).
40. William Kerr, Earl of Lothian, *A True Representation of the Proceedings of the Kingdom of Scotland; Since the late Pacification &c.* (Edinburgh, 1640), p. 88.
41. Quoted by Albert J. Loomie, 'Alonso de Cárdenas and the Long Parliament, 1640–1648', *English Historical Review*, 97:383 (1982), p. 292.
42. Quoted by O'Neill, 'Charles I and the Spanish Plot', p. 438 (16 June 1640).
43. Quoted by J. H. Elliott, 'The Year of the Three Ambassadors' in Hugh Lloyd-Jones, Valerie Pearl and Blair Worden (eds), *History and Imagination. Essays in Honour of H. R. Trevor-Roper* (London, 1981), p. 171 (6 March 1640).
44. Quoted by J. H. Elliott, *The Revolt of the Catalans. A Study in the Decline of Spain (1598–1640)* (Cambridge, 1963), pp. 400, 401, 489.
45. James Balfour, *The Historical Works of Sir James Balfour of Denmylne and Kinnaird, Knight and Baronet &c.*, 4 vols (Edinburgh, 1825), Vol. II, p. 379.
46. Quoted by David Scott, '"Hannibal at our Gates": Loyalists and Fifth-columnists during the Bishops' Wars – the Case of Yorkshire', *Historical Research*, 70:173 (1997), p. 282 (14 August 1640).
47. Quoted by Jeremy Goldsmith, 'Charles I and Chess', *Notes and Queries*, 61:3 (2014), p. 360.
48. Collins (ed.), *Letters and Memorials*, Vol. II, p. 658 (11/21 September 1640).
49. *CSP Venice, Volume XXV: 1640–1642*, p. 77 (15 September 1640).
50. *CSP Domestic ... Charles I, 1640–1641*, p. 53 (12/22 September 1640); Drummond added his hope 'to see them all hanged, or die a more shameful death that say it or wish it'.
51. Steve Murdoch, *Britain, Denmark-Norway and the House of Stuart, 1603–1660: A Diplomatic and Military Analysis* (East Linton, 2003), pp. 96–8.
52. Rushworth, *Historical Collections*, Vol. III, pp. 1335, 1336.
53. *CSP Venice, Volume XXV: 1640–1642*, p. 97 (30 November 1640).
54. Thomas Hobbes, *On the Citizen*, Richard Tuck (trans. and ed.) (Cambridge, 1998), pp. 93, 92.
55. Perez Zagorin, 'Thomas Hobbes's Departure from England in 1640: An Unpublished Letter', *Historical Journal*, 21:1 (1978), p. 160.

56. Finch had been presented by MPs with a letter, in his handwriting, confirming Henrietta Maria's intention to raise funds from English Catholics to fight Charles's Scottish critics during the Bishops' Wars.
57. Quoted by O'Neill, 'Charles I and the Spanish Plot', pp. 456, 461–2 (30 November 1640 and 15 February 1641).
58. *CSP Venice, Volume XXV: 1640–1642*, pp. 129, 132 (8 and 29 March 1641).
59. Pérez Tostado, *Irish Influence*, p. 66n. (21 March 1641).
60. Quoted by Thomas Pert, 'Pride and Precedence: The Rivalry of the House of Orange-Nassau and the Palatine Family at the Anglo-Dutch Wedding of 1641', *The Seventeenth Century* (published online September 2020), p. 8.
61. Quoted by Pieter Geyl, *Orange and Stuart, 1641–1672* (London, 2001), pp. 32–3; *CSP Venice, Volume XXV: 1640–1642*, p. 147n (16 May 1641: 'les rideaux du lit furent toujours ouverts').
62. *CSP Venice, Volume XXV: 1640–1642*, p. 129 (8 March 1641).
63. Quoted by William R. Stacy, 'Matter of Fact, Matter of Law, and the Attainder of the Earl of Strafford', *American Journal of Legal History*, 29:4 (1985), p. 326.
64. Oliver St John, *An Argument of Law concerning the Bill of Attainder of High-Treason of Thomas, Earl of Strafford* (London, 1641), p. 72.
65. Samuel Rawson Gardiner (ed.), *The Constitutional Documents of the Puritan Revolution, 1625–1660* (Oxford, 1906), pp. 156–7 (Act for the Attainder of the Earl of Strafford).
66. Quoted by Helmers, *Royalist Republic*, p. 181.
67. Akkerman (ed.), *Correspondence* 2, p. 957 (28 May 1641).
68. *CSP Venice, Volume XXV: 1640–1642*, p. 130 (15 March 1641).
69. [Charles I], *His Majesty's Manifestation Concerning the Palatine Cause* ([London], 1641), pp. 3, 5.
70. *A Speech Delivered in the House of Commons, July 7, 1641 being resolved into a Committee . . . in the Palatine Cause. By Sir Simonds D'Ewes* (London, 1641), pp. 3–4, 8.
71. *CSP Venice, Volume XXV: 1640–1642*, p. 200 (23 August 1641).
72. *News from Scotland. His Majesty's Manifest touching the Palatine Cause and Act of Parliament Concerning the Same: Read, Voiced, and Passed in the Parliament of Scotland, the 6 Day of September, 1641* (London, 1641), p. 5.
73. John Campbell, earl of Loudoun, *A Second Speech made by the Lord Loudoun, in the Parliament of Scotland the 24 of September 1641. Being in Answer to some Objections made against the Honourable Design of the Palatinate* (London, 1641), pp. 6–7.
74. *CSP Domestic . . . Charles I, 1641–1643*, p. 141 (18/28 October 1641).
75. *CSP Venice, Volume XXV: 1640–1642*, p. 223 (4 October 1641).

11 EARTHQUAKES OF STATE, 1641–1644

1. 'G. L. V.', *British Lightning, or Sudden Tumults in England, Scotland and Ireland; To Warn the United Provinces to Understand the Dangers and the Causes Thereof . . . Translated for the Benefit of Britain* (Amsterdam, 1643), sig. A3r.
2. Quoted by Geoffrey Parker, 'The Crisis of the Spanish and the Stuart Monarchies in the Mid-Seventeenth Century: Local Problems or Global Problems?' in Ciarán Brady and Jane Ohlmeyer (eds), *British Interventions in Early Modern Ireland* (Cambridge, 2005), p. 253.
3. 'H. G.', *England's Present Distractions, Paralleled with those of Spain and other Foreign Countries &c.* (London, 1642), sig. A2r.
4. Peter H. Wilson, 'Was the Thirty Years War a "Total War"?' in Erica Charters, Eve Rosenhaft and Hannah Smith (eds), *Civilians and War in Europe, 1618–1815* (Liverpool, 2012), p. 26.
5. 'G. L. V.', *British Lightning*, sig. B2v.
6. Anonymous, *England's Division and Ireland's Distraction* (London, 1642), pp. 3–4.
7. Sir Benjamin Rudyerd, *His Speech in the High Court of Parliament, the 17 of February, for a speedy Treaty of Peace with His Majesty* (London, 1643), pp. 4–5.
8. Richard Bulstrode, *Memoirs and Reflections upon the Reign and Government of King Charles the First and King Charles the Second* (London, 1721), p. 84.
9. Eliot Warburton (ed.), *Memoirs of Prince Rupert and the Cavaliers: including their Private Correspondence, now first published from the Original Manuscripts*, 3 vols (London, 1849), Vol. III, p. 173 (3 September 1645).
10. [James Howell], *The True Informer, who in the following Discourse or Colloquy, discovers unto the World the chief causes of the sad Distempers in Great Britain and Ireland &c.* ([London, 1643]), p. 22.
11. Quoted by Pérez Tostado, *Irish Influence*, p. 66.
12. Cornelius Burges, *Another Sermon Preached to the Honourable House of Commons, now assembled in Parliament, November the Fifth 1641* (London, 1641), p. 8.
13. James Balfour, *The Historical Works of Sir James Balfour of Denmylne and Kinnaird, Knight and Baronet &c.*, 4 vols (Edinburgh, 1825), Vol. III, p. 120.
14. Quoted by Jason White, *Militant Protestantism and British Identity, 1603–1642* (London, 2012), p. 189n.
15. [Henry Jones et al.], *A Remonstrance of Diverse Remarkable Passages Concerning the Church and Kingdom of Ireland* (London, 1642), pp. 7–10.
16. Historical Manuscripts Commission, *Fourth Report of the Royal Commission on Historical Manuscripts. Part I: Report and Appendix* (London, 1874), p. 113.

17. Joseph Cope, *England and the 1641 Irish Rebellion* (Woodbridge, 2009), p. 80.
18. Akkerman (ed.), *Correspondence* 2, p. 1015 (2 December 1641).
19. 'G. L. V.', *British Lightning*, sig. A3r.
20. Hiram Morgan, 'News from Ireland: Catalan, Portuguese and Castilian Pamphlets on the Confederate War in Ireland' in Micheál Ó'Siochrú and Jane Ohlmeyer (eds), *Ireland, 1641: Contexts and Reactions* (Manchester, 2013), pp. 130, n. 11, 122.
21. Quoted by Pérez Tostado, *Irish Influence*, p. 73. The anonymous *Relaçam Sumaria & Verdadeira do estado presente do Reyno de Irlanda &c* was published in Lisbon in 1644.
22. Anonymous, *England's Comfort and London's Joy expressed in the Royal Triumphant and Magnificent Entertainment of our Dread Sovereign Lord, King Charles &c.* (London, 1641), p. 3.
23. Quoted by Siobhan Keenan, *The Progresses, Processions and Royal Entries of King Charles I, 1625–1642* (Oxford, 2020), p. 188.
24. *CSP Domestic . . . Charles I, 1641–1643*, pp. 217–18 (30 December 1641).
25. Quoted by Conrad Russell, *The Fall of the British Monarchies 1637–1642* (Oxford, 1991), p. 454 ('si c'estoit une autre nation que celle cy, je croirois que la ville seroit à feu et à sang dans 24 heures: il sera pourtant malaisé que l'affaire se passe sans scandale').
26. Sophie Crawford Lomas (ed.), Historical Manuscripts Commission, *Report on the Manuscripts of Lord Montagu of Beaulieu* (London, 1900), p. 141 (7 January 1642). The peer was Lord Mandeville.
27. *CSP Domestic . . . Charles I, 1641–1643*, p. xxvii ('J'avois prévenu mes amis').
28. House of Commons, *The Declaration agreed upon by the Committee of the House of Commons appointed to sit in The Guildhall, to consider of the Safety of the Kingdom &c.* ([London], 1642), single-sheet folio.
29. Lomas (ed.), HMC, *Report on the Manuscripts of Lord Montagu of Beaulieu*, p. 141 (7 January 1642).
30. Russell, *Fall of the British Monarchies*, p. 452.
31. HMC *Franciscan*, pp. 116, 120 (1 and 22 February 1642).
32. [Samuel Butler], *A Letter from Mercurius Civicus to Mercurius Rusticus: Or London's Confession but not Repentance &c.* ([Oxford], 1643), pp. 3, 33, 19.
33. Edward, Earl of Clarendon, *The History of the Rebellion: A New Selection*, Paul Seaward (ed.) (Oxford, 2009), p. 126.
34. *CSP Venice, Volume XXVI: 1642–1643*, p. 74 (13 June 1642).
35. Charles I, *His Majesty's Answer to the Nineteen Propositions of both Houses of Parliament* (Cambridge, 1642), pp. 5, 14, 10.
36. Willson H. Coates, Anne Steele Young and Vernon F. Snow (eds), *The Private Journals of the Long Parliament. Volume 1: 3 January to 5 February 1642* (New Haven, CT, 1982), Vol. I, p. 72.
37. *CSP Venice, Volume XXVI: 1642–1643*, p. 90 (4 July 1642).

38. Quoted by David Cressy, *England on Edge: Crisis and Revolution 1640–1642* (Oxford, 2006), p. 416.
39. Anonymous, *The Beginning of Civil Wars in England, or, a Skirmish between the Lord Strange and the Inhabitants of Manchester in Lancashire, July 4* (London, 1642), sig. A4r.
40. Quoted by Mark Stoyle, *Soldiers and Strangers. An Ethnic History of the English Civil War* (New Haven, CT, 2005) p. 116.
41. See John Morrill, 'An Irish Protestation? Oaths and the Confederation of Kilkenny' in Michael J. Braddick and Phil Withington (eds), *Popular Culture and Political Agency in Early Modern England and Ireland: Essays in Honour of John Walter* (Woodbridge, 2017), pp. 252–3.
42. Quoted by Eamon Darcy, 'The Confederate Catholics of Ireland and Popular Politics' in Patrick Little (ed.), *Ireland in Crisis: War, Politics and Religion, 1641–50* (Manchester, 2019), p. 181.
43. Quoted by Pérez Tostado, *Irish Influence*, p. 99 (27 November 1641); *CSP Domestic . . . Charles I, 1641–1643*, p. 190 (3/13 December 1641).
44. Quoted by Parker, 'The Crisis of the Spanish and Stuart Monarchies', p. 269.
45. The Spanish text is reproduced in Eamon Darcy, 'The Spanish-language "Manifesto" of the Catholic Confederation of Ireland, 1642', *Archivium Hibernicum*, 67 (2014), p. 30 ('las mismas condiciones y articulos, que los Escoceses subditos de su Magestad pidieron y alcançaron con su reciente invasion en Inglaterra').
46. Morgan, 'News from Ireland', p. 126.
47. HMC *Franciscan*, pp. 124, 122, 124, 138 (5 and 1 March 1642 and 10 May 1642).
48. Quoted by Jane Ohlmeyer, 'Ireland Independent: Confederate Foreign Policy and International Relations during the Mid-Seventeenth Century' in Jane H. Ohlmeyer (ed.), *Ireland from Independence to Occupation 1641–1660* (Cambridge, 1995), pp. 90, 103.
49. HMC *Franciscan*, p. 138 (10 May 1642).
50. William Seymour, Duke of Somerset, *The Lord Marquess of Hertford, His Letter, Sent to the Queen in Holland &c.* (London, 1642), p. 6.
51. Charles Louis, Prince Palatine, *A Declaration of the Prince Paltsgrave, to the High Court of Parliament, concerning the cause of his Departure out of England in these times of Distraction &c.* (London, 1642), pp. 1–2.
52. *CSP Venice, Volume XXVI: 1642–1643*, p. 148 (12 September 1642).
53. Anonymous, *An Item to his Majesty concerning Prince Rupert and his Cavaliers, or a Looking-Glass wherein His Majesty may see his Nephew's Love &c.* (n.p., 1642), pp. 4–5.
54. *Prince Robert's Message to my Lord of Essex with an Answer to his Desires Touching the Construction of the Laws and Certain Other Points &c.* (London, 1642), p. 5.

55. Helmers, *Royalist Republic*, p. 30.
56. Quoted by Michelle Anne White, *Henrietta Maria and the English Civil Wars* (Aldershot, 2006), p. 71, n. 59.
57. 'G. L. V.', *British Lightning*, p. 61.
58. White, *Henrietta Maria*, pp. 84–5.
59. Anonymous, *Secrets Discovered. In England's Complaint or Outcry against the High and Mighty Lords, the States General of the United Provinces, for their Perfidious, Deceitful, and Unthankful proceedings against the Welfare of this Kingdom &c.* (London, 1643), p. 24.
60. *The King of Great Britain's Declaration to the High and Mighty Lords, the States General of the United Provinces &c.* (n.p., 1643), sig. A3r [presented June 1643].
61. *CSP Venice, Volume XXVI: 1642–1643*, p. 70 (6 June 1642).
62. Quoted by D. A. Bigby, *Anglo-French Relations, 1641 to 1649* (London, 1933), p. 39.
63. *CSP Venice, Volume XXVII: 1643–1647*, p. 52 (18 December 1643).
64. Cárdenas, *Revolución Inglesa*, p. 126.
65. Robert Baillie, *The Letters and Journals of Robert Baillie, 1637–1662*, D. Laing (ed.), 3 vols (Edinburgh, 1841–2), Vol. II, pp. 79–80.
66. *Stuart Royal Proclamations* 2, pp. 988–9 (22 December 1643).
67. Fotheringham (ed.), *Diplomatic Correspondence*, Vol. II, pp. 554, 556 (November 1643).
68. Charles I, *His Majesty's Speech delivered the Twenty-Second of January 1643 [1644] to the Members of the Two Houses of Parliament at Oxford* ([Oxford], 1644), pp. 3–4.
69. Quoted by Andrew Hopper, *Turncoats and Renegadoes: Changing Sides during the English Civil Wars* (Oxford, 2012), p. 55.
70. *CSP Venice, Volume XXVII: 1643–1647*, p. 76 (26 February 1644).
71. [James Howell], *The True Informer*, pp. 33, 43.
72. Quoted by Stoyle, *Soldiers and Strangers*, p. 66.
73. Mark Stoyle, 'Pagans or Paragons? Images of the Cornish during the English Civil War', *English Historical Review*, 111:441 (1996), pp. 309–10.
74. Quoted by Stoyle, *Soldiers and Strangers*, p. 84.
75. Anonymous, *The Earl of Strafford's Ghost Complaining, of the Cruelties of his Countrymen, in Killing One Another* (London, 1644), pp. 3, 7.
76. *CSP Domestic . . . Charles I, 1644*, p. 259 (21 June 1644).
77. *CSP Venice, Volume XXVII: 1643–1647*, pp. 145, 149 (14 October and 4 November 1644).
78. *Motives and Reasons, concerning His Highness the Prince Elector Palatine's Coming into England. Presented to Both the Honourable Houses of Parliament by his Said Highness, on Saturday the 14 of September 1644* (London, 1644), pp. 2, 3.

79. *CSP Venice, Volume XXVII: 1643–1647*, pp. 116, 130, 135, 139 (15 July, 26 August, 16 and 23 September 1644).
80. *CSP Domestic ... Charles I, 1644–1645*, p. 151 (November 1644).
81. William Bray (ed.), *Diary and Correspondence of John Evelyn F.R.S., to which is subjoined the Private Correspondence between King Charles I and Sir Edward Nicholas &c.*, 4 vols (London, 1850–52), Vol. IV, p. 137 (5 February 1644); for Uxbridge Propositions, see Samuel Rawson Gardiner (ed.), *The Constitutional Documents of the Puritan Revolution, 1625–1660* (Oxford, 1951), pp. 275–86.

12 THE MEDIATION OF STRANGERS, 1644–1648

1. 'The Rebel Scot' in Brian Morris and Eleanor Withington (eds), *The Poems of John Cleveland* (Oxford, 1967), pp. 29, 31. The Parliamentarian leader John Pym had died in December 1643. 'Pig-wiggin' is another term for very small; 'myrmidon' denotes a subordinate and 'truckle' means to act in a subordinate manner (from truckle beds).
2. Meikle (ed.), *Correspondence*, p. 78 (27 May 1645). The prospect of establishing garrisons provoked particular nervousness; in March 1607, James VI & I had tried to explain Scots' fears regarding potential subjugation in a closer Anglo-Scottish union by warning English MPs that he trusted they did not envisage that he 'should set garrisons over them, as the Spaniards do over Sicily and Naples' (James VI & I, 'Speech ... Last Day of March 1607' in Johann P. Sommerville (ed.), *King James VI and I. Political Writings* (Cambridge, 1994), pp. 172–3).
3. Quoted by Albert J. Loomie, 'Alonso de Cárdenas and the Long Parliament, 1640–1648', *English Historical Review*, 97:383 (1982), p. 295.
4. *CSP Venice, Volume XXVII: 1643–1647*, p. 111 (24 June 1644).
5. [Richard Kilvert], *A Discourse of a True Englishman, Free from Self-Interest, concerning the Interest England hath in the Siege of Gravelines* (London, 1644), p. 6.
6. Quoted by Loek Luiten, 'The Dutch Republic and the English Civil War: Consensus or Conflict?', *Dutch Crossing: Journal of Low Countries Studies*, 42:2 (2018), p. 116, n. 89.
7. Meikle (ed.), *Correspondence*, p. 13 (19 March 1644).
8. 'Articles of the Charge against Lady Henrietta Maria, Queen of England, 3 January 1644'; <https://legalhistorymiscellany.com/2017/10/09/impeaching-the-queen-of-england/#_ftn11>; transcribed by Krista Kesselring from Parliamentary Archives HL/PO/JO/10/3/180/29 (accessed 30 April 2020).
9. Charles I, *The King's Cabinet Opened; or, certain Packets of Secret Letters and Papers, written with the King's Own Hand, and taken in his Cabinet at Naseby-Field, June 14, 1645* (London, 1645), pp. 44, 7, 43, sigs A3r–A3v.

10. Quoted by Michelle Anne White, *Henrietta Maria and the English Civil Wars* (Aldershot, 2006), p. 176.
11. Charles I, *King's Cabinet Opened*, p. 1.
12. Meikle (ed.), *Correspondence*, pp. 102, 156–7 (2 August 1645 and 31 January 1646).
13. Jacques du Perron, *A Warning to the Parliament of England ... In an Oration made to the General Assembly of the French Clergy in Paris* (London, 1647), pp. 3, 7, 6.
14. *CSP Venice, Volume XXVII: 1643–1647*, p. 185 (2 May 1645).
15. Lisa Shapiro (ed.), *The Correspondence between Princess Elisabeth of Bohemia and René Descartes* (Chicago, IL, 2007), p. 127 (30 November 1645).
16. Quoted by J. R. Tanner, *English Constitutional Conflicts of the Seventeenth Century 1603–1689* (Cambridge, 1928), p. 135.
17. 'I. W.', *The Bloody Prince, or A Declaration of the Most Cruel Practices of Prince Rupert, and the rest of the Cavaliers, in fighting against God, and the true members of His Church* (London, 1643), p. 10.
18. Eliot Warburton (ed.), *Memoirs of Prince Rupert and the Cavaliers: including their Private Correspondence, now first published from the Original Manuscripts*, 3 vols (London, 1849), Vol. III, p. 28 (16 October 1644).
19. Warburton (ed.), *Memoirs of Prince Rupert*, Vol. III, pp. 172–4 (3 September 1645).
20. *CSP Venice, Volume XXVII: 1643–1647*, p. 217 (5 October 1645).
21. Warburton (ed.), *Memoirs of Prince Rupert*, Vol. III, p. 189 (20 September 1645).
22. Henry Cary, *Memorials of the Great Civil War in England From 1646 to 1652*, 2 vols (London, 1842), Vol. I, p. 130 (30 June 1646).
23. C. H. Firth (ed.), 'The Journal of Prince Rupert's Marches, 5 Sept. 1642 to 4 July 1646', *English Historical Review*, 13:52 (1898), pp. 730–41; Ian Roy, 'Rupert, Prince and Count Palatine of the Rhine and Duke of Cumberland (1619–1682)', *Oxford Dictionary of National Biography* (Oxford, 2004).
24. Quoted by Jason Peacey, 'The Struggle for *Mercurius Britanicus*: Factional Politics and the Parliamentarian Press, 1643–1646', *Huntington Library Quarterly*, 68:3 (2005), pp. 529, 530.
25. *CSP Venice, Volume XXVII: 1643–1647*, pp. 207–8 (17 August 1645).
26. Quoted by Joyce Macadam, '*Mercurius Britanicus* on Charles I: An Exercise in Civil War Journalism and High Politics, August 1643 to May 1646', *Historical Research*, 84:225 (2011), p. 470. (The 4 August 1645 issue of *Mercurius Britanicus* became known as the 'Hue and Cry' edition, after the editorial continued, 'it were best to send Hue and Cry after him'.)
27. *CSP Venice, Volume XXVII: 1643–1647*, p. 169 (6 January 1645).

28. Quoted by Albert J. Loomie, 'New Light on the Spanish Ambassador's Purchases from Charles I's Collection 1649–53', *Journal of the Warburg and Courtauld Institutes*, 52 (1989), pp. 258–9.
29. Geraldine M. Phipps, 'The Russian Embassy to London of 1645–46 and the Abrogation of the Muscovy Company's Charter', *Slavonic and East European Review*, 68:2 (1990), p. 268.
30. *The Lord George Digby's Cabinet and Dr Goff's Negotiations; Together with His Majesty's, the Queen's, and the Lord Jermyn's and other Letters, taken at the Battle of Sherburn in Yorkshire about the 15th of October last. Also Observations upon the Said Letters* (London, 1646), p. 2.
31. Quoted by John Lowe, 'The Glamorgan Mission to Ireland, 1645–1646', *Studia Hibernica*, 4 (1964), p. 175.
32. Quoted by Jane H. Ohlmeyer, *Civil War and Restoration in the Three Stuart Kingdoms: The Career of Randal MacDonnell, Marquis of Antrim, 1609–1683* (Cambridge, 1993), p. 162.
33. *CSP Venice, Volume XXVII: 1643–1647*, p. 253 (21 April 1646).
34. Fotheringham (ed.), *Diplomatic Correspondence*, Vol. I, pp. 118, 106 (22 January/1 February and 15/25 January 1646).
35. Bruce (ed.), *Charles I*, pp. 19, 6 (19 February and 8 January 1646).
36. Clarendon, *State Papers*, Vol. II, pp. 226–7 (2 March 1646).
37. Bruce (ed.), *Charles I*, pp. 36, 37, 38 (21 and 22 April 1646). Charles added that Montereul was now 'confessing my knowledge of that nation to be much better than his' (p. 37).
38. *CSP Domestic . . . Charles I: 1645–1647*, p. 433 (5 May 1646). As the Commissioners continued, they would negotiate nothing that might 'encroach upon our League and Covenant or weaken the union and confidence between the two kingdoms'.
39. 'The King's Disguise' in Brian Morris and Eleanor Withington (eds), *The Poems of John Cleveland* (Oxford, 1967), pp. 6, 9.
40. *Journal of the House of Lords: Volume 8, 1645–1647* (London, 1767–1830), pp. 419–21; British History Online: <http://www.british-history.ac.uk/lords-jrnl/vol8/pp419-421> (accessed 16 December 2020).
41. Bruce (ed.), *Charles I*, p. 45 (10 June 1646).
42. Fotheringham (ed.), *Diplomatic Correspondence*, Vol. I, p. 208 (28 May/7 June 1646).
43. Bruce (ed.), *Charles I*, pp. 48, 44 (17 and 3 June 1646).
44. Fotheringham (ed.), *Diplomatic Correspondence*, Vol. II, p. 587 (June 1646).
45. Quoted by Philip A. Knachel, *England and the Fronde: The Impact of the English Civil War and Revolution on France* (Ithaca, NY, 1967), p. 113.
46. Bruce (ed.), *Charles I*, pp. 53–4 (8 July 1646).
47. Fotheringham (ed.), *Diplomatic Correspondence*, Vol. I, pp. 244, 256 (30 July/9 August 1646; 31 August/10 September 1646).

48. Quoted by Tadhg Ó hAnnracháin 'The Strategic Involvement of Continental Powers in Ireland, 1596–1691' in Padraig Lenihan (ed.), *Conquest and Resistance: War in Seventeenth Century Ireland* (Leiden, 2001), p. 42.
49. Quoted by Knachel, *England and the Fronde*, p. 30.
50. Fotheringham (ed.), *Diplomatic Correspondence*, Vol. I, pp. 322, 335 (2/12 November and 22 November/2 December 1646).
51. Meikle (ed.), *Correspondence*, p. 218 (3 October 1646).
52. *The House of Commons, The Answer of the Commons assembled in Parliament, to the Scots Commissioners' Papers of the 20th, and their Letter of the 24th of October last, 28 November 1646* (London, 1646), pp. 59, 61.
53. David Scott, *Politics and War in the Three Stuart Kingdoms, 1637–49* (Basingstoke, 2004), p. 127.
54. Anonymous, *Lex Talionis. Or, A Declamation against Mr. Challener, the Crimes of the Times, and the Manners of You Know Whom* (London, 1647), pp. 2, 5, 8.
55. Bruce (ed.), *Charles I*, p. 86 (19 December 1646).
56. Fotheringham (ed.), *Diplomatic Correspondence*, Vol. I, pp. 365, 375 (21/31 December 1646 and 24 December 1646/3 January 1647).
57. Quoted by Scott, *Politics and War in the Three Stuart Kingdoms*, p. 129; Fotheringham (ed.), *Diplomatic Correspondence*, Vol. I, p. 445 (12 February 1647).
58. Quoted by Guillaume Van Gemert, 'Between Disregard and Political Mobilization – Vondel as a Playwright in Contemporary European Context: England, France and the German Lands' in Jan Bloemendal and Frans-Willem Korsten (eds), *Joost van den Vondel (1587–1679): Dutch Playwright in the Golden Age* (Leiden, 2012), p. 185n.
59. Fotheringham (ed.), *Diplomatic Correspondence*, Vol. II, p. 55 (21 March 1647).
60. *CSP Venice, Volume XXVIII: 1647–1652*, p. 17 (12 September 1647).
61. Quoted by Thomas Pert, '"The Prince Elector is going from hence to London, I imagine for no good": The Elector Palatine, Parliament, and the Civil War, *c.*1638–1644' (unpublished seminar paper). I am grateful to Dr Pert for supplying me with a copy of this paper before publication.
62. Edward Whalley, *Joyful News of the Kings Majesty's Safe Arrival in the Isle of Wight with Mr. John Ashburnham, and Sir John Barclay &c.* (London, 1647), p. 2.
63. David Cressy, *England's Islands in a Sea of Troubles* (Oxford, 2020), p. 240.
64. Quoted by Tadhg Ó hAnnracháin, *Catholic Reformation in Ireland: The Mission of Rinuccini, 1645–1649* (Oxford, 2002), p. 146.
65. Quoted by Ohlmeyer, *Civil War and Restoration in the Three Stuart Kingdoms*, p. 202.
66. Quoted by Pérez Tostado, *Irish Influence*, p. 132.

67. Quoted by Davide Boerio, 'The "Trouble of Naples" in the Political Information Arena of the English Revolution' in Joad Raymond and Noah Moxham (eds), *News Networks in Early Modern Europe* (Leiden, 2016), p. 797.
68. *A Declaration of the Commons of England in Parliament Assembled; expressing their Reasons and Grounds of passing the late Resolutions touching No Farther Addresses or Application to be made to the King* [11 February 1648] (London, 1648), pp. 7, 37, 17.
69. Oliver Cromwell to Robert Jenner and John Ashe, 20 November 1648, Knottingley; <http://www.olivercromwell.org/Letters_and_speeches/letters/Letter_83.pdf> (accessed 16 December 2020).

13 ENGLAND SHALL BECOME HELL, 1648–1650

1. *CSP Venice, Volume XXVIII: 1647–1652*, p. 87 (26 February 1649).
2. Quoted by Gilles Bertheau, 'Representing Charles I's Death in some Mazarinades: The Limits of the Aristotelian Tragic Model', *Études Épistémè*, 20 (2011), fn. 19.
3. Anonymous, *Les Dernières Parole du Roy d'Angleterre* (Paris, 1649), p. 3 ('la premiere fois qu'ils on exercé leur cruauté sur la personne sacrée de leurs roys').
4. Quoted by Bertheau, 'Representing Charles I's Death', fn. 22.
5. Quoted by Imogen Peck, 'Remembering – and Forgetting – Regicide: The Commemoration of the 30th January, 1649–1660' in Estelle Paranque (ed.), *Remembering Queens and Kings of Early Modern England and France: Reputation, Reinterpretation, and Reincarnation* (Cham, 2019), p. 138.
6. Quoted by Dirk Wiemann, 'Spectacles of Astonishment: Tragedy and the Regicide in England and Germany, 1649–1663' in Gaby Mahlberg and Dirk Wiemann (eds), *European Contexts for English Republicanism* (Farnham, 2013), p. 45.
7. Quoted by Robert Ashton, *Counter-Revolution. The Second Civil War and its Origins, 1646–1648* (New Haven, CT, 1994), p. 440.
8. Bernard Capp, *Cromwell's Navy: The Fleet and the English Revolution, 1648–1660* (Oxford, 1989), pp. 23–4.
9. Quoted by Nigel Smith, *Literature and Revolution in England, 1640–1660* (New Haven, CT, 1994), pp. 61–2.
10. Quoted by Barbara Donagan, *War in England, 1642–1649* (Oxford, 2010), p. 9.
11. Samuel Rawson Gardiner (ed.), *The Hamilton Papers: Being Selections from Original Letters in the Possession of His Grace, The Duke of Hamilton and Brandon, Relating to the Years 1638–1650* (London, 1880), pp. 167–8 (18 March 1648).
12. Clarendon, *State Papers*, Vol. II, p. 416 (September 1648).

13. James Howell, *The Instruments of a King, Or a Short Discourse of the Sword, the Sceptre, the Crown* (London, 1648), pp. 9–11.
14. 'Theodorus Vorax' [Clement Walker], *Anarchia Anglicana: or The History of Independency, with Observations Historical and Politique upon this present Parliament &c.* (London, 1648), p. 32.
15. See <http://www.olivercromwell.org/Letters_and_speeches/letters/Letter_65.pdf> (Oliver Cromwell to William Lenthall, 20 August 1648; accessed 6 February 2021).
16. Cárdenas, *Revolución Inglesa*, p. 133.
17. *A Remonstrance of His Excellency Thomas Lord Fairfax, Lord General of the Parliament's Forces. And of the General Council of Officers held at St Albans the 16 of November* (London, 1648), pp. 62, 64.
18. Clarendon, *State Papers*, Vol. II, pp. 448–9 (25 November 1648).
19. William Prynne, *A Brief Memento to the present Unparliamentary Junto Touching their Present Intentions and Proceedings to Depose and Execute Charles Stewart, their Lawful King* (London, 1649), pp. 12–13.
20. Carte (ed.), *Collection*, Vol. I, pp. 195–7 ('The Declaration of his most Christian Majesty').
21. *A Letter from the Commissioners of the Kingdom of Scotland residing here at London to William Lenthall Esq. Speaker of the House of Commons &c.* (London, 1649), p. 4.
22. *Letter from the Commissioners of the Kingdom of Scotland*, pp. 7, 8.
23. K. J. Kesselring (ed.), *The Trial of Charles I* (Peterborough, ON, 2016), pp. 37, 36.
24. Kesselring (ed.), *Trial of Charles I*, p. 66.
25. Kesselring (ed.), *Trial of Charles I*, p. 74.
26. Charles I, *Eikon Basilike. The Portraiture of His Sacred Majesty, in his Solitudes and Sufferings, With Selections from Eikonoklastes*, Jim Daems and Holly Faith Nelson (eds) (Peterborough, Ontario, 2006), pp. 321–2 ('King Charles His Speech').
27. Quoted by Martin A. S. Hume, *The Court of Philip IV: Spain in Decadence* (London, 1928), p. 254.
28. [John Warner], *The Devilish Conspiracy, Hellish Treason, Heathenish Condemnation, and Damnable Murder committed and executed by the Jews against . . . Christ their King &c.* (London, 1649), pp. 17, 40, 20–21.
29. F. H. Blackburne Daniell (ed.), Historical Manuscripts Commission, *The Manuscripts of His Grace the Duke of Portland, preserved at Welbeck Abbey* (London, 1891), Vol. I, p. 512 (28 February 1649).
30. *CSP Venice, Volume XXVIII: 1647–1652*, p. 93 (10 April 1649). Henrietta Maria learned of her husband's death ten days after the event.
31. *CSP Venice, Volume XXVIII: 1647–1652*, p. 91 (11 March 1649).
32. Carte (ed.), *Collection*, Vol. I, p. 198 (1/11 February 1649).

33. *Narration des Procédures de la Haute Court de Justice en l'Examen du Roy Charles* ([London], 1649); *Relation Générale et Veritable de Tout ce qui c'est fait au Procez du Roy de la Grand Bretagne* ([London], 1649), p. 2 ('une chose inoüie & un catastrophe de plus estranges don't vous ayez jamais oüy parler').
34. Quoted by Davide Boerio, 'The "Trouble of Naples" in the Political Information Arena of the English Revolution' in Joad Raymond and Noah Moxham (eds), *News Networks in Early Modern Europe* (Leiden, 2016), p. 785.
35. Guizot, *Oliver Cromwell*, Appendix I, pp. 383, 399 (4 March 1649 and 5 July 1649).
36. Charles I, 'Eikon Basilike' in Daems and Nelson (eds), *Eikon Basilike*, pp. 88, 122.
37. John Milton, 'The Tenure of Kings and Magistrates' in Martin Dzelzainis (ed.), *John Milton. Political Writings* (Cambridge, 1991), pp. 4, 30, 31; see Martin Dzelzainis, 'Milton, *Macbeth* and Buchanan', *The Seventeenth Century*, 4:1 (1989), pp. 55–66.
38. John Milton, 'Selections from *Eikonoklastes*' in Daems and Nelson (eds), *Eikon Basilike*, pp. 224, 225, 281, 280, 283.
39. *CSP Venice, Volume XXVIII: 1647–1652*, p. 89 (5 March 1649).
40. Quoted by Helmers, *Royalist Republic*, p. 103; see also Paul R. Sellin and Margriet Lacy-Bruijn, 'Royalist Propaganda and Dutch Poets on the Execution of Charles I: Notes towards an Inquiry', *Dutch Crossing*, 24: 2 (2000), pp. 241–64.
41. Jason T. Peacey, 'Order and Disorder in Europe: Parliamentary Agents and Royalist Thugs, 1649–1650', *Historical Journal*, 40:4 (1997), p. 955.
42. Quoted by P. Alessandra Maccioni and Marco Mostert, 'Isaac Dorislaus (1595–1649): The Career of a Dutch Scholar in England', *Transactions of the Cambridge Bibliographical Society*, 8:4 (1984), pp. 439, 440.
43. *CSP Venice, Volume XXVIII: 1647–1652*, p. 100 (18 May 1649).
44. Anonymous, *A Salt Tear or, the Weeping Onion, at the Lamentable Funeral of Dr Dorislaus* ([London], 1649), single sheet.
45. Helmer J. Helmers, '"The Cry of the Royal Blood": Revenge Tragedy and the Stuart Cause in the Dutch Republic, 1649–1660' in Jan Bloemendal, Arjan Van Dixhoorn and Elsa Strietman (eds), *Literary Cultures and Public Opinion in the Low Countries, 1450–1650* (Leiden, 2011), p. 230.
46. Quoted by Cesare Cuttica, 'The English Regicide and Patriarchalism: Representing Commonwealth Ideology and Practice in the Early 1650s', *Renaissance and Reformation/Renaissance et Réforme*, 36:2 (2013), pp. 137, 148.
47. John Milton, 'A Defence of the People of England' in Dzelzainis (ed.), *Milton. Political Writings*, pp. 244, 69, 197, 77.
48. Clarendon, *State Papers*, Vol. II, p. 479 (Hyde to Lord Hatton, 12 April 1649).

49. John Bramhall, *A Fair Warning, to take Heed of the Scottish Discipline: as being of all others most Injurious to the Civil Magistrate, most Oppressive to the Subject, most Pernicious to Both* ([London, 1649), pp. 3, 24, 17, 6.
50. Robert Baillie, *A Review of the Seditious Pamphlet lately published in Holland by Dr. Bramhell, pretended Bishop of London-Derry; entitled, His Fair Warning against the Scots Discipline* (Delft, 1649), sigs a2r, a4v.
51. Warner (ed.), *Nicholas Papers*, Vol. I, p. 124 (6 April 1649).
52. Clarendon, *State Papers*, Vol. II, pp. 507, 512; P. Alessandra Maccioni and Marco Mostert, 'Isaac Dorislaus (1595–1649): the career of a Dutch Scholar in England', *Transactions of the Cambridge Bibliographical Society*, 8:4 (1984), Vol. III, p. 16 (3 and 31 January and 18 March 1650). In April, Hyde protested anew that the Spanish were 'a wretched, miserable, proud, senseless people, and as far from the wise men I expected, as can be imagined; and if some miracle do not preserve them, this Crown must be destroyed' (Vol. III, p. 17; 14 April 1650).
53. *CSP Venice, Volume XXVIII: 1647–1652*, pp. 137, 138, 139, 140 (14 February 1650).
54. Warner (ed.), *Nicholas Papers*, Vol. I, p. 183 ('Relation of the Lord Culpeper's Reception').
55. Anonymous, *A Declaration of His Imperial Majesty, the Most High and Mighty Potentate Alexei, Emperor of Russia, and Great Duke of Muscovy, &c.* ([London], 1650), pp. 1, 3 5.
56. Clarendon, *State Papers*, Vol. II, pp. 499–500 (3 December 1649).
57. Samuel Rawson Gardiner (ed.), *Letters and Papers Illustrating the Relations between Charles the Second and Scotland in 1650* (Edinburgh, 1894), p. 33.
58. E. K. Purnell (ed.), Historical Manuscripts Commission, *Report on the Pepys Manuscripts, Preserved at Magdalene College, Cambridge* (London, 1911), p. 250 (February 1649).
59. Gardiner (ed.), *Letters and Papers*, pp. 5–6; quoted by Steve Murdoch, *Britain, Denmark-Norway and The House of Stuart 1603–1660: A Diplomatic and Military Analysis* (East Linton, 2003), p. 147.
60. Gardiner (ed.), *Letters and Papers*, pp. 74, 46, 74, 75.
61. Clarendon, *State Papers*, Vol. II, p. 533 (13 April 1650).
62. *CSP Domestic . . . Interregnum, 1650*, p. 155 (10 May 1650).
63. *CSP Venice, Volume XXVIII: 1647–1652*, pp. 147, 148 (4 and 8 June 1650). The book cited was Ascham's *A Discourse, Wherein is Examined, What is Particularly Lawfull during the Confusions and Revolutions of Government* (London, 1648); see Igor Pérez Tostado, 'Murder as a Weapon of Exile: English Politics at the Spanish Court (1649–1652)' in David Worthington (ed.), *British and Irish Emigrants and Exiles in Europe 1603–1688* (Leiden, 2010), pp. 141–60.

64. See A. J. Loomie, 'The Publication of Sir Edward Hyde's *Consideraciones* at Madrid in June 1650', *Recusant History*, 19 (1989), pp. 447–59.
65. Clarendon, *State Papers*, Vol. II, Appendix, pp. lxviii–lxix.
66. Frederic George Stephens and M. Dorothy George (eds), *Catalogue of Prints and Drawings in the British Museum. Division I: Political and Personal Satires* (London, 1877), p. 444 (Hugo Allard the Elder, 'The Crowning of Charles II at Scone, 1651').

14 HERE *WAS* YE KING'S HEAD, 1650–1654

1. John Adamson, 'Policy and Pomegranates: Art, Iconography and Counsel in Rubens's Anglo-Spanish Diplomacy of 1629–1630' in Luc Duerloo and R. Malcolm Smuts (eds), *The Age of Rubens. Diplomacy, Dynastic Politics and the Visual Arts in Early Seventeenth-Century Europe* (Turnhout, 2016), p. 154.
2. Jerry Brotton, *The Sale of the Late King's Goods. Charles I and his Art Collection* (London, 2017), pp. 237–8.
3. Quoted by Maija Jansson, 'Remembering Marston Moor: The Politics of Culture' in Susan D. Amussen and Mark A. Kishlansky (eds), *Political Culture and Cultural Politics in Early Modern Europe: Essays Presented to David Underdown* (Manchester, 1995), p. 257.
4. Quoted by Brotton, *Sale of the Late King's Goods*, p. 263.
5. *Diary of Alexander Jaffray, Provost of Aberdeen, one of the Scottish Commissioners to Charles II &c.* (London, 1834), p. 32.
6. Anonymous, *The King of Scotland's Negotiations at Rome, for Assistance against the Commonwealth of England, in certain Propositions there made, for, and on his Behalf* (London, 1650), p. 5.
7. See <http://www.olivercromwell.org/Letters_and_speeches/letters/Letter_129.pdf>. Cromwell to the General Assembly of the Church of Scotland, Musselburgh, 3 August 1650 (accessed 11 May 2020).
8. David Hay Fleming (ed.), *Diary of Sir Archibald Johnston of Wariston. Volume II: 1650–1654* (Edinburgh, 1919), pp. 14–15 (9 August 1650).
9. Charles II, *A Declaration by the Kings Majesty, to his Subjects of the Kingdoms of Scotland, England, and Ireland* (Edinburgh, 1650), pp. 1, 2–3 (16 August 1650).
10. Quoted by Benjamin Woodford, 'From Tyrant to Unfit Monarchy: Marchamont Nedham's Representation of Charles Stuart and Royalists during the Interregnum', *History*, 100:339 (2015), p. 8.
11. Robert Douglas, *The Form and Order of the Coronation of Charles the II, King of Scotland, together with the Sermon then Preached, by Mr. Robert Dowglas &c.* (Aberdeen, 1660), pp. 8, 15.
12. Philip A. Knachel, *England and the Fronde: The Impact of the English Civil War and Revolution on France* (Ithaca, NY, 1967), p. 146 (13 October 1650).

13. Cárdenas, *Revolución Inglesa*, p. 65.
14. Alonso de Cárdenas, *The Address of Alonso de Cardenas, Lord Ambassador for the King of Spain, to the Parliament of the Commonwealth of England &c.* (Edinburgh, 1650), sig. A2r.
15. Sir Richard Fanshawe, *Original Letters of his Excellency Sir Richard Fanshaw, during his Embassies in Spain and Portugal &c.* (London, 1701), p. 465 ('Transactions between England and Spain, from the year 1650').
16. *CSP Venice, Volume XXVIII: 1647–1652*, pp. 169–70 (8 February 1651).
17. Thurloe, *State Papers*, Vol. I, p. 176 (27 March 1651).
18. *CSP Venice, Volume XXVIII: 1647–1652*, p. 187 (21 June 1651).
19. Robert Thomas Fallon, *Milton in Government* (University Park, PA, 1993), p. 46.
20. John Nickolls (ed.), *Original Letters and Papers of State, Addressed to Oliver Cromwell: Concerning the Affairs of Great Britain . . . Found among the Political Collections of John Milton* (London, 1743), p. 41 (28 December 1650).
21. Knachel, *England and the Fronde*, p. 84.
22. Robert Mentet de Salmonet, *The History of the Troubles of Great Britain: containing a particular Account of the most Remarkable Passages in Scotland, from the Year 1633 to the year 1650 &c.* (London, 1735), 'Preface', p. ii.
23. *CSP Venice, Volume XXVIII: 1647–1652*, p. 192 (15 July 1651).
24. John Milton, 'Preface' to 'A Defence of the People of England' in Martin Dzelzainis (ed.), *John Milton. Political Writings* (Cambridge, 1991), p. 57.
25. Blair Worden, *Literature and Politics in Cromwellian England. John Milton, Andrew Marvell, Marchamont Nedham* (Oxford, 2009), pp. 119–20.
26. Quoted by Pincus, *Protestantism*, p. 36.
27. Thurloe, *State Papers*, Vol. I, p. 186 (June 1651).
28. Quoted by Pincus, *Protestantism*, pp. 29–30.
29. Thurloe, *State Papers*, Vol. I, p. 190 (20/30 June 1651).
30. Quoted by Helmers, *Royalist Republic*, p. 159.
31. See Helmers, *Royalist Republic*, p. 163; John Milton, 'Preface' to 'A Defence of the People of England' in Dzelzainis (ed.), *Milton. Political Writings*, p. 64.
32. Anonymous, *A New and True Declaration of the False Treachery of the Scots against England from time to time. Wherein the manifold Inroads, and bloody Invasions of the Scots into England are fully Discovered* (London, 1651), p. 8.
33. Thurloe, *State Papers*, Vol. I, p. 195 (8 August 1651).
34. See <https://www.pubnames.co.uk/top100.php> (accessed 14 May 2020).
35. William Matthews (ed.), *Charles II's Escape from Worcester. A Collection of Narratives Assembled by Samuel Pepys* (London, 1967), p. 50 ('The King's Own Account'); see Jerome de Groot, 'Fugitives, Fields, Pubs and Trees', *The Seventeenth Century*, 32:4 (2017), pp. 493–512.

36. *By the Parliament. A Proclamation for the Discovery and Apprehending of Charles Stuart &c.* (London, 1651), single sheet.
37. Matthews (ed.), *Charles II's Escape*, pp. 52, 54 ('The King's Own Account').
38. *CSP Venice, Volume XXVIII: 1647–1652*, p. 202 (7 November 1651).
39. Quoted by Austin Woolrych, *Britain in Revolution, 1625–1660* (Oxford, 2002), p. 499.
40. Peter Sterry, *England's Deliverance from the Northern Presbytery, Compared with its Deliverance from the Roman Papacy* (Leith, 1652), pp. 14, 23.
41. David Cressy, *England's Islands in a Sea of Troubles* (Oxford, 2020), p. 165.
42. A. G. H. Bachrach and R. G. Collmer (eds), *Lodewijk Huygens. The English Journal 1651–1652* (Leiden, 1982), pp. 109, 105 (11 April and 25 March 1652).
43. *CSP Venice, Volume XXVIII: 1647–1652*, pp. 226, 227, 227–8 (2 May 1652).
44. Knachel, *England and the Fronde*, p. 43n.
45. Quoted by Roger Bigelow Merriman, *Six Contemporaneous Revolutions* (Oxford, 1938), pp. 180, 181.
46. J. W., *Brandy-Wine, in the Hollanders Ingratitude. Being a Serious Expostulation of an English Soldier with the Dutch: wherein he debates with them of former kindness received from England &c.* (London, 1652), title-page, p. 2.
47. Thurloe, *State Papers*, Vol. I, p. 292 (24 June 1653).
48. Owen Felltham, *A Brief Character of the Low Countries under the States being Three Weeks' Observation of the Vices and Virtues of the Inhabitants* (London, 1652), pp. 1–2, 5, 41.
49. Elizabeth Staffell, 'The Horrible Tail-Man and the Anglo-Dutch Wars', *Journal of the Warburg and Courtauld Institutes*, 63 (2000), p. 181.
50. Helen Pierce, *Unseemly Pictures. Graphic Satire and Politics in Early Modern England* (New Haven, CT, 2008), p. 201.
51. Thurloe, *State Papers*, Vol. I, p. 214 (27 August 1652).
52. Quoted by Eva Scott, *The King in Exile. The Wanderings of Charles II from June 1646 to July 1654* (London 1905), p. 369.
53. Thurloe, *State Papers*, Vol. I, p. 246 (28 May 1653). Even if practical support was not forthcoming, Charles's representatives at the Imperial Diet enjoyed more creature comforts than the impoverished exiled court in Paris. In late 1653, a correspondent in Regensburg admitted to Hyde's secretary that 'You will hardly believe me, but I assure you it is true, we have had this Christmas plum puddings, mince pies, brawn and have sometimes been merry and laughed, though at ourselves' (quoted by Scott, *King in Exile*, pp. 373–4).
54. Quoted by Andrew B. Pernal, '"Ready to Lay Down His Person and Fortune at Her Feet": Prince Bogusław Radziwiłł's Proposal for Marriage with Mary Stuart, Princess Royal of England, and Princess of Orange in 1653–1654', *Canadian Slavonic Papers*, 48:1–2 (2006), p. 68n.
55. Thurloe, *State Papers*, Vol. I, pp. 249, 250 (23 May 1653).
56. Staffell, 'The Horrible Tail-Man', p. 176.

57. Quoted by Robert Lloyd Haan, 'The Treatment of England and English Affairs in the Dutch Pamphlet Literature 1640–1660' (University of Michigan PhD thesis, 1959), p. 194.
58. Thurloe, *State Papers*, Vol. I, pp. 309, 366 (30 June 1653 and 31 July 1653).
59. Quoted by Pincus, *Protestantism*, p. 138.
60. Quoted by Herbert H. Rowen, *John de Witt, Grand Pensionary of Holland 1625–1672* (Princeton, NJ, 1978), p. 202.
61. Thurloe, *State Papers*, Vol. I, pp. 422, 438 (23 August and 5 September 1653).
62. Thurloe, *State Papers*, Vol. I, p. 386 (29 July 1653). The charge of drunkenness was seemingly justified, since another envoy, van Jongestal, complained to William Frederick of Nassau in November that Beverning, 'being drunk, at last told me, that he could no longer endure the proceedings of the Lord Nieupoort, that he always contradicted him, and corrected him, that he could never do anything to his mind, etc., so that I perceive well enough, that they do not agree' (Thurloe, *State Papers*, Vol. I, p. 600; 28 November 1653).
63. Thurloe, *State Papers*, Vol. I, pp. 511–12 ('Declaration of His Majesty's Forces, now on foot within the Kingdom of Scotland').
64. *A Declaration Concerning the Government of the Three Nations of England, Scotland, and Ireland, by His Highness the Lord Protector Cromwell &c.* (London, 1653), p. 6.
65. Thurloe, *State Papers*, Vol. I, p. 651 (28 December 1653).
66. *CSP Venice, Volume XXIX: 1653–1654*, pp. 159, 167 (23 December 1653 and 6 January 1654).
67. Henry Reeve (ed.), *A Journal of the Swedish Embassy in the Years 1653 and 1654. Impartially written by the Ambassador Bulstrode Whitelocke*, 2 vols (London, 1855), Vol. I, pp. 202 (13 December 1653).
68. Reeve (ed.), *A Journal of the Swedish Embassy*, Vol. I, pp. 203, 247, 285, 318, 327 (13 and 26 December 1653 and 5, 13 and 17 January 1654).
69. Reeve (ed.), *A Journal of the Swedish Embassy*, Vol. I, pp. 437, 441–2 (21 and 23 February 1654).
70. Quoted by Helmers, *Royalist Republic*, p. 229.
71. Thurloe, *State Papers*, Vol. II, p. 345 (June 1654).
72. *CSP Venice, Volume XXIX: 1653–1654*, p. 235 (14 July 1654).

15 CASTLES IN THE AIR, 1654–1658

1. Abraham de Wicquefort, *The Embassador and his Functions: Written by Monsieur de Wicquefort, Privy-Counsellor to the Duke of Brunswick and Lunenburg, Zell &c.* (London, 1716), p. 17.
2. Thurloe, *State Papers*, Vol. II, p. 144 (6 March 1654).
3. *CSP Venice, Volume XXIX: 1653–1654*, p. 224 (17 June 1654).

4. *CSP Venice, Volume XXX: 1655–1656*, p. 77, 80 (6 and 13 July 1655).
5. *CSP Venice, Volume XXX: 1655–1656*, pp. 302, 308 ('Relation').
6. Warner (ed.), *Nicholas Papers*, Vol. II, p. 14 (19/29 May 1653); Thurloe, *State Papers*, Vol. I, p. 366 (31 July 1653).
7. Thurloe, *State Papers*, Vol. II, p. 275; Vol. III, p. 658 (May 1654 and 8 July 1655).
8. James Welwood, *Memoirs of the Most Material Transactions in England, for the last Hundred Years, preceding the Revolution in 1688* (London, 1702), p. 109.
9. Evelyn, *Diary*, p. 358 (9 April 1655).
10. H. M. Margoliouth (ed.), *The Poems and Letters of Andrew Marvell*, 2 vols (Oxford, 1971), Vol. I, p. 118 ('The First Anniversary of the Government under O. C.').
11. Thurloe, *State Papers*, Vol. II, pp. 421, 567 (12 July and 8 September 1654).
12. Quoted by Catriona Murray, *Imaging Stuart Family Politics. Dynastic Crisis and Continuity* (Abingdon, 2017), p. 51.
13. Quoted by Nicole Greenspan, 'Public Scandal, Political Controversy, and Familial Conflict in the Stuart Courts in Exile: The Struggle to Convert the Duke of Gloucester in 1654', *Albion: A Quarterly Journal Concerned with British Studies*, 35:3 (2003), pp. 412, 420–21.
14. Thurloe, *State Papers*, Vol. I, p. 661 (10 November 1654).
15. *The Victory of Truth for the Peace of the Church to the King of Great Britain to Invite him to Embrace the Roman Catholic Faith, by Monsieur de la Militière, Counsellour-in-Ordinary to the King of France; With an Answer Thereunto, written by the Right Reverend John Bramhall, D.D. and Lord Bishop of London-Derry* (The Hague, 1653), pp. 8, 34, 55, 115–16, 128.
16. Thurloe, *State Papers*, Vol. II, p. 351 (5 June 1654).
17. Wilbur Cortez Abbott (ed.), *The Writings and Speeches of Oliver Cromwell. With an Introduction, Notes and an Account of His Life*, 4 vols (Oxford, 1988), Vol. III, pp. 347, 348 (29 June 1654).
18. *CSP Venice, Volume XXIX: 1653–1654*, p. 232 (7 July 1654).
19. Quoted by Linda Frey and Marsha Frey, 'The Bounds of Immunity: the Sá Case. Politics, Law and Diplomacy in Commonwealth England', *Canadian Journal of History*, 25:1 (1990), p. 49.
20. Wicquefort, *Embassador and his Functions*, p. 269.
21. Thurloe, *State Papers*, Vol. II, p. 685; Vol. III, p. 49 (30 October 1654 and 8 January 1655).
22. Thurloe, *State Papers*, Vol. III, p. 477 (4 June 1655).
23. Abbott (ed.), *Writings and Speeches of Oliver Cromwell*, Vol. III, p. 729 (25 May 1655).
24. Quoted by Benjamin Woodford, 'From Tyrant to Unfit Monarch: Marchamont Nedham's Representation of Charles Stuart and Royalists during the Interregnum', *History*, 100:339 (2015), p. 14.

25. Arthur Bryant (ed.), *The Letters, Speeches and Declarations of King Charles II* (London, 1935), p. 37 (3/13 June 1655).
26. *Miscellanea Aulica: or, a Collection of State-Treatises, Never Before Published, Containing Letters by King Charles and King James II in their Exile &c.* (London, 1702), p. 113 (8 June 1655).
27. Thurloe, *State Papers*, Vol. IV, pp. 301, 182 (20 December and 10 November 1655).
28. Thurloe, *State Papers*, Vol. IV, p. 88 (n.d. [1655]).
29. *CSP Venice, Volume XXIX: 1653–1654*, p. 108 (9 August 1653).
30. Tommaso Campanella, *A Discourse Touching the Spanish Monarchy. Wherein we have a Political Glasse, Representing Each Particular Country, Province, Kingdom, and Empire of the World, With Ways of Government by which They may be Kept in Obedience* (London, 1653), pp. 155, 161.
31. C. H. Firth (ed.), *The Clarke Papers: Selections from the Papers of William Clarke, Secretary to the Council of the Army, 1647–1649, and to General Monck and the Commanders of the Army in Scotland 1651–1660*, 4 vols (London, 1889–1901), Vol. III, p. 197.
32. Quoted by Carla Gardina Pestana, *The English Conquest of Jamaica. Oliver Cromwell's Bid for Empire* (Cambridge, MA, 2017), p. 36.
33. *CSP Venice, Volume XXX: 1655–1656*, pp. 74, 85 (3 and 24 July 1655).
34. Michael Roberts (trans. and ed.), *Swedish Diplomats at Cromwell's Court, 1655–1656. The Missions of Peter Julius Coyet and Christer Bonde* (London, 1988), p. 177 (19 October 1655).
35. Cárdenas, *Revolución Inglesa*, p. 148.
36. *A Declaration of His Highness, By the Advice of his Council; Setting Forth, On the Behalf of this Commonwealth, the Justice of Their Cause against Spain* (London, 1655), sig. A3r, p. 18.
37. *Sir Francis Drake Revived. Who is or may be a Pattern to Stir up all Heroic and Active Spirits of these Times &c.* (London, 1653), p. 1.
38. *CSP Venice, Volume XXX: 1655–1656*, p. 94 (15 August 1655).
39. Warner (ed.), *Nicholas Papers*, Vol. III, p. 58 (24 September 1655).
40. Roberts (trans. and ed.), *Swedish Diplomats*, p. 166 (28 September 1655).
41. *Miscellanea Aulica*, pp. 117–18 (17 August 1655).
42. Abbott (ed.), *Writings and Speeches of Oliver Cromwell*, Vol. III, p. 858 (October 1655).
43. Julian de Castilla, *The English Conquest of Jamaica: An Account of what happened in the Island of Jamaica*, trans. Irene A. Wright, *Camden Miscellany*, 13, Third Series, 31 (1924), pp. 5, 19.
44. Roberts (trans. and ed.), *Swedish Diplomats*, pp. 125, 208–9 (23 August and 30 November 1655).
45. Thurloe, *State Papers*, Vol. IV, pp. 336, 525 (1 January and 21 February 1656).
46. Thurloe, *State Papers*, Vol. IV, p. 704 (26 April 1656).

47. Abbott (ed.), *Writings and Speeches of Oliver Cromwell*, Vol. IV, p. 139 (27 July 1655).
48. Thurloe, *State Papers*, V, 263 (11 August 1656); see David L. Smith, 'Diplomacy and the Religious Question: Mazarin, Cromwell and the Treaties of 1655 and 1657', *E-Rea: Revue Électronique D'Études sur le Monde Anglophone*, 11:2 (2014).
49. Clarke (ed.), *Life of James the Second*, Vol. I, pp. 278, 277 (September 1656).
50. Thurloe, *State Papers*, Vol. V, p. 369 (1/11 September 1656).
51. Warner (ed.), *Nicholas Papers*, Vol. III, pp. 35, 36 (24 August 1655).
52. Quoted by Eva Scott, *The Travels of the King. Charles II in Germany and Flanders 1654–1660* (London, 1907), pp. 194, 212.
53. Thurloe, *State Papers*, Vol. V, p. 45 (20 May 1656).
54. Thurloe, *State Papers*, Vol. V, pp. 125, 344, 602 (17 June, 3 September and 18 November 1656).
55. *CSP Venice, Volume XXXI: 1657–1659*, p. 8 (19 January 1657).
56. Thurloe, *State Papers*, Vol. V, p. 774 (9 January 1657).
57. *CSP Venice, Volume XXXI: 1657–1659*, p. 58 (25 May 1657).
58. *CSP Venice, Volume XXX: 1655–1656*, p. 124 (22 October 1655).
59. 'J. H.', *An Admonition to my Lord Protector and his Council, of their Present Danger, with the Means to Secure him and his Posterity in their Present Greatness &c.* (London, 1654), p. 8.
60. Abbott (ed.), *Writings and Speeches of Oliver Cromwell*, Vol. III, p. 787 (27 July 1655).
61. Warner (ed.), *Nicholas Papers*, Vol. II, p. 42 (8 January 1654).
62. Abbott (ed.), *Writings and Speeches of Oliver Cromwell*, Vol. IV, p. 412.
63. Anonymous, *A Copy of a Letter written to an Officer of the Army by a true Commonwealths-man, and No Courtier, concerning the right and settlement of our present Government and Governors* (London, 1656), pp. 4, 32; see Jonathan Fitzgibbons, 'Hereditary Succession and the Cromwellian Protectorate: The Offer of the Crown Reconsidered', *English Historical Review*, 128:534 (2013), 1095–1128.
64. Abbott (ed.), *Writings and Speeches of Oliver Cromwell*, Vol. IV, pp. 473, 514 (13 April and 8 May 1657).
65. Quoted by C. H. Firth, 'Killing No Murder', *English Historical Review*, 17:66 (1902), p. 308; [Edward Sexby], *Killing No Murder. Briefly Discoursed in Three Questions. By William Allen* ([Holland, 1657]), sig. B2v; Charles I, *Eikon Basilike. The Portraiture of His Sacred Majesty, in his Solitudes and Sufferings, With Selections from Eikonoklastes*, Jim Daems and Holly Faith Nelson (eds) (Peterborough, ON, 2006), p. 146. Information supplied in May 1657 by John Coltman of the Tower of London cited 'seven parcels of books, entitled *Killing No Murder &c.* containing about 200 in each parcel' (Thurloe, *State Papers*, Vol. VI, p. 315).

66. Chad Schrock, 'Plain Styles: Disillusioned Rhetoric in Edward Sexby's *Killing Noe Murder*', *Modern Language Review*, 105:2 (2010), pp. 343–4.
67. Quoted by Laura Lunger Knoppers, *Constructing Cromwell. Ceremony, Portrait, and Print, 1645–1661* (Cambridge, 2000), p. 125.
68. *CSP Venice, Volume XXXI: 1657–1659*, p. 64 (8 June 1657).
69. *CSP Venice, Volume XXXI: 1657–1659*, p. 115 (5 October 1657).
70. Clarke (ed.), *Life of James the Second*, Vol. I, p. 327; having evidently provoked suspicion by his actions, Reynolds was recalled to London, but drowned en route when his vessel was shipwrecked on Goodwin Sands in December 1657.
71. *Journal of the House of Commons: Volume 7, 1651–1660* (London, 1802), p. 586 (25 January 1658).
72. Thurloe, *State Papers*, Vol. VII, pp. 246, 272, 334 (17 July 1658, undated and 23 August 1658).
73. Quoted by Susan Broomhall and Jacqueline Van Gent, 'The Queen of Bohemia's Daughter: Managing Rumour and Reputation in a Seventeenth-Century Dynasty' in Heather Kerr and Claire Walker (eds), *Fama and Her Sisters. Gossip and Rumour in Early Modern Europe* (Turnhout, 2015), p. 162.
74. Quoted by Nicole Greenspan, 'Charles II, Lucy Walter and the Stuart Courts in Exile', *English Historical Review*, 131:553 (2016), p. 1410.
75. Clarendon, *State Papers*, Vol. III, pp. 382, 384 (6, 10 and 22 December 1657).
76. Sir Thomas Morgan, *A True and Just Relation of Maj. Gen. Sir Thomas Morgan's Progress in France and Flanders with the Six Thousand English, in the Years 1657 and 1658, at the Taking of Dunkirk and other Important Places, as it was Delivered by the General Himself* (London, 1699), p. 7.
77. Thurloe, *State Papers*, Vol. VII, pp. 174, 198 (24 June and 3 July 1658).
78. Jean François Paul de Gondi de Retz, *France No Friend to England. Or, The Resentments of the French upon the success of the English. As it is expressed in a most Humble and Important Remonstrance to the King of France, upon the Surrendering of the Maritime Ports of Flanders into the Hands of the English* (London, 1659), pp. 5, 10, 11, 23.

16 NOW IN ANOTHER WORLD, 1658–1660

1. Thurloe, *State Papers*, Vol. VII, pp. 364, 376 and 372 (30 August, 8 and 4 September 1658).
2. Quoted by N. H. Keeble, *The Restoration. England in the 1660s* (Oxford, 2002), p. 5.
3. Frances Henderson (ed.), *The Clarke Papers. Further Selections from the Papers of William Clarke &c.* (Camden Society, Fifth Series, 27, Cambridge,

2005), p. 272 (6 September 1658); a newsletter contained in the Clarke papers claims that Oliver 'did not declare the Lord Richard to be his successor till about 2 days before he died' (p. 272).

4. Quoted by Jonathan Fitzgibbons, '"Not in any Doubtfull Dispute?" Reassessing the Nomination of Richard Cromwell', *Historical Research*, 83:220 (2010), p. 288; as Fitzgibbons shows, Cromwell cited, to support his view, the text from Ecclesiastes: 'Who knoweth whether he may beget a fool or wise?' For the political influences of Cromwell's extended family, see Patrick Little, 'Cromwell and Sons. Oliver Cromwell's *Intended* Legacy?' in Jane A. Mills (ed.), *Cromwell's Legacy* (Manchester, 2012), pp. 17–32.
5. Quoted by Peter Gaunt, 'Richard Cromwell (1626–1712)', *Oxford Dictionary of National Biography* (Oxford, 2004).
6. Carte (ed.), *Collection*, Vol. II, p. 156.
7. Clarendon, *State Papers*, Vol. III, pp. 412, 413 (20 September 1658).
8. Thurloe, *State Papers*, Vol. VII, pp. 381, 374 (20 and 7 September 1658).
9. Quoted by Alistair Malcolm, 'Pretending to be Catholic? Sir Henry Bennet, the Alliance with Spain and Stuart Dalliance with Rome, 1656–62' in Robin Eagles and Coleman A. Dennehy (eds), *Henry Bennet, Earl of Arlington, and his World. Restoration Court, Politics and Diplomacy* (Abingdon, 2020), p. 40.
10. Guizot, *Richard Cromwell*, Vol. II, p. 442 (16 September 1658).
11. Edward Vallance, *Loyalty, Memory and Public Opinion in England, 1658–1727* (Manchester, 2019), p. 46.
12. Guizot, *Richard Cromwell*, Vol. II, p. 276 (23 December 1658).
13. Quoted by Patrick Little and David L. Smith, *Parliaments and Politics during the Cromwellian Protectorate* (Cambridge, 2007), pp. 259–60.
14. Quoted by Fitzgibbons, '"Not in any Doubtfull Dispute?"', p. 299.
15. Clarendon, *State Papers*, Vol. III, p. 440 (18 March 1659).
16. Guizot, *Richard Cromwell*, Vol. I, pp. 389, 390 (29 May 1659).
17. Peter Gaunt (ed.), *The Correspondence of Henry Cromwell, 1655–1659* (Camden Society, Fifth Series, 31, Cambridge, 2007), p. 516 (17 May 1659).
18. 'F. B.', *Considerations and Proposals Presented to his Late Highness Oliver, Lord Protector of England, Touching the not Warring with Spain &c.* (London, 1659), p. 1.
19. Thurloe, *State Papers*, Vol. VII, p. 586 (3 December 1658).
20. Guizot, *Richard Cromwell*, Vol. I, p. 437 (31 July 1659).
21. *CSP Venice, Volume XXXII: 1659–1661*, p. 82 (26 October 1659).
22. Quoted by Jonathan Scott, *Algernon Sidney and the English Republic, 1623–1677* (Cambridge, 1988), pp. 132–3.
23. The Council's advice referred to an envoy from 'una Republica Tirana, que con acto tan destestable quito en publico cadalso juntamente la caveza y la corona a su Rey' (cited in F. J. Routledge, *England and the Treaty of the Pyrenees* (Liverpool, 1953), p. 32n).

24. Clarendon, *State Papers*, Vol. III, pp. 545, 550 (22 August and 1 September 1659).
25. Quoted by Eva Scott, *The Travels of the King. Charles II in Germany and Flanders 1654–1660* (London, 1907), p. 423 (4 November 1659).
26. Anonymous, *Certamen Britannicum, Gallico Hispanicum. A True Relation of a Conference held between Charles Stuart, King of Scots, Don Lewis de Haro, and the Cardinal Mazarin, the two Grand Favourites of the Courts of France and Spain* (London, 1659), pp. 6, 7.
27. Clarendon, *State Papers*, Vol. III, pp. 546, 547 (26 August 1659).
28. F. J. Routledge (ed.), *Calendar of The Clarendon State Papers Preserved in the Bodleian Library, Volume IV 1657–1660* (Oxford, 1932), p. 235 (15/25 June 1659)
29. Mary Coate (ed.), *The Letter-Book of John Viscount Mordaunt 1658–1660* (London, 1945), pp. 43, 129 (undated and 18 December 1659).
30. William L. Sachse (ed.), *The Diurnal of Thomas Rugg, 1659–1661* (London, 1961), p. 4.
31. Evelyn, *Diary*, p. 399 (12 October 1659).
32. *CSP Venice, Volume XXXII: 1659–1661*, pp. 83–4 (31 October 1659).
33. [Thomas Flatman], *Don Juan Lamberto, or a Comical History of the Late Times* (London, 1661), sig. F3v.
34. James D. Ogilvie (ed.), *The Diary of Sir Archibald Johnston of Wariston. Volume III: 1655–1660* (Edinburgh, 1940), p. 162.
35. Anonymous, *The Court Career Death Shadowed to Life, Or Shadows of Life and Death. A Pasquil Dialogue seriously perused and highly approved by the clearest judgements* (London, 1659), pp. 15, 13, 9.
36. *Anonymous, A Dialogue Betwixt the Ghosts of Charles the I, Late King of England, and Oliver, the Late Usurping Protector* (London, 1659), p. 8.
37. Rachel Willie, *Staging the Revolution: Drama, Reinvention and History, 1647–1672* (Manchester, 2015), p. 69.
38. Clarendon, *State Papers*, Vol. III, pp. 479, 413, 414 (3 June 1659 and 20 September 1658).
39. Thurloe, *State Papers*, Vol. VII, p. 573 (18 December 1658).
40. *CSP Venice, Volume XXXII: 1659–1661*, p. 91 (21 November 1659).
41. Clarendon, *State Papers*, Vol. III, pp. 619, 641, 681–2 (2 December 1659; 10 January 1660 and 17 February 1660).
42. Quoted by Blair Worden, '1660: Restoration and Revolution' in Janet Clare (ed.), *From Republic to Restoration. Legacies and Departures* (Manchester, 2018), p. 24.
43. *CSP Venice, Volume XXXII: 1659–1661*, p. 114 (13 February 1660).
44. Quoted by Gary S. De Krey, *London and the Restoration, 1659–1683* (Cambridge, 2005), p. 49.
45. Clarendon, *State Papers*, Vol. III, p. 681 (17 February 1660).

46. Quoted by Worden, '1660: Restoration and Revolution' in Clare (ed.), *From Republic to Restoration*, p. 41.
47. Carte (ed.), *Collection*, Vol. II, pp. 312–13 (9 March 1660).
48. [Marchamont Nedham], *News from Brussels, In a Letter from a Near Attendant on His Maiesty's Person &c.* (London, 1660), pp. 4–5.
49. [John Evelyn], *The Late News, or, Message from Brussels Unmasked and His Majesty Vindicated from the Base Calumny and Scandal therein fixed on him* (London, 1660), pp. 1, 3, 6; for other communications issued in Charles's name, see Carolyn A. Edie, 'News from Abroad: Advice to the People of England on the Eve of the Stuarts Restoration', *Bulletin of the John Rylands University of Manchester Library*, 67 (1984), pp. 382–407.
50. Andrew Browning (ed.), *English Historical Documents 1660–1714* (London, 1953), pp. 57–8 (Declaration of Breda, 1660).
51. Quoted by Scott, *Travels of the King*, p. 458.
52. Quoted by Christine Stevenson, *The City and the King: Architecture and Politics in Restoration London* (New Haven, CT, 2013), p. 82.
53. Guizot, *Richard Cromwell*, Vol. II, p. 395 (12 April 1660).
54. Carte (ed.), *Collection*, Vol. II, p. 344 (20 May 1660).
55. *CSP Venice, Volume XXXII: 1659–1661*, p. 146 (21 May 1660); as Giavarina recalled, on earlier occasions, Bordeaux 'used to make the most splendid displays . . . after the French humour which always runs to excess' (p. 146).
56. Pepys, *Diary*, Vol. I, p. 143 (16 May 1660).
57. Sir William Lower, *A Relation in Form of Journal, of the Voyage and Residence which the Most Excellent and Most Mighty Prince Charles II . . . hath made in Holland from the 25 of May to the 2 of June, 1660 &c.* (The Hague, 1660), pp. 72–3.
58. Quoted by Pincus, *Protestantism*, p. 195.
59. Pepys, *Diary*, Vol. I, p. 158 (25 May 1660).
60. Historical Manuscripts Commission, *The Manuscripts of S. H. Le Fleming Esq., of Rydal Hall* (London, 1890), p. 25 (4 June 1660).
61. Ruth Norrington (ed.), *My Dearest Minette. The Letters between Charles II and his sister, Henrietta, Duchesse d'Orleans* (London, 1996), p. 37 (26 May 1660).
62. Evelyn, *Diary*, p. 406 (29 May 1660).
63. *An Act for a Perpetual Anniversary Thanksgiving on the Nine and Twentieth Day of May*, 12 Car. 11, c.14.
64. *Journal of the House of Lords: Volume 11, 1660–1666* (London, 1767–1830), p. 303 (8 July 1661).
65. Quoted by Paulina Kewes, 'Acts of Remembrance, Acts of Oblivion: Rhetoric, Law, and National Memory in Early Restoration England' in Lorna Clymer (ed.), *Ritual, Routine, and Regime: Institutions of Repetition in Euro-American Cultures 1650–1832* (Toronto, 2006), p. 114.

66. Anonymous, *The English Devil: or, Cromwell and his Monstrous Witch Discovered at White-Hall* (London, 1660), title-page and sig. A2r.
67. Anonymous, *Englands Redemption: or, A Pathway to Peace: plainly demonstrating, that we shall never have any Settled state, until Charles II (whose right it is) enjoy the Crown* (London, 1660), pp. 3, 7, 4, 5.
68. Quoted by B. J. Cook, '"Stampt with your own Image": The Numismatic Dimension of Two Stuart Successions' in Paulina Kewes and Andrew McRae (eds), *Stuart Succession Literature. Moments and Transformations* (Oxford, 2019), pp. 311, 314.
69. See Laura L. Knoppers, 'Imagining the Death of the King: Milton, Charles I and Anamorphic Art' in Elizabeth Jane Bellamy, Patrick Cheney and Michael Schoenfeldt (eds), *Imagining Death in Spenser and Milton* (Basingstoke, 2003), pp. 151–70.
70. Edward Hyde, *The Life of Edward, Earl of Clarendon, Lord High Chancellor of England &c.*, (Oxford, 1759), p. 29 ('Continuation of the Life').
71. *CSP Venice, Volume XXXII: 1659–1661*, p. 235 (7 January 1661).
72. *CSP Venice, Volume XXXII: 1659–1661*, pp. 227, 193, 229, 241 (22 December, 8 September and 24 December 1660 and 26 January 1661).
73. Arthur Bryant (ed.), *The Letters, Speeches and Declarations of King Charles II* (London, 1935), pp. 104, 112 (November/December 1660 and 8 May 1661).
74. *CSP Venice, Volume XXXII: 1659–1661*, p. 270 (29 March 1661); Anonymous, *Hell's Higher Court of Justice, or the Trial of the Three Politick Ghosts, viz. Oliver Cromwell, King of Sweden and Cardinal Mazarine* (London, 1661).
75. *CSP Venice, Volume XXXII: 1659–1661*, pp. 155, 182 (11 June and 13 August 1660).
76. Quoted by David R. Evans, 'Charles II's "Grand Tour": Restoration Panegyric and the Rhetoric of Travel Literature', *Philological Quarterly*, 72:1 (1993), p. 60.
77. Evans, 'Charles II's "Grand Tour"', p. 64.
78. *CSP Venice, Volume XXXIII: 1661–1664*, pp. 27, 75 (11 August and 9 December 1661).

17 HELL, FRANCE, ROME OR AMSTERDAM, 1661–1667

1. Pepys, *Diary*, Vol. II, p. 88 (23 April 1661).
2. François Duchatel, *The Entry of the Prince de Ligne into London* (1660) and Gillis van Tilborch, *The Reception of the Prince de Ligne, 1660*; Anonymous, *Relation de l'Entrée Magnifique, de Monsieur le Prince de Ligne, Dans la Ville de Londres. En Qualité d'Ambassadeur Extraordinaire de Sa Majesté Catholique &c.* (London, 1660).

3. Historical Manuscripts Commission, *The Manuscripts of S. H. Le Fleming, Esq., of Rydal Hall*, p. 26 (25 September 1660).
4. Inge Broekman and Helmer Helmers, '"Het hart des Offraers" – The Dutch Gift as an Act of Self-Representation', *Dutch Crossing*, 31:2 (2007); such newfound dynastic loyalism discomfited anti-Orangist republicans. One pamphleteer imagined Charles and his brother York debating whether or not to accept the gift, given the Dutch Republic's reluctance to support the Stuarts during the 1650s. As 'York' acknowledged to 'Charles', since 'many bad and unjust things are done with gifts', receiving 'gifts from those with whom one has to negotiate, cannot but create injurious effects' (pp. 239, 240).
5. *CSP Venice, Volume XXXIII: 1661–1664*, p. 19 (29 July 1661).
6. Pepys, *Diary*, Vol. III, p. 297 (29 December 1662).
7. *CSP Venice, Volume XXXIII: 1661–1664*, p. 226 (19 January 1663).
8. See Jan Hennings, 'The Failed Gift: Ceremony and Gift-Giving in Anglo-Russian Relations (1662–1664)' in Tracey Sowerby and Jan Hennings (eds), *Practices of Diplomacy in the Early Modern World, c.1410–1800* (London, 2017), pp. 237–53.
9. Pepys, *Diary*, Vol. II, pp. 188, 189 (30 September 1661).
10. Jusserand, *French Ambassador*, p. 28 (13 October 1661).
11. R. C. Anderson (ed.), *The Journal of Edward Montagu, First Earl of Sandwich, Admiral and General at Sea 1659–1665* ([London], 1929), p. 125.
12. Arthur Bryant (ed.), *The Letters, Speeches and Declarations of King Charles II* (London, 1935), pp. 125–6 (*c.* April 1662).
13. T. H. Lister (ed.), *Life and Administration of Edward, First Earl of Clarendon; with Original Correspondence, and Authentic Papers never before Published*, 3 vols (London, 1838), Vol. III, p. 197 (25 May 1662).
14. Evelyn, *Diary*, pp. 438, 443 (30 May and 23 August 1662).
15. Pepys, *Diary*, Vol. III, p. 175 (23 August 1662).
16. John Tatham, *Aqua Triumphalis, Being a True Relation of the Honourable the City of London's Entertaining their Sacred Majesties Upon the River of Thames and Welcoming Them from Hampton Court to Whitehall* (London, 1662), pp. 10, 11, 6.
17. Lister (ed.), *Life and Administration . . . of Clarendon*, Vol. III, 202 (*c.* June 1662).
18. Jusserand, *French Ambassador*, p. 90 (August 1663).
19. Edward Combe (ed.), *The Sale of Dunkirk to the Late French King Lewis XIV. In the year 1662. Taken from the Letters, Memoirs, &c of Count d'Estrades &c.* (London, 1728), pp. 43, 109 (21 August; 3 October 1662).
20. Combe (ed.), *The Sale of Dunkirk to the Late French King Lewis XIV*, pp. 116, 137, 141 (27 October and 6 November 1662).

21. *CSP Venice, Volume XXXIII: 1661–1664*, pp. 204, 220 (1 November and 15 December 1662).
22. Quoted by Jonathan Scott '"Good Night Amsterdam": Sir George Downing and Anglo-Dutch State-Building', *English Historical Review*, 118:476 (2003), p. 349.
23. See Paul Seaward, 'A Restoration Publicist: James Howell and the Earl of Clarendon, 1661–1666', *Historical Research*, 61 (1988), p. 127.
24. [James Howell], *A Discourse of Dunkirk, with some Reflexes upon the Late Surrender Thereof, &c.* (London, 1664), p. 12.
25. Combe (ed.), *Sale of Dunkirk*, sig. A3r.
26. *CSP Domestic . . . Charles II, 1663–1664*, p. 72 (10 March 1663).
27. Quoted by R. A. Stradling, *Spain's Struggle for Europe, 1598–1668* (London, 1994), p. 286.
28. Quoted by Pincus, *Protestantism*, p. 200.
29. Jusserand, *French Ambassador*, pp. 125, 105, 106 (12 February and 23 July 1663).
30. Samuel de Sorbière, *A Voyage to England, containing many things relating to the State of Learning, Religion, and other Curiosities of that Kingdom &c.* (London, 1709), pp. 51, 54, 55.
31. S. Konovalov, 'England and Russia: Three Embassies, 1662–1665', *Oxford Slavonic Papers*, 10 (1962), p. 92 (14 June 1664).
32. Guy Miège, *A Relation of Three Embassies from his Sacred Majesty, Charles II to the Great Duke of Muscovy, the King of Sweden and the King of Denmark* (London, 1669), pp. 254, 303–4, 304. Six years later, before undertaking a second diplomatic mission to Denmark, Sweden and Hamburg in 1669, Carlisle added his personal endorsement to Miège's *Relation* of the turbulent Moscow embassy, which was published in English and French in London, Amsterdam and Rouen (see Jan Hennings and Edward Holberton, 'Andrew Marvell in Russia: Secretaries, Rhetoric, and Public Diplomacy', *Journal of Medieval and Early Modern Studies*, 50:3 (2020), p. 580).
33. *CSP Venice, Volume XXXIV: 1664–1666*, p. 19 (25 May 1664).
34. Sir Richard Fanshawe, *Original Letters of his Excellency Sir Richard Fanshaw, during his Embassies in Spain and Portugal &c.* (London, 1701), pp. 148–9, 252, 351 (13 June, 22 September and 21 October 1664).
35. Quoted by Jonathan Scott, *How the Old World Ended. The Anglo-Dutch-American Revolution, 1500–1800* (New Haven, CT, 2019), p. 180.
36. Quoted by Pincus, *Protestantism*, p. 237.
37. D'Estrades, *Letters and Negotiations*, Vol. I, p. 345 (19 December 1664).
38. *CSP Venice, Volume XXXIV: 1664–1666*, p. 61 (12 December 1664); D'Estrades, *Letters and Negotiations*, Vol. I, p. 346 (19 December 1664).

39. Anonymous, *Europae Modernae Speculum: Or, A View of the Empires, Kingdoms, Principalities, Seigneuries, and Commonwealths of Europe &c.* (London, 1665), pp. 67, 62.
40. John Crouch, *Belgica Caracteristica, Or, The Dutch Character: being News from Holland: A Poem* (London, 1665), p. 7.
41. Pepys, *Diary*, Vol. VI, p. 78 (12 April 1665).
42. Jusserand, *French Ambassador*, p. 141 (23 April 1665).
43. Quoted by Roger Downing and Gijs Rommelse, *A Fearful Gentleman. Sir George Downing in The Hague, 1658–1672* (Hilversum, 2011), p. 140; see the opening to John Dryden's 'An Essay of Dramatic Poesy' (*c.*1666) at <https://www.poetryfoundation.org/articles/69377/an-essay-of-dramatic-poesy>(accessed 5 June 2020).
44. *CSP Domestic . . . Charles II, 1664–1665*, p. 408 (4 June 1665).
45. John Crouch, *The Dutch Armado, A Meer Bravado* (London, 1665), single-sheet broadside.
46. Jusserand, *French Ambassador*, pp. 148, 149 (22 June 1665).
47. See *Orders Conceived and Published by the Lord Mayor and Aldermen of the City of London, Concerning the Infection of the Plague* (London, 1665).
48. Pepys, *Diary*, Vol. VI, pp. 201, 224 (22 August and 14 September 1665).
49. Anonymous, *The Shutting Up Infected Houses as it is Practised in England Soberly Debated. By Way of Address from the Poor Souls that are visited, to their Brethren that are Free* (London, 1665), pp. 8–9, 11.
50. W[illiam] Kemp, *A Brief Treatise of the Nature, Causes, Signs, Preservation from, and Cure of the Pestilence* (London, 1665), p. 5, sig. A2v, p. 5.
51. *CSP Venice, Volume XXXIV: 1664–1666*, pp. 168, 147 (31 July and 3 July 1665).
52. Jusserand, *French Ambassador*, pp. 172–3 (13 October 1665).
53. D'Estrades, *Letters and Negotiations*, Vol. II, p. 103 (18 September 1665).
54. *CSP Venice, Volume XXXIV: 1664–1666*, p. 262 (23 February 1666).
55. D'Estrades, *Letters and Negotiations*, Vol. II, p. 530 (8 July 1666). Fortunately for Charles, D'Estrades had simply assured de Witt, 'I would inform you of this proposal'.
56. Anonymous, *Sir Robert Holmes his Bonfire: or, The Dutch Doomsday* ([London], 1666), single-sheet.
57. Quoted by Hazel Forsyth, *Butcher, Baker, Candlestick Maker: Surviving the Great Fire of London* (London, 2016), p. 24.
58. George Percy Elliott (ed.), 'Autobiography and Anecdotes by William Taswell D. D.' in *Camden Miscellany. Volume II* (London, 1853), p. 11.
59. Anonymous, *A Poem on the Burning of London* (York, 1667), single-sheet.
60. *CSP Venice, Volume XXXV: 1666–1668*, pp. 76, 77 (28 September 1666).
61. Evelyn, *Diary*, p. 497 (6 September 1666).
62. Bryant (ed.), *Letters, Speeches*, p. 193 (13 September 1666).

63. Quoted by K. H. D. Haley, *An English Diplomat in the Low Countries. Sir William Temple and John De Witt, 1665–1672* (Oxford, 1986), p. 97; see also p. 98.
64. *CSP Venice, Volume XXXV: 1666–1668*, pp. 93, 92 (20 October 1666).
65. Quoted by Pincus, *Protestantism*, p. 292.
66. D'Estrades, *Letters and Negotiations*, Vol. II, p. 611 (17 September 1666).
67. D'Estrades, *Letters and Negotiations*, Vol. II, p. 469 (6 May 1666).
68. Quoted by Haley, *English Diplomat*, p. 99. In late-December, D'Estrades, who was approaching sixty, described joining De Witt and the teenage prince on the tennis court where he had 'played six games, which I won'. Although it was 'thirty years ago since I last played at tennis', D'Estrades reassured Lionne 'that I have still arms and legs to be employed in the king's service' (D'Estrades, *Letters and Negotiations*, Vol. II, p. 728; 30 December 1666).
69. [François-Paul de Lisola], *The Buckler of State and Justice against the Design manifestly discovered of the Universal Monarchy, under the vain pretext of the Queen of France, her pretensions* (London, 1667), sigs A6r, A7r, p. 294; see Mark Goldie and Charles-Édouard Levillain, 'François-Paul de Lisola and English Opposition to Louis XIV', *Historical Journal* 63:3 (2020), pp. 559–80.
70. Anonymous, *A Free Conference Touching the Present State of England both at Home and Abroad, in order to the Designs of France* (London, 1668), pp. 14, 24, 29, 32, 62.
71. Evelyn, *Diary*, p. 510 (11 June 1667).
72. Pepys, *Diary*, Vol. VIII, pp. 265, 345 (13 June and 19 July 1667).

18 TRIBUTARY TO THE FRENCH, 1667–1677

1. Quoted by J. D. Davies, '"Great Neptunes of the Main": Myths, Mangled Histories and "Maritime Monarchy" in the Stuart Navy, 1603–1714' in J. D. Davies, Alan James and Gijs Rommelse (eds), *Ideologies of Western Naval Power, c.1500–1815* (London, 2019), p. 106.
2. Pepys, *Diary*, Vol. VIII, p. 181 (26 April 1667).
3. Pepys, *Diary*, Vol. VIII, p. 269 (14 June 1667).
4. *CSP Venice, Volume XXXV: 1666–1668*, pp. 201, 202 (20 December 1667).
5. See Jean Bérenger, 'An Attempted *Rapprochement* between France and the Emperor: The Secret Treaty for the Partition of the Spanish Succession of 19 January 1668' in Ragnhild Hatton (ed.), *Louis XIV and Europe* (London, 1976), pp. 133–53.
6. Quoted by Herbert H. Rowen, 'John De Witt and the Triple Alliance', *Journal of Modern History*, 26:1 (1954), pp. 1–2.
7. Quoted by Paul Sonnino, *Louis XIV and the Origins of the Dutch War* (Cambridge, 1988), p. 23.

8. Temple, *Works*, Vol. III, p. 110 (24 January 1668).
9. Quoted by Sonnino, *Louis XIV*, p. 25.
10. Quoted by William James Roosen, 'The Ambassador's Craft: A Study of the Functioning of French Ambassadors under Louis XIV' (University of Southern California PhD thesis, 1967), p. 145 (March 1669).
11. *CSP Venice, Volume XXXVI: 1669–1670*, p. 76 (12 July 1669); *CSP Venice, Volume XXXV: 1666–1668*, p. 314 (13 November 1668).
12. Quoted by K. H. D. Haley, *An English Diplomat in the Low Countries. Sir William Temple and John De Witt, 1665–1672* (Oxford, 1986), pp. 237, 248.
13. Waldemar Westergaard (ed.), *The First Triple Alliance. The Letters of Christopher Lindenov, Danish Envoy to London, 1668–1672* (New Haven, CT, 1947), p. 57 (18 December 1668).
14. Quoted by Annabel Patterson, '*The Country Gentleman*: Howard, Marvell and Dryden in the Theater of Politics', *Studies in English Literature, 1500–1900*, 25:3 (1985), pp. 504, 503, 504, 501.
15. HMC *Buccleuch*, p. 22 (3 May 1669); cited by Sonya M. Wynne, 'The Mistresses of Charles II and Restoration Court Politics, 1660–1685' (University of Cambridge PhD thesis, 1997), p. 166.
16. Ruth Norrington (ed.), *My Dearest Minette. The Letters between Charles II and his sister Henrietta, Duchesse d'Orleans* (London, 1996), pp. 163, 167 (21 September and 14 December 1668).
17. Clarke (ed.), *Life of James the Second*, Vol. I, p. 442.
18. Jacques Truchet (ed.), *Oraisons Funèbres de Bossuet* (Paris, 1961), pp. 126–7.
19. M. Beryl Curran (ed.), *The Despatches of William Perwich, English Agent in Paris, 1669–1677* (London, 1903), p. 45 (23 October 1669); Cardinal Barberini, to whom Perwich attributed the sermon, was bishop of Reims.
20. In later years, the cardinal de Bouillon, Turenne's nephew, relayed the duke of York's description of the (formerly Huguenot) Marshal General as 'the greatest and most perfect man he had ever known and the best friend he had ever had' (quoted by Susan Rosa, '"Il était possible aussi que cette conversion fût sincère": Turenne's Conversion in Context', *French Historical Studies*, 18:3 (1994), p. 650n).
21. See Gabriel Glickman, 'Christian Reunion, the Anglo-French Alliance and the English Catholic Imagination, 1660–1672', *English Historical Review*, 128:531 (2013), pp. 263–91.
22. *CSP Venice, Volume XXXV: 1666–1668*, p. 269 (21 September 1668).
23. W. E. Knowles Middleton (ed.), *Lorenzo Magalotti at the Court of Charles II. His Relazione d'Inghilterra of 1668* (Waterloo, ON, 1980), p. 65.
24. *CSP Venice, Volume XXXVI: 1669–1670*, p. 58 (24 May 1669).
25. Westergaard (ed.), *First Triple Alliance*, p. 219 (12 April 1670). Meeting Henrietta Anne en route to England in Flanders, however, the experienced French

diplomat Pomponne was impressed by her knowledge and command of foreign affairs: as he recalled 'j'avoue que je fus estonnné de trouver tant d'estendue, d'ésprit et de capacité pour les affaires dans une jeune princesse qui paroissoit née seulement pour les grâces qui font l'ornement de son sexe' (Herbert H. Rowen (ed.), *Pomponne's "Rélation de Mon Ambassade en Hollande" 1669–1671* (Utrecht, 1955), p. 130).

26. Curran (ed.), *Despatches of William Perwich*, p. 12 (18 May 1669).
27. Curran (ed.), *Despatches of William Perwich*, p. 97 (21 and 26 June/1 and 6 July 1670).
28. Quoted by Thomas Worcester, 'The Classical Sermon' in Joris Van Eijnatten (ed.), *Preaching, Sermon and Cultural Change in the Long Eighteenth Century* (Leiden, 2009), p. 148; see *Oraison Funèbre de Henriette-Anne, d'Angleterre, duchesse d'Orléans, pronouncée at Saint-Denis, le 21 jour d'août 1670.*
29. Temple, *Works*, Vol. III, p. 487 (September 1670).
30. Westergaard (ed.), *First Triple Alliance*, p. 291 (30 August 1670).
31. *CSP Venice, Volume XXXVI: 1669–1670*, p. 288 (17 October 1670).
32. *His Majesties Most Gracious Speech to both Houses of Parliament, with the Lord Keepers on Tuesday, October 19, 1669* (Edinburgh, 1669), p. 7; see Clare Jackson, 'The Anglo-Scottish Union Negotiations of 1670' in Tony Claydon and Thomas N. Corns (eds), *Religion, Culture and National Community in the 1670s* (Cardiff, 2011), pp. 35–65.
33. Sir George Mackenzie, *Memoirs of the Affairs of Scotland from the Restoration of King Charles II. A.D.M.DC.LX* [Thomas Thomson (ed.)] (Edinburgh, 1821), p. 141.
34. Osmund Airy (ed.), *The Lauderdale Papers*, 3 vols (London, 1884–5), Vol. II, p. 154 (2 November 1669).
35. Mackenzie, *Memoirs of the Affairs of Scotland*, p. 181.
36. Westergaard (ed.), *First Triple Alliance*, p. 201 (4 March 1670).
37. Quoted by Barbara J. Shapiro, *John Wilkins, 1614–1672. An Intellectual Biography* (Berkeley, CA, 1969), p. 187.
38. H. M. Margoliouth (ed.), *The Poems and Letters of Andrew Marvell*, 2 vols (Oxford, 1971), Vol. II, p. 317.
39. *CSP Venice, Volume XXXVI: 1669–1670*, p. 175 (4 April 1670).
40. *CSP Venice, Volume XXXVII: 1671–1672*, pp. 38, 115 (17 April and 23 October 1671). Pressure from Catherine to recognize the ambassador, however, ultimately ensured de Melo's admittance.
41. *CSP Venice, Volume XXXVII: 1671–1672*, p. 167 (17 February 1672).
42. Quoted and translated by Wynne, 'The Mistresses of Charles II', p. 169 (8 October 1671).
43. Quoted by Esmond S. De Beer, 'King Charles II's Own Fashion: An Episode in Anglo-French Relations 1666–1670', *Journal of the Warburg and Courtauld Institutes*, 2:2 (1938), pp. 111–12.

44. Quoted by Michel Reinders, *Printed Pandemonium. Popular Print and Politics in the Netherlands 1650–72* (Leiden, 2013), p. 85.
45. Evelyn, *Diary*, p. 568 (12 March 1672).
46. Quoted by Harold A. Hansen, 'Opening Phase of the Third Dutch War described by the Danish Envoy in London, March–June 1672', *Journal of Modern History*, 21:2 (1949), p. 100 (29 March 1672).
47. Charles II, *His Majesties Declaration Against the States General of the United Provinces of the Low Countries* (London, 1672), p. 6.
48. [Henry Stubbe], *A Justification of the Present War Against the United Netherlands* (London, 1672), p. 40.
49. Quoted by Reinders, *Printed Pandemonium*, p. 91.
50. Quoted by David Onnekink, 'The Ideological Context of the Dutch War (1672)' in David Onnekink and Gijs Rommelse (eds), *Ideology and Foreign Policy in Early Modern Europe (1650–1750)* (Farnham, 2011), p. 140.
51. Herbert H. Rowen, *John De Witt, Grand Pensionary of Holland 1625–1672* (Princeton, NJ, 2015), p. 839.
52. Quoted by K. H. D. Haley, *William of Orange and the English Opposition, 1672–1674* (Oxford, 1953), p. 89.
53. Basil Duke Henning (ed.), *The Parliamentary Journal of Sir Edward Dering 1670–1673* (New Haven, CT, 1940), pp. 107, 128–9.
54. [Pierre Du Moulin], *England's Appeal from the Private Cabal at Whitehall to the Great Council of the Nation, the Lords and Commons in Parliament assembled. By a True Lover of his Country* ([London], 1673), pp. 33, 36.
55. Anonymous, *The Anatomy of Popery, or a Catalogue of Popish Errors in Doctrine, and Corruptions in Worship, Together with the Agreement between Paganism, Pharisaism, and Popery* (London, 1673), sig. A7r.
56. C. D. Chandaman, *The English Public Revenue, 1660–1688* (Oxford, 1975), p. 274.
57. Quoted by Haley, *William of Orange*, p. 114.
58. Joseph Hill, *The Interest of these United Provinces: Being a Defence of the Zeelanders Choice &c.* (Middelburg, 1673), sigs M3v, Lr.
59. *CSP Venice, Volume XXXVIII: 1673–1675*, p. 121 (20 September 1673).
60. Grey (ed.), *Debates*, Vol. II, p. 189.
61. Quoted by Steven C. A. Pincus, 'From Butterboxes to Wooden Shoes: The Shift in English Popular Sentiment from Anti-Dutch to Anti-French in the 1670s', *Historical Journal*, 38:2 (1995), p. 350.
62. Edward Maunde Thompson (ed.), *Correspondence of the Family of Hatton: Being Chiefly Letters Addressed to Christopher, First Viscount Hatton, A.D. 1601–1704*, 2 vols (London, 1878), Vol. I, p. 118 (28 October 1673).
63. Osmund Airy (ed.), *Essex Papers. Volume 1: 1672–1679* (London, 1890), pp. 154, 155 (25 December 1673).
64. *His Majesty's Most Gracious Speech, Together with the Lord Keeper's, To both Houses of Parliament, January 7, 1673/4* (London, 1675), p. 4.

65. Airy (ed.), *Essex Papers*, p. 161 (10 January 1674).
66. *CSP Domestic ... Charles II, 1673–1675*, p. 132 ('*Verbum Sapienti*, or a short memorandum' [January 1674]).
67. *CSP Venice, Volume XXXVIII: 1673–1675*, p. 206 (2 February 1674).
68. Margoliouth (ed.), *Poems and Letters of Andrew Marvell*, Vol. I, pp. 195, 198 ('Britannia and Rawleigh'). The poem was first printed in 1689, but probably written in early 1674 and variously attributed to John Ayloffe and Andrew Marvell.
69. *The Miscellaneous Works of John Dryden, Esq., Containing all his Original Poems, Tales and Translations*, 4 vols (London, 1767), Vol. II, p. 233 ('Prologue Spoken at the Opening of the New House, March 26, 1674').
70. John Dryden, *Marriage A-la-Mode. A Comedy. As it is Acted at the Theatre-Royal* (London, 1673), pp. 68, 7, 63. Citing popular French terms, the character 'Philotis' referred to 'foible, chagrin, grimace, embarrasse, double entendre, équivoque, ésclaircissement, suittè, béveue, façon, panchant, coup d'étourdy, and ridicule' (p. 36).
71. Lorraine Madway, 'Majesty and Mockery: Representations of Royal Power in the Reign of Charles II, 1660–1685' (Yale University PhD thesis, 1999), pp. 208–10.
72. Clement Edwards Pike (ed.), *Selections from the Correspondence of Arthur Capel, Earl of Essex, 1675–1677* (London, 1913), p. 11 (11 May 1675).
73. Temple, *Works*, Vol. I, pp. 305, 306, 341 ('Memoirs of what passed in Christendom').
74. Quoted by Ronald Hutton, *Charles the Second, King of England, Scotland, and Ireland* (Oxford, 1989), p. 346.
75. For suggestions that the baby prince was 'potentially purposefully infected with smallpox', see Troy Heffernan, 'Protecting England and its Church: Lady Anne and the Death of Charles Stuart', *The Seventeenth Century*, 31:1 (2016), p. 58.
76. Quoted by Catriona Murray, 'An Inflammatory Match? Public Anxiety and Political Assurance at the Wedding of William III and Mary II', *Historical Research*, 89:246 (2016), p. 733.

19 DEVILS WHO INTEND MY RUIN, 1678–1683

1. Quoted by R. A. Beddard, 'Wren's Mausoleum for Charles I and the Cult of the Royal Martyr', *Architectural History*, 27 (1984), pp. 37, 38; Waller is quoted at p. 47, n. 70. Since the death of Queen Anna of Denmark in 1619, all royal Stuarts, apart from Charles I, had been buried in Mary, Queen of Scots's sepulchre, including twelve since 1660 (Elizabeth of Bohemia; Henry, duke of Gloucester; Mary, Princess of Orange; and eight children of James, duke of York and his first wife, Anne Hyde (pp. 42, 46, n. 54).

2. Quoted by Mark Knights, *Politics and Opinion in Crisis, 1678–81* (Cambridge, 1994), p. 154.
3. Grey (ed.), *Debates*, Vol. VIII, p. 199 (20 December 1680).
4. John Dryden, 'To the King' in *The History of the League Written in French by Monsieur Maimbourg; Translated into English by His Majesty's Command by Mr. Dryden* (London, 1684), sig. Ar; 'Monsieur Maimbourg' was the Jesuit Louis Maimbourg.
5. Quoted by Paulina Kewes, '"The Idol of State Innovators and Republicans": Robert Persons's *A Conference About the Next Succession* (1594/5) in Stuart England' in Paulina Kewes and Andrew McRae (eds), *Stuart Succession Literature. Moments and Transformations* (Oxford, 2019), p. 173.
6. Andrew Browning (ed.), *Thomas Osborne, Earl of Danby and Duke of Leeds, 1632–1712*, 3 vols (Glasgow, 1944), Vol. II, p. 263 (4 April 1677). Convened on a plenary basis, the Nijmegen talks differed from the bilateral negotiations that had generated the Peace of Westphalia in 1648 when Protestant powers had convened in Osnabrück and their Catholic counterparts had met in Münster.
7. Dalrymple, *Memoirs*, Vol. II, p. 127 (1 November 1677).
8. *Ninth Report of the Royal Commission on Historical Manuscripts. Part I Report and Appendix* (London, 1883), p. 453 (29 December 1677).
9. Quoted and translated by Sonya M. Wynne, 'The Mistresses of Charles II and Restoration Court Politics, 1660–1685' (University of Cambridge PhD thesis, 1997), p. 183 (31 January 1678).
10. Osmund Airy (ed.), *The Lauderdale Papers*, 3 vols (London, 1884–5), Vol. III, p. 146 (11 May 1678).
11. Temple, *Works*, Vol. IV, pp. 389, 390 (1 August 1678); for unusual celestial activity in 1678, see David Ogg, *England in the Reign of Charles II* (Oxford, 1967), p. 559.
12. Temple, *Works*, Vol. I, p. 371 ('Memoirs of what passed in Christendom'); see J. A. H. Bots, *The Peace of Nijmegen, 1676–1678/9* (Amsterdam, 1980).
13. Arthur Bryant (ed.), *The Letters, Speeches and Declarations of King Charles II* (London, 1935), p. 299 (21 October 1678).
14. William Lloyd, *A Sermon at the Funeral of Sr Edmund-Bury Godfrey, one of His Majesty's Justices of the Peace who was Barbarously Murdered &c.* (London, 1678), p. 40.
15. Quoted by Melinda S. Zook, *Radical Whigs and Conspiratorial Politics in Late Stuart England* (University Park, PA, 1999), p. xi.
16. William Lawrence, *Marriage by the Moral Law of God Vindicated against all Ceremonial Laws of Popes and Bishops destructive to Filiation, Aliment and Succession and the Government of Families and Kingdoms* ([London], 1680), p. 280.
17. *CSP Domestic … Charles II, March 1st, 1678, to December 31st, 1678 &c.*, pp. 562, 563 (9 December 1678).

18. Samuel Clarke, *England's Remembrancer, A True and Full Narrative of those two never to be forgotten deliverances: One from the Spanish Invasion in 88. The other from the Hellish Powder Plot, November 5. 1605 ... to which is newly added a brief account of the Late Horrid Plot discovered, 1678* (London, 1679), p. 25.
19. Titus Oates, *A True Narrative of the Horrid Plot and Conspiracy of the Popish Party Against the Life of his Sacred Majesty, The Government and The Protestant Religion &c.* (London, 1679), p. 65.
20. Quoted by Ronald Hutton, *Charles the Second, King of England, Scotland, and Ireland* (Oxford, 1989), p. 362.
21. Dalrymple, *Memoirs*, Vol. II, p. 200.
22. *The History and Proceedings of the House of Commons from the Restoration to the Present Time*, 14 vols (London, 1742), Vol. I, pp. 316–17.
23. Quoted by Edward Charles Metzger, 'Ralph Montagu, first Duke of Montagu (bap. 1638–1709)', *Oxford Dictionary of National Biography* (Oxford, 2004).
24. Dalrymple, *Memoirs*, Vol. I, pp. 239, 241 (24 October 1678).
25. Quoted by Jonathan Scott, *Algernon Sidney and the Restoration Crisis 1677–1683* (Cambridge, 1991), p. 104.
26. Anonymous, *A Letter from Amsterdam to a Friend in England* (London, 1678), p. 2; for the information about Sidney's payments, see Scott, *Algernon Sidney and the Restoration Crisis*, p. 109.
27. Grey (ed.), *Debates*, Vol. VI, p. 350 (19 December 1678).
28. Alan Macfarlane (ed.), *The Diary of Ralph Josselin, 1616–1683* (London, 1976), p. 619. Ten days earlier, Josselin had alarmed himself by imagining 'the King of France was likely the little horn and that England was one kingdom he should, or that horn pull up by the root' (p. 619).
29. Temple, *Works*, Vol. I, p. 396 ('Memoirs of what passed in Christendom').
30. *Charles II, His Majesty's Most Gracious Speech, Together with the Lord Chancellor's, To Both Houses of Parliament, On Thursday the 6th of March, 1678/9* (London, 1679), pp. 4, 7, 17.
31. Quoted by Leanna Hope McLaughlin, '"Poetick Rage" to Rage of Party: English Political Verse 1678–1685' (University of California, Riverside, PhD thesis, 2018), pp. 80, 81.
32. Quoted by Odai Johnson, 'Pope-Burning Pageants: Performing the Exclusion Crisis', *Theatre Survey*, 37:1 (1996), p. 39.
33. Grey (ed.), *Debates*, Vol. VII, pp. 238, 258, 259, 257 (11 May 1679).
34. Dalrymple, *Memoirs*, Vol. II, pp. 219, 220, 221 (29 May and 8 June 1679).
35. Quoted by Scott, *Algernon Sidney and the Restoration Crisis*, p. 62, n. 47.
36. R. W. Blencowe (ed.), *Diary of the Times of Charles the Second, by the Honourable Henry Sidney &c.*, 2 vols (London, 1843), Vol. I, pp. 141, 99, 176 (11 and 2 September and 29 October 1679).

37. Tim Harris, *London Crowds in the Reign of Charles II. Propaganda and Politics from the Restoration until the Exclusion Crisis* (Cambridge, 1987), p. 104.
38. [Charles Blount], *An Appeal from the Country to the City, For the Preservation of His Majesty's Person, Liberty, Property and the Protestant Religion* (London, 1679), pp. 2, 25.
39. See Nancy Klein Maguire, 'The Duchess of Portsmouth: English Royal Consort and French Politician, 1670–85' in R. Malcolm Smuts (ed.), *The Stuart Court and Europe. Essays in Politics and Political Culture* (Cambridge, 1996), pp. 254–6.
40. Quoted by Ogg, *England in the Reign of Charles II*, p. 594 (11/21 March 1680).
41. Blencowe (ed.), *Diary of the Times of Charles the Second*, Vol. II, pp. 335, 336, 342 (24 May 1680).
42. *CSP Domestic ... Charles II, January 1st, 1679, to August 31st, 1680*, p. 509 (11 June 1680).
43. Blencowe (ed.), *Diary of the Times of Charles the Second*, Vol. II, p. 86 (24 July 1680).
44. Knights, *Politics and Opinion in Crisis*, p. 159 (8/18 September 1680).
45. Charles II, *His Majesty's Gracious Speech to Both Houses of Parliament, on Thursday the 21st October, 1680* (London, 1680), pp. 6, 7.
46. *An Exact Collection of the Most Considerable Debates in the Honourable House of Commons, at the Parliament held at Westminster, the One and Twentieth of October 1680 &c.* (London, 1681), p. 11.
47. Grey (ed.), *Debates*, Vol. VII, pp. 402, 407, 419, 420 (29 October 1680).
48. Quoted by Dalrymple, *Memoirs*, Vol. II, pp. 290–91 (21 November 1680).
49. Bryant (ed.), *Letters, Speeches*, p. 311 (6 January 1679).
50. See Mark Goldie, 'Contextualizing Dryden's Absalom: William Lawrence, the Laws of Marriage and the Case for King Monmouth' in Donna B. Hamilton and Richard Strier (eds), *Religion, Literature, and Politics in Post-Reformation England, 1540–1688* (Cambridge, 1996), pp. 208–30.
51. Anonymous, *A True Narrative of the Duke of Monmouth's Late Journey into the West in a Letter from an Eyewitness thereof, to his Correspondent in London* (London, 1680), p. 2.
52. Quoted by Knights, *Politics and Opinion in Crisis*, p. 159 (1 November 1680).
53. *An Intimation of the Deputies of the States General, in a late Discourse with Mr. Sidney, Extraordinary Envoy from His Majesty of Great Britain* (London, 1680), p. 3.
54. Pedro Ronquillo, *The Last Memorial of the Spanish Ambassador Faithfully Translated into English* (London, 1681), p. 2.

55. Quoted by Charles Findlay Scott, 'Don Pedro Ronquillo and Spanish–British Relations (1674–91)' (University of St Andrews PhD thesis, 1955), p. 176 (4 November 1680).
56. Clarke (ed.), *Life of James the Second*, Vol. I, pp. 635, 659–60.
57. Dalrymple, *Memoirs*, Vol. II, p. 307 (10 December 1680).
58. Quoted by J. P. Kenyon, *Robert Spencer, Earl of Sunderland, 1641–1702* (London, 1958), p. 63 (5 November 1680).
59. *His Majesty's Most Gracious Speech to both Houses of Parliament, At the Opening of the Parliament at Oxford, Monday the 21st Day of March 1680/1* (Oxford, 1681), pp. 3–4.
60. W. E Buckley (ed.), *Memoirs of Thomas, Earl of Ailesbury, Written by Himself*, 2 vols (London, 1890), Vol. I, p. 57.
61. Bryant (ed.), *Letters, Speeches*, p. 321 (8 April 1681).
62. [John Dryden], *His Majesty's Declaration Defended: In a Letter to a Friend &c.* (London, 1681), pp. 19, 13.
63. Quoted by Grant Tapsell, *The Personal Rule of Charles II, 1681–1685* (Woodbridge, 2007), p. 151.
64. Charles II, *The Kings Majesties Gracious Letter to his Parliament of Scotland &c.* (London, 1681), p. 7.
65. Quoted by Tapsell, *Personal Rule of Charles II*, p. 165.
66. Dalrymple, *Memoirs*, Vol. II, p. 10 (28 June 1681).
67. Edward Maunde Thompson (ed.), *Correspondence of the Family of Hatton: Being Chiefly Letters Addressed to Christopher, First Viscount Hatton, A.D. 1601–1704*, 2 vols (London, 1878), Vol. II, p. 4 (2 August 1681).
68. Anonymous, *Oliver Cromwell's Ghost, Dropt from the Clouds* (London, 1681), p. 1.
69. Anonymous, *Plain Dealing, or A Dialogue between Humphrey and Roger about Choosing the Next Parliament* (London, 1681), p. 1.
70. [Jean-Paul de Cerdan], *Europe a Slave, Unless England Break her Chains: Discovering the Grand Designs of the French-Popish Party in England for Several Years Past* (London, 1681), pp. 33–4, 46, 54.
71. Dalrymple, *Memoirs*, Vol. II, pp. 20–21, 15 (17 November and 22 December 1681).
72. Charles II, *His Majesties Declaration to all his Loving Subjects, Concerning the Treasonable Conspiracy against his Sacred Person and Government, Lately Discovered* (London, 1683), pp. 3, 6.
73. William, Lord Russell, *The Speech of the Late Lord Russel to the Sheriffs together with the Paper Delivered by Him to Them at the Place of Execution, on July 21, 1683* (London, 1683), p. 3.
74. *The Judgment and Decree of the University of Oxford, passed in their Convocation, July 21, 1683, against certain pernicious Books and Damnable*

Doctrines destructive to the Sacred Persons of Princes, their State and Government ([Oxford], 1683), p. 7.

75. F. Elrington Ball (ed.), HMC *Ormonde ... Volume VII* (London, 1912), p. 22 (8 May 1683).
76. Quoted by Hutton, *Charles the Second*, p. 426.
77. Quoted by Anders Ingram, 'The Ottoman Siege of Vienna, English Ballads, and the Exclusion Crisis', *Historical Journal*, 57:1 (2014), pp. 72, 54, 76.
78. Quoted by Tristan Stein, 'Tangier in the Restoration Empire', *Historical Journal*, 54:4 (2011), p. 997; Pepys, *Diary*, Vol. IV, p. 319 (28 September 1663).
79. W. O. Hewlett (ed.), Historical Manuscripts Commission, *The Manuscripts of the Earl of Dartmouth, Volume 1: 1660–1843* (London, 1887), p. 96 (8 October 1683).
80. Quoted by Margarette Lincoln, 'Samuel Pepys and Tangier, 1662–1684', *Huntington Library Quarterly*, 77:4 (2014), pp. 433–4.
81. Dalrymple, *Memoirs*, Vol. II, p. 55 (7 December 1683).
82. Algernon Sidney, *The Very Copy of a Paper Delivered to the Sheriffs Upon the Scaffold on Tower-Hill on Friday, December 7, 1683* (London, 1683), pp. 1–2.

20 A NEW MAGNA CARTA, 1683–1687

1. Richard Bulstrode, *Memoirs and Reflections upon the Reign and Government of King Charles the First and King Charles the Second* (London, 1721), pp. 424–5, 356.
2. Dalrymple, *Memoirs*, Vol. II, pp. 56, 57 (4 January and 6 June 1684).
3. Jean-Antoine de Mesme, Count d'Avaux, *The Negotiations of Count d'Avaux, Ambassador from his Most Christian Majesty to the States General of the United Provinces &c.*, 4 vols (London, 1754–5), Vol. III, p. 132.
4. Dalrymple, *Memoirs*, Vol. II, pp. 95, 97, 98 (18 February 1685).
5. James Wright, *A Compendious View of the Late Tumults and Troubles in this Kingdom By Way of Annals for Seven Years* (London, 1685), p. 208.
6. James II, *An Account of what His Majesty said at his First Coming to Council* (London, 1685), single-sheet folio.
7. Clarke (ed.), *Life of James the Second*, Vol. II, pp. 4–6 (February 1685).
8. Quoted by Cristina Bravo Lozano, *Spain and the Irish Mission, 1609–1707* (New York, 2019), p. 164, n.3 (26 February 1685).
9. Quoted by Steve Pincus, *1688: The First Modern Revolution* (New Haven, CT, 2009), p. 104.
10. Dalrymple, *Memoirs*, Vol. II, p. 103 (19 February 1685).
11. Francis Turner, *A Sermon Preached Before Their Majesties King James II and Queen Mary at their Coronation in Westminster Abbey, April 23, 1685.*

By Francis, Lord Bishop of Ely and Lord Almoner to His Majesty (London, 1685), pp. 14–15.

12. R. Lowman, *An Exact Narrative and Description of the Wonderful and Stupendous Fireworks in honour of Their Majesties' Coronations, and for the High Entertainment of Their Majesties, the Nobility, and City of London . . . on April the 24, 1685* (London, 1685), p. 2; for the coronation feast, see Carolyn A. Edie, 'The Public Face of Royal Ritual: Sermons, Medals and Civic Ceremony in Later Stuart Coronations', *Huntington Library Quarterly*, 53:4 (1990), p. 318.
13. *The Records of the Parliaments of Scotland to 1707*, Keith M. Brown et al. (eds) (St Andrews, 2007–2020), 1685/4/16. Date accessed: 8 July 2020.
14. James II, *His Majesty's most Gracious Speech to Both Houses of Parliament, On Friday the 22th of May, 1685* (London, 1685), pp. 3–4.
15. *His Majesty's most Gracious Speech to Both Houses of Parliament, On Saturday the 30th of May, 1685* (London, 1685), p. 4.
16. Quoted by Richard L. Greaves, *Secrets of the Kingdom. British Radicals from the Popish Plot to the Revolution of 1688–1689* (Stanford, CA, 1992), p. 278.
17. Walter Macleod (ed.), *Journal of the Hon. John Erskine of Carnock 1683–1687* (Edinburgh, 1893), pp. 113, 114.
18. Archibald Campbell, Earl of Argyll, *The Declaration and Apology of the Protestant People that is, of the Noblemen, Barons, Gentlemen, Burgesses, and Commons of all sorts, now in Arms within the Kingdom of Scotland* ([?Edinburgh], 1685), p. 5.
19. James Scott, Duke of Monmouth, *The Declaration of James Duke of Monmouth, & the Noblemen, Gentlemen & Others, Now in Arms, for Defence & Vindication of the Protestant Religion, & the Laws, Rights, & Privileges of England, from the Invasion made upon them, & for Delivering the Kingdom from the Usurpation & Tyranny of James, Duke of York* (London, 1685), pp. 4, 7.
20. Quoted by Helmer Helmers, '1685 and the Battle for Dutch Public Opinion: Succession Literature from a Transnational Perspective' in Paulina Kewes and Andrew McRae (eds), *Stuart Succession Literature. Moments and Transformations* (Oxford, 2019), p. 105.
21. Quoted by Greaves, *Secrets of the Kingdom*, p. 286.
22. Augustine Frezer, *The Wickedness and Punishment of Rebellion. A Sermon Preached the 26 July 1685 (being the Day of Thanksgiving appointed by His Majesty for the Defeat of the Rebels) before the Right Worshipful the Fellowship of Merchants Adventurers of England residing at Dordrecht* (Rotterdam, 1686), sig. *2r, pp. 18, 31.
23. Anonymous, *Relacion de las Fiestas, que celebro en esta muy noble Villa de Bilbao . . . en la Gloriosa Ocasion de aueisse Coronado en Inglaterra por*

Rey de la Gran Bretaña el muy Catholico, Jacobo Estuardo segundo de este nombre, y del memorable Triumfo, que alcanzo de los Rebeldes (Bilbao, 1685).

24. James II, *His Majesty's Most Gracious Speech to Both Houses of Parliament on Monday the 9th of November, 1685* (London, 1685), p. 3; Grey (ed.), *Debates*, Vol. VIII, p. 356 (12 November 1685).
25. Brent S. Sirota, *The Christian Monitors. The Church of England and the Age of Benevolence, 1680–1730* (New Haven, CT, 2014), p. 35.
26. Quoted by D. E. C. Yale, 'Sir Thomas Jones (1614–1692)', *Oxford Dictionary of National Biography* (Oxford, 2004).
27. Dalrymple, *Memoirs*, Vol. II, p. 172 (11 March 1686).
28. James II, *His Majesty's Most Gracious Letter to the Parliament of Scotland, together with the Parliament's Dutiful Answer to His Majesty's Letter* ([London], 1686), pp. 2, 6.
29. Sir John Lauder of Fountainhall, *Historical Notices of Scottish Affairs*, David Laing (ed.), 2 vols (Edinburgh, 1848), Vol. II, p. 719.
30. Morrice, *Entring Book*, Vol. III, p. 221 (14 August 1686).
31. *To the Most Reverend Fathers in God, William Lord Archbishop of Canterbury, Primate of all England and Metropolitan, and John Lord Archbishop of York, Primate of England and Metropolitan* (London, 1686), p. 5.
32. Sirota, *The Christian Monitors*, p. 42.
33. Morrice, *Entring Book*, Vol. III, p. 180 (17 July 1686).
34. Cristina Bravo Lozano, 'Popular Protests, the Public Sphere and Court Catholicism. The Insults to the Chapel of the Spanish Embassy in London, 1685–1688', *Culture & History*, 6:1 (2017).
35. Anna Keay, *The Magnificent Monarch. Charles II and the Ceremonies of Power* (London, 2008), p. 177.
36. Quoted by Tim Harris, *Revolution. The Great Crisis of the British Monarchy, 1685–1720* (London, 2006), p. 99.
37. Clarke (ed.), *Life of James the Second*, Vol. II, p. 621.
38. Anonymous, 'Reasons for Abrogating the Penal Statutes' in Robert Wodrow, *The History of the Sufferings of the Church of Scotland from the Restoration to the Revolution*, Robert Burns (ed.), 4 vols (Glasgow, 1885), Vol. IV, p. 373.
39. Evelyn, *Diary*, p. 833 (3 November 1685).
40. Jean Claude, *An Account of the Persecution and Oppressions of the Protestants in France* (London, 1686), pp. 1, 29, 47; Evelyn, *Diary*, p. 844 (25 April 1686).
41. Quoted by Carolyn Lougee Chappell, '"The Pains I Took to Save My/His Family": Escape Accounts by a Huguenot Mother and Daughter after the Revocation of the Edict of Nantes', *French Historical Studies*, 22:1 (1999), pp. 56, 60.
42. Quoted by Pincus, *1688*, p. 333 (1 May 1686).

43. Quoted by A. A. Hanham, 'Sir William Trumbull' in Eveline Cruickshanks, Stuart Handley and D. W. Hayton (eds), *The History of Parliament: The House of Commons, 1690–1715. Volume V: Members O–Z* (Cambridge, 2002), p. 692; the reference to flattering courtiers is quoted by Stéphane Jettot, 'The Court of Louis XIV and the English Public Sphere: Worlds Set Apart?' in Tony Claydon and Charles-Édouard Levillain (eds), *Louis XIV Outside In. Images of the Sun King beyond France, 1661–1715* (Farnham, 2015), p. 80.
44. Anonymous, *The Designs of France Against England and Holland* ([n.p.], 1686), pp. 2, 7.
45. *A Form of Prayer and Thanksgiving to Almighty God for the Prosperity of the Christian Arms Against the Turks and especially for Taking the City of Buda to be used Publicly on Sunday the Twelfth of September in His Majesty's Free Chapel of St. Georges Windsor &c.* ([London, 1686]), sig. A4r.
46. John Childs, *The Army, James II, and the Glorious Revolution* (Manchester, 1980), p. 96.
47. Quoted by Wout Troost, *William III, the Stadholder-King. A Political Biography* (Aldershot, 2005), p. 182 (13 September 1686).
48. Lozano, 'Popular Protests', p. 13, n. 48.
49. Dalrymple, *Memoirs*, Vol. II, p. 176 (16 July 1685).
50. Morrice, *Entring Book*, Vol. IV, p. 5 (9 April 1687).
51. Eoin Lorcan Devlin, 'England's Encounters with Papal Rome in the late Counter-Reformation, *c.*1685– *c.*1697' (University of Cambridge PhD thesis, 2010), pp. 145, 149.
52. John Michael Wright, *An Account of his Excellence Roger, Earl of Castlemaine's Embassy from his Sacred Majesty James the IId, King of England, Scotland, France and Ireland &c. to His Holiness Innocent XI* (London, 1688), pp. 50, 55, 73, 74.
53. Quoted by Thomas M. McCoog, S. J., 'A Letter from a Jesuit of Liège (1687)?', *Recusant History*, 30:1 (2010), pp. 88, 89, 90.
54. James VII & II, *By the King. A Proclamation. James the Seventh, By the Grace of God, King of Scotland, England, France and Ireland &c.* (Edinburgh, 1687), single-sheet.
55. [Gilbert Burnet], *Some Reflections on His Majesty's Proclamation of the 12th of February 1686/7 for a Toleration in Scotland, together with the said Proclamation* (n.p., 1687), pp. 1–2.
56. N. Japikse (ed.), *Correspondentie van Willem III en van Hans Willem Bentinck ... Deel II* (The Hague, 1928), pp. 13, 17, 20–21.
57. J. P. Kenyon (ed.), *The Stuart Constitution 1603–1608. Documents and Commentary* (Cambridge, 1986), pp. 389, 390 (Declaration of Indulgence, 1687).

58. [Robert Ferguson], *A Representation of the Threatening Dangers, Impending over Protestants in Great Britain, With an Account of the Arbitrary and Popish Ends, Unto which the Declaration for Liberty of Conscience in England, and the Proclamation for a Toleration in Scotland, are Designed* ([Edinburgh, 1687]), p. 21.
59. Dalrymple, *Memoirs*, Vol. II, pp. 299–300 (13 March 1687).
60. Quoted by Scott Sowerby, 'Of Different Complexions: Religious Diversity and National Identity in James II's Toleration Campaign', *English Historical Review*, 124:506 (2009), p. 32.
61. [William King], *The State of the Protestants of Ireland under the Late King James's Government, in which their Carriage towards him is Justified, and the Absolute Necessity of their Endeavouring to be Freed from his Government, of Submitting to their Present Majesties is Justified* (London, 1691), p. 18.
62. Quoted by Harris, *Revolution*, p. 109.
63. Samuel Weller Singer (ed.), *The Correspondence of Henry Hyde, Earl of Clarendon and his brother, Laurence Hyde, Earl of Rochester: With the Diary of Lord Clarendon from 1687 to 1690*, 2 vols (London, 1828), Vol. I, pp. 270, 291, 474, 464, 448 and 451.
64. S. J. Connolly, *Religion, Law and Power. The Making of Protestant Ireland 1660–1760* (Oxford, 1992), p. 33.
65. Singer (ed.), *Correspondence of Henry Hyde, Earl of Clarendon*, Vol. I, pp. 357, 534.
66. F. H. Blackburne Daniell (ed.), Historical Manuscripts Commission, *Calendar of the Stuart Papers belonging to His Majesty the King, Preserved at Windsor Castle. Volume VI* (London, 1916), pp. 8, 9.
67. Singer (ed.), *Correspondence of Henry Hyde, Earl of Clarendon*, Vol. II, p. 88.
68. Quoted by James Muilenburg, 'The Embassy of Everaard Van Weede, Lord of Dykvelt, to England in 1687', *University Studies* (University of Nebraska), 20:3–4 (1920), p. 101, n. 62.
69. Dalrymple, *Memoirs*, Vol. II, pp. 184–5, 185 (17 June and 16 June 1687).
70. George Savile, Marquis of Halifax, *A Letter to a Dissenter, Upon Occasion of His Majesty's Late Gracious Declaration of Indulgence* (London, 1687), pp. 3, 9.
71. Dalrymple, *Memoirs*, Vol. II, p. 197 (31 May 1687).
72. Gaspar Fagel, *A Letter Writ By Mijn Heer Fagel, Pensioner of Holland, to Mr. James Stewart, Advocate, Giving an Account of the Prince and Princess of Orange's Thoughts Concerning the Repeal of the Test and Penal Laws* (Amsterdam, 1688), p. 1.
73. Dalrymple, *Memoirs*, Vol. II, p. 213.
74. Emma Bergin, 'Defending the True Faith: Religious Themes in Dutch Pamphlets on England, 1688–1689' in David Onnekink (ed.), *War and Religion after Westphalia, 1648–1713* (Farnham, 2009), pp. 232–3.

21 THE DUTCH DESIGN ANATOMIZED, 1687–1690

1. Thomas Pennant, *The History of the Parishes of Whiteford, and Holywell* ([London], 1796), p. 230.
2. John Weldon, 'To the High and Mighty Prince James II' in *The Second Nativity of Jesus ... written in French by a Learned Capuchin. Translated into English, Augmented and Divided into Six Parts by John Weldon of Raffin* (Antwerp, 1686), sig. A4v. With 'the lily' denoting France, 'the lion' the Dutch Republic and 'the harp' Ireland, forms of similar prophecy reappeared in various forms throughout the seventeenth century.
3. *A Form of Prayer with Thanksgiving for the Safe Delivery of the Queen; and Happy Birth of the young Prince. To be used on Sunday next, being the Seventeenth Day of this instant, June, in all Churches and Chapels within the Cities of London and &c.* (Edinburgh, 1688), sigs A4r, A3r.
4. James Macpherson (ed.), *Original Papers; Containing the Secret History of Great Britain, from the Restoration, to the Accession of the House of Hannover*, 2 vols (London, 1775), Vol. I, p. 264 (16/26 June 1688).
5. David Worthington, 'The 1688 Correspondence of Nicholas Taaffe, second earl of Carlingford (?–1690), from the Imperial Court in Vienna', *Archivium Hibernicum*, 58 (2004), p. 192.
6. Catriona Murray, *Imaging Stuart Family Politics. Dynastic Crisis and Continuity* (Abingdon, 2017), p. 32, n. 114.
7. John-Paul Ghobrial, *The Whispers of Cities. Information Flows in Istanbul, London, and Paris in the Age of William Trumbull* (Oxford, 2013), p. 80; Michael Talbot, *British-Ottoman Relations 1661–1807. Commerce and Diplomatic Practice in Eighteenth-Century Istanbul* (Martlesham, 2017), p. 166.
8. Anonymous, *Englands Triumphs for the Prince of Wales: or, A Short Description of the Fireworks, Machines, &c. which were represented on the Thames before Whitehall, to the King and Queen, Nobility and Gentry, Foreign Ministers, and many Thousands of Spectators, on Tuesday-night, July 17 1688* (London, 1688).
9. Quoted by Paul Hoftijzer, '"Such Onely as Are Very Honest, Loyall and Active": English Spies in the Low Countries, 1660–1688' in Paul Hoftijzer and C. C. Barfoot (eds), *Fabrics and Fabrications. The Myth and Making of William and Mary* (Amsterdam, 1990), p. 92.
10. Dalrymple, *Memoirs*, Vol. II, pp. 300, 303, 305–6 (14 March; 18 June 1688 and 'Questions', 21 July 1688).
11. Macpherson (ed.), *Original Papers*, Vol. I, p. 270 (30 October 1688).
12. Anonymous, *Revolution Politicks: Being a Compleat Collection of all the Reports, Lyes, and Stories, which were the Forerunners of the Great*

Revolution in 1688; Commencing from the Death of King Charles II and from thence regularly continued to the Settlement of the Prince and Princess of Orange upon the Throne (London, [1733]), pp. 47–8.

13. Aphra Behn, *A Congratulatory Poem to His Most Sacred Majesty on the Happy Birth of the Prince of Wales by Mrs A. Behn* (London, 1688), p. 4.
14. Andrew Browning (ed.), *English Historical Documents 1660–1714* (London, 1953), pp. 120, 121 (Letter of Invitation to William of Orange, 1688).
15. Quoted by Henry Horwitz, *Revolution Politicks. The Career of Daniel Finch, Second Earl of Nottingham, 1647–1730* (Cambridge, 1968), p. 52.
16. David Onnekink, *The Anglo-Dutch Favourite: The Career of Hans Willem Bentinck, 1st Earl of Portland (1649–1709)* (Aldershot, 2007), p. 61 (20 July 1688).
17. Quoted by K. H. D. Haley, 'The Dutch, the Invasion of England, and the Alliance of 1689' in Lois G. Schwoerer (ed.), *The Revolution of 1688–1689. Changing Perspectives* (Cambridge, 1992), pp. 29–30.
18. Quoted by Charles-Édouard Levillain, 'French Diplomacy and the Run-up to the Glorious Revolution (1688): A Critical Reading of Jean-Antoine d'Avaux's Correspondence as Ambassador to the States General', *Journal of Modern History*, 88:1 (2016), p. 140.
19. Quoted by Emma Theresa Bergin, 'The Revolution of 1688 in Dutch Pamphlet Literature: A Study in the Dutch Public Sphere in the late Seventeenth Century' (University of Hull PhD thesis, 2006), pp. 163–7.
20. Worthington, 'The 1688 Correspondence of Nicholas Taaffe', pp. 200–201, 205, 206 (9/19 September and 7/17 October 1688).
21. Quoted by Steve Pincus, 'The European Catholic Context of the Revolution of 1688–89: Gallicanism, Innocent XI, and Catholic Opposition' in Allan I. Macinnes and Arthur H. Williamson (eds), *Shaping the Stuart World 1603–1714. The Atlantic Connection* (Brill, 2006), p. 79.
22. James II, *By The King. A Proclamation. We have Received Undoubted Advice, That a Great and Sudden Invasion from Holland, with an Armed Force of Foreigners, &c.* (London, 1688).
23. Quoted by Jonathan I. Israel, 'Propaganda in the Making of the Glorious Revolution' in *Conflicts of Empires. Spain, the Low Countries and the Struggle for World Supremacy, 1585–1713* (London, 1997), p. 362.
24. David Onnekink, 'The Revolution in Dutch Foreign Policy (1688)' in Femke Deen, David Onnekink and Michel Reinders (eds), *Pamphlets and Politics in the Dutch Republic* (Leiden, 2011), p. 146.
25. *The Declaration of His Highness, William Henry, by the Grace of God, Prince of Orange &c, of the Reasons inducing him, to appear in arms in the Kingdom of England, for preserving of the Protestant Religion, and for restoring the Laws and Liberties of England, Scotland and Ireland* (The Hague, 1688), pp. 4, 3.

26. *The Declaration of His Highness William by the Grace of God, Prince of Orange &c, of the Reasons inducing him to appear in arms for preserving of the Protestant Religion, and for restoring the Laws and Liberties of the Ancient Kingdom of Scotland* (The Hague, 1688), sig. A2r.
27. *Extract of the States General, their Resolution, Thursday, 28th October 1688* ([London, 1688]), single-sheet.
28. Macpherson (ed.), *Original Papers*, Vol. I, pp. 285, 268 (26 November and 30 October 1688).
29. H. Manners Sutton (ed.), *The Lexington Papers; or, Some Account of the Courts of London and Vienna; at the Conclusion of the Seventeenth Century* (London, 1851), pp. 328, 330, 338.
30. Onnekink, *Anglo-Dutch Favourite*, pp. 50–51.
31. John Whittel, *An Exact Diary of the Late Expedition of His Illustrious Highness, the Prince of Orange, now King of Great Britain, from his Palace at The Hague, to his landing at Torbay, and from thence to his Arrival at Whitehall &c.* (London, 1689), p. 14.
32. [Edmund Bohun], *The History of the Desertion, or, An Account of all the Publick Affairs in England, from the Beginning of September 1688, to the Twelfth of February following &c.* (London 1689), p. 35.
33. Whittel, *Exact Diary*, p. 31.
34. Quoted by Steve Pincus, *1688: The First Modern Revolution* (New Haven, CT, 2009), p. 230.
35. R. Bentley (ed.), *The Life, Journals, and Correspondence of Samuel Pepys, Esq. F.R.S., Secretary to the Admiralty in the Reigns of Charles II and James II*, 2 vols (London, 1841), Vol. II, p. 336 (11 November 1688).
36. Anonymous, *The Dutch Design Anatomized, or, A Discovery of the Wickedness and Unjustice of the Intended Invasion and a Clear Proof that it is the Interest of all the King's Subjects to Defend His Majesty and Their Country Against it* (London, 1688), pp. 11–12, 15, 38.
37. James II, *By the King. A Declaration. James R. As We Cannot Consider this Invasion of our Kingdoms by the Prince of Orange, without Horror &c.* (London, 1688), single-sheet (6 October 1688).
38. *Letters Written during the Years 1686, 1687, 1688 and Addressed to John Ellis, Esq., Secretary to the Commissioners of His Majesty's Revenue in Ireland &c.*, 2 vols (London, 1831), Vol. II, p. 296 (15 November 1688).
39. Anonymous, *A True and Exact Relation of the Prince of Orange his Publick Entrance into Exeter* ([London], 1688); single-sheet.
40. Quoted by Lothar Höbelt, 'Imperial Diplomacy and the "Glorious Revolution"', *Parliaments, Estates and Representation*, 11:1 (1991), p. 61.
41. *Prince George's Letter to the King* ([London, 1688]), single-sheet; see Julie Farguson, 'Dynastic Politics, International Protestantism and Royal Rebellion: Prince George of Denmark and the Glorious Revolution', *English Historical Review*, 131:550 (2016), pp. 559–60.

42. Historical Manuscripts Commission, *Report on the Manuscripts of F. W. Leyborne-Popham, Esq. of Littlecote, Co. Wilts.* (London, 1899), p. 267. As Clarke added of James VII & II, 'it was the last time I ever saw him'.
43. Evelyn, *Diary*, pp. 894–5 (2 December 1688).
44. [Hugh Speke], *The Prince of Orange His Third Declaration* (n.p., [1688]), p. 3.
45. Dalrymple, *Memoirs*, Vol. II, p. 326 (29 November 1688).
46. Historical Manuscripts Commission, *Eleventh Report, Part V. The Manuscripts of the Earl of Dartmouth* (London, 1887) pp. 276, 278 (3 and 6 December 1688).
47. Clarke (ed.), *Life of James the Second*, Vol. II, p. 241.
48. Quoted by Cristina Bravo Lozano, 'Popular Protests, the Public Sphere and Court Catholicism. The Insults to the Chapel of the Spanish Embassy in London, 1685–1688', *Culture & History*, 6:1 (2017), pp. 9, 11.
49. Quoted by Pincus, 'The European Catholic Context', p. 105.
50. Morrice, *Entring Book*, Vol. IV, p. 383 (December 1688).
51. Quoted by Robert Beddard, 'The Loyalist Opposition in the Interregnum: a Letter of Dr. Francis Turner, Bishop of Ely, on the Revolution of 1688', *Bulletin of the Institute of Historical Research*, 40:101 (1967), p. 106.
52. Morrice, *Entring Book*, Vol. IV, p. 384 (December 1688); George Hilton Jones, 'The Irish Fright of 1688: Real Violence and Imagined Massacre', *Bulletin of the Institute of Historical Research*, 55:132 (1982), pp. 149, 151.
53. Quoted by Jones, 'The Irish Fright of 1688', p. 152.
54. Quoted by W. A. Speck, *James II* (Harlow, 2002), p. 79.
55. Clarke (ed.), *Life of James the Second*, Vol. I, pp. 262–3.
56. James II, *His Majesty's Letter to the Lords and Others of His Privy Council* (London, 1689); single-sheet folio.
57. Quoted by Charles-Édouard Levillain, 'London Besieged? The City's Vulnerability during the Glorious Revolution' in Jason McElligott, *Fear, Exclusion and Revolution: Roger Morrice and Britain in the 1680s* (Aldershot, 2006), p. 101.
58. Gilbert Burnet, *A Sermon Preached in the Chapel of St. James's Before His Highness the Prince of Orange, the 23rd of December, 1688 by Gilbert Burnet* (London, 1689), pp. 3, 4, 33, 22–3.
59. Anonymous, *A Dialogue Between Dick and Tom; Concerning the Present Posture of Affairs in England* (London, 1689), p. 7.
60. Quoted by Charles-Édouard Levillain, 'Cromwell Redivivus? William III as Military Dictator: Myth and Reality' in Esther Mijers and David Onnekink (eds), *Redefining William III. The Impact of the King-Stadholder in International Context* (Aldershot, 2007), p. 163.
61. Anonymous, *News from Sherburn-Castle, being an Accidental Discovery of a Private Conference lately held there. Wherein the Prince of O's Third*

Declaration is Truly Stated. In a Familiar Dialogue between Frank a Protestant and Tom a R. Catholick (London, 1688), p. 2.

62. Grey (ed.), *Debates*, Vol. IX, pp. 3, 5 (22 January 1689), 17, 21 (28 January 1689).
63. Quoted by Howard Nenner, *The Right to be King. The Succession to the Crown of England, 1603–1714* (Basingstoke, 1995), p. 184.
64. Gilbert Burnet, *Bishop Burnet's History of His Own Time. Volume 1: From the Restoration of King Charles II to the Settlement of King William and Queen Mary at the Revolution*, 2 vols (London, 1724), Vol. I, p. 820.
65. El Duque de Maura (ed.), *Correspondencia Entre Dos Embajadores. Don Pedro Ronquillo y el Marqués de Cogolludo 1689–1691*, 2 vols (Madrid, 1951), Vol. I, p. 86 (11 February 1689: 'ha dicho que, como vino a reintegrar la Religión, las Leyes y las libertades del pueblo inglés, no vino a quitar las de la Corona').
66. Robert Beddard, 'Introduction; the Protestant Succession; the Unexpected Whig Revolution of 1688' in Robert Beddard (ed.), *The Revolutions of 1688 (The Andrew Browning Lectures 1988)* (Oxford, 1991), p. 99.
67. Evelyn, *Diary*, p. 902 (22 February 1689).
68. Grey (ed.), *Debates*, Vol. IX, p. 95 (20 February 1689).
69. Lois G. Schwoerer, 'The Transformation of the 1689 Convention into a Parliament', *Parliamentary History*, 3:1 (1984), p. 71.
70. Anonymous, *Observations Upon the Late Revolution in England* ([?Edinburgh], 1689), p. 2.
71. Quoted by Tim Harris, *Revolution. The Great Crisis of the British Monarchy, 1685–1720* (London, 2006), p. 394.
72. Anonymous, *A Letter From a Gentleman in the Country to his Correspondent in the City, Concerning the Coronation Medal, Distributed April 11, 1689* (n. p., 1689), p. 1.
73. Gilbert Burnet, *A Sermon Preached at the Coronation of William III and Mary II, King and Queen of England, France and Ireland, Defenders of the Faith, in the Abby-Church of Westminster, April 11, 1689* (London, 1689), p. 28.
74. Quoted by Emilie Dosquet, '"We have been Informed that the French are Carrying Desolation Everywhere": The Desolation of the Palatinate as a European News Event' in Joad Raymond and Noah Moxham (eds), *News Networks in Early Modern Europe* (Leiden, 2016), pp. 662–3.
75. Anonymous, *A True Account of the Barbarous Cruelties committed by the French in the Palatinate, in January and February last, Faithfully Translated from the High-Dutch Copy* (London, 1689), p. 2.
76. Quoted by John A. Lynn, 'A Brutal Necessity? The Devastation of the Palatinate, 1688–1689' in Mark Grimsley and Clifford J. Rogers (eds), *Civilians in the Path of War* (Lincoln, NE, 2002), pp. 87, 79.

77. Quoted by David Onnekink, 'Primacy Contested: Foreign and Domestic Policy in the Reign of William III' in William Mulligan and Brendan Simms (eds), *The Primacy of Foreign Policy in British History, 1660–2000. How Strategic Concerns Shaped Modern Britain* (Basingstoke, 2010), p. 32.
78. Quoted by John M. Stapleton, Jr, 'The Dual Monarchy in Practice: Anglo-Dutch Alliance and War in the Spanish Netherlands 1689–1697' in Mijers and Onnekink (eds), *Redefining William III*, p. 69.
79. See D. W. Hayton, 'Louis XIV, James II and Ireland' in Tony Claydon and Charles-Édouard Levillain (eds), *Louis XIV Outside In. Images of the Sun King beyond France, 1661–1715* (Farnham, 2015), pp. 114–15.
80. HMC *Ormonde ... Volume VIII* (London, 1920), pp. 389, 390 (Address presented ... at Kilkenny on 22 March 1689).
81. Anonymous, *Two Letters Discovering the Designs of the Late King James in Ireland Written from a Person of Quality to a Noble Peer sitting in the House of Lords* (London, 1689), p. 2.
82. Browning (ed.), *English Historical Documents 1660–1714*, pp. 747–8 ([Irish] Act of Recognition, 1689).
83. William King, *The State of the Protestants of Ireland under the late King James's Government in which their Carriage towards him is Justified, and the Absolute Necessity of their Endeavouring to be Freed from his Government, and of Submitting to their Present Majesties is Demonstrated* (London, 1691), p. 396.
84. Quoted by J. G. Simms, *Jacobite Ireland 1685–91* (London, 1969), p. 92.
85. Quoted by Edward Gregg, 'France, Rome and the Exiled Stuarts, 1689–1713' in Edward Corp (ed.), *A Court in Exile: The Stuarts in France, 1689–1718* (Cambridge, 2004), p. 23.
86. Anonymous, *K. William or K. Lewis, wherein is set forth the inevitable necessity these nations lye under: of submitting wholly to one or other of these kings, and that the matter in controversie is not now between K. William and K. James, but between K. William and K. Lewis of France, for the Government of these Nations* (London, 1689), p. 7.
87. Lilian Tate (ed.), 'Letter-book of Richard Talbot', *Analecta Hibernica*, 4 (1932), pp. 104, 127, 121 (27 November 1689, 20 May and 30 April 1690).
88. Quoted by Wout Troost, 'Ireland's Role in the Foreign Policy of William III' in Onnekink and Mijers (eds), *Redefining William III*, p. 53.
89. Quoted by Meredith McNeill Hale, *The Birth of Modern Political Satire. Romeyn de Hooghe and the Glorious Revolution* (Oxford, 2020), p. 101.
90. Quoted by Rudolf Dekker, *Family, Culture and Society in the Diary of Constantijn Huygens Jr., Secretary to Stadholder-King William of Orange* (Leiden, 2013), p. 41.
91. Quoted by Philip Mansel, *King of the World. The Life of Louis XIV* (London, 2019), p. 339.
92. Evelyn, *Diary*, p. 927 (6 July 1690).

93. Quoted by Pincus, *1688*, p. 358.
94. J. F. Bosher, 'The Franco-Catholic Danger, 1660–1715', *History*, 79:255 (1994), p. 20.
95. Hayton, 'Louis XIV, James II and Ireland' in Claydon and Levillain (eds), *Louis XIV Outside In*, pp. 122–3. Following William's eventual victory in Ireland, around 12,000–15,000 Jacobite soldiers (known as the 'Wild Geese') were granted safe passage from Ireland to join the French army.

EPILOGUE: A HEAP OF CONSPIRACIES

1. Quoted by W. A. Speck, 'William – and Mary?' in Lois G. Schwoerer (ed.), *The Revolution of 1688–1689. Changing Perspectives* (Cambridge, 1992), p. 133.
2. Quoted by Rudolf Dekker, *Family, Culture and Society in the Diary of Constantijn Huygens Jr., Secretary to Stadholder-King William of Orange* (Leiden, 2013), p. 35.
3. Anonymous, *The Dutch Design Anatomized, or, A Discovery of the Wickedness and Unjustice of the Intended Invasion and a Clear Proof that it is the Interest of all the King's Subjects to Defend His Majesty and Their Country Against it* (London, 1688), p. 40.
4. *Lettres de Madame de Sévigné, avec les Notes de Tous les Commentateurs*, 6 vols (Paris, 1843), Vol. V, p. 321 (23 February 1689).
5. William King, *Europe's Delivery from France and Slavery: A Sermon preached at St. Patrick's Church, Dublin, on the 16th of November 1690 . . . Being the Day of Thanksgiving for the Preservation of His Majesty's Person, His Good Success in our Deliverance, and his Safe and Happy Return into England* (Dublin, 1691), p. 20.
6. Quoted by Rachel Weil, *A Plague of Informers. Conspiracy and Political Trust in William III's England* (New Haven, CT, 2013), p. 38.
7. Samuel Weller Singer (ed.), *The Correspondence of Henry Hyde, Earl of Clarendon and his brother, Laurence Hyde, Earl of Rochester: With the Diary of Lord Clarendon from 1687 to 1690*, 2 vols (London, 1828), Vol. II, p. 300 (7 January 1690).
8. *CSP Domestic . . . William and Mary, 13th February 1689–April 1690*, p. 257 (16 September 1689).
9. Quoted by Weil, *Plague of Informers*, p. 85.
10. Quoted by Alan Marshall, *Intelligence and Espionage in the Reign of Charles II, 1660–1685* (Cambridge, 1994), pp. 29–30, 1.
11. Quoted by Henry Horwitz, *Parliament, Policy and Politics in the Reign of William III* (Manchester, 1977), p. 42.
12. Alexander Peterkin (ed.), *Records of the Kirk of Scotland: containing the Acts and Proceedings of the General Assemblies, from the year 1638 &c.* ([Edinburgh], 1838), p. 70 (25 June 1638).

13. Quoted by Horwitz, *Parliament, Policy and Politics*, p. 42.
14. Steve Pincus, *1688: The First Modern Revolution* (New Haven, CT, 2009), p. 351.
15. [Nathaniel Johnston], *The Dear Bargain. Or, A True Representation of the State of the English Nation under the Dutch. In a Letter to a Friend* ([London, 1690]), pp. 1–2.
16. [Sir James Montgomery of Skelmorlie], *Great Britain's Just Complaint for her Late Measures, Present Sufferings, and the Future Miseries she is Exposed To* (Oxford, 1692), p. 34.
17. Joanna Craigwood, 'Diplomacy, Poetry, and Publics in the Late Seventeenth Century: Elegies for Mary II by George Stepney and Matthew Prior', *Huntington Library Quarterly*, 82:4 (2019), pp. 624–5.
18. Historical Manuscripts Commission, *Calendar of the Manuscripts of the Marquess of Bath, Preserved at Longleat, Wiltshire*, 3 vols (London, 1904–8), Vol. III, pp. 47, 49 (25 February/4 March and 8/18 March 1695).
19. Quoted by Matthias Range, *British Royal and State Funerals. Music and Ceremonial since Elizabeth I* (Martlesham, 2016), p. 110.
20. Narcissus Luttrell, *A Brief Historical Relation of State Affairs from September 1678 to April 1714*, 6 vols (Oxford, 1857), Vol. IV, p. 21 (25 February 1696); *CSP Domestic ... William and Mary: January 1st–December 31st 1696*, p. 59 (29 February 1696).
21. Andrew Browning (ed.), *English Historical Documents 1660–1714* (London, 1953), p. 75 (Act for the Security of the Crown, 1696).
22. Evelyn, *Diary*, p. 1008 (24 May 1696).
23. Quoted by Horwitz, *Parliament, Policy and Politics*, p. 169.
24. Quoted by Ian Higgins, *Swift's Politics. A Study in Disaffection* (Cambridge, 1994), p. 63.
25. Quoted by Howard Nenner, *The Right to be King. The Succession to the Crown of England, 1603–1714* (Basingstoke, 1995), pp. 228–9.
26. Daniel Defoe, 'The Two Great Questions Consider'd' in *A True Collection of the Writings of the Author of the True Born English-man* (London, 1703), pp. 362, 354.
27. Quoted by Nenner, *The Right to be King*, p. 231.
28. John M. Simpson, 'John Ker, first duke of Roxburghe', *Oxford Dictionary of National Biography* (Oxford, 2004).
29. James VI & I, 'Speech ... 19 Day of March &c.' in Johann P. Sommerville (ed.), *King James VI and I. Political Writings* (Cambridge, 1994), p. 136.
30. [Daniel Defoe], *A Fourth Essay, at Removing National Prejudices; With Some Reply to Mr. H—dges and Some Other Authors &c.* ([Edinburgh], 1706), p. 43.
31. Quoted by Julian Hoppit, *A Land of Liberty? England 1689–1727* (Oxford, 2000), p. 253.

32. Hoppit, *Land of Liberty?*, p. 384.
33. Dalrymple, *Memoirs*, Vol. II, p. 280 (4 November 1680).
34. Quoted by Paul Langford, *Englishness Identified. Manners and Character 1650–1850* (Oxford, 2000), p. 11.
35. Jonathan Swift, *Gulliver's Travels*, Claude Rawson (ed.) (Oxford, 2005), p. 120.

Select Bibliography

PRIMARY SOURCES

'A. Ar.', *The Practise of Princes* (Amsterdam, 1630).

Wilbur Cortez Abbott (ed.), *The Writings and Speeches of Oliver Cromwell. With an Introduction, Notes and an Account of His Life*, 4 vols (Oxford, 1988).

Osmund Airy (ed.), *The Lauderdale Papers*, 3 vols (London, 1884–5).

Nadine Akkerman (ed.), *The Correspondence of Elizabeth Stuart, Queen of Bohemia. Volume 2: 1632–1642* (Oxford, 2011).

Nadine Akkerman (ed.), *The Correspondence of Elizabeth Stuart, Queen of Bohemia. Volume 1: 1603–1631* (Oxford, 2015).

G. P. V. Akrigg (ed.), *Letters of King James VI & I* (Berkeley, CA, 1984).

Anonymous, *A Free Conference Touching the Present State of England both at Home and Abroad, in order to the Designs of France* (London, 1668).

Anonymous, *The Dutch Design Anatomized, or, A Discovery of the Wickedness and Unjustice* [sic] *of the Intended Invasion and a Clear Proof that it is the Interest of all the King's Subjects to Defend His Majesty and Their Country Against it* (London, 1688).

A. G. H. Bachrach and R. G. Collmer (eds), *Lodewijk Huygens. The English Journal 1651–1652* (Leiden, 1982).

Robert Bell (trans. and ed.), *Extract from the Despatches of M. de Courcelles, French Ambassador at the Court of Scotland, 1586–1587* (Edinburgh, 1828).

[Thomas Birch (ed.)], *The Court and Times of James the First; Illustrated by Authentic and Confidential Letters, from Various Public and Private Collections*, 2 vols (London, 1848).

[Thomas Birch (ed.)], *The Court and Times of Charles I; Illustrated by Authentic and Confidential Letters, from Various Public and Private Collections &c.*, 2 vols (London, 1848).

R. W. Blencowe (ed.), *Diary of the Times of Charles the Second, by the Honourable Henry Sidney &c.*, 2 vols (London, 1843).

Antoine le Fèvre de la Boderie, *Ambassades de Monsieur de la Boderie en Angleterre sous le Regne d'Henri IV & la Minorité de Louis XIII depuis les années 1606 jusqu'en 1611*, 5 vols (Paris, 1750).

Robert Bowyer, *The Parliamentary Diary of Robert Bowyer, 1606–1607*, David Harris Willson (ed.) (New York, 1971).

Andrew Browning (ed.), *English Historical Documents 1660–1714* (London, 1953).

John Bruce (ed.), *Letters of Queen Elizabeth and King James of Scotland &c.* (London, 1849).

John Bruce (ed.), *Charles I in 1646: Letters of King Charles the First to Queen Henrietta Maria* (London, 1855).

Arthur Bryant (ed.), *The Letters, Speeches and Declarations of King Charles II* (London, 1935).

Richard Bulstrode, *Memoirs and Reflections upon the Reign and Government of King Charles the First and King Charles the Second* (London, 1721).

Gilbert Burnet, *Bishop Burnet's History of His Own Time. Volume 1: From the Restoration of King Charles II to the Settlement of King William and Queen Mary at the Revolution*, 2 vols (London, 1724).

Alonso de Cárdenas, *La Revolución Inglesa (1638–1656) / The English Revolution (1638–1656)*, Ángel Alloza and Glyn Redworth (eds) (Madrid, 2011).

Dudley Carleton, *Letters from and to Sir Dudley Carleton, Knight During his Embassy in Holland, from January 1615/16, to December 1620* (London, 1775).

Julian de Castilla, *The English Conquest of Jamaica: An Account of what happened in the Island of Jamaica*, trans. Irene A. Wright, *Camden Miscellany*, 13, Third Series, 31 (1924).

John Chamberlain, *The Letters of John Chamberlain*, Norman E. McClure (ed.), 2 vols (Philadelphia, PA, 1939).

Charles I, *His Majesty's Declaration to all his Loving Subjects, of the Causes which moved him to Dissolve the last Parliament* (London, 1629).

Charles I, *The King's Cabinet Opened; or, certain Packets of Secret Letters and Papers, written with the King's Own Hand, and taken in his Cabinet at Naseby-Field, June 14, 1645* (London, 1645).

Charles I, *Eikon Basilike. The Portraiture of His Sacred Majesty, in his Solitudes and Sufferings, With Selections from Eikonoklastes*, Jim Daems and Holly Faith Nelson (eds) (Peterborough, ON, 2006).

H. J. Chaytor (trans. and ed.), 'Embajada Española: An Anonymous Contemporary Spanish Guide to Diplomatic Procedure in the Last Quarter of the Seventeenth Century', *Camden Miscellany. Vol. XIV* (London, 1926).

Arthur Collins (ed.), *Letters and Memorials of State, in the Reigns of Queen Mary, Queen Elizabeth, King James, King Charles the First, Part of the Reign of King Charles the Second, and Oliver's Usurpation*, 2 vols (London, 1746).

Edward Combe (ed.), *The Sale of Dunkirk to the Late French King Lewis XIV. In the year 1662. Taken from the Letters, Memoirs, &c. of Count d'Estrades &c.* (London, 1728).

Esther S. Cope and Willson H. Coates (eds), *Proceedings of the Short Parliament of 1640* (London, 1977).

Allan J. Crosby and John Bruce (eds), *Accounts and Papers Relating to Mary, Queen of Scots* (London, 1867).

M. Beryl Curran (ed.), *The Despatches of William Perwich, English Agent in Paris, 1669–1677* (London, 1903).

Eamon Darcy (ed.), 'The Spanish- language "Manifesto" of the Catholic Confederation of Ireland, 1642', *Archivium Hibernicum*, 67 (2014).

Elizabeth I, *Elizabeth I: Collected Works*, Leah S. Marcus, Janel Mueller and Mary Beth Rose (eds) (Chicago, IL, 2000).

Gaspar Fagel, *A Letter Writ By Mijn Heer Fagel, Pensioner of Holland, to Mr. James Stewart, Advocate, Giving an Account of the Prince and Princess of Orange's Thoughts Concerning the Repeal of the Test and Penal Laws* (Amsterdam, 1688).

Sir Richard Fanshawe, *Original Letters of his Excellency Sir Richard Fanshaw, During his Embassies in Spain and Portugal &c.* (London, 1701).

Sir John Finet, *Finetti Philoxenis: Some Choice Observations of Sir John Finet Knight . . . touching the Reception, and Precedence, the Treatment and Audience, the Punctilios and Contests of Foreign Ambassadors in England* (London, 1656).

Elizabeth Read Foster (ed.), *Proceedings in Parliament, 1610*, 2 vols (New Haven, CT, 1966).

Bruce R. Galloway and Brian P. Levack (eds), *The Jacobean Union. Six Tracts of 1604* (Edinburgh, 1985).

Samuel Rawson Gardiner (ed.), *Letters and other Documents Illustrating the Relations between England and Germany at the Commencement of the Thirty Years War* (London, 1865).

Samuel Rawson Gardiner (ed.), *Letters and other Documents Illustrating the Relations between England and Germany at the Commencement of the Thirty Years War. Second Series* (London, 1868).

Samuel Rawson Gardiner (ed.), *Prince Charles and the Spanish Marriage: 1617–1623: A Chapter of English History &c.*, 2 vols (London, 1869).

Samuel Rawson Gardiner (trans. and ed.), *El Hecho de los Tratados del Matrimonio Pretendido por el Principe de Gales con la Serenissima Infante de España . . . por F. Francisco de Jesus* [*Narrative of the Spanish Marriage Treaty*] (London, 1869).

Samuel Rawson Gardiner (ed.), *The Hamilton Papers: Being Selections from Original Letters in the Possession of His Grace, The Duke of Hamilton and Brandon, Relating to the Years 1638–1650* (London, 1880).

Samuel Rawson Gardiner (ed.), *Letters and Papers illustrating the Relations between Charles the Second and Scotland in 1650* (Edinburgh, 1894).

Edmund Garrard, *The Country Gentleman Moderator. Collections of such Intermarriages as have been between the two Royal Lines of England and Spain, since the Conquest &c.* (London, 1624).

James Orchard Halliwell (ed.), *The Autobiography and Correspondence of Sir Simonds D'Ewes Baronet &c.*, 2 vols (London, 1845).

T. E. Hartley (ed.), *Proceedings in the Parliaments of Elizabeth I. Volume II: 1584–1589* (London, 1995).

Historical Manuscripts Commission, *Fourth Report of the Royal Commission on Historical Manuscripts. Part I: Report and Appendix* (London, 1874).

James Howell, *Epistolæ Ho-Elianæ. Familiar Letters Domestic and Foreign. Divided into Sundry Sections Partly Historical, Political, Philosophical* (London, 1655).

James Howell, *Proedria Vasilikē: A Discourse concerning the Precedency of Kings . . . whereunto is also adjoined a Distinct Treatise of Ambassadors &c.* (London, 1664).

James VI & I, *King James VI and I. Political Writings*, Johann P. Sommerville (ed.) (Cambridge, 1994).

Maija Jansson (ed.), *Proceedings in Parliament 1614 (House of Commons)* (Philadelphia, PA, 1988).

Maija Jansson and William B. Bidwell (eds), *Proceedings in Parliament 1625* (New Haven, CT, 1987).

N. Japikse (ed.), *Correspondentie van Willem III en van Hans Willem Bentinck*, 5 vols (The Hague, 1927–37).

Robert C. Johnson, Mary Frear Keeler, Maija Jansson Cole and William B. Bidwell (eds), *Commons Debates 1628*, 6 vols (New Haven, CT, 1977).

J.-J. Jusserand, A *French Ambassador at the Court of Charles II. Le Comte de Cominges from his Unpublished Correspondence* (London, 1912).

J.-J. Jusserand (ed.), *Recueil des Instructions Données aux Ambassadeurs et Ministres de France. Volume XXV* (Paris, 1929).

J. P. Kenyon (ed.), *The Stuart Constitution 1603–1608. Documents and Commentary* (second edition, Cambridge, 1986).

K. J. Kesselring (ed.), *The Trial of Charles I* (Peterborough, ON, 2016).

William Knowler (ed.), *The Earl of Strafforde's Letters and Dispatches: With an Essay Towards his Life by Sir George Radcliffe*, 2 vols (London, 1739).

W. E. Knowles Middleton (ed.), *Lorenzo Magalotti at the Court of Charles II. His Relazione d'Inghilterra of 1668* (Waterloo, ON, 1980).

John Knox Laughton (ed.), *State Papers Relating to the Defeat of the Spanish Armada*, 2 vols (London, 1895).

Maurice Lee Jr (ed.), *Dudley Carleton to John Chamberlain 1603–1624. Jacobean Letters* (New Brunswick, NJ, 1972).

Pierre de L'Estoile, *Mémoires-Journaux de Pierre de L'Éstoile*, 11 vols (Paris, 1875–83).

[François-Paul de Lisola], *The Buckler of State and Justice against the Design manifestly discovered of the Universal Monarchy, under the vain pretext of the Queen of France, her pretensions* (London, 1667).

Albert J. Loomie (ed.), *Spain and the Jacobean Catholics*, 2 vols (London, 1973).

Albert J. Loomie (ed.), *Ceremonies of Charles I. The Notebooks of John Finet 1628–1641* (New York, 1987).

Sir George Mackenzie, *Memoirs of the Affairs of Scotland from the Restoration of King Charles II. A.D.M.DC.LX* [Thomas Thomson (ed.)] (Edinburgh, 1821).

Ruth Saunders Magurn (trans. and ed.), *The Letters of Peter Paul Rubens* (Cambridge, MA, 1955).

Andrew Marvell, *The Poems and Letters of Andrew Marvell*, H. M. Margoliouth (ed.), 2 vols (Oxford, 1971).

William Matthews (ed.), *Charles II's Escape from Worcester. A Collection of Narratives assembled by Samuel Pepys* (London, 1967).

Henry W. Meikle (ed.), *Correspondence of the Scots Commissioners in London 1644–1646* (Edinburgh, 1917).

Thomas Middleton, *A Game at Chess. Thomas Middleton*, T. H. Howard-Hill (ed.) (Manchester, 1993).

Guy Miège, *A Relation of Three Embassies from his Sacred Majesty, Charles II to the Great Duke of Muscovy, the King of Sweden and the King of Denmark* (London, 1669).

John Milton, *John Milton. Political Writings*, Martin Dzelzainis (ed.) (Cambridge, 1991).

[Pierre du Moulin], *England's Appeal from the Private Cabal at Whitehall to the Great Council of the Nation, the Lords and Commons in Parliament assembled. By a True Lover of his Country* ([London], 1673).

Giovan Battista Nani, *The History of the Affairs of Europe in the Present Age, but more particularly of the Republic of Venice*, translated by Sir Robert Honywood (London, 1673).

John Nichols (ed.), *The Progresses, Processions and Magnificent Festivities of King James the First &c.*, 4 vols (London, 1828).

Ruth Norrington (ed.), *My Dearest Minette. The Letters between Charles II and his sister Henrietta, Duchesse d'Orléans* (London, 1996).

[Robert Persons], *A Conference about the Next Succession to the Crown of England, divided into Two Parts &c.* ([Antwerp, 1595]).

Robert Pitcairn (ed.), *Collections Relative to the Funerals of Mary, Queen of Scots* (Edinburgh, 1822).

Henry Reeve (ed.), *A Journal of the Swedish Embassy in the Years 1653 and 1654. Impartially written by the Ambassador Bulstrode Whitelocke*, 2 vols (London, 1855).

Pedro de Ribadeneyra, *Pedro de Ribadeneyra's Ecclesiastical History of the Schism in the Kingdom of England. A Spanish Jesuit's History of the English Reformation*, Spencer J. Weinreich (ed.) (Leiden, 2017).

Michael Roberts (trans. and ed.), *Swedish Diplomats at Cromwell's Court, 1655–1656. The Missions of Peter Julius Coyet and Christer Bonde* (London, 1988).

John Rushworth, *Historical Collections of Private Passages of State, Weighty Measures in Law, Remarkable Proceedings in Five Parliaments &c.*, 8 vols (London, 1721–2).

R. Scrope and T. Monkhouse (eds), *State Papers Collected by Edward, Earl of Clarendon, Commencing from the Year MDCXXI*, 3 vols (Oxford, 1767–86).

Alan G. R. Smith (ed.), *The Last Years of Mary, Queen of Scots. Documents from the Cecil Papers at Hatfield House* (London, 1990).

Samuel de Sorbière, *A Voyage to England, containing many things relating to the State of Learning, Religion, and other Curiosities of that Kingdom &c.* (London, 1709).

H. Manners Sutton (ed.), *The Lexington Papers; or, Some Account of the Courts of London and Vienna; at the Conclusion of the Seventeenth Century* (London, 1851).

Lilian Tate (ed.), 'Letter-book of Richard Talbot', *Analecta Hibernica*, 4 (1932).

William Temple, *The Works of Sir William Temple Bart. In Four Volumes. To which is Prefixed, The Life and Character of the Author*, 4 vols (Edinburgh, 1754).

Edward Maunde Thompson (ed.), *Correspondence of the Family of Hatton: Being Chiefly Letters Addressed to Christopher, First Viscount Hatton, A.D. 1601–1704*, 2 vols (London, 1878).

John Thurloe, *A Collection of the State Papers of John Thurloe Esq.; Secretary, First to the Council of State, and Afterwards to the Two Protectors, Oliver and Richard Cromwell*, John Thurloe (ed.), 7 vols (London, 1742).

Eliot Warburton (ed.), *Memoirs of Prince Rupert and the Cavaliers: including their Private Correspondence, now first published from the Original Manuscripts*, 3 vols (London, 1849).

James Welwood, *Memoirs of the Most Material Transactions in England, for the last Hundred Years, preceding the Revolution in 1688* (London, 1704).

Waldemar Westergaard (ed.), *The First Triple Alliance. The Letters of Christopher Lindenov, Danish Envoy to London, 1668–1672* (New Haven, CT, 1947).

John Whittel, *An Exact Diary of the Late Expedition of His Illustrious Highness, the Prince of Orange, now King of Great Britain, from his Palace at The Hague, to his landing at Torbay, and from thence to his Arrival at Whitehall &c.* (London, 1689).

Abraham de Wicquefort, *The Embassador and his Functions: Written by Monsieur de Wicquefort, Privy-Counsellor to the Duke of Brunswick and Lunenburg, Zell &c.* (London, 1716).

Ralph Winwood, *Memorials of Affairs of State in the Reigns of Q. Elizabeth and K. James I, Collected Chiefly from the Original Papers of the Right Honourable Sir Ralph Winwood Kt., Sometime one of the Principal Secretaries of State*, [Edmund Sawyer (ed.)], 3 vols (London, 1725).

David Worthington, 'The 1688 Correspondence of Nicholas Taaffe, second earl of Carlingford (?–1690), from the Imperial Court in Vienna', *Archivium Hibernicum*, 58 (2004).

Sir Henry Wotton, *Reliquiæ Wottonianæ; or a Collection of Lives, Letters, Poems, with characters of Sundry Personages: and other incomparable pieces of Language and Art* (London, 1651).

SECONDARY SOURCES

Paul C. Allen, *Philip III and Pax Hispanica, 1598–1621. The Failure of Grand Strategy* (New Haven, CT, 2000).

Rayne Allison, 'The Queen's Three Bodies: Gender, Criminality and Sovereignty in the Execution of Mary, Queen of Scots' in Megan Cassidy Welch and Peter Sherlock (eds), *Practices of Gender in Late Medieval and Early Modern Europe* (Turnhout, 2008).

Ronald G. Asch, *Sacral Kingship between Disenchantment and Re-enchantment: The French and English Monarchies, 1587–1688* (Oxford, 2014).

Ian Atherton, *Ambition and Failure in Stuart England. The Career of John, First Viscount Scudamore* (Manchester, 1999).

Alastair Bellany and Thomas Cogswell, *The Murder of King James I* (New Haven, CT, 2015).

Cristina Bravo Lozano, *Spain and the Irish Mission, 1609–1707* (New York, 2019).

Jerry Brotton, *The Sale of the Late King's Goods. Charles I and his Art Collection* (London, 2017).

Valentina Caldari and Sara J. Wolfson (eds), *Stuart Marriage Diplomacy. Dynastic Politics in their European Context, 1604–1630* (Woodbridge, 2018).

Marie-Claude Canova-Green and Sara J. Wolfson (eds), *The Wedding of Charles I and Henrietta Maria, 1625. Celebrations and Controversy* (Turnhout, 2020).

John Carswell, *The Descent on England. A Study of the English Revolution of 1688 and its European Background* (London, 1969).

Janet Clare (ed.), *From Republic to Restoration. Legacies and Departures* (Manchester, 2018).

Tony Claydon, *Europe and the Making of England, 1660–1760* (Cambridge, 2007).

Tony Claydon, *The Revolution in Time: Chronology, Modernity, and 1688–1689 in England* (Oxford, 2020).

Tony Claydon and Charles-Édouard Levillain (eds), *Louis XIV Outside In. Images of the Sun King beyond France, 1661–1715* (Farnham, 2015).

Stephen Clucas and Rosalind Davies (eds), *The Crisis of 1614 and The Addled Parliament: Literary and Historical Perpectives* (Farnham, 2003).

David Coast, *News and Rumour in Jacobean England. Information, Court Politics and Diplomacy, 1618–1625* (Manchester, 2014).

Thomas Cogswell, *The Blessed Revolution: English Politics and the Coming of War, 1621–1624* (Cambridge, 1989).

Thomas Cogswell, '"Published by Authoritie": Newsbooks and the Duke of Buckingham's Expedition to the Île de Ré', *Huntingdon Library Quarterly*, 67:1 (2004).

Thomas Cogswell, 'John Felton, Popular Culture and the Assassination of the Duke of Buckingham, *Historical Journal*, 49:2 (2006).

Joseph Cope, *England and the 1641 Irish Rebellion* (Woodbridge, 2009).

David Cressy, *Bonfires and Bells. National Memory and the Protestant Calendar in Elizabethan and Stuart England* (Stroud, 2004).

David Cressy, *England on Edge: Crisis and Revolution 1640–1642* (Oxford, 2007).

David Cressy, *England's Islands in a Sea of Troubles* (Oxford, 2020).

Eamon Darcy, *The Irish Rebellion of 1641 and the Wars of the Three Kingdoms* (Woodbridge, 2013).

H. Neville Davis, 'The Limitations of Festival: Christian IV's State Visit to England in 1606' in J. R. Mulryne and Margaret Shewring (eds), *Italian Renaissance Festivals and their European Influence* (Lewiston, NY, 1992).

Rudolf Dekker, *Family, Culture and Society in the Diary of Constantijn Huygens Jr., Secretary to Stadholder-King William of Orange* (Leiden, 2013).

Barbara Donagan, *War in England, 1642–1649* (Oxford, 2010).

Susan Doran, 'Revenge her Foul and Unnatural Murder? The Impact of Mary Stewart's Execution on Anglo-Scottish Relations', *History*, 85:280 (2000).

Susan Doran and Paulina Kewes (eds), *Doubtful and Dangerous: The Question of Succession in late Elizabethan England* (Manchester, 2014).

Robin Eagles and Coleman A. Dennehy (eds), *Henry Bennet, Earl of Arlington, and his World. Restoration Court, Politics and Diplomacy* (Abingdon, 2020).

Jemma Field, *Anna of Denmark. The Material and Visual Culture of the Stuart Courts, 1589–1619* (Manchester, 2020).

David Finnegan, Éamonn Ó Ciardha and Marie-Claire Peters (eds), *The Flight of the Earls. Imeacht na nIarlaí* (Derry, 2010).

Jonathan Fitzgibbons, '"Not in any Doubtfull Dispute?" Reassessing the Nomination of Richard Cromwell', *Historical Research*, 83:220 (2010).

Linda Frey and Marsha Frey, 'The Bounds of Immunity: the Sá Case. Politics, Law and Diplomacy in Commonwealth England', *Canadian Journal of History*, 25:1 (1990).

Robert von Friedeburg and John Morrill (eds), *Monarchy Transformed. Princes and their Elites in Early Modern Western Europe* (Cambridge, 2017).

Richard L. Greaves, *Secrets of the Kingdom. British Radicals from the Popish Plot to the Revolution of 1688–1689* (Stanford, CA, 1992).

Nicole Greenspan, 'Public Scandal, Political Controversy, and Familial Conflict in the Stuart Courts in Exile: The Struggle to Convert the Duke of Gloucester in 1654', *Albion: A Quarterly Journal Concerned with British Studies*, 35:3 (2003).

Nicole Greenspan, 'Charles II, Lucy Walter and the Stuart Courts in Exile', *English Historical Review*, 131:553 (2016).

Erin Griffey (ed.), *Henrietta Maria. Piety, Politics and Patronage* (Farnham, 2008).

Meredith McNeill Hale, *The Birth of Modern Political Satire. Romeyn de Hooghe and the Glorious Revolution* (Oxford, 2020).

K. H. D. Haley, *William of Orange and the English Opposition, 1672–1674* (Oxford, 1953).

K. H. D. Haley, *An English Diplomat in the Low Countries. Sir William Temple and John De Witt, 1665–1672* (Oxford, 1986).

Tim Harris, *Restoration. Charles II and his Kingdoms, 1660–1685* (London, 2005).

Tim Harris, *Revolution. The Great Crisis of the British Monarchy, 1685–1720* (London, 2006).

Helmer J. Helmers, *The Royalist Republic. Literature, Politics and Religion in the Anglo-Dutch Public Sphere, 1639–1660* (Cambridge, 2015).

Jan Hennings and Edward Holberton, 'Andrew Marvell in Russia: Secretaries, Rhetoric and Public Diplomacy', *Journal of Medieval and Early Modern Studies*, 50:3 (2020).

Caroline M. Hibbard, *Charles I and the Popish Plot* (Chapel Hill, NC, 1983).

Andrew Hopper, *Turncoats and Renegadoes: Changing Sides during the English Civil Wars* (Oxford, 2012).

Henry Horwitz, *Parliament, Policy and Politics in the Reign of William III* (Manchester, 1977).

Ronald Hutton, *Charles the Second, King of England, Scotland, and Ireland* (Oxford, 1989).

Jonathan I. Israel (ed.), *The Anglo-Dutch Moment: Essays on the Glorious Revolution and its World Impact* (Cambridge, 1991).

Nathan Johnstone, *The Devil and Demonism in Early Modern England* (Cambridge, 2006).

Siobhan Keenan, *The Progresses, Processions and Royal Entries of King Charles I, 1625–1642* (Oxford, 2020).

Paulina Kewes and Andrew McRae (eds), *Stuart Succession Literature. Moments and Transformations* (Oxford, 2019).

Philip A. Knachel, *England and the Fronde: The Impact of the English Civil War and Revolution on France* (Ithaca, NY, 1967).

Mark Knights, *Politics and Opinion in Crisis, 1678–81* (Cambridge, 1994).

Laura Lunger Knoppers, *Constructing Cromwell. Ceremony, Portrait, and Print, 1645–1661* (Cambridge, 2000).

Laura L. Knoppers, 'Imagining the Death of the King: Milton, Charles I and Anamorphic Art' in Elizabeth Jane Bellamy, Patrick Cheney and Michael Schoenfeldt (eds), *Imagining Death in Spenser and Milton* (Basingstoke, 2003).

Paul Langford, *Englishness Identified: Manners and Character 1650–1850* (Oxford, 2000).

Charles-Édouard Levillain, 'London Besieged? The City's Vulnerability during the Glorious Revolution' in Jason McElligott, *Fear, Exclusion and Revolution: Roger Morrice and Britain in the 1680s* (Aldershot, 2006).

Charles-Édouard Levillain, 'French Diplomacy and the Run-up to the Glorious Revolution (1688): A Critical Reading of Jean-Antoine d'Avaux's Correspondence as Ambassador to the States General', *Journal of Modern History*, 88:1 (2016).

Albert J. Loomie, 'Alonso de Cárdenas and the Long Parliament, 1640–1648', *English Historical Review*, 97:383 (1982).

Loek Luiten, 'The Dutch Republic and the English Civil War: Consensus or Conflict?', *Dutch Crossing: Journal of Low Countries Studies*, 42:2 (2018).

Catharine MacLeod (ed.), *The Lost Prince. The Life & Death of Henry Stuart* (London, 2012).

Noel Malcolm, *Reason of State, Propaganda, and the Thirty Years' War. An Unknown Translation by Thomas Hobbes* (Oxford, 2007).

Philip Mansel, *King of the World. The Life of Louis XIV* (London, 2019).

Alan Marshall, *Intelligence and Espionage in the Reign of Charles II, 1660–1685* (Cambridge, 1994).

Margaret M. McGowan (ed.), *Dynastic Marriages, 1612/1615. A Celebration of the Habsburg and Bourbon Unions* (Farnham, 2013).

Esther Mijers and David Onnekink (eds), *Redefining William III. The Impact of the King-Stadholder in International Context* (Aldershot, 2007).

Noah Millstone, 'Evil Counsel: *The Propositions to Bridle the Impertinency of Parliament* and the Critique of Caroline Government in the Late 1620s', *Journal of British Studies*, 50:4 (2011).

Noah Millstone, *Manuscript Circulation and the Invention of Politics in Early Stuart England* (Cambridge, 2016).

Hiram Morgan (ed.), *The Battle of Kinsale* (Wicklow, 2004).

Hiram Morgan, 'News from Ireland: Catalan, Portuguese and Castilian Pamphlets on the Confederate War in Ireland' in Micheál Ó'Siochrú and Jane Ohlmeyer (eds), *Ireland, 1641: Contexts and Reactions* (Manchester, 2013).

Steve Murdoch, *Britain, Denmark-Norway and the House of Stuart 1603–1660: A Diplomatic and Military Analysis* (East Linton, 2003).

Catriona Murray, *Imaging Stuart Family Politics. Dynastic Crisis and Continuity* (Abingdon, 2017).

Howard Nenner, *The Right to be King. The Succession to the Crown of England, 1603–1714* (Basingstoke, 1995).

Jane H. Ohlmeyer, *Civil War and Restoration in the Three Stuart Kingdoms: The Career of Randal MacDonnell, Marquis of Antrim, 1609–1683* (Cambridge, 1993).

Jane H. Ohlmeyer, 'Ireland Independent: Confederate Foreign Policy and International Relations during the Mid-Seventeenth Century' in Jane H. Ohlmeyer (ed.), *Ireland from Independence to Occupation 1641–1660* (Cambridge, 1995).

Eduardo Olid Guerrero and Esther Fernández (eds), *The Image of Elizabeth I in Early Modern Spain* (Lincoln, NE, 2019).

David Onnekink, *The Anglo-Dutch Favourite: The Career of Hans Willem Bentinck, 1st Earl of Portland (1649–1709)* (Farnham, 2013).

Geoffrey Parker, *Global Crisis: War, Climate Change and Catastrophe in the Seventeenth Century* (New Haven, CT, 2013).

Geoffrey Parker, 'The Crisis of the Spanish and the Stuart Monarchies in the Mid-Seventeenth Century: Local Problems or Global Problems?' in Ciarán Brady and Jane Ohlmeyer (eds), *British Interventions in Early Modern Ireland* (Cambridge, 2005).

Igor Pérez Tostado, *Irish Influence at the Court of Spain in the Seventeenth Century* (Dublin, 2008).

Carla Gardina Pestana, *The English Conquest of Jamaica. Oliver Cromwell's Bid for Empire* (Cambridge, MA, 2017).

James Emerson Phillips, *Images of a Queen. Mary Stuart in Sixteenth-Century Literature* (Los Angeles, CA, 1964).

Geraldine M. Phipps, 'The Russian Embassy to London of 1645–46 and the Abrogation of the Muscovy Company's Charter', *Slavonic and East European Review*, 68:2 (1990).

Steven C. Pincus, *Protestantism and Patriotism. Ideologies and the Making of English Foreign Policy, 1650–1688* (Cambridge, 1996).

Steve Pincus, 'The European Catholic Context of the Revolution of 1688–1689: Gallicanism, Innocent XI, and Catholic Opposition' in Allan I. Macinnes and Arthur H. Williamson (eds), *Shaping the Stuart World 1603–1714. The Atlantic Connection* (Leiden, 2006).

Steve Pincus, *1688. The First Modern Revolution* (New Haven, CT, 2009).

Brennan C. Pursell, *The Winter King. Frederick V of the Palatinate and the Coming of the Thirty Years' War* (Farnham, 2003).

Michael Questier, *Dynastic Politics and the British Reformations 1558–1630* (Oxford, 2019).

Joad Raymond and Noah Moxham (eds), *News Networks in Early Modern Europe* (Leiden, 2016).

Óscar Recio Morales, *Ireland and the Spanish Empire 1600–1825* (Dublin, 2010).

Glyn Redworth, *The Prince and the Infanta: The Cultural Politics of the Spanish Match* (London, 2003).

Michel Reinders, *Printed Pandemonium. Popular Print and Politics in the Netherlands 1650–1672* (Leiden, 2013).

Diane Roussel, '"Several Fanatics who talked only of Killing Kings": Conspirators and Regicides before the *Parlement de Paris* in the Wake of the Assassination of Henri IV, 1610', *French History*, 30:4 (2016).

F. J. Routledge, *England and the Treaty of the Pyrenees* (Liverpool, 1953).

Herbert H. Rowen, *John de Witt, Grand Pensionary of Holland 1625–1672* (Princeton, NJ, 1978).

Robert E. Ruigh, *The Parliament of 1624. Politics and Foreign Policy* (Harvard, MA, 1971).

Conrad Russell, *The Fall of the British Monarchies 1637–1642* (Oxford, 1991).

Alexander Samson (ed.), *The Spanish Match. Prince Charles's Journey to Madrid, 1623* (Aldershot, 2006).

David Scott, *Politics and War in the Three Stuart Kingdoms, 1637–49* (Basingstoke, 2004).

Eva Scott, *The King in Exile. The Wanderings of Charles II from June 1646 to July 1654* (London 1905).

Eva Scott, *The Travels of the King. Charles II in Germany and Flanders 1654–1660* (London, 1907).

Jonathan Scott, *Algernon Sidney and the English Republic, 1623–1677* (Cambridge, 1988).

Jonathan Scott, *Algernon Sidney and the Restoration Crisis 1677–1683* (Cambridge, 1991).

Jonathan Scott, *England's Troubles: England's Seventeenth–Century Political Instability in European Context* (Cambridge, 2000).

Jonathan Scott, *How the Old World Ended. The Anglo-Dutch-American Revolution, 1500–1800* (New Haven, CT, 2018)

Kevin Sharpe, *The Personal Rule of Charles I* (New Haven, CT, 1992).

Brent S. Sirota, *The Christian Monitors. The Church of England and the Age of Benevolence, 1680–1730* (New Haven, CT, 2014).

Sara Smart and Mara R. Wade (eds), *The Palatine Wedding of 1613: Protestant Alliance and Court Festival* (Wiesbaden, 2013).

David L. Smith, 'Diplomacy and the Religious Question: Mazarin, Cromwell and the Treaties of 1655 and 1657', *E-Rea: Revue Électronique d'Études sur le Monde Anglophone*, 11:2 (2014).

R. Malcolm Smuts (ed.), *The Stuart Court and Europe. Essays in Politics and Political Culture* (Cambridge, 1996).

Paul Sonnino, *Louis XIV and the Origins of the Dutch War* (Cambridge, 1988).

Elizabeth Staffell, 'The Horrible Tail-Man and the Anglo-Dutch Wars', *Journal of the Warburg and Courtauld Institutes*, 63 (2000).

Christine Stevenson, *The City and the King: Architecture and Politics in Restoration London* (New Haven, CT, 2013).

Mark Stoyle, *Soldiers and Strangers. An Ethnic History of the English Civil War* (New Haven, CT, 2005).

Fabio Troncarelli and Igor Pérez Tostado, 'A Plot without *Capriccio*: Irish Utopia and Political Activity in Madrid, 1639–1640' in Declan M. Downey and Julio Crespo MacLennan (eds), *Spanish–Irish Relations through the Ages* (Dublin, 2008), pp. 123–36.

Wout Troost, *William III, the Stadholder-King. A Political Biography* (Aldershot, 2005).

Sarah Waurechen, 'Imagined Polities, Failed Dreams, and the Beginnings of an Unacknowledged Britain: English Responses to James VI and I's Vision of Perfect Union', *Journal of British Studies*, 52:3 (2013).

Rachel Weil, *A Plague of Informers. Conspiracy and Political Trust in William III's England* (New Haven, CT, 2013).

Jason White, *Militant Protestantism and British Identity, 1603–1642* (London, 2012).

Michelle Anne White, *Henrietta Maria and the English Civil Wars* (Aldershot, 2006).

Dirk Wiemann, 'Spectacles of Astonishment: Tragedy and the Regicide in England and Germany, 1649–1663' in Gaby Mahlberg and Dirk Wiemann (eds), *European Contexts for English Republicanism* (Farnham, 2013).

Alexander S. Wilkinson, *Mary, Queen of Scots and French Public Opinion, 1542–1600* (Basingstoke, 2004).

Robert Zaller, *The Parliament of 1621. A Study in Constitutional Conflict* (Berkeley, CA, 1971).

Unpublished PhD Theses

Emma Theresa Bergin, 'The Revolution of 1688 in Dutch Pamphlet Literature: A Study in the Dutch Public Sphere in the late Seventeenth Century' (University of Hull PhD thesis, 2006).

Victoria Jane Buckley, 'Patterns of Mischief: The Impact of the Gunpowder Plot on the Jacobean Stage, 1605–1616' (University of Sussex PhD thesis, 2012).

Robert Stuart Davis Cross, 'To Counterbalance the World: England, Spain, and Peace in the early 17th century' (Princeton University PhD thesis, 2012).

Eoin Lorcan Devlin, 'England's Encounters with Papal Rome in the late Counter-Reformation, *c.*1685– *c.*1697' (University of Cambridge PhD thesis, 2010).

Robert Lloyd Haan, 'The Treatment of England and English Affairs in the Dutch Pamphlet Literature 1640–1660' (University of Michigan PhD thesis, 1959).

Lorraine Madway, 'Majesty and Mockery: Representations of Royal Power in the Reign of Charles II, 1660–1685' (Yale University PhD thesis, 1999).

Albert Henry Marshall, 'Sir Dudley Carleton and English Diplomacy in the United Provinces, 1616–1628' (Rutgers State University of New Jersey PhD thesis, 1978).

Leanna Hope McLaughlin, '"Poetick Rage" to Rage of Party: English Political Verse 1678–1685' (University of California, Riverside, PhD thesis, 2018).

Patrick Ignacio O'Neill, 'Charles I and the Spanish Plot: Anglo-Habsburg Relations and the Outbreak of the War of the Three Kingdoms, 1630–1641' (University of California, Riverside, PhD thesis, 2015).

William James Roosen, 'The Ambassador's Craft: A Study of the Functioning of French Ambassadors under Louis XIV' (University of Southern California PhD thesis, 1967).

Charles Findlay Scott, 'Don Pedro Ronquillo and Spanish–British Relations (1674–91)' (University of St Andrews PhD thesis, 1955).

Thomas Vernon Thoroughman, 'Some Political Aspects of Anglo-French Relations, 1610–1619' (University of North Carolina at Chapel Hill PhD thesis, 1968).

Sonya M. Wynne, 'The Mistresses of Charles II and Restoration Court Politics, 1660–1685' (University of Cambridge PhD thesis, 1997).

Unpublished Seminar Paper

Thomas Pert, '"The Prince Elector is going from hence to London, I imagine for no good": The Elector Palatine, Parliament, and the Civil War, *c.*1638–1644'.

Acknowledgements

By coincidence, *Devil-Land* was commissioned by Penguin in the week that followed the referendum held on 23 June 2016 in which a majority of the United Kingdom's electorate voted to leave the European Union and was completed in the week after the UK's final departure from the EU, following the expiry of the 'transition period' on 31 December 2020. Written in the shadow of Brexit speculation and debate, *Devil-Land*'s focus on the contingent mutability of seventeenth-century England's relations with its Continental neighbours provides perspective, if scant comfort, for its readers.

Devil-Land's inspiration was, however, sparked by five television films I made for BBC Scotland in two series entitled *The Stuarts* (2014) and *The Stuarts in Exile* (2015). Seeds for the book's argument were sown while reappraising the impact of Stuart rule in locations ranging from a windswept Aberdeenshire beach that once hosted an invading Jacobite force, to Derry's city walls, Breda's cobbled streets, Madrid's monumental Plaza Mayor, Versailles's Hall of Mirrors and the Vatican City tomb of the Jacobite 'Old Pretender'. Working with a talented production team was a huge privilege and I remain indebted to Richard Downes, Clara Glynn, Neil MacDonald, Ross Leven, Colin Murray, Tim Neil and Andy Twaddle. Lively conversations with my former literary agent Peter Robinson helped those ideas to germinate into a book proposal into which was injected Simon Winder's infectious enthusiasm at Penguin. Simon's combination of gusto and patience has been invaluable, while Natasha Fairweather assumed the agent's mantle on Peter's retirement. I am grateful for the keen editorial eyes of Eva Hodgkin and Jane Robertson and was also delighted to be able to draw, once more, on Cecilia Mackay's expertise with regard to *Devil-Land*'s illustrations.

To let seventeenth-century contemporaries speak for themselves,

Devil-Land's text eschews historiographical overlay, but the endnotes and select bibliography document the extensive corpus of illuminating scholarship on which it is based. I am especially indebted to the cohort of nineteenth- and early twentieth-century editors of state papers and diplomatic correspondence; the lives of these knowledgeable scholars, many of whom were women, lie dwarfed by their colossal publications. From 1908 onwards, for example, Allen B. Hinds published over twenty calendared volumes of manuscript material relating to seventeenth-century England, from repositories in Venice and northern Italy. Necessarily obliged to halt his research in 1940, Hinds poignantly acknowledged 'the deep regret I feel that those with whom I have been pleasantly associated for so many years in preparing these Calendars must now be reckoned among the enemies of my country'.

In much lighter days, I am very grateful to Amy Blakeway, Susan Doran, Martin Dzelzainis, Paul Seaward and David Smith for commenting on draft chapters of *Devil-Land*. I am also indebted to Eoin Devlin and Gijs Rommelse for supplying copies of works during library closures; Tom Pert for sending an unpublished seminar paper and Isabelle McNeill for advice regarding French translations. I would like to have discussed *Devil-Land*'s arguments with the late Jenny Wormald, with whom lunches were always convivial; the fifth chapter's title is taken from an article by Jenny in the *Journal of British Studies* (1985). Colleagues with whom I wish there was simply more time to discuss history include John Baker, John Cairns, Paul Cavill, Steve Murdoch, David Parrott, Jane Partner, Pedro Ramos Pinto, Jan-Melissa Schramm and Richard Serjeantson. Especial thanks are owed to Tony Claydon whose biennial Bangor conferences on the Restoration are models of interdisciplinary insight, as well as facilitating summer holidays on Anglesey's stunning west coast. I have also derived rich stimulus from Liberty Fund colloquia, enjoying eclectic conversations about the writings of Cervantes, Conrad, Dickens, Forster, Hayek, Hume, Oakeshott, Shakespeare, Smith, Swift and Toqueville, among others. On this front, I am especially grateful to Steve Davies, Christine Henderson, Catherine Marshall, Seamus Perry, Adam Tomkins, David Wootton and David Womersley. Among many stimulating supervision discussions in Cambridge, a particular debt is owed to current and recent PhD students including Alexander Campbell, Will Ferguson, Ian King, Alice O'Driscoll, Elly Robson and Tom Tyson.

Cambridge's bookshops, libraries and coffee-shops are catalysts of creativity and inspiration. Having long marvelled at the University Library's phenomenal resources, I did not need its prolonged closure – on account of the coronavirus pandemic – to reinforce my deep appreciation. But *Devil-Land*'s navigation of plague outbreaks, past and present, has provided precedents for a new world of fragmented community and social distancing. As Stephen Bradwell's *A Watch-Man for the Pest* advised in 1625, 'if you stand to talk with another, be distant from him the space of two yards. But if you suspect the party to have the infection, let the space of four yards at the least part you'. *Devil-Land* has been written while I have been Senior Tutor of Trinity Hall – a College founded in 1350 in the immediate aftermath of the Black Death. For helping me to juggle College and University administration, teaching and research, I am indebted to my PA Julie Powley, the Tutorial Registrar Rosie Ince, and the dedicated Tutorial Office team. I am also grateful to Tim Harvey-Samuel, Glen Sharp and Daniel Tyler for supportive fortitude and encouragement as this book neared completion.

Years ago, I was struck by Hermione Lee's description of Virginia Woolf continually asking 'herself why she so much wants to read, and wants to read so much'. From childhood, I've always craved time to read and I remain constantly inspired, diverted and sustained by authors' creative imaginations. I am very grateful to my mother Margaret Storrie for keenly encouraging my early historical enthusiasms and infusing my interest in England's past with a critical Scots perspective. For decades of camaraderie, company and counsel, I warmly thank Emma Harding, Patricia Glennie, Celia Joicey and Jo Lambert. With Susanna Mitchell I enjoyed what felt like a series of unbroken conversations over nearly thirty years, sustained by laughter, long lunches and art exhibitions; sadly, she did not live to see this book's publication. I cherish Christopher Dandeker's longstanding friendship, kindness and thoughtful sagacity, while Jane Clarke provides a model of vibrant energy and liberal hospitality. For providing welcome distraction, generous childcare and lively rapport, I owe much to Rachel Begbie, Carolyn Dunn, Carley Gibbens, Kelly Mawby, Zoe Oram, Laura Owen, Ania Pine, Beth Robinson and Sophie Song.

Finally, my greatest debt is to Mark Goldie and our son Julius. As well as commenting on drafts of *Devil-Land* and readily discussing finer points of Stuart detail, Mark has supplied unwavering encouragement, calm reassurance and immense practical support. Equally unstinting in his enthusiasm, Julius's construction of an elaborate pulley-system for coffee deliveries to my study expedited *Devil-Land*'s completion, alongside diversions to discuss cacti, current affairs and Norwich City performances at Carrow Road. *Devil-Land* is dedicated to Mark and Julius, with love, gratitude and admiration.

Index

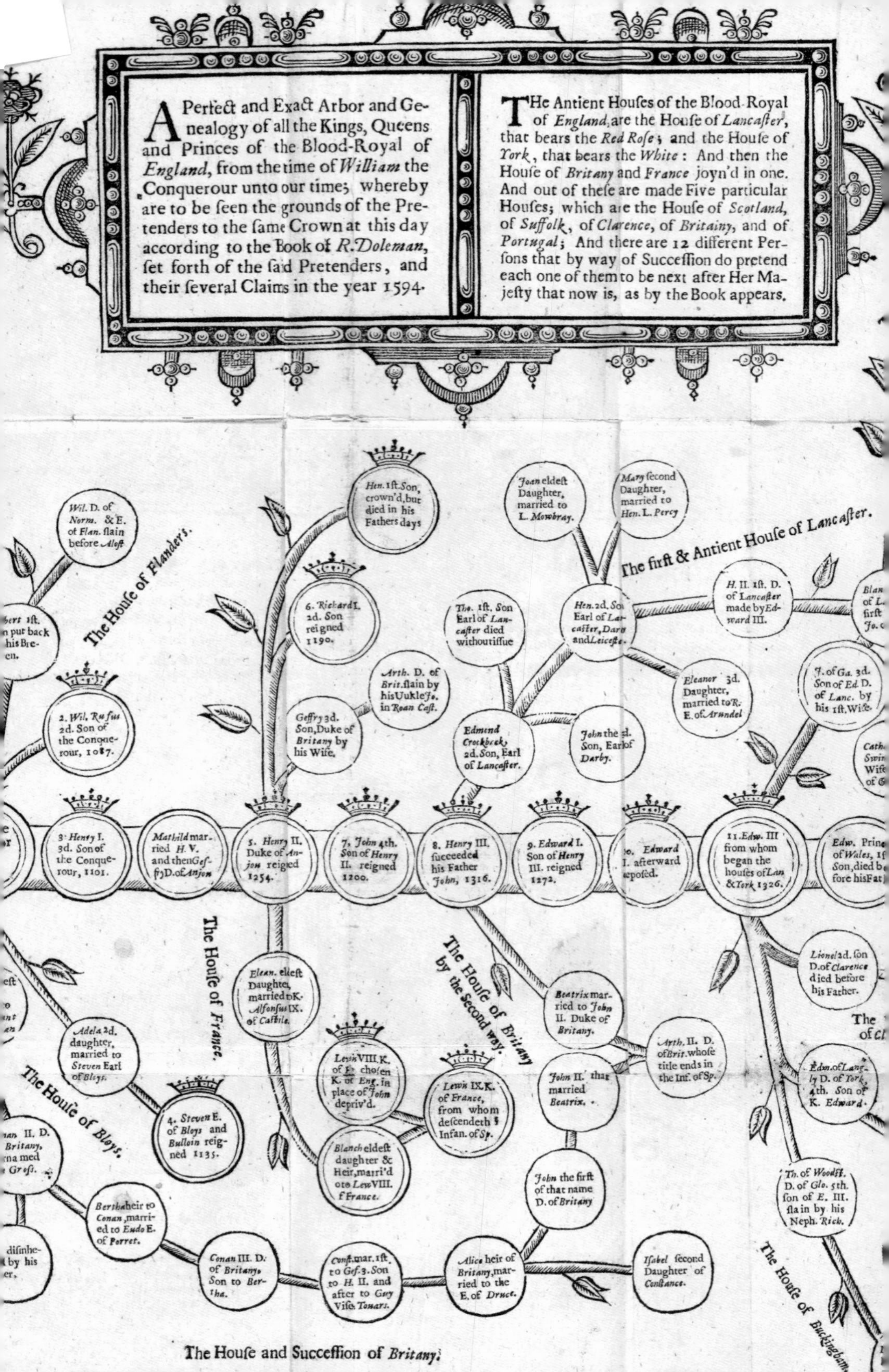
A Perfect and Exact Arbor and Genealogy of all the Kings, Queens and Princes of the Blood-Royal of England, from the time of William the Conquerour unto our time; whereby are to be seen the grounds of the Pretenders to the same Crown at this day according to the Book of R. Doleman, set forth of the said Pretenders, and their several Claims in the year 1594.
The Antient Houses of the Blood-Royal of England, are the House of Lancaster, that bears the Red Rose; and the House of York, that bears the White: And then the House of Britany and France joyn'd in one. And out of these are made Five particular Houses; which are the House of Scotland, of Suffolk, of Clarence, of Britainy, and of Portugal; And there are 12 different Persons that by way of Succession do pretend each one of them to be next after Her Majesty that now is, as by the Book appears.
The House of Flanders.
Wil. D. of Norm. & E. of Flan. slain before Alost
2. Wil. Rufus 2d. Son of the Conquerour, 1087.
3. Henry I. 3d. Son of the Conquerour, 1101.
Mathild married H. V. and then Geffry D. of Anjou
Hen. 1st. Son, crown'd, but died in his Fathers days
6. Richard I. 2d. Son reigned 1190.
Geffry 3d. Son, Duke of Britany by his Wife.
Arth. D. of Brit. slain by his Uukle Jo. in Roan Cast.
5. Henry II. Duke of Anjou reigned 1254.
7. John 4th. Son of Henry II. reigned 1200.
8. Henry III. succeeded his Father John, 1316.
9. Edward I. Son of Henry III. reigned 1272.
10. Edward I. afterward deposed.
11. Edw. III from whom began the houses of Lan & York 1326.
Joan eldest Daughter, married to L. Mowbray.
Mary second Daughter, married to Hen. L. Percy
The first & Antient House of Lancaster.
Tho. 1st. Son Earl of Lancaster died without issue
Hen. 2d. Son Earl of Lancaster, Darby and Leicester.
H. II. 1st. D. of Lancaster made by Edward III.
Eleanor 3d. Daughter, married to R. E. of Arundel
Edmond Crookback, 2d. Son, Earl of Lancaster.
John the 3d. Son, Earl of Darby.
J. of Ga. 3d. Son of Ed. D. of Lanc. by his 1st. Wife.
Edw. Prince of Wales, 1st Son, died before his Father
Lionel 2d. Son D. of Clarence died before his Father.
Edm. of Langly D. of York, 4th. Son of K. Edward.
Th. of Woodst. D. of Glo. 5th. son of E. III. slain by his Neph. Rich.
The House of Buckingham.
The House of France.
Elean. eldest Daughter, married to K. Alfonsus IX. of Castile.
Lewis VIII. K. of Fr. chosen K. of Eng. in place of John depriv'd.
Lewis IX. K. of France, from whom descendeth y Infan. of Sp.
Blanch eldest daughter & Heir, marri'd to Lew VIII. of France.
The House of Britany by the Second way.
Beatrix married to John II. Duke of Britany.
Arth. II. D. of Brit. whose title ends in the Inf. of Sp.
John II. that married Beatrix.
John the first of that name D. of Britany
Adela 2d. daughter, married to Steven Earl of Bloys.
4. Steven E. of Bloys and Bulloin reigned 1135.
The House of Bloys.
Bertha heir to Conan, married to Eudo E. of Porret.
Conan III. D. of Britany, Son to Bertha.
Const. mar. 1st to Gef. 3. Son to H. II. and after to Guy Visc. Tonars.
Alice heir of Britany, married to the E. of Druce.
Isabel second Daughter of Constance.
The House and Succession of Britany.